Regulating Tobacco, Alcohol and Unhealthy Foods

The need to reduce disability and premature deaths from non-communicable diseases ('NCDs') is increasingly engaging international organisations and national and sub-national governments. In this book, experts from a range of backgrounds provide insights into the legal implications of regulating tobacco, alcohol and unhealthy foods, all of which are risk factors for NCDs. As individual countries and the international community move to increase targeting of these risk factors, affected industries are turning to national and international law to challenge the resulting regulations.

This book explores how the effective regulation of tobacco, alcohol and unhealthy foods can be achieved within the context of international health law, international trade and investment law, international human rights law, international intellectual property law and domestic laws on constitutional and other matters. Its contributors consider the various tensions that arise in regulating NCD risk factors, as well as offering an original analysis of the relationship between evidence and health regulation.

Covering a range of geographical areas, including the Americas, the European Union, Africa and Oceania, the book offers lessons for health and policy practitioners and scholars in navigating the complex legal fields in which the regulation of tobacco, alcohol and unhealthy foods takes place.

Tania Voon is Professor at Melbourne Law School and a former Legal Officer of the Appellate Body Secretariat of the World Trade Organization.

Andrew D Mitchell is Professor at Melbourne Law School and Australian Research Council Future Fellow.

Jonathan Liberman is Director of the McCabe Centre for Law and Cancer, a joint initiative of Cancer Council Victoria and the Union for International Cancer Control.

Regulating Tobacco, Alcohol and Unhealthy Foods

The Legal Issues

Edited by
Tania Voon, Andrew D Mitchell and Jonathan Liberman

Routledge
Taylor & Francis Group

LONDON AND NEW YORK

First published 2014
by Routledge
2 Park Square, Milton Park, Abingdon, Oxfordshire OX14 4RN

and by Routledge
711 Third Avenue, New York, NY 10017

First issued in paperback 2016

Routledge is an imprint of the Taylor & Francis Group, an informa business

British Library Cataloguing in Publication Data
A catalogue record for this book is available from the British Library

Library of Congress Cataloging-in-Publication Data
Library of Congress Cataloging-in-Publication Data
Regulating tobacco, alcohol, and unhealthy foods : the legal issues /
edited by Tania Voon, Andrew Mitchell, Jonathan Liberman.
pages cm
Includes bibliographical references and index.
ISBN 978-0-415-72234-6 (hardback) -- ISBN 978-1-315-84976-8 (ebk)
1. Tobacco--Law and legislation. 2. Alcohol--Law and legislation.
3. Tobacco industry--Government policy. 4. Tobacco use--Health aspects.
5. Chronic diseases. I. Voon, Tania, editor of compilation. II. Mitchell, Andrew,
editor of compilation. III. Liberman, Jonathan, editor of compilation.
K3593.5.T63R44 2014
344.04--dc23
2014001735

ISBN 13: 978-1-138-68647-2 (pbk)
ISBN 13: 978-0-415-72234-6 (hbk)

Typeset in 10/12 Baskerville MT by
Servis Filmsetting Ltd, Stockport, Cheshire

Contents

PART III
National and Regional Perspectives of NCD
Risk Regulation

PART IV
Case Study of a Legal Dispute

For
Rebecca, Millie and Alice
Max and Zoe

Acknowledgements

This volume was produced with generous funding provided for independent research by the Australian National Preventive Health Agency (Grant ID 203MIT2011) and the Australian Research Council pursuant to the Linkage Project scheme (project number LP120200028). Support was also provided by Melbourne Law School at the University of Melbourne and the McCabe Centre for Law and Cancer, a joint initiative of Cancer Council Victoria and the Union for International Cancer Control.

Devon Whittle provided valuable research and editorial assistance with numerous chapters, for which we are very grateful. We also appreciate the research and editorial assistance provided by Georgina Dimopoulos, James Munro, Stephen Lloyd and Shawn Rajanayagam. Thanks also to Thijs De Jong for extensive assistance in compiling the bibliography.

Figure 3.1 first appeared in Jean Bae et al, 'Child Passenger Safety Laws in the United States, 1978–2010: Policy Diffusion in the Absence of Strong Federal Intervention' (2014) *Social Science & Medicine* (forthcoming) and is reproduced with permission of Elsevier.

Figure 3.10 first appeared in Brian Flay and Marc Schure, 'The Theory of Triadic Influence' in Alexander Wagenaar and Scott Burris (eds) *Public Health Law Research: Theories and Methods* (2013) and is reproduced with permission of John Wiley & Sons, Inc.

The opinions expressed in each chapter of this volume are those of the relevant authors and are not necessarily shared by the editors or any employer or other entity. The chapters were written at various times throughout 2013 (and January 2014 in the case of Chapters 1 and 5).

Notes on contributors

Alberto Alemanno is the Jean Monnet Professor of EU Law and Risk Regulation at HEC Paris, Global Clinical Professor at NYU Law School, where he is the faculty director of the HEC–NYU EU Regulatory Policy Clinical program, and Adjunct Professor at Georgetown Law. Alberto was formerly *référendaire* (clerk) at the Court of Justice of the European Union, Teaching Assistant at the College of Europe in Bruges and attorney at law in New York. He is the author of *Trade in Food: Regulatory and Judicial Approaches in the EU and the WTO* (Cameron May, 2007), editor of *Governing Disasters: The Challenges of Emergency Risk Regulation* (Edward Elgar, 2011), co-editor of *Better Business Regulation in a Risk Society* (Springer, 2013) and *Foundations of EU Food Law & Policy* (Ashgate, 2013). Together with Amandine Garde, he is editing *Regulating Lifestyle Risks: Europe, Alcohol, Tobacco and Unhealthy Diets* (Cambridge University Press, 2014). Originally from Italy, Alberto earned a Laurea in Giurisprudenza *cum laude* from the Università degli Studi di Torino, LLM degrees from Harvard Law School and the College of Europe, and a PhD in International Law & Economics from Bocconi University. He is the founder and editor of the *European Journal of Risk Regulation* and a member of the editorial boards of the *Revue du Droit de l'Union Européenne*, and the *European Food and Feed Law Review*. Alberto is the founder and scientific director of the Summer Academy in Global Food Law & Policy. He regularly provides advice to a variety of international organisations, such as the Organisation for Economic Cooperation and Development, the United Nations International Trade Center and the European Commission, on various aspects of European Union law, WTO law and tobacco, alcohol, food and gambling regulation.

Fernanda Alonso is a Research Assistant at the Center for Economic Research and Teaching ('CIDE') and head of the Substance Control Area of the Right to Health Program. Fernanda studied law at the Instituto Tecnológico Autónomo de Mexico ('ITAM'). She has worked as a researcher in areas such as drug policy, tobacco control, pharmaceutical regulation and health care. She has also worked as a research assistant in areas of health and regulation with other international organisations such as the O'Neill Institute for National and Global Health Law at Georgetown Law and the Instituto Tecnológico

Autónomo de Mexico as well as NGOs such as Oxfam International and Oxfam Mexico.

Evan Anderson is a Senior Fellow at the Center for Public Health Initiatives at the University of Pennsylvania. He was previously Senior Legal Fellow at Public Health Law Research, a Robert Wood Johnson Foundation program, and a faculty member at the Johns Hopkins Bloomberg School of Public Health. His current research interests lie at the intersection of law and epidemiology, and particularly how law influences population health. His prior research has focused on emergency preparedness, access to essential medicines and regulation of blood products.

Tanya E Baytor is a trained attorney who earned her law degree in her home country of Canada, and her Master of Laws (LLM) in Global Health Law from Georgetown University Law Center. Before starting her Master's Degree Program, Tanya worked for several years as an Associate at the Canadian law firm Torys LLP, where she practised health regulatory and intellectual property law. She has been involved in health and security projects with the Global Health Policy Center at the Center for Strategic and International Studies and was also a member of the Georgetown Human Rights Action/Georgetown Human Rights Institute team that researched US trade policy and access to medicines in the Dominican Republic. At the O'Neill Institute, Tanya has worked on a number of global health law and policy projects with the World Health Organization, the World Bank and the InterAmerican Heart Foundation, among other organisations. She has studied and is interested in various health law related fields, such as the intersection between global health and human rights, non-communicable diseases, access to medicines, and the implementation of the World Health Organization's revised International Health Regulations.

Enrico Bonadio is Senior Lecturer in Law at City University London (City Law School), where he teaches Intellectual Property Law and EU Law. He holds a PhD in international and European Union law from the University of Florence. He is Associate Editor and Intellectual Property Correspondent of the *European Journal of Risk Regulation*. Enrico is a solicitor qualified to practise in England and Wales as well as Italy. He regularly publishes, lectures and advises in the fields of international and European intellectual property law. He recently published a book on the Agreement on Trade-Related Aspects of Intellectual Property Rights ('TRIPS') and genetic resources (Jovene, 2008). Enrico is a Visiting Professor at Université Jean Moulin Lyon (France), Université Catholique de Lyon and University of Turku (Finland), as well as lecturer in intellectual property law at the LLM in intellectual property offered by the World Intellectual Property Organization and the University of Turin. He has also taught at Universidad San Carlos de Guatemala, Université de Toulouse (France), University of Wroclaw (Poland), Moscow State Law Academy (Russia) and the University of Pisa (Italy).

Scott Burris is Professor of Law at Temple University, where he directs the Center for Health Law, Policy and Practice, and the Robert Wood Johnson Foundation's Public Health Law Research program. His work focuses on how law influences public health, and what interventions can make laws and law enforcement practices healthier in their effects. He is the author of more than 100 books, book chapters, articles and reports on issues including urban health, HIV/AIDS, research ethics, global health governance, and the health effects of criminal law and drug policy. His work has been supported by organisations including the Open Society Institute, the National Institutes of Health, the Bill and Melinda Gates Foundation, the UK Department for International Development and the US Centers for Disease Control and Prevention. He has served as a consultant to numerous US and international organisations including the WHO, the United Nations Office on Drugs and Crime, and the United Nations Development Program. Burris is a graduate of Washington University in St Louis and Yale Law School.

Oscar A Cabrera is Executive Director of the O'Neill Institute for National and Global Health Law and a Visiting Professor of Law at Georgetown University Law Center, Washington, DC, United States. He earned his law degree in his home country of Venezuela (Universidad Católica Andrés Bello), and his Master of Laws (LLM), with concentration in Health Law and Policy, at the University of Toronto. Before starting his Masters Degree program, Oscar worked as an Associate at a Venezuelan law firm (d'Empaire Reyna Bermúdez). Oscar has worked on projects with the World Health Organization, the Centers for Disease Control and Prevention, and the Campaign for Tobacco Free Kids, among other organisations. He has studied and is interested in various health law related fields, such as health and human rights, sexual and reproductive rights, global tobacco litigation and health systems law and policy.

Mark Davison is Professor in the Faculty of Law at Monash University, where he teaches and researches primarily in the area of intellectual property. He is the first author of all three editions of Shanahan's *Australian Law of Trade Marks and Passing Off* that have been published since the introduction of the *Trade Marks Act 1995* (Cth). The work is the leading Australian reference work on trade mark law. His other publications include a monograph on the legal protection of databases published by Cambridge University Press, co-authorship of *Australian Intellectual Property Law*, also published by Cambridge University Press, and co-authorship with Sam Ricketson and Megan Richardson of a casebook on Australian Intellectual Property Law. He is a member of the Intellectual Property Committee of the Law Council of Australia, special counsel with Knightsbridge Lawyers, and a member of the Australian government's Expert Advisory Group on Plain Packaging of Tobacco Products.

Sondra Davoren is a Senior Legal Policy Advisor at Cancer Council Victoria, working on alcohol law and policy, and the role of law in cancer treatment and supportive care. She is a member of Australia's National Preventive Health Agency's Expert Committee on Alcohol, the National Alliance for Action on Alcohol and the Victorian Alcohol Policy Coalition. She has published papers on alcohol advertising regulation and legal and regulatory interventions to reduce alcohol-related cancers. Prior to joining Cancer Council Victoria, Sondra worked as legal advisor to the Victorian Legal Services Board and in multi-party litigation for Irwin Mitchell Solicitors (UK), specialising in product liability claims. Sondra studied law at the University of Canterbury, New Zealand and the University of Sheffield, UK.

Susy Frankel is Professor and Director of the New Zealand Centre of International Economic Law at Victoria University of Wellington, New Zealand. She is also Chair of the Copyright Tribunal, New Zealand. Susy qualified as Barrister and Solicitor of the High Court of New Zealand in 1988 and as a Solicitor of England & Wales in 1991. She has been a Visiting Professor at the University of Western Ontario and University of Iowa and Fellow of Clare Hall and visitor to the Centre for Intellectual Property and Information Law, University of Cambridge. She is a member of the Executive Committee of the Association for the Advancement of Teaching and Research in Intellectual Property ('ATRIP') and of the editorial boards of the *Journal of World Intellectual Property*, *Queen Mary Journal of Intellectual Property* and the *University of Western Australia Law Review*. Susy holds an appointment as a Neutral for the World Intellectual Property Organization Arbitration and Mediation Centre, Geneva, Switzerland. She has previously been an Assistant Commissioner of Trade Marks, Patents and Designs for the Intellectual Property Office of New Zealand, 1998–2006. In that capacity she acted as an independent Hearings Officer, mostly relating to trade mark oppositions. She has published widely on the nexus between international intellectual property and trade law.

Amandine Garde is a Professor in the School of Law and Social Justice, University of Liverpool, UK. Before joining the university in April 2013, she lectured at King's College London, the Faculty of Law in Cambridge (where she was also a Fellow of Selwyn College), the University of Exeter, and the University of Durham. Her research interests lie in the fields of European Union trade, consumer, advertising, food and public health law. She specialises more specifically in the role legal instruments can play in improving public health and the wellbeing of children as a group of particularly vulnerable consumers. Her book *EU Law and Obesity Prevention* is the first to offer a critical analysis of the obesity prevention strategy of the European Union. She recently won a grant from the Economic and Social Research Council to continue her work on the regulation of food marketing to children. She has spent part of her research leave at the World Health Organization and has provided technical assistance to several States and regions worldwide in the implementation of the WHO Recommendations on food marketing to children. She also spent a year as a postdoctoral Jean Monnet Fellow at the European University Institute in

Florence in 2005–2006 and is a qualified solicitor, having trained at Simmons & Simmons in their London and Paris offices.

Alexandra Jones is a Senior Legal Policy Advisor at the McCabe Centre for Law and Cancer, Australia, a joint initiative of Cancer Council Victoria and the Union for International Cancer Control ('UICC'), engaged in research, policy development and advocacy on the role of law in prevention of cancer. Her current focus is global tobacco control. Prior to joining the McCabe Centre, Alexandra was a Fellow and Associate of the O'Neill Institute for National and Global Health Law in Washington, DC, where she worked on projects related to non-communicable diseases, international trade and health law, and HIV prevention policy. She has also worked as a human rights advocate and educator in Cambodia, and as a solicitor in a corporate practice. Alexandra holds a Masters of Global Health Law (Dist) from Georgetown University Law Center, and a BA/LLM (Hons I) from Sydney University.

Rachel Kitonyo-Devotsu is the Project Coordinator of The Africa Tobacco Control Consortium ('ATCC'), which is a coalition of six public health organisations focused on preventing a tobacco epidemic in Africa (the American Cancer Society, the Africa Tobacco Control Regional Initiative, the Africa Tobacco Control Alliance, the Framework Convention Alliance, the Campaign for Tobacco-Free Kids and the International Union Against Tuberculosis and Lung Disease). Rachel holds a Bachelor of Laws degree from the University of Nairobi and has nine years' experience in tobacco control ranging from drafting and lobbying for tobacco control legislation in Kenya, working on enforcement campaigns of tobacco control legislation in Kenya, and training government enforcement officers and media advocacy to create awareness about the dangers of tobacco use and the contents of tobacco control legislation. She has also served as amicus curiae in two court cases filed by the tobacco industry challenging the Kenyan tobacco control legislation. Under the African Tobacco Control Consortium, Rachel works with six staff and grantees in ten countries in sub-Saharan Africa to support national and regional advocacy campaigns for the implementation of the Framework Convention on Tobacco Control in sub-Saharan Africa. In recognition of her work at national and regional level, in 2009 Rachel was awarded the Judy Wilkenfeld Award for International Tobacco Control Excellence by the Campaign for Tobacco Free Kids based in Washington, DC.

Jonathan Liberman is Director of the McCabe Centre for Law and Cancer, Australia, a joint initiative of Cancer Council Victoria and the Union for International Cancer Control ('UICC'), engaged in research, policy development and advocacy on the role of law in the prevention and treatment of cancer. Jonathan has over a decade of experience in legal and policy research, advice and advocacy on issues relating to cancer prevention and treatment at both domestic and global levels. His work has covered a wide range of issues across tobacco, alcohol and food regulation, access to medicines, international trade law, international investment law, international drug control law and international human rights law. He is a member of the Australian Government's Expert Advisory Group on Plain Packaging of Tobacco Products and the Standing Committee on Tobacco to the Intergovernmental Committee on Drugs. Together with Professors Andrew Mitchell and Tania Voon, he is the recipient of research grants from the Australian National Preventive Health Agency and the Australian Research Council to examine the relationship between international trade and investment law and regulation of tobacco, alcohol and unhealthy foods.

Alejandro Madrazo is Professor and Researcher at the Center for Economic Research and Teaching ('CIDE'), Mexico, where he coordinates the Right to Health Program. Before and after joining CIDE faculty full-time he undertook strategic litigation and legislative projects involving the right to health, including same sex marriage and adoption, abortion, local tobacco control legislation and federal tobacco control bills. Alejandro obtained his Bachelor of Laws at the Instituto Tecnológico Autónomo de México ('ITAM') in Mexico City and then undertook his Master of Laws and JSD at Yale Law School. He has published in the areas of sexual and reproductive rights, substance control and freedom of speech, legal education and the history of legal thought. On tobacco control he has published *Human Rights as a Tool for Tobacco Control in Latin America* (Salud Pública de Mexico, Vol 52/2010, Mexico with O Cabrera) and *Estrategias de la industria tabacalera en México para interferer en las políticas de control de tabaco* (Salud Pública de Mexico, Vol. 54/2011, Mexico with A Guerrero). He has provided expertise to organisations such as the Inter-American Heart Foundation, the Campaign for Tobacco Free Kids, and the International Union Against Tuberculosis and Lung Disease.

Benn McGrady is Project Director of the Initiative on Trade, Investment and Health and Adjunct Professor at the O'Neill Institute for National and Global Health Law, Georgetown University Law Center. He is the author of *Trade and Public Health: The WTO, Tobacco, Alcohol and Diet* (Cambridge University Press, 2011). Benn teaches courses exploring the intersection between trade and investment agreements and health at Georgetown and advises governmental, inter-governmental and non-governmental bodies on these issues. Originally from Australia, Benn holds a Bachelor of Arts, a Bachelor of Laws (Hons) and a doctorate from Monash University in Melbourne, as well as a Master of Laws (Dist) (Global Health Law) from the Georgetown University Law Center.

Caroline Mills is a Legal Policy Adviser with the Obesity Policy Coalition in Melbourne, a coalition between Cancer Council Victoria, Diabetes Australia – Victoria, VicHealth and the World Health Organization Collaborating Centre for Obesity Prevention at Deakin University. She holds a Bachelor of Science and Bachelor of Laws from Monash University and is currently undertaking a Masters of Public and International Law at the University of Melbourne, with a particular interest in medical ethics and philosophy of international law.

Caroline has previously practised as a barrister at the Victorian Bar, primarily in medical and injuries law, as well as practising as a solicitor in insurance litigation.

Andrew D Mitchell is Professor at Melbourne Law School, Australia, having joined the faculty in 2006. He is also currently an Australian Research Council Future Fellow, Director of the Global Economic Law Network, and Assistant Director Research at the Melbourne School of Government. In 2007, following a nomination by the Australian government, the World Trade Organization's Dispute Settlement Body added him to the Indicative List of Governmental and Non-Governmental Panelists to hear WTO disputes. He has law degrees from Melbourne Law School, Harvard Law School and the University of Cambridge. His previous employers include the International Monetary Fund, the Organization for Economic Cooperation and Development, Davis Polk & Wardwell and Allens Arthur Robinson (now Allens Linklaters). Andrew also consults for the private sector and governmental and non-governmental organisations, including Telstra and the World Health Organization. He has over 90 academic publications and has taught at numerous law schools in Canada, the US and Australia.

Stephanie Palmer is Senior Lecturer at the University of Cambridge, Faculty of Law. She has degrees in law from Harvard University and the University of Adelaide and teaches a range of courses in public law and human rights to undergraduates and postgraduates at the University of Cambridge. Stephanie is Fellow and Director of Legal Studies at Girton College, Cambridge, and a member of the editorial board of the *European Human Rights Law Review* and the *International Journal of Constitutional Law* based in New York and published by Oxford University Press. She is a barrister and a member of Blackstone Chambers, Temple, London.

Matthew Rimmer is an Australian Research Council Future Fellow, working on Intellectual Property and Climate Change. He is an Associate Professor at the Australian National University College of Law and an Associate Director of the Australian Centre for Intellectual Property in Agriculture. He holds a Bachelor of Arts (Hons) and a University Medal in literature and a Bachelor of Laws (Hons) from the Australian National University. Matthew received a PhD in law from the University of New South Wales for his dissertation on *The Pirate Bazaar: The Social Life of Copyright Law*. He is a member of the Australian National University Climate Change Institute and a director of the Australian Digital Alliance. Matthew has published widely on copyright law and information technology, patent law and biotechnology, access to medicines, clean technologies, and traditional knowledge. His work is archived at Social Science Research Network Abstracts and Bepress Selected Works.

Stephen D Sugarman is Roger J Traynor Professor of Law at the University of California Berkeley School of Law, US. He is the co-editor of *Regulating Tobacco* (Oxford, 2001) and *Smoking Policy: Law, Politics and Culture* (Oxford, 1993) and has authored numerous articles and book chapters on tobacco, diet and public health. He has been a Visiting Professor at the London School of Economics; University College, London; the University of Paris; the European University Institute, Florence; Kobe University Faculty of Law; Kyoto University Faculty of Law; Tel Aviv University Faculty of Law; and Columbia University Law School.

Barbara von Tigerstrom is Professor and Associate Dean (Research and Graduate Studies) at the University of Saskatchewan College of Law, Canada, where she teaches health law, administrative law and international law. She holds a Master of Arts and Bachelor of Laws from the University of Toronto and a PhD in law from the University of Cambridge. Before joining the University of Saskatchewan, she worked at the Supreme Court of Canada, University of Alberta and University of Canterbury. Her current research focuses on legal issues in chronic disease prevention and the regulation of drugs and medical devices. She has acted as principal investigator on projects funded by the Canadian Institutes of Health Research, examining the impact of tax credits to encourage physical activity and the role of law in preventing obesity and chronic disease. She has also been an investigator and collaborator on several projects funded by the Stem Cell Network relating to ethical, legal, and social issues in stem cell research. Her recent publications include articles and book chapters on the regulation of stem cell-based products and on public health law and policy, including tobacco control, disease surveillance and control, and legal strategies to promote healthy eating and physical activity.

Tania Voon is Professor and Associate Dean (Research) at Melbourne Law School, University of Melbourne, Australia. She is a former Legal Officer of the Appellate Body Secretariat of the World Trade Organization ('WTO') and has previously practised law with Mallesons Stephen Jaques and the Australian Government Solicitor, and taught law at Georgetown University, the University of Western Ontario, the Australian National University, Monash University, and Bond University. Tania undertook her Master of Laws at Harvard Law School and her PhD in Law at the University of Cambridge. She has published widely in the areas of public international law and international economic law. She is the author of *Cultural Products and the World Trade Organization* (Cambridge: Cambridge University Press, 2007), a member of the Editorial Board of the *Journal of International Economic Law*, and a member of the Indicative List of Governmental and Non-Governmental Panelists for resolving WTO disputes. Tania has provided expert advice and training to entities such as Telstra, the Australian Department of Foreign Affairs and Trade, the WTO, and the World Health Organization, and NGOs such as Cancer Council Victoria.

Part I

Challenges of Non-Communicable Diseases

1 Introduction: Law and the Growing Burden of Non-Communicable Diseases

Tania Voon

Non-communicable diseases ('NCDs') are estimated to account for close to two thirds of the deaths occurring globally, with the burden of NCDs increasing and falling predominantly on low- and middle-income countries.[1] Cardiovascular diseases, cancers, chronic respiratory diseases and diabetes together 'make the largest contribution to morbidity and mortality' due to NCDs.[2] In turn, 'four shared behavioural risk factors' can be identified for these types of NCDs: 'tobacco use, unhealthy diet, physical inactivity and harmful use of alcohol'.[3] These diseases and risk factors form the core of international action that has developed over the last two decades to combat the growing problem of NCDs around the world.

Regulation forms a central part of national and international strategies to combat NCD morbidity and mortality, particularly regulation regarding the risk factors of tobacco use, unhealthy diet and harmful use of alcohol. The law is thus a crucial tool in targeting NCDs. Yet, at the same time, local, national and international laws have been used to challenge NCD risk factor regulation, for example, on the grounds that it infringes freedom of speech or property rights or that it discriminates against foreign investors or imported products. This book is designed to explore the interaction between the law and NCDs, and specifically the legal issues surrounding the regulation of tobacco, alcohol and unhealthy foods.

1 Developments on NCDs in the World Health Organization and the United Nations

In 1998, the World Health Assembly – the decision-making body of the World Health Organization ('WHO') – adopted a resolution calling on WHO member states 'to collaborate with WHO in developing a global strategy for the prevention and control' of NCDs.[4] This resolution was followed in 2000 by the World Health Assembly adoption of a *Global Strategy for the Prevention and Control of Noncommunicable Diseases*[5] and another resolution on NCDs.[6] In order to implement the global strategy, in 2008, the World Health Assembly endorsed an action plan for the period 2008 to 2013.[7]

Progress has accelerated, moving beyond the WHO to the broader United Nations ('UN') in recent years. In 2010, the UN General Assembly adopted a resolution on NCDs, noting that:

the conditions in which people live and their lifestyles influence their health and quality of life and that the most prominent non-communicable diseases are linked to common risk factors, namely, tobacco use, alcohol abuse, an unhealthy diet, physical inactivity and environmental carcinogens, being aware that these risk factors have economic, social, gender, political, behavioural and environmental determinants, and in this regard stressing the need for a multisectoral response to combat non-communicable diseases …[8]

In recognition of the urgency and significance of NCDs, the General Assembly decided to convene a high-level meeting of the General Assembly in 2011 and requested the UN Secretary-General to submit a report on the global status of NCDs.[9]

In his report presented to the General Assembly in May 2011, the Secretary-General Ban Ki-moon noted that '[t]he rapidly growing magnitude of such diseases is driven in part by population ageing, the negative impact of urbanization and the globalization of trade and marketing … particularly for tobacco, food and alcohol'.[10] Referring to NCDs as representing 'a global epidemic',[11] the Secretary-General noted their adverse impact on the Millennium Development Goals[12] and recommended that UN member states '[i]mplement cost-effective population-wide interventions, including through regulatory and legislative actions, for the non-communicable disease-related risk factors of tobacco use, unhealthy diet, lack of physical activity and harmful alcohol use'.[13]

Following the high-level meeting of heads of state and government and other state and government representatives, held in September 2011, the General Assembly adopted a resolution adopting the political declaration generated in the meeting, recognising 'the primary role and responsibility of Governments in responding to the challenge of non-communicable diseases'[14] and that 'the rising prevalence, morbidity and mortality of non-communicable diseases worldwide can be largely prevented and controlled through collective and multisectoral action by all Member States and other relevant stakeholders at the local, national, regional and global levels'.[15] This political declaration encapsulated the growing recognition of the NCD epidemic and the significant role of governments in addressing it, including through regulation.

In May 2013, the World Health Assembly endorsed[16] the *Global Action Plan for the Prevention and Control of Noncommunicable Diseases 2013–2020*,[17] with the overarching goal being:

To reduce the preventable and avoidable burden of morbidity, mortality and disability due to noncommunicable diseases by means of multisectoral collaboration and cooperation at national, regional and global levels, so that populations reach the highest attainable standards of health and productivity at every age and those diseases are no longer a barrier to well-being or socioeconomic development.[18]

These multilateral developments present an opportune time for research and reflection on the way that law can be used to promote the prevention and control of NCDs around the world.

2 The role of law and evidence in NCD risk regulation

Part I of this book sets out overarching principles that inform the rest of the volume. In Chapter 2, Jonathan Liberman continues the discussion of the global architecture for NCD governance, explaining the various mechanisms and agencies involved in implementing the current action plan within the broader context of global health. He demonstrates how law can be used both 'as a proactive intervention to reduce exposure to NCD risk factors' (for example through regulation establishing smoke-free public areas) and 'as setting the context within which power is exercised and constraints on the exercise of that power' (for example through constitutional provisions that provide for the creation of legislation and constitutional guarantees that set limits on legislation). Liberman provides several suggestions for using law effectively to prevent NCDs, despite the fact that efforts to do so 'are liable to face legal challenges (or threats of such challenges) in both domestic and international fora'. He emphasises the need for expertise in relevant areas of law throughout relevant stages of policy-making, and the differences and similarities between the three risk factors addressed in this book.

In the sphere of NCD risk factor regulation, strong evidence can be used to defend policy measures that are subject to legal challenge in domestic or international tribunals. Moreover, evidence is essential in the development of appropriate and effective measures to combat NCD risk factors. Recognising that NCD risk factor regulation may require innovative policy-making, in Chapter 3, Evan Anderson and Scott Burris provide an in-depth analysis of the ways in which research can be used to enhance the development of policy in a manner that is properly informed by and based on evidence. Using concrete examples from US laws, for example regarding the use of child restraints in motor vehicles and the incidence of concussion in sports, they illustrate the importance of the definition of a given policy problem to the subsequent success of the policy response, and the different ways in which knowledge can be used to identify and select appropriate legal interventions. Anderson and Burris highlight the different ways that evidence can be used in the three stages of problem definition, identification of intervention strategies and selection of regulatory interventions.

Seeking and using evidence from the earliest stages of policy-making may assist both in ensuring that the most appropriate regulatory strategies are used from a health perspective and in enhancing confidence that those strategies will survive a legal challenge. Lessons about the interaction between evidence, law and health are therefore valuable at domestic, regional and international levels in addressing NCD risk factors.

3 International aspects of NCD risk regulation

Part II of this book examines key areas of international law that affect NCD risk factor regulation, as well as offering insights into the interaction of these laws with domestic laws and comparison of certain common legal principles in different jurisdictions. This part provides a solid basis for understanding the international context in which domestic laws and regulations on NCD risk factors are operating.

The international focus on NCDs has brought into focus the right to health, with the UN General Assembly recognising the 'urgent need for greater measures at the global, regional and national levels to prevent and control non-communicable diseases in order to contribute to the full realization of the right of everyone to the highest attainable standard of physical and mental health'.[19] In Chapter 4 of this book, Tanya Baytor and Oscar Cabrera explain the relationship between health and international human rights law and the impact of NCD risk factor regulation on the right to health, the right to food and freedom of information. They recognise the potential for tension between the right to health and various other rights, such as those championed by the tobacco industry in resisting tobacco control, while emphasising the common judicial recognition of proportionality in assessing restrictions on particular rights:

> In order for a restriction to be lawful, the proposed restriction must be imposed through the law. It must respond to a legitimate aim to raise a social interest or to preserve the general well-being in a democratic society. The restriction must be necessary and must use the least restrictive measures. Finally, the restriction must be proportional. It is under this prong of the test that the right to health trumps the rights of smokers or the rights of the tobacco industry …

In conclusion, the authors recognise the potential for NCD risk factor regulation to contribute to 'the full realisation of the highest attainable standard of health'.

In Chapter 5, Andrew Mitchell and I consider an area in which the tobacco and alcohol industries in particular have been active in resisting regulation: international trade law. Focusing on the law of the World Trade Organization ('WTO') in connection with trade in goods, this chapter elucidates the core obligations of (i) tariff bindings (preventing import duties above an agreed amount); (ii) the prohibition on import bans and limits on other trade-restrictive measures; and (iii) non-discrimination (eg not discriminating against or between imported products). We highlight the existing disputes concerning tobacco regulation in the WTO (concerning the United States' ban on flavoured cigarettes and the Australian laws mandating standardised packaging of tobacco products) and past disputes on taxation of alcohol. In relation to unhealthy food, we acknowledge both the difficulties faced by countries such as Samoa in acceding to the WTO with its ban on fatty turkey tail products, as well as the opportunities provided by WTO law to combat subsidisation of unhealthy foods. Like Baytor and Cabrera in Chapter 4, we emphasise the importance of evidence-based policy as well as multilateral action in advancing NCD risk factor regulation in the context of international trade law.

Chapter 6 addresses the related field of international investment law, with Benn McGrady explaining the ways in which bilateral investment treaties, investment chapters in preferential trade agreements and investment contracts intersect with health law in the form of NCD risk factor regulation. McGrady highlights the risks associated with contracts between states and foreign investors, particularly contracts that include stabilisation clauses, which 'can constrain the regulatory autonomy of a state in a number of different ways'. He also explains certain common obligations found in international investment agreements that may create difficulties for states seeking to engage in NCD risk factors: fair and equitable treatment; expropriation; and non-discrimination. The principle of non-discrimination is also seen in the trade law field (as addressed in Chapter 5), and notions of expropriation also arise in some constitutional settings (see eg Chapters 9 and 17). In relation to fair and equitable treatment, which is less obviously reflected in other legal contexts, McGrady warns against states making representations to induce investment that may give rise to legitimate expectations on the part of the investor regarding the future regulatory framework.

In Chapter 7, Mark Davison addresses international aspects of intellectual property law, a field that intersects with both international trade law and international investment law. Davison focuses on trademark rights under the WTO's *Agreement on Trade-Related Aspects of Intellectual Property Rights*,[20] using the ongoing challenges brought in the WTO against Australia's 'plain' packaging laws as a case study for assessing how that agreement would apply to regulation of alcohol and unhealthy foods. Enrico Bonadio continues the discussion of intellectual property in Chapter 8, arguing that commonly used measures to reduce consumption of tobacco, alcohol and unhealthy foods do not infringe on intellectual property rights as commonly conceived in national, regional and international law, even though these measures affect manufacturers' ability to 'produce, present, advertise and market their products as they wish'. Bonadio then proposes certain reforms to intellectual property regimes to encourage healthier food and beverage production and consumption.

Chapter 9 provides a link between Parts II and III of the book, offering a comparative perspective of constitutional issues arising from NCD risk factor regulation in the United Kingdom and South Africa. In a chapter building on the human rights discussion in Chapter 4 and foreshadowing some of the constitutional issues that have arisen in particular jurisdictions discussed in Part III, Stephanie Palmer explains factors of jurisdiction, freedom of expression, the right to property and the right to health that have arisen in legal challenges to NCD risk factor regulation in the United Kingdom and South Africa. She explains the different constitutional frameworks in which the various challenges have arisen in these two jurisdictions and includes in her analysis an assessment of the future for plain packaging in the United Kingdom. While recognising the tension that may arise between different rights in connection with NCD risk factor regulation, Palmer concludes that, to date, '[t]he objectives based on public health have outweighed competing interests'.

4 National and regional approaches and challenges

Part III of this book comprises seven chapters that examine in detail the role of the law in regulating NCD risk factors in specific countries and regions around the world. While not providing a comprehensive overview of NCD risk factor regulation in every continent, these chapters are intended to provide a flavour of the different ways in which countries have approached regulation in this field and the strategies that have proven most effective and resilient to challenge.

Stephen Sugarman's chapter on the United States presents a sobering picture of how a litigious culture and wariness of interference with commercial interests has led to some success in challenging NCD risk factor regulation on constitutional or other grounds. Elsewhere in the Americas, Barbara von Tigerstrom explains the complex structure of federal and provincial NCD risk factor regulation in Canada, highlighting the difficulties with industry-led initiatives and concluding that Canadian governments have further space to regulate in this area, despite the constraints of Canadian constitutional law including the *Canadian Charter of Rights and Freedoms*.

In Chapter 12, on Latin America, Fernanda Alonso and Alejandro Madrazo provide examples of difficulties with the regulation of unhealthy food and alcohol before turning to focus on tobacco control, given that the greatest advances have been made in this context of NCD risk factor regulation in the region. The authors explain the expansive tobacco control laws that exist throughout many countries in Latin America, while highlighting continuing difficulties with tobacco industry interference, tobacco litigation and enforcement.

Turning to the European Union ('EU'), in Chapter 13, Alberto Alemanno and Amandine Garde explain the history of the EU's NCD policy and its integration within the framework of EU law, including an evaluation of constitutional principles affecting EU powers in this field. They note that although 'the constitutional structure of the EU as a union of member states adds a further level of complexity to the already difficult process of translating research into effective policies', EU law can be used to promote relevant rights to health, life, a clean environment, information and nutritious food.

In Chapter 14, Rachel Kitonyo-Devotsu explains that, primarily due to the *WHO Framework Convention on Tobacco Control* ('WHO FCTC'),[21] tobacco control is more advanced in Africa than regulation of alcohol or unhealthy foods. Her chapter therefore focuses on the African experience of tobacco control, using case studies from Kenya, Mauritius and Chad. She provides insights into the types of challenges faced in taxing tobacco, mandating pictorial health warnings on tobacco packaging and raising the priority of tobacco control within national health and development agendas in Africa. Kitonyo-Devotsu also provides an extended examination of the interference of the tobacco industry in efforts to regulate tobacco in Africa. She concludes that although tobacco control has advanced in Africa, significant obstacles remain.

Chapters 15 and 16 deal with New Zealand and Australia respectively. Susy Frankel explains the New Zealand regulation of tobacco, alcohol and unhealthy foods as a basis for discussing the trade relationship between New Zealand and Australia, emphasising the need for coordination between the two countries in developing appropriate regulatory mechanisms, particularly in the area of unhealthy foods. Sondra Davoren, Caroline Mills and Alexandra Jones compare Australia's recognised leadership in tobacco control with its limited progress in enacting evidence-based laws directed at alcohol consumption and obesity, highlighting the need for cooperation within and between different levels of government in responding to powerful industry groups.

5 Conclusions

In Part IV of this book, Matthew Rimmer provides a fitting conclusion by offering a detailed illustration of how the Australian government successfully defended its plain tobacco packaging measure against a challenge by tobacco companies in the High Court of Australia. Although this was a domestic dispute involving Australian constitutional law, the chapter provides hope for the ongoing trade and investment challenges against the Australian laws (discussed in Chapters 5 and 6 respectively) and corresponding investment treaty arbitration against Uruguay (discussed by Benn McGrady in Chapter 6), in which some of the same considerations are likely to arise. Reflecting on issues of intellectual property and the acquisition of property on just terms (which may be seen as broadly comparable to issues arising under expropriation in international investment law), Rimmer explains the development of the measure and the perception of it by Australia's highest court. He concludes that the Australian decision will lend support to efforts in other countries to adopt similar measures, a conclusion that seems supported by recent developments in the United Kingdom and New Zealand as discussed in Chapters 9 and 15 respectively.

The nuances of different areas of law in different jurisdictions hinder generalisations about the future of NCD risk factor regulation. Similarly, the differences between tobacco, alcohol and unhealthy food mean that each regulation must be carefully examined on its merits in view of the relevant legal framework. Nevertheless, the various chapters in this book develop certain themes and lead to several common conclusions. First, tobacco control regulation is more advanced, particularly in some regions, than regulation of alcohol and unhealthy foods. Legal defences of tobacco control measures may therefore offer pertinent lessons for future regulation of the latter two risk factors. Second, the development and appropriate use of evidence is crucial in developing, implementing and defending regulation of NCD risk factors. Particularly in this regard, interdisciplinary collaboration is required involving law, health and policy experts from within and across countries and regions. Third, and perhaps most importantly, the industries affected by this kind of regulation are powerful and well-resourced and can be expected to pursue any available legal avenue to prevent it.

Against this background, knowledge and effective use of the relevant domestic and international laws provide a necessary tool of resistance in targeting NCD risk factors through effective regulation. The increasing unity of the international community in the contexts of the UN and the WHO offers a valuable opportunity for states to work together in developing the necessary legal and evidentiary base to continue to combat the global NCD epidemic.

Notes

1 World Health Assembly, *Follow-up to the Political Declaration of the High-level Meeting of the General Assembly on the Prevention and Control of Non-communicable Diseases*, WHA Res WHA66.10, 66th sess, 9th plen mtg, Agenda Items 13.1 and 13.2 (27 May 2013) annex, *Global Action Plan for the Prevention and Control of Noncommunicable Diseases 2013–2020* [6].
2 Ibid [2].
3 Ibid [6].
4 World Health Assembly, *Noncommunicable Disease Prevention and Control*, WHA Res WHA51.18, 51st sess (11–16 May 1998).
5 World Health Organization, *Global Strategy for the Prevention and Control of Noncommunicable Diseases: Report by the Director-General*, WHO Doc A53/14 (22 March 2000), adopted by the World Health Assembly in WHA Res WHA53.14, 53rd sess (May 2000).
6 World Health Assembly, *Prevention and Control of Noncommunicable Diseases*, WHA Res WHA 53.17, 53rd sess, 8th plen mtg, Agenda Item 12.11, WHO Doc A53/VR/8 (20 May 2000).
7 World Health Assembly, *Action Plan for the Global Strategy for the Prevention and Control of Noncommunicable Diseases*, WHO Doc A61/8 (18 April 2008), endorsed by World Health Assembly, *Prevention and Control of Noncommunicable Diseases: Implementation of the Global Strategy*, WHA Res WHA61.14, 61st sess, 8th plen mtg, WHO Doc A61/VR/8 (24 May 2008) [1].
8 *Prevention and Control of Non-communicable Diseases*, GA Res 64/265, UN GAOR, 64th sess, 86th plen mtg, Agenda Item 114, UN Doc A/RES/64/265 (20 May 2010, adopted 13 May 2010) 2.
9 Ibid [1], [4].
10 *Prevention and Control of Non-communicable Diseases: Report of the Secretary-General*, UN GAOR, 66th sess, UN Doc A/66/83 (19 May 2011) [3], [6].
11 Ibid [9].
12 Ibid [29].
13 Ibid [68].
14 *Political Declaration of the High-level Meeting of the General Assembly on the Prevention and Control of Non-communicable Diseases*, GA Res 66/2, UN GAOR, 66th sess, 3rd plen mtg, Agenda Item 117, UN Doc A/RES/66/2 (24 January 2012, adopted 19 September 2011), annex [3].
15 Ibid [3].
16 World Health Assembly, *Follow-up to the Political Declaration of the High-level Meeting of the General Assembly on the Prevention and Control of Non-communicable Diseases*, WHA Res WHA66.10, 66th sess, 9th plen mtg, Agenda Items 13.1 and 13.2 (27 May 2013) [1(1)].
17 Ibid annex, *Global Action Plan for the Prevention and Control of Noncommunicable Diseases 2013–2020*.
18 Ibid 7.

19 *Political Declaration of the High-level Meeting of the General Assembly on the Prevention and Control of Non-communicable Diseases*, GA Res 66/2, UNGAOR, 66th sess, 3rd plen mtg, Agenda Item 117, UN Doc A/RES/66/2 (24 January 2012, adopted 19 September 2011), annex [6].
20 *Marrakesh Agreement Establishing the World Trade Organization*, opened for signature 15 April 1994, 1867 UNTS 3 (entered into force 1 January 1995) annex 1C ('*Agreement on Trade-Related Aspects of Intellectual Property Rights*').
21 Opened for signature 16 June 2003, 2302 UNTS 166 (entered into force 27 February 2005). As at June 2013, the six countries within the WHO Afro region that are not party to the WHO FCTC are Ethiopia, Eritrea, Malawi, Mozambique, South Sudan and Zimbabwe.

2 Making Effective Use of Law in the Global Governance of NCD Prevention

*Jonathan Liberman**

1 Background

The World Health Organization ('WHO') estimates that in 2008 36 million deaths, or 63 per cent of the 57 million deaths that occurred globally, were due to non-communicable diseases ('NCDs'), primarily cardiovascular diseases, cancers, chronic respiratory diseases and diabetes.[1] Approximately 80 per cent of these deaths (29 million) occurred in low- and middle-income countries, with a higher proportion (48 per cent) of the deaths in these countries being premature (under the age of 70) compared to high-income countries (26 per cent).[2] The WHO projects that the total annual number of deaths from NCDs will increase to 55 million by 2030 if 'business as usual' continues.[3]

The continuation of 'business as usual' will also result in a loss of productivity and an escalation of health care costs in all countries.[4] Losses to low- and middle-income countries from the four major NCDs are estimated to surpass US$7 trillion over the period 2011–25, an average of nearly US$500 billion per year.[5] This yearly loss is equivalent to approximately 4 per cent of these countries' current annual output.[6] For all countries, the cost of inaction far outweighs the cost of taking action.[7] Affordable interventions provide a good return on investment. The total cost of implementing a combination of very cost-effective population-wide and individual interventions, in terms of current health spending, amounts to 4 per cent in low-income countries, 2 per cent in lower middle-income countries and less than 1 per cent in upper-middle-income and high-income countries.[8]

After being long neglected as a global health, economic and political priority, the case for attention and action on NCDs has become irresistible. The last few years have seen the steady rise of NCDs on the global agenda, highlighted by the landmark September 2011 United Nations ('UN') General Assembly High-level Meeting on the Prevention and Control of NCDs and the substantial series of follow-up activities that the High-level Meeting has generated. In the *Political Declaration* adopted at the High-level Meeting ('Political Declaration'), the 193 member states of the UN acknowledged that:

> the global burden and threat of non-communicable diseases constitutes one
> of the major challenges for development in the twenty-first century, which

undermines social and economic development throughout the world, and threatens the achievement of the internationally agreed development goals.[9]

While also underlining the importance of providing treatment to people with NCDs – and making commitments to do so – states '[r]ecognize[d] that prevention must be the cornerstone of the global response to non-communicable diseases'.[10] They recognised that the most prominent NCDs 'are linked to common risk factors, namely tobacco use, harmful use of alcohol, an unhealthy diet, and a lack of physical activity',[11] and the 'critical importance of reducing the level of exposure of individuals and populations' to these common modifiable risk factors, and their determinants.[12]

As the Director-General of the WHO, Dr Margaret Chan, recently noted, socioeconomic progress is creating the conditions that favour the rise of NCDs.[13] This reality contrasts sharply with many other diseases, the burden of which tends to reduce as living conditions improve. Economic growth, modernisation and urbanisation 'have opened wide the entry point for the spread of unhealthy lifestyles'.[14] 'Unhealthy commodities industries' – including tobacco, alcohol and ultra-processed food and drink – are now 'major drivers of NCD epidemics worldwide';[15] 'the vectors of spread are not biological agents, but transnational corporations'.[16]

These realities have major implications for the governance of NCDs, and the role of law in that governance. First, perhaps more than for any other global health priority, progress will be limited if NCDs are addressed solely as a health issue, through the health sector. As recognised in the Political Declaration, 'a whole-of-government and a whole-of-society effort' is required.[17] Leadership and multi-sectoral approaches are needed across such sectors as health, education, energy, agriculture, sports, transport, communication, urban planning, environment, labour, employment, industry and trade, finance and social and economic development.[18]

The *Global Action Plan for the Prevention and Control of Noncommunicable Diseases 2013–2020* ('Global Action Plan'), endorsed by the World Health Assembly at its May 2013 session, expands this list of sectors to also cover food, foreign affairs, housing, justice and security, legislature, social development, tax and revenue and youth affairs.[19]

This underlines the sheer complexity and political challenge of addressing NCDs, and explains why NCDs merited a UN General Assembly High-Level Meeting. NCDs cannot be addressed by the WHO, and the constituencies with which it most directly engages, alone.

Second, efforts to prevent NCDs conflict with the interests of powerful commercial operators.[20] Large and well-resourced corporations, and the interest groups that represent them, work hard to resist the adoption and implementation of measures that will affect their bottom lines. They can exert significant power, lobbying, advocating and campaigning both behind the scenes and in prominent public view, substantially increasing the political costs to governments of taking action.

Measures adopted to combat NCDs are also liable to face legal challenge by these powerful interests and their supporters, whether in domestic courts or in international fora. The lawfulness of measures adopted to promote and protect public health is being adjudicated upon in non-health fora, in which health norms, instruments and values are not the predominant considerations. In addition to the uncertainty that such challenges – or their threat (or mere possibility) – create, they can dramatically increase the implementation costs of measures that would otherwise be inexpensive.

This chapter attempts to offer some observations about the effective use of law in reducing exposure to tobacco, alcohol and unhealthy foods,[21] recognising that the effective use of law is indispensable to global NCD governance. Part 2 sets out the current political and institutional context of global NCD governance, briefly sketching its evolving architecture. Part 3 locates the challenges of global NCD governance within three of the broader themes of global health governance, namely its ever-increasing complexity and the inter-relationships between global health and foreign policy, and global health and development. Part 4 focuses on the role of law, outlining both its use as a proactive intervention and its role in setting the context in which power is exercised. It offers a number of observations relating to the important role of legal capacity within the NCD workforce, and through policy research, development and implementation; the power of treaties and of non-binding instruments; challenges involved in dealing with existing international trade and investment treaties; the need for deference to public health imperatives and governments' regulatory choices in trade and investment adjudication; and managing the similarities and differences between tobacco, alcohol and unhealthy foods within the NCD agenda. Part 5 offers some concluding thoughts. It suggests that the 'law and NCD prevention' endeavour requires speaking, listening and learning across different disciplines, which make sense of and explain the world in different ways. Interdisciplinary respect and patience are key to its success.

2 The evolving global NCD governance architecture

A substantial global NCD governance architecture is being developed to steer the global response called for by the Political Declaration. The arrangements affirm the WHO's 'leadership and coordination' role, as the 'primary specialized agency for health',[22] but the approach underlines that effectively combating NCDs is beyond the power, mandate and capacity of the WHO alone.

The key components of this evolving global NCD architecture are:

- targets and indicators to allow for monitoring and assessment of progress;
- a new WHO Global Action Plan on NCDs;
- a new UN Interagency Task Force on the Prevention and Control of NCDs; and
- a new global coordination mechanism for NCDs.

2.1 *Targets and indicators adopted by the World Health Assembly in May 2013*

The Political Declaration initiated a process that led to the adoption by the World Health Assembly – the WHO's governing body – at its May 2013 session of a 'comprehensive global monitoring framework'[23] including:

1. A set of nine voluntary targets for achievement by 2025 for the prevention and control of NCDs, including:
   a. an overarching target of a 25 per cent relative reduction in the overall mortality from cardiovascular diseases, cancer, diabetes, or chronic respiratory diseases; and
   b. targets for behavioural risk factors (harmful use of alcohol, physical inactivity, salt/sodium intake, and tobacco use).[24]
2. A set of 25 indicators that, inter alia, track the nine targets.[25]

The aim of the Global Monitoring Framework is to 'monitor trends and to assess progress made' in the implementation of national strategies and plans on NCDs.[26]

2.2 *The WHO Global Action Plan on NCDs 2013–20*

The new Global Action Plan, endorsed by the World Health Assembly at its May 2013 session, aims to 'operationalize the commitments of the Political Declaration'.[27] Its vision is '[a] world free of the avoidable burden of [NCDs]'.[28]

The Global Action Plan focuses on the four major NCDs and their four shared behavioural risk factors.[29] It 'provides a road map and a menu of policy options for all Member States and other stakeholders, to take coordinated and coherent action, at all levels, to attain the nine voluntary global targets'.[30]

2.3 *Establishment of the UN Interagency Task Force on the Prevention and Control of NCDs*

On 12 July 2013, the UN Economic and Social Council ('ECOSOC') requested the UN Secretary-General to establish the UN Interagency Task Force on the Prevention and Control of NCDs (the 'Task Force').[31] The Task Force is to be established by way of expanding the mandate of the existing United Nations Ad Hoc Interagency Task Force on Tobacco Control ('IATFTC'), established by the Secretary-General in 1999 to coordinate the tobacco control work being carried out by different UN agencies.[32] It is to be convened and led by the WHO, report to the ECOSOC through the Secretary-General and incorporate the work of the IATFTC. The new Task Force will be mandated to coordinate the activities of relevant UN funds, programs and specialised agencies and other intergovernmental organisations to support the realisation of the commitments made in the Political Declaration, in particular through the implementation of the Global Action Plan.

2.4 Establishment of a global coordination mechanism for NCDs

The Global Action Plan foreshadows the development by the WHO Secretariat, in consultation with WHO member states, of a global mechanism to coordinate the activities of the UN system and promote engagement, international cooperation and accountability among all stakeholders.[33] WHO member states have requested the WHO Director-General to develop draft terms of reference for a global coordination mechanism, aimed at facilitating engagement among member states, UN funds, programs and agencies and other international partners and non-state actors, while safeguarding the WHO and public health from undue influence by any form of real, perceived or potential conflicts of interest.[34]

3 Understanding the challenges of NCD governance within the broader context of global health governance

The challenges and opportunities facing global NCD governance are best understood within the context of those of global health governance more broadly. They touch upon larger questions and themes that underscore the ever-increasing complexity of global health governance, and the inter-relationship between global health, foreign policy and sustainable development.

3.1 The ever-increasing complexity of global health governance

Global health governance has become increasingly fragmented.[35] It is no longer seen as being solely about 'health governance' or 'governance *of* health', but as including 'governance *for* health'.[36] The WHO describes 'governance *for* health' as an advocacy and public policy function that seeks to influence governance in other sectors in ways that positively impact on human health,[37] recognising that many of the areas in which change can have a positive impact on health are those in which existing rules and regimes are managed by different international institutions.[38] This evolution in global health governance has seen it become, as David Fidler observes, 'more political and less dominated by humanitarian-focused technical experts applying the tools of science, medicine and epidemiology'.[39]

Indeed, the WHO views work on NCDs as 'illustrat[ing] the importance of governance for health'.[40] While many health conditions are influenced by governance decisions in other sectors, NCDs 'have a particularly wide and multi-layered range of interrelated social, economic and environmental determinants'.[41] These are linked to income, housing, employment, transport, agricultural and education policies, which in turn are influenced by patterns of international commerce, trade, finance, advertising, culture and communications.[42] While policy levers can be identified for these factors individually, 'orchestrating a coherent response across societies remains one of the most prominent governance challenges in global health'.[43]

3.2 *Increasing recognition of global health as a foreign policy issue*

Global health – including the NCD challenge – is now increasingly understood as interacting with the core functions of foreign policy: achieving security, creating economic wealth, supporting development in low-income countries and protecting human dignity.[44] The UN General Assembly's December 2012 resolution on global health and foreign policy welcomed the Political Declaration and acknowledged that 'many of the underlying determinants of health and risk factors of both non-communicable and communicable diseases … are associated with social and economic conditions, the improvement of which is a social and economic policy issue'.[45] The General Assembly acknowledged the need to continue to promote, establish or support and strengthen multi-sectoral national policies and plans for the prevention and control of NCDs and to take steps to implement such policies and plans.[46]

3.3 *Health and NCDs in the sustainable development agenda: now and post-2015*

The first objective of the Global Action Plan is to 'raise the priority accorded to the prevention and control of non-communicable diseases in global, regional and national agendas and internationally agreed development goals, through strengthened international cooperation and advocacy'.[47] Without the prevention and control of NCDs, health cannot be attained as a result of human development, nor can it serve as a means to achieve that development.[48] NCDs impose enormous costs on families, households, communities and economies. They contribute to inequity and have a disproportionate effect on poor people, who are more likely to be exposed to NCD risk factors and consequently bear a higher burden of disease, yet have fewer resources to deal with them.[49] The burden of NCDs is increasing fastest in low-and-middle income countries ('LMICs').[50]

It has often been noted that NCDs have been largely absent from the development agenda. This, too, is changing.[51] In the Outcome Document to the June 2012 Rio+20 UN Conference on Sustainable Development, 'The Future We Want', states recognised[52] that 'health is a precondition for and an outcome and indicator of all three dimensions of sustainable development' – economic, social and environmental – and that the goals of sustainable development 'can only be achieved in the absence of a high prevalence of debilitating communicable and non-communicable diseases'.[53] Echoing the Political Declaration, they acknowledged that 'the global burden and threat of non-communicable diseases constitutes one of the major challenges for sustainable development in the twenty-first century'[54] and committed to establish or strengthen multi-sectoral national policies for the prevention and control of NCDs.[55]

The first report of the UN System Task Team on the Post-2015 Development Agenda, *Realizing the Future We Want for All*,[56] identifies the increase in NCDs as one of the issues not adequately addressed by the Millennium Development Goals ('MDGs').[57] It includes NCDs as one of the priorities for social development.[58] NCDs were also recognised in the final report of the UN High-Level Panel convened to make recommendations on the content of a framework to replace the MDGs.[59] The report suggests 12 goals including '[e]nsuring healthy lives'.[60] Five illustrative targets are offered for this goal: ending preventable infant and under five deaths; increasing the proportion of people vaccinated; decreasing maternal mortality; ensuring universal sexual and reproductive health rights; and reducing the burden of disease from HIV/AIDS, tuberculosis, malaria, neglected tropical diseases and *priority non-communicable diseases*.[61]

Building on these developments, the Global Action Plan includes among its policy options for WHO member states the dissemination of information about the effectiveness of interventions or policies to intervene positively on linkages between NCDs and sustainable development,[62] and the integration of NCD prevention and control into national health-planning processes and broader development agendas and processes.[63] Proposed actions for international partners and the private sector include 'encouraging the continued inclusion of [NCDs] in development cooperation agendas and initiatives, internationally-agreed development goals, economic development policies, sustainable development frameworks and poverty-reduction strategies'.[64]

4 Law and NCD prevention

4.1 Law as a proactive intervention and as setting the context in which power is exercised

As the individual chapters of this book show, the law is relevant to the regulation of the NCD risk factors of tobacco, alcohol and unhealthy foods in multiple ways and at multiple levels. Its role and function can broadly be seen as falling into two categories: law as a proactive intervention to reduce exposure to NCD risk factors, and law as setting the context in which power is exercised and constraints on the exercise of that power.

4.1.1 Law as a proactive intervention to reduce exposure to NCD risk factors

In the Political Declaration, states committed to:

> [a]dvance the implementation of multisectoral, cost-effective, population-wide interventions in order to reduce the impact of the common non-communicable disease risk factors ... through the implementation of relevant international agreements and strategies, and education, *legislative, regulatory* and fiscal measures.[65]

The Global Action Plan recognises the role of regulatory measures and laws in creating supportive environments that protect physical and mental health and promote healthy behaviour.[66]

Interventions to reduce exposure to tobacco, alcohol and unhealthy food that can, or must, be implemented through the use of legislation or regulation are outlined in Table 2.1.

Table 2.1 Legal/regulatory interventions to reduce exposure to tobacco, alcohol and unhealthy food.

	Tobacco	Alcohol	Unhealthy food
Recognised in	WHO FCTC, the Political Declaration and the Global Action Plan	Political Declaration, the WHO Global Strategy to Reduce the Harmful Use of Alcohol and the Global Action Plan	Political Declaration, the WHO Global Strategy on Diet, Physical Activity and Health, the WHO set of recommendations on the marketing of foods and non-alcoholic beverages to children and the Global Action Plan

Regulatory measures	• protection of public health policies relating to tobacco control from the commercial and other vested interests of the tobacco industry
	• price and tax measures
	• protection against exposure to tobacco smoke
	• regulation of tobacco product contents and emissions
	• regulation of disclosure of information about contents and emissions
	• packaging and labelling measures, including health warnings and bans on misleading packaging
	• bans on tobacco advertising, promotion and sponsorship
	• measures to combat illicit trade in tobacco products
	• bans on sales to and by children
	• bans on the manufacture and sale of sweets, snacks, toys or any other objects in the form of tobacco products which appeal to children
	• bans on the distribution of free tobacco products
	• bans on the sale of individual cigarettes and cigarettes in small packets
	• bans or restrictions on sale through vending machines
		• regulation of the availability of alcohol including:
		  • limitations on the distribution of alcohol and the operation of alcohol outlets (including retailer licensing schemes)
		  • regulation of the number and location of outlets
		  • regulation of days and hours of retail sales
		  • regulation of modes of retail sales
		  • regulation of retail sales in certain places or during special events
		  • minimum purchase or consumption age
		  • prevention of sales to intoxicated persons
		  • seller and server liability
		  • regulation of drinking in public places or at certain functions
		• combating illicit production, sale and distribution
		• regulation of alcohol advertising, promotion and sponsorship
		• price and tax measures
			• regulation of consumer information, including product labelling
			• regulation of unhealthy food advertising, promotion and sponsorship, including in settings where children gather (including nurseries, schools, school grounds and pre-school centres, playgrounds, family and child clinics and paediatric services and during any sporting and cultural activities that are held on these premises)
			• regulation of health claims
			• regulation of salt, sugar and saturated fat content
			• replacement of trans fats with unsaturated fats
			• regulation of the provision and availability of healthy food in public institutions including schools, other educational institutions and the workplace
			• availability of fruit and vegetables and other healthy food products
			• regulation of portion size
			• regulation of energy density

4.1.2 Law as setting the context in which power is exercised and constraints on the exercise of that power

In both its domestic and international forms, law provides a framework within which power is exercised. Law confers power, and requires or supports its exercise. For example:

- constitutions conferring legislative, executive and judicial power and responsibilities on parliaments, executive governments and courts;
- legislation or regulation empowering regulatory or administrative action; and
- international instruments requiring, encouraging or supporting governments to take legislative or other action.

Law also constrains the exercise of that power. For example:

- constitutional or other domestic protections of expression (personal, political and, in some jurisdictions, commercial) or private property;
- international (including regional) instruments requiring, encouraging or supporting governments to protect expression or private property;
- distribution and/or separation of powers between different levels or branches of government (whether within individual states or through supranational arrangements);
- regulation of the processes or procedures through which law is developed or implemented; and
- regulation of the adoption and implementation of 'discriminatory' or 'trade restrictive' regulatory measures.

4.1.3 Law and NCD prevention – a complex interplay of domestic and international powers, duties and constraints

The field of 'law and NCD prevention' thus involves a complex interplay of legal powers, duties and constraints, and of relationships between national (and subnational) and international law, and between different international instruments adopted through different processes and institutions, and having different kinds of legal (and political) status. At the international level, 'law and NCD prevention' involves relationships between:

- instruments adopted or endorsed through the WHO/World Health Assembly including the *WHO Framework Convention on Tobacco Control* ('WHO FCTC'),[67] the Global Action Plan, the WHO *Global Strategy to Reduce the Harmful Use of Alcohol*,[68] the WHO *Global Strategy on Diet, Physical Activity and Health*,[69] and the WHO *Set of Recommendations on the Marketing of Foods and Non-alcoholic Beverages to Children*;[70]
- instruments adopted in other multilateral fora such as the Political Declaration, the Moscow Declaration of the First Global Ministerial

Conference on Healthy Lifestyles and Noncommunicable Disease Control[71] and the Outcome Document to the Rio+20 UN Conference on Sustainable Development;[72]

- international human rights law, particularly the right to the highest attainable standard of health enshrined in the *International Covenant on Economic, Social and Cultural Rights*;[73]
- the World Trade Organization ('WTO') agreements, including the *Agreement on Technical Barriers to Trade* ('TBT'),[74] the *Agreement on Trade-Related Aspects of Intellectual Property Rights* ('TRIPS'),[75] the *General Agreement on Tariffs and Trade* ('GATT')[76] and the *General Agreement on Trade in Services* ('GATS');[77]
- other agreements applying to the trade in goods or services and to the protection of intellectual property (whether regional, plurilateral or bilateral); and
- agreements applying to foreign investments (whether in regional, plurilateral or bilateral investment treaties, or investment chapters in trade agreements).

At the domestic level, the interplay can take very different forms in different countries, which have different laws, legal systems, procedures, traditions and values.[78] For example, domestic legal challenges to identical measures brought in different jurisdictions can engage very different substantive laws (eg the right to life, the right to health, the right to information, private property rights, freedom of expression), be resolved through very different processes and engage with evidence in very different ways.[79]

4.2 Doing 'law and NCD prevention' well

Against this background, the remainder of this part attempts to offer some observations and suggestions about how those interested in reducing the burden of NCDs might think about some of the challenges and opportunities that the use of law presents.

4.2.1 Strong legal capacity is essential to an effective NCD workforce

Strong legal capacity is an essential component of an effective NCD workforce. It is no less important today to know what the TBT Agreement is, or whether a domestic constitution protects private property rights, or what 'fair and equitable treatment' means in international investment law, than it is to know how to run an effective healthy living education program or how to estimate the economic costs of NCDs.

The Global Action Plan acknowledges the importance of legal training for NCD prevention. Its second objective addresses the need to 'strengthen institutional capacity and the workforce', and notes the value of addressing law within public health institutions.[80] But much more can be done.

Stronger interdependent collaborations between public health and legal institutions should be pursued. For example, 'law and NCD prevention' should be integrated into law school curricula, whether as a standalone subject or taught within broader health law subjects, or identified as it intersects with more specific subjects, such as constitutional law, human rights law, international trade law, international investment law and intellectual property law. Interdisciplinary research opportunities that reflect the multi-sectoral nature of the NCD challenge should be supported and pursued. Law students should be encouraged and assisted to undertake internships with health organisations that work on NCDs – something that is common in many countries for human rights education and training.

'Law and NCD prevention' raises a large number of fascinating domestic and international legal questions that will engage and stimulate legal academics and law students, offering rich opportunities for research and interdisciplinary collaboration. The NCD community needs to think systematically about how to develop the 'law and NCD prevention' workforce of today and tomorrow, both through academic institutions and the creation of stable and rewarding career paths.

4.2.2 *The need for legal expertise to be engaged across all stages of policy research, development and implementation*

The effective development, implementation and defence of laws and regulations designed to reduce exposure to NCD risk factors requires the ongoing engagement of legal expertise. The role of lawyers should not be seen as limited to legal drafting, or being called upon when a legal challenge is threatened or initiated. Rather, lawyers have a valuable role to play in all stages of policy development and implementation.

Involvement of legal expertise in the design of research can contribute to the formulation of research questions that precisely address the issues likely to be litigated in the event of a challenge, increasing the utility of the research findings in the event of such litigation. An intricate understanding of likely or possible legal challenges, and the substantive issues on which their resolution is likely to turn, can inform the drafting of legislation to enhance its potential to withstand legal challenge.

Similarly, when the implementation of measures is being monitored and evaluated, the involvement of lawyers in research design can contribute to the collection of useful and meaningful 'evidence' (in the legal sense). This is not to suggest that lawyers should dictate or vet research, but that they have important contributions to make to its design, conduct and use.

In addition, the involvement of lawyers throughout the policy process will help to foster interdisciplinary understanding and trust, which will be critical in the event that measures do need to be defended before a court or tribunal. Lawyers and public health researchers should not be learning to understand each other's languages and disciplines for the first time under the pressures of defending large-scale litigation.

4.2.3 *Contextualising the power of treaties and of non-binding instruments*

It is often pointed out that tobacco is the only NCD risk factor currently the subject of an international treaty. Doubtless, this puts tobacco on a different legal and political plane from other NCD risk factors. I have suggested elsewhere that, through its terms and the institutions and processes it has generated, the WHO FCTC has: raised the global profile of tobacco control; strengthened governments in their fight against the tobacco industry politically and legally; reinforced the view that tobacco products are not normal consumer products, contributing to the ongoing global denormalisation of the tobacco industry; catalysed the formation and deepening of transnational civil society coalitions; facilitated the sharing of experiences, expertise and capacity among and between governments and non-governmental organisations (NGOs); and brought new resources – political, financial and human – into the field.[81] This is an impressive list of achievements, and it is little wonder that commentators and advocates have called for similar framework conventions on alcohol and obesity.[82]

The relative legal and political strengths and weaknesses of treaties and 'softer' international instruments have been much discussed and debated.[83] Without question, treaties do tend to indicate a higher degree of political commitment than other kinds of instruments. This is both reflected in the decision to negotiate, adopt and then ratify treaties, and then further reinforced by these acts. This is likely to have important implications in many countries for the implementation of domestic measures to address the subject matter of an international instrument. And it is also true that in the interplay of international instruments mentioned earlier, a binding treaty is 'stronger' than other instruments.

Nevertheless, other instruments need not be seen as 'weak' or meaningless. The collective normative, political and legal weight (even if not 'legally binding') of the instruments listed earlier should be championed rather than downgraded or devalued. The propensity to downgrade or devalue these instruments may reflect a number of matters including:

- First, a tendency among some advocates to apply their experiences at domestic level – where (binding) legislation is often essential to ensure activity, and anything less is often regarded dismissively – to an international context that is not analogous.[84] Whereas corporations may often adopt measures that would be effective to reduce exposure to NCD risk factors, and that would affect their bottom lines, only when legally required to do so, or under threat of regulation, governments do not take action only where legally bound under international law to do so.
- Second, a sometimes exaggerated sense of the constraints that existing trade and investment agreements pose to the capacity of governments to regulate in the public interest, including public health.
- Third, and relatedly, a sense that these agreements are in 'conflict' with health measures and values, meaning that 'binding' instruments are needed to 'trump' them. This view may reflect in part a conflation of conflict seen at the (more superficial) level of narrative (eg trade *versus* health) with conflict in a strict legal sense. Assumption of conflict in the legal sense may understandably give rise to a perception that a 'competing' binding instrument is needed if health interests are to be asserted and respected. But if no such conflict

exists, non-binding normative instruments can be understood as having the capacity to significantly inform the way in which trade and investment treaties, with all of their flexibilities, are interpreted and applied.[85]

4.2.4 Dealing with the reality of existing trade and investment agreements

Public health advocates are becoming increasingly engaged with, and concerned about, the implications of international trade and investment treaties for NCD prevention, and, in particular, the ways in which such agreements may constrain governments' capacity to regulate NCD risk factors. This concern has been galvanised by Philip Morris Switzerland's challenge to Uruguay's tobacco packaging measures under a bilateral investment treaty between Switzerland and Uruguay,[86] Philip Morris Asia's challenge to Australia's plain tobacco packaging measures under a bilateral investment treaty between Australia and Hong Kong[87] and complaints against Australia's plain packaging measures initiated in the WTO by Ukraine, Honduras, the Dominican Republic, Cuba and Indonesia.[88] The level of concern has been heightened by the fact that Philip Morris Asia acquired its interest in Philip Morris Australia some 10 months after Australia's plain packaging measures were announced[89] – giving rise to fears about the multinational tobacco industry's ability to endlessly restructure in order to take advantage of investment treaties to bring litigation against governments – and the tobacco industry's openness about its support for the bringing of WTO complaints by states.[90] However strong the legal ground on which Uruguay and Australia stand might be, these challenges are expensive and resource-intensive to defend. The initiation of these challenges presumably has a collateral objective, namely to dissuade other governments considering the adoption of similar measures from doing so – the well-known concept of 'regulatory chill'.[91]

While public health advocates may, quite justifiably, believe that governments should not have to defend their tobacco control measures under such agreements and in such fora, a balance must be struck between efforts to change the system that allows this to happen – understanding the political and legal difficulties of doing so, particularly within the WTO's consensus decision-making processes[92] – and efforts to proceed with strong and effective measures within the existing system. A further complication is that new trade and investment agreements are being negotiated – including, most prominently at the moment, the *Trans-Pacific Partnership Agreement* ('TPP')[93] – and many advocates have legitimate concerns about how such agreements may impact on national policy space.[94] This all creates a very delicate context for advocacy.

In my view, a number of advocates campaigning against new agreements such as the TPP – either in their entirety or in relation to their potential impacts on tobacco control or public health more broadly – have advanced their concerns in ways that undermine the power of governments to act within their existing international obligations. In painting worst case scenarios of the ways in which such agreements might be interpreted and applied so as to diminish governments' capacity to regulate to protect and promote public health – including terms and concepts that are in the WTO Agreements and in many other trade and invest-ment treaties by which governments are already bound – such advocates at times say things that are strikingly similar to things the tobacco industry routinely says to governments in its efforts to dissuade them from implementing tobacco control measures. In these circumstances, regulatory chill is being contributed to by both the tobacco industry and (purported) tobacco control advocates. I put the word 'purported' in brackets here, because at times it can appear that tobacco control is used as a convenient, politically powerful 'lightning rod' issue by some who have broader complaints about international trade and investment agreements, and may not particularly care whether governments do or do not implement effective tobacco control measures. Strong views about the constraints that trade and investment agreements purportedly impose on tobacco control are at times offered in analyses that appear to diminish the WHO FCTC and show very little awareness of, or regard for, the contents of the treaty, its guidelines or other critical decisions of its Conference of the Parties ('COP').

In contrast, the approach taken with respect to the relationship between the WHO FCTC and WTO agreements by the WHO FCTC's COP and by the WHO has reflected a belief that the WTO agreements do not represent a threat to WHO FCTC implementation. At its 2010 and 2012 sessions, the COP adopted decisions promoting cooperation between the Convention Secretariat and the WTO[95] and between the Convention Secretariat, the WHO, the WTO and the United Nations Conference on Trade and Development.[96] The 2012 *Ad Hoc Interagency Task Force on Tobacco Control Report* stated that: 'It should be clarified at global trade forums that World Trade Organization agreements and implementa-tion of the Convention are not incompatible so long as the Convention is imple-mented in a non-discriminatory fashion and for reasons of public health'.[97] The former Director-General of the WTO, Pascal Lamy, also explained that WTO rules and the implementation of the WHO FCTC are not incompatible.[98]

It is, however, important to distinguish between the WTO agreements and other international agreements regulating international trade or investment, and particularly the large number of bilateral investment treaties into which states have entered.[99] A WHO report prepared for the fifth session of the WHO FCTC's Conference of the Parties in relation to cooperation with the WTO on trade-related tobacco-control issues evinces a different view of the latter, noting that '[i]nternational investment agreements are of particular concern in the context of challenges being made to the tobacco-control measures of Parties'.[100] Unlike WTO dispute settlement, which is state-to-state, many international investment agreements allow challenges to be brought directly by foreign investors against states. In addition, dispute settlement under international investment agreements takes place through ad hoc tribunals that are not part of a unified system, where no unified substantive law is applied, cases are conducted in a less transparent manner than is ordinarily applied in domestic litigation and tribunal decisions are not generally subject to appeal. This makes for an uncertain system, and these uncertainties can be, and are, exaggerated and exploited by those who have an interest in persuading governments that they are unable to act.

The point here is not that public health advocates should be unconcerned with existing trade and investment agreements, or the negotiation of new ones. I share the view that governments should not be forced to defend bona fide public health measures before international trade and investment tribunals, with all of the political, financial and resource implications of having to do so, and all of the incentives for industry to threaten legal action as a way of dissuading governments from regulating, and to bring such legal action, however spurious a claim might be. However, advocates have a responsibility to engage in a nuanced and sophisticated way, understanding that the things they say in one forum – where their intention is to portray the constraints of trade and investment agreements as crippling – may prove highly damaging in others.

4.2.5 *The need for respect, sensitivity and deference in trade and investment adjudication*

Generally speaking, international trade and investment treaties do, in my view, afford significant space to states to regulate in the public interest in general, and for the protection and promotion of public health in particular. Nevertheless, decisions ultimately fall to be made in particular cases by individual panels and tribunals, composed of individuals who tend not to have great experience of, or knowledge about, public health imperatives, values and approaches to the collection, understanding and use of evidence in policy-making, implementation and evaluation. It is unrealistic to expect trade and investment panelists and tribunal members to become overnight public health experts, but it is perfectly reasonable to expect them both to appreciate the limitations of their own expertise and to show an appropriate degree of deference to public health imperatives, values and approaches and to governments' regulatory choices.[101]

Three areas in which such deference can (and should) be exhibited are: engagement with scientific evidence, articulation of the objective or objectives against which challenged measures should be assessed and the standards of 'proof' or 'persuasion' applied to governments' explanations or justification of their challenged measures. As Andrew Higgins, Andrew Mitchell and James Munro argue,[102] the WTO's Appellate Body has tended to show considerable deference in all three respects. For example, it has:

- recognised that there may be a degree of uncertainty regarding scientific evidence.[103] In *Canada – Continued Suspension*, it held that, in seeking to justify a measure as 'necessary to protect human health', a Member may rely 'on scientific sources which … may represent a divergent, but qualified and respected, opinion';[104]
- recognised that gaps in scientific knowledge are inevitable, and that such gaps do not necessarily render available knowledge insufficient;[105]
- held that a given measure need only contribute to the achievement of the objective at issue, rather than comprehensively achieve the objective, in order to satisfy the 'necessity' test. WTO jurisprudence acknowledges that certain complex public health and environmental problems require 'a comprehensive

policy comprising a multiplicity of interacting measures', individual elements of which cannot be examined in isolation from one another;[106]

- permitted the use of quantitative projections or qualitative reasoning to demonstrate that a measure is 'apt to produce a material contribution to the achievement of its objective'.[107] Such evidence can be relied on in lieu of evidence of 'actual contribution' to the objective; and
- held that results obtained from certain actions, including certain preventive actions to reduce the incidence of diseases that may manifest themselves only after a certain period of time, can be evaluated only with the benefit of time.[108]

If public health measures generally, and NCD prevention measures in particular, are to be challenged under trade and investment treaties, it is essential that panels and tribunals exhibit this kind of respect, sensitivity and deference. Indeed, international legal challenges to measures implemented by governments to reduce exposure to NCD risk factors represent one of the key coalfaces of the multi-sectoral nature of NCD governance (and global health governance more broadly), at which cross-sectoral policy coherence must be realised. Trade and investment panels should be expected to view their exercise of power within the political and legal context of the increasingly urgent global efforts to combat NCDs.

4.2.6 *Managing the similarities and differences between tobacco, alcohol and unhealthy foods within the NCD agenda*

The bundling together of tobacco, alcohol and unhealthy foods into a single global NCD prevention agenda makes a good deal of conceptual and governance sense. Much can be learned across the three different risk factors, and a number of common and overlapping challenges (and opportunities) arise in addressing them. At the global level in particular, health governance needs to be broken down into a limited number of agendas and processes if it is to remain manageable.

Yet this bundling does not always make for a comfortable fit. For all of their commonalities, each product category (not to mention sub-category) is different, causes different kinds and degrees of harm and is used in different ways and for different reasons. They cannot be treated in an identical fashion. In addition, at the domestic level, tobacco, alcohol and unhealthy foods may not be grouped together within an NCD governance framework. For example, tobacco and alcohol may be regulated within the context of a drug strategy that includes both licit and illicit drugs (and not unhealthy foods).

These tensions can play out in a number of ways. Some tobacco control advocates view the NCD agenda as (at least partially) a threat to progress in tobacco control, by diluting the uniqueness of tobacco, diffusing the political attention it currently receives and weakening the power of the WHO FCTC by grouping tobacco with other risk factors within more nebulous governance arrangements than exist for the treaty. Advocates for progress in combating other risk factors may wish for stronger governance for these risk factors at global and domestic levels, expressing frustration at the unique treatment that tobacco receives, and at the continued indulgence of the unhealthy food and alcohol industries compared to the tobacco industry. The tobacco industry, in its resistance to the introduction of stronger tobacco control measures such as plain tobacco packaging, uses 'thin end of the wedge' scaremongering – 'tobacco today, alcohol tomorrow, fast food the day after'.[109]

It is clear that tobacco and the tobacco industry are regarded, and treated, very differently from alcohol and unhealthy food. Most obviously, tobacco has its own treaty. Echoing art 5.3 of the WHO FCTC and its implementation guidelines,[110] the Political Declaration '[r]ecognize[s] the fundamental conflict of interest between the tobacco industry and public health'.[111] Concerns about the role of, and engagement with, other industries finds expression only through the inclusion of the words 'where appropriate' and 'as appropriate' in conjunction with references to the role of the 'private sector'.[112] The difference in approach is also reflected in the Global Action Plan. While one of its overarching principles and approaches is '[m]anagement of real, perceived or potential conflicts of interest',[113] the tobacco industry is singled out, with 'non-State actors' to be engaged being defined to 'include academia and relevant nongovernmental organizations, as well as selected private sector entities as appropriate, *excluding the tobacco industry*'.[114]

If NCD governance is to work effectively, it will need to be able to capture all of the risk factors within a single sensible and manageable framework, allowing for necessary streamlining in governance and the learning of lessons across the risk factors, while concurrently allowing each to be treated on its health, political and legal merits. This will require civil society organisations with mandates that focus on only one risk factor to be conscious of the way in which their policy and advocacy work might affect progress on other risk factors. For example, might efforts to respond to the risks that trade and investment agreements under negotiation pose to tobacco control solely by advocating that tobacco should be treated differently from all other products[115] have adverse implications for the treatment of other risk factors? Might differential treatment of tobacco legally or politically weaken, even to some small degree, the general exceptions available to governments to defend other measures, by suggesting that these exceptions do not give governments sufficient room to regulate for the protection and promotion of public health?[116] The problems for global health governance arising from foreign investors being able to sue governments under investment agreements over public health measures are much broader than tobacco, and would ideally be addressed at that broader level. While tobacco should be treated differently from other products as a matter of regulatory *choice*, governments should have no less regulatory *autonomy* to deal with these other products. On the other side of the coin, those who work on other risk factors will need to respect what is different about tobacco, and what is unique and powerful about the global governance of tobacco, as enshrined in the WHO FCTC.

The new UN Interagency Task Force on the Prevention and Control of NCDs may well be a test of this challenge. The work of the Task Force, being established by way of expanding the mandate of the Ad Hoc Interagency Task Force on Tobacco Control, must enhance global coordination of activities on tobacco control, and uphold and strengthen the power of the WHO FCTC, rather than dilute or undermine them. The World Health Assembly acknowledged this, recognising the need to 'ensur[e] that tobacco control continues to be duly addressed and prioritized in the new task force mandate'.[117]

5 Conclusion

The conception of this book recognises that the effective use and understanding of law, both domestic and international, are critical to making progress in combating NCDs. While the effective use of law is essential to global health governance generally, as this chapter has argued, it is particularly so in the case of NCDs. NCDs cannot be combated solely as a health issue, through the health sector. Efforts to prevent NCDs represent a threat to the commercial interests of powerful industries, meaning that measures adopted by governments are liable to face legal challenges (or threats of such challenges) in both domestic and international fora.

The field of 'law and NCD prevention' is rapidly developing. At its heart lies the challenge of speaking, listening and learning across different disciplines, each with its own language, values, concerns, priorities, institutions and ways of managing conflict and uncertainty.

Key to the success of the 'law and NCD prevention' endeavour is interdisciplinary respect and patience. Lawyers need to understand the limitations of their expertise and training, and be respectful of the way other disciplines make sense of and explain the world. Lawyers need to learn how to understand and value the way in which evidence is generated by other disciplines, and treat that evidence with respect in legal fora.[118] Lawyers need to do their best to demystify the law, complex as it undoubtedly can be. At the same time, other disciplines need to accept that many critical policy issues cannot be resolved at the level of theme or narrative or value, but only through detailed, technical legal analysis. Lawyers are often criticised for refusing to give straight 'yes' or 'no' answers to questions, preferring to qualify their responses. In their defence, this does not necessarily reflect an unwillingness to take a position, but rather a sense that questions are often asked at a level of generality that does not lend itself to a meaningful legal answer.

In the complex web of domestic and international law described in this chapter, questions about *what* governments can do, and *how* they can do it, often fall to be answered in highly specific circumstances. If we are going to answer these questions in a way that advances our collective efforts to reduce the burden of NCDs, and encourages others to do so, we are going to have to answer them collectively. This is not an easy undertaking, but it is essential, and it can be immensely rewarding, both intellectually and, more importantly, in health outcomes ultimately achieved.

Notes

* My thanks to Caroline Henckels, Alexandra Jones, Laura Perriam, Tania Voon and Devon Whittle for very helpful comments, suggestions and editorial assistance.
1 World Health Assembly, *Global Action Plan for the Prevention and Control of Noncommunicable Diseases 2013–2020, Follow-up to the Political Declaration of the High-Level Meeting of the General Assembly on the Prevention and Control of Non-communicable Diseases*, WHA Res WHA66.10, 66th sess, 9th plen mtg, Agenda Items 13.1 and 13.2, WHO Doc A66/VR/9 (27 May 2013) annex ('Global Action Plan') [2].
2 Ibid.
3 Ibid.
4 Ibid [12].
5 World Health Organization and World Economic Forum, *From Burden to 'Best Buys': Reducing the Economic Impact of Non-Communicable Diseases in Low- and Middle-Income Countries* (2011) <http://www.who.int/nmh/publications/best_buys_summary.pdf>.
6 Ibid.
7 Global Action Plan [12].
8 Ibid.
9 *Political Declaration of the High-level Meeting of the General Assembly on the Prevention and Control of Non-communicable Diseases*, GA Res 66/2, UN GAOR, 66th sess, 3rd plen mtg, Agenda Item 117, UN Doc A/RES/66/2 (24 January 2012, adopted 19 September 2011) annex ('Political Declaration').
10 Ibid [34].
11 Ibid [20].
12 Ibid [35].
13 Dr Margaret Chan, Director-General of the World Health Organization, 'Opening Address' (Speech delivered at the 8th Global Conference on Health Promotion, Helsinki, Finland, 10 June 2013) <http://www.who.int/dg/speeches/2013/health_promotion_20130610/en/index.html>.
14 Ibid.
15 Rob Moodie et al, 'Profits and Pandemics: Prevention of Harmful Effects of Tobacco, Alcohol, and Ultra-processed Food and Drink Industries' (2013) 381 *The Lancet* 670, 670.
16 Ibid 671.
17 Political Declaration [33].
18 Ibid [36].
19 Global Action Plan [18].
20 Dr Margaret Chan, Director-General of the World Health Organization, *Opening Address* (Speech delivered at the 8th Global Conference on Health Promotion, Helsinki, Finland, 10 June 2013) <http://www.who.int/dg/speeches/2013/health_promotion_20130610/en/index.html>.
21 While law also has an important role to play in promoting physical activity, this book focuses on tobacco, alcohol and unhealthy foods.
22 Political Declaration [13], [51]; see also World Health Assembly, *Follow-up to the Political Declaration of the High-Level Meeting of the General Assembly on the Prevention and Control of Non-communicable Diseases*, WHA Res WHA66.10, 66th sess, 9th plen mtg, Agenda Items 13.1 and 13.2 (27 May 2013) ('*Follow-up to the Political Declaration*') 2.
23 *Follow-up to the Political Declaration* preamble.
24 See Global Action Plan [36], [37], [40], [42]. The framework also includes targets for biological risk factors (raised blood pressure, and diabetes and obesity), and national system responses (drug therapy to prevent heart attacks and strokes, and essential NCD disease medicines and basic technologies to treat major NCDs).
25 *Follow-up to the Political Declaration* [1(2)].

26   Ibid.

27   Global Action Plan [3].

28   Ibid [16].

29   Ibid [6], though it recognises that there are many other conditions of public health importance that are closely associated with the four major NCDs.

30   Global Action Plan [5].

31   *United Nations Interagency Task Force on the Prevention and Control of Non-communicable Diseases*, ESC Res 2013/L.23, Agenda Item 7(g), UN Doc E/2013/L.23 (12 July 2013).

32   See World Health Organization, *United Nations Ad Hoc Interagency Task Force on Tobacco Control* <http://www.who.int/tobacco/about/partners/un_taskforce/en/>.

33   Global Action Plan [14].

34   *Follow-up to the Political Declaration* [3(2)].

35   Jonathan Liberman and Andrew Mitchell, 'In Search of Coherence Between Trade and Health: Inter-Institutional Opportunities' (2010) 25 *Maryland Journal of International Law* 143, 153–5. See also Jonathan Liberman, 'Combating Counterfeit Medicines and Illicit Trade in Tobacco Products: Minefields in Global Health Governance' (2012) 40 *Journal of Law, Medicine & Ethics* 326, 326–8; Allyn Taylor, 'Governing the Globalization of Public Health' (2004) 32 *Journal of Law, Medicine & Ethics* 500; Lawrence Gostin and Allyn Taylor, 'Global Health Law: A Definition and Grand Challenges' (2008) 1 *Public Health Ethics* 53.

36   World Health Organization, *WHO's Role in Global Health Governance*, Executive Board, 132nd sess, Provisional Agenda Item 5, WHO Doc EB132/5 Add 5 (18 January 2013) [5] ('*WHO's Role in Global Health Governance*').

37   Ibid [15].

38   Ibid [22].

39   David Fidler, 'The Challenges of Global Health Governance' (Working Paper, Council on Foreign Relations, International Institutions and Global Governance Program, May 2010) 6.

40   *WHO's Role in Global Health Governance*, WHO Doc EB132/5 Add 5 [15].

41   Ibid.

42   Ibid.

43   Ibid.

44   *Global Health and Foreign Policy: Strategic Opportunities and Challenges: Note by the Secretary-General*, General Assembly 54th sess, Agenda Item 123, UN Doc A.64.365 (23 September 2009). See also Fidler, above n 39, 5.

45   *Global Health and Foreign Policy*, GA Res 67/81, UN GAOR, 67th sess, 53rd plen mtg, Agenda Item 123, UN DOC A/RES/67/81* (14 March 2013, adopted 12 December 2012).

46   Ibid.

47   Global Action Plan, objective 1.

48   George Alleyne et al, 'Embedding Non-communicable Diseases in the Post-2015 Development Agenda' (2013) *The Lancet Non-Communicable Diseases Series* 4, 7.

49   Ibid 10–12.

50   World Health Organization, *Global Status Report on Noncommunicable Diseases 2010* (World Health Organization, 2011) <http://www.who.int/nmh/publications/ncd_report_full_en.pdf>.

51   Helen Clark, 'NCDs: A Challenge to Sustainable Human Development' (2013) *The Lancet Non-Communicable Diseases Series* 4, 2.

52   *The Future We Want*, GA Res 66/288, UN GAOR, 66th sess, 123rd plen mtg, Agenda Item 19, UN Doc A/RES/66/288* (11 September 2012, adopted 27 July 2012) annex.

53   Ibid [138].

54   Ibid [141].

55 Ibid.
56 UN System Task Team, *Realizing the Future We Want for All: Report to the Secretary General* (2012)   <http://www.un.org/en/development/desa/policy/untaskteam_undf/report.shtml>
57 Ibid [19].
58 Ibid [67].
59 United Nations, *A New Global Partnership: Eradicate Poverty and Transform Economies Through Sustainable Development: The Report of the High-Level Panel of Eminent Persons on the Post-2015 Development Agenda* <http://www.un.org/sg/management/beyond2015.shtml>.
60 Ibid.
61 Ibid.
62 Global Action Plan [21(a)].
63 Ibid [21(b)].
64 Ibid [23(a)]. Note that the need for integration into the development agenda and its programs has been recognised for some time in respect of tobacco control: see, eg, WHO FCTC Conference of the Parties, *FCTC/COP4(17) Financial Resources, Mechanisms of Assistance and International Cooperation*, WHO Doc FCTC/COP/4/DIV/6, 4th sess, 10th plen mtg (6 December 2010, adopted 20 November 2010).
65 Political Declaration [43] (emphasis added).
66 Global Action Plan [34].
67 *WHO Framework Convention on Tobacco Control*, opened for signature 21 May 2003, 2302 UNTS 116 (entered into force 27 February 2005) ('WHO FCTC').
68 World Health Assembly, *Global Strategy to Reduce the Harmful Use of Alcohol*, WHA Res 63.13, 63rd sess, 8th plen mtg, WHO Doc WHA63/2010/REC/1 (21 May 2010).
69 World Health Assembly, *Global Strategy on Diet, Physical Activity and Health: Report by the Secretariat*, WHA Res 57.17, 57th sess, 8th plen mtg, WHO Doc A57/2004/REC/1 (22 May 2004).
70 World Health Organization, *Set of Recommendations on the Marketing of Foods and Non-alcoholic Beverages to Children* (World Health Organization, 2010).
71 World Health Organization, *First Global Ministerial Conference on Healthy Lifestyles and Noncommunicable Disease Control: Moscow Declaration* (28–29 April 2011) <http://www.who.int/nmh/events/moscow_ncds_2011/conference_documents/en/>.
72 *The Future We Want*, GA Res 66/288, UN GAOR, 66th sess, 123rd plen mtg, Agenda Item 19, UN Doc A/RES/66/288* (11 September 2012, adopted 27 July 2012) annex.
73 *International Covenant on Economic, Social and Cultural Rights*, opened for signature 16 December 1966, 993 UNTS 3 (entered into force 3 January 1976).
74 *Marrakesh Agreement Establishing the World Trade Organization*, opened for signature 15 April 1994, 1867 UNTS 3 (entered into force 1 January 1995) annex 1A ('Agreement on Technical Barriers to Trade') ('TBT Agreement').
75 *Marrakesh Agreement Establishing the World Trade Organization*, opened for signature 15 April 1994, 1867 UNTS 3 (entered into force 1 January 1995) annex 1C ('Agreement on Trade-Related Aspects of Intellectual Property Rights') ('TRIPS Agreement').
76 *Marrakesh Agreement Establishing the World Trade Organization*, opened for signature 15 April 1994, 1867 UNTS 3 (entered into force 1 January 1995) annex 1A ('General Agreement on Tariffs and Trade') ('GATT').
77 *Marrakesh Agreement Establishing the World Trade Organization*, opened for signature 15 April 1994, 1869 UNTS 183 (entered into force 1 January 1995) annex 1B ('General Agreement on Trade in Services') ('GATS').
78 Jonathan Liberman, 'Plainly Constitutional: The Upholding of Plain Tobacco Packaging by the High Court of Australia' (2013) 39 *American Journal of Law & Medicine* 361, 381.

79 Ibid.
80 Global Action Plan [30(h)].
81 Jonathan Liberman, 'Four COPs and Counting: Achievements, Underachievements and Looming Challenges in the Early Life of the WHO FCTC Conference of the Parties' (2012) 21 *Tobacco Control* 215.
82 See, eg, Robin Room et al, 'International Regulation of Alcohol' (2008) *British Medical Journal* 337; The Lancet, 'A Framework Convention on Alcohol Control' (2007) 370 *The Lancet* 1102; Sally Casswell, 'Current Status of Alcohol Marketing Policy – an Urgent Challenge for Global Governance' (2012) 107 *Addiction* 478; The Lancet, 'Urgently Needed: A Framework Convention for Obesity Control' (2011) 378 *The Lancet* 741.
83 See, eg, Allyn Taylor and Ibadat Dhillon, 'An International Legal Strategy for Alcohol Control: Not a Framework Convention – at Least Not Yet' (2013) 108 *Addiction* 450; Jonathan Liberman, 'Alternative Legal Strategies for Alcohol Control: Not a Framework Convention – at Least Not Right Now' (2013) 108 *Addiction* 456; Steven Hoffman and John-Arne Røttingen, 'Dark Sides of the Proposed Framework Convention on Global Health's Many Virtues: A Systematic Review and Critical Analysis' (2013) 15(1) *Health & Human Rights Journal* 117.
84 Jonathan Liberman, 'Alternative Legal Strategies for Alcohol Control', above n 83.
85 However, if advocates are looking for 'binding' instruments to introduce into the interplay, international human rights law seems to me to have been somewhat neglected. The 160 parties to the *International Covenant on Economic, Social and Cultural Rights* (opened for signature 16 December 1966, 993 UNTS 3 (entered into force 3 January 1976)) 'recognize the right of everyone to the enjoyment of the highest attainable standard of physical and mental health': art 12.1. This is one of the rights in relation to which states agree 'to take steps, individually and through international assistance and co-operation, especially economic and technical, to the maximum of [their] available resources' to progressively achieve the full realisation, 'by all appropriate means, including particularly the adoption of legislative measures': art 2. Under art 12.2, steps to be taken include 'those necessary for … [t]he prevention … of epidemic, endemic, occupational and other diseases'. See also Chapter 4 of this volume.
86 *Philip Morris Brand Sàrl v Uruguay (Decision on Jurisdiction)* (ICSID Arbitral Tribunal, Case No ARB/10/7, 2 July 2013).
87 *Philip Morris Asia Ltd v Australia (Procedural Order)* (Permanent Court of Arbitration, Case No 2012-12, 31 December 2012).
88 *Australia – Certain Measures Concerning Trademarks and Other Plain Packaging Requirements Applicable to Tobacco Products and Packaging*, WTO Doc WT/DS434/11 (17 August 2012) (Request for the Establishment of a Panel by Ukraine); *Australia – Certain Measures Concerning Trademarks, Geographical Indications and Other Plain Packaging Requirements Applicable to Tobacco Products and Packaging*, WTO Doc WT/DS435/16 (17 October 2012) (Request for the Establishment of a Panel by Honduras); *Australia – Certain Measures Concerning Trademarks, Geographical Indications and Other Plain Packaging Requirements Applicable to Tobacco Products and Packaging*, WTO Doc WT/DS441/15 (9 November 2012) (Request for the Establishment of a Panel by Dominican Republic); *Australia – Certain Measures Concerning Trademarks, Geographical Indications and Other Plain Packaging Requirements Applicable to Tobacco Products and Packaging*, WTO Doc WT/DS458/1 (7 May 2013) (Request for Consultations by Cuba); *Australia – Certain Measures Concerning Trademarks, Geographical Indications and Other Plain Packaging Requirements Applicable to Tobacco Products and Packaging*, WTO Doc WT/DS467/1 (25 September 2013) (Request for Consultations by Indonesia).
89 *Philip Morris Asia Ltd v Australia*, Australia's Response to the Notice of Arbitration, 21 December 2011 [30].

90   Christopher Thompson, 'Big Tobacco Backs Australian Law Opposers', *Financial Times*, 29 April 2012; Andrew Martin, 'Philip Morris Leads Plain Packs Battle in Global Trade Arena', *Bloomberg*, 22 August 2013.

91   Liberman and Mitchell, above n 35, 165–6.

92   *Marrakesh Agreement Establishing the World Trade Organization*, opened for signature 15 April 1994, 1867 UNTS 3 (entered into force 1 January 1995) art IX:1.

93   See Department of Foreign Affairs and Trade, *Trans-Pacific Partnership Agreement Negotiations* <http://www.dfat.gov.au/fta/tpp/>.

94   See, eg, Gary Fooks and Anna Gilmore, 'International Trade Law, Plain Packaging and Tobacco Industry Political Activity: The Trans-Pacific Partnership' (2013) *Tobacco   Control*   <http://tobaccocontrol.bmj.com/content/early/2013/06/19/tobaccocontrol-2012-050869.full>.

95   WHO FCTC Conference of the Parties, *FCTC/COP4(18) Cooperation between the Convention Secretariat and the World Trade Organization*, 4th sess, 10th plen mtg, WHO Doc FCTC/COP/4/DIV/6 (6 December 2010, adopted 20 November 2010).

96   WHO FCTC Conference of the Parties, *FCTC/COP5(15) Cooperation between the Convention Secretariat, the World Health Organization, the World Trade Organization and the United Nations Conference on Trade and Development*, 5th sess, 4th plen mtg WHO Doc FCTC/COP5(15) (17 November 2012).

97   *Ad Hoc Inter-Agency Task Force on Tobacco Control Report of the Secretary-General*, Prov Agenda Item 7(g), UN Doc E/2012/70 (9 May 2012) [58].

98   WHO Framework Convention on Tobacco Control, *WTO Rules and the Implementation of the WHO FCTC are not Incompatible* (2011) <http://www.who.int/fctc/wto_fctc/en/>.

99   United Nations Conference on Trade and Development, *World Investment Report 2012: Towards a New Generation of Investment Policies* (2012).

100 World Health Organization, *FCTC/COP5(18) Cooperation with the World Trade Organization on Trade-related Tobacco-control Issues – Report by the WHO Secretariat*, 5th sess, WHO Doc FCTC/COP/5/18 (20 September 2012) [10].

101 Caroline Henckels, 'Balancing Investment Protection and the Public Interest: The Role of the Standard of Review and the Importance of Deference in Investor-State Arbitration' (2013) 4 *Journal of International Dispute Settlement* 197.

102 Andrew Higgins, Andrew Mitchell and James Munro, 'Australia's Plain Packaging of Tobacco Products: Science and Health Measures in International Economic Law' in Bryan Mercurio and Kuei-Jung Ni (eds), *Science and Technology in International Economic Law: Balancing Competing Interests* (Routledge, 2013), draft available at <http://ssrn.com/abstract=2280071>.

103 Ibid 8.

104 Appellate Body Report, *Canada – Continued Suspension of Obligations in the EC – Hormones Dispute*, WTO Doc WT/DS321/AB/R (adopted 14 November 2008) [529].

105 Higgins, Mitchell and Munro, above n 102, 5.

106 Ibid 6; Appellate Body Report, *Brazil – Measures Affecting Imports of Retreaded Tyres*, WTO Doc WT/DS332/AB/R (adopted 17 December 2007) [151].

107 Ibid.

108 Appellate Body Report, *Brazil – Measures Affecting Imports of Retreaded Tyres*, WTO Doc WT/DS332/AB/R (adopted 17 December 2007) [151].

109 British American Tobacco Australia's campaign against plain tobacco packaging included an advertisement with the caption 'What company would stand for this?' depicting a can of cola, and an advertisement about compensation for the taking of intellectual property rights depicting a bottle of beer.

110 WHO FCTC Conference of the Parties, *Guidelines for Implementation of Article 5.3 of the WHO Framework Convention on Tobacco Control*, WHO Doc FCTC/COP3(7) (22 November 2008).

111 Political Declaration [38]. Though note that the art 5.3 guidelines refer to 'funda-mental *and irreconcilable* conflict between the tobacco industry's interests and public health policy interests', see World Health Organization, *WHO Framework Convention on Tobacco Control: Guidelines for Implementation* (2011) 5 (emphasis added).

112 Political Declaration [37], [44], [45(i)], [54].

113 Global Action Plan [18].

114 Ibid [15] nn 3, [33] nn 1 (emphasis added).

115 See, eg, Robert Stumberg, 'Safeguards for Tobacco Control: Options for the TPPA' (2013) 39 *American Journal of Law & Medicine* 382.

116 See, eg, Jamie Strawbridge, 'Cigarettes, TPP and the Wisdom of Product-Specific Rules in Trade Deals' (2012) 5 *Transnational Dispute Management* <http://www.trans-national-dispute-management.com/article.asp?key=1873>.

117 *Follow-up to the Political Declaration* [2(8)].

118 Jonathan Liberman, 'On the Balance of Probabilities' on World Cancer Research Fund International, *Cancer Prevention Research & Policy Blog* (10 April 2013) <http://www.wcrf.org/blog/on-the-balance-of-probabilities>.

3 Researchers and Research Knowledge in Evidence-Informed Policy Innovation

Evan Anderson and Scott Burris

1 Introduction

Law has played an indispensable role in public health's successes over the last hundred years, and remains one of the most potent and popular levers for increasing the quality and length of life.[1] The important role of policy is well-recognised in the worldwide effort to reduce the burden of non-communicable disease ('NCD').[2] There are certainly legal interventions of proven effectiveness, such as tobacco excise taxes and smoke-free-air laws.[3] Efforts to legislatively address causally complex phenomena such as cardiovascular disease, cancer, chronic respiratory diseases and diabetes will inevitably also require innovation – new legal interventions that have not been previously tried. When deployed effectively, law promotes healthy behaviour and reduces exposure to harmful products and environments. Like other health interventions, however, promising public health laws can turn out to be ineffective or even harmful. In the long run, research names the winners and losers, so a preference for 'evidence-based' interventions makes as much sense in law as it does in other domains of public health.[4] Research synthesis, research translation and a vigorous practice of public health law research are all crucial to inform the refinement (and, sometimes, the retirement) of policy.[5]

In the second part of this chapter, we describe the primary contemporary strategies researchers and research institutions use for getting evidence into policy: (i) developing tools for credibly synthesising evidence as it accumulates; and (ii) adopting the individual and institutional research practices that best promote the timely translation of research evidence into actionable, salient and available knowledge for policy actors. Both strategies seem to be effective in increasing the uptake of evidence in areas where the evidence base is reasonably thick. Recently we have also seen progress in developing evidence synthesis and impact assessment strategies designed for emerging policies not yet assessed by a body of strong evidence.

While this work is essential to disseminating interventions of established effectiveness (or at least promise and feasibility), policy-makers and public health advocates facing new problems with new legal interventions are, by definition, working without directly evidence-tested options. This early stage of the policy cycle is too often neglected in the conversation about evidence-based policy.

In the third part, we use an example from our United States ('US') experience (and perspective) to discuss how evidence about the problem law-makers are addressing, combined with widely used analytic tools and an understanding of the generic mechanisms through which law influences behaviour and outcomes, can bring existing research knowledge into the crafting of even very innovative legal interventions for newly perceived problems. By participating in policy innovation, researchers have an opportunity to help advocates devise better policy proposals and law-makers identify more and better options for action.

2 Evidence tools and translation in public health policy

2.1 The policy learning process

In response to growing awareness of the toll of motor vehicle crashes on children, every state in the US adopted a law between 1978 and 1986 requiring at least some child passengers be restrained in safety devices.[6] There was wide political and social recognition of a problem, but no widely shared sense of exactly which children needed to be protected, how to protect them or how stringent the rules should be. The first generation of laws varied considerably across a number of dimensions including the age, height and weight of children subject to the law, whether the law was enforceable as a primary or secondary offence and the amount and type of penalty for violations.[7] It was clear almost immediately that many of these laws had struck a less than optimal balance.[8]

Variation like this is common in the formative stages of policy. The meaning and intensity of concern about emerging problems often differ across juris-dictions. These and other factors (different leaders, different levels of industry influence, different legislative processes)[9] determine how great an intrusion into current practice is politically feasible. The fact that an intervention is labelled 'public health' does not mean that it poses no trade-offs or value judgements upon which people may reasonably differ. Variation in policy can be frustrat-ing and confusing for public health practitioners, but it has benefits for policy learning: variants represent natural experiments, observing which researchers are often able to identify the effects of different policy choices. The work of states as fertile 'laborator[ies]' for 'try[ing] novel social and economic experiments'[10] remains indispensable to an 'experimenting society' capable of dealing with complex emerging problems.[11]

Evidence helped move states to act on child motor vehicle injury, even if imper-fectly. A longer view observes evidence guiding initially diverse policies towards a more effective form. Evaluations of child restraint laws began immediately after their adoption in the early 1980s. The first results were single-state pre-post evaluations,[12] showing that legal action was saving lives. Following quickly there-after, evaluators designed more sophisticated studies incorporating comparisons not only over time, but across states with and without similar laws,[13] a technique capable of providing much stronger inferences about the true effect of the laws.[14] By the end of the 1980s, the evidence supporting the general effectiveness of child restraint laws was clear and the impetus in policy-making and research shifted towards identifying the most effective variations. In ensuing decades, researchers explored the effectiveness of requiring the use of different safety devices, the placement and location of children and enforcement procedures (eg, primary versus secondary). As the evidence base evolved, so too did state policies; since their initial adoption, US states have amended their child restraint laws an average of six times to bring them into line with current evidence (see Figure 3.1).[15]

In reasonably effective regulatory systems, this policy learning process occurs constantly. Evidence informs the dissemination and refinement of effective policies and the repeal of unsuccessful ones. While a particular study rarely produces immediate policy results, accumulating evidence seeps into the policy process through a number of information channels, including advocacy, legislative staff work, expert testimony and the media – all providing a backdrop of information that influences policy.[16] One need only consider the dramatic increases in the safety of motor vehicles, consumer products, workplaces and other frequent targets of regulation to understand the value of the policy learning dynamic.[17] Of course, the process does not always work perfectly and seldom works quickly. Most importantly, it does not work automatically. Happy stories like that of child restraints are the products of hard political work and the social investment in research and advocacy.

Speeding the adoption of the most effective policy models is a high stakes game for public health, in which the costs of delay can be measured in preventable death, injury and expenditure. The reasons for the lag between evidence and action have been explored in a rich and still-growing literature. Policy-makers face a 'glut' of information[18] and almost always lack the time, resources, and expertise to make sense of it.[19] It is not just the daunting amount of information that matters, but also how it is produced and received. Significant differences in culture, training and experience between researchers and policy-makers often hinder the effective creation and exchange of information.[20] Researchers in a scientific culture and policy-makers in a political culture think differently, on different timelines, shaped by different constituencies and priorities.[21] The size of the gap is reflected in the fact that those who specialise in bridging it no longer speak of 'communication', but of 'translation'.

The effort in public health to speed the uptake of evidence in policy has followed two main strategies. The first is the development of tools (and sponsoring institutions) for credibly synthesising evidence as it accumulates. The second is the study and adoption of individual and institutional practices aimed at strengthening the relationship between researchers and policy-makers. We address each strategy in turn below.

2.2 *Synthesis tools*

For a given intervention (eg, child restraint laws), there are often many evaluations differing in design, analytic techniques, sample sizes and, not infrequently, findings and interpretations. A systematic review is a study that reviews such a

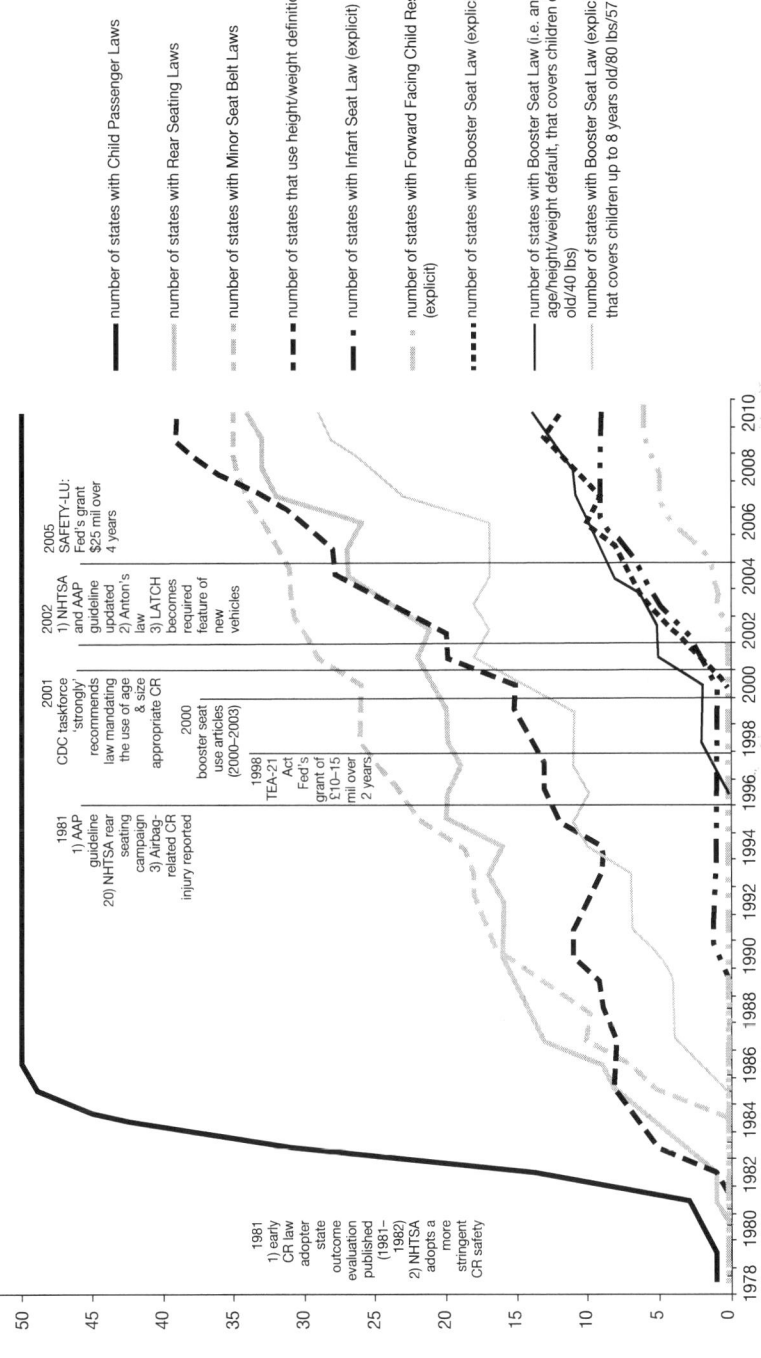

Figure 3.1 Evolution of US state child restraint laws.

Source: Jean Bae et al, 'Child Passenger Safety Laws in the United States, 1978–2010: Policy Diffusion in the Absence of Strong Federal Intervention' (2014) 100 *Social Science & Medicine* 30. This material is reproduced with permission of Elsevier.

collection of evidence according to an explicit, rigorous and transparent method-ology.[22] In the past three decades there has been an enormous acceleration in the production of systematic reviews.[23] By collecting, filtering and appraising studies through robust and transparent methods, systematic reviews assess the effective-ness of an intervention based on the overall weight of the evidence available, taking into account not just study results but also the methods that yielded them. Although they are too dense and complicated to be an ideal communications tool in the era of the one-pager (or the tweet), systematic reviews serve the goal of translation by distilling evidence from many sources into one.

In recent decades, important institutions have emerged to foster the systematic review of evidence in health and related fields. The Cochrane Collaborative grew out of Archibald Cochrane's observations in the early 1970s about the fragmented and often misleading state of knowledge on the effectiveness of maternal health interventions.[24] The Collaborative quickly became an international force in the promotion of rigorous and methodologically consistent reviews. There are cur-rently over 5000 systematic reviews covering a wide range of health interventions in the Cochrane collection, each following a standard protocol detailing how the research question was defined, the relevant studies identified and the overall body of evidence characterised.[25] The Campbell Collaboration, founded in 2000, provides a similar service with an equally robust collection of systematic reviews covering a broad range of social science subjects including, among others, educa-tion and criminology.[26] The Community Guide for Preventive Services publishes the findings from the US Preventive Services Task Force, which was created by the US government in 1996 to systematically identify effective and economi-cally efficient public health interventions.[27] Like Cochrane and Campbell, the Community Guide follows well-defined and transparent processes for conducting and reporting reviews.[28]

In 2009, Moulton and colleagues identified over 60 systematic reviews of the effectiveness of public health laws.[29] At least 10 additional systematic reviews on interventional public health laws have been conducted since. These reviews produce policy-relevant guidance that is important to disseminate, and policy-makers regard them as a valuable resource,[30] but even a quick scan of the topics[31] reveals that the production of a quantity of evidence sufficient to ground confident conclusions about the effectiveness of an intervention usually only happens after wide adoption. The reviews can help push late adopters, promote fine-tuning or support repeal of ineffective policies,[32] but they are of no use earlier in the process, when many durable policy decisions are made. Recently, we have seen action in recognition of this problem that adopts criteria and evidence standards more suitable for the intermediate stage of policy development. Brennan and colleagues devised a four-tier hierarchy of evidence for obesity policies. Their scheme gives greatest weight to systematic reviews and high quality empirical studies, but also includes evidence that would not qualify for a systematic review but that nonethe-less can shed light on 'promising' policies (ie, tested by relatively less rigorous and preliminary research) and even 'emerging' strategies (ie, newly implemented and with high face validity, but not yet subject to evaluation research).[33] This is hugely important, but it still does not address the very earliest stages of innovation, the challenge we take up in the third part of this chapter.

2.3 Dissemination and implementation science as practice

Systematic reviews (and other less formal syntheses of established evidence of the 'policy brief' type) are only part of a broader movement to narrow the 'chasm between science and policy'.[34] To add value to policy, researchers must explore policy-relevant issues in ways that yield policy-relevant information. And policy-makers must want, value and believe in the information being produced, and have access to it when it matters. That sort of correspondence requires overcoming cultural and institutional differences between policy-makers and researchers, long recognised as primary impediments to evidence-based policy.[35]

In the last two decades, researchers from multiple areas of health practice have been working to understand and ameliorate these impediments.[36] This work began with a focus on knowledge transfer – getting evidence from researchers to practitioners – as exemplified in the work of Archibald Cochrane in the 1970s and more system-oriented work in the evidence-based medicine movement of the 1990s.[37] Gradually, however, and particularly in research on policy-making, there has been a move away from thinking about evidence problems exclusively or even primarily in terms of moving evidence from one group (researchers) to another (policy-makers), to an emphasis on relationships that foster the bi-directional understanding and exchange of information.[38] In a systematic review of 24 studies including over 2000 interviews with health policy-makers, personal contact with researchers was identified as the most important facilitator of the use of research in policy-making.[39] Trust and ready access to researchers turn out to be very important for policy-makers and tend to influence their view and use of evidence.[40]

Policy-makers will rely on researchers, when they are available, for 'outside the box' thinking and fresh ideas.[41] Researchers, in turn, benefit from learning from policy-makers about the problems and the sort of evidence most likely to resonate in current policy debate. To increase researcher interest in such strategies and reduce obstacles tied to professional advancement (eg, tenure systems that privilege publications over practical influence), there is increasing funding for translational research. Programs like the Robert Wood Johnson Foundation Clinical Scholars Program and Centers for Disease Control and Prevention ('CDC') Research Fellows require participation in community-based participatory research, emphasising the importance of contact with evidence-consumers.[42] At the institutional level, the literature recommends creating points or modes of connection at which members of each group can learn about and from each other.[43] Examples include practice-based research networks,[44] partnership initiatives that systematise collaboration between researchers and policy-makers like the Canadian Metropolis Project,[45] provincial knowledge exchange health initiatives,[46] and a wide range of variously named arrangements between academic centres and communities.[47]

For all the value of these efforts, a practical paradox confronts exponents of evidence-based public health law: if a legal intervention is truly innovative, there will not yet be direct evidence of its impact. There will be no studies for systematic reviews and syntheses to digest. Researchers who have established relationships with policy players will be in a good position to find out what to study next – the innovation – but they will not have evaluated the policy options under consideration, and so will have no directly applicable study results to share. It is plain to see why this phase of the policy-making cycle gets relatively less attention in discussions of evidence-based policy. Yet direct evidence from policy evaluations hardly exhausts the supply of researcher knowledge relevant to a policy decision, even under conditions of novelty and uncertainty.

When a new threat to health emerges on to the legislative agenda as a 'problem', law-makers and advocates who are sincerely looking for a promising intervention face several common challenges. First, they have to get a good grip on the problem for both political and practical reasons. Problems, after all, define solutions. It is not uncommon for an inaccurate characterisation of a problem to lead to ineffective legislation. Second, they have to choose a legal approach to address the problem. The set of intervention options is likely to emerge quickly, and reflect a variety of interests and ideological and psychological factors. As a result, even policy actors starting with a reasonably accurate framing of the problem may fail to identify promising options for action. Finally, crafting a new legal intervention entails many choices of regulatory strategy, each of which has the potential to enhance or diminish its impact.

Policy-makers face and overcome these challenges every day. Active involvement of researchers, and the use of simple tools to support systematic use of relevant knowledge, could help them do better at avoiding the pitfalls of problem path dependency, missed options and errors of regulatory design. In the next section, we sketch out an approach for enhancing the translation of research knowledge at the policy innovation stage. We will illustrate the approach with a case study of one policy cascade, the US legislative response to a rising concern about concussion in youth sports. Though not an NCD, as a population harm, sports concussions share many of the same attributes of and challenges for legal intervention raised by NCDs. These include uncertainties in the epidemiology, a complicated clinical course, a latency between exposure and effect (for many of the associated harms), the presence of a powerful industry and risk behaviour that is seen as individually rewarding and culturally significant.

3 Linking tacit and explicit knowledge in policy innovation

3.1 Defining policy problems

For decades epidemiologists and medical researchers knew that head injuries were a common risk of contact sports like American football, that these injuries could be serious and that they required care. Both doctors and epidemiologists understood that traumatic brain injuries ('TBIs') could have a long term impact on cognitive ability. Players, parents, coaches and fans, too, were all more or less aware that concussion occurred among young athletes. Most treated it, however, as a normal if unfortunate part of the game. As late as 2006, a systematic review carried the title 'Pediatric Sport-related Concussion: A Review of the Clinical Management of an Oft-neglected Population'.[48] Then, suddenly, 'youth sports concussion' took shape as a policy problem. Between 2009 and 2012, 44 states adopted youth 'sports concussion laws', often mandating education about sports concussion risks and treatment, removal from competition for youth athletes with suspected concussion or clearance by a health professional before an athlete could return to competition (see Figure 3.2).[49]

The drivers of this change were a familiar mix of evidence, anecdote and advocacy. Annual incidence estimates for high school athletes grew from 63,000[50] to 136,000[51] in less than a decade as diagnostic understanding of head trauma sharpened and surveillance improved; current estimates of sports concussions across all youth ages run as high as 3 million or more.[52] Anecdote and evidence combined in the cases of National Football League ('NFL') alumni suffering dementia, cognitive problems and depression, some of whom contributed their remains to brain researchers at Boston University. Their symptoms, and the physiological damage observed post-mortem, were indistinguishable from *dementia pugilistica*, the longstanding clinical description of neuropsychological degeneration among boxers.[53] A public discussion began about the possibility that repeated head injuries in football could cause serious, even life-threatening brain damage later in life. Players, parents, fans and coaches began to wonder whether the hits kids were taking in 'Pop Warner' youth football or high school could be enough to produce the terrible damage seen in retired professionals or boxers like Muhammad Ali.[54] The question spread to other contact sports including soccer, where the effect of repeated heading of the ball has long been a concern.[55] The tipping point into advocacy came after a junior high football player in Washington state named Zackery Lystedt suffered multiple concussions in a single game, with catastrophic results. His parents took up a campaign for legislation, and in fairly short order the NFL and a variety of public health and social organisations were supporting them.[56] In 2009, Washington became the first state to enact youth sports concussion regulations, in the aptly named Zackery Lystedt Law.[57]

Political scientist John Kingdon's familiar model of legislation posits that a bill will pass with the merging of three distinct streams representing how a problem is defined, the availability of a policy response and the politics of action.[58] It is evident from the rapid spread of the law that the politics were right, and why not? This was a bill to protect kids from readily imagined harm, supported by parents, health experts and the major industry involved. Countervailing ideological concerns about the 'nanny state' did not take hold, and the budget implications of the proposed law were slight.

The policy problem was very well constructed for avoiding trouble in the politics stream: as defined on the website of USA Football, the official youth football partner of the NFL, 'Zackery's 2006 injury stemmed from returning to a game too soon after suffering a concussion'.[59] As this campaign moved towards legislation, it did not define the problem as the rules of the game, the age of the participants, the equipment or the field conditions, but the fact that after his first concussion

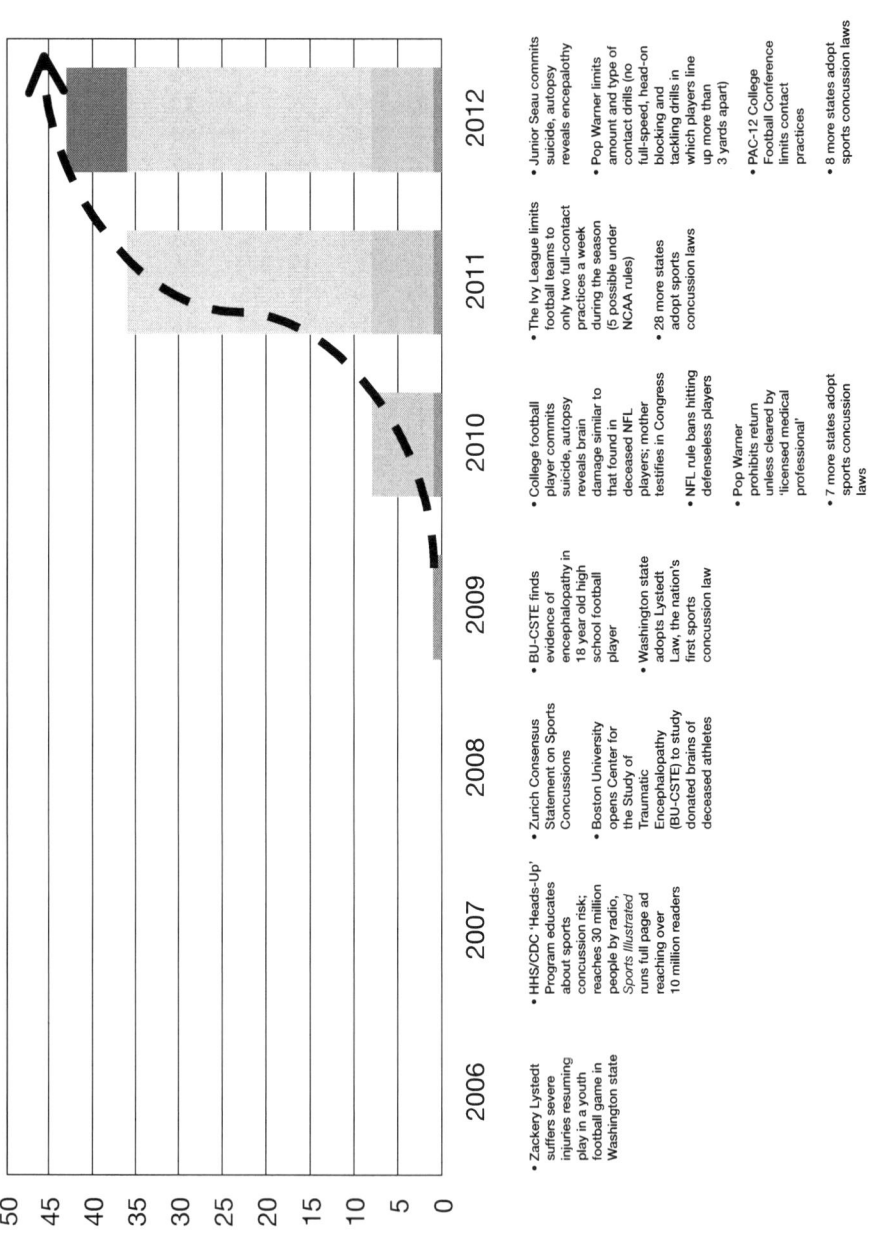

Figure 3.2 Adoption of state 'sports concussion laws' and timeline of related events.

Zach did not stop playing. With Zach, the impact of concussion was immediate and acute; his version of the problem did not evoke images of long term chronic exposure that might have come up if the emblem of harm had been a middle-aged NFL veteran with depression and early-stage dementia. This meant that the hardest issues, and greatest potential opposition, were defined out of the problem – and the solution. If premature return to play was the problem, the policy stream had a perfectly matched answer: increase awareness and promote proper medical management and time for recovery. There was no need to vote on the rules of popular sports. The policy is only triggered once a concussion has occurred, and its focus is on proper care of the injured child.

Though some commentators have worried that the Lystedt Law approach was more the result of NFL lobbying than serious attention to youth sports concussion,[60] we take a more sanguine view. Without any existing policy models for dealing with concussion, let alone evidence of policy impact, advocates and legislators addressed a real problem with a plausible legal intervention. Whether it works or not, or how to refine the regulatory strategy for greatest impact, is now in the realm of evaluation research, research synthesis and evidence translation. That is the end of the story; here we go back to the beginning, using concussion policy as an example of policy innovation under uncertainty. There was no direct evidence of the effectiveness of the Lystedt Law approach, but we will show how three straightforward tools could have been used by researchers, on their own or in collaboration with evidence brokers or policy actors, to add valuable research knowledge to the policy-making process.

3.2 Step 1: bringing evidence to the problem

Scholars from all over the disciplinary map agree that the single most powerful factor in policy-making is the definition of the problem[61] – and that's not even asking practitioners. Problems define solutions, and can be framed to flow with, rather than against, the political stream. Some staffer or lobbyist did a good day's work for football by describing the concussion problem as premature return to play, taking the game itself off the table, but that move may also have made rapid action across the country possible. Defining solvable problems is part of the politician's job description, and an art in itself.

Researchers also define problems, but they do so by methods and for reasons that are usefully different than those of policy professionals. Epidemiological statistics and clinical knowledge are often eagerly collected by policy entrepreneurs as they define problems for action, but researchers can do more than supply raw statistical and anecdotal material for the constructions of others. Researchers can promote the framing of problems in a manner that is consistent with the available direct evidence and applicable theoretical models. Researchers can make implicit causal models explicit, and then add greater complexity and uncertainty. They can attach proximate events to more distal causes, and link attributions of individual control to contingencies in the social and physical environment. Not all of these contributions will be salient or acceptable or effective in the policy world, but all will tend to promote more robust problem description to the extent that they are influential in any given case.

Causal mapping is a practical way for researchers to enrich the problem with or for non-scientists. We use the term 'mapping' here to embrace any visual tool that purports to depict how one variable influences another or changes over time. In health policy-making, causal diagrams 'can help to describe ("how things are now…"), classify ("why things go together…"), explain ("how things really work…"), predict ("what will happen if…"), and decide ("what you should do now…")'.[62] Pictures are a well-established tool for simplifying the complicated,[63] and the *exercise* of trying to do so is itself a useful intervention for making the implicit explicit. Here we will demonstrate how causal mapping can first explain, and then raise some questions about, the Lystedt Law model.

One can easily draw the causal diagram of youth sport concussion as explained by USA Football:

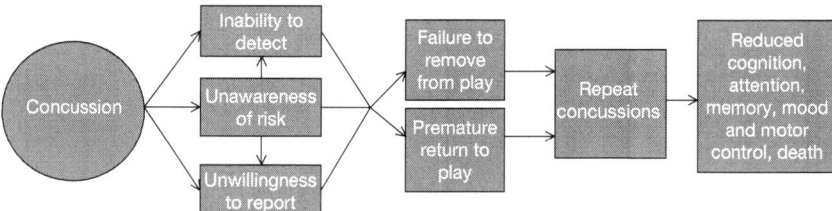

Figure 3.3 'The problem' according to USA Football.

Here the problems to be solved lie between initial and repeat concussion, and consist in improving the detection of concussions and ensuring that kids who suffer them are removed from play and given adequate time to recover. A researcher in public health would see this as secondary prevention, and might add a little more on the left:

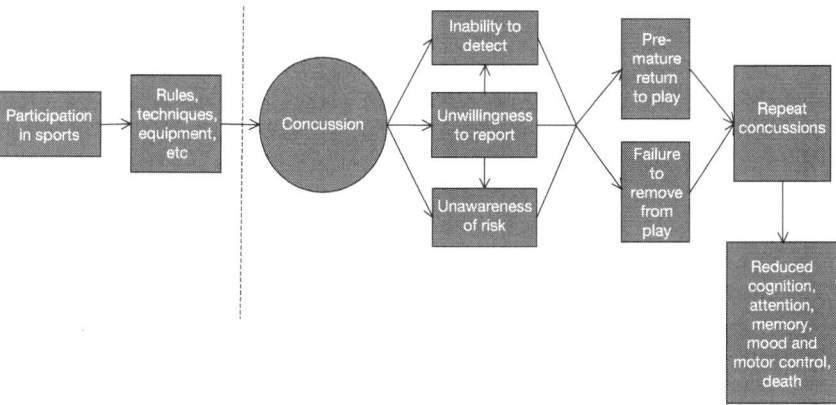

Figure 3.4 Expanding the 'problem'.

The dotted line here represents what may have been perceived by many participants as the border of political reality. Research knowledge may be able to change the definition of the problem in real time, expanding the range of conceivable interventions. Even if it can't, problem-definition, practised well, is not simply about finding an actionable solution under present political circumstances, but also about building a foundation for future action. With the initial concussion as a given, the logic of the Lystedt approach becomes apparent (see Figure 3.5): education addresses the factors that lead to non-detection and continued play, while new rules define the required response. If the education part succeeds (and research continues to expand understanding of the drivers of concussion risk), the dotted line of political reality could move. (Thus, Figure 3.2 notes that, in 2012, the youth Pop Warner football program instituted rule changes aimed at reducing youth TBI.)

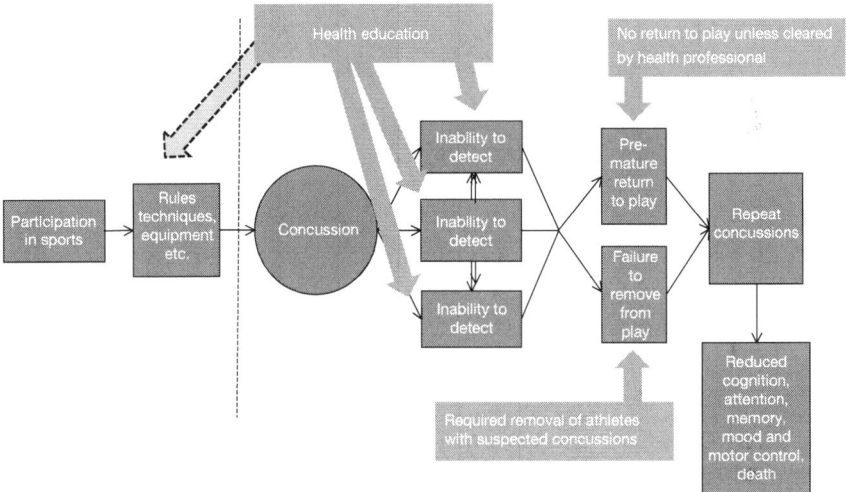

Figure 3.5 The Lystedt Law: how it works.

As Figure 3.6 indicates, research knowledge could have and almost certainly did influence the evolution of this problem and solution. Clinical and epidemiological evidence helped people see that Zach Lystedt was not the only child suffering concussion injury, even if his was unusually severe. Clinical, if not epidemiological, knowledge supported concern about the risks of returning to play 'too soon'. Studies confirmed the severe cumulative effects of repeat concussions in young athletes and identified a range of harms other than the acute trauma witnessed with Zach.[64] Observational and survey research found that many high school football players who suffer a concussion return to play the same day[65] and the reasons why (unaware of the seriousness of the injury or fearful of being removed from competition).[66]

Even if we accept the current line of political reality, there is research knowledge available to usefully complicate the problem. One place to start is with the term 'concussion'. The Centers for Disease Control and Prevention defines it simply

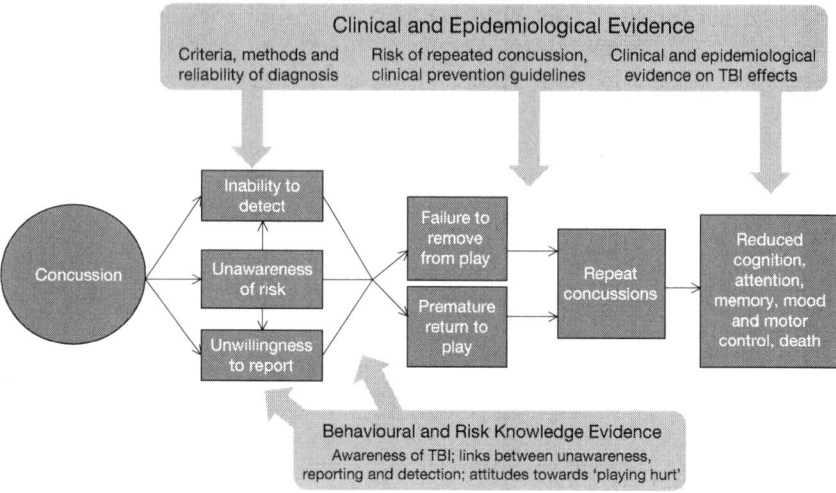

Figure 3.6 Bringing evidence into the picture.

as a type of TBI caused by 'a bump, blow, or jolt to the head that can change the way your brain normally works'.[67] For the purposes of health education, this teaches that any head injury is potentially important. As the cornerstone of health intervention or general policy planning in the area, however, it may be a little *too* simple. Concussion (from the Latin for 'shaking') often occurs without any external contact to the head through inertial forces transmitted through the body that jostle the brain within the skull. This explains why, as a recent international consensus statement on sports concussion reminds, helmets are not proven to reduce incidence.[68] The focus on concussion, traditionally associated with rare severe hits, may obscure the potential harms of more frequent and slight head impacts as with soccer head-balls and routine contact between football linemen. Research about this chronic brain jostling – depicted in Figure 3.7 – is just emerging in the form of studies that track exposure to sub-concussive hits, explore risk relationships and detail potentially related neurological harm.[69]

Available research also adds some complexity to the 'rest and medical care' model for solving the problem. It is actually not clear from existing evidence that the legislatively prescribed recuperation periods, or clinical practices for determining adequate periods of recuperation, are appropriate.[70] One large study found that many concussed high school athletes did not wait for symptoms to resolve before resuming play, and those that did were no less likely to suffer another concussion that year or to exhibit more lingering sequelae 45 and 90 days after their premature return.[71] How much do we know about the time period needed for recovery for various ages and genders? How reliable are clinical measures of recovery? The fact that we don't have answers to these questions is an important kind of knowledge for policy-makers to consider. It does not make the Lystedt Law approach wrong, but it does make it fragile.

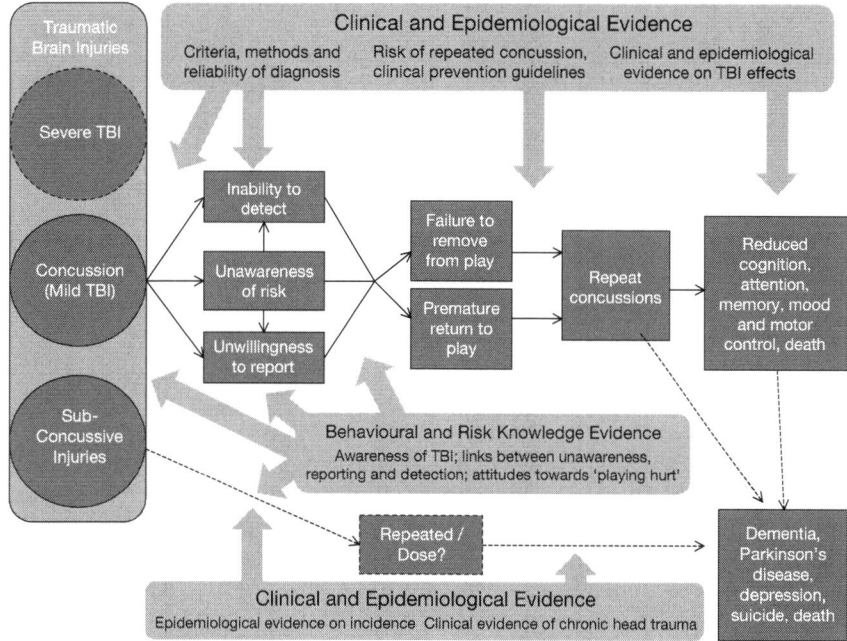

Figure 3.7 Considering alternate causal mechanisms and more distal harms.

There are good political reasons for staying away from the rules, the equipment, playing field design and other factors that implicate fundamental aspects of the game or the culture, and research is not yet pointing confidently to solutions in those realms. Premature return to play seems like a sensible pressure point for reducing harm to young people in sports. But perhaps we should be a bit worried about the gaps in our knowledge about what the right 'return to play' practice should be, and also more open to options for primary prevention. In the next part we illustrate how established public health theories and strategies can be used to identify a broader range of legal interventions and consider the likely strengths and weaknesses of their respective designs. None of these can be sure to have replaced or modified the Lystedt model, but they might have, and they represent important options for the future.

3.3 Step 2: identifying intervention strategies

As in the process of defining the problem and its pathology, mapping is a valuable tool for organising evidence and systematically thinking about plausible intervention strategies. Given the impetus of a politically effective problem definition, the stage of devising an intervention offers a second chance to understand the problem more capaciously. Researchers have at hand well-tested tools for these purposes. An excellent one was created by William Haddon, a pioneer in the science of injury prevention. Haddon recognised that all harms can be considered in terms of the interaction between a host, an agent and the social and physical environment over time. The resulting typology supports a matrix of approaches to addressing population harms.[72] A completed matrix helps identify what to target (hosts, agents and environments) and when (before, during and after the event).

Figure 3.8 is a representative Haddon Matrix for youth sports concussion. The host is the athlete who suffers the head injury, and the agent of harm is participation in sport. Important attributes of athletes that are known to influence concussion risk include age, size, gender and genetics.[73] Rules and volume of play are obvious risk factors for sports as an agent of harm. The physical environment encompasses fields, equipment, size and speed of other players and the nature of contact within the sport and the availability of coaches and others educated in concussion risk and diagnosis. The socioeconomic environment is shaped by a broader range of social norms including the meaning of concussion risks, aggressive play and 'playing hurt'. The event phase is when head contact or another jarring force to the body occurs. The pre-event phase represents conditions that may be targeted for primary prevention; the post-event phase refers to possibility of reducing the harmfulness of inertial forces on the brain after impact occurs, and secondary prevention.

The Haddon Matrix is a good tool for re-examining preconceived notions of a problem and looking for alternate intervention strategies. In Figure 3.9, the shaded sections designate the three event phases. In each phase, important modifiable attributes of the agent, host and environment are noted.

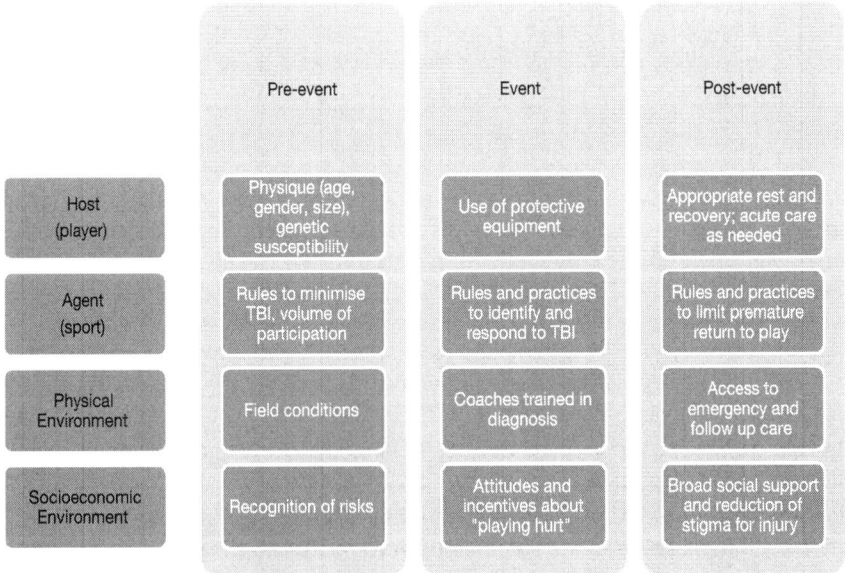

Figure 3.8 Haddon Matrix for sports concussions.

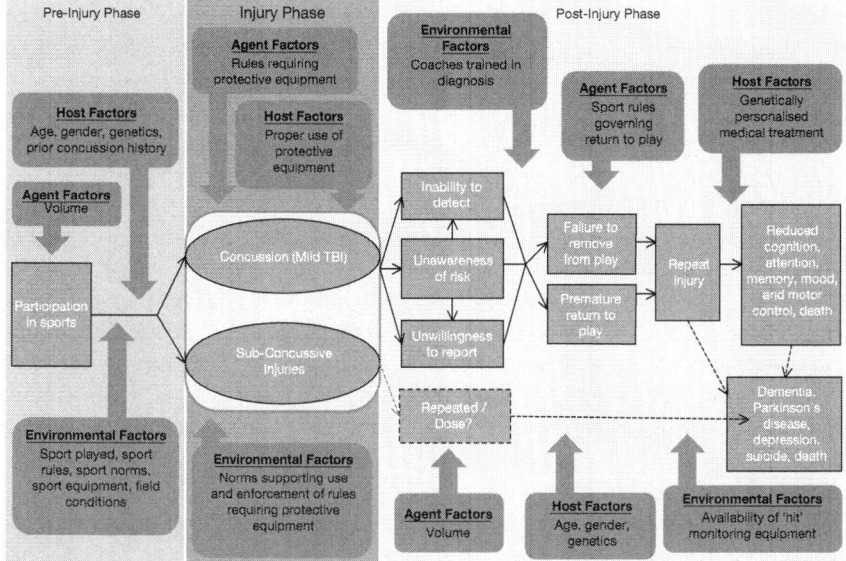

Figure 3.9 Using the Haddon Matrix to revise a sports concussion model.

The Haddon Matrix helps draw attention to things that might be important to try. Although not all of these actions are suitable to be taken through law, a tool like Figure 3.9 can nevertheless be useful to a policy-maker or advocate as a guide for how to use the power at their disposal. The value of changing public perceptions of sports concussion cannot be overstated, and in legislating to address what happens after a concussion, policy-makers can influence environmental factors that in turn influence the risk of primary concussion. Legislative signals, and changing public perceptions, probably had something to do with rule changes in youth and college sports, and with the decisions of the NFL and the National Institutes of Health to invest more in concussion research.

3.4 Step 3: selecting legal interventions by using evidence of 'how law works'

Once a consensus developed around the Lystedt approach, choices remained about how to implement each of its three primary elements. These choices raise questions about regulatory authority: who will be required to do what? This is in one sense a technical legal matter, but in the case of youth sports and many other public health problems, sources of legal authority are typically available and apparent. Lawyers and policy-makers knew they could order state and local agencies to create and distribute information, require licensed coaches to receive information or demonstrate competencies, place conditions on sports participation, establish rules of behaviour and set penalties for non-compliance. New legal interventions like the Lystedt Law are, by definition, innovations not tried before with a particular problem. But the mechanisms through which they change behaviour have almost always been deployed and evaluated in other contexts.[74] Researchers can add value by bringing evidence to bear on how well these generic strategies generally work and under what conditions – knowledge that can illuminate decisions about how to design the regulatory system for concussion. Evidence about these *mechanisms of legal effect* therefore provides a helpful guide for the initial formulation, subsequent testing and ongoing refinement of regulatory designs.

Mandated health education is a common legal intervention; there is no doubt that law can ensure that a sign is posted, a document transmitted and received, a training process completed. Regulatory designers in this instance could have chosen from a range of well-established models, ranging from simply requiring that information be posted in schools and locker rooms, to requiring that the licensure requirements for coaches be changed to include training and demonstrated competency in concussion diagnosis and management. In the Lystedt Law, Washington's legislature barely pushed its available regulatory levers. It did not specify any route or amount of training for coaches, leaving the design and provision to individual school districts and the Interscholastic Athletic Association. For parents and players, it required the annual receipt, signature and return of an information form.[75] Most other states also used this informed consent model with parents, but 29 states have explicitly required some kind of coach training.[76] The laws vary, but generally delegate the task of creating and providing the training to a health department, school district or interscholastic athletic organisation. Connecticut seems to push hardest, requiring completion of a training course in concussion management as a condition of licensure, with a refresher course every five years.[77]

Posting health and safety information has long been used with good effect to transmit basic health and safety information and rules,[78] and sports concussion awareness mailings to paediatricians have been found to increase knowledge.[79] However, regulations aimed at promoting complex competencies (such as identifying and managing a concussion) typically use more demanding mechanisms like certification or licensure based on specified curricula or passage of examinations.[80] Likewise, evidence from medicine and human research subject protection[81] casts some doubt on the effectiveness of the determination of informed consent the law created for parents and students, especially when both are motivated to continue participation in the game. From a researcher perspective, framers of Lystedt-type laws have done about as little as they could to ensure that the right information was received and understood by the right people.

Law is a reliable way to organise the provision of specified information to a specified class of recipients, but of course the real challenge is to convert knowledge into behaviour change.[82] Commonly, law's special advantage over other modes of behaviour change is thought to be the power of punishment, which uses the mechanism of deterrence to secure compliance with a stated standard of behaviour.[83] If anything, however, many state sports concussion laws have disclaimed deterrence, going so far as to create immunity from tort liability for those who followed minimal requirements.[84] Pennsylvania law-makers, by contrast, were willing to give deterrence a chance: coaches who fail to remove players from the game after a possible concussion can be punished by temporary (and in repeat cases, permanent) suspension.[85] Which is right? Deterrence as a mechanism for promoting compliance with legal standards has been studied extensively, and we know that it depends upon three key perceptions in the actor's mind: that non-compliance will be detected, that punishment will be quick, and that it will be more unpleasant than non-compliance is rewarding.[86] From this perspective, we can see some problems in the Lystedt case. In most states, there are no penalties, nor is any agency given the job of watching over compliance. Even in Pennsylvania, no enforcement system beyond parental complaint was established. And in all states, deterrence runs into a problem that the rewards of non-compliance (winning for the coaches, staying in the game for the students and parents) may be perceived as more valuable than the sanctions are costly.

Do the modest education requirements, the lack of punishment and the absence of an enforcement system mean the Lystedt model is toothless and not intended to work? Not necessarily. Deterrence is only one mechanism for getting people to obey the law, and one that is perhaps relied on more often than it deserves.[87] In many if not most cases, law works best (and most efficiently) when people obey the law voluntarily, without state enforcement. Indeed, there is some evidence that deterrence, if mechanically applied, can actually decrease this sort of internal motivation to comply.[88] The Washington Lystedt model's mechanism of effect can best be understood, and consciously enhanced, as working through a psychosocial mechanism of social normative change well-grounded in behavioural theory and research.

We will illustrate with the Theory of Triadic Influence, which integrates well-established theories of change along three 'streams': cultural, interpersonal and intrapersonal.[89] The Lystedt Law changes the sociocultural environment (depicted in Figure 3.10) by establishing a new behavioural standard for coaches. Coaches see the new rules being operationalised in institutions, changing their sense of what will happen to them if they don't change their practices with respect to concussions, and of how likely they are to run into trouble. These experiences can change their attitudes towards their prior behaviour and give them a more positive view of the behaviour mandated by the law.

The influence of law is also felt in the interpersonal and intrapersonal streams. In the interpersonal stream, the law and its factual premises can become a feature of the individual's community, peer and family relationships, manifested not only in attitudes but also in the behaviour of others. These change the individual's perceptions of what is normative in the community, and triggers the desire to please others to whom the individual is bonded. The law thus changes interpersonal relations as norms begin to reshape the context and social negotiations of 'playing hurt' and other risk behaviours. What was once accepted as good or normal begins to be seen by some as deviant, and these changing group norms influence coaches' understanding of how their decisions will be viewed by parents and professional peers. Intrapersonally, a clear rule of behaviour, recognised as at least a possible social norm, can increase an individual's ability to follow the

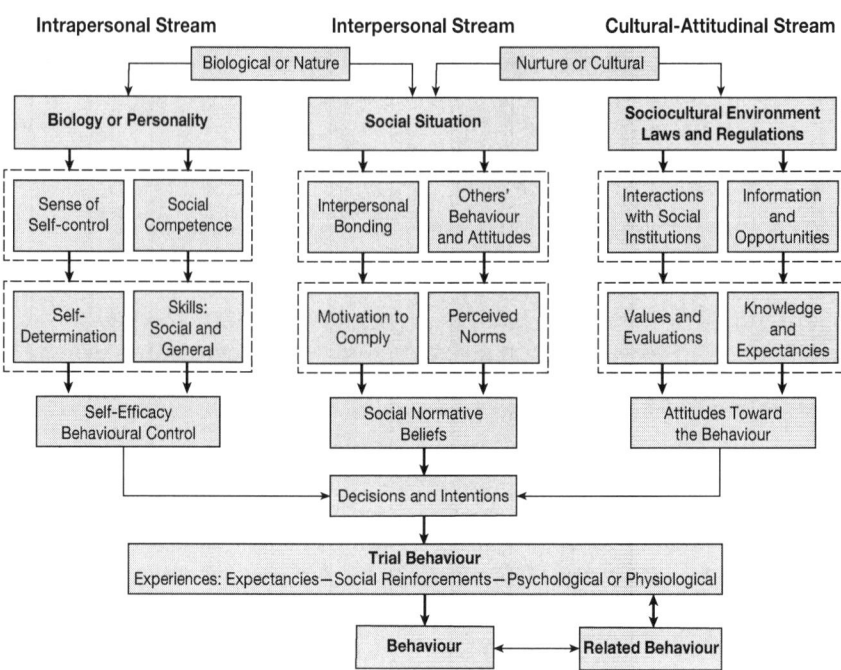

Figure 3.10 The theory of triadic influence.

Source: Brian Flay and Marc Schure, 'The Theory of Triadic Influence' in Alexander Wagenaar and Scott Burris (eds) *Public Health Law Research: Theories and Methods* (2013) © John Wiley and Sons, Inc. This material is reproduced with permission of John Wiley & Sons, Inc.

rule, supporting self-control or giving the individual a pro-social justification for the new behaviour. On this view, law works through social, institutional and individual affective processes to produce 'voluntary' compliance without overt government oversight or threats of government sanctions.

Deliberately or not, the drafters of the Lystedt Law chose to rely on a social normative mechanism to induce voluntary behaviour change. In so doing, they were choosing a mechanism of legal effect that has a solid evidence base in experiences like drink driving and limits on public smoking.[90] A researcher drawing on knowledge of this mechanism could point to the importance of the social marketing component of the law (mandated information) and of a robust social marketing effort outside and beyond the law. There is no formal government oversight of compliance in many instances for the removal and return to play components, but if parental education works, the stands will be full of 'police'. Likewise, even if no actual legally stipulated penalties exists, a social-normative model like the Theory of Triadic Influence ultimately contemplates some 'punishment': under the Lystedt model, if it works, coaches who fail to identify potential injuries or enforce a waiting period may be subject to social disapproval, expressed in interpersonal situations or through secondary channels of state enforcement – ie, complaints to the school administration. These kinds of social sanctions, for most people, are quite powerful. In sum, then, an understanding of how legal rules actually produce changes in behaviour can help reassure us that the Lystedt approach, which stipulates no enforcement or punishment, can actually have powerful behavioural effects – but only if community norms change.[91]

4 Discussion and conclusion: three actions in search of a practice

The translation of research evidence into information that lawmakers will use is a high public health priority. Research focused on evidence translation and a growing set of credible synthesis tools aim to promote evidence-based (or at least evidence-informed) public policies. For all the value of these efforts, the more truly innovative a legal intervention, the less likely there is to be an evidence base defining its capacity for impact. In this chapter, aimed primarily at researchers and brokers of evidence-informed policies, we have drawn attention to opportunities to bring research knowledge to bear in policy innovation – opportunities not explicitly addressed, let alone thoroughly considered, in the current literature on research translation. Our approach is a mix of the descriptive and the prescriptive. While scientific and critical in spirit, the reasoning process we describe is substantially intuitive and heuristic in practice, and reflects what lawmakers and advocates do every day. Our prescription consists in making the tacit explicit, and the spontaneous systematic.

What we have presented may strike even a charitable reader as an extended excursion through the obvious, with occasional detours to the well-known. Precisely. The steps we have described, and set out here in Figure 3.11, *must* be taken by anyone moving between the mere desire for a law and the creation of a concrete bill. In that light, anyone who has watched or participated or studied the lawmaking process will recall instances in which the various steps were taken mindfully, with as much information as possible. And anyone can also call to mind instances in which the three steps were taken in a heedless sprint. Figure 3.11 summarises generic forms of research-based knowledge (ie 'evidence') that are often available to inform the lawmaking process even when the particular intervention or target is novel. It is pretty obvious, for example, that epidemiological data have a big influence on defining a phenomenon as a health problem, and that regulatory expertise can help drafters design a rule that will work in practice. Here, too, what happens in practice sometimes but not always matches what is possible.

As the child restraint story suggests, the work is seldom done with the initial adoption of law. Legal interventions, like youth sports concussion laws, are constantly being refined, reflecting both the political constraints on early action and the related evolution of understanding of problems and solutions. Especially at an early stage of understanding and action, legislators might plausibly regard doing *something* as the best way to proceed towards figuring out and building support for the *right thing* down the road. The policy learning process is capable of moving us towards optimal laws. But how quickly we arrive there, and therefore how much harm we avoid along the way, depends on the quality of both the experimentation and subsequent evaluation. The process we sketch serves both interests. On the experimentation side it helps bring evidence to bear on the specific regulatory choices associated with emerging solutions. Specifying these choices and their underlying logic in turn provides a map to guide evaluators in deciphering whether laws are working as expected.

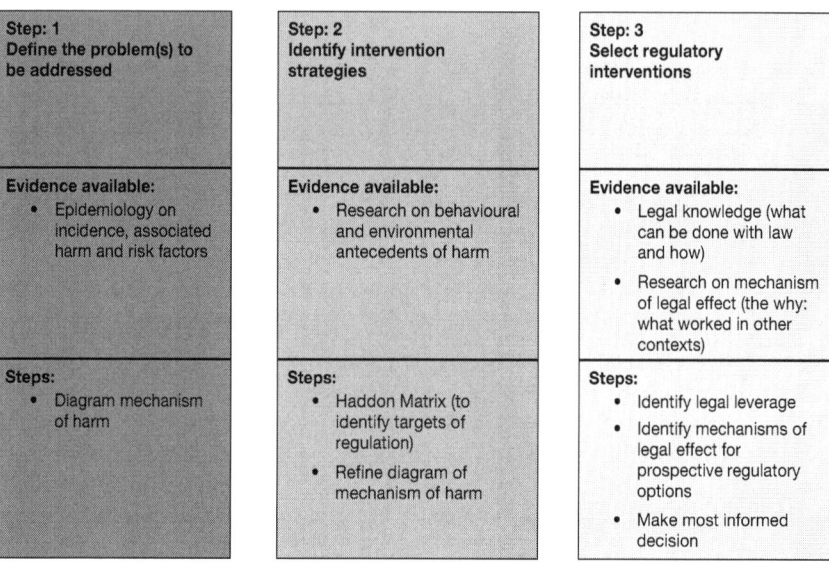

Figure 3.11 A simple process.

The implications of our inquiry are modest but useful. We highlight the fact that evidence can have a decisive impact on policy, even at the problem-definition stage. We make the less often recognised point that mechanisms of legal intervention have an informative evidence base even when specific uses of those mechanisms do not. And we show how simple heuristic diagrams and matrices can help organise this evidence and promote more systematic thinking, even in the innovation stage of policy-making. The result is a clearer picture of the role that researchers and research can play in policy innovation, and a set of tools that policy-makers can use to innovate better.

Notes

1 Scott Burris and Evan Anderson, 'Legal Regulation of Health-related Behavior: A Half-century of Public Health Law Research' (2013) 39 *Annual Review of Law and Social Science* 95; Stephanie Morain and Michelle Mello, 'Survey Finds Public Support for Legal Interventions Directed at Health Behavior to Fight Noncommunicable Disease' (2013) 32(3) *Health Affairs* 486.

2 *Global Action Plan for the Prevention and Control of Noncommunicable Diseases 2013–2020*, WHO Doc A66/VR/9.

3 Ibid 67.

4 Ross Brownson, Graham Colditz and Enola Proctor (eds), *Dissemination and Implementation Research in Health: Translating Science to Practice* (Oxford University Press, 2012).

5 Scott Burris et al, 'Making the Case for Laws that Improve Health: A Framework for Public Health Law Research' (2010) 88(2) *The Milbank Quarterly* 169.

6 Jin Yung Bae et al, 'Child Passenger Safety Laws in the United States, 1978–2010: Policy Diffusion in the Absence of Strong Federal Intervention' (2014) 100 *Social Science & Medicine* 30.

7 Ibid.

8 Stephen Teret et al, 'Child Restraint Laws: An Analysis of Gaps in Coverage' (1986) 76(1) *American Journal of Public Health* 31.

9 Charles Shipan and Craig Volden, 'Policy Diffusion: Seven Lessons for Scholars and Practitioners' (2012) *Public Administration Review* 788.

10 *New State Ice Co v Liebmann* 285 US 262, 311 (1932).

11 Donald Campbell and Laurence Ross, 'The Connecticut Crackdown on Speeding: Time-series Data in Quasi-experimental Analysis' (1968) 3(1) *Law and Society Review* 33.

12 Allan Williams and JoAnn Wells, 'Evaluation of the Rhode Island Child Restraint Law' (1981) 71(7) *American Journal of Public Health* 742; Allan Williams and JoAnn Wells, 'The Tennessee Child Restraint Law in its Third Year' (1981) 71(2) *American Journal of Public Health* 163; C Mack Sewell et al, 'Child Restraint Law Effects on Motor Vehicle Accident Fatalities and Injuries: the New Mexico Experience' (1986) 78(6) *Pediatrics* 1079.

13 Diana Guerin and David MacKinnon, 'An Assessment of the California Child Passenger Restraint Requirement' (1985) 75(2) *American Journal of Public Health* 142; Alexander Wagenaar, Daniel Webster and Richard Maybee, 'Effects of Child Restraint Laws on Traffic Fatalities in Eleven States' (1987) 27(7) *Journal of Trauma, Injury, Infection and Critical Care* 726.

14 Alexander Wagenaar and Kelli Komro, 'Natural Experiments: Research Design Elements for Optimal Causal Inference Without Randomization' in Alexander Wagenaar and Scott Burris (eds), *Public Health Law Research: Theory and Methods* (Wiley, 2013) 307.

15 Bae et al, above n 6.

16 Carol Weiss, 'Research for Policy's Sake: the Enlightenment Function of Social Research' (1977) 3 *Policy Analysis* 531; Ross Brownson, Jamie Chriqui and Katherine Stamatakis, 'Understanding Evidence-based Public Health Policy' (2009) 99(9) *American Journal of Public Health* 1576.

17 Centers for Disease Control and Prevention, 'Ten Great Public Health Achievements – United States, 1900–1999' (1999) 48(12) *Morbidity and Mortality Weekly Report* 241; Burris and Anderson, above n 1.

18 David Colby et al, 'Research Glut and Information Famine: Making Research Evidence More Useful for Policymakers' (2008) 27(4) *Health Affairs* 1177.

19 Ross Brownson et al, 'Researchers and Policymakers: Travelers in Parallel Universes' (2006) 30(2) *American Journal of Preventive Medicine* 164; Christopher Jewell and Lisa Bero, 'Developing Good Taste in Evidence: Facilitators of and Hindrances to Evidence-informed Health Policymaking in State Government' (2008) 86(2) *The Milbank Quarterly* 177.

20 Brownson, Chriqui and Stamatakis, above n 16.

21 Brownson et al, above n 19.

22 Trisha Greenhalgh et al, 'Diffusion of Innovations in Service Organizations: Systematic Review and Recommendations' (2004) 82(4) *The Milbank Quarterly* 581.

23 David Moher et al, 'Epidemiology and Reporting Characteristics of Systematic Reviews' (2007) 4(3) *PLoS Medicine* e78.

24 Archibald Cochrane, *Effectiveness and Efficiency: Random Reflections on Health Services* (1972) <http://www.nuffieldtrust.org.uk/sites/files/nuffield/publication/Effectiveness_and_Efficiency.pdf>.

25 *Cochrane Collaborative* (2013) Cochrane Collaborative <http://www.cochrane.org/cochrane-reviews>.

26 *The Campbell Collaboration* (2013) Campbell Collaboration <http://www.campbell collaboration.org/>.

27 Vilma Carande-Kulis et al, 'Methods for Systematic Reviews of Economic Evaluations for the Guide to Community Preventive Services: Task Force on Community Preventive Services' (2000) 18 (supplement 1) *American Journal of Preventive Medicine* 75; Stephanie Zaza et al, 'Data Collection Instrument and Procedure for Systematic Reviews in the Guide to Community Preventive Services: Task Force on Community Preventive Services' (2000) 18 (supplement 1) *American Journal of Preventive Medicine* 44.

28 Peter Briss et al, 'Developing an Evidence-based Guide to Community Preventive Services – Methods: The Task Force on Community Preventive Services' (2000) 18 (supplement 1) *American Journal of Preventive Medicine* 35.

29 Anthony Moulton et al, 'The Scientific Basis for Law as a Public Health Tool' (2009) 99(1) *American Journal of Public Health* 17.

30 John Lavis et al, 'How Can Research Organizations More Effectively Transfer Research Knowledge to Decision Makers?' (2003) 81(2) *The Milbank Quarterly* 221; Jonathan Fielding and Peter Briss, 'Promoting Evidence-based Public Health Policy: Can We Have Better Evidence and More Action?' (2006) 25(4) *Health Affairs* 969; Melissa Sweet and Ray Moynihan, 'Improving Population Health: The Uses of Systematic Reviews' (2007) *The Milbank Quarterly* 1.

31 *Evidence Briefs* (2013) Public Health Law Research <http://www.phlr.org/evidence-briefs>.

32 Sweet and Moynihan, above n 30.

33 Laura Brennan et al, 'Accelerating Evidence Reviews and Broadening Evidence Standards to Identify Effective, Promising, and Emerging Policy and Environmental Strategies for Prevention of Childhood Obesity' (2011) 32 *Annual Review Public Health* 199.

34 Brownson et al, above n 19.

35 Carol Weiss, 'The Powers of Problem Definition: The Case of Government Paperwork' (1989) 22(2) *Policy Sciences* 97; John Kingdon, *Agendas, Alternatives, and Public Policies* (Pearson, 2nd ed, 2010).

36 Brownson, Colditz and Proctor, above n 4.

37 Lawrence Green et al, 'Diffusion Theory and Knowledge Dissemination, Utilization, and Integration in Public Health' (2009) 30 *Annual Review of Public Health* 151.

38 Lavis et al, above n 30; Craig Mitton et al, 'Knowledge Transfer and Exchange: Review and Synthesis of the Literature' (2007) 85(4) *The Milbank Quarterly* 729.

39 Simon Innvaer et al, 'Health Policy-makers' Perceptions of Their Use of Evidence: A Systematic Review' (2002) 7(4) *Journal of Health Services Research and Policy* 239.

40 Lavis et al, above n 30; Jewell and Bero, above n 19.

41 Abby Haynes et al, 'Galvanizers, Guides, Champions, and Shields: the Many Ways that Policymakers Use Public Health Researchers' (2011) 89(4) *The Milbank Quarterly* 564.

42 Brownson, Colditz and Proctor, above n 4.

43 John Lavis, 'Research, Public Policymaking, and Knowledge-translation Processes: Canadian Efforts to Build Bridges' (2006) (26) *The Journal of Continuing Education in the Health Professions* 37.

44 James Mold and Kevin Peterson, 'Primary Care Practice-based Research Networks: Working at the Interface between Research and Quality Improvement' (2005) 3(Suppl 1) *The Annals of Family Medicine* S12.

45 John Shield and Bryan Evans, 'Building a Policy-oriented Research Partnership for Knowledge Mobilization and Knowledge Transfer: The Case of the Canadian Metropolis Project' (2012) 2(4) *Administrative Science* 250.

46 Donna Murnaghan, 'Knowledge Exchange Systems for Youth Health and Chronic Disease Prevention: A Tri-provincial Case Study' (2013) 4 *Chronic Diseases and Injuries in Canada* 257.

47 Lorraine Johnston, Sarah Robinson and Nigel Lockett, 'Recognising "Open Innovation" in HEI-industry Interaction for Knowledge Transfer and Exchange' (2010) 16(6) *International Journal of Entrepreneurial Behaviour & Research* 540.

48 Michael Kirkwood, Keith Yeates and Pamela Wilson, 'Pediatric Sport-related Concussion: A Review of the Clinical Management of an Oft-neglected Population' (2006) 117(4) *Pediatrics* 1359.

49 Hosea Harvey, 'Reducing Traumatic Brain Injuries in Youth Sports: Youth Sports Traumatic Brain Injury State Laws: January 2009–December 2012' (2013) 103(7) *American Journal of Public Health* 1249.

50 John Powell and Kim Barber-Foss, 'Traumatic Brain Injury in High School Athletes' (1999) 282(10) *Journal of the American Medical Association* 958.

51 Luke Gessel et al, 'Concussions among United States High School and Collegiate Athletes' (2007) 42(4) *Journal of Athletic Training* 495.

52 Jean Langlois, Wesley Rutland-Brown and Marlena Wald, 'The Epidemiology and Impact of Traumatic Brain Injury: A Brief Overview' (2006) 21(5) *Journal of Head Trauma Rehabilitation* 375.

53 Steven DeKosky, Milos Ikonomovic and Sam Gandy, 'Traumatic Brain Injury: Football, Warfare, and Long-term Effects' (2010) 93(12) *New England Journal of Medicine* 46.

54 See, eg, Dave D'Allesandro, 'Historic Decline in Youth Football Enrollment Suggests Parents Are Concerned' (2013) *New Jersey Star-Ledger* (online) <http://www.nj.com/ledger-dalessandro/index.ssf/2013/11/dalessandro_historic_decline_in_youth_football_enrollment_suggests_parents_are_catching_on.html>.

55 See, eg, Ann Punnoose, 'Study Raises Concerns about "Heading" in Soccer, but Jury is Still Out on Risks' (2012), 307(10) *Journal of the American Medical Association* 1012.

56 See, eg, Centers for Disease Control and Prevention, *The Lystedt Law: A Concussion Survivor's Journey* (2010) <http://www.cdc.gov/media/subtopic/matte/pdf/031210-Zack-story.pdf>.

57 *Youth Sports – Concussion and Head Injury Guidelines – Injured Athlete Restrictions*, Washington Revised Statutes 28A.600.190, 2009, ch 475 § 2 (2009).

58 Kingdon, above n 35.

59 Joe Frollo Thu, 'Three Years Later, Lystedt Law Protects Young Athletes in 34 States and DC' (2012) *USA Football* (online) <http://usafootball.com/news/featured-articles/three-years-later-lystedt-law-protects-young-athletes-34-states-and-dc>.

60 Hosea Harvey, 'Refereeing the Public Health' 14(1) *Yale Journal of Health Policy, Law, and Ethics* (Winter 2014) (forthcoming).

61 Timur Kuran and Cass Sunstein, 'Availability Cascades and Risk Regulation' (1999) 51(4) *Stanford Law Review* 683; Kingdon, above n 35; Carol Baicchi, 'Why Study Problematizations? Making Politics Visible' (2010) 2 *Open Journal of Political Science* 1; Geoffrey Rose, *The Strategy of Preventive Medicine* (Oxford University Press, 1992); Graham Burchell, Colin Gordon and Peter Miller (eds), *The Foucault Effect: Studies in Governmentality* (University of Chicago Press, 1991).

62 Jeffrey Swanson and Jennifer Ibrahim, 'Picturing Public Health Law Research: The Value of Causal Diagrams' in Wagenaar and Burris, above n 14, 217, 234.

63 Kay Bartholomew, Guy Parcel and Gerjo Kok, 'Intervention Mapping: A Process for Developing Theory – and Evidence-based Health Education Programs' (1998) 25(5) *Health Education and Behavior* 545; Kellogg Foundation, 'Using Logic Models to Bring

Together Planning, Evaluation, and Action: Logic Model Development Guide' (WK Kellogg Foundation, 1998).

64   Michael Collins et al, 'Cumulative Effects of Concussion in High School Athletes' (2002) 51(5) *Neurosurgery* 1175.

65   Kevin Guskiewicz et al, 'Epidemiology of Concussion in Collegiate and High School Football Players' (2000) 28(5) *American Journal of Sports Medicine* 643.

66   Michael McCrea et al, 'Unreported Concussion in High School Football Players: Implications for Prevention' (2004) 14(1) *Clinical Journal of Sports Medicine* 13.

67   *Concussion in Sports* (2013) Center for Disease Control <http://www.cdc.gov/concussion/sports/>.

68   Paul McCrory et al, 'Consensus Statement on Concussion in Sport: The 4th International Conference on Concussion in Sport Held in Zurich, November 2012' (2013) 47(5) *British Journal of Sports Medicine* 250, 255.

69   Andrew Gardner, Grant Iverson and Paul McCrory, 'Chronic Traumatic Encephalopathy in Sport: A Systematic Review' (26 June 2013) *British Journal of Sports Medicine* (online first) doi:10.1136/bjsports-2013-092646.

70   McCrory et al, above n 68.

71   Michael McCrea et al, 'Effects of a Symptom-free Waiting Period on Clinical Outcome and Risk of Reinjury after Sport-related Concussion' (2009) 65(5) *Neurosurgery* 876.

72   William Haddon, Jr, 'Advances in the Epidemiology of Injuries as a Basis for Public Policy' (1980) 95(5) *Public Health Reports* 411.

73   Thomas Terrell et al, 'Genetic Polymorphisms, Concussion Risk, and Post Concussion Neurocognitive Deficits in College and High School Athletes' (2013) 47 *British Journal of Sports Medicine* E1; Kirkwood, Yeates and Wilson, above n 48.

74   Ray Pawson, 'Evidence-based Policy: The Promise of "Realist Synthesis"' (2002) 8(3) *Evaluation* 340.

75   *Youth Sports – Concussion and Head Injury Guidelines – Injured Athlete Restrictions*, Washington Revised Statutes 28A.600.190, 2009, ch 475 § 2 (2009).

76   See, eg, Harvey, 'Reducing Traumatic Brain Injuries', above n 49.

77   *Training Courses for Coaches Re Concussions and Head Injuries – Development or Approval by State Board of Education – Revocation of Coaching Permit*, Connecticut General Statutes 10-149-b, 2010, Public Act 10-62 § 1 (2009).

78   Gabriel Rousseau and Michael Wogalter, 'Research on Warning Signs' in Michael Wogalter (ed), *Handbook of Warnings* (CRC Press, 2006).

79   Sara Chrisman, Melissa Schiff and Frederick Rivara, 'Physician Concussion Knowledge and the Effect of Mailing the CDC's "Heads Up" Toolkit' (2011) 50(11) *Clinical Pediatrics* 1031.

80   Herve Maisonneuve et al, 'Continuing Medical Education and Professional Revalidation in Europe: Five Case Examples' (2009) 29(1) *The Journal of Continuing Education in the Health Professions* 58; Linda Young and Reynold Willie, 'Effectiveness of Continuing Education for Health Professionals: A Literature Review' (1984) 13(2) *Journal of Allied Health* 112; Bernard Bloom, 'Effects of Continuing Medical Education on Improving Physician Clinical Care and Patient Health: a Review of Systematic Reviews' (2005) 21(3) *International Journal of Technology Assessment in Health Care* 380; Louise Forsetlund et al, 'Continuing Education Meetings and Workshops: Effects on Professional Practice and Health Care Outcomes' (2009) (2) *Cochrane Database Systematic Review* CD003030.

81   See, eg, Tanja Treschan et al, 'The Influence of Protocol Pain and Risk on Patients' Willingness to Consent for Clinical Studies: A Randomized Trial' (2003) 96 *Anesthesia and Analgesia* 498; Oonagh Corrigan, 'Empty Ethics: The Problem with Informed Consent' (2003) 25 *Sociology of Health and Illness* 768.

82   Lawrence Gostin, *Public Health Law: Power, Duty, Restraint* (University of California Press, 2nd ed, 2008), 334.

83 Wesley Jennings and Tom Mieczkowski, 'Criminological Theories' in Wagenaar and Burris, above n 14, 109, 110.

84 Harvey, 'Reducing Traumatic Brain Injuries', above n 49, e4.

85 *Concussions and Traumatic Brain Injuries*, Pennsylvania Statutes 24-5323, 2013, Pub L 411, § 3 (2011).

86 Jennings and Mieczkowski, above n 83, 119.

87 Tom Tyler, *Why People Obey the Law* (Princeton University Press, 2006).

88 Tom Tyler and Avital Mentovich, 'Procedural Justice Theory' in Wagenaar and Burris, above n 14, 131, 133.

89 Brian Flay and Marc Shure, 'The Theory of Triadic Influence' in Wagenaar and Burris, above n 14, 169, 179.

90 See, eg, Dale Berger and William Marelich, 'Legal and Social Control of Alcohol-Impaired Driving in California: 1983–1994' (1997) 58(5) *Journal of Studies on Alcohol and Drugs* 519; Alison Albers et al, 'Relation between Local Restaurant Smoking Regulations and Attitudes towards the Prevalence and Social Acceptability of Smoking: A Study of Youths and Adults Who Eat Out Predominantly at Restaurants in Their Town' (2004) 13(4) *Tobacco Control* 347.

91 For a more detailed review of different disciplinary perspectives (eg, law and economics, psychosocial, criminological, socio-legal) on mechanisms of legal effect, refer to Wagenaar and Burris, above n 14.

Part II

NCD Risk Regulation under International and Comparative Law

4 International Human Rights Law

Tanya E Baytor and Oscar A Cabrera

1 Introduction

International human rights law and regulatory efforts to address the risk factors for non-communicable diseases ('NCDs') share the common laudable goal of advancing the right to the highest attainable standard of health. At the 2011 United Nations ('UN') General Assembly high-level meeting on NCDs, a number of cost-effective and evidence-based regulatory interventions that could reduce the burden of disease were discussed.[1] Confronted with the looming NCDs crisis, public health advocates are increasingly turning to the human rights framework to both advance and defend such regulatory interventions. With the world's most vulnerable populations bearing the unequal burden of NCDs, recognising the epidemic's human rights dimension is crucial in formulating a just and effective global response. The challenge of tackling NCDs may also present an opportunity for the evolving field of human rights law. As the international community is galvanised to develop a coordinated public health strategy, newly shaped global norms help inform and provide content for the state's international human rights obligations under the right to health.

This chapter examines the implications of international human rights law on strategies to address NCDs and the key risk factors for NCDs, which include tobacco consumption, alcohol consumption and unhealthy diets. Part 2 of the chapter gives a brief introduction to international human rights law and the human right to health. Part 3 examines the relationship between human rights law and the regulation of tobacco, alcohol and unhealthy food and the ways in which human rights law and the regulation of unhealthy products are mutually reinforcing. Regulatory frameworks that address the risk factors for NCDs are a vital component of the right to health. International human rights law can play a fundamental role in advocating for stronger regulation in the interest of public health. The *WHO Framework Convention on Tobacco Control* ('WHO FCTC')[2] provides an example of an international, legally binding instrument that establishes obligations with respect to tobacco control and helps define a state's obligations in promoting the right to health. To date, there are no international binding instruments comparable to the WHO FCTC that address the regulation of alcohol or unhealthy food. However, we suggest that non-binding, international instruments can be equally effective in advancing the right to health when the content of these instruments represents globally accepted norms and standards. Part 4 explores the rights that can come into tension when governments seek to regulate tobacco, alcohol and unhealthy food. In Part 5, we examine how to measure the right to health and the impact of regulatory interventions such as tobacco and alcohol control on health outcomes. Devising tools to measure human rights is critical in formulating effective policies and interventions regulating unhealthy products to fully realise the right to health.

2 Overview of international human rights law and the right to health

2.1 The nature of human rights

Broadly, human rights may be defined as a range of entitlements and protections that inhere in all people as a consequence of being human and are founded on respect for the dignity and worth of each person.[3] Fundamental characteristics of human rights include that they are universal (meaning that they apply equally and without discrimination and they are not subject to national or cultural interpretation), indivisible and interdependent. All human rights are of equal importance, and the respect of all rights equally is viewed as essential to the dignity and worth of every person. A body of human rights law legally guarantees human rights and sets out the obligations of the state to protect individuals and groups against actions that interfere with fundamental freedoms and human dignity. International human rights law is expressed in treaties, customary international law and other sources of law.

Adopted by the UN in 1948, the *Universal Declaration of Human Rights* ('UDHR')[4] is considered the cornerstone document in the field of international human rights. The UDHR, together with the *International Covenant on Civil and Political Rights* ('ICCPR')[5] – and its Optional Protocols[6] – and the *International Covenant on Economic, Social and Cultural Rights* ('ICESCR'),[7] make up what is referred to as the International Bill of Human Rights. Although technically the UDHR is not legally binding, it has gained legitimacy through state practice. Both the ICCPR and the ICESCR create legally binding obligations on states that have become parties to them. While the UDHR elaborates on the rights and freedoms referenced in the *Charter of the United Nations*, the ICCPR and the ICESCR provide additional content and detail to the rights enumerated under the UDHR.

Traditionally, human rights were bifurcated into two broad categories: positive rights and negative rights.[8] Negative rights were deemed to be those rights that impose obligations on states to refrain from certain conduct. Civil and political rights such as the right to life and freedom from torture were considered negative rights. Positive rights require that states take affirmative measures and actions to comply with human rights, including the expenditure of resources. Economic, social and cultural rights such as the right to health and the right to education were historically regarded as positive rights. This rights dichotomy was strongly supported by the political climate of the Cold War, in which the United States championed civil and political rights and the Eastern Bloc promoted economic, social and cultural rights.

As the human rights discourse evolved, this traditional classification has been criticised as inadequate and failing to capture the full dimension of each human right obligation.[9] For example, a positive right, such as the right to education, requires a state to take affirmative steps to provide access to schools, but it also demands that the state refrain from discriminating in intent or effect against marginalised populations. Conversely, rights that are typically considered negative, such as the right to a fair trial, also oblige the state to provide infrastructure and expend resources to create the infrastructure and court system necessary to realise this right.

The modern human rights approach adopts a threefold classification of human rights obligations that emphasises the *type* of state obligation. Under this typology, states have obligations to respect, protect and fulfil all human rights.[10] The obligation to respect requires states that have ratified human rights treaties to respect and refrain from interfering with the enjoyment of human rights. The obligation to protect requires states to implement mechanisms to prevent violation of rights by non-state or third-party actors. The obligation to fulfil requires states to take positive action and measures to establish the necessary infrastructure to facilitate the full enjoyment of human rights. This contemporary understanding of human rights has been particularly instrumental in the evolution of the right to health because it emphasises the state's duties both to refrain from violating the right to health and, more importantly, to create the conditions that are necessary to fulfil the right to health.

2.2 *The relationship between health and human rights*

The relationship between health and human rights is expansive; 'human rights implicate fundamental rights to a wide range of entitlements and protections that are relevant to health'.[11] Traditionally, however, public health has been viewed as colliding with human rights largely due to historical efforts to control infectious diseases, which often interfered with or necessitated the limitation of human rights. Coercive measures such as mandatory testing, quarantine and isolation cast the relationship between health and human rights with an antagonistic hue.[12] It was not until the HIV/AIDS pandemic in the 1980s that the structural relationship between health and human rights was recognised. The HIV/AIDS movement acted as a catalyst for the use of a response that embraced a comprehensive human rights approach and advanced a public health strategy aligned with human rights.[13] The relationship between health and human rights is complex and multifaceted. The violation of a number of diverse human rights, including the right to liberty and security of person and freedom from torture or cruel, inhuman or degrading treatment may have health impacts. Health is also now recognised as both a fundamental human right in and of itself and a necessary element for the full enjoyment of other human rights.[14]

The human right to health finds legal expression in a number of key international instruments. Article 25.1 of the UDHR affirms: 'Everyone has the right to a standard of living adequate for the health of himself and of his family, including food, clothing, housing and medical care and necessary social services'. The most comprehensive article on the right to health in international human rights law is enshrined in the ICESCR. In accordance with art 12.1 of the ICESCR, states parties recognise 'the right of everyone to the enjoyment of the highest attainable standard of physical and mental health', while art 12.2 enumerates, by way of illustration, a number of 'steps to be taken by the states parties … to achieve the full realization of this right'. Included in the steps to be taken by states to achieve the full realisation of the right to health in the ICESCR are those necessary for:

(a)   the provision for the reduction of the stillbirth-rate and of infant mortality and for the healthy development of the child;
(b)   the improvement of all aspects of environmental and industrial hygiene; the prevention, treatment and control of epidemic, endemic, occupational and other diseases.[15]

Additionally, the right to health is recognised, inter alia, in art 5(e)(iv) of the *International Convention on the Elimination of All Forms of Racial Discrimination* of 1965,[16] arts 11.1(f) and 12 of the *Convention on the Elimination of All Forms of Discrimination against Women* of 1979[17] and art 24 of the *Convention on the Rights of the Child* ('CRC') of 1989.[18] Several regional human rights instruments also recognise the right to health, such as the *European Social Charter* of 1961 as revised (art 11),[19] the *African Charter on Human and Peoples' Rights* of 1981 (art 16)[20] and the *Additional Protocol to the American Convention on Human Rights in the Area of Economic, Social and Cultural Rights* of 1988 (art 10).[21]

The UN Committee on Economic, Social and Cultural Rights ('CESCR' or 'Committee') is the body in charge of interpreting the content of the human rights provisions enshrined in the ICESCR. The normative content of the right to health is outlined in General Comment 14 of the CESCR.[22] Although not legally binding, the CESCR provides guidance as to the interpretation of the right to health. The CESCR stresses that the right to health is not merely the right to be healthy and recognises that health is unique in that it must consider both an individual's biological and socioeconomic preconditions and a state's available resources.[23] The right to health is understood to include both freedoms and entitlements. Freedom from government interference in the right to health includes the right to be free from torture and non-consensual medical treatment. Entitlements under the right to health include the right to a health system that provides equality of opportunity for all people to enjoy the right to health.[24]

In accordance with the ICESCR, the obligation of the right to health is subject to progressive realisation and constraints due to resource limitations. This concept was clarified by the CESCR in its General Comment 3:

the concept of progressive realization constitutes recognition of the fact that full realization of all economic, social and cultural rights will generally not be able to be achieved in a short period of time. ... Nevertheless, the fact that realization over time, or in other words progressively, is foreseen under the Covenant should not be misinterpreted as depriving the obligation of all meaningful content.[25]

States have an obligation to move as expeditiously and effectively as possible to fulfil the right to health. Moreover, any deliberately retrogressive measures require justification. While the ICESCR allows for progressive realisation, it also imposes various obligations on states parties, which are of immediate effect. States parties have direct obligations in relation to the right to health, such as the guarantee that the right will be exercised without discrimination of any kind (art 2.2) and the obligation to take steps (art 2.1) towards the full realisation of art 12. Such steps must be deliberate, concrete and targeted towards the full realisation of the right to health.

3 The relationship between human rights and the regulation of tobacco, alcohol and unhealthy food

3.1 The right to health, the right to food and freedom of information

Human rights have been used to both advocate for and attack the regulation of tobacco, alcohol and unhealthy foods. Human rights arguments crafted to challenge tobacco, alcohol and food regulation are assessed in Part 4 below, while the majority of this part will focus on how human rights arguments can promote regulatory interventions to address NCDs. There is a growing recognition that a human rights approach to address the major risk factors for NCDs will be vital in stemming the tide of the epidemic. Ultimately, 'the goal of linking health and human rights is to contribute to advancing human well-being beyond what could be achieved through an isolated health or human rights based approach'.[26] International human rights law not only provides normative and analytical guidance but can also draw upon other human rights principles, including transparency, equality, non-discrimination, participation and accountability.[27] These are critical principles to consider when developing and evaluating government proposals for stronger regulation.

The relationship between international human rights and the regulation of unhealthy products can be examined from two different lenses. First, we will look at how, in the context of the regulation of tobacco, alcohol and unhealthy food, the human rights system can strengthen efforts to regulate. Secondly, we will examine how international legal efforts to regulate unhealthy products can reciprocally help to define a state's obligation to promote the right to health.

General Comment 14 lends specific support to an understanding that the right to health includes the obligation to regulate unhealthy products. The CESCR emphasises in that comment that the right to health extends beyond the right to access health services and encompasses the socioeconomic determinants of health, including the right to clean water and an adequate supply of safe food, nutrition and housing.[28] In articulating that content of art 12.2(b), the right to healthy natural and workplace environments, the Committee states that this obligation 'also embraces adequate housing and safe and hygienic working conditions, an adequate supply of food and proper nutrition, and discourages the abuse of alcohol, and the use of tobacco, drugs and other harmful substances'.[29]

Perhaps most relevant to a discussion of the regulation of tobacco, alcohol and unhealthy foods, General Comment 14 also explores the state's duty to *protect* individuals from infringement of their rights by third parties. A violation of the obligation to protect the right to health includes:

> the failure to regulate the activities of individuals, groups or corporations so as to prevent them from violating the right to health of others; the failure to protect consumers and workers from practices detrimental to health, e.g. by employers and manufacturers of medicines or food.[30]

This obligation extends beyond traditional considerations of food safety and food contamination to the need to consider regulation of products that may be harmful to health, including tobacco, alcohol and foods of poor nutritional value. If these products are being consumed in a manner hazardous to health, an obligation is placed on the state to intervene to protect the right to health. A policy response is required to reduce the detrimental effects on health by altering the market or consumption patterns in some manner.

General Comment 14 also supports the argument that states have an obligation to regulate unhealthy products in order to *fulfil* the right to health. Fulfilment of the right to health requires states to take positive measures 'that enable and assist individuals and communities to enjoy the right to health'.[31] This can be interpreted as including the obligation to create an enabling environment for healthy lifestyle choices.

While a human rights argument to support tobacco control is well established, using a human rights framework to support stronger regulation of alcohol and unhealthy foods is still relatively novel and challenging. Tobacco is unique in that it is the only legal product that is lethal when consumed as directed.[32] Making the argument that the state is obliged under the right to health to regulate the food and alcohol industry is more complex and presents important distinctions. Alcohol in moderation has minimally deleterious effects on health.[33] Food and beverages must be consumed daily, and physical activity may limit some of the detrimental effects of consuming high-caloric foods.[34] Smoking is not a necessary activity, and no amount of cigarettes is safe to consume.[35]

In addition to the right to health, the regulation of unhealthy food also invokes the fundamental right to food. The right to food is anchored in art 11 of the ICESCR, which recognises the right of everyone to an adequate standard of living.[36] This includes, but is not limited to, the right to adequate food, clothing and housing and the continuous improvement of living conditions. The right to food is not only a right to a minimum level of calories but an inclusive 'right to all nutritional elements that a person needs to live a healthy and active life, and the means to access them'.[37] The Report Submitted to the Human Rights Council by the Special Rapporteur on the Right to Food explicitly expresses concern over the marketing of unhealthy food and beverages to children and recommends that states: (i) adopt national strategies on diets and physical activity; (ii) provide accurate and balanced information to consumers; and (iii) align food and agricultural policies with the requirements of public health in accordance with their obligation to respect, protect and fulfil the right to health.[38] Specific policy recommendations in the report include: (i) imposing taxes on soft drinks and on foods high in saturated fats, sugar and sodium; (ii) transposing into domestic legislation the World Health Organization ('WHO') recommendations on the marketing of foods and non-alcoholic beverages to children; and (iii) adopting a plan for complete replacement of trans-fatty acids with polyunsaturated fats.[39]

Effective interventions to reduce the consumption of cigarettes, alcohol and unhealthy foods also implicate the right to freedom of information, which is a component of the right to freedom of expression enshrined in art 19 of the ICCPR.[40] In order to meet obligations under the right to freedom of information, governments are required to take actions to ensure that consumers are informed of the health risks of smoking and of consuming alcoholic beverages and diets high in saturated fats, sugar and sodium. Deceptive marketing and promotional activities of these products, such as the tobacco and alcohol industries' sponsorship of sporting and music events, may also be viewed as interfering with the individual's right to freedom of information. Public health professionals posit that these tactics compel individuals to ignore the health hazards associated with consuming these products by associating smoking and alcohol with healthy activities, professional athletes and celebrities.[41]

3.2 Corporations and international human rights law

Because the regulation of tobacco, alcohol and food involves restricting or intervening in the activities of the corporations that manufacture, sell and distribute these products, it is important to examine how international human rights law relates to the actions of corporations. Over the last decade, there has been considerable work on businesses and human rights. The UN has adopted a framework based on three foundational principles addressing businesses and human rights – the 'Protect, Respect, Remedy' framework ('Ruggie Framework').[42] This framework specifies that states have a duty to protect human rights, businesses have a responsibility to respect human rights and individuals need better access to both judicial and non-judicial remedies for human rights violations.[43] Accompanying the Ruggie Framework is a set of Guiding Principles adopted by the United Nations Human Rights Council ('Guiding Principles').[44]

The Ruggie Framework and Guiding Principles do not create new legal obligations but rather are intended to elaborate on existing obligations set out in international human rights treaties and how they impact the actions of businesses and state regulation of these businesses.[45] The Guiding Principles explain that the 'failure to enforce existing laws that directly or indirectly regulate business respect for human rights is often a significant gap in State practice'.[46] Moreover, 'it is equally important for States to review whether these laws provide the necessary coverage in light of evolving circumstances and whether, together with relevant policies, they provide an environment conducive to business respect for human rights'. [47]

The Ruggie Framework also provides foundational principles and sets out the corporate responsibility to respect human rights. The responsibility to respect human rights is a global standard expected of all business enterprises, regardless of where they operate. In addition, 'business enterprises should not undermine States' abilities to meet their own human rights obligations'.[48] The responsibility to respect human rights also demands that businesses 'seek to prevent or mitigate adverse human rights impacts that are directly linked to their operations, products or services by their business relationships, even if they have not contributed to those impacts'.[49] The Ruggie Framework may apply to the right to health in so far as it explicitly recognises the responsibility of businesses to respect human rights including the right to health as distinct from issues of legal liability and enforcement. By elaborating on human rights obligations and acknowledging that there is a corporate responsibility to respect human rights, these Guiding Principles may serve as further support for a range of policy interventions to regulate tobacco, alcohol and unhealthy foods. For example, the Ruggie Framework suggests that corporations involved in manufacturing foods should consider the impact of their products on consumers' right to health. This may be a useful tool, particularly when governments are proposing voluntary agreements with industry to address the health impacts of their products.

The contemporary conception of human rights and its twin challenges of limiting state intrusion on human rights and ensuring state promotion of human rights implicates a number of stakeholders. The Ruggie Framework represents a growing awareness that other actors including transnational businesses may significantly influence the state's capacity for the realisation of rights. This development is promising in strengthening the relationship between human rights and NCDs, particularly as states seek to implement stronger legal and regulatory interventions to address NCD risk factors that require support from the alcohol and food industries.

3.3 The WHO FCTC as an international, legally binding standard

The right to health has been criticised for its ambiguity and for being 'so broad that it lacks coherent meaning and is qualified by the principle of progressive realization'.[50] However, connecting international human rights law with international legal instruments like the WHO FCTC can help inform and provide content for the right to health.[51] As has been examined in greater detail in previous chapters, the ratification of the WHO FCTC has encouraged states to implement certain measures to control the tobacco epidemic. It represents an international commitment that calls for the interpretation of the right to health to include clear tobacco control standards and policies including smoke-free environments, prohibitions on tobacco advertising, promotion and sponsorship and health warnings. By ratifying the WHO FCTC, states recognise that tobacco is a significant threat to public health and that there are evidence-based measures and policies that can be implemented to protect the public's health and result in a palpable reduction in the incidence and overall prevalence of smoking. In this manner, the WHO FCTC acts as an international legal standard offering concrete obligations under the right to health with respect to tobacco control. Some judicial bodies have even gone as far as to claim that the WHO FCTC is not merely a health law treaty but also a human rights treaty, creating human rights obligations.[52] In upholding the constitutionality of a tobacco control law, for example, the Constitutional Tribunal of Peru stated that 'the FCTC is a human rights treaty, because although it does not recognize the right to health protection as a "new right" … it obliges State Parties clearly and directly to take steps that contribute to optimizing its effectiveness'.[53]

Further strengthening the connection between the WHO FCTC and international human rights law is a series of recommendations from UN treaty monitoring bodies stressing that states have an obligation to implement the WHO FCTC's measures. Through UN human rights mechanisms, human rights law serves as a tool to monitor and enforce a country's obligations under the WHO FCTC. Access to the UN system is particularly helpful for tobacco control advocates because the WHO FCTC does not include any formal monitoring provisions or avenues for civil society to formally participate.[54] Human rights treaty bodies have now firmly established that tobacco control is an integral component of advancing the right to health. In its 2009 review of Brazil, the CESCR expressly drew the connection between the right to health and compliance with the WHO FCTC. The CESCR 'welcomed the Brazilian government's ratification of the FCTC' but was concerned that it was 'still permissible to promote the use of tobacco through advertising in the State party [Brazil] and that … smoking is permitted in areas specially designed for the purpose'.[55] The CESCR in this instance explicitly referenced tobacco control measures stipulated under the WHO FCTC: developing smoke-free places (WHO FCTC, art 8) and banning advertising, promotion and sponsorship of tobacco products (WHO FCTC, art 13) to provide a standard by which to measure Brazil's compliance with its obligations under the right to health.

The human rights discourse, coupled with the international norms and legal standards created by the WHO FCTC, is also being used to encourage even those countries that have not yet ratified the WHO FCTC to implement its tobacco measures in order to meet human rights obligations. In the CESCR's 2011 periodic review of Argentina (which is a signatory but not a party to the WHO FCTC), the Committee recommended that 'the State party [Argentina] ratify and implement the WHO Framework Convention on Tobacco Control and develop effective public awareness and tax and pricing policies to reduce tobacco consumption, in particular targeting women and youth'.[56] In its review of Argentina, the United Nations Committee on the Elimination of the Discrimination Against Women ('CEDAW Committee') noted that Argentina was not meeting its international obligations under CEDAW in failing to address the tobacco industry's promotional strategies targeting women.[57] This example of a UN body using the WHO FCTC as a standard to measure a country's compliance with the right to health is significant as the international community contemplates the regulation of alcohol and unhealthy food. It suggests that there may be scope to assert that international legal instruments that are not binding on particular countries (or not binding in general) may nevertheless inform the content of the right to health and that the normative content of the right to health should not be limited to standards set out in legally binding instruments.

The imprint of international human rights law on tobacco control is also visible at the domestic level through tobacco control rights-based litigation. This is particularly evident in countries that have enshrined human rights obligations under international treaties in their domestic constitutions, or in countries where international human rights law is regarded as a source of law in domestic adjudication. Implementing the international human rights framework at the domestic level is integral in advancing tobacco control through litigation because it creates the potential for alleging the violation of a legal *right* through the absence of effective tobacco control measures.[58] Legal action cannot arise based on allegations that the government has neglected a public good, but instead requires the violation of a legal right. In India in 1999, the High Court of the State of Kerala issued a ground-breaking decision stating that second hand smoke violates the right to life under art 21 of the *Indian Constitution* and ordered that smoking be banned in public places.[59] This judgment was in response to a claim brought by a woman complaining of severe health problems due to exposure to second hand smoke.

In other examples of domestic litigation, the right to health is invoked to defend against challenges to tobacco control. The Peruvian Constitutional Tribunal dismissed a suit against the government claiming that a tobacco control law that prohibits smoking in certain places violated the claimants' rights to personal autonomy and economic freedom. In its decision, the Tribunal applied a proportionality test and determined that the right to health outweighs the right to personal autonomy and economic freedom.[60]

3.4 Non-binding instruments and the right to health: regulating alcohol and unhealthy food

Although there have been recent calls from public health advocates to promulgate binding international legal instruments to address alcohol and obesity, there are not yet comprehensive legally binding treaties comparable to the WHO FCTC.[61] Proponents of legally binding instruments to address obesity and alcohol highlight the parallels between tobacco, alcohol and even unhealthy foods: these products are considered major global health problems and the primary risk factors for non-communicable diseases; they are aggressively marketed to children; and the challenges of regulating these products are increasingly transnational in scope.[62] However, such proposals are currently challenged as being politically unfeasible and premature. Moreover, there are striking differences between tobacco, alcohol and unhealthy foods that make global regulation of alcohol and unhealthy foods extraordinarily challenging. Critics contend that non-binding legal instruments, including guidelines and codes, may be more appropriate and have more impact in creating international legal norms and standards for alcohol control and food regulation.[63] Assessing the viability of international treaties to regulate alcohol and obesity is outside the purview of this chapter. It may be suggested, however, that international non-binding instruments may, like the WHO FCTC, serve as tools to help inform the content of its obligations to regulate tobacco, alcohol and unhealthy food under the right to health. Non-binding instruments can create norms that guide state behaviour. As the NCD crisis looms, there may be vast, unexplored potential for public health advocates to connect non-binding instruments relating to unhealthy food and alcohol to the binding international human rights framework.

With respect to alcohol control, the *Global Strategy to Reduce the Harmful Use of Alcohol*, adopted by the World Health Assembly in May 2010, provides policy options, including pricing options, drink-driving policies and countermeasures, and the availability and marketing of alcoholic beverages.[64] On efforts to regulate unhealthy foods, the key international documents to date that provide standards to regulate unhealthy food include the Codex Alimentarius, the WHO's *Set of Recommendations on the Marketing of Foods and Non-alcoholic Beverages to Children* ('Set of Recommendations'),[65] and the 2004 *Global Strategy on Diet, Physical Activity and Health*.[66] As efforts are made to implement these strategies and non-binding instruments, and as consensus in the global public health community emerges as to the legal and regulatory interventions necessary to respond to the NCDs epidemic, these standards may become a tool like the WHO FCTC to guide policy makers, courts and civil society in defining the state's obligations under the right to health.

3.5 Case study: applying the human rights framework to the regulation of marketing of unhealthy foods to children

Applying the human rights framework to the issue of regulating the marketing of unhealthy foods to children presents an illuminating case study of the potential for expanding the use of human rights arguments beyond tobacco control in the NCDs crisis. The childhood obesity epidemic is emerging as one of the world's most pressing public health challenges, with a staggering 170 million children estimated to be overweight globally.[67] Obesity places children and adolescents at risk of a range of serious health problems including cardiovascular disease, diabetes and depression, making obesity second only to smoking as a cause of preventable death.[68] Although childhood obesity is a complex problem that requires a multifaceted approach, there is increasing evidence that food marketing to children influences eating behaviour.[69] Research shows that even when children have been educated about the benefits of maintaining a healthy diet, they do not yet have the highly developed behavioural control mechanisms required to self-regulate their consumption when they are constantly inundated with junk food advertising.[70] Young children under the age of 12 are particularly affected by food marketing, and research suggests that they are unable to view advertising critically and have difficulty comprehending its persuasive intent.[71]

In addition to the right to health under the ICESCR, the CRC is a legally binding international human rights instrument that may be used to advocate for policy and legal measures to promote and protect a child's right to health. In 1989, the UN General Assembly decided that, as a vulnerable population, children are entitled to special care and assistance that necessitates a separate human rights convention to address a child's particular needs.[72] The CRC was founded on human dignity and the development of every child and explicitly commits governments to develop and take all necessary measures for the best interests of the child.[73]

Article 24 of the CRC addresses the right to the highest attainable standard of health. It states:

1. States Parties recognize the right of the child to the enjoyment of the highest attainable standard of health and to facilities for the treatment of illness and rehabilitation of health. States Parties shall strive to ensure that no child is deprived of his or her right of access to such health care services.

2. States Parties shall pursue full implementation of this right and, in particular, *shall take appropriate measures*:

   …

   (c) *To combat disease and malnutrition*, including within the framework of primary health care, through, inter alia, the application of readily available technology *and through the provision of adequate nutritious foods* and clean drinking-water, taking into consideration the dangers and risks of environmental pollution;

   …

   (e) *To ensure that all segments of society, in particular parents and children, are informed, have access to education and are supported in the use of basic knowledge of child health and nutrition*, the advantages of breastfeeding, hygiene and environmental sanitation and the prevention of accidents.[74]

As highlighted above, there is some direct support in the text of the CRC for government obligations with regards to health and nutrition. While these may generally be used to advance efforts on undernourishment and malnutrition, they could also be used to highlight government obligations to ensure children have access to healthy food choices and information on healthy diets, such as nutritious diets and choices, to reduce the risks of NCDs.

Article 17 of the CRC provides further support for government regulation of marketing that may adversely impact children, as it deals with the right to information and the role of the media:

States Parties recognize the important function performed by the mass media and shall ensure that the child has access to information and material from a diversity of national and international sources, especially those aimed at the promotion of his or her social, spiritual and moral well-being and physical and mental health. To this end, States Parties shall:

> …
>
> (e) *Encourage the development of appropriate guidelines for the protection of the child from information and material injurious to his or her well-being*, bearing in mind the provisions of articles 13 and 18.[75]

This provision could be used to argue that states have obligations to protect children from the marketing of unhealthy foods and beverages because the foods can have a detrimental impact on health when eaten excessively and are, therefore, 'materially injurious' to children's well-being. Protection could take the form of adequate safeguards and regulation.

The Committee on the Rights of the Child has issued a general comment on the right of the child to the enjoyment of the highest attainable standard of health.[76] General Comment 15 elaborates on the state's obligations to ensure access to nutritionally adequate and safe food. Paragraph 47 provides that children's exposure to 'fast foods' that are high in fat, sugar or salt, energy-dense and micronutrient-poor should be limited. In addition, the marketing of these substances – especially when such marketing is focused on children – should be regulated and their availability in schools and other places controlled.

The human rights obligations embedded in the CRC to regulate the marketing of unhealthy foods are broadly framed, but it may be argued that other international instruments, such as the WHO's Set of Recommendations, can inform states of the content of policies and necessary policy actions in order to meet these obligations. Although the Set of Recommendations is not binding, it represents recommendations developed by WHO member states and other stakeholders and endorsed by the World Health Assembly. The Set of Recommendations is structured as 12 recommendations under the following sub-headings: rationale; policy development; policy implementation; policy monitoring and evaluation; and research with the aim of preparing mechanisms for 'promoting the responsible marketing of foods and non-alcoholic beverages to children'.[77] Recommendation 5, for example, expressly states that settings where children gather, such as schools, childcare and other educational institutions, should be free from all forms of marketing of foods high in saturated fats, trans-fatty acids, free sugars or salt.[78] Like the obligations set out in the WHO FCTC, the policy standards agreed upon in the Set of Recommendations guide states in fulfilling their obligation to respect, protect and promote the right to health. The right to health can be used by public health advocates and policy makers to support legal and policy interventions to address the deleterious effects of unhealthy food marketing to children. Just as human rights and tobacco control can be mutually reinforcing, so too can human rights and the promotion of responsible marketing to children. Imposing restrictions on the marketing of unhealthy food, however, may also result in a potential tension between the right to health and the right to freedom of expression or commercial speech rights. This possible tension is explored in more detail in the following section.

4 Human rights in tension

When governments seek to regulate the tobacco, alcohol and food industries, different fundamental human rights are placed in tension. The use of a human rights approach in tobacco is a relatively recent tool employed by the tobacco control movement. Indeed, traditionally the tobacco industry has been more proactive in using human rights law arguments to attack tobacco control laws and policies.[79] The fundamental rights to economic and personal freedom, private property, free speech and equal protection comprise the tobacco industry's arsenal of human rights arguments.[80]

The central argument used by opponents of controlling consumption of tobacco, alcohol and unhealthy food is that government regulation of these products is paternalistic and interferes with personal autonomy. Indoor smoking bans, for example, are cast as unjust intrusions on the liberty of smokers and business owners. The tobacco industry has championed 'smokers' rights' and asserts that there is a fundamental human right to smoke.[81] 'Fat taxes' on foods high in salt, sugar or fat are said to restrict an individual's personal liberty and the freedom to choose what products they wish to consume.[82] The industry's early arguments challenging a proposed tobacco regulation (in both Mexico City's local Congress and Federal Congress during the second half of 2007) even went as far as claiming that a ban on smoking in public spaces constituted discrimination on the grounds of health because smokers are addicts with a health condition.[83]

In tackling industry's human rights arguments, the legal merit of these claims should first be carefully examined. The 'right to smoke', for example, is not grounded in law, and governments reserve the right to regulate hazardous substances.[84] When confronted with duelling human rights with a valid legal basis in the context of tobacco control, many courts have embraced a doctrine of balancing the competing rights within an analytical framework of proportionality. For example, the Inter-American Commission on Human Rights has elaborated on the components of this proportionality test. In order for a restriction to be lawful, the proposed restriction must be imposed through the law. It must respond to a legitimate aim to raise a social interest or to preserve the general well-being in a democratic society. The restriction must be necessary and must use the least restrictive measures. Finally, the restriction must be proportional. It is under this prong of the test that the right to health trumps the rights of smokers or the rights of the tobacco industry:

> Under any reasonable understanding of 'proportionality', the interests of the public in being protected from the inherent dangers of tobacco smoke in indoor places and work places and on public transport, at a minimum, outweigh whatever interests the industry has in marketing and encouraging the consumption of a lethal product.[85]

An examination of the rights arguments used by the tobacco industry against bans on advertising, promotion and sponsorship underlines the inherent weakness of these claims. The tobacco industry asserts that bans on advertising, promotion and sponsorship violate its rights to freedom of commerce and freedom of expression.[86] A restriction on advertising, however, does not constitute an infringement of the right to freedom of commerce because it does not interfere with the economic activity of buying, producing and selling tobacco products.[87] The industry is free to engage in these activities, but governments reserve the right to regulate these activities in order to protect the population's health.[88] The industry's arguments that advertising bans violate the fundamental freedom of expression also fall short. In making these claims, tobacco companies are conflating commercial advertising with social and political speech, which has traditionally been protected as a fundamental human right.[89] Commercial speech typically receives a lower level of protection than political and social speech because its primary purpose is to sell a product and to obtain a profit.[90] Conversely, political, social and artistic expression is protected under international human rights law because of its value in a democratic society.[91] The human right to health argument supporting advertising bans is therefore far more compelling than the industry's claims to commercial speech, as courts are willing to provide less protection to commercial speech than to other forms of expression.

Strong evidence of the health impact and effectiveness of the regulatory measure is critical when justifying limits on human rights and applying the proportionality test. In the case of tobacco, evidence supporting tobacco control policies has been well established and built into the WHO FCTC. As governments seek to introduce regulatory interventions to address alcohol and unhealthy food, courts will demand evidence of the effectiveness of these measures to justify restrictions on other rights such as freedom of expression. The following section considers the availability of such evidence in the context of measuring the implementation of the right to health.

5 Measuring the implementation of the right to health

Although the international human rights framework offers a robust argument to support the regulation of unhealthy foods and alcohol, the linkage of human rights to the regulation of unhealthy products has focused primarily on the issue of tobacco control. A cardinal factor in both the creation of the WHO FCTC and the success of a human rights approach to tobacco control has been the availability of strong, scientific evidence supporting tobacco control policies and interventions. In fact, tobacco control has been lauded as 'one of the most rational, evidence-based policies in health care'.[92] In order to facilitate the use of human rights as a tool for stronger regulation of unhealthy products beyond just tobacco control, strong empirical evidence that links regulatory interventions to positive health outcomes will be crucial.

An analysis of the connection between international human rights law and the regulation of tobacco, alcohol and food would be incomplete without a discussion of the role of human rights indicators and the measuring of the right to health. There is a growing movement for the development of human rights indicators to assess the implementation and realisation of human rights; to measure human rights and:

> to manage a process of change directed at meeting certain socially desirable objectives, there is a need to articulate targets consistent with those objectives, mobilize the required means, as well as identify policy instruments and mechanisms that translate those means into desired outcomes.[93]

The importance of identifying specific indicators rather than general statistics is now recognised as integral in advancing human rights claims but may also help clarify the content of human rights standards and ensure that the interpretative phase is well informed. The UN Office of the High Commissioner for Human Rights ('OHCHR') has produced *Human Rights Indicators: A Guide to Measurement and Implementation* which defines a human rights indicator as:

> specific information on the state or condition of an object, event, activity or outcome that can be related to human rights norms and standards; that addresses and reflects human rights principles and concerns; and that can be used to assess and monitor the promotion and implementation of human rights.[94]

Indicators used for human rights assessments may be categorised as quantitative, qualitative, fact-based and judgment-based.[95] In the context of the right to health, for example, indicators may include the prevalence of overweight children under the age of 12, or whether national policies that limit saturated fatty acids and hydrogenated vegetable oils in the food supply have been adopted.

Following the Political Declaration on NCDs adopted by the UN General Assembly in 2011,[96] the WHO developed the *NCD Global Monitoring Framework* ('Monitoring Framework'), adopted in 2013.[97] The Monitoring Framework is designed to track global progress in preventing and controlling NCDs and their key risk factors. It includes a set of nine targets to be achieved by 2025 along with 25 indicators, including short-term outcomes addressing behavioural risk factors to measure progress. Although it does not create human rights obligations, the Monitoring Framework does suggest a global consensus on the comparative priorities with respect to NCDs and what is achievable for states by 2025. Targets and specific indicators relating to tobacco, alcohol and unhealthy foods (salt/sodium, micronutrients and saturated fats) are established. The Monitoring Framework sets out a target of a 30 per cent reduction in prevalence of current tobacco smoking and provides two specific indicators: (i) the age standardised prevalence of current tobacco use among persons aged 15 years and older; and (ii) prevalence of current tobacco use among adolescents. On the issue of alcohol, a targeted 10 per cent relative reduction in overall consumption of alcohol (including hazardous and harmful drinking) along with a reduction of specific indicators such as alcohol related morbidity and mortality among adolescents and adults, as appropriate within the national context, are provided. An example of a specific indicator relating to the issue of unhealthy food is the age-standardised mean proportion of total energy intake from saturated fatty acids in persons aged 18 years and older. Again, although they are non-binding, these indicators and targets can be utilised by policy makers and advocates to assess regulatory interventions and to measure a state's progress in achieving the right to health. Effectively measuring the right to health and the state's obligation to prevent and respond to NCDs will be vital in sustaining the relationship between human rights and the regulation of tobacco, alcohol and unhealthy food.

6 Conclusion

Human rights law and the regulation of products that are pernicious to health are intimately intertwined. Human rights treaties can provide an opportunity and framework for advancing interventions in the NCDs epidemic, which will allow policy makers and advocates to take collaborative action documented in international health instruments to the state obligation level and even into domestic courts. In this sense, human rights law may function as a vehicle for the implementation of evidence-based policies derived from binding and non-binding international instruments to regulate tobacco, alcohol and unhealthy foods. The relevance of a human rights approach to tobacco control has been firmly established, with the WHO FCTC providing international legal standards to inform the state's obligations under the right to health. With obesity rates soaring, it remains to be seen whether the human rights approach will also be used in domestic courts and by policy makers to advance regulatory interventions to address the issue of unhealthy eating and alcohol abuse. Although not without challenges, contemporary human rights law offers promising potential to translate its success with the tobacco control movement to tackle other risk factors for NCDs and progress towards the full realisation of the highest attainable standard of health.

Notes

1 See generally *Political Declaration of the High-level Meeting of the General Assembly on the Prevention and Control of Non-communicable Diseases*, GA Res 66/2, UN GAOR, 66th sess, 3rd plen mtg, Agenda Item 117, UN Doc A/RES/66/2 (24 January 2012, adopted 19 September 2011) annex; Kavita Sivaramakrishnan and Richard Parker, 'The United Nations High Level Meeting on the Prevention and Control of Noncommunicable Diseases: A Missed Opportunity?' (2012) 102 (11) *American Journal of Public Health* 2010.
2 *WHO Framework Convention on Tobacco Control*, opened for signature 16 June 2003, 2302 UNTS 166 (entered into force 27 February 2005) ('WHO FCTC').
3 UN Office of the High Commissioner for Human Rights, *Vienna Declaration and Programme of Action* (25 June 1993) <http://www.ohchr.org/en/professionalinterest/pages/vienna.aspx>.
4 *Universal Declaration of Human Rights*, GA Res 217A (III), UN GAOR, 3rd sess, 183rd plen mtg, UN Doc A/710 (10 December 1948).
5 *International Covenant on Civil and Political Rights*, opened for signature 16 December 1966, 999 UNTS 171 (entered into force 23 March 1976).
6 See, eg, *Optional Protocol to the International Covenant on Civil and Political Rights*, opened for signature 16 December 1966, 999 UNTS 171 (entered into force 23 March 1976).

7 *International Covenant on Economic, Social and Cultural Rights*, opened for signature 16 December 1966, 993 UNTS 3 (entered into force 3 November 1976).

8 Philip Alston, Ryan Goodman and Henry Steiner, *International Human Rights in Context: Law, Politics, Morals* (Oxford University Press, 2008) 256.

9 Ibid 282.

10 Ida Koch, 'Dichotomies, Trichotomies or Waves of Duties?' (2005) 5(1) *Human Rights Law Review* 81.

11 Peter Jacobson and Soheil Soliman, 'Co-opting the Health and Human Rights Movements' (2000) 30(4) *Journal of Law, Medicine & Ethics* 605, 705.

12 Jonathan Mann et al, 'Health and Human Rights' (1994) 1 *Health and Human Rights* 6, 13.

13 Ibid.

14 Helena Nygren-Krug, 'A Human Rights-based Approach to Non-communicable Diseases' in Andrew Clapham and Mary Robinson (eds), *Realizing the Right to Health* (Rüffer & Rub, 2009) 263.

15 See ICESCR art 12.

16 *International Convention on the Elimination of All Forms of Racial Discrimination*, opened for signature 21 December 1965, 660 UNTS 195 (entered into force 4 January 1969).

17 *Convention on the Elimination of All Forms of Discrimination against Women*, opened for signature 1 March 1980, 1249 UNTS 13 (entered into force 3 September 1981).

18 *Convention on the Rights of the Child*, opened for signature 20 November 1989, 1577 UNTS 3 (entered into force 2 September 1990) ('CRC').

19 *European Social Charter*, opened for signature 27 June 1981, 1520 UNTS 217 (entered into force 21 October 1986).

20 *African Charter on Human and Peoples' Rights*, opened for signature 26 February 1965, 529 UNTS 89 (entered into force 21 October 1991).

21 *Additional Protocol to the American Convention on Human Rights in the Area of Economic, Social and Cultural Rights*, opened for signature 11 November 1988, OAS Treaty Series No 69 (entered into force 16 November 1999).

22 UN Economic and Social Council Committee on Economic, Social and Cultural Rights, *General Comment No 14: The Right to the Highest Attainable Standard of Health*, UN Doc E/C.12/2000/4 (11 August 2000) ('General Comment 14').

23 Ibid 9.

24 Ibid 8.

25 UN Economic and Social Council Committee on Economic, Social and Cultural Rights, *General Comment No 3: The Nature of States Parties' Obligations (Art 2, Para 1, of the Covenant)*, UN Doc E/1991/23 ('General Comment 3').

26 See Mann et al, above n 12, 11.

27 Nygren-Krug, above n 14.

28 General Comment 14, [4].

29 Ibid [15].

30 Ibid [51].

31 Ibid [37].

32 Richard Doll et al, 'Mortality in Relation to Smoking: 40 Years' Observations on Male British Doctors' (1994) 309 *British Medical Journal* 901.

33 See generally Michael Collins et al, 'Alcohol in Moderation, Cardioprotection, and Neuroprotection: Epidemiological Considerations and Mechanistic Studies' (2009) 33(2) *Alcoholism: Clinical & Experimental Research* 206.

34 Miriam Reiner et al, 'Long-term Health Benefits of Physical Activity – A Systematic Review of Longitudinal Studies' (2013) 13 *BMC Public Health* 813.

35 See Doll, above n 32.

36 ICESCR art 11.

37 UN Office of the High Commissioner for Human Rights, *Fact Sheet No 34: The Right to Adequate Food* (2012) 2 <http://www.ohchr.org/Documents/Publications/FactSheet34en.pdf>.

38 Ibid.

39 Ibid.

40 ICCPR art 19.

41 Melissa Crow, 'Smokescreens and State Responsibilities: Using Human Rights Strategies to Promote Global Tobacco Control' (2004) 29 *Yale Journal of International Law* 209, 219.

42 John Ruggie, *Report of the Special Representative of the Secretary-General on This Issue of Human Rights and Transnational Corporations and Other Business Enterprises,* UN GAOR, 11th sess, Agenda Item 3, UN Doc A/HRC/17/31/Add.3 (25 May 2011) 5.

43 Ibid 7.

44 United Nations Office of the High Commissioner on Human Rights, *Guiding Principles on Business and Human Rights: Implementing the United Nations 'Protect, Respect and Remedy' Framework* (2011) <http://www.ohchr.org/Documents/Publications/GuidingPrinciplesBusinessHR_EN.pdf>

45 Ibid.

46 Ibid 5.

47 Ibid.

48 Ibid 13.

49 Ibid 14.

50 David Fidler, *International Law and Infectious Diseases* (Clarendon Press, 1999) 197.

51 Oscar Cabrera and Lawrence Gostin, 'Human Rights and the Framework Convention on Tobacco Control: Mutually Reinforcing Systems' (2011) 7(3) *International Journal of Law in Context* 285.

52 O'Neill Institute for National and Global Health Law, *Tobacco Industry Strategy in Latin American Courts – A Litigation Guide* (2012) 16.

53 Peruvian Constitutional Tribunal, *Jaime Barco Rodas contra el Articulo 30 de la ley N 28705 – Ley general para la prevencion y control de los riesgos del consump de tabaco,* unconstitutionality proceeding, July 2011, 69.

54 Cabrera and Gostin, above n 51, 294.

55 Oscar Cabrera and Alejandro Madrazo, 'Human Rights as a Tool for Tobacco Control in Latin America' (2010) 52 *Salud Publica de Mexico* 288.

56 CESCR, *Concluding Observations of the Committee on Economic, Social and Cultural Rights on Argentina,* UN Doc C.12/ARG/CO/3 (2011) [23].

57 Ibid [8].

58 Oscar Cabrera and Juan Carballo, 'Tobacco Control Litigation: Broader Impacts on Health Rights Adjudication' (2013) 41(1) *Global Health and the Law* 147, 150.

59 Ibid 151. *Ramakrishnan v State of Kerala,* OP No 24160/1998-A (23 February 1999, Supreme Court of India, unreported).

60 See Peruvian Constitutional Tribunal, *Jaime Barco Rodas contra el Articulo 30 de la ley N 28705 – Ley general para la prevencion y control de los riesgos del consump de tabaco,* unconstitutionality proceeding, July 2011, 69.

61 The Lancet, 'Urgently Needed: A Framework Convention for Obesity Control' (2011) 378(9793) *The Lancet* 741.

62 Allyn Taylor and Ibadat Dhillon, 'An International Legal Strategy for Alcohol Control: Not a Framework Convention – At Least Not Yet' (2012) 108(3) *Addiction* 450, 451.

63 Ibid.

64 World Health Assembly, *Global Strategy to Reduce the Harmful Use of Alcohol,* WHA Res 63.13, 63rd sess, 8th plen mtg, WHO Doc WHA63/2010/REC/1 (21 May 2010).

65 World Health Organization, *Set of Recommendations on the Marketing of Foods and Non-alcoholic Beverages to Children* (World Health Organization, 2010).

66 World Health Assembly, *Global Strategy on Diet, Physical Activity and Health: Report by the Secretariat*, WHA Res 57.17, 57th sess, 8th plen mtg, WHO Doc A57/2004/REC/1 (22 May 2004).

67 Ibid.

68 Katherine Flegal et al, 'Excess Deaths Associated with Underweight, Overweight, and Obesity' (2005) 293(15) *Journal of the American Medical Association* 1861.

69 Jennifer Harris and Samantha Graff, 'Protecting Young People from Junk Food Advertising: Implications of Psychological Research for First Amendment Law' (2012) 102(2) *American Journal of Public Health* 214.

70 Ibid 218.

71 Lawrence Gostin, *Public Health Law: Power, Duty, Restraint* (University of California Press, 2nd ed, 2008) 356.

72 *Convention on the Rights of the Child*, opened for signature 20 November 1989, 1577 UNTS 3 (entered into force 2 September 1990) preamble.

73 Ibid.

74 Ibid art 24 (emphasis added).

75 Ibid art 17 (emphasis added).

76 Committee on the Rights of the Child, *General Comment No 15 (2013) on the Right of the Child to the Enjoyment of the Highest Attainable Standard of Health (art 24)*, UN Doc CRC/C/GC/15 (17 April 2013).

77 World Health Organization, *Set of Recommendations*, above n 65, 6.

78 Ibid 9.

79 See generally, eg, Cabrera and Madrazo, above n 55.

80 Ibid 293.

81 Ibid.

82 Patrick Basham and John Luik, 'Kicking the Soda Can: Hard Truths about Soft Drink Taxes' (2010) 25(21) *Washington Legal Foundation: Legal Backgrounder*.

83 Cabrera and Gostin, above n 51, 295.

84 Ibid.

85 Instituto Brasileiro de Defensa do Consumidor, 'Amicus Curiae Brief in Support of the Respondents', in Supreme Tribunal Federal (Brazil) [Supreme Court of Brazil], *Confederacao Nacional da Industria v Presidente da Republica*, ADI/3311 (2008) 3.

86 Unconstitutionality Claim Brief for Nobleza Piccardo SAICYF, *Nobleza Piccardo SAICYF v Provincia de Santa Fe* (No 188/2006, Supreme Court of Argentina).

87 Constitutional Court of Guatemala, *Chamber of Commerce v Government of Guatemala*, Docket No 2158-2009 (2010) Brief as Amicus Curiae Supporting Respondents Provincia de Sante Fe, 4.2.

88 Gostin, above n 71, 26.

89 Cabrera and Gostin, above n 51, 300.

90 Ibid. See generally *Chaplinsky v New Hampshire*, 315 US 568 (1942); *Miller v California*, 413 US 15 (1973).

91 Cabrera and Gostin, above n 51, 300.

92 Ibid 227.

93 UN Office of the High Commissioner for Human Rights (OHCHR), *Human Rights Indicators: A Guide to Measurement and Implementation*, UN Doc HR/PUB/12/5 (2012) <http://www.refworld.org/docid/51a739694.html> 1.

94 Ibid 16.

95 Ibid.

96 *Political Declaration of the High-level Meeting of the General Assembly on the Prevention and Control of Non-communicable Diseases*, GA Res 66/2, UN GAOR, 66th sess, 3rd plen mtg, Agenda Item 117, UN Doc A/RES/66/2 (24 January 2012, adopted 19 September 2011) annex.

97 World Health Organization, *Follow-up to the Political Declaration of the High-level Meeting*

of the General Assembly on the Prevention and Control of Non-communicable Diseases, WHA Res WHA66.10, 66th sess, 9th plen mtg, Agenda Items 13.1 and 13.2, WHO Doc A66/ VR/9 (27 May 2013) annex, app 2 ('Comprehensive global monitoring framework, including 25 indicators, and a set of nine voluntary global targets for the prevention and control of noncommunicable diseases').

5 International Trade Law

*Tania Voon and Andrew D Mitchell**

1 Introduction

The liberalisation of international trade pursuant to the World Trade Organization ('WTO') and preferential trade agreements ('PTAs') offers the potential for considerable welfare benefits at national and global levels, through economic growth, fairer competition among producers, increased access to a wider range of better quality products and services, and the transfer of technology and knowledge.[1] But trade liberalisation also has the potential to increase certain unhealthy habits such as smoking and over-consumption of alcohol and unhealthy foods, leading to a corresponding increase in non-communicable diseases ('NCDs').[2]

A range of measures designed to reduce consumption of these products may implicate international trade rules. For example, NCD risk factors may be addressed through: product bans; packaging and labelling requirements; import tariffs; sales taxes; subsidies; licences; restrictions on advertising, promotion or sponsorship; regulation of product content through disclosure or restriction of ingredients; restrictions on ages of sale or purchase; exclusion areas (eg no smoking or no alcohol areas); and education. To a greater or lesser degree, each of these measures could potentially infringe international trade rules and therefore needs to be crafted with those rules in mind. A key aim of this chapter is therefore to provide insights for public health officials and policy-makers in countries around the world on how regulation of NCD risk factors can be optimised to accord with the requirements of international trade law without compromising public health objectives. Despite some problematic examples of recent clashes between international trade law and NCD risk factor regulation (particularly in connection with tobacco), we firmly believe as international trade law scholars that international trade law need not impede sound health policy.

At the time of writing, the number of WTO members is 159,[3] with Yemen set to become the 160th member in 2014,[4] and 23 other states and customs territories engaged in the process of WTO accession.[5] PTAs provide preferential treatment – for example, lower tariffs – to specified countries only, typically with provisions mirroring and sometimes going beyond WTO law. PTAs that include a WTO member must be notified to the WTO: 379 PTAs have been notified to the WTO (or its predecessor the *General Agreement on Tariffs and Trade 1947* ('GATT 1947'))[6] and are in force.[7] This number has risen exponentially since the 1990s,[8] providing one reason for increasing concern about the impact of international trade law on health policy. Unlike in international investment law (as discussed in Chapter 6 of this volume), international trade law does not entail investor-state dispute settlement ('ISDS'). Thus, only a WTO member (which would be a state or a state-like entity such as the European Union or Hong Kong, China) may bring a formal legal dispute against another WTO member under the WTO dispute settlement system. Similarly, only a PTA party may bring a formal dispute against another PTA party to enforce compliance with the international trade rules of the PTA (although a separate investment chapter within the PTA might include an ISDS mechanism). Although this structure precludes direct international trade law challenges to NCD risk factor regulation by affected industries, those industries may nevertheless support or lobby their governments to take action[9] and may also form a part of the government delegation in supporting the claim.[10]

In Part 2 of this chapter, we outline some of the core obligations of the WTO agreements and PTAs, which affect the design of NCD risk factor regulation by WTO members and other PTA parties. In Part 3, we outline the various forms of 'flexibility' that are available in international trade law to allow public policy measures such as health regulations even where they may interfere with the usual trade obligations. We then turn in Part 4 to explore some of the ways in which international trade law has come to interact with NCD risk factor regulation to date, drawing lessons for the future in Part 5 as to how best to minimise potential conflicts and resist industry calls to retreat from such regulation to avoid costly legal challenges.

This chapter focuses on two WTO agreements, which are among the most relevant to this area of regulation: the *General Agreement on Tariffs and Trade 1994* ('GATT 1994')[11] and the *Agreement on Technical Barriers to Trade* ('TBT Agreement').[12] The WTO's *Agreement on Trade-Related Aspects of Intellectual Property Rights* ('TRIPS Agreement')[13] is also significant for NCD risk factor regulation and is separately addressed in Chapter 7 of this volume. The WTO's *Agreement on Subsidies and Countervailing Measures* ('SCM Agreement')[14] may also be relevant to subsidisation of relevant goods, along with the *Agreement on Agriculture*,[15] which relates to the subsidisation of tobacco[16] as well as subsidisation of agricultural products connected with alcoholic beverages or unhealthy food. Others have discussed the potential relevance of the WTO's *Agreement on the Application of Sanitary and Phytosanitary Measures*[17] for NCD risk factor regulation.[18] Finally, the *General Agreement on Trade in Services*[19] could be relevant to WTO members' regulation of NCD risk factors to the extent that such regulation relates to, for example, advertising services, distribution services, wholesale services, or retail services.[20]

Much of the discussion below focuses on WTO rules as interpreted pursuant to the WTO dispute settlement system, under which claims are initially heard by a three-person panel composed on an ad hoc basis,[21] and appeals are heard by a division of three from the standing seven-member Appellate Body.[22] The decisions of panels or the Appellate Body become binding – only on the parties to the dispute and only with respect to that dispute[23] – upon their adoption by the WTO's Dispute Settlement Body,[24] which comprises representatives of all WTO members.[25] These decisions do not contain authoritative interpretations of the WTO agreements (which can be made only by the WTO's Ministerial Conference or General Council)[26] and cannot 'add to or diminish the rights and obligations' in the WTO agreements.[27] Nevertheless, panels are generally expected to follow the reasoning of the Appellate Body,[28] and adopted panel and Appellate Body reports are routinely referred to in subsequent cases and are seen as persuasive or offering relevant guidance,[29] particularly given the need for security and predictability in international trade.[30]

2 Core obligations of international trade law

Several core obligations of international trade law are important in understanding the relationship between NCD risk factor regulation and international trade law. These obligations are found in a variety of contexts in international trade law, with the examples below focusing on their reflection in the GATT 1994 and the TBT Agreement. Health advocates and policy-makers can learn to be alert to proposed regulatory measures that contain factors that may raise difficulties under international trade law by understanding the nature of these kinds of core obligations. Below we discuss in turn: (i) tariff bindings, which relate to trade in goods; (ii) import bans and other trade-restrictive measures, which relate to both goods and services and extend to packaging and labelling requirements; and (iii) non-discrimination, which takes the primary forms of the 'national treatment' and 'most-favoured-nation treatment' obligations, which appear in a range of WTO agreements including others not discussed here, such as the TRIPS Agreement. These obligations are subject to specific and general exceptions, according to which members may be able to retain measures inconsistent with the core obligations, as discussed further in Part 3 of this chapter below.

2.1 Tariff bindings

Under the GATT 1994, each WTO member must refrain from imposing tariffs (that is, customs duties) on products imported from other WTO members in excess of those set out in the importing member's GATT schedule.[31] Tariffs are not to be confused with 'internal' taxes such as goods and services taxes or sales taxes, which are imposed after a product has crossed the border and must be applied on a non-discriminatory basis as discussed further below. Tariff bindings presently apply only to physical goods.[32] The effect of a tariff is typically to increase the price of the imported product, because the amount of the tariff is incorporated into the price paid by the consumer,[33] thereby reducing the competitiveness of the imported product in comparison to local (ie domestically produced) products. Thus, one way of reducing consumption of unhealthy products might be to increase tariffs on imports of such products. However, if consumers respond simply by purchasing cheaper local versions of the same unhealthy product, from a health perspective nothing has changed.

2.2 *Import bans and other trade-restrictive measures*

Under the GATT 1994, WTO members are generally precluded from imposing

> prohibitions or restrictions other than duties, taxes or other charges ... on the importation of any product of the territory of any other Member or on the exportation or sale for export of any product destined for the territory of any other Member.[34]

Essentially this means that WTO members cannot ban the importation of particular goods or impose quotas on such imports (although either might be possible under an exception such as those discussed below).

Under the TBT Agreement, art 2.1 provides ('[w]ith respect to ... central government bodies')[35] that:

> Members shall ensure that *technical regulations* are not prepared, adopted or applied with a view to or with the effect of creating *unnecessary obstacles to international trade*. For this purpose, technical regulations shall not be *more trade-restrictive than necessary* to fulfil a *legitimate objective*, taking account of the risks non-fulfilment would create. Such legitimate objectives are, inter alia: ... protection of *human health* or safety ... In assessing such risks, relevant elements of consideration are, inter alia: available scientific and technical information, related processing technology or intended end-uses of products.[36]

A 'technical regulation' for the purposes of this provision and the TBT Agreement as a whole (in contrast to a 'standard' as discussed in section 5.2 of this chapter below) is defined as a:

> [d]ocument which lays down product characteristics or their related processes and production methods, including the applicable administrative provisions, with which compliance is *mandatory*. It may also include or deal exclusively with terminology, symbols, packaging, marking or labelling requirements as they apply to a product, process or production method.[37]

Accordingly, in preparing mandatory product characteristics (eg content requirements) or packaging or labelling regulations with respect to tobacco, alcohol or unhealthy foods, states need to bear in mind the requirements of the TBT Agreement. In particular, in order to ensure compliance with TBT art 2.2, states should be wary of NCD risk factor regulations that create 'obstacles to international trade' or are 'trade-restrictive'.[38] States should be clear about the precise objective of the measure (with 'protection of human health' being explicitly recognised as a 'legitimate objective' in art 2.2), the relationship between the measure and the objective, available scientific information about the two and any alternatives that could be used.

Recent WTO cases on the TBT Agreement offer some comfort to WTO members concerned about ensuring sufficient policy space with respect to their

NCD risk factor regulations under that agreement. The cases demonstrate that the mere existence of some trade-restrictiveness arising from a particular measure is insufficient to demonstrate its violation of TBT art 2.2.[39] Indeed, while discrimination was found contrary to TBT art 2.1 (discussed further below), in none of the recent cases did the complainants succeed in establishing a violation of TBT art 2.2.[40] These outcomes arguably demonstrate the significant degree of deference that WTO panels and the Appellate Body are likely to show under TBT art 2.2 towards WTO members' legitimate policy objectives in constructing technical regulations.

2.3 Non-discrimination

The principle of non-discrimination in international trade law is most often given effect through the twin obligations to provide 'national treatment' and 'most-favoured-nation' ('MFN') treatment. These obligations are reflected in various WTO agreements in different ways. In the GATT 1994, the national treatment obligation essentially precludes WTO members from imposing higher internal taxes or other internal charges on products imported from another WTO member compared to those imposed on 'like' products that are domestically produced,[41] or from according less favourable treatment to such imported products through regulations affecting sale, purchase, transportation, distribution or use.[42] The MFN obligation in the GATT 1994 essentially precludes WTO members from providing products imported from or exported to any country with an advantage – with respect to tariffs or regulations affecting importation, exportation, sale, purchase, transportation, distribution or use – unless that advantage is also given to 'like' products imported from or exported to all WTO members.[43] In addition to other general exceptions discussed in Part 3 below, exceptions to the MFN obligation apply for PTAs allowed under GATT art XXIV[44] and for tariff preferences granted to developing countries pursuant to the WTO's 'Enabling Clause'.[45]

The obligations to accord national treatment and MFN treatment are also contained in TBT art 2.1, which states:

> Members shall ensure that in respect of technical regulations, products imported from the territory of any Member shall be accorded treatment no less favourable than that accorded to like products of national origin and to like products originating in any other country.

The meaning of 'like products' under the national treatment and MFN treatment obligations in the GATT 1994 varies but takes account of factors including: (i) the products' properties, nature and quality; (ii) end-uses; and (iii) tariff classification; as well as (iv) consumer tastes and habits.[46] These traditional criteria are also likely to be used in determining whether products are 'like' for the purposes of TBT art 2.1.[47] Under both the GATT 1994 and the TBT Agreement, the question of likeness focuses on the 'competitive relationship' between the products and not on the regulatory purpose of the challenged measure,[48] except to the extent that this purpose impacts on the traditional likeness criteria or otherwise affects the products' competitive relationship.[49] Accordingly, in devising NCD risk factor regulations, WTO members must attempt to ensure that products treated in different ways under the regulations are not the same, for example, in their nature and the way they are used, or in the sense that a consumer would be likely to substitute one for the other.

Assuming that two relevant products are 'like' (be they an imported product and a domestic product, or two imported products), the basic question arises in assessing an allegedly discriminatory regulation whether the regulation treats one product less favourably than the other. The recent TBT cases have made clear that, at least with respect to TBT art 2.1, the fact that a regulation operates 'to the detriment of the group of imported products' from the complaining WTO member does not necessarily mean that the regulation violates the non-discrimination obligation.[50] If the 'detrimental impact … stems exclusively from a legitimate regulatory distinction' then the regulation does not entail less favourable treatment contrary to TBT art 2.1.[51] Thus, although regulatory purpose is not directly relevant in assessing product likeness, it is central in assessing less favourable treatment. This approach enhances the possibility for WTO members to highlight their health objectives in targeting NCD risk factors through regulation.

The Panel Report in the recent case against the European Union's seal product ban suggests that the approach taken to assessing less favourable treatment under TBT art 2.1 will not be replicated in subsequent cases concerning the national treatment or MFN treatment obligations in the GATT 1994. Rather, less favourable treatment under the GATT 1994 may be shown simply by demonstrating a detrimental impact on the group of imported products.[52] This distinction is based on the fact that the GATT 1994, unlike the TBT Agreement, contains an express exception for public health measures,[53] as we discuss in the following section. That Panel Report is likely to be appealed, and the Appellate Body may shed further light on this matter in due course.

3 General exception for health measures

The GATT 1994 contains an exception for health measures that is often duplicated in PTAs.[54] GATT art XX(b) provides:

> Subject to the requirement that such measures are not applied in a manner which would constitute a means of arbitrary or unjustifiable *discrimination* between countries where the same conditions prevail, or a disguised *restriction on international trade*, nothing in this Agreement shall be construed to prevent the adoption or enforcement by any Member of measures: …
> (b) *necessary* to protect *human*, animal or plant *life or health* …[55]

The so-called 'chapeau' to GATT art XX, preceding paragraph (b), incorporates the principles of non-discrimination and limiting trade-restrictiveness found in the core obligations discussed in Part 2 above. Accordingly, a WTO member will have difficulty in justifying under GATT art XX(b) a health measure that discriminates in law or fact against or between imported products. In addition, the word 'necessary' in paragraph (b) requires a respondent WTO member to demonstrate that no less trade-restrictive alternative was reasonably available that could have made a contribution to the member's health objective equal to that of the contested measure.[56] The exception therefore does not give WTO members free rein in devising their NCD risk factor regulations. As already noted above, careful attention must be paid to the contribution the measure makes to its objective, the evidence supporting that objective and its relationship to the contribution, any discriminatory aspect of the measure and whether alternatives exist that would impose less of a burden on international trade.

4 Existing interaction of international trade law with NCD risk factor regulation

4.1 Current tobacco disputes in the WTO

Two high profile disputes have arisen in the WTO in recent years in connection with tobacco control and have been subject to extensive discussion elsewhere. In the 2012 case of *United States – Measures Affecting the Production and Sale of Clove Cigarettes* ('*US – Clove Cigarettes*'),[57] the United States' tobacco flavouring ban was found consistent with TBT art 2.2[58] but inconsistent with TBT art 2.1 because the ban extends to clove cigarettes (primarily imported from Indonesia) but excludes menthol cigarettes (primarily domestically produced).[59] This case remains in dispute regarding the United States' implementation of the WTO ruling against it.[60] An obvious means for the United States to bring its flavoured cigarette ban into conformity with WTO law would have been to remove the exemption for menthol, although this would not have benefited the complainant Indonesia and would likely have been difficult politically. Alternatively – worse from a public health perspective – the United States could have repealed the flavoured cigarette ban altogether. Either approach would have ended the less favourable treatment of imported clove cigarettes. Instead, the United States alleges that it has implemented the adverse ruling by taking steps such as further investigation of the health impact of menthol cigarettes in comparison to other cigarettes through the United States Food and Drug Administration.[61] Jamie Strawbridge characterises this approach to implementation as strengthening rather than weakening the United States' law.[62]

During 2012 and 2013, five countries initiated complaints against Australia regarding Australia's introduction of laws standardising tobacco product packaging.[63] The so-called 'plain' packaging laws preclude the use of promotional colours, graphics and logos on tobacco products and allow the identification of brand and variant only in a standardised font, colour and size. The majority of the package is taken up with graphic and textual health warnings against a specified 'drab dark brown' colour background.[64] These laws apply on a non-discriminatory basis to all tobacco products from all countries including Australia. The staggered timing of the complaints and differences between them have created procedural difficulties as the case slowly proceeds.[65] Although some debate exists over the legality of the Australian laws (particularly under the TRIPS Agreement),[66] we have previously expressed our view that Australia will prevail in these disputes.[67]

4.2 Alcohol disputes in the GATT 1947 and the WTO

A number of disputes concerning alcohol have been decided since the establishment of the WTO in 1995, but these have generally related to discriminatory taxes and have not been focused on health objectives.[68] Some GATT 1947 cases were similarly not focused on health.[69] However, two cases brought under GATT 1947 related more explicitly to public health. One 1998 case found GATT-inconsistent import restrictions and protection akin to tariffs in the administration of Canadian provincial marketing boards for alcoholic beverages,[70] despite the inclusion of health among the objectives of these monopolies.[71] This case may be instructive for states that maintain monopolies on the sale or distribution of alcohol or other health-damaging products. Additional WTO rules apply to these kinds of bodies.[72]

In the 1992 case of *United States – Measures Affecting Alcoholic and Malt Beverages*,[73] a GATT Panel found several federal and state measures of the United States inconsistent with the national treatment obligation in GATT art III because they were discriminatory, eg offering exemptions or preferential tax treatment to domestically produced but not imported products.[74] However, the measures challenged also included the application by certain states of 'restrictions on points of sale, distribution and labelling based on the alcohol content of beer above 3.2 per cent by weight'.[75] The United States argued that 'states encouraged the consumption of low alcohol beer over beer with a higher alcohol content specifically for the purposes of protecting human life and health and upholding public morals'.[76] Although Canada disputed that argument,[77] the Panel found that 'low alcohol content beer and high alcohol content beer need not be considered like products in terms of Article III:4'[78] and that 'the alcohol content of beer has not been singled out as a means of favouring domestic producers over foreign producers'.[79] While the United States was successful in relation to the alcohol content measures, this decision reinforces the need for WTO members to be able to justify distinctions drawn between similar products on health grounds.

4.3 Unhealthy foods in WTO disputes and WTO accession

International trade law is not simply a barrier that public health policy needs to overcome. As we have discussed elsewhere, legal challenges to the subsidisation of unhealthy food products have already been made in the WTO,[80] demonstrating the possibility of using international trade law to combat unhealthy diets around the world by addressing the artificially low prices of such products.[81]

Nevertheless, WTO law may appear to pose some challenges to members' policies in combating unhealthy food and obesity. For example, when Samoa acceded to the WTO, under pressure from existing WTO members, Samoa agreed to remove its ban on the importation and distribution of turkey tails and turkey tail products,[82] which are high fat products that are relatively cheap and therefore popular in Samoa.[83] Some commentators have promoted these kinds of bans on the grounds of health,[84] and Samoa explained during the accession process that the ban was designed 'to help curb the rise in diseases such as diabetes, high blood pressure and heart and kidney failure'.[85] In response to other members' concerns, Samoa indicated that it was developing 'a public education plan to combat bad dietary choices that promoted obesity and its attendant problems of ill health and disease in Samoa'[86] and that Samoa would seek assistance from 'the World Health Organization and other development partners ... to undertake a detailed study ... of practical and realistic options to combat Samoa's health problems'.[87] Samoa also agreed to a transition period of three years: in the first 12 months, the ban on imports would be revoked and replaced with import tariffs of 300 per cent; and after an additional two years the ban on domestic sales would be 'eliminated and replaced with an import duty of 100 per cent or other tax regulation, and the recommendations from the study'.[88]

The impact of Samoa's accession to the WTO on its policy regarding turkey tails might be seen as an indictment of international trade law and, specifically, WTO law and its accession process. On the other hand, the ability of Samoa to convert its import ban to a high tariff (as occurred generally in the creation of the WTO, in a process known as 'tariffication')[89] and to consider the availability of non-discriminatory measures such as education and evidence-based regulation may also be seen as confirmation that health objectives can be optimally addressed through regulation that also happens to comply with the obligations of international trade law. Putting political considerations to one side, just as a non-discriminatory approach to regulating flavoured cigarettes would arguably best serve both health and trade goals in the United States, so too may removing the import ban (often identified as the most trade-restrictive measure possible)[90] prove appropriate in Samoa.

5 Promoting optimal health regulation

5.1 Pursuing evidence-based policy

Chapter 3 of this volume provides valuable analysis of the relationship between research and evidence on the one hand and policy development on the other. Evidence can clearly enhance the effectiveness of health policy, including in facing new health challenges or in developing new policy responses, for example by analysing the causal relationships between different kinds of behaviours, or by assessing strategies after their implementation. Evidence can equally enhance the legality of health policy in international trade law, for example by supporting a state's assertion of the legitimacy of its health objectives, the connection between its health objectives and its chosen regulations or the connection between its NCD risk factor regulations and consumer behaviour. Evidence could also be used to confirm that a regulation that distinguishes between different products does so on health grounds rather than as a result of discrimination against or between imported products. Relevant evidence need not be created specifically by the state for the purpose of devising or testing its regulatory proposals; rather, evidence from other countries or from international organisations may provide a basis for local health policy. By relying on a broad, international evidence base, states with fewer resources may be able to obtain support for their measures without having to engage directly in lengthy and expensive research.

In the WTO, the Appellate Body has accepted that both quantitative and qualitative evidence may be used to justify a given measure (in the context of GATT art XX)[91] and that some problems are best addressed through a series of complementary measures operating together over an extended period of time:

> We recognize that certain complex public health or environmental problems may be tackled only with a comprehensive policy comprising a multiplicity of interacting measures. In the short-term, it may prove difficult to isolate the contribution to public health or environmental objectives of one specific measure from those attributable to the other measures that are part of the same comprehensive policy. Moreover, the results obtained from certain actions – for instance, measures adopted in order to attenuate global warming and climate change, or certain preventive actions to reduce the incidence of diseases that may manifest themselves only after a certain period of time – can only be evaluated with the benefit of time.[92]

This recognition by the Appellate Body is particularly significant for NCD risk factor regulation, which may precisely target unhealthy behaviours that may not give rise to NCDs for several years or even decades. States may continue to educate WTO panels and the Appellate Body on the limits and various forms of relevant evidence, for example through the provision of technical or expert evidence in their written or oral submissions or pursuant to a request by a panel.[93] In *US – Clove Cigarettes*, the United States seemed to have insufficient evidence to support its distinction between menthol cigarettes and other flavoured cigarettes on the grounds of health, and in the absence of such evidence the Appellate Body drew its own conclusions about the likely effect of including menthol in the flavouring ban. Additional evidence indicating a health basis for that distinction might have prevented the finding of a violation on the basis of discrimination as discussed above. Further evidence specifically on tobacco control is likely to arise in the ongoing WTO disputes against Australia,[94] should they proceed to a panel hearing.

5.2 Supporting multilateral guidelines and standards

The development of multilateral guidelines and standards, whether through or in association with treaties such as the *WHO Framework Convention on Tobacco Control* ('WHO FCTC')[95] or through independent instruments, may assist in defending NCD risk factor regulations in international trade law fora. Article 2.4 of the TBT Agreement creates a general obligation to use relevant standards:

> Where technical regulations are required and relevant international standards exist or their completion is imminent, Members shall use them, or the relevant parts of them, as a basis for their technical regulations except when such international standards or relevant parts would be an ineffective or inappropriate means for the fulfilment of the legitimate objectives pursued, for instance because of fundamental climatic or geographical factors or fundamental technological problems.

In addition, pursuant to TBT art 2.5, a technical regulation that is 'prepared, adopted or applied for one of the legitimate objectives explicitly mentioned in [art 2.2], and is in accordance with relevant international standards' is 'rebuttably presumed not to create an unnecessary obstacle to international trade' (ie presumed not to violate TBT art 2.2).

Lukasz Gruszczynski has argued that the WHO FCTC or its related implementing guidelines could constitute an 'international standard' for the purpose of the TBT Agreement.[96] Further insights into this question may be offered in the plain packaging case against Australia in the WTO,[97] if Australia raises such documents as a defence to the claims of violation of the non-discrimination obligation in TBT art 2.1. In any case, the following criteria for establishing the existence of a relevant international standard are worth keeping in mind as international health law evolves in connection with NCD risk factors, in case opportunities arise to develop such a standard to support states' health goals.

The TBT Agreement does not define the term 'international standard' but specifies in annex 1.2 that a 'standard' is a:

> Document approved by a recognized body, that provides, for common and repeated use, rules, guidelines or characteristics for products or related processes and production methods, with which compliance is not mandatory. It may also include or deal exclusively with terminology, symbols, packaging, marking or labelling requirements as they apply to a product, process or production methods.

The explanatory note to this provision makes clear that a standard for the purpose of the TBT Agreement is *voluntary* rather than mandatory and that it need not necessarily be 'based on consensus'.

According to the WTO Appellate Body, a standard has to be adopted by an 'international standardizing *body*',[98] which is 'not necessarily … an organisation'[99] but is a body:

(a)   'that has recognized activities in standardization';[100] and
(b)   'whose membership is open to the relevant bodies of at least all [WTO] Members'[101] on a non-discriminatory basis throughout the development of the standard.[102]

The Appellate Body has explained that the requirement of having activities in standardisation 'does not necessarily imply that a body is, or has been, involved in the development of more than one standard … [A] body simply has to be "active" in standardization in order to have "activities in standardization"'.[103] The requirement that these standardisation activities be *recognised* involves both 'factual' and 'normative' considerations.[104] The 'factual dimension … would appear to require, at a minimum, that WTO Members are aware, or have reason to expect, that the international body in question is engaged in standardization activities'.[105] In this regard, 'evidence of recognition by WTO Members as well as evidence of recognition by national standardizing bodies would be relevant'.[106] The 'normative dimension' would be more easily satisfied to the extent that the body 'complies with the principles and procedures that WTO Members have decided "should be observed" in the development of international standards',[107] which are contained in a decision by the WTO's TBT Committee.[108] That decision includes principles such as:

> All essential information regarding current work programmes, as well as on proposals for standards, guides and recommendations under consideration and on the final results should be made easily accessible to at least all interested parties in the territories of at least all WTO Members …[109]

> Any interested member of the international standardizing body, including especially developing country Members, with an interest in a specific standardization activity should be provided with meaningful opportunities to participate at all stages of standard development.[110]

> Consensus procedures should be established that seek to take into account the views of all parties concerned and to reconcile any conflicting arguments.[111]

> Impartiality should be accorded throughout all the standards development process …[112]

> Whenever possible, international standards should be performance based rather than based on design or descriptive characteristics.[113]

> [I]nternational standards … should not distort the global market, have adverse effects on fair competition, or stifle innovation and technological development.[114]

> Cooperation and coordination with other relevant international bodies is essential.[115]

> Constraints on developing countries, in particular, to effectively participate in standards development, should be taken into consideration in the standards development process.[116]

In summary, in order to maximise the likelihood of a particular body being recognised as an international standardisation body, or a particular document being recognised as a standard, for the purposes of the TBT Agreement, states and international bodies would need to promote – in the course of standardisation-type activities – principles of non-discrimination, openness to new members, transparency and fairness in decision-making, recognition of the particular needs of developing countries and coordination with other relevant international bodies including the WTO. Consistency with these principles may enable relevant health-related or NCD-related documents to be recognised as international standards in appropriate circumstances, supporting the defence of a regulation concerning NCD risk factors under the TBT Agreement when necessary.

5.3 *Crafting international trade agreements*

The progress made as part of the WTO's Doha Development Agenda in Bali, Indonesia, in December 2013[117] may foreshadow future positive steps being taken in this round of WTO negotiations (which have dragged on since their commencement in 2001),[118] meaning that the WTO may be reinvigorated as a locus for international trade activity beyond the dispute settlement realm.[119] Further amendments and agreements reached in the WTO may affect NCD risk regulation directly or indirectly. WTO members should therefore keep their health ministries informed of likely developments and seek input from them early enough to ensure that the negotiations do not unintentionally hinder health regulation. Coalitions of governments on health-related issues, as already exist in various forms within the WTO,[120] may further assist particularly those members that may have limited presence at the WTO in Geneva or limited resources or expertise to devote to these issues.

  Health ministries must also remain abreast of negotiations towards PTAs, whether bilateral or plurilateral. The increasing number of PTAs includes 'next generation' agreements such as the *Trans-Pacific Partnership Agreement* ('TPP'),[121] which may present novel negotiating approaches and ambitions for liberalising trade and therefore potentially invasive commitments from a health perspective. In order to retain sufficient regulatory autonomy in connection with NCD risk factors, states should be aware of the range of mechanisms available to address health in trade and investment treaties, including:

a) mention of importance of health objectives in the preamble and in any provisions regarding legitimate objectives or public policy;

b) exclusions or 'carve-outs' of particular unhealthy products – as we have discussed elsewhere in relation to the proposed exclusion of tobacco from the TPP,[122] these must be carefully examined on a case-by-case basis, taking account of the likely implications of the exclusion of one product for other products and for other treaties (eg WTO agreements, PTAs or bilateral investment treaties as discussed further in Chapter 6);

c)   exceptions from all obligations or from key obligations for measures that are related to, designed to protect or necessary for public health or for human life or health (taking account of the different implications of these various formulations); and

d)   side letters dealing with specific products or issues such as health, noting that health objectives and health measures are generally better dealt with in the main text to avoid ambiguities about the relationship between the main text and the side letter or the legal significance of the side letter.

In addition to these discrete strategies for addressing health in international trade agreements, states should maintain awareness of the possibilities under treaty law to advance health through: (i) declining to negotiate new agreements where the benefits would not outweigh any costs to health; (ii) promoting the interpretation of existing agreements so as to allow legitimate regulation on health grounds; and (iii) modifying or terminating existing agreements to better accord with health goals.

   The customary rules of interpretation of treaties under public international law are largely codified in the *Vienna Convention on the Law of Treaties* ('VCLT').[123] Article 31(1) of the VCLT requires a treaty interpreter to consider not only the 'ordinary meaning' of treaty terms but also their 'context' and the 'object and purpose of the treaty', both of which may be reflected in the preamble to the treaty or other treaty provisions. In addition, under art 31(3)(c) of the VCLT, a treaty interpreter should take account of 'any relevant rules of international law applicable in the relations between the parties'. In a dispute arising between the two parties to a bilateral PTA, the PTA would therefore need to be interpreted taking account of other treaties to which the PTA parties are party, such as the WHO FCTC. In the context of a WTO dispute, art 31(3)(c) of the VCLT might be understood as referring to relevant rules of international law applicable between all WTO members (which would include, at least, customary international law but not the WHO FCTC, to which most but not all WTO members are party), rather than rules applicable between the parties to the dispute. However, this matter remains unresolved at the WTO.[124] In any case, the WHO FCTC or other relevant WHO guidelines or other documents might be relevant aids to interpretation of a PTA or a WTO agreement in identifying the 'ordinary meaning' of a treaty term pursuant to VCLT art 31(1) or as factual references similar to other evidence even if not falling within VCLT art 31(3)(c).[125] The Panel and Appellate Body in *US – Clove Cigarettes* referred to the WHO FCTC and WHO respectively in these kinds of ways.[126]

   The VCLT also contains rules on modifying and terminating treaties. Subject to the rules within the treaty itself, the parties to a treaty such as a PTA may agree to amend[127] or terminate[128] the treaty. This provides additional options for states to consider in reviewing their existing suite of PTAs for compliance with health policy objectives. The WTO agreements have their own provisions on amendment,[129] which is extremely difficult to achieve. For example, an amendment to enhance access to medicines under the TRIPS Agreement has still not yet secured sufficient acceptances (the required two-thirds of the WTO membership)[130] to enter into force following its approval at the end of 2005.[131] However, other possibilities for reform exist within WTO law to ensure sufficient autonomy in the area of NCD risk factor regulation, should this be required. For example, WTO jurisprudence may evolve through the resolution of WTO disputes regarding health or other measures, as has happened to provide greater nuance in the interpretation and application of the general exceptions in GATT art XX or the non-discrimination obligation in TBT art 2.1. The WTO Ministerial Conference and General Council also have 'the exclusive authority to adopt interpretations' of the WTO agreements, and the Ministerial Conference may '[i]n exceptional circumstances … waive an obligation imposed on a Member'.[132] Although interpretations and waivers are also subject to a high threshold (requiring agreement by three-quarters of the WTO members), these mechanisms do provide additional avenues for states to consider should health-related reform be necessary.

5.4 Resisting regulatory chill

Defending regulation in international litigation is likely to impose heavy resource burdens on governments. Countries might therefore back down from a proposed regulation in the face of a formal legal complaint. Regulatory chill may also arise in the absence of formal dispute settlement proceedings. Countries might simply choose to regulate tobacco, alcohol and processed foods less intensely rather than risk a legal challenge in the WTO or through investment treaty arbitration. Informal complaints or media statements by particular countries (or companies) might also dissuade a country from adopting a novel public health measure. For example, WTO members may impose pressure on governments by expressing concerns in the TBT Committee, as several governments have done in relation to Thailand's proposed pictorial warning labels on alcoholic beverages,[133] Canada's restrictions on tobacco flavouring[134] and proposed Brazilian measures limiting additives in tobacco products.[135]

Increasing the expertise that governments may draw on in relevant legal areas, including international trade law, will assist in enabling countries to assess objectively the potential for a successful international legal claim being brought against a given health measure designed to combat NCD risk factors. That increased expertise need not come at great expense, although it is likely to require a commitment of time and energy. Aside from formal legal qualifications or expensive training courses, governments may be assisted by:

a) various NGOs, such as the Union for International Cancer Control, the Framework Convention Alliance for Tobacco Control and the Campaign for Tobacco Free Kids;

b) the World Health Organization and the Convention Secretariat of the WHO FCTC, which have been providing technical support to WHO member states specifically in relation to trade-related tobacco control issues;[136]

c)   the Advisory Centre on WTO Law, which is funded by 11 developed country members of the WTO and provides services to its 31 developing country members and all least-developed country members of the WTO;[137] and

d)   the WTO Secretariat, which offers technical cooperation services to WTO members pursuant to art 27(2) and (3) of the WTO's *Understanding on Rules and Procedures Governing the Settlement of Disputes* ('DSU')[138] and the Doha Development Agenda.[139]

Institutional and scholarly publications such as the present volume are also increasingly available to provide insights into the intersection between international trade law and regulation of NCD risk factors.[140]

Compliance with trade or investment rulings may also weaken regulation of NCD risk factors, whether or not the challenged measure was initially directed at public health. For example, WTO rulings against discriminatory taxation of imported alcoholic beverages may be expected to lead to lower taxes on those products in order to cure the discrimination, rather than increased taxes on domestically produced alcoholic beverages, because the domestic industry would object to such a change.[141] However, as discussed elsewhere, a review of three key WTO cases against Chile, Korea and Japan[142] in respect of alcoholic beverage taxation indicates that countries may find feasible and politically acceptable ways of raising taxes on domestic alcoholic beverages in some circumstances.[143] The United States' implementation of the adverse ruling against it in *US – Clove Cigarettes*, although still the subject of dispute as discussed above, may also confirm the ability of WTO members to reconcile health and trade objectives even in the face of political controversy.

The sources of expertise listed above may similarly assist in determining how best to comply with an adverse trade or investment law ruling against an NCD risk factor regulation while maximising the achievement of health objectives. A whole of government approach will also be essential, meaning that health ministries must remain engaged with the regulation and other relevant ministries during the implementation of the regulation and in the course of any legal defence. In most cases the ideal solution from the perspective of both health and trade will be non-discrimination against or between imports or foreign producers, although this may be difficult to achieve in practice as demonstrated by the WTO dispute in *US – Clove Cigarettes*. In that case, more creative solutions may be required rather than simply abandoning a valued health measure due to its imperfections. The continuous development of the evidence base for a particular measure, as discussed above, may also assist in justifying any distinctions drawn on health grounds between different products or suppliers.

6 Conclusion

International trade law presents a complex web of obligations and exceptions that can be difficult to navigate, even for the seasoned international trade law scholar. Yet the complexity and ambiguity of this area of law should not be allowed to undermine the objectives of states in regulating NCD risk factors on the basis that such regulation cannot be crafted in a manner consistent with international trade agreements. On the contrary, WTO panels and the Appellate Body have shown an ability to understand the importance of health objectives (indeed, describing them as 'vital and important in the highest degree')[144] and of the impossibility of regulating all health problems through a single measure or expecting an immediate health benefit from a given regulation.[145] The field of international trade law becomes even more variable and uncertain if the continuing proliferation of PTAs is taken into account. Nevertheless, this chapter has offered suggestions for enhancing the likelihood of compliance between NCD risk factor regulation and international trade law, by highlighting the importance of evidence and multilateral instruments, as well as the need for increased awareness of the details of international trade law and its impact on health regulation. Perhaps the most important lessons for states engaged in NCD risk factor regulation in the face of potential international trade law challenges is to minimise discrimination against or between imports to the greatest extent possible, and to ensure that measures are buttressed by comprehensive research of their contribution to the stated health objective and their superiority to available alternatives.

Notes

* We gratefully acknowledge the generous financial support provided for this independent research by the Australian National Preventive Health Agency (Grant ID 203MIT2011) and the Australian Research Council (Linkage Project LP120200028). Thank you also to Caroline Henckels and Catherine Gascoigne for research assistance. The opinions expressed here are our personal views as academics and are not necessarily shared by any employer or other entity. Any errors or omissions are ours.
1 See generally, eg, Alan Sykes, 'Comparative Advantage and the Normative Economics of International Trade Policy' (1998) 1 *Journal of International Economic Law* 49.
2 See the discussion and sources cited in Tania Voon, 'WTO Law and Risk Factors for Non-Communicable Diseases: A Complex Relationship' in Geert van Calster and Denise Prévost (eds), *Research Handbook on Environment, Health and the WTO* (Edward Elgar Publishing, 2013) 390, 391–3.
3 *Members and Observers* (2 March 2013) WTO <http://www.wto.org/english/thewto_e/whatis_e/tif_e/org6_e.htm>.
4 WTO, 'Ministerial Conference approves Yemen's WTO membership' (WTO News Item, 4 December 2013).
5 *Accessions* (2013) WTO <http://www.wto.org/english/thewto_e/acc_e/acc_e.htm>.
6 *General Agreement on Tariffs and Trade*, signed 30 October 1947, 55 UNTS 187 (entered into force 1 January 1948) ('GATT 1947').
7 *Regional trade agreements* (31 July 2013) WTO <http://www.wto.org/english/tratop_e/region_e/region_e.htm>.
8 World Trade Organization, *World Trade Report 2011 – The WTO and Preferential Trade Agreements: From Co-existence to Coherence* (2011) 55.
9 See, eg, Christopher Thompson, 'Big Tobacco Backs Australian Law Opposers', *Financial Times* (online), 29 April 2012; Stephanie Nebehay, 'Australia Says Big Tobacco Aiding WTO Challengers', *Reuters* (online), 23 May 2012; Peter Martin, 'Hidden Hand of Big Tobacco Leads to WTO Challenge', *The Sydney Morning Herald* (online) 20 August 2012.

10 See, eg, Panel Report, *Korea – Anti-Dumping Duties on Imports of Certain Paper from Indonesia*, WTO Doc WT/DS312/R (adopted 28 November 2005) [7.11].

11 GATT 1947 as incorporated in *Marrakesh Agreement Establishing the World Trade Organization*, opened for signature 15 April 1994, 1867 UNTS 3 (entered into force 1 January 1995) annex 1A ('*General Agreement on Tariffs and Trade 1994*') ('GATT 1994').

12 *Marrakesh Agreement Establishing the World Trade Organization*, opened for signature 15 April 1994, 1867 UNTS 3 (entered into force 1 January 1995) annex 1A ('*Agreement on Technical Barriers to Trade*') ('TBT Agreement').

13 *Marrakesh Agreement Establishing the World Trade Organization*, opened for signature 15 April 1994, 1867 UNTS 3 (entered into force 1 January 1995) annex 1C ('*Agreement on Trade-Related Aspects of Intellectual Property Rights*') ('TRIPS Agreement').

14 *Marrakesh Agreement Establishing the World Trade Organization*, opened for signature 15 April 1994, 1867 UNTS 3 (entered into force 1 January 1995) annex 1A ('*Agreement on Subsidies and Countervailing Measures*') ('SCM Agreement').

15 *Marrakesh Agreement Establishing the World Trade Organization*, opened for signature 15 April 1994, 1867 UNTS 3 (entered into force 1 January 1995) annex 1A ('*Agreement on Agriculture*').

16 Tobacco products appear in Chapter 24 of the Harmonized System (being the nomenclature set out in the annex to the *International Convention on the Harmonized Commodity Description and Coding System*, signed 14 June 1983, 1503 UNTS 167 (entered into force 1 January 1988)), which is covered by the *Agreement on Agriculture*, as stated in its annex 1.

17 *Marrakesh Agreement Establishing the World Trade Organization*, opened for signature 15 April 1994, 1867 UNTS 3 (entered into force 1 January 1995) annex 1A ('*Agreement on the Application of Sanitary and Phytosanitary Measures*').

18 See, eg, Benn McGrady, *Trade and Public Health: The WTO, Tobacco, Alcohol, and Diet* (Cambridge University Press, 2011) ch 5.

19 *Marrakesh Agreement Establishing the World Trade Organization*, opened for signature 15 April 1994, 1867 UNTS 3 (entered into force 1 January 1995) annex 1B ('*General Agreement on Trade in Services*').

20 See WTO, *Services Sectoral Classification List: Note by the Secretariat*, WTO Doc MTN. GNS/W/120 (10 July 1991).

21 *Marrakesh Agreement Establishing the World Trade Organization*, opened for signature 15 April 1994, 1867 UNTS 3 (entered into force 1 January 1995) annex 2 ('*Understanding on Rules and Procedures Governing the Settlement of Disputes*') ('DSU') art 8.

22 DSU art 17.1.

23 Appellate Body Report, *United States – Final Anti-Dumping Measures on Stainless Steel from Mexico*, WTO Doc WT/DS344/AB/R (adopted 20 May 2008) ('*US – Stainless Steel (Mexico)*') [158].

24 DSU arts 16.4, 17.14.

25 DSU art 2.1; *Marrakesh Agreement Establishing the World Trade Organization*, opened for signature 15 April 1994, 1867 UNTS 3 (entered into force 1 January 1995) ('*Marrakesh Agreement*') arts IV:2, IV:3.

26 *Marrakesh Agreement* art IX:2.

27 DSU arts 3.2, 19.2.

28 Appellate Body Report, *US – Stainless Steel (Mexico)*, [160]–[161].

29 Appellate Body Report, *Japan – Taxes on Alcoholic Beverages*, WTO Docs WT/DS8/AB/R, WT/DS10/AB/R, WT/DS11/AB/R (adopted 1 November 1996) ('*Japan – Alcoholic Beverages II*') 14; Appellate Body Report, *United States – Import Prohibition of Certain Shrimp and Shrimp Products – Recourse to Article 21.5 of the DSU By Malaysia*, WTO Doc WT/DS58/AB/RW (adopted 21 November 2001) [109].

30 Appellate Body Report, *US – Stainless Steel (Mexico)*, [160]–[161].

31 GATT 1994 art II:1.

32 See WTO Ministerial Conference, *Ministerial Declaration Adopted on 14 November 2001*, WTO Doc WT/MIN(01)/DEC/1 (20 November 2001) [34].
33 See Sykes, above n 1, 65.
34 GATT 1994 art XI:1.
35 TBT Agreement art 2.
36 Emphasis added; italics in original omitted.
37 TBT Agreement annex 1.1 (emphasis in original).
38 TBT Agreement art 2.2.
39 Appellate Body Report, *United States – Measures Affecting the Production and Sale of Clove Cigarettes*, WTO Doc WT/DS406/AB/R (adopted 24 April 2012) ('*US – Clove Cigarettes*'); Appellate Body Report, *United States – Measures Concerning the Importation, Marketing and Sale of Tuna and Tuna Products*, WTO Doc WT/DS381/AB/R (adopted 13 June 2012) ('*US – Tuna II (Mexico)*') [212], [319]; Appellate Body Report, *United States – Certain Country of Origin Labelling (COOL) Requirements*, WTO Doc WT/DS384/AB/R, WT/DS386/AB/R (adopted 23 July 2012) ('*US – COOL*') [268], [375].
40 Panel Report, *US – Clove Cigarettes*, WTO Doc WT/DS406/R (adopted 24 April 2012) [7.332] (finding not appealed); Appellate Body Report, *US – Tuna II (Mexico)*, [407(b)]–[407(e)]; Appellate Body Report, *US – COOL*, [350], [491]; Panel Report, *European Communities – Measures Prohibiting the Importation and Marketing of Seal Products*, WTO Docs WT/DS400/R, WT/DS401/R (circulated 25 November 2013, not yet adopted) ('*EC – Seal Products*') [7.505] (case not yet appealed at the time of writing). For further discussion see Tania Voon, Andrew Mitchell and Catherine Gascoigne, 'Consumer Information, Consumer Preferences and Product Labels under the TBT Agreement' in Michael Trebilcock and Tracey Epps (eds), *Research Handbook on the WTO and Technical Barriers to Trade* (Edward Elgar Publishing, 2013) 454, 455, 458–61, 473.
41 GATT 1994 art III:2.
42 GATT 1994 art III:4.
43 GATT 1994 art I:1.
44 See generally Andrew Mitchell and Nicolas Lockhart, 'Legal Requirements for FTAs under the WTO' in Simon Lester and Bryan Mercurio (eds), *Bilateral and Regional Trade Agreements: Commentary and Analysis* (Cambridge University Press, 2009) 81.
45 GATT Contracting Parties, *Decision on Differential and More Favourable Treatment, Reciprocity, and Fuller Participation of Developing Countries*, GATT Doc L/4903, BISD 26S/203 (28 November 1979), incorporated into the WTO agreements through the language of annex 1A incorporating the GATT 1994 into the *Marrakesh Agreement* [1(b)(iv)]: Appellate Body Report, *European Communities – Conditions for the Granting of Tariff Preferences to Developing Countries*, WTO Doc WT/DS46/AB/R (adopted 20 April 2004) [90].
46 See, eg, Appellate Body Report, *European Communities – Measures Affecting Asbestos and Asbestos-containing Products*, WTO Doc WT/DS135/AB/R (adopted 5 April 2001) ('*EC – Asbestos*') [101], referring to GATT Working Party Report, *Border Tax Adjustments*, GATT Doc L/3464, BISD 18S/97 (adopted 2 December 1970).
47 Appellate Body Report, *US – Clove Cigarettes*, [104], [121].
48 Ibid [112].
49 Ibid [117], [119]–[120].
50 Ibid [180]–[181]; Appellate Body Report, *US – Tuna II (Mexico)*, [215]. See also Appellate Body Report, *US – COOL*, [271]; Panel Report, *EC – Seal Products*, [7.131].
51 Appellate Body Report, *US – Clove Cigarettes*, [182] (quoted in Appellate Body Report, *US – Tuna II (Mexico)*, [215], see also [231]); Appellate Body Report, *US – COOL*, [271]; Panel Report, *EC – Seal Products*, [7.131].
52 Panel Report, *EC – Seal Products*, [7.585]–[7.586] (referring to Appellate Body Report, *US – Clove Cigarettes*, [180]–[182], [215]; Appellate Body Report *US – Tuna II (Mexico)*, [215]).

53 Panel Report, *EC – Seal Products*, [7.585]–[7.586].

54 See, eg, *Singapore-Australia Free Trade Agreement*, signed 17 February 2003, 2257 UNTS 103 (entered into force 28 July 2003) art 12.

55 Emphasis added.

56 Appellate Body Report *Brazil – Measures Affecting Imports of Retreaded Tyres*, WTO Doc WT/DS332/AB/R (adopted 17 December 2007) ('*Brazil – Retreaded Tyres*'), [156]. See subsequently, eg, Appellate Body Report, *China – Measures Affecting Trading Rights and Distribution Services for Certain Publications and Audiovisual Entertainment Products*, WTO Doc WT/DS363/AB/R (adopted 19 January 2010) [241]–[242].

57 See generally Tania Voon, 'International Decision: *United States – Measures Affecting the Production and Sale of Clove Cigarettes*' (2012) 106(4) *American Journal of International Law* 824, 827–8; Tania Voon, 'The WTO Appellate Body Outlaws Discrimination in US Flavored Cigarette Ban' (30 April 2012) 16(15) *ASIL Insights* (online); Todd Tucker, '"One of These Things is not Like the Other": Likeness and Detrimental Impacts in *US – Clove Cigarettes*' in Andrew Mitchell and Tania Voon (eds), 'Special Issue: Legal Issues in Tobacco Control' (November 2012) 9(5) *Transnational Dispute Management* (online).

58 Panel Report, *United States – Measures Affecting the Production and Sale of Clove Cigarettes*, WTO Doc WT/DS406/R (adopted 24 April 2012) ('*US – Clove Cigarettes*') [7.432] (this finding not appealed: Appellate Body Report, *US – Clove Cigarettes*, WTO Doc WT/DS406/AB/R (adopted 24 April 2012) [9]).

59 Appellate Body Report, *US – Clove Cigarettes*, [224], [226].

60 WTO, *United States – Measures Affecting the Production and Sale of Clove Cigarettes: Recourse to Article 22.2 of the DSU by Indonesia*, WTO Doc WT/DS406/12 (13 August 2013).

61 *Menthol in Cigarettes, Tobacco Products; Request for Comments*, 78 Fed Reg 44484 (24 July 2013).

62 Jamie Strawbridge, 'US Implementation of Adverse WTO Rulings: A Closer Look at the Tuna-Dolphin, COOL, and Clove Cigarettes Cases' (30 October 2013) 17(23) *ASIL Insights* (online).

63 *Australia – Certain Measures Concerning Trademarks and Other Plain Packaging Requirements Applicable to Tobacco Products and Packaging: Request for the Establishment of a Panel by Ukraine*, WTO Doc WT/DS434/11 (17 August 2012); *Australia – Certain Measures Concerning Trademarks, Geographical Indications and Other Plain Packaging Requirements Applicable to Tobacco Products and Packaging: Request for the Establishment of a Panel by Honduras*, WTO Doc WT/ DS435/16 (17 October 2012); *Australia – Certain Measures Concerning Trademarks, Geographical Indications and Other Plain Packaging Requirements Applicable to Tobacco Products and Packaging: Request for the Establishment of a Panel by the Dominican Republic*, WTO Doc WT/DS441/15 (14 November 2012); *Australia – Certain Measures Concerning Trademarks, Geographical Indications and Other Plain Packaging Requirements Applicable to Tobacco Products and Packaging: Request for Consultations by Cuba*, WTO Doc WT/DS458/1 (7 May 2013); *Australia – Certain Measures Concerning Trademarks, Geographical Indications and Other Plain Packaging Requirements Applicable to Tobacco Products and Packaging: Request for Consultations by Indonesia*, WTO Doc WT/DS467/1 (25 September 2013).

64 *Tobacco Plain Packaging Act 2011* (Cth); *Competition and Consumer (Tobacco) Information Standard 2011* (Cth) ss 9.13.1, 9.19.1; *Tobacco Plain Packaging Regulations 2011* (Cth) regs 2.2.1(2), 2.3.4(1).

65 The minutes of the relevant meetings of the WTO's Dispute Settlement Body on these issues are not yet publicly available at the time of writing.

66 See, eg, Mark Davison, 'Plain Packaging and the TRIPS Agreement: A Response to Professor Gervais' (2013) 23 *Australian Intellectual Property Journal* 160; Susy Frankel and Daniel Gervais, 'Plain Packaging and the Interpretation of the TRIPS Agreement' (2013) 46(5) *Vanderbilt Journal of Transnational Law* 1149.

67 Tania Voon and Andrew Mitchell, 'Implications of WTO Law for Plain Packaging

of Tobacco Products' in Tania Voon, Andrew Mitchell and Jonathan Liberman with Glyn Ayres (eds), *Public Health and Plain Packaging of Cigarettes: Legal Issues* (Edward Elgar Publishing, 2012) 109.

68   See generally Appellate Body Report, *Japan – Alcoholic Beverages II*; Appellate Body Report, *Korea – Taxes on Alcoholic Beverages*, WTO Docs WT/DS75/AB/R, WT/DS84/AB/R (adopted 17 February 1999); Appellate Body Report, *Chile – Taxes on Alcoholic Beverages*, WTO Docs WT/DS87/AB/R, WT/DS110/AB/R (adopted 12 January 2000); Appellate Body Report, *Philippines – Taxes on Distilled Spirits*, WTO Docs WT/DS396/AB/R, WT/DS403/AB/R (adopted 20 January 2012). See also Appellate Body Report, *India – Additional and Extra-Additional Duties on Imports from the United States*, WTO Doc DS360/AB/R (adopted 17 November 2008).

69   GATT Panel Report, *Japan – Customs Duties, Taxes and Labelling Practices on Imported Wines and Alcoholic Beverages*, GATT Doc L/6216, BISD 34S/83 (adopted 10 November 1987); GATT Panel Report, *Canada – Import, Distribution and Sale of Certain Alcoholic Drinks by Provincial Marketing Agencies*, GATT Doc DS17/R, BISD 39S/27 (adopted 18 February 1992).

70   GATT Panel Report, *Canada – Import, Distribution and Sale of Alcoholic Drinks by Canadian Provincial Marketing Agencies*, GATT Doc L/6304, BISD 35S/37 (adopted 22 March 1988) [4.4], [4.19], [4.25], [4.36(a)].

71   Ibid [2.3], [4.29].

72   See, eg, GATT 1994 arts II:4, XVII.

73   GATT Panel Report, *United States – Measures Affecting Alcoholic and Malt Beverages*, GATT Doc DS23/R, BISD 39S/206 (adopted 19 June 1992).

74   Ibid [6.1].

75   Ibid [5.70].

76   Ibid [5.74].

77   Ibid.

78   Ibid [5.75].

79   Ibid [5.74].

80   See, eg, Appellate Body Report, *European Communities – Export Subsidies on Sugar*, WTO Docs WT/DS265/AB/R, WT/DS266/AB/R, WT/DS283/AB/R (adopted 19 May 2005); WTO, *United States – Subsidies and Other Domestic Support for Corn and Other Agricultural Products: Request for the Establishment of a Panel by Canada*, WTO Docs WT/DS357/12 (9 November 2007) and WT/DS357/12/corr.1 (16 November 2007).

81   Andrew Mitchell and Tania Voon, 'Implications of the World Trade Organization in Combating Non-Communicable Diseases' (2011) 125 *Public Health* 832, 836–7. See also Voon, 'WTO Law and Risk Factors', above n 2, 395; Anne Marie Thow and Shishir Priadarshi, 'Aid for Trade: An Opportunity to Increase Fruit and Vegetable Supply' (2013) 91 *Bulletin of the World Health Organization* 57.

82   WTO, *Report of the Working Party on the Accession of Samoa to the World Trade Organization*, WTO Docs WT/ACC/SAM/30, WT/MIN(11)/1 (1 November 2011) ('*Working Party Report – Samoa*') [106]. Pursuant to [254] of this document, [106] forms part of Samoa's accession obligations on the basis that it is incorporated in WTO, *Access of Samoa: Decision of 17 December 2011*, WTO Docs WT/MIN(11)/27, WT/L/840 (17 December 2011) 'Protocol on the Accession of Samoa' [2].

83   *Working Party Report – Samoa*, [103].

84   See, eg, Anne Marie Thow and Wendy Snowdon, 'The Effect of Trade and Trade Policy on Diet and Health in the Pacific Islands' in Corinna Hawkes et al (eds), *Trade, Food, Diet and Health: Perspectives and Policy Options* (Wiley-Blackwell, 2010) 147, 161.

85   *Working Party Report – Samoa*, [91].

86   Ibid [103].

87   Ibid [105].

88   Ibid [106].

89   See, eg, Gilbert Winham, 'The Evolution of the World Trading System – The Economic and Policy Context' in Daniel Bethlehem et al (eds), *The Oxford Handbook of International Trade Law* (Oxford University Press, 2009) 5, 7–8.

90   Appellate Body Report, *Brazil – Retreaded Tyres*, [150].

91   Appellate Body Report, *EC – Asbestos*, [167]; Appellate Body Report, *Brazil – Retreaded Tyres*, [146]–[147], [151].

92   Appellate Body Report, *Brazil – Retreaded Tyres*, [151] (see also [211]).

93   DSU art 13.

94   See above n 63.

95   *WHO Framework Convention on Tobacco Control*, opened for signature 21 May 2003, 2302 UNTS 116 (entered into force 27 February 2005) ('WHO FCTC').

96   Lukasz Gruszczynski, 'The WHO Framework Convention on Tobacco Control as an International Standard under the TBT Agreement?' in Mitchell and Voon, 'Special Issue', above n 57.

97   See above n 63.

98   Appellate Body Report, *United States – Measures Concerning the Importation, Marketing and Sale of Tuna and Tuna Products*, WTO Doc WT/DS381/AB/R (adopted 13 June 2012) [356] (emphasis in original).

99   Ibid.

100   Ibid [359].

101   Ibid [359] (see also [351], which refers to the corresponding definition of an 'international body or system' in TBT Agreement annex 1.4: 'Body or system whose membership is open to the relevant bodies of at least all Members').

102   Appellate Body Report, *United States – Measures Concerning the Importation, Marketing and Sale of Tuna and Tuna Products*, WTO Doc WT/DS381/AB/R (adopted 13 June 2012) [374]–[375] (referring to 'Decision of the Committee on Principles for the Development of International Standards, Guides and Recommendations with relation to Articles 2, 5 and Annex 3 of the Agreement' [6] in WTO, *Decisions and Recommendations Adopted by the WTO Committee on Technical Barriers to Trade Since 1 January 1995: Note by the Secretariat*, WTO Doc G/TBT/1/Rev.9 (8 September 2008) annex B, 37–9, WTO Doc G/TBT/1/Rev.10 (9 June 2011) annex B, 46–8.

103   Appellate Body Report, *United States – Measures Concerning the Importation, Marketing and Sale of Tuna and Tuna Products*, WTO Doc WT/DS381/AB/R (adopted 13 June 2012) [360].

104   Ibid [361].

105   Ibid [362].

106   Ibid [363].

107   Ibid [376].

108   'Decision of the Committee on Principles for the Development of International Standards, Guides and Recommendations with relation to Articles 2, 5 and Annex 3 of the Agreement' in WTO, *Decisions and Recommendations Adopted by the WTO Committee on Technical Barriers to Trade Since 1 January 1995: Note by the Secretariat*, WTO Doc G/TBT/1/Rev.9 (8 September 2008) annex B, 37–9, WTO Doc G/TBT/1/Rev.10 (9 June 2011) annex B, 46–8 ('TBT Committee Decision'). The Appellate Body identified this decision as a 'subsequent agreement' for the purposes of *Vienna Convention on the Law of Treaties*, opened for signature 23 May 1969, 1155 UNTS 331 (entered into force 27 January 1980) art 31(3)(a). That treaty is discussed further below.

109   TBT Committee Decision [3].

110   Ibid [7].

111   Ibid [8].

112   Ibid [9].

113   Ibid [10].

114   Ibid.

115 Ibid [12].
116 Ibid [13].
117 WTO Ministerial Conference, *Bali Ministerial Declaration Adopted on 7 December 2013*, WTO Doc WT/MIN(13)/DEC (11 December 2013).
118 WTO Ministerial Conference, *Ministerial Declaration Adopted on 14 November 2001*, WTO Doc WT/MIN(01)/DEC/1 (20 November 2001).
119 See, eg, 'Unaccustomed Victory: Global Trade Talks Yield a Deal for the First Time in Almost 20 Years', *The Economist* (online), 14 December 2013; Alan Kohler, 'WTO Deal in Bali Keeps Doha Round Alive', *The Australian* (online), 10 December 2013; Roberto Azevêdo, 'Introduction' (Speech delivered at diplomatic seminar, Lisbon, 6 January 2014) <http://www.wto.org/english/news_e/spra_e/spra4_e.htm>.
120 See *Groups in the negotiations*, WTO <http://www.wto.org/english/tratop_e/dda_e/negotiating_groups_e.htm>.
121 See generally Tania Voon (ed), *Trade Liberalisation and International Co-operation: A Legal Analysis of the Trans-Pacific Partnership Agreement* (Edward Elgar Publishing, 2013); CL Lim, Deborah Elms and Patrick Low (eds), *The Trans-Pacific Partnership: A Quest for a Twenty-first Century Trade Agreement* (Cambridge University Press, 2012); Jane Kelsey (ed), *No Ordinary Deal: Unmasking the Trans-Pacific Partnership Free Trade Agreement* (Allen & Unwin, 2010).
122 Andrew Mitchell, Tania Voon and Devon Whittle, 'Public Health and the Trans-Pacific Partnership Agreement' (under review).
123 *Vienna Convention on the Law of Treaties*, opened for signature 23 May 1969, 1155 UNTS 331 (entered into force 27 January 1980) ('VCLT').
124 See Panel Report, *European Communities – Measures Affecting the Approval and Marketing of Biotech Products*, WTO Docs WT/DS291/R, WT/DS292/R, WT/DS293/R (adopted 21 November 2006) [7.68]; Appellate Body Report, *European Communities and Certain Member States – Measures Affecting Trade in Large Civil Aircraft*, WTO Doc WT/DS316/AB/R (adopted 1 June 2011) [844], [846].
125 In relation to WTO law, see, eg, Joost Pauwelyn, *Conflict of Norms in Public International Law: How WTO Law Relates to Other Rules of International Law* (Cambridge University Press, 2003) 263; Appellate Body Report, *United States – Import Prohibition of Certain Shrimp and Shrimp Products – Recourse to Article 21.5 of the DSU by Malaysia*, WTO Doc WT/DS58/AB/RW (adopted 21 November 2011) [130]; Appellate Body Report, *European Communities – Conditions for the Granting of Tariff Preferences to Developing Countries*, WTO Doc WT/DS246/AB/R (adopted 20 April 2004) [163].
126 Appellate Body, *US – Clove Cigarettes*, [235]; Panel Report, *US – Clove Cigarettes*, [7.414].
127 VCLT art 39.
128 VCLT art 54.
129 *Marrakesh Agreement* art X.
130 *Members accepting amendment of the TRIPS Agreement* (21 October 2013) WTO <http://www.wto.org/english/tratop_e/trips_e/amendment_e.htm>: 77 of the WTO's 159 members (including all the European Union member states counted separately from the European Union) have accepted the amendment – that is, close to half. See also Andrew Mitchell and Tania Voon, 'Patents and Public Health in the WTO, FTAs and Beyond: Tension and Conflict in International Law' (2009) 43(3) *Journal of World Trade* 571.
131 WTO, *Amendment of the TRIPS Agreement: Decision of 6 December 2005*, WTO Doc WT/L/641 (8 December 2005).
132 *Marrakesh Agreement* arts IX:2, IX:3. See, eg, WTO General Council, *Implementation of Paragraph 6 of the Doha Declaration on the TRIPS Agreement and Public Health: Decision of 30 August 2003*, WTO Doc WT/L/540 (2 September 2003).
133 See, eg, WTO Committee on Technical Barriers to Trade, *Minutes of the Meeting of 23–24 June 2010: Note by the Secretariat*, WTO Doc G/TBT/M/51 (1 October 2010) [237]–[251].

134 Ibid [181]–[216].
135 WTO Committee on Technical Barriers to Trade, *Minutes of the Meeting of 24–25 March 2011: Note by the Secretariat*, WTO Doc G/TBT/M/53 (26 May 2011) [3]–[55].
136 See, eg, WHO FCTC Conference of the Parties, *Cooperation with the World Trade Organization on Trade-related Tobacco-control Issues: Report by the Secretariat*, WHO Doc FCTC/COP/5/18 (20 September 2012) [8].
137 *Members: Introduction* (2013) Advisory Centre on WTO Law <http://www.acwl.ch/e/members/Introduction.html>.
138 See above n 20.
139 WTO Ministerial Conference, *Ministerial Declaration Adopted on 14 November 2001*, WTO Doc WT/MIN(01)/DEC/1 (20 November 2001) [38]–[41]; WTO Ministerial Conference, *Doha Work Programme: Ministerial Declaration Adopted on 18 December 2005*, WTO Doc WT/MIN(05)/DEC (22 December 2005) [52]–[54].
140 See, eg, Benn McGrady, *Confronting the Tobacco Epidemic in a New Era of Trade and Investment Liberalization* (World Health Organization, 2012); Mitchell and Voon, 'Special Issue', above n 57.
141 See, eg, Thomas Babor et al, *Alcohol: No Ordinary Commodity – Research and Public Policy* (Oxford University Press, 2nd ed, 2010) 90; World Bank, *Public Policy and the Challenge of Chronic Noncommunicable Diseases* (2007) 86.
142 WTO, *Japan – Taxes on Alcoholic Beverages: Mutually Acceptable Solution on Modalities for Implementation – Addendum*, WTO Docs WT/DS8/17/Add.1, WT/DS10/17/Add.1, WT/DS11/15/Add.1 (12 January 1998) annex A (European Communities); WTO, *Japan – Taxes on Alcoholic Beverages: Mutually Acceptable Solution on Modalities for Implementation*, WTO Docs WT/DS8/19, WT/DS10/19, WT/DS11/17 (12 January 1998) annex A (United States); WTO, *Japan – Taxes on Alcoholic Beverages: Mutually Acceptable Solution on Modalities for Implementation*, WTO Docs WT/DS8/20, WT/DS10/20, WT/DS11/18 (12 January 1998) annex 1 (Canada); WTO, *Korea – Taxes on Alcoholic Beverages: Status Report by Korea*, WTO Docs WT/DS75/18, WT/DS84/16 (17 January 2000) 2; WTO, *Chile – Taxes on Alcoholic Beverages: Status Report by Chile*, WTO Docs WT/DS87/17/Add.2, WT/DS110/16/Add.2 (27 February 2001).
143 Voon, 'WTO Law and Risk Factors', above n 2, 403–7.
144 Appellate Body Report, *EC – Asbestos*, [172].
145 See above n 92 and corresponding text.

6 International Investment Law

Benn McGrady

1 Introduction

Investment claims by Philip Morris against Australian and Uruguayan tobacco packaging regulations[1] signal the opening of a new front in tobacco litigation. That Philip Morris has taken questions of tobacco regulation out of the hands of domestic courts has heightened controversy over the legitimacy of investor state arbitration. However, for the public health community to be fixated on these two claims would be a mistake. The broader political context suggests that states are accelerating efforts to address the major risk factors for non-communicable diseases ('NCDs'), which include tobacco consumption, alcohol consumption and unhealthy diets. Moreover, in many respects, tobacco control may prove to be a model for regulation of alcoholic beverages and unhealthy foods.

These accelerating efforts to address NCDs follow a period of time during which foreign direct investment ('FDI') has increased significantly in the tobacco, alcohol and food industries. This increase follows trends like privatisation of state run industries, trade liberalisation and the global consolidation of firms in those sectors. These efforts to address NCDs also coincide with foreign investors showing an increasing willingness to bring claims under international investment agreements ('IIAs').

The merits of the Philip Morris claims have been examined in detail elsewhere.[2] Accordingly, this chapter examines the broader question of how international investment law governs action to address NCDs. With the exception of the Philip Morris claims, there are no publicly reported challenges to public health measures addressing NCDs. Nonetheless, some points of tension between IIAs and efforts to control NCDs include: the fact that investment instruments seek to incentivise investment, whereas measures to reduce risk factors for NCDs seek to discourage consumption of particular products; the fact that host states may induce investment only to take downstream steps that restrict the profitability of that investment; and the difficulty associated with drawing regulatory distinctions between investments.

This chapter examines the legal issues in further detail. Part 2 gives a brief description of the range of international legal instruments relevant to the intersection of investment law and NCDs. Part 3 examines state contracts under international investment law. It is argued that host states are most vulnerable to legal claims in this context and that lessons can be learned from past mistakes. Part 4 examines the core standards of protection found in IIAs governing expropriation and fair and equitable treatment. Although these standards of treatment offer host states a wide degree of regulatory autonomy, there are particular risks associated with attempts to incentivise investment. Part 4 also examines national treatment under IIAs and the implications of drawing regulatory distinctions, such as between unhealthful and healthful foods.

2 Relevant international investment and health laws

A variety of legal instruments make up the field of international investment law. These include bilateral investment treaties ('BITs'), investment chapters in free trade agreements ('FTAs') (together IIAs) and investment contracts. Unlike the trade regime discussed in Chapter 5 of this volume, international investment law is not governed by a single unifying international agreement or institution. Rather, IIAs form what is often referred to as a 'spaghetti bowl' of primarily bilateral agreements.

IIAs protect the investments and investors of each contracting party in the territory of the other contracting parties. For example, the Philip Morris claim against Uruguay is made under the Switzerland-Uruguay BIT,[3] which protects Swiss investors and their investments in Uruguay and Uruguayan investors and investments in Switzerland. Although IIAs differ in their terms, they often provide substantially similar standards of protection for investors and their investments. Typically, IIAs protect investors and their investments against discrimination by the host state in favour of its nationals or nationals of another state and against treatment that is unfair or inequitable. IIAs also provide investors with a right to compensation where an investment is nationalised or expropriated, or where action of the host state has an equivalent effect.

Most IIAs provide investors with standing to bring claims on their own behalf. In this way, BITs and then FTAs replaced the law of diplomatic protection, which permitted a state to bring a claim on behalf of its nationals under customary international law. Today, claims are made directly by investors under arbitral rules such as the International Centre for Settlement of Investment Disputes ('ICSID') Convention and United Nations Commission on International Trade Law ('UNCITRAL') Arbitration Rules. A panel of three independent arbitrators, one of which is appointed by each of the parties, usually decides claims. The arbitral rules in question permit enforcement of arbitral awards in the domestic courts of the parties to the rules, ensuring enforceability in a significant number of countries. Although investors may bring claims for specific performance, such as an order that a state withdraw a regulatory measure, such orders are difficult to enforce, meaning that compensation is usually the remedy of choice.

Beyond treaties such as BITs and FTAs, an investor may protect its investments through a contract with the host state. This is particularly common when an investor purchases state-owned assets, or agrees to invest in the territory of the host state in the context of inducements offered by the state.

Beyond the investment context, various international instruments govern the protection of human health. In the specific context of NCDs, these instruments include the *WHO Framework Convention on Tobacco Control* ('WHO FCTC'),[4] the *Global Strategy for the Prevention and Control of NCDs*,[5] the *Political Declaration of the High-level Meeting of the General Assembly on the Prevention and Control of Non-communicable Diseases*,[6] the *Global Strategy on Diet, Physical Activity and Health*,[7] the *Global Strategy to Reduce the Harmful Use of Alcohol*,[8] and the WHO Action Plan for the Control and Prevention of NCDs for 2013–2020.[9] Because these instruments have been discussed in earlier chapters, they will not be examined in detail here. Nonetheless, there are two important points to note.

First, international instruments governing health might be relevant to the interpretation of investment treaties. Such instruments might be relevant to questions of fact, such as the merits of regulating particular risks or of particular approaches to risk, or to questions of law, such as in interpreting exceptions in investment treaties. These instruments could also be important in mixed questions of fact and law, such as in determining the 'legitimate expectations' of an investor.

Second, these instruments suggest that there is an international consensus that the state has a valid role in intervening to reduce risk factors for disease. For example, art 3 (Objective) of the WHO FCTC refers to the goal of reducing the prevalence of tobacco use and exposure to tobacco smoke continually and substantially. This suggests that the role of the state extends not only to correcting market failures, but also to shaping the behaviour of individuals in order to influence health outcomes at the individual and population levels.

3 State contracts and inducements

3.1 Contracts and risk

In some sectors, such as extractive industries, contracts between a host state and a foreign investor are the norm. These contracts constitute an important means of allocating risk, including risks associated with regulation. State contracts also exist in the tobacco, alcohol and food sectors, although it is difficult to assess how many because they are ordinarily confidential. The Washington Consensus saw large-scale privatisation of public assets, including in the tobacco, alcohol and food production sectors. This process necessarily involved contracting between the state and investors, some of which were foreign. These contracts included contracts for the sale of assets and contracts for the operation of public assets such as water utilities.

In some countries, state-owned enterprises in the tobacco, alcohol and food sectors continue to exist. Some of these enterprises are partly state-owned with the rights and obligations of the private owner governed by contract between the investor and state (as well as other domestic laws).[10] Fully state-owned enterprises also exist.[11] In some cases, these state-owned enterprises contract with investors through joint venture agreements and other legal instruments. Like contracts directly between the state and an investor, contracts between a state-owned enterprise and an investor can create legal liability for the state. One important difference, however, is that the conduct of a state-owned enterprise must be attributable to the state in order for liability to ensue under international law.[12]

Where a state is not a contracting party to a relevant IIA, a contract between the state and a foreign investor containing an arbitration clause may remove the resolution of contractual disputes from the host state's courts. This does not, in and of itself, constrain domestic regulatory autonomy, but it does provide a neutral forum for the settlement of disputes in place of the domestic courts of the host state. Similarly, a state contract may contain a choice of law clause, which alters the applicable law from that of the host state, for example by reference to general principles of law. Such a clause limits the ability of the host state to legislate its way out of liability for breach.

Two legal risks associated with state contracts stand out. First, a contract creates a set of legal obligations that may alter the legal implications of regulation. The most prominent example of this is found in the form of stabilisation clauses, which seek to prevent the host state from changing its laws, or provide a remedy for the investor in the event of particular changes being made.

Second, a contract may also increase the risk of liability under IIAs. In this respect, umbrella clauses in IIAs may oblige the host state to respect commitments made to investors, such as those in an investment contract. The legitimate expectations of an investor, which may be established by reference to a contract or inducements to invest, are also relevant in the application of provisions in IIAs governing fair and equitable treatment, and to a lesser extent indirect expropriation.

3.2 Contracts and stabilisation clauses

Stabilisation clauses in investment contracts come in a number of different forms. In the strict sense, stabilisation clauses prevent a change in domestic law affecting a contract or investment. These clauses are also often referred to as 'freezing clauses' because they seek to freeze the domestic law of the host state as at the time the investment was made. By contrast, economic equilibrium clauses provide compensation to the investor for damage caused as a result of measures taken by the host state that upset the economic equilibrium of an investment. These clauses are often present in contracts involving fixed tariffs, such as the operation of public utilities. Finally, hybrid clauses contain a mixture of obligations, including freezing commitments and commitments for compensation in the context of specified governmental activities affecting the value of an investment.

Stabilisation clauses are used in combination with arbitration clauses and often with choice of law clauses. When these clauses are also in place, the host state may be less able to change domestic law in a way that overrides the contract. This is not to suggest that stabilisation clauses will always be valid. For example, controversy surrounds freezing clauses and whether a state can fetter its legislature in this way, as well as how an arbitral tribunal might enforce a specific commitment of this type. There is less controversy surrounding the validity of economic equilibrium clauses and hybrid clauses that provide compensation as a remedy.

In recent years, the implications of stabilisation clauses for human rights and sustainable development have received attention. A research project conducted jointly by the International Finance Corporation ('IFC') and United Nations Special Representative to the Secretary-General on Business and Human Rights found that stabilisation clauses included in state contracts posed a variety of risks for human rights, including in the context of environmental and health regulation.[13] The sample of contracts examined also suggested that developing countries were more likely to agree to freezing clauses than Organisation for Economic Co-operation and Development ('OECD') countries. This attention culminated in John Ruggie, the Special Representative of the Secretary-General, proposing a set of principles for responsible contracts to the United Nations Human Rights Council.[14]

Stabilisation clauses can constrain the regulatory autonomy of a state in a number of different ways. Freezing clauses, if enforced through specific performance, provide the greatest restraint on the sovereign right to regulate. Economic equilibrium clauses provide a lesser constraint, but do require payment of compensation. This could lead to situations where the host state elects not to regulate in ways it otherwise might, or elects to exempt certain investments or investors from regulation.[15] In either case, the regulatory outcome may be sub-optimal.

The commercial in confidence nature of most state contracts means that they are not in the public domain. Nonetheless, some state contracts in the tobacco sector have come to light. For example, the government of Laos used an investment contract to sell a partial share in a newly privatised Laotian tobacco company to a French investor. The investment contract provided the investor with a 5-year profit tax holiday and fixed the excise tax rate for a 25-year period (2002–26).[16] Under the contract, the investor is entitled to compensation in the event that excise taxes are increased. Accordingly, Laos is obliged under the contract to compensate the investor for implementation of tax measures notwithstanding the widespread recognition that excise taxes lower tobacco consumption and thereby reduce morbidity and mortality.[17] Although this does not prevent Laos from implementing the measure, it does have short-term budgetary implications that alter the political feasibility of implementing such measures.

Large sporting events offer another example of state contracts that affect implementation of health measures, such as restrictions on advertising, promotion and sponsorship. For example, during a public debate about banning tobacco advertising at the Melbourne Formula One Grand Prix, government figures revealed that the Australian state of Victoria had a contract to host the Grand Prix with the organising body. The contract obliged the state to pay a fee in return for the right to host the event. The contract also provided that the fee would increase in the event that the state restricted tobacco advertising.[18] Hence, the government had to elect between not restricting advertising, not hosting the Grand Prix or paying compensation. Similar contractual commitments are made in the context of hosting the Olympic Games. In that context, the International Olympic Committee is sponsored by companies such as Coca-Cola and McDonalds, ensuring that marketing by those firms is present during Olympic Games.[19]

As noted above, joint venture agreements between state entities and foreign investors provide another type of relevant contract. For example, the China National Tobacco Corporation, a state-owned enterprise, has committed to a number of joint venture agreements with foreign tobacco companies seeking to build a foothold in the Chinese market.[20] Although disputes concerning the impact of health regulation on an investment might not always fall within the scope of a contract, the investor may still be able to bring a claim at the international level where recourse to an investment treaty is possible. Depending on the circumstances, the ability of the investor to bring a claim might also be enhanced by the presence of an umbrella clause. Typically, umbrella clauses require the host state to respect commitments made to investors. In some claims, umbrella clauses have been interpreted to include commitments found in contracts.[21] Where this is not the case, or an umbrella clause is not present, the investor might argue that a contract provides a legitimate expectation that founds the basis for a claim under another provision of an investment treaty.

The role of state contracts highlights the importance of state behaviour (other than of a regulatory character) in determining the potential legal liability of a state for action to address NCDs. Most obviously, state contracts create legal obligations and the potential for legal liability that would otherwise not exist. In this respect, states should be particularly careful when it comes to stabilisation clauses, as is shown by the examples of the privatisation of the Laotian tobacco monopoly and contracts to host large sporting events.

Leaving aside the risk of legal liability, state contracts may be used in ways that are counter-productive to public health goals. In particular, fiscal incentives designed to lower costs of production may ultimately facilitate the sale of harmful products at lower retail prices than was previously possible. For example, in 2002 the Uruguayan government granted tobacco companies exemptions from surtaxes associated with importation of cigarette manufacturing equipment and value-added-tax in association with acquisition of materials required for works.[22] Similarly, Coca-Cola has recently made a direct investment in Myanmar after the government reformed its investment law and offered fiscal incentives such as tax holidays to attract foreign investment.[23]

Furthermore, for products that are not produced domestically and are subjected to customs duties at importation, an investment from a foreign investor in local manufacturing and distribution facilities may permit an investor to lower retail prices from behind a tariff wall. In each of these examples, the morbidity and mortality associated with particular products may increase where lower prices stimulate consumer demand.

Policy coherence is a central issue with respect to the risks associated with inducing investment and legal liability under state contracts. These risks are likely to be lower if a state is able to take a whole-of-government approach to policymaking, or to incorporate health in all policies. However, at least three concerns are raised by the fact that policy coordination is central to managing legal risks.

First, from an organisational perspective, policy coherence is logistically difficult, particularly in low resource settings. Second, policies and policy priorities change over time as new information comes to light, including information concerning health risks. Since state contracts involve an exercise in hand tying (often over long periods of time) there is an inevitable risk that even a well-coordinated state cannot anticipate its future policy preferences. Third, although the state is a unitary actor for purposes of liability under international law, liberal theories of international relations suggest that different actors within the state may work at cross-purposes. Investment and health authorities within a single state may face not just coordination problems, but broader cooperation problems that are associated with competing incentives and roles.

When viewed together, these three concerns suggest that there may be points at which it is not possible to reconcile the goals of attracting FDI and protecting human health. In such circumstances, trade-offs and policy prioritisation will be necessary. This is the case in the tobacco context, where guidelines to art 5.3 of the WHO FCTC establish the principle that '[b]ecause their products are lethal, the tobacco industry should not be granted incentives to establish or run their businesses'.[24] Whether alcohol should be treated in the same way is open to question, but there is little doubt that food provides a far more complex policy environment. In this context, governments have a legitimate interest in promoting food security and rural development. These and other political interests often result in the offering of incentives for investment, such as subsidies, some of which are tied to production levels. This can have negative impacts in terms of NCDs, the classic example being the subsidisation of corn in the United States ('US') that is then converted to high-fructose corn syrup ('HFCS'), a caloric sweetener often used in beverages. Beyond government programs of a general character, states may have an interest in attracting investors in the food supply chain. There may be policy trade-offs made in the process, but a whole of government approach to policymaking is necessary to manage the risk of legal liability under investment contracts.

4 International investment agreements

When an investor challenges host state action under an IIA, it is common for the investor to argue that a number of standards of treatment have been violated. Most often, this includes an argument that an investment has been expropriated indirectly and that the investor has not been accorded 'fair and equitable treatment'. These standards of protection differ, but each is relevant to host state action that seeks to discourage the consumption of particular products.

Besides the Philip Morris claims, investors in the tobacco, alcohol and food sectors have made a number of investment treaty claims. For example, in the tobacco context, *Grand River* concerned the application of the Master Settlement Agreement (discussed below) in the US to a Canadian investor.[25] *Feldman Karpa* concerned a claim by a grey market exporter for tax rebates paid by the Mexican government in respect of exported products.[26] Discussed further below, neither of these claims represented a challenge to public health regulation likely to be implemented on a widespread basis. Similarly, *RJ Reynolds Tobacco Company v Iran* concerned enforcement of a licensing agreement between RJ Reynolds and an Iranian state-run tobacco company in which the claimant alleged that the state company failed to pay for a purchase of tobacco products.[27]

In the food context, *Canadian Cattlemen* concerned a challenge by a Canadian investor to US import restrictions on beef designed to prevent the spread of bovine spongiform encephalopathy.[28] In *Chemtura*, measures prohibiting the use of particular pesticides in order to protect human health were challenged.[29] In *Archer Daniels Midland* and *Cargill*, US investors challenged a tax on HFCS but not other sweeteners, which had been imposed to protect Mexico's cane sugar industry from unfair competition.[30] To date, however, there have not been any publicly reported challenges to public health nutrition measures under IIAs. It also does not appear that there has been a relevant publicly reported claim concerning health regulation in the context of alcoholic beverages.[31]

Again, these disputes are discussed further below. There is no formal doctrine of precedent in investment treaty arbitration, and many of the disputes are decided under different treaties. Nonetheless, these and other cases highlight the standards of treatment applicable to measures to prevent and control NCDs. As the discussion will show, these standards of treatment each demand a fact-specific analysis. This limits the capacity to generalise about the application of these standards to whole classes of measures to address NCDs. Although it is possible to identify key principles in the case law and their general relevance to public health, it would also be possible to conceive of measures structured in unique and unexpected ways, or implemented in unique contexts. Just like the conduct of a host state, the unique and unexpected features of individual measures moderate the general conclusions drawn in the analysis below.

Although it is a trite observation, each investment dispute is decided in light of the evidence presented by the parties. Accordingly, the importance of evidence, including evidence of risk, evidence of the effects of measures and evidence of the intentions of a host state should not be underestimated. This necessarily draws tribunals as fact finders into a complex intersection between public health, scientific evidence and the law.[32] At this intersection, the question of which standard of proof should be applied becomes crucial because standards of proof determine the extent to which tribunals defer to domestic scientific and regulatory processes and to international consensus.

4.1 Fair and equitable treatment

Clauses requiring the host state to provide an investor with fair and equitable treatment come in different forms and are often interpreted differently by arbitral tribunals.

Some clauses specify, or are interpreted to require, that the host state provide the investor with the international 'minimum standard of treatment' under customary international law. This standard of treatment is often associated with the *Neer* claim, in which it was stated that:

[t]he treatment of an alien, in order to constitute an international delin-
quency, should amount to an outrage, to bad faith, to wilful neglect of duty,
or to an insufficiency of government action so far short of international
standards that every reasonable and impartial man would readily recognize
its insufficiency.[33]

More recently, the tribunal in *Glamis* reviewed the case law and stated that:

an act must be sufficiently egregious and shocking – a gross denial of justice,
manifest arbitrariness, blatant unfairness, a complete lack of due process,
evident discrimination, or a manifest lack of reasons – so as to fall below
accepted international standards.[34]

In contrast to the approach taken in *Glamis*, some tribunals have viewed the customary standard as an evolving one that requires a higher standard of treatment
today than it did in the past. For example, in *Merrill*, the tribunal concluded that
customary international law may be violated by acts that are merely unfair, inequitable or unreasonable.[35] Thus, even when it is clear that a treaty requires application of the international minimum standard found in customary international
law, there remains some uncertainty concerning what that standard requires.

Leaving the content of the customary standard to one side, some clauses have
been interpreted to require a standard of treatment that is not linked to that standard, but that reflects a stand-alone treaty obligation. The standard articulated in
Tecmed, and quoted above, is arguably the high water mark not just for the concept
of legitimate expectations, but also for the fair and equitable treatment standard
more generally. Under this approach, investors would be entitled to relief for
a very wide variety of host state acts. In that claim, the arbitral tribunal had to
interpret art 4(1) of the Mexico-Spain BIT,[36] which simply states that '[e]ach
Contracting Party shall guarantee fair and equitable treatment in its territory
pursuant to international law for investments made by investors from another
Contracting Party'. The tribunal stated that the provision:

requires the Contracting Parties to provide to international investments treatment that does not affect the basic expectations that were taken into account
by the foreign investor to make the investment. The foreign investor expects
the host State to act in a consistent manner, free from ambiguity and totally
transparently in its relations with the foreign investor, so that it may know
beforehand any and all rules and regulations that will govern its investments,
as well as the goals of the relevant policies and administrative practices or
directives, to be able to plan its investment and comply with such regulations.
Any and all State actions conforming to such criteria should relate not only to
the guidelines, directives or requirements issued, or the resolutions approved
thereunder, but also to the goals underlying such regulations.[37]

The sweeping character of this pronouncement and the breadth of the obligation
it implies have been both criticised and endorsed.[38]

Leaving aside controversy concerning the standard, and the fact that a diversity of clauses and interpretations makes it difficult to generalise, claims tend to fall into one of the following categories:

- failure to provide a transparent and stable environment and to observe an investor's legitimate expectations;
- arbitrary, discriminatory or unreasonable treatment;
- denial of due process or procedural fairness;
- bad faith; or
- government coercion and harassment.[39]

The most relevant issues are now examined in further detail.

4.1.1 Contracts and inducements as a source of legitimate expectations

A contract itself and other inducements, whether included in a contract or not, may form the basis for reasonable expectations that are relied upon in non-contractual claims under an investment treaty. In bringing claims under provisions governing fair and equitable treatment and indirect expropriation, investors often argue that contracts and other inducements to invest form the basis of legitimate expectations that the host state will behave in a particular way. Investors also often rely on statements or representations by the host state. As the argument goes, those expectations are relevant in determining whether an investor has been accorded fair and equitable treatment and whether indirect expropriation has occurred.

A state contract may create non-contractual expectations above and beyond its terms.[40] As was described above, contractual claims can be brought under the terms of a contract[41] or under an investment treaty where an umbrella clause permits. In addition, contracts may provide the basis for non-contractual expectations with respect to sovereign (non-contractual) acts. This is more likely to occur where a contract has been made in a broader context of non-contractual inducements or representations that a host state does not subsequently uphold. Inducements might include tax holidays, subsidies and privileges associated with manufacturing in free zones or other tax free zones. Representations might also be made with respect to these matters or with respect to the general regulatory environment.

MTD v Chile provides a contemporary example of how a lack of policy coordination can lead to violation of the fair and equitable treatment standard. In that case, Chilean investment authorities agreed to an investment contract for a construction project with a foreign investor only for the project to fail because it was inconsistent with domestic zoning regulations. In finding against Chile the tribunal stated that 'Chile has an obligation to act coherently and apply its policies consistently, independently of how diligent an investor is'.[42]

In the discussion of state contracts above, concerns relating to policy coherence and long-term government hand tying were identified. The potential for a contract to form the basis for non-contractual expectations raises an additional concern of a similar character in the context of the fair and equitable treatment standard.

4.1.2 Providing a stable and predictable regulatory environment in light of the investor's legitimate expectations

In the absence of an investment contract between the host state and the investor, there is an additional question of what legitimate expectations an investor might have.

Arguably, the high point of the concept of legitimate expectations came in *Tecmed*, as quoted above. Other tribunals have suggested that the legitimate expectations of an investor are narrower. Tribunals in disputes under the *North American Free Trade Agreement* ('NAFTA'),[43] such as *Glamis* and *Thunderbird*, have stressed the notion of 'reasonable reliance'. For example, in *Glamis*, the tribunal emphasised that a 'State may be tied to the objective expectations that it creates in order to induce investment'.[44] Similarly, in *Thunderbird*, the tribunal stated that the concept of legitimate expectations relates:

> to a situation where a Contracting Party's conduct creates reasonable and justifiable expectations on the part of an investor (or investment) to act in reliance on said conduct, such that a failure by the NAFTA party to honor those expectations could cause the investor (or investment) to suffer damages.[45]

Other tribunals have highlighted that investors are not entitled to a legitimate expectation that the regulatory environment affecting an investment will remain unchanged. In *El Paso*, the tribunal stated:

> if the often repeated formula to the effect that 'the stability of the legal and business framework is an essential element of fair and equitable treatment' were true, legislation could never be changed: the mere enunciation of that proposition shows its irrelevance. Such a standard of behaviour, if strictly applied, is not realistic, nor is it the BITs' purpose that States guarantee that the economic and legal conditions in which investments take place will remain unaltered ad infinitum.[46]

It is also quite clear that the concept of fair and equitable treatment does not entitle an investor to expectations that are not legitimate or reasonable. For example, the tribunal in *Grand River*, referring specifically to the tobacco industry, noted that '[a]n investor entering an area traditionally subject to extensive regulation must do so with awareness of the regulatory situation'.[47] Similarly, the dispute in *Methanex* concerned a fuel additive that California prohibited due to environmental risks. In considering whether an indirect expropriation had arisen under NAFTA, the tribunal stated that the investor entered a political economy in which it was widely known, if not notorious, that governmental environmental and health protection institutions at the federal and state level, operating under the vigilant eyes of the media, interested corporations, non-governmental organizations and a politically active electorate, continuously monitored the use and impact of chemical compounds and commonly prohibited or restricted the use of some of those compounds for environmental and/or health reasons.[48]

More recently, in *Glamis*, a claim concerning open pit gold mining, the tribunal noted that the claimant was operating in an environment that was becoming more and more sensitive to the environmental consequences of open pit mining.[49] Like *Grand River* and *Methanex*, this dispute suggests that an investor is not entitled to a general expectation of an unchanging regulatory environment in the absence of some representation or agreement to the contrary. This line of case law might be reconciled with *Tecmed* and other cases that stress the need for predictability and stability on the basis that it is only 'legitimate' or 'reasonable' expectations that are relevant to the fair and equitable treatment standard. Alternatively, it might be argued that increased regulation is 'predictable' in sectors posing risks to health and does not in itself reflect instability.

For present purposes, the key point is that investors in sectors such as tobacco, alcohol and food should expect government intervention, partly because those sectors are already highly regulated, and partly because of the risks to health associated with tobacco, alcohol and food products.

4.1.3 Arbitrary and unreasonable measures

Many investment treaties include language prohibiting arbitrary and unreasonable measures or arbitrary and discriminatory measures. Often, this language is found in clauses governing fair and equitable treatment. In some cases, obligations to avoid arbitrary and unreasonable measures have been interpreted separately to the fair and equitable treatment standard.[50] In other cases, such as under the NAFTA, where arbitrary and unreasonable measures are not mentioned in the treaty, the fair and equitable treatment standard has been considered broad enough to encompass the issues.[51]

In its claims against Australia and Uruguay, Philip Morris is arguing that the challenged tobacco-packaging measures are arbitrary and unreasonable. In the Australian context, Philip Morris argues that there is insufficient evidence that 'plain packaging' of tobacco products[52] will have a positive effect on the protection of human health.[53] Similarly, Philip Morris argues that a Uruguayan prohibition on misleading branding on tobacco packaging has been applied in an arbitrary way after Uruguayan authorities judged Philip Morris branding to be misleading and indicated that only one variant per brand would be permitted in the Uruguayan market.[54]

Given the potential invocation of these types of arguments by investors, it is worth identifying the standards applied. In this respect, it must first be noted that arbitrariness and unreasonableness have been equated as interchangeable, and as something done capriciously, without reason.[55] The International Court of Justice offered what is perhaps the most widely quoted definition of arbitrariness in the *ELSI* case, where it stated that '[a]rbitrariness is not so much something opposed to a rule of law, as something opposed to the rule of law … It is a willful disregard of due process of law, an act which shocks, or at least surprises a sense of judicial propriety'.[56] In *AES v Hungary*, the tribunal articulated a rational relationship test requiring the existence of a rational policy and a reasonable relationship between that rational policy and the act of the state in question.[57]

In the context of measures to address NCDs, the concepts of arbitrariness and unreasonableness are most likely to be relevant to unique measures implemented for the first time, to circumstances where risk is difficult to measure and to circumstances where the effects of a measure are difficult to assess in the short term. In each context, the quality of the reasoning and scientific evidence underlying a measure will be important. It should be noted, however, that the investor must satisfy a very high threshold in order to prevail. This threshold is so high that it concerns only measures unlikely to be of value from a public health perspective.

Beyond arbitrariness, claims may also arise on the basis of discrimination. Clauses governing arbitrary and discriminatory treatment usually exist in addition to prohibitions on discrimination based on nationality (discussed below). Clauses governing arbitrary and discriminatory treatment are more likely to be invoked by an investor on other grounds, such as racial discrimination, religious discrimination or discrimination based on political affiliation. However, these clauses do not ordinarily restrict or specify the grounds on which they can be invoked.

In the context of NCDs, clauses governing arbitrary and discriminatory treatment might be invoked where regulatory distinctions are drawn between comparable products. For example, in the food and beverage sector, it is not uncommon to observe selective approaches to regulation that single out particular product categories, such as soft drinks. In such a situation, it is conceivable that an investor in the soft drinks industry, for example, might argue that the effect of selective regulation is to discriminate against that investor or its investment in favour of other foods or beverages with similar nutritional content. The merits of such a claim would turn first on the legal question of whether these types of treaty clauses can be stretched to cover discrimination of this type. If so, the issues would appear to turn on whether the product categories treated differently are comparable, whether the treatment is actually less favourable to the investor or investment and whether there is a sufficient justification for the regulatory distinction in question. These issues are considered in further detail below in the discussion of nationality-based discrimination.

4.2 Expropriation

It is common for IIAs to provide protection for investors against expropriation and nationalisation of investments and measures having equivalent effect. Clauses governing expropriation tend to be similar across agreements and are interpreted in largely the same manner. In general, it is permissible for the host state to expropriate or nationalise investments provided it is done for a public purpose, on a non-discriminatory basis and compensation is paid.

In the case of measures to address NCDs, it would only be in rare cases that a host state would take formal title of an investment or nationalise an investment. This might occur, for example, if a state decided to nationalise the tobacco or alcohol industries so as to create a state-run monopoly and control the industry directly.[58] Alternatively, an act of direct transfer of property rights might occur with mixed motives that extend beyond prevention or treatment of NCDs. For example, a host state might nationalise a private water utility to ensure access to potable water or nationalise a private hospital to ensure access to medical treatment. Although these acts would be relevant to the prevention and treatment of NCDs, this is likely to be only one of many purposes. In any case, these formal acts of expropriation or nationalisation would require the host state to pay compensation to an investor.

The legal question of greater interest is when action by the host state can be considered equivalent to expropriation or nationalisation (indirect expropriation). For example, claims brought by Philip Morris against Australia and Uruguay argue that tobacco packaging and labelling measures result in indirect expropriation by interfering with trademark rights.[59] Similarly, investors might argue that product bans or regulations governing content have an effect on their investments equivalent to expropriation and that specific measures negatively affect their goodwill and market share.

A good deal of case law suggests that in order for an indirect expropriation to arise there must be substantial interference with an investment. As one NAFTA tribunal put it, there must be 'a substantially complete deprivation of the economic use and enjoyment of rights to the property, or of identifiable distinct parts thereof (i.e. it approaches total impairment)'.[60] A number of factors might be taken into account in determining whether this is the case, including whether the investor maintains control of an investment, the duration of interference, whether the state had taken proceeds of sales other than through taxation and whether the state had interfered with management.[61]

Chemtura illustrates this requirement. That claim concerned a Canadian ban on lindane, a pesticide harmful to human health and the environment. The investor argued, among other things, that the ban constituted an indirect expropriation of its lindane business in Canada, including goodwill and customer/market share. The tribunal found that sales of the prohibited product represented only a relatively small part of the claimant's overall sales and that consequently interference with the investment could not be considered substantial.[62] Similarly, in *Feldman Karpa*, the tribunal rejected an indirect expropriation claim on the basis that the investor continued to run a successful business.[63] Each of these outcomes illustrates how difficult it might be for investors in the tobacco, alcohol and food sectors to demonstrate that individual actions by a host state amount to indirect expropriation while their investments continue to be profitable.

Although there is a line of case law suggesting that it is only the effect of the state action that matters,[64] the better view appears to be that substantial interference is necessary but not sufficient for indirect expropriation to arise. This view is reflected in another line of case law, which emphasises that tribunals often have to draw a line between compensable indirect expropriation and legitimate host state activity for which compensation need not be paid. In drawing this line tribunals consider a number of factors, including whether the host state action is a valid exercise of its 'police powers', the public purpose and effect of the measure, whether the action is discriminatory, proportionality between the means and ends and whether the action is bona fide.[65] In addition, tribunals sometimes consider the legitimate expectations of the investor.[66]

Without examining these factors in detail, it is important to note that a significant line of case law recognises an established principle that the state may act within its sovereign police powers, including the power to protect health, without incurring an obligation to compensate an investor for expropriation. The state cannot invoke this principle if its conduct is discriminatory or designed to cause a foreign investor to abandon property to the state or sell it at a distress price.[67] As the tribunal in *Saluka* noted, the concept of police powers is derived from customary international law.[68]

Notwithstanding recognition of the principle of police powers, the tribunal in *Saluka* also noted that:

> international law has yet to identify in a comprehensive and definitive fashion precisely what regulations are considered 'permissible' and 'commonly accepted' as falling within the police or regulatory power of States and, thus, noncompensable. In other words, it has yet to draw a bright and easily distinguishable line between non-compensable regulations on the one hand and, on the other, measures that have the effect of depriving foreign investors of their investment and are thus unlawful and compensable in international law.[69]

Accordingly, the common approach is to conduct a fact-specific analysis and draw analogies with prior cases where relevant. In *Chemtura*, after rejecting the claim on grounds of insufficient interference with property rights, the tribunal noted that in any case the measure constituted a valid exercise of Canada's police powers in that the Canadian regulator had taken measures within its mandate, on a non-discriminatory basis and motivated by increasing awareness of the risks posed by lindane to human health and the environment.[70]

The concept of police powers confirms the broad scope of host state power to engage in product regulation. This is in line with state-practice, which sees states prohibit the offering for sale of various types of products without that conduct attracting liability under investment treaties. Where measures of a regulatory character do have substantial effects on an investor or investment there remains a line between indirect expropriation and non-compensable regulation that gives host states a wide margin within which to regulate in the interests of health. That line will be drawn on a case-by-case basis, which suggests the importance of evidence and sound reasoning in regulation.

4.3 Non-discrimination

Typically, IIAs include provisions governing national treatment and most favoured nation ('MFN') treatment. National treatment provisions prohibit less favourable treatment of foreign investors and investments (of a contracting party) than like domestic investors and investments. MFN provisions prohibit less favourable treatment of foreign investors and investments (of a contracting party) than like foreign investors or investments from another state. National treatment obligations are most relevant to regulatory measures of the type contemplated to address NCDs.

National treatment provisions prohibit de jure and de facto discrimination, also known as discrimination in form and effect. Because the public health grounds for discriminating between investors or investments on the basis of origin are few and far between in the context of NCDs, it is discrimination through the effect of a measure that is most relevant. In this respect, there is a concern that regulatory distinctions drawn by a host state might inadvertently treat foreign investors or investments less favourably than domestic investors in like circumstances. In considering claims, tribunals usually examine: (i) whether the relevant investors/investments are like; (ii) whether the investor or its investment has been treated less favourably than like investors/investments of domestic nationality; and (iii) whether the differential treatment is justified.

Successful claims of discrimination in the context of the tobacco and food industries have been made in the past. For example, in *Feldman Karpa*, Mexico was found to have violated the national treatment standard with respect to treatment of a grey market exporter of cigarettes. The investor argued that he was entitled to tax rebates under Mexican law for cigarettes exported from Mexico and that occasional denial of those rebates resulted in less favourable treatment than that accorded to a like Mexican firm. Similarly, in *Archer Daniels Midland*, Mexico was found to have discriminated against a US investor when it applied a tax on HFCS that was not also applied to sugar. The tax was not applied on health grounds, but instead was applied for the purpose of protecting the domestic sugar industry from competition with foreign HFCS producers because HFCS had benefited from unlawful production subsidies in the US.[71] The same outcome was reached in *Cargill*, another dispute arising out of the same measure.[72]

To date, claims concerning the legitimacy of regulatory distinctions drawn for purposes of protecting health in the tobacco, alcohol and food sectors have not arisen. In the event that they do, the case law suggests that tribunals will compare the treatment of similarly situated investors (such as investors in a particular sector) and that the justification given for differential treatment may be central in determining whether discrimination has arisen. This again highlights the importance of scientific evidence and/or rational reasoning serving as the basis for such distinctions.

5 Conclusion

It is difficult to generalise about the implications of international investment law for action to address NCDs. Earlier chapters in this volume have detailed the variety of risk factors for NCDs and the great variety of approaches available to addressing each of those risk factors. Where the potential liability of a host state depends on that state's behaviour and on a fact-specific analysis, there is limited value in using one or two case studies to explore the issues. Rather, this chapter has outlined the applicable principles, illustrated their application in relevant cases and discussed the implications for action in general terms. Although this approach has some limitations, it is preferable to drawing conclusions about case studies with so many caveats that the very conclusions become meaningless or misleading.

The field of international investment law comprises a variety of legal instruments, including investment contracts and IIAs. IIAs are standing agreements in the sense that they govern treatment of investors and investments generally. Although the standards of treatment in IIAs may differ slightly from agreement to agreement, those standards are at least transparent and relatively fixed in their content. In contrast, investment contracts involving the state create legal obligations in addition to the standing arrangements reflected in IIAs. These additional obligations can result in the state tying its own hands to a degree that is greater than under typical IIAs. For example, stabilisation clauses might compel payment of compensation for host state action to address NCDs that would not be compelled by an IIA. The investment contract governing the former Laotian tobacco monopoly provides an example of this, with Laos committing to compensate the investor if the government raises tobacco excises.

From a public health perspective, the need for policy coherence around investment and NCDs raises concerns because coordination of government agencies is logistically difficult, policy preferences cannot always be identified in advance and different government bodies do not always cooperate with one another. These problems make negotiation of investment contracts fraught with legal risk. Moreover, coherence between investment and health policies would mean states not offering incentives for investment in production of harmful goods such as tobacco and alcohol. In the food context, where food security and rural livelihoods are also concerns, policy coherence would see states incentivising production of healthful foods, but not items such as nutrient poor energy dense foods.

In the context of IIAs, it is also clear that the conduct of a host state in inducing investment is relevant to the question of which actions are compensable. State contracts and representations may form the basis of legitimate expectations that are relied upon in claims relating to fair and equitable treatment. In the absence of such interaction between the host state and investor, investors in the tobacco, alcohol and food sectors are unlikely to have legitimate expectations that they can avoid host state action to address NCDs. There is a spectrum in the sense that some measures may be more expected than others. In this respect, the rationality of the host state's reasoning, evidence of the risk being addressed and evidence of the effects of a measure will all be relevant to the legitimacy of an investor's expectations. These same factors will be relevant to whether a measure is arbitrary, unreasonable or discriminatory.

In the context of claims for indirect expropriation, interaction between the investor and host state may also be relevant, but is likely to play a lesser role. The core questions are likely to concern whether the extent of interference with an investor or investment is sufficiently substantial and, if so, whether the conduct is properly characterised as expropriation or non-compensable regulation. The case law on each of these issues suggests that it will ordinarily be difficult for investors in the tobacco, alcohol and food sectors to prevail on these issues.

In the context of claims concerning nationality-based discrimination, the primary concern is that measures might have an effect that inadvertently discriminates in favour of domestic investors or investments. The prospects of this type of claim succeeding are limited by the fact that tribunals use their own discretion to determine which investors and investments to compare and also consider whether there is a sufficient justification for the different treatment accorded to investors or investments of one category compared to those of another. This approach to analysis limits the prospects of inadvertent discrimination provided that regulatory distinctions between investors and investments are legitimate.

Notes

1 *Philip Morris Brands Sàrl v Uruguay (Notice of Arbitration)* (ICSID Arbitral Tribunal, Case No ARB/10/7, 19 February 2010); Allens Arthur Robinson, *Notice of Arbitration: Australia /Hong Kong Agreement for the Promotion and Protection of Investments* (21 November 2011) Attorney-General's Department <http://www.ag.gov.au/Internationalrelations/ InternationalLaw/Documents/Philip%20Morris%20Asia%20Limited%20 Notice%20of%20Arbitration%2021%20November%202011.pdf>.

2 Tania Voon and Andrew Mitchell, 'Implications of International Investment Law for Plain Tobacco Packaging: Lessons from the Hong Kong–Australia BIT' in Tania Voon, Andrew Mitchell and Jonathan Liberman with Glyn Ayres (eds), *Public Health and Plain Packaging of Cigarettes: Legal Issues* (Edward Elgar Publishing, 2012) 137; Benn McGrady, 'Implications of Ongoing Trade and Investment Disputes: Philip Morris v Uruguay' in Tania Voon, Andrew Mitchell and Jonathan Liberman with Glyn Ayres (eds), *Public Health and Plain Packaging of Cigarettes: Legal Issues* (Edward Elgar Publishing, 2012) 173.

3 *Agreement between the Swiss Confederation and the Oriental Republic of Uruguay concerning the reciprocal promotion and protection of investments*, signed 7 October 1988 (entered into force 22 April 1991).

4 *WHO Framework Convention on Tobacco Control*, opened for signature 16 June 2003, 2302 UNTS 166 (entered into force 27 February 2005) ('WHO FCTC').

5 World Health Organization, *Global Strategy for the Prevention and Control of Noncommunicable Diseases: Report by the Director-General*, WHO Doc A53/14 (22 March 2000), adopted by the World Health Assembly in WHA Res WHA53.14, 53rd sess (May 2000). See also World Health Assembly, *Prevention and Control of Noncommunicable Diseases*, WHA Res 53.17, 53rd sess, 8th plen mtg, Agenda Item 12.11, WHO Doc A53/VR/8 (20 May 2000).

6 *Political Declaration of the High-level Meeting of the General Assembly on the Prevention and Control*

of Non-communicable Diseases, GA Res 66/2, UN GAOR, 66th sess, 3rd plen mtg, Agenda Item 117, UN Doc A/RES/66/2 (24 January 2012, adopted 19 September 2011), annex.

7   World Health Assembly, *Global Strategy on Diet, Physical Activity and Health: Report by the Secretariat*, WHA Res 57.17, 57th sess, 8th plen mtg, WHO Doc A57/2004/REC/1 (22 May 2004).

8   World Health Assembly, *Global Strategy to Reduce the Harmful Use of Alcohol*, WHA Res 63.13, 63rd sess, 8th plen mtg, WHO Doc WHA63/2010/REC/1 (21 May 2010).

9   World Health Assembly, *Follow-up to the Political Declaration of the High-Level Meeting of the General Assembly on the Prevention and Control of Non-communicable Diseases*, WHA Res WHA66.10, 66th sess, 9th plen mtg, Agenda Items 13.1 and 13.2 (27 May 2013) annex, *Global Action Plan for the Prevention and Control of Noncommunicable Diseases 2013–2020*.

10 For example, Lao Tobacco Limited is a corporation owned by the Lao People's Democratic Republic and by Imperial Tobacco.

11 The China National Tobacco Corporation is an example.

12 See generally Michael Feit, 'Responsibility of the State under International Law for the Breach of Contract Committed by a State Owned Entity' (2010) 28 *Berkeley Journal of International Law* 142.

13 International Finance Corporation and the United Nations Special Representative of the Secretary-General on Business and Human Rights, *Stabilization Clauses and Human Rights* (27 May 2009) International Finance Corporation <http://www1.ifc.org/wps/wcm/connect/9feb5b00488555eab8c4fa6a6515bb18/Stabilization%2BPaper.pdf?MOD=AJPERES>; Audley Sheppard and Antony Crockett, 'Are Stabilization Clauses a Threat to Sustainable Development?' in Marie-Claire Cordonier Segger, Markus Gehring and Andrew Newcombe (eds), *Sustainable Development in World Investment Law* (Wolters Kluwer, 2011).

14 John Ruggie, *Report of the Special Representative of the Secretary-General on the Issue of Human Rights and Transnational Corporations and Other Business Enterprises*, UN GAOR, 17th sess, Agenda Item 3, UN Doc A/HRC/17/31/Add.3 (25 May 2011).

15 See generally Lorenzo Cotula, 'Reconciling Regulatory Stability and Evolution of Environmental Standards in Investment Contracts: Towards a Rethink of Stabilization Clauses' (2008) 1(2) *Journal of World Energy Law & Business* 158.

16 Isra Sarntisart, *Tax Policies for Tobacco Industry in Lao PDR* (July 2008) Southeast Asia Tobacco Control Alliance <http://www.seatca.org/dmdocuments/13_tax_policies_for_tobacco_industry_in_lao_pdr.pdf>.

17 Ibid.

18 See Jane Holroyd, 'Tobacco Ad Ban Won't Jeopardise GP: Bracks', *The Age* (online), 30 March 2006 <http://www.theage.com.au/news/national/tobacco-ad-ban-wont-jeopardise-gp-bracks/2006/03/29/1143441216042.html>.

19 See, for discussion, 'IOC Chief Jacques Rogge Admits Question Mark Over McDonalds and Coca-Cola Sponsoring Olympics', *The Telegraph* (online), 9 July 2002 <http://www.telegraph.co.uk/sport/olympics/news/9385751/IOC-chief-Jacques-Rogge-admits-question-mark-over-McDonalds-and-Coca-Cola-sponsoring-Olympics.html>.

20 A joint venture agreement with Philip Morris provides one example: see Philip Morris International, 'Agreements Provide for the Licensed Manufacture and Sale of Marlboro Cigarettes in China and Establishment of International Equity Joint Venture Company in Switzerland' (News Release, 21 December 2005) <http://www.pmi.com/eng/media_center/press_releases/pages/200512210000.aspx>.

21 See, eg, *Noble Ventures Inc v Romania (Award)* (ICSID Arbitral Tribunal, Case No ARB/01/11, 12 October 2005); although see *contra SGS Société Générale de Surveillance SA v Pakistan (Jurisdiction)* (2003) 42 ILM 1290.

22 *Philip Morris Brands Sàrl v Uruguay (Decision on Jurisdiction)* (ICSID Arbitral Tribunal, Case No ARB/10/7, 2 July 2013) [172].

23 See http://www.oneillinstituteblog.org/health-implications-of-coca-cola-investment-in-myanmar.

24 World Health Organization, *WHO Framework Convention on Tobacco Control: Guidelines for Implementation* (2011) 5.

25 *Grand River Enterprises Six Nations Ltd v United States (Award)* (2011) IIC 481 (*'Grand River'*).

26 *Marvin Roy Feldman Karpa v Mexico (Award and Separate Opinion)* (2003) 18(2) ICSID Review 488 (*'Feldman Karpa'*).

27 *RJ Reynolds Tobacco Company v Iran* (1984) 7 Iran–US CTR 181.

28 *Canadian Cattlemen for Fair Trade v United States (Jurisdiction)* (2008) IIC 316 (*'Canadian Cattlemen'*).

29 *Chemtura Corporation v Canada (Award)* (2010) IIC 451 (*'Chemtura'*).

30 *Archer Daniels Midland Company v Mexico (Award and Separate Opinion)* (2007) IIC 329 (*'Archer Daniels Midland'*); *Cargill Inc v Mexico (Award)* (2009) 11C 479.

31 Based on a search for the term 'alcohol' on www.investmentclaims.com.

32 Marcos Orellana, 'Science, Risk and Uncertainty: Public Health Measures and Investment Disciplines' in Philippe Kahn and Thomas Walde (eds), *New Aspects of International Investment Law* (The Hague Academy of International Law, 2007) 672. See also Chapter 3 of this volume.

33 *LFH Neer & Pauline Neer (USA) v Mexico (Award and Separate Opinion)* (1926) 4 RIAA 60 (*'Neer'*).

34 *Glamis Gold Ltd v United States (Award)* (2009) IIC 380 [616] (*'Glamis'*).

35 *Merrill & Ring Forestry LP v Canada (Award)* (2010) IIC 427 [210] (*'Merrill'*).

36 *Agreement on the Reciprocal Promotion and Protection of Investments between the Kingdom of Spain and the United Mexican States*, signed 23 June 1995 (entered into force 18 December 1996).

37 *Técnicas Medioambientales Tecmed SA v Mexico (Award)* (2003) 10 ICSID Rep 130 [154] (*'Tecmed'*).

38 See Michele Potestà, 'Legitimate Expectations in Investment Treaty Law: Understanding the Roots and Limits of a Controversial Concept' (2013) 28(1) *ICSID Review* 88–122.

39 See generally, Ioana Tudor, *The Fair and Equitable Treatment Standard in the International Law of Foreign Investment* (Oxford University Press, 2008) 154–81.

40 For a detailed examination of these issues see ibid 163–9; Potestà above note 38, 88.

41 As a general rule, contractual expectations will not found a legitimate expectation under international law: see, eg, *Parkerings-Compagniet AS v Lithuania (Award)* (2007) IIC 302 [344].

42 *MTD Equity Sdn Bhd v Chile (Award)* (2004) 12 ICSID Rep 6 [165] (*'MTD v Chile'*).

43 *North American Free Trade Agreement*, signed 17 December 1992, 32 ILM 289 (entered into force 1 January 1994).

44 *Glamis Gold Ltd v United States (Award)* (2009) IIC 380 [799].

45 *International Thunderbird Gaming Corporation v Mexico (Award)* (NAFTA Arbitral Tribunal, 26 January 2006) [147]–[148] (*'Thunderbird'*).

46 *El Paso Energy International Company v Argentina (Award)* (2011) IIC 519 [350] (*'El Paso'*).

47 *Grand River Enterprises Six Nations Ltd and Others v United States (Award)* (2011) IIC 481 [144].

48 *Methanex Corporation v United States of America (Award)* (2005) 44 ILM 1345, Part IV, Chapter D, [9] (*'Methanex'*).

49 *Glamis Gold Ltd v United States (Award)* (2009) IIC 380 [767].

50 For discussion see Rudolf Dolzer and Christoph Schreuer, *Principles of International Investment Law* (Oxford University Press, 2nd ed, 2013) 191–5.

51 *SD Myers Inc v Canada (Partial Award)* (NAFTA Arbitral Tribunal, 13 November 2000) [263].

52 The *Tobacco Plain Packaging Act 2011* (Cth) prohibits branding on packaging other than brand and variant names displayed in a standardised font, style and size.

53 *Philip Morris Asia Limited v The Commonwealth of Australia (Notice of Arbitration)* (Ad Hoc Arbitral Tribunal, UNCITRAL Rules, PCA Case No 2012-12, 21 November 2011).

54 *Philip Morris Brands Sàrl v Uruguay (Notice of Arbitration)* (ICSID Arbitral Tribunal, Case No ARB/10/7, 19 February 2010) [78]–[80].

55 *National Grid plc v Argentina (Award)* (Arbitral Tribunal, Case No 1:09-cv-00248-RBW, 3 November 2008) [197].

56 *Elettronica Sicula SpA (ELSI) (United States of America v Italy)* [1989] ICJ Rep 15, 76 ('*ELSI*').

57 *AES Summit Generation Limited v Hungary (Award)* (ICSID Arbitral Tribunal, Case No ARB/07/22, 23 September 2010) [10.3.7]–[10.3.9] ('*AES v Hungary*').

58 For a discussion of this approach see Ron Borland, 'A Strategy for Controlling the Marketing of Tobacco Products: a Regulated Market Model' (2003) 12(4) *Tobacco Control* 374; Jonathan Liberman, 'The Future of Tobacco Regulation: A Response to a Proposal for Fundamental Institutional Change' (2006) 15(4) *Tobacco Control* 333.

59 See for example, Allens Arthur Robinson, above n 1, [7.2].

60 *Fireman's Fund Insurance Company v Mexico (Award)* (2006) IIC 291 [176(c)]; cited in *Corn Products International Inc v Mexico (Decision on Responsibility)* (2008) IIC 373, [91].

61 *Pope & Talbot Inc v Canada (Interim Award)* (NAFTA Arbitral Tribunal, 26 June 2000) [100].

62 *Chemtura Corporation v Canada (Award)* (2010) IIC 451 (2010) [263].

63 *Marvin Roy Feldman Karpa v Mexico (Award and Separate Opinion)* (2003) 18(2) *ICSID Review* 488, [152].

64 *Metalclad Corporation v Mexico (Award)* (2000) IIC 161 [103].

65 *Corn Products International Inc v Mexico (Decision on Responsibility)* (2008) IIC 373 [87(j)].

66 *Metalclad Corporation v Mexico (Award)* (2000) IIC 161 [209].

67 *Emmanuel Too v Greater Modesto Insurance Associates (Award)* (1989) 23 Iran–US CTR 378; American Law Institute, *Restatement of the Law (Third) of the Foreign Relations Law of the United States* (1987).

68 *Saluka Investments BV (The Netherlands) v Czech Republic (Partial Award)* (Permanent Court of Arbitration, 17 March 2006) [262] ('*Saluka*').

69 Ibid [263].

70 *Chemtura Corporation v Canada (Award)* (2010) IIC 451 [266].

71 *Archer Daniels Midland Company v Mexico (Award and Separate Opinion)* (2007) IIC 329 [210]–[213].

72 *Cargill*, above n 30.

7 International Intellectual Property Law

Mark Davison

1 Introduction

In Chapter 8 of this volume, Enrico Bonadio sets out a number of types of regulation that may affect intellectual property. Potentially, any government regulation of the creation, sale or promotion of tobacco, alcohol or unhealthy foods could conflict with international intellectual property law obligations, especially those relating to trademarks and possibly geographical indications, which have a similar function to trademarks.

Issues relating to intellectual property regimes other than trademarks are less likely to arise and can be dealt with briefly for that reason. After dealing with those other regimes, the majority of this chapter will focus on the international trademark law obligations that may affect the marketing and promotion of tobacco, alcohol and unhealthy foods.

The nature of trademarks is that they are a key means by which to differentiate one product from another. They are used to acquire and maintain market share. They are also a key aspect of the promotion of both individual brands of those products and the promotion of the product generally. They are a means of increasing the overall size of the market. Part of the clash between those who support trademark rights and those who support public health initiatives is that the former claim to be more concerned with the impact on the capacity to distinguish brands while the latter group is more concerned about the use of branding to promote products that are directly or indirectly responsible for non-communicable diseases or other public harm.

Restrictions on advertising such as bans on the use of mass media or partial bans such as prohibiting advertisements at certain times of the day, bans on sponsorship of sporting events, and restrictions on the display of branded products at the point of sale all affect the capacity to use trademarks as owners would like. Probably the harshest form of regulation from a trademark owner's perspective is plain packaging, such as the plain packaging for tobacco products introduced by the Australian legislation.[1]

The current disputes before the World Trade Organization ('WTO') concerning Australia's plain packaging legislation for tobacco will obviously clarify a number of issues about the nature and extent of permissible regulation of products that are considered to contribute to very significant public health problems.[2] The discussion to date about plain packaging legislation has been focused to some extent on a too simplistic analysis of the question of whether or not the legislation complies with international trademark law. The real issue is more nuanced. If the legislation does comply with international trademark law, the real question will be why it complied with international trademark law. If the hurdle for compliance with the WTO agreements set by the WTO is relatively low,[3] the opportunity, as a matter of law as opposed to politics, to introduce more stringent regulation of packaging of other products will be greater than if the hurdle is set high.

Alternatively, in the highly unlikely event that the legislation is found not to comply with international trademark law, the real question will be why it did not do so and what measures short of plain packaging can be applied, to which goods, and on what grounds.

2 What is plain packaging?

Detailed descriptions of the Australian legislation have been provided elsewhere.[4] A brief summary here will suffice. The plain packaging legislation has three major effects on retail packaging of tobacco products in Australia. The first effect is that it bans non-word trademarks and signs altogether.[5] There can be no use of colours, artistic devices, or fancy script of any kind. The basic colour of the packaging is a drab brown, which takes up the space previously occupied by the get-up of packaging.[6] The second effect is that it permits the use of word trademarks, but the particular use is heavily prescribed. They can only occupy a small percentage of the front of the packaging, in no more than 14 point font, and the colour and font face are dictated by the legislation.[7] The third effect of the legislation is to very significantly increase the percentage of the packaging that is taken up by text and graphic warnings. Ninety per cent of the back of a cigarette packet is taken up with warnings, as is 75 per cent of the front.[8] Consequently, some trademarks are totally prohibited (non-word trademarks), others are heavily regulated (word trademarks), and the space available for trademarks is restricted by the requirement that warnings take up the majority of the packaging.

The WTO may face some difficulty in establishing general principles that give clear guidance as to which rules relating to packaging would be permissible and which would not. If plain packaging is ruled to violate the *Agreement on Trade-Related Aspects of Intellectual Property Rights* ('TRIPS'),[9] the question then remains whether the pre-existing requirements for such warnings are also invalid. Alternatively, can the Australian government increase the size of the warnings to 100 per cent and, say, 90 per cent respectively, thus allowing tobacco companies to do what they wish but only with the remaining 10 per cent of the front of their packets? Or can the government restrict the use of, say, colours by tobacco companies but not require what might be considered to be excessively large graphic and textual warnings? The potential combinations and permutations relating to both warnings and limits on the use of trademarks is obviously infinite.

This chapter considers the relationship between regulation of marketing of some products for public health purposes and international trademark law. Unsurprisingly, it does so primarily through the lens of the issues surrounding the WTO disputes concerning Australia's plain packaging legislation for tobacco. However, as just indicated, the potential implications of the WTO's decision, whatever that decision may be, need to be considered. To that extent, it is necessary to consider the nature of the products that are being regulated and the similarities and differences between those products. Part of the difficulty in this area is that some of the legal analysis does not grapple directly with the nature of the public health concerns with tobacco as opposed to the nature of the concerns with other products such as alcohol and unhealthy foods and the potential implications of those differences from a legal perspective. As already indicated, before proceeding to address trademark issues, the other intellectual property regimes and their relationship to regulation of the promotion of tobacco, alcohol and unhealthy foods will be briefly addressed.

3 Relevant forms of intellectual property

3.1 Copyright

In the course of creating branding for various products, a variety of original artworks are created, and that artwork receives copyright protection pursuant to art 9 of TRIPS, which, in turn, incorporates relevant provisions of the *Berne Convention for the Protection of Literary and Artistic Works*.[10] The rights of an owner of copyright in such artworks include the rights to authorise the reproduction of those artworks. While this right exists, it does not carry with it a right to place reproductions on any item of commerce that the copyright owner deems fit and to offer those items of commerce for sale on such terms as the copyright owner deems fit. The matter is not being pursued as part of the current disputes between Australia on the one hand and Ukraine, the Dominican Republic and Honduras on the other.

3.2 Designs

Packaging of goods may involve industrial designs that are new or original. Design rights or copyright or both forms of protection must be conferred on such designs.[11] The owner of a protected industrial design has the right to prevent unauthorised third parties from making, selling or importing articles bearing or embodying a design that is a copy, or substantially a copy, of the protected design.[12]

Again, the difficulty is that the right to prevent others from using one's intellectual property does not necessarily translate into a positive right to use it oneself. The issue is discussed in more detail in the context of trademarks, where there is an argument that there is an entitlement to use trademarks under art 20 of TRIPS.

3.3 Patents

As Bonadio has explained in Chapter 8, there may be some circumstances in which patentability may be an issue in regards to alcohol, tobacco or unhealthy foods. However, those circumstances are limited and, at this point, there are no substantive proposals in relation to them. Most of the detrimental health effects of those products are not attributable to their patentability, especially as most of those products are not actually protected by patents. There are some patents in respect of innovative packaging, but they are not a major consideration in this area.[13]

As with copyright and designs, patent owners have the exclusive rights to prevent third parties from making, using, offering for sale, selling or importing for those purposes a patented product.[14] However, they do not have a positive right to sell their patented product if the relevant governments decide they should not be offered for sale.

3.4 Geographical indications

A similar situation exists in relation to geographical indications as that in relation to patents, designs and copyright. The basic right provided by TRIPS is a right to prevent others from wrongly using geographical indications, rather than a positive right to use them, and no TRIPS provision may be interpreted as providing an entitlement to use.[15]

The complaints may rely on the proposition that the legislation that does not prevent 'any use which constitutes an act of unfair competition', but the details of that part of the complaint are not yet elucidated. In addition, TRIPS art 24(3) provides that:

> In implementing this Section, a Member shall not diminish the protection of geographical indications that existed in that Member immediately prior to the date of entry into force of the WTO Agreement.

Australia's protection of geographical indications for products other than wine and spirits are either via trademark law and the registration of collective or certification trademarks, or via general laws preventing misleading or deceptive conduct in trade or commerce. Again, the details of the claim that there has been a diminution of protection for geographical indications are not yet available.

4 The nature of the WTO complaints

Three complaints have been launched at the WTO against the plain packaging legislation. The complaints have been brought by Ukraine, Honduras and the Dominican Republic.[16] At this point in time, only a general indication of the basis of the complaints has been given.[17]

Further details supporting the complaints will be provided in due course. The complaints relate to a relatively broad range of provisions within TRIPS, the *Agreement on Technical Barriers to Trade* ('TBT Agreement')[18] and the *General Agreement on Tariffs and Trade 1994* ('GATT').[19] Whether all of the provisions in question receive equal attention in the dispute resolution process remains to be seen, and it may be possible that the disputes will eventually focus on one or two key provisions. For the purposes of this chapter, the key provision is art 20 of TRIPS, but other provisions of TRIPS, including but not limited to the other trademark provisions, are important in themselves and as part of the context in which art 20 is to be interpreted.

5 Interpreting TRIPS

5.1 National treatment and most favoured nation status

Two key principles and requirements of TRIPS are those of national treatment and most favoured nation status. Article 3(1) provides in relation to national treatment that:

> Each Member shall accord to the nationals of other Members treatment no less favourable than that it accords to its own nationals with regard to the protection[3] of intellectual property …

Footnote 3 to that article provides that:

> For the purposes of Articles 3 and 4, 'protection' shall include matters affecting the availability, acquisition, scope, maintenance and enforcement of intellectual property rights as well as those matters affecting the use of intellectual property rights specifically addressed in this Agreement.

Article 4 provides for most favoured nation status by stating that:

> With regard to the protection of intellectual property, any advantage, favour, privilege or immunity granted by a Member to the nationals of any other country shall be accorded immediately and unconditionally to the nationals of all other Members.

Neither of these requirements is subject to any exception or limitation in TRIPS other than quite precise and limited exceptions that are clearly set out in art 3. They are absolute requirements that must be met at all times. For example, art 8, which permits measures necessary for public health in some circumstances, would not and does not override the requirements.

The plain packaging of tobacco legislation would appear to be entirely consistent with both requirements. The legislation applies to all tobacco products, regardless of their origin, and has the same effect on all trademarks.

One possible argument pursuant to these provisions is that the legislation makes it more difficult for new entrants into the tobacco market in Australia as they are not able to easily differentiate their new brands from existing brands. In some respects, the legislation may 'fossilise' the market share of particular brands, as consumers with a pre-existing knowledge of particular brands are less likely to be exposed to new brands. They are then more likely to continue to smoke their previous brand than to experiment with a new brand. If pre-existing brands come from one or other particular nations, the argument might be made that the legislation gives an advantage or favour to those pre-existing brands.

There are two difficulties with this argument. The first is that clearly the legislation applies equally to all tobacco products, and there can be no argument of direct discrimination. The argument of indirect discrimination is also difficult to make out. If such an approach was taken, almost any alteration of intellectual property rights, favours and privileges could be argued to constitute a breach of the requirement because it would result in conferring a market advantage on pre-existing trademark owners vis-à-vis new trademark owners.

Two examples might suffice to demonstrate the point. In 2006, the United States amended its trademark legislation as it related to dilution of trademarks. In some respects, it became easier for the owner of a well known trademark to demonstrate dilution because the requirements imposed by case law which interpreted the previous anti-dilution legislation provided that a plaintiff had to demonstrate actual dilution of the distinctiveness of its trademark from the alleged dilution.[20] The amending legislation provides that it is sufficient to demonstrate a likelihood of dilution.[21] The effect is to provide greater protection for pre-existing, senior trademarks than was previously the case and to necessarily make it harder for new, junior trademarks. Obviously, the new laws apply in respect of all trademarks and, in that regard, clearly do not breach the requirements of national treatment or most favoured nation status. But if making an alteration to laws that has the effect of favouring existing entrants over new entrants contravenes the national treatment requirements, this legislation would so contravene that requirement. It seems unlikely that there would be a finding to that effect.

The second example relates to amendment of s 60 of the Australian trademark legislation.[22] Prior to the amendment, a trademark with a reputation in Australia could be the basis of opposing a later trademark registration application if the two trademarks were substantially identical or deceptively similar and the reputation of the earlier trademark would result in a likelihood of confusion in the event of use of the latter trademark for which registration was being sought. Section 60 was amended to delete the requirement that the senior trademark be substantially identical with or deceptively similar to the junior trademark.[23] Again, as with the American anti-dilution legislation, the effect was to increase the capacity of the earlier trademark to prevent use of the later trademark and to therefore favour pre-existing trademarks. Similarly, it is difficult to see how these requirements of national treatment and most favoured nation status have been breached by the plain packaging legislation unless almost any alteration of intellectual property legislation might be regarded as breaching them.

However, the two requirements do have some potential implications for other products, especially unhealthy products. While tobacco products and alcohol products can be defined and identified relatively easily, there is an issue about the definition and identification of unhealthy foods. The imposition of severe packaging and labelling requirements or prohibitions on one type of unhealthy food or beverage might prompt a legitimate query as to the basis upon which that food or beverage has been targeted while others have not. For example, regulation of soft drinks but a lack of regulation of energy drinks may lead to questions being asked about why vendors of the latter retain the privileges of use of trademarks that are taken away from vendors of the former. The issue is somewhat similar to that addressed in the dispute between the United States and Indonesia under the TBT Agreement.[24] That decision is discussed in more detail in Chapter 5 of this volume. Briefly, the United States banned clove flavoured cigarettes while permitting the continued sale of other flavoured cigarettes, such as menthol cigarettes. Ultimately, the decision to prohibit the ban was based on the proposition that clove and menthol cigarettes are substitutes and should be treated equally. A similar argument may be run in relation to unhealthy foods and labelling requirements, which may complicate attempts to regulate one product rather than another.

5.2 *Article 20*

The major provision for consideration in the plain packaging disputes is art 20, which reads, in part:

> The use of a trademark in the course of trade shall not be unjustifiably encumbered by special requirements, such as use with another trademark, use in a special form or use in a manner detrimental to its capability to distinguish the goods or services of one undertaking from those of other undertakings.

Article 20 and the interpretation placed on it by the WTO in the plain packaging disputes is likely to be the fulcrum on which pivots the nature and extent of permissible regulation of packaging and labelling of unhealthy products. For that reason, a close examination of it generally and in the context of the plain packaging legislation is necessary.

Some of the initial debate in relation to plain packaging laws and art 20 surrounded claims that there is a right to use a trademark[25] and the laws contravene that right. In turn, this argument about the existence of such a right has resulted in a 'yes, there is a right to use', 'no, there isn't a right to use' binary approach to the debate.[26] As with the other intellectual property regimes already considered above, the express rights conferred on trademark owners are expressed in negative terms. TRIPS art 16(1) provides, in part, that:

> The owner of a registered trademark shall have the exclusive right to prevent all third parties not having the owner's consent from using in the course of trade identical or similar signs for goods or services which are identical or similar to those in respect of which the trademark is registered where such use would result in a likelihood of confusion.

The incorporation of art 6*bis* of the *Paris Convention for the Protection of Industrial Property* ('Paris Convention')[27] into TRIPS via art 2(1) also confers rights on well known trademarks via TRIPS. The relevant part of art 6*bis* provides that:

> The countries of the Union undertake … to prohibit the use, of a trademark which constitutes a reproduction, an imitation, or a translation, liable to create confusion, of a mark considered by the competent authority of the country of registration or use to be well known in that country as being already the mark of a person entitled to the benefits of this Convention and used for identical or similar goods.

Other rights are conferred on well known trademarks, whether or not they are registered, by arts 16(2) and 16(3), although art 16(2) relates to service trademarks and is therefore not relevant in this context.

The fact that the trademark rights in TRIPS have been expressed in purely negative terms of excluding certain types of use by third parties has been confirmed by a WTO panel report that rejected an argument that there is a positive right to use trademarks conferred by TRIPS.[28] However, this fact is but one relevant consideration in the interpretation of art 20, and there are conflicting views on the nature of that relevance.

For example, Frankel and Gervais in a recent article[29] have argued that the issue of the nature of property held by a trademark owner requires a more nuanced discussion about the nature of property and trademark property in particular than a simple focus on the existence or non-existence of an express right to use. In particular, they argue that the negative nature of the rights conferred by art 16 does not mean that there is therefore no legitimate interest of trademark owners in the positive use of trademarks.

5.3 *The more restrictive interpretation*

With the brief discussion above in mind, we can proceed with a more detailed discussion of the meaning of art 20. From a government perspective, the most restrictive interpretation of art 20 or, from the perspective of trademark owners, the most generous interpretation is as follows. Article 20 needs to be interpreted in the light of the international norms concerning the use of trademarks and the surrounding articles of TRIPS.[30] The purpose of the registration system is to facilitate use of trademarks, and trademarks are a critical aspect of commerce.[31] Article 15 defines a trademark, and defines it quite broadly, as just about any sign that is capable of being used to distinguish goods or services. For current purposes, the discussion will be limited to goods. Article 16(1) then confers a right on registered owners to prevent the use of their trademarks by others in certain circumstances, in particular, where the use by others would be likely to cause confusion relating to the goods. Article 2(1), which incorporates art 6*bis* of the Paris Convention, and arts 16(2) and 16(3) confer some protection on well known trademarks, whether or not they are registered, and a right on the owners of those trademarks to exclude others from using those trademarks. These provisions reinforce the concept of use as being the primary reason for trademarks to exist.[32] Article 17 permits limited exceptions to the rights conferred on trademarks, which means it applies in respect of registered trademarks and well known trademarks, whether registered or not.

The exceptions must have regard to the legitimate interests of registered trademark owners and third parties. Consequently, trademark owners have both rights of exclusion under arts 16 and 2(1) and legitimate interests, which are something separate from the exclusive rights.[33] Legitimate interests include the interest in using a trademark.[34] The legitimate interests of trademark owners are advanced and protected by the rights of exclusion conferred by arts 16 and 2(1).[35]

Other provisions within TRIPS also deal with the question of use of a trademark. For example, art 19 deals with removal of a trademark for non-use, which further demonstrates the connection between registration, the right of exclusion and the legitimate interest in use of a trademark. Article 19 provides some protection from removal from registration for non-use. However, it is primarily if not exclusively aimed at temporary non-use rather than permanent non-use. The purpose of being immune from losing registration for temporary non-use is to retain registration so that the right to exclude is maintained and, in due course, use will occur.[36] Consequently, TRIPS contemplates use of a registered trademark as a normal state of affairs and art 20 needs to be interpreted with that in mind.

Article 20 is aimed at providing further protection for the legitimate interests of trademark owners. The argument then proceeds on the basis that the very purpose of the rights of exclusion is to facilitate the legitimate interest in using a trademark.[37] For various reasons, including the need to give a meaningful purpose to the rights to exclude under arts 16 and 2(1), the legitimate interests of trademark owners require some positive entitlement to use those trademarks.[38]

In addition to considering the purpose of the rights of exclusion under arts 16 and 2(1) and other provisions in TRIPS, the Paris Convention clearly envisages an entitlement to registration in defined circumstances, and the purpose of registration is use. The relevant Paris Convention provisions concerning registration are also incorporated into TRIPS via art 2(1). A prohibition on use of trademarks is the greatest of restrictions on the legitimate interest in using a trademark and therefore art 20 should be interpreted to include prohibitions on use within the meaning of 'encumbered by special requirements' rather than being interpreted by reference to other interpretations of the words of art 20 that have been proposed by others to the effect that art 20 does not apply to prohibitions on use.[39]

The only circumstance permitted by art 20 in which governments can restrict the legitimate interest of trademark owners in using a trademark is where the encumbrance on use proposed by government is justifiable. In the context of art 20, an obvious possible justification provided by TRIPS is art 8.

Article 8(1) provides in part that:

> Members may, in formulating or amending their laws and regulations, adopt measures necessary to protect public health and nutrition, provided that such measures are consistent with the provisions of this Agreement.

Article 8 is described as a basic principle of TRIPS. It will apply to the interpretation of 'justifiability' for the purpose of art 20 because, if the measures are necessary for public health, they will be consistent with the discretion given to governments by the reference to the concept of justification in art 20. Since public health concerns are the only justification advanced to date for plain packaging, art 8(1) appears to be the only relevant justification available. If the Australian government is relying on art 8(1) as its justification for the encumbrances that would otherwise contravene art 20, the onus is on it to actually prove that the measures are in fact necessary for public health within the meaning of that expression in art 8(1). The onus is not on a complaining member to prove that they are not necessary.[40] The WTO jurisprudence on what does and does not constitute measures necessary for public health is discussed later in this chapter.

5.4 The broadest interpretation

The most generous interpretation from the government perspective, and therefore the least generous from a trademark owner's perspective, is that a prohibition on use of trademarks is not within the scope of art 20, although provisions that mandate the form of use are within the scope of art 20. The basis of this proposition is that there is no right to use a trademark, and an encumbrance on use does not include a prohibition, which is a denial of a right to use.[41]

It is important to remember that the plain packaging legislation does both. It bans the use of non-word trademarks at the retail level and mandates the form of use in respect of word trademarks. The consequence is that, even on this broad interpretation, the mandated form of use of word trademarks must, at the least, not be unjustifiable. The awkwardness of the double negative is created by the actual wording of art 20, which refers to 'not be unjustifiably', and this wording also affects the question of onus of proof. In any event, it is important to focus on the concept of 'justifiability' – or absence or lack of justifiability – within the meaning of art 20. The broad view that art 20 does not apply to prohibitions on use has been discussed elsewhere.[42] Many of the reasons advanced for such an interpretation are also relevant to the third possible interpretation of art 20, which is discussed below.

5.5 A third way

A detailed response to the arguments for a restrictive interpretation of art 20 based on property law concepts is beyond the scope and size of this chapter.

To date, in terms of justifiability within the meaning of art 20, the justification proposed and advanced could be described in broad terms as a justification for public health reasons. If that general statement is the sole justification for the measures, one view is that the issue must be mediated by the application and adjudication of that justification via the precise test in art 8(1) of TRIPS of 'necessary for public health'.[43] An alternative view is that art 8(1) establishes a basic principle of the importance of public health generally. Public health concerns are a valid justification for encumbrances within the meaning of art 20,[44] and the wording of art 20 imposes an obligation on a nation complaining about an encumbrance to demonstrate that it is unjustifiable.[45]

Part of this approach between the most and least restrictive interpretations of art 20 is that while art 20 may apply to all encumbrances on the use of trademarks in the course of trade, the justification for such encumbrances can involve reference to a number of principles that are either expressly or implicitly part of the TRIPS agreement that should be recognised in the context of interpreting 'justification' within the meaning of art 20. Hence, 'justifiability' of an encumbrance embraces significantly more than necessity for public health. In short, the scope of government power to regulate the use of trademarks and thus to limit any legitimate interest to use that may be relevant, for the purposes of art 20, is significantly greater than that suggested by the most restrictive interpretation.

The nature of the possible justifications for plain packaging for the purpose of art 20 include the following individual justifications, which also constitute justification in combination with each other and the public health issues that have been addressed in some detail elsewhere. A brief summary of those potential additional justifications is provided below:

a. The plain packaging legislation is intended to prevent the misleading use of tobacco trademarks. The purpose of trademark use is to avoid a likelihood of confusion. When trademarks are used so as to generate confusion, the limitation of their use to that end may be justifiable, especially having regard to the consequences of the misleading behaviour. The issue is expressly addressed in the *WHO Framework Convention on Tobacco Control* ('WHO FCTC')[46] and its guidelines relating to arts 11 and 13 of the Convention.

b. The use of trademarks in a manner likely to lead to confusion may be an abuse of the rights of a trademark owner although that proposition in itself raises the issue of the precise rights held by trademark owners. It may be the case that the relevant abuse is abuse of the privilege of use of trademarks or simply an abuse of the privilege of use of signs. In any event, prevention of the abuse of intellectual property rights is a basic principle espoused in art 8(2) of TRIPS. As with the arguments concerning the applicability of art 8(1), the reference to the concept of justifiability in art 20 means that measures designed to prevent the abuse of trademark rights are consistent with TRIPS and art 20 in particular.

c. One of the uses of trademarks is to promote a product rather than to just differentiate one product from another. The former role of trademarks is not considered or protected by the trademark provisions in TRIPS. The point that trademarks are also used for promotion has been expressly conceded by British American Tobacco Australia Ltd in pleadings before the High Court of Australia.[47] It was also accepted by Justice Crennan in her judgment in the same case.[48] Measures targeted at the promotional aspect of trademarks may be justified on that basis, especially if some entitlement to use of trademarks is retained for the purposes of differentiating products. In the case of plain packaging, word trademarks remain in use as an important means of differentiating cigarettes, but the promotional aspect of non-word trademarks is removed, and some promotional aspects of word trademarks are reduced by the prescription on the manner of their use and the surrounding packaging requirements such as warnings and the background colour. In other words, there is a justifiable balance between curtailing the promotion of cigarettes and permitting the differentiation of cigarettes.

d.   Article 20 is only relevant to the use of trademarks in the course of trade. The primary impact of plain packaging is on the use of trademarks in a social setting by smokers after the retail sale of cigarettes.[49] Existing advertising bans and point of sale display bans already severely limit the use of non-word trademarks at the retail level, especially at the point of sale.

5.6 The onus of proof

If the justification pursuant to art 20 is something other than necessity for public health within the meaning of art 8(1), the onus of proof issue comes into starker relief. At this point, it is not the Australian government that is asserting that the measures are necessary for public health within the meaning of art 8 and therefore justified within the meaning of art 20, but the complainant nation asserting that the encumbrances are unjustifiable. The onus may therefore be on it to prove the measures unjustifiable.

The issue of the onus of proof is complex.[50] However, it would seem that art 20 does not apply unless an encumbrance is unjustifiable and the complainants have to establish that to be so. In any event, it is highly unlikely that the Australian government (or any government defending any regulatory measures) would simply stand mute and rely purely on the onus of proof to defend itself. A likely outcome would be that all parties would submit their evidence and the Panel would have to make a final determination by reference to an obligation on the complainants to demonstrate that the evidence shows that any relevant encumbrances are unjustifiable.[51] It is also the case that a later complaint could be brought if the measures were ultimately found to be unjustifiable in light of actual evidence once they had been in place for some time. This possibility may itself support the proposition that the onus is on the complainant given that it can re-litigate the matter at a later point but, if the measures are not implemented, the defendant cannot, and would be consistent with the reference in art 20 to 'justifiability' rather than 'justification'.[52] The resolution of the issue of onus of proof is one of the outcomes of the plain packaging disputes that will affect any future measures that might be scrutinised under WTO agreements.

5.7 Article 8: necessary for public health

If the most restrictive interpretation of art 20 is adopted, a careful discussion of necessity for public health within the meaning of art 8(1) is required. There are no decisions of the WTO directly on the interpretation of art 8 of TRIPS. However, there are a number of decisions of the WTO in relation to art XX of the GATT which has a similar provision that provides an exception in relation to measures necessary for human health.[53]

While there is some dispute about a number of aspects of the interpretation and application of the provision, there appears to be a certain amount of agreement on some key principles.[54] The first principle is that each Member nation has very great autonomy to determine its own health objectives.[55] Hence, if Australia adopts as a health objective an extremely low rate of tobacco consumption by its citizens, it is entitled to take measures designed to achieve that objective.

The second principle is that the measures in question need to make a material contribution to the objective in question.[56] This proposition becomes more problematic in a context where the efficacy of particular measures cannot be determined with any precision unless and until they are actually implemented. For example, while it is possible to determine that the banning of asbestos altogether will result in a lower death rate from asbestos-related disease in advance of the implementation of such a ban, the precise impact of restricting the promotion of a product cannot be ascertained until the restriction is actually imposed. It cannot be the case that a measure cannot be implemented unless it is already known with certainty in advance that it will contribute to the relevant objective.

In that situation, the question is one of assessing the evidence of the likelihood that the proposed measures will make a material contribution to the objective.[57] The jurisprudence suggests that it is sufficient for the nation alleging a measure is necessary for public health to demonstrate that there is credible evidence to support the introduction of the measures rather than there being overwhelming proof of their efficacy.[58]

A related issue to this requirement of making a material contribution to the desired objective is that the prospects of measures doing so depends to some extent on how narrowly or broadly one defines the objective. Defining the objectives narrowly will usually make it easier to demonstrate that the measures will contribute to that objective.[59]

For example, the stated objectives of the plain packaging legislation are defined relatively narrowly and include:

- discouraging people from taking up smoking, or using tobacco products; and
- encouraging people to give up smoking, and to stop using tobacco products.[60]

The legislation aims to achieve these objectives by regulating packaging of tobacco to:

- reduce the appeal of tobacco products to consumers; and
- reduce the ability of the retail packaging of tobacco products to mislead consumers about the harmful effects of smoking or using tobacco products.[61]

In other words, plain packaging is intended to contribute to the suite of public health measures that are aimed at collectively reducing smoking rates in Australia.

It is the synergy between plain packaging and other measures that gives plain packaging its efficacy, and plain packaging contributes to the efficacy of those other measures. For example, there has been a prolonged government advertising campaign highlighting the dangers of smoking and exhorting smokers to give up, coupled with support in the form of government subsidies for nicotine patches and government funding of organisations to assist smokers to quit. Other measures designed to reduce the appeal of tobacco products include long standing bans on advertising in mass media, prohibitions on smoking in many public places and bans on display of cigarettes at point of sale. In addition, high government taxes have been imposed on cigarettes. The combination of these measures is designed to lead to a reduction in tobacco consumption.

No single measure is or is intended to be a 'silver bullet' that will, by itself, result in significant reductions in tobacco consumption. Nor does the WTO jurisprudence on measures necessary for human health require this to be the case. The jurisprudence clearly acknowledges the use of complementary measures designed to assist the measures being considered to achieve their objective.[62] There is no requirement to choose either this measure or that measure but not both. On the other hand, a complementary measure would be one that has already been implemented or, at the least, is implemented simultaneously with the relevant measures under consideration, rather than a measure that has yet to be implemented. The latter would be an alternative measure.

A third principle is that there is no alternative measure, as opposed to a complementary measure, that is less trade restrictive and could achieve the same or a greater contribution to the objectives in question.[63] This requirement brings into even starker focus the previous point about defining the objective. If the objective is defined narrowly, it is likely to be specifically served by the measures in question and it is more difficult to develop alternative measures. On the other hand, if the objective is defined broadly as reducing smoking rates, this definitional process would, in theory, bring more alternative measures into play.

It is difficult to see how the stated objectives of the plain packaging legislation would be achieved by less trade restrictive alternatives than plain packaging, although various hypothetical arguments could be considered here. For example, it might be argued that graphic and text warnings might be just as effective with a background of any colour chosen by the vendor rather than a prescribed colour, or that smaller warnings would be just as effective as larger ones.

6 Application to alcohol and unhealthy foods

One can start to see the potential implications for regulation of other products of the requirements to be met in order to demonstrate that measures are necessary for public health. For example, if we try to transpose the objectives of the plain packaging legislation into similar legislation for alcohol or unhealthy foods or transpose the means of achieving those objectives, some issues arise that suggest plain packaging might be more than one bridge too far, at least in the foreseeable future.

For example, there would be at the very least significant political difficulties with governments deciding as a matter of policy to discourage people from drinking any alcohol or consuming any fat or sugar. There would need to be evidence that any consumption, as opposed to excessive consumption, of those products is a serious health risk. A government may be very reluctant to publicly declare that it has adopted a health objective of its population abstaining altogether from alcohol or sugar or fat. If a government abjures that objective and aims for a lesser one of responsible drinking or restricted intake of fat and sugar, the possibilities of alternative measures that would make an equal or greater contribution to the stated objective while having a less trade restrictive impact on trademarks would appear to present themselves. If the objective is to minimise excessive drinking, numerous measures are available including increasing taxes, reducing the opening hours of licensed premises, and reducing the number of outlets for selling alcohol to be consumed off the premises.

There would be similar issues with governments identifying the nature of the harm flowing from consumption of the product in question. In the context of tobacco, there is only one general regulatory response that is available to governments. They have little choice but to pursue a policy of abstinence due to the addictive nature of the product which is on a par with cocaine and heroin according to the Royal College of Physicians[64] and the US Surgeon General[65] and the fact that use itself is harmful. It is not feasible to run a public education campaign that says 'Smoke responsibly'. In turn, these aspects of tobacco dictate the regulatory response and the alternatives that are available.

With a product such as alcohol, the nature of the harm flowing from its use is different. First, some degree of use is probably safe for most people, or at least the risks associated with consumption at low levels are low for most people.[66] Second, different types of harm flow from wrongful or excessive use. For example, one possible harm from excessive alcohol consumption is drink driving. Increased surveillance via measures such as increased random breath testing and increased penalties may well have a greater effect than labelling changes. Harm from street violence due to alcohol might be reduced by measures such as reducing opening hours of licensed premises and policing policies such as zero tolerance. Harm from binge drinking might be attributable to pricing policies that facilitate the easy purchase of large volumes of cheap alcohol. Tax policies may have a significant role to play in that situation. All these alternatives would need to be considered.

Similar issues might arise with unhealthy foods. There are many measures that have not yet been adopted that would be far short of plain packaging such as greater public information campaigns, and greater information or more readily processed information on packaging about the potential health risks of the products. Until those alternative measures are first implemented and some assessment of their effectiveness undertaken, the far more severe measures such as plain packaging would be difficult to justify.

7 Consequences of the different interpretations

There are some obvious implications of the various interpretations for future regulatory action. If the narrowest interpretation applies and the only available justification is that measures are necessary for public health, a relatively heavy onus may fall on governments. As already indicated, the possibility of alternative, less trade restrictive measures needs to be considered in detail and basically excluded before introducing measures. In addition, existing measures may not meet the necessary onus of proof if relatively strict evidentiary requirements have not been met. It is quite conceivable that the narrowest interpretation would result in rolling back existing and possibly long standing regulatory controls on unhealthy products if the evidence of their efficacy is equivocal or lacking. The latter is entirely possible in nations where government resources are limited and a comprehensive assessment of measures cannot occur for that reason. The government of a developed country such as Australia may well have the necessary resources to fund public research of that nature but many developing countries may not. The manner in which regulatory measures might be targeted might be by, for example, asserting that graphic warnings for a particular product do not have to be 75 per cent of the front of a package to be effective and that they do not have to be coupled with a uniform background colour as opposed to one chosen by a trademark owner. As each individual restriction is 'picked off' as not having been proved to be necessary as opposed to a (slightly) less restrictive alternative, the combination of measures may well be rolled back. The actual response of governments may not be the subject of adjudication at the WTO, as the mere threat of such action may chill the ardour of governments to attempt regulatory measures because of the micro analysis of those measures that might flow from a test of necessity.

If the test of justifiability or lack of justifiability, depending on the onus of proof issue, is broader than that of necessity for public health, the scope for government action becomes correspondingly broader. The precise details of how easy or difficult it becomes to do so will depend on the precise findings of the WTO and the requirements for the provision of evidence on issues such as the misleading use of trademarks. The concept of justification would seem to involve a balancing of considerations. Hence, the degree of an encumbrance or the degree to which it diminishes the capacity to distinguish goods would need to be weighed against the justification given. The application of the bases of justification discussed above in relation to tobacco may well lead to a different result in relation to other products. For example, the nature, degree and effect of any misleading or promotional use of trademarks, if any, may be less significant for other products. In this regard, the evidence of such misleading behaviour may be less than is the case for tobacco which has been the subject of intense scrutiny for some decades. For example, there is no international convention or framework on alcohol or unhealthy foods that has stated that misleading uses of trademarks have occurred or could occur or recommends particular labelling or packaging restrictions to counter such a possibility. Nor is there a publicly available bank of documentation from the industries themselves of their use of packaging and labelling to convey misleading impressions about the attributes of their products as is the case with tobacco.[67] At the high dollar end of the alcohol market, the health risks of excess consumption may be significantly less because of the price of the product in question. So any 'abuse' of the use of trademarks in that sector of the market may have significantly less harmful effects. In addition, the question of the extent, if any, to which the products are physiologically addictive and the nature of the harm from excessive use is relevant to the extent of the justification to limit promotion of the goods or to limit the use of promotion in a social setting. While a broad test of 'justifiability' would obviously be an easier test to meet than necessity for public health, it is not a free pass for any government regulation of any product for any reason nominated by government.

Notes

1 'TPP' refers to an act of parliament, the regulations to that act and information standards imposed pursuant to the *Competition and Consumer Act 2010* (Cth). The relevant act is the *Tobacco Plain Packaging Act 2011* (Cth) ('TPP Act') and the regulations to that act are the *Tobacco Plain Packaging Regulations 2011* (Cth) (as amended by the *Tobacco Plain Packaging Amendment Regulations 2012* (Cth)) ('TPP Regulations'). The TPP Act and the TPP Regulations prescribe the nature of tobacco packaging and create the restrictions on the use of trademarks. The relevant information standard is the *Competition and Consumer (Tobacco) Information Standard 2011*, which imposes the requirements for text and graphic warnings on tobacco packaging.

2 See *Australia – Certain Measures Concerning Trademarks and Other Plain Packaging Requirements Applicable to Tobacco Products and Packaging: Request for the Establishment of a Panel by Ukraine*, WT/DS434/11 (17 August 2012); *Australia – Certain Measures Concerning Trademarks, Geographical Indications and Other Plain Packaging Requirements Applicable to Tobacco Products and Packaging; Request for the Establishment of a Panel by Honduras*, WTO Doc WT/DS435/16 (17 October 2012); *Australia – Certain Measures Concerning Trademarks, Geographical Indications and Other Plain Packaging Requirements Applicable to Tobacco Products and Packaging; Request for the Establishment of a Panel by Dominican Republic*, WTO Doc WT/DS441/15 (9 November 2012). Cuba has also sought consultations on Australia's measures: *Australia – Certain Measures Concerning Trademarks, Geographical Indications and Other Plain Packaging Requirements Applicable to Tobacco Products and Packaging: Request for Consultations by Cuba*, WTO WT/DS458/1 (3 May 2013).

3 *Marrakesh Agreement Establishing the World Trade Organization* ('WTO Agreement'), opened for signature 15 April 1994, 1867 UNTS 3 (entered into force 1 January 1995).

4 Jonathan Liberman, 'Plainly Constitutional: The Upholding of the Plain Tobacco Packaging by the High Court of Australia' (2013) 39(2) *American Journal of Law & Medicine* 361.

5 TPP Act s 20; TPP Regulations regs 2.3.1-2.3.9.

6 TPP Act s 19; TPP Regulations reg 2.2.1(2) requires that 'All outer surfaces of primary packaging and secondary packaging must be the colour known as Pantone 448C'.

7 TPP Act s 21; TPP Regulations reg 2.3.2.

8 *Competition and Consumer (Tobacco) Information Standard 2011* (Cth) pt 2 sets out the location of health warnings on a retail packaging of a tobacco product and pts 3–8 set out various warning statements and accompanying graphics.

9 *Marrakesh Agreement Establishing the World Trade Organization*, opened for signature 15 April 1994, 1867 UNTS 3 (entered into force 1 January 1995) annex 1C ('*Agreement on Trade-Related Aspects of Intellectual Property Rights*') ('TRIPS').

10 *Berne Convention for the Protection of Literary and Artistic Works*, opened for signature 14 July 1967, 828 UNTS 222 (entered into force 29 January 1970).

11 TRIPS art 25(1).

12 TRIPS art 26(1).

13 British American Tobacco Investments Ltd owns an Australian patent in respect of cigarette packaging, Patent No 2001258572.

14 TRIPS art 28.

15 TRIPS art 22(2): 'In respect of geographical indications, Members shall provide the legal means for interested parties to prevent: (a) the use of any means in the designation or presentation of a good that indicates or suggests that the good in question originates in a geographical area other than the true place of origin in a manner which misleads the public as to the geographical origin of the good; (b) any use which constitutes an act of unfair competition within the meaning of art 10*bis* of the Paris Convention (1967)'.

16 See above n 2.

17 Ibid.

18 *Marrakesh Agreement Establishing the World Trade Organization*, opened for signature 15 April 1994, 1867 UNTS 3 (entered into force 1 January 1995) annex 1A ('*Agreement on Technical Barriers to Trade*').

19 *General Agreement on Tariffs and Trade*, signed 30 October 1947, 55 UNTS 187 (entered into force 1 January 1948), as incorporated in *Marrakesh Agreement Establishing the World Trade Organization*, opened for signature 15 April 1994, 1867 UNTS 3 (entered into force 1 January 1995) annex 1A ('*General Agreement on Tariffs and Trade 1994*').

20 *Moseley v V Secret Catalogue Inc* 537 US 418 (2003).

21 *The Trademark Dilution Revision Act of 2006* (HR 683).

22 *Trade Marks Act 1995* (Cth) s 60.

23 *Trade Marks Amendment Act 2006* (Cth).

24 Appellate Body Report, *United States – Measures Affecting the Production and Sale of Clove Cigarettes*, WTO Doc WT/DS406/AB/R (adopted 24 April 2012).

25 Memorandum from LaLive to Philip Morris International Management SA, *Why Plain Packaging is in Violation of WTO Members' International Obligations under TRIPS and the Paris Convention*, 23 July 2009, [20].

26 Ibid; see also Mark Davison, 'The Legitimacy of Plain Packaging Under International Intellectual Property Law: Why There is No Right to Use a Trademark Under Either the Paris Convention or the TRIPS Agreement' in Tania Voon, Andrew Mitchell and Jonathan Liberman with Glyn Ayres (eds), *Public Health and Plain Packaging of Cigarettes: Legal Issues* (Edward Elgar Publishing, 2012) 81, 94–5.

27 *Paris Convention for the Protection of Industrial Property*, opened for signature 14 July 1967, 828 UNTS 306 (entered into force 26 April 1970) ('Paris Convention').

28 Panel Report, *European Communities – Protection of Trademarks and Geographical Indications for Agricultural Products and Foodstuffs, Complaint by Australia*, WTO Doc WT/DS290/R (adopted 20 April 2005) [7.610]–[7.611]. The WTO complaint by the Dominican Republic alleges that art 16(1) is breached because plain packaging deprives trademark owners of the benefit or enjoyment of the rights granted by the section. This argument may need to be addressed via art 20.

29 Susy Frankel and Daniel Gervais, 'Plain Packaging and the Interpretation of the TRIPS Agreement' (2013) 46(5) *Vanderbilt Law Journal* 1148, 28. References in this chapter are to a pre-publication version available on SSRN (26 April 2013): <http://ssrn.com/abstract=2234580>.

30 Ibid 13–17.

31 Ibid 25–6.

32 Ibid 28.

33 Ibid 39, 41. See also Panel Report, *European Communities – Protection of Trademarks and*

Geographical Indications for Agricultural Products and Foodstuffs, Complaint by the United States, WTO Doc WT/DS174/R (adopted 20 April 2005).

34 Frankel and Gervais, above n 29, 23, 41.

35 Ibid 39.

36 Ibid 25.

37 Ibid 41.

38 Ibid.

39 Ibid 20–1.

40 Ibid 44.

41 See Davison, above n 26.

42 Ibid.

43 Frankel and Gervais, above n 29, 42; see also Mark Davison and Patrick Emerton, 'Rights, Privileges, Legitimate Interests, and Justifiability: Article 20 of TRIPS and Plain Packaging of Tobacco' (2014) *American University International Law Review* (forthcoming) <http://papers.ssrn.com/sol3/papers.cfm?abstract_id=2322043>.

44 Tania Voon and Andrew Mitchell, 'Implications of WTO Law for Plain Packaging of Tobacco Products' in Voon et al, above n 26, 109, 121–5.

45 Ibid 124–5.

46 2302 UNTS 166 (adopted 21 May 2003, entered into force 27 February 2005) arts 11(1) and 13(4).

47 See the Reply of British American Tobacco Australasia in its case of *British American Tobacco Australasia Limited v The Commonwealth of Australia* (No S389 of 2011, filed in the High Court of Australia on 24 February 2012). At paragraph 7 of the Reply, BATA states that it uses its packaging for the purposes of a. distinguishing its cigarettes in the course of trade from other brands of cigarettes; and b. promoting its cigarettes.

48 See *JT International SA v Commonwealth of Australia* (2012) 291 ALR 669 [286] (Crennan J): 'Whilst the prime concern of the Trade Marks Act is with the capacity of a trade mark to distinguish the goods of the registered owner from those of another trader, trade marks undoubtedly perform other functions. For example … it may be accepted that distinctive marks can have a capacity to advertise, and therefore to promote sales of products sold under or by reference to them. The advertising function of a trade mark is much more readily appreciated than it once was, and that function may be of great commercial value'.

49 See, eg, RP Ferris, *Communication of Novel Product Features* (29 April 1981) Legacy Tobacco Documents Library <http://legacy.library.ucsf.edu/tid/tdz75a99/pdf?search=%22 packaging%20colour%20perception%22>.

50 See generally Michelle Grando, *Evidence, Proof, and Fact-Finding in WTO Dispute Settlement* (Oxford University Press, 2009) ch 4.

51 Ibid ch 5.

52 See Daniel Gervais, 'Plain packaging and the TRIPS Agreement: A Response to Professors Davison, Mitchell and Voon' (2013) 23 *Australian Intellectual Property Journal* 96, 109.

53 See Voon and Mitchell, above n 44, 126.

54 For differing views on the interpretation of art 8(1), see, eg, Daniel Gervais, 'Analysis of the Compatibility of Certain Tobacco Product Packaging Rules with the TRIPS Agreement and the Paris Convention' (Report for Japan Tobacco International, 30 November 2010); Voon and Mitchell above n 44.

55 Voon and Mitchell, above n 44, 126.

56 Ibid 126–7.

57 Ibid 127.

58 Ibid 126–8.

59 See Benn McGrady, 'Necessity Exceptions in WTO Law: Retreaded Tyres, Regulatory

Purpose and Cumulative Regulatory Measures' (2009) 12(1) *Journal of International Economic Law* 153.

60 TPP Act s 3.

61 Ibid.

62 Voon and Mitchell above n 44, 128.

63 Ibid 125–8.

64 Royal College of Physicians of London, *Nicotine Addiction in Britain: A Report of the Tobacco Advisory Group of the Royal College of Physicians* (2000) xiv, 77, 98–9.

65 See, eg, United States Department of Health and Human Services, *The Health Consequences of Smoking: Nicotine Addiction: A Report of the Surgeon General* (1988) 25. See also United States Department of Health and Human Services, *Preventing Tobacco Use Among Youth and Young Adults* (2012).

66 <http://www.nhmrc.gov.au/your-health/alcohol-guidelines>.

67 The Legacy Tobacco Documents Library has over 14 million documents created by tobacco companies relating to issues such as their marketing activities and their knowledge of the detrimental effects of their products. <http://legacy.library.ucsf.edu/>.

8 Interaction with Domestic Intellectual Property Law

*Enrico Bonadio**

1 Introduction

This chapter aims to highlight the impact of certain recent regulatory measures on intellectual property ('IP') regimes. The measures I will be focusing on have the common purpose of reducing the consumption of products that are increasingly perceived as harmful to people. The products that have come under attack are, in particular, tobacco, alcohol and unhealthy foodstuffs. Indeed, tobacco use, abuse of alcohol and unhealthy diets are among the most important risk factors of non-communicable diseases ('NCDs'), which constitute the main cause of death on our planet and are one of the major challenges for social and economic development in the 21st century. Most regulatory measures targeting these risk factors have been prompted by international moves, namely the adoption of the *WHO Framework Convention on Tobacco Control* ('WHO FCTC'),[1] an international treaty that entered into force in 2005 under the auspices of the World Health Organization ('WHO'),[2] and the 2011 United Nations ('UN') Political Declaration on NCDs.[3]

The above mentioned measures are analysed in the second part of the chapter. They can be grouped into four categories: (i) measures related to the presentation of products (for example, plain packaging requirements and display bans on cigarettes and other tobacco products); (ii) measures related to advertising (for example, advertising prohibitions or restrictions, or bans on aggressive marketing strategies, especially those targeting minors); (iii) measures related to the supply of the products (for example, sales restriction to and by minors, or bans of vending machines dispensing alcohol or cigarettes); (iv) measures related to the manufacturing of the products (for example, bans on the use of certain ingredients including trans-fat in foodstuffs, bans on the use of additives in tobacco such as flavouring or colouring agents, or rules prohibiting certain shapes of tobacco packaging).

The common denominator of these measures is the fact that their aim is to reduce the consumption of products considered harmful and thus protect consumers' health. Yet these measures also have the effect of reducing the ability of tobacco, alcohol and food manufacturers to produce, present, advertise and market their products as they wish, and to make them appealing to consumers. More importantly, all these measures impair the ability of manufacturers to fully exploit their IP assets, whether they are: (a) trademarks affixed on products and packaging; (b) copyrighted works displayed on products or packaging; (c) distinctive trade dress and get-up for products; (d) registered or unregistered designs incorporated in products or packaging; or (e) patented inventions related to ingredients and constituents or related to packaging. In the third part of the chapter I will look at whether the inability of tobacco, alcohol and food manufacturers to fully use their IP assets due to the introduction of the measures at issue also entails a violation of the rights offered by IP legislation to IP owners: I will argue that the measures in question do not entail infringement of IP rights. Finally, in the last part of the chapter I will discuss if, and to what extent, IP legislation, and in particular patent procedures, could be amended with a view to incentivising companies to produce and market healthy products in the field of foodstuff and beverages. In this regard I will put forward three proposals.

2 Regulatory measures affecting IP in the fields of tobacco, alcohol and foodstuffs

Regulatory measures often have a negative impact on business and trade, as they make it more expensive and cumbersome for companies to produce and market their products. This is particularly true of industries that have been traditionally (and heavily) regulated, such as tobacco, alcohol and food. Recently, in many countries there has been an increase in the regulatory burden on companies in these fields. Indeed, in the past years a wave of new regulatory measures have restricted the freedom of tobacco, alcohol and food companies to produce, present, offer for sale, advertise and supply their products as they wish. Such a limitation of commercial freedom is perceived by several governments and international organisations, as well as non-governmental organisations (including anti-smoking and anti-alcohol pressure groups), as necessary to protect an overriding public interest – that is, human health. The underlying idea behind most of these policies is that states should take care of their citizens' health and therefore prohibit or restrict commercial and industrial activities that could be harmful to people.

We will see in the following paragraphs that all these measures – which affect most phases of the production chain bringing the products into the hands of final consumers (from manufacturing to supply) – have an impact on manufacturers' freedom to conduct their business and, as mentioned, restrict the ability of tobacco, alcohol and food manufacturers to fully exploit their intangible assets.

2.1 Measures relating to product presentation

The first category of measures relates to the presentation of tobacco, alcohol and food products. Generally speaking, all companies tend to present their goods in such a way as to induce consumers to make purchase decisions. Packaging is often the means to communicate such messages to prospective purchasers: trademarks, logos, colours, designs and even smells increasingly pervade the packaging in several industries. It therefore does not come as a surprise that more and more regulators and policymakers around the world have started targeting the packaging of products perceived to be harmful to people's health.

The case of tobacco is particularly relevant. Regulatory measures have recently been adopted in some countries that aim to prevent tobacco companies from using their usual brands and other fancy elements, especially on packaging. In particular, regulations have prohibited companies from displaying trademarks, designs, drawings, colours and other ornamental elements, or from presenting a single brand in multiple forms. The aim of these measures is to discourage consumption of what are considered to be harmful products, on the assumption that less exposure of existing and potential customers to tobacco brands and other fancy elements reduces the chance of purchase. The most striking examples within this category of measures, as detailed below, are plain packaging and display bans on tobacco products, as well as the so-called single presentation requirement. I will also briefly comment on a recent dispute regarding a packaging appropriation measure adopted by Iceland in the field of alcohol.

2.1.1 Plain packaging requirements: Australia's experience

Also known as generic or standardised packaging, plain packaging requires that all forms of tobacco branding be labelled exclusively with simple, unadorned text. This entails that trademarks, graphics and logos be removed from cigarette packs, except for the brand name and variant, which are displayed in a standard font (identical for all brands in the market). The pack is also required to be in a neutral colour and shape and to include only the content and consumer information (for example, toxic ingredient information) and health warnings required by law. In essence, plain packaging aims at standardising the appearance of all cigarette boxes in order to make them unappealing, especially for adolescents, thus reducing the prevalence and up-take of smoking.[4] Indeed, some scientific evidence shows that this measure – by eliminating logos, designs and other elements that are capable of inducing people to start smoking – is likely to reduce tobacco consumption.[5]

The practical effect of this measure is thus to prevent tobacco producers from showing some characterising features of their trademarks, as well as designs and copyrighted works on cigarette packs. To the eyes of tobacco majors, this is a strong limitation on their commercial freedom, especially in those countries where almost all forms of tobacco advertising are prohibited and thus packaging has become their ultimate marketing tool. Indeed, cigarette packs, once opened, remain in the hands of final consumers and constitute a powerful means of 'mobile' advertising.

This new measure is endorsed by the WHO FCTC, and more precisely by the guidelines to arts 11 and 13 to this treaty, which expressly recommend that states consider adopting such measures.[6] These guidelines are intended to assist countries in implementing their obligations under the WHO FCTC and therefore must be taken into account when interpreting this treaty. As has been noted, they constitute 'subsequent agreement[s] between the parties regarding the interpretation of the treaty or the application of its provisions',[7] pursuant to art 31(3)(a) of the *Vienna Convention on the Law of Treaties*.[8]

Generic packaging has already been implemented by Australia (other states are considering it as an option, especially those at the forefront in the battle against tobacco consumption, such as Norway, Canada, New Zealand and the United Kingdom). The Australian legislation was introduced in November 2011 and has been fully implemented since 1 December 2012. It mandates that all surfaces of tobacco packaging be drab dark brown and that no trademark or other logo can appear on the packaging save for the brand, business or variant name.[9]

The Australian legislation has been challenged by leading tobacco majors such as British American Tobacco Australasia Limited ('BAT') and Philip Morris Asia Limited before both the High Court of Australia and an arbitral panel constituted pursuant to a bilateral investment treaty ('BIT') between Australia and Hong Kong.[10] A dispute is also currently pending at the World Trade Organization ('WTO'), with Ukraine requesting and obtaining the establishment of a panel to assess the compatibility of the Australian measure with several provisions of the *Agreement on Trade-Related Aspects of Intellectual Property Rights* ('TRIPS Agreement').[11] In August 2012, the domestic proceedings came to an end with the High Court confirming that the measure does not amount to an expropriation of the tobacco companies' (intellectual) property and is thus compliant with the Australian Constitution.[12]

Thus far, legislation on plain packaging has been passed or proposed with reference to tobacco products. Yet there are speculations that plain packaging legislation may, in the not too distant future, spread to alcohol and other products perceived to be harmful, thus enlarging the range of IP rights owners hit by this marketing restriction.

2.1.2 Alcohol packaging regulations: Iceland's experience

Packaging appropriation measures aimed at reducing the attractiveness of unhealthy products have also recently been adopted or proposed in industries other than tobacco. Alcoholic products are a good example. A recent decision of the European Free Trade Association Court ('EFTA Court') in *HOB-vín ehf* – which found the measure in question was not compliant with the *Agreement on the European Economic Area* ('EEA Agreement')[13] – is relevant here.[14] The most interesting part of this dispute regards the refusal by the State Alcohol and Tobacco Company of Iceland ('ÁTVR') to authorise the marketing and sale of three cider cans that had been legally manufactured and sold in Denmark. The reason for such refusal was that their packaging bore text and visual imagery in violation of a provision adopted by ÁTVR. That provision states that the text and images on alcoholic packaging and labelling should not: contain loaded or unrelated information; suggest that the product enhances physical, mental, social or sexual functions; or offend people's general sense of propriety, for example by referring to violence, religion, pornography, illegal drugs, political views, discrimination or criminal conduct. ÁTVR stressed that the packaging of the products in question – which were marketed in stylish cans, featuring artful drawings including colourful illustrations of women's legs with some apparently naked skin – were 'evidently intended to make the products sensually appealing and challenging'.[15]

The importer of the cans challenged this decision. The case was then referred to the EFTA Court, which was asked to give an advisory opinion about the compatibility of the Icelandic provision with the EEA Agreement[16] (a treaty that extends portions of European Union ('EU') law to European Economic Area ('EEA') countries including Iceland). The EFTA Court noted that the refusal by ÁTVR had been based exclusively on a specific part of the rule in question, namely the part of the provision that prohibits the use of texts or visual imagery that offends people's general sense of propriety. Accordingly, it was found that the measure in question could not be justified under the EEA Agreement by a stringent public interest objective such as the protection of public health (ÁTVR had claimed in the proceedings that the ban in question could be justified by invoking the protection of consumers' health).

Even though the Icelandic provision has been condemned for being contrary to the EEA Agreement, this case shows that policymakers have started targeting the packaging of alcoholic products, and they have done so with a view to reducing the market appeal of such products and therefore their consumption. Yet such measures inevitably restrict the ability of manufacturers to fully exploit their logos, designs or copyrighted drawings.

2.1.3 The 'single presentation requirement': Uruguay's experience

Another measure related to the presentation of tobacco products (and believed to have a negative impact on manufacturers' ability to use their IP) is in force in Uruguay. Uruguayan legislation prohibits misleading or deceptive tobacco packaging.[17] Initially this provision was invoked to outlaw descriptors including 'mild', 'light' and 'ultra-light'. After Philip Morris began using different brands differentiated by colours and terms referring to such colours instead of the above descriptors (such as 'Gold', 'Blue', 'Silver'), the Uruguayan Ministry of Public Health interpreted the ban on deceptive and misleading packaging as also outlawing the use of colours. Philip Morris challenged this provision under the BIT between Uruguay and Switzerland,[18] claiming that the effect of the way the Uruguayan provision on deceptive and misleading packaging had been interpreted and applied entailed that just one product from a brand family can be marketed in that country,[19] with the result that tobacco manufacturers would be unable to fully use their trademark portfolio.[20] Some commentators have labelled this measure the 'single presentation requirement', as it bans the presentation of a single brand in multiple forms if such forms are capable of misleading consumers about the risk of smoking.[21] In the eyes of the challenger, Philip Morris, this measure is arbitrary and not reasonably justified by a public health objective and thus amounts to an unlawful expropriation of (intellectual) property.[22] The dispute is still pending.

2.1.4 Display bans of tobacco products: Norway's experience

Display bans of tobacco products are another measure that prevents tobacco companies from fully exploiting their trademarks, designs and other elements affixed to packaging. This measure entails a ban on displaying tobacco products at points of sale, which means that tobacco companies are prevented from showing their packs to potential purchasers.[23] Display bans have been adopted by several countries such as Norway, Iceland, Ireland and Finland in the context of policies aimed at protecting public health.[24] The Norwegian measure, in particular, has been given a green light by the EFTA Court. On 12 September 2011, the EFTA Court delivered an advisory opinion confirming the compatibility of the Norwegian measure with the EEA Agreement. The court found that the Norwegian display ban amounts to a restriction on the free movement of goods within the EEA, but that such a restriction is justified as it protects public health by limiting the consumption of tobacco products.[25]

2.2 Measures restricting advertising

A second category of IP restrictive measures relate to advertising.[26] Several countries have already passed legislation prohibiting or restricting advertising of tobacco, alcohol and unhealthy food: for example, bans on tobacco sponsorships in sporting events; bans on product placement;[27] bans on aggressive marketing strategies, especially those targeting minors;[28] and bans on brand stretching and brand sharing.[29] In the field of tobacco many of these measures have been adopted pursuant to the WHO FCTC, which defines tobacco advertising and promotion as 'any form of commercial communication, recommendation or action with the aim, effect or likely effect of promoting a tobacco product or tobacco use either directly or indirectly'.[30] Bans on advertising on television, on radio, in cinemas and at sporting events have also been recently proposed in the field of alcohol. Russia, for example, has introduced a prohibition on alcohol advertising on radio, television, the internet, public transport, billboards and even in print media.[31] Again, the effect of these measures is to prevent owners of IP rights from using their signs, designs or copyrighted works in advertising. They thus constitute a limitation on the IP owners' commercial freedom.

In the past, IP owners have challenged restrictions on advertising and marketing strategies by invoking trademark rights. An old Guatemalan food related measure is relevant here. This case regarded marketing of infant formula milk. In 1983, Guatemala implemented the WHO's *International Code of Marketing of Breastmilk Substitutes*, which prohibited the use of images of babies on foods destined for children under the age of two.[32] The goal of this legislative move was to protect the lives of infants by promoting breast-feeding over breast milk substitutes and, particularly, to thwart aggressive marketing by baby food companies aimed at convincing mothers that their products were superior to breast milk. The law specifically banned images that idealised the products in question. Facing its implementation, the United States' ('US') children's food company Gerber claimed that the law infringed its trademark, which included the image of a healthy baby. Gerber then began threatening Guatemala that the company would lobby the US State Department to encourage it to impose trade sanctions under the *General Agreement on Tariffs and Trade 1947* ('GATT')[33] and other trade measures (in particular, the withdrawal of most-favoured-nation trading status).[34] This move prompted the Guatemalan Supreme Court to exclude products imported into Guatemala, including those marketed by Gerber, from the application of the legislation.[35]

2.3 Limiting supply of products to consumers

Other restrictive measures relate to the supply of the products to final consumers. For example, states often limit the times during which alcoholic products may be sold, or use authorisation systems to limit the number of shops and places that can sell such products.[36] This category also includes measures that prohibit or make it more difficult to sell tobacco and alcohol to minors, for example bans of tobacco or alcohol vending machines[37] or bans on the sale of tobacco with or in sweets, snacks, toys or any other objects that appeal to minors.[38]

All these measures restrict the freedom of manufacturers/IP rights owners, and their distributors, to sell their IP-protected products or to choose innovative ways of supplying their products, and limit the number of final consumers available to such companies by excluding a category of potential purchasers. This also restricts the ability of such companies to fully use and exploit their trademarks and other IP assets.

2.4 Measures impacting patents and designs

Another category of restrictive measures relate to the manufacturing of the products in question. Take the bans or restrictions on the use of certain ingredients, including trans-fats, in foodstuffs (recently introduced in several US states and cities); or the bans on the use of flavouring or colouring agents in tobacco and alcoholic products,[39] which help make them more attractive.[40] For example, the US recently prohibited the sale of clove-flavoured cigarettes with the aim of discouraging young people from smoking (this measure was found by a WTO Panel to be discriminatory as similar products, menthol cigarettes, could still be sold in the US).[41] Brazil also recently banned the use of additives in tobacco products, including chocolate, mint, fruit and cinnamon.[42] It is believed that such additives hide the bad taste of tobacco, reduce coughing, facilitate drag and thus contribute to smokers developing dependence. Moreover, several countries are considering bans on high-caffeine content in alcoholic beverages as a tool for fighting alcohol-related violence.[43]

Having said that, if a product or manufacturing process that includes the prohibited ingredient is patented, such a ban would basically make the patent meaningless as the producer/IP right owner would be prevented from properly using the invention. Concerns are growing, as patents covering food products and processes, and food and beverage recipes, are more and more frequently granted. Patent applications also show that some ingredients associated with energy and vitality, such as caffeine and taurine (which are increasingly viewed with suspicion by regulators) have also been considered for use in tobacco products.[44]

Plain packaging of tobacco products may also make pack-related patents and three-dimensional designs meaningless. For example, new Australian legislation requires that cigarette packs not contain an opening, such as a flip-top lid, that can be re-closed or re-sealed after the pack is first opened.[45] It also requires the outer faces of retail packaging to not have any decorative ridges, embossing, bulges or other irregularities of shape or texture.[46] As noted by Gummow J in the decision of the High Court of Australia, which confirmed the lawfulness of plain packaging under the Australian Constitution, this regulatory measure denies the exploitation of the patent owned by BAT.[47] BAT's patent covers an invention titled 'Smoking article packaging' and refers to a method of re-sealing the contents in that packaging.[48] It also makes meaningless – added the court – BAT's registered design protecting the so-called 'ribbed pack', the characteristic features of which resided in its particular shape and configuration.[49]

3 Measures with an indirect impact on IP rights

A category that does not have a direct impact on IP is measures governing the consumption of the products in question. Examples include bans on smoking in public spaces (already adopted in many jurisdictions) and bans on drinking in public (adopted in several Muslim countries), as well as price increases and consumption taxes (which are introduced by governments to make unhealthy products such as alcohol and tobacco less affordable).[50]

It seems clear that such measures do not jeopardise the ability of IP rights owners to use their intangible assets, but they limit the use of the products by final consumers.[51] However, these measures might have an indirect impact on IP as they may cause manufacturers/IP rights owners to lose sales. This in turn makes it more difficult for them to recoup the investments needed to come up with the relevant logos, designs or inventions and/or obtain the relevant IP protection (that is, trademark or patent registration).

4 The compatibility of the regulatory measures with IP rights

As we have seen, the measures aimed at restricting the manufacture, presentation, advertising and supply of tobacco, alcohol and unhealthy food and beverages jeopardise the ability of manufacturers to exploit their IP. They do so in different phases of the production chain that eventually brings the product into the hands of consumers, from the manufacturing process to the supply to end-users.

Do such interferences violate IP rights?[52] On the one hand, manufacturers may stress that as these restrictive measures prevent them from fully using their IP assets, they encroach upon the rights offered to them by trademark, patent and design registration law, as well as copyright law provisions.

Yet, I believe that these measures do not encroach upon the rights offered to IP rights owners and therefore cannot be considered legally incompatible with the IP rights system. A look at most national and international provisions on the scope of IP protection reinforces such a belief.[53] Such provisions clarify that IP rights holders do not have a positive right to actually use the IP assets – they are just given a *ius excludendi alios*, that is, the negative right to prevent third parties from using the asset.[54] The use of trademarks, designs, inventions and copyrighted works can thus be prohibited or restricted by measures adopted on public interest grounds, such as the ones analysed in this chapter. This is exactly what has occurred in many jurisdictions as far as tobacco products are concerned. Indeed many countries, in the context of public health protection programs, have adopted advertising restrictions entailing a prohibition of the use of tobacco trademarks under certain circumstances. For example, as we have seen, several states passed legislation prohibiting tobacco sponsorship of international events such as bans on tobacco sponsorships of sporting events, and motorcycle and Formula 1 races in particular.[55] These measures have not raised any doubts about their compatibility with national and international provisions protecting trademarks and other IP rights. This is due, I believe, to the fact that the TRIPS Agreement, and most IP laws, do not offer IP rights holders any positive right to use their protected assets.[56]

The above argument is disputed by some commentators, who consider it too formalistic and mistaken in permitting a right of registration but at the same time denying a right of use. Such an interpretation is argued to risk undermining the IP system and to be contrary to the spirit of IP legislation.[57] According to this school of thought, therefore, IP registrations confer an implied positive right to use the protected asset.[58] This reasoning seems flawed though. Indeed, the right to commercially use a sign or an invention arises not from the registration,[59] but is rather a characteristic intrinsic to the freedom to carry out commercial activities in the market,[60] such freedom being capable of being restricted on public interest grounds, such as the protection of public health.

After all, that IP rights, and in particular trademarks, offer their owners negative rights has been reaffirmed by both a WTO Panel in *EC – Trademarks and Geographical Indications (Australia)*[61] and Advocate General Geelhoed in his *Opinion on the Validity of the Directive 2001/37 on the Manufacture, Presentation and Sale of Tobacco Products*.[62] In that opinion the Advocate General stated that:

> [T]he essential substance of a trademark right does not consist in an entitlement as against the authorities to use a trademark unimpeded by provisions of public law. On the contrary, a trademark right is essentially a right enforceable against other individuals if they infringe the use made by the holder.[63]

Following this interpretation, it seems that the restrictive measures highlighted in this chapter[64] – that is, 'provisions of public law' – would not breach IP rights as they do not authorise third parties to exploit IP protected assets; they merely consist of restrictions on the ability of rights owners to use their own signs, logos or copyrighted works. Yet, despite this limitation, rights holders could still exercise the right to prohibit the misappropriation of their assets by unauthorised third parties.

The fact that IP rights are essentially negative rights should therefore permit states to adopt measures aimed at protecting people's health, including the ones analysed in this chapter, even where such measures jeopardise the ability of IP rights holders to use their intangible assets. This conclusion seems reinforced by the WTO Panel Report in the above mentioned dispute *EC – Trademarks*,[65] a case between the US and the EU regarding the latter's geographical indications and trademarks regimes. In that case the Panel held that a

> fundamental feature of intellectual property protection inherently grants Members freedom to pursue legitimate public policy objectives since many measures to attain those public policy objectives lie outside the scope of intellectual property rights and do not require an exception under the TRIPS Agreement.[66]

5 How to use IP regimes for encouraging the production of healthier food and beverages: three proposals

In the previous paragraphs I have analysed the (negative) impact on IP of certain regulatory measures aimed at discouraging the manufacture, sale and consumption of harmful products, whether they be cigarettes, alcohol or unhealthy food or beverages. We have also seen that, despite being negative, such an impact entails no violation of IP rights.

It is now time to verify if, and to what extent, IP regimes may be amended with a view to incentivising companies to manufacture and market healthier products in the fields of food and beverages. Indeed, the need to supply customers with healthier food and beverages constitutes an urgent need as many people in both industrialised and developing countries struggle with obesity (which is mostly caused by unhealthy diets), its related diseases, and other illnesses caused by consumption of unhealthy products. Some recent data will help make clear why it is important to take action urgently. According to a recent report published in *The Economist*, two-thirds of US citizens are overweight and, more alarmingly, 36 per cent of adults and 17 per cent of children are not just overweight but obese (this is probably due to the fact that in the US junk-food calories are often less expensive than healthy ones and therefore manufacturers tend to prefer using such unhealthy ingredients).[67] It is foreseen that by 2030 almost half of US adults might be obese.[68] The scenario is not brighter in other areas of the world. In the United Kingdom 25 per cent of women and 25 per cent of men are obese, and in the Czech Republic the figure reaches 30 per cent. In Brazil 53 per cent of adults were overweight in 2008. Even in China, a nation scourged by famine for many years, one in four adults is obese or at least overweight. Overall, in 2008, about 1.5 billion adults, which amounts to one-third of the planet's adult population, were obese or at least overweight and by 2030 the total number of obese and overweight persons could reach 3.3 billion.[69] These data are self-explanatory and complemented by other data confirming that obesity has increasingly become the cause of chronic diseases. As estimated by the WHO, excess fat in food is the cause of 44 per cent of cases of diabetes, 23 per cent of ischaemic heart disease and over 40 per cent of cancers. It is also a fact that since 1990 obesity has grown much faster than any other cause of illness and that in the US obesity-related diseases amounted to one-fifth of overall health-care costs in 2005.[70]

Having said that, I believe that the IP system may play a role in fighting obesity and related illnesses. I therefore put forward three proposals. The first one would require food and beverage manufacturers that want to patent their products or processes to show that the products or processes contain or use healthy ingredients. The same burden is the focal point of the second and third proposals: yet in these cases fulfilling such requirement would not constitute the *sine qua non* condition for patent protection – it would just aim at speeding up or facilitating the patenting process for foods and beverages that are considered healthy.

5.1 Requiring food and beverage patent applicants to demonstrate use of healthy ingredients

The first proposal would be to make the patenting of inventions related to foodstuff and beverages subject to both (i) the presence in the relevant products or processes of macronutrients including proteins, vitamins and carbohydrates; and (ii) the reduction of unhealthy ingredients such as salt, fat and sugar. In other words, this proposal would require applicants to show that their foodstuffs and beverages are healthy and do not contain harmful ingredients or components. Further, a patent covering an invention that does not satisfy the proposed condition should be invalidated. Such a requirement could be justified by relying on a provision contained in many international, regional and national patent legislation that states that countries are allowed to exclude from patentability inventions that are contrary to *ordre public* and morality.[71] It could indeed be argued that inventions related to unhealthy food and beverages (whose excessive use can cause mortal diseases) should be excluded from patentability on the above grounds. The proposal also seems to be in line with the very purpose of the patent system, which is to incentivise the realisation of products that are really useful to societies.

From a procedural perspective, I would propose that applicants make a reasonable, written assertion that the products or processes for which they seek a patent are healthy. Food and beverage products and processes for which health benefits are immediately clear would just need a simple statement. More detailed clarifications should be required for less obviously healthy inventions – and their healthiness should be confirmed by the patent office.[72]

Having said that, one might say that this proposal would be contrary to art 62(1) of the TRIPS Agreement, which states that 'Members may require, as a condition of the acquisition or maintenance of the intellectual property rights ... compliance with *reasonable* procedures and formalities'.[73] Thus, it may be argued that making the patenting of food and beverage related inventions subject to the above mentioned requirement would amount to an unreasonable condition on the acquisition or maintenance of the relevant patent. Also, it may be noted that introducing this condition only with reference to food and beverage related inventions would violate the principle of non-discrimination between fields of technology pursuant to art 27(1) of the TRIPS Agreement. This provision clarifies that 'patents shall be available and patent rights enjoyable without discrimination as to … the field of technology'.

Yet I believe that this proposal would not constitute an unreasonable condition on the acquisition of patents on food and beverage related inventions as it would not place excessively heavy burdens on patent offices and applicants. The objection that patent offices and judges would not be well equipped to verify whether the product or process in question is healthy (indeed one may note that such task exceeds the skills of patent offices) could be overcome. For example, patent officers could be partnered with experts (such as professors in food safety) who could be questioned about technical issues. The latest developments in food safety would certainly help overcome the scientific uncertainties that have thus far surrounded the distinction between healthy and unhealthy food. Also, the proposal in question should be considered reasonable because it aims at pursuing an overriding public interest, that is, to incentivise the production of healthy food and beverages and thus fight obesity and related illnesses. As is well known, the furtherance of public interests is one of the objectives pursued by the TRIPS Agreement, art 8 of which states that:

> Members may, in formulating or amending their laws and regulations, adopt measures necessary to protect *public health* and *nutrition*, and to promote the public interest in sectors of vital importance to their socio-economic and technological development.[74]

It could be further argued that the proposed measure does not constitute discriminatory treatment vis-à-vis the food and beverage sector, but that it boils down to lawful differential treatment that is necessary to meet a socially sensitive objective in specific fields – that is, the protection of public health. The distinction between unlawful 'discrimination' and lawful 'differential treatment' in the field of IP rights has already been stressed by the WTO Panel in *Canada – Patent Protection of Pharmaceutical Products*.[75] In that case the Panel stated that 'Article 27 does not prohibit bona fide exceptions to deal with problems that may exist only in certain product areas'.[76] In this respect, Frederick Abbott points out that if specific rules applicable only to pharmaceutical patents are necessary to address important public interests such as the protection of public health: 'this does not constitute "discrimination" against the field of pharmaceutical technology. It constitutes recognition of legitimate public interests in differential treatment'.[77] This statement has been made in relation to pharmaceutical inventions, but it might also be invoked, I believe, when it comes to food and beverage related products and processes. Indeed the proposed condition aims to meet socially relevant aims in the field of public health, especially the fight against obesity and related diseases.

5.2 *Fast track procedures for healthy food and beverage patent applications*

The second proposal is to set up a fast track procedure for patent applications covering foodstuffs and beverages containing macronutrients or other healthy ingredients so as to provide an expedited examination of the relevant patentability requirements. This proposal would thus again aim at protecting public health. Analogous procedures are being or have been established in the field of green technologies in Canada, Israel, Japan, South Korea, the United Kingdom and the US.[78]

Applicants that ask for this fast track procedure should show that their products or processes both contain healthy ingredients and lack unhealthy components, and in the case that the health benefits are clear a brief statement by the claimant would satisfy this requirement.

It would be wise to devise this fast track procedure in the context of an international treaty. This would be recommended in order to overcome possible differences between national procedures (which could vary widely in their rules and requirements). As a matter of fact, such disparities would make participation in multiple fast track programs expensive and lengthy, as applicants who want to protect their inventions in multiple jurisdictions would have to comply with different rules. An international, harmonised fast track program, with similar rules and requirements, would instead eliminate substantial burdens on applicants and thus speed up and make cheaper the patenting process for healthy food and beverage products. It would therefore also boost participation. A similar proposal has already been put forward with reference to fast track programs for green technology-based inventions.[79]

What should be avoided is to set up a fast track program based on a rigid classification system that 'crystallises' the categories of inventions that are eligible for fast track procedures. The risk of such a system might be that foodstuffs or beverages containing healthy ingredients or constituents not mentioned in a particular category may not be eligible as they do not fall into one of the pre-selected classifications. Also, additional burdens on applicants should be avoided, such as conducting prior art searches and analysis. In such a way the entire process would be accelerated.[80] Such a system and such requirements would amount to 'reasonable procedures and formalities', as required by art 62(1) of the TRIPS Agreement, as they would speed up and make less costly and time-consuming the whole patent procedure for food and beverage related inventions. Again, in order to overcome the objection that patent offices would not be well equipped to verify whether a food or beverage related invention is really healthy, it would be recommendable to partner patent officers with technical experts. Also, the proposed system would not violate the above mentioned art 27(1) of the TRIPS Agreement for the reasons already highlighted in the previous section.

5.3 Exempting healthy food and beverage patent applications from fees

The third proposal would entail exempting applicants for patents covering healthy food and beverage related inventions from paying the patent procedures fees – or at least significantly reducing them (again, applicants should demonstrate the healthiness of their products and processes). This proposal would therefore aim at facilitating the patent protection of healthy foodstuff and beverages. Indeed, patent fees may sometimes be unaffordable, especially for small and medium sized enterprises. Take, for instance, the high number of fees required by the European Patent Office, for example filing fees, search fees, fees per designated state, fees per claim over ten claims, examination fees and a fee for the patent grant and printing.

This proposal could also be 'merged' with the previous one. For example, countries particularly keen on protecting their people's health could both set up a fast track patent procedure for healthy food and beverages and exempt such applicants from paying the relevant fees (or greatly reduce them).

6 Conclusion

We have seen that in the past years new regulatory actions have restricted the freedom of tobacco, alcohol and food companies to produce, present, offer for sale, advertise and supply their products as they wish, limiting their commercial freedom. Yet, such measures are considered by many governments and international and non-governmental organisations as necessary to protect an overriding public interest, that is, human health. We have also seen that the measures in question – which affect the presentation, advertising, supply and manufacture of tobacco, alcohol and foodstuffs – jeopardise the ability of producers to fully use and exploit their IP assets. However, such inability does not necessarily signify that these measures encroach upon IP rights. Indeed, the negative nature of these rights – which give their owners the power to prevent unauthorised uses of their assets – allows states to take regulatory actions on public interest grounds.

We have also seen that patent law could be modified in such a way as to protect public health, especially in the field of foodstuffs and beverages. The proposals put forward in this chapter aim at amending patent procedures with a view to eventually encouraging the realisation and entry into the market of foodstuffs and beverages that contain healthy ingredients and constituents. These proposals seem to be compliant with the aim of the patent system and with several provisions, including patent-related rules, of the TRIPS Agreement.

Notes

* An earlier version of this chapter was presented at the Second Paris École des Hautes Études Commerciales Paris Workshop on Regulation (Regulating Lifestyle Risks in Europe: The Case of Alcohol, Tobacco and Unhealthy Diets), 20–1 September 2012, Paris (France).
1 *WHO Framework Convention on Tobacco Control*, opened for signature 16 June 2003, 2302 UNTS 166 (entered into force 27 February 2005) ('WHO FCTC').
2 See Chapter 2 of this volume for discussion of the WHO FCTC.
3 See *Political Declaration of the High-level Meeting of the General Assembly on the Prevention and Control of Non-communicable Diseases*, GA Res 2, UN GAOR, 66th sess, 3rd plen mtg, UN Doc A/Res/66/2 (2012).
4 See Becky Freeman, Simon Chapman and Matthew Rimmer, 'The Case for the Plain Packaging of Tobacco Products' (2007) 103(4) *Addiction* 580; Alberto Alemanno and

Enrico Bonadio, 'The Case of Plain Packaging for Cigarettes' (2010) 3 *European Journal of Risk Regulation* 268.

5   See Melanie Wakefield et al, 'Do Larger Pictorial Health Warnings Diminish the Need for Plain Packaging of Cigarettes?' (2012) 107(6) *Addiction* 1159; David Hammond, Samantha Daniel and Christine White, 'The Effect of Cigarette Branding and Plain Packaging on Female Youth in the United Kingdom' (2013) 52(2) *Journal of Adolescent Health* 151.

6   World Health Organization, *WHO Framework Convention on Tobacco Control: Guidelines for Implementation* (2011) 59, 95–6 ('*Guidelines to the WHO FCTC*').

7   See Jonathan Liberman et al, 'Plain Tobacco Packaging in Australia: the Historical and Social Context' in Tania Voon, Andrew Mitchell and Jonathan Liberman with Glyn Ayres (eds), *Public Health and Plain Packaging of Cigarettes: Legal Issues* (Edward Elgar Publishing, 2012) 30, 39.

8   *Vienna Convention on the Law of Treaties*, opened for signature on 23 May 1969, 1155 UNTS 331 (entered into force on 27 January 1980).

9   *Tobacco Plain Packaging Act 2011* (Cth) ch 2.

10   See the *Agreement between the Government of Hong Kong and the Government of Australia for the Promotion and Protection of Investments*, signed on 15 September 1993, 1748 UNTS 385 (entered into force 15 October 1993).

11   *Marrakesh Agreement Establishing the World Trade Organization*, opened for signature 15 April 1994, 1867 UNTS 3 (entered into force 1 January 1995) annex 1C ('*Agreement on Trade-Related Aspects of Intellectual Property Rights*') ('TRIPS Agreement'). See Chapter 7 of this volume.

12   *JT International SA v Commonwealth* [2012] HCA 43. See Jonathan Liberman, 'Plainly Constitutional: The Upholding of Plain Tobacco Packaging by the High Court of Australia' (2013) 39(2) *American Journal of Law and Medicine* 361.

13   Signed 2 May 1993, 1801 UNTS 3 (entered into force 1 January 1994) ('EEA Agreement').

14   *HOB-vín ehf v The State Alcohol and Tobacco Company of Iceland (ÁTVR)* (EFTA Court, E-2/12, 11 December 2012). For a timely comment on this case see Alberto Alemanno, 'The HOB-vín Judgment: A Failed Attempt to Standardise the Visual Imagery, Packaging and Appeal of Alcohol Products' (2013) 1 *European Journal of Risk Regulation* 101.

15   *HOB-vín ehf v The State Alcohol and Tobacco Company of Iceland (ÁTVR)* (EFTA Court, E-2/12, 11 December 2012) [26].

16   The EFTA Court has the task of interpreting the EEA Agreement with regard to the EFTA countries that are party to it, namely Iceland, Liechtenstein and Norway. EFTA is a free trade organisation grouping Iceland, Liechtenstein, Norway and Switzerland. Though not EU member states, Iceland, Liechtenstein and Norway are part of the EU internal market through the EEA Agreement. Switzerland instead opted to enter into bilateral agreements with the EU covering many areas, such as movement of persons, transport and technical barriers to trade.

17   See *Law No 18,256* (2008) (Uruguay) 29 February 2008.

18   *Agreement between the Swiss Confederation and the Oriental Republic of Uruguay Concerning the Reciprocal Promotion and Protection of Investments*, signed 7 October 1988, 1976 UNTS 413 (entered into force 7 October 1988).

19   Benn McGrady, 'Implications of Ongoing Trade and Investment Disputes Concerning Tobacco: Philip Morris v Uruguay' in Voon et al, above n 7, 173, 178.

20   Ibid.

21   See also Benn McGrady, *Confronting the Tobacco Epidemic in a New Era of Trade and Investment Liberalization* (World Health Organization, 2012) 59–60.

22   See also Benn McGrady, 'Philip Morris v. Uruguay: The Punta del Este Declaration on the Implementation of the WHO Framework Convention on Tobacco Control' (2011) 2 *European Journal of Risk Regulation* 254.

23 Display of tobacco products at the point of sale also constitutes a powerful means of advertising and promotion. As stressed by the *Guidelines to the WHO FCTC*, above n 6, 94, display of products is a major tool for their promotion, including by stimulating impulse purchases, giving the impression that tobacco consumption is socially acceptable and making it more difficult for smokers to quit smoking.

24 Iceland was the first country to introduce a display ban of tobacco products in August 2001. Norway followed by introducing the same measure on 1 January 2010, through an amendment to *Act No 14 of 9 March 1973 Relating to Prevention of the Harmful Effects of Tobacco (the Tobacco Control Act)* (Norway). Ireland did the same in July 2009 and Finland in January 2012.

25 *Philip Morris Norway AS v Staten/Helse-og omsorgsdepartementet* (EFTA Court, E-16/10, 12 September 2011). See Alberto Alemanno, 'The Legality, Rationale and Science of Tobacco Display Bans after the Philip Morris Judgment' (2011) 4 *European Journal of Risk Regulation* 591.

26 I am talking here about *stricto sensu* advertising. Indeed, the many ways in which companies present their products can also be considered as advertising in its widest sense.

27 Product placement is a form of advertisement where branded products are placed in a context usually devoid of advertising messages, such as movies. The placement is not disclosed at the time the product is shown.

28 See also World Health Assembly, *Global Strategy on Diet, Physical Activity and Health Diet: Report by the Secretariat*, WHA Res 57.17, 57th sess, 8th plen mtg, WHO Doc A57/2004/REC/1 (22 May 2004) ('*Global Strategy Diet*'), which recommends that states ensure that sponsorship, promotion and advertising targeting children are appropriate. Its aim is to address unhealthy diet and physical inactivity, two of the major risk factors responsible for the growing burden of chronic diseases, including heart disease, stroke, diabetes and cancer, which are responsible for 60 per cent of all global deaths. It has also been noted that states should prohibit the advertising of energy-dense, nutrient-poor foods directed at children: see National Preventative Health Taskforce, *Australia: The Healthiest Country by 2020* (30 June 2009) <http://www.preventativehealth.org.au/internet/preventativehealth/publishing.nsf/Content/nphs-roadmap/$File/nphs-roadmap-1.pdf> 16.

29 Brand stretching means using an established brand name in order to introduce unrelated products (for example, a tobacco company may introduce non-tobacco products in order to circumvent advertising restrictions). Brand sharing is a similar marketing strategy that occurs when, for example, a brand of a non-tobacco product is connected with a tobacco product in such a way that the two products are likely to be associated.

30 See WHO FCTC art 1. Bans and restrictions on tobacco advertising had been adopted even before the entry into force of the WHO FCTC. See also Ulf Bernitz, 'Logo Licensing of Tobacco Products – Can It Be Prohibited?' (1990) 4 *European Intellectual Property Review* 137.

31 See inter alia *Federal Law No 119* (Russia) 20 July 2012.

32 The World Health Organization, *International Code of Marketing of Breast-milk Substitutes*, WHA Res 34.22, 33rd sess (21 May 1981). This was implemented in Guatemala by the *Law on the Marketing of Breastmilk Substitutes* (Guatemala) 7 June 1983, Presidential Decree 66-83; *Guatemalan Government Agreement No 841-87* (Guatemala) 30 September 1987.

33 Signed 30 October 1947, 55 UNTS 187 (entered into force 1 January 1948).

34 See Russell Mokhiber, 'Gerber Uses Threats of GATT Sanctions to Gain Exemption from Guatemalan Infant Health Law' (1996) 10(14) *Corporate Crime Reporter* 6.

35 Ibid; Robert Mayer, 'Protectionism, Intellectual Property and Consumer Protection: Was the Uruguay Round Good for Consumers?' (1998) 21 *Journal of Consumer Policy* 195, 209.

36 See Benn McGrady, *Trade and Public Health: The WTO, Tobacco, Alcohol, and Diet* (Cambridge University Press, 2011) 115.

37 Vending machines also constitute a means of advertising or promotion (see WHO FCTC art 16).

38 These measures are recommended by art 16 of the WHO FCTC.

39 Examples of flavouring substances in tobacco products include benzaldehyde, maltol, menthol and vanillin: see *Guidelines to the WHO FCTC*, above n 6, 39. Examples of colouring agents in tobacco products include inks (for example, imitation cork pattern on tipping paper) and pigments (for example titanium dioxide in filter material): 40. In 2009 Canada introduced the *Cracking Down on Tobacco Marketing Aimed at Youth Act*, SC 2009, c 27, which bans the use of additives, including some flavours in cigarettes, little cigars and blunt wraps. Bans on flavouring agents in alcoholic products, such as the so-called alcopops, have also been introduced in some countries. Alcopops are flavoured alcoholic beverages that – according to advocates of tighter restrictions on alcoholic consumption – fool drinkers into believing they are harmless drinks.

40 As noted by the *Guidelines to the WHO FCTC*, above n 6, 39, some tobacco products also contain added sugars and sweeteners (such as glucose, molasses, honey and sorbitol), which improve the palatability of tobacco products to tobacco users. The *Guidelines to the WHO FCTC* also encourage states to introduce bans on ingredients in tobacco products that help to create the impression that they have health benefits or to create the impression that they present reduced health hazard (such as vitamin C and vitamin E, fruit and vegetables as well as amino acids and essentially fatty acids): 40.

41 See Panel Report, *United States – Measures Affecting the Production and Sale of Clove Cigarettes*, WTO Doc WT/DS406/R (adopted 24 April 2012). For a timely comment on this decision see Benn McGrady, 'Panel Report US – Clove Cigarettes' (2011) 4 *European Journal of Risk Regulation* 600.

42 See *Resolução – RDC No 14 de 15 de Março de 2012* [Resolution – RDC No 14 of 15 March 2012] (Brazil) 15 March 2012.

43 See McGrady, above n 36, 172 n 10.

44 See *Guidelines to the WHO FCTC*, above n 6, 40.

45 *Tobacco Plain Packaging Regulations 2011* (Cth) reg 2.1.1.

46 *Tobacco Plain Packaging Act 2011* (Cth) s 18(1)(a).

47 *JT International SA v Commonwealth* [2012] HCA 43, [93].

48 British American Tobacco (Investments) Limited, *Smoke Article Packaging*, Australian Patent No 2001258572 (22 May 2001).

49 *JT International SA v Commonwealth* [2012] HCA 43, [260].

50 See WHO FCTC art 6, which recognises that price and tax measures are an effective and important means of reducing tobacco consumption (the categories of taxes are sales tax, value-added tax and excise tax). See also World Health Assembly, *Global Strategy to Reduce the Harmful Use of Alcohol*, WHA Res 63.13, 63rd sess, 8th plen mtg, WHO Doc WHA63/2010/REC/1 (21 May 2010); *Global Strategy Diet*, above n 28.

51 Yet we have seen that tobacco packaging also constitutes a form of 'mobile advertising' so that restricting the use of the relevant products by end consumers also indirectly restricts the ability of manufacturers to convey their brand image and related messages.

52 We have already seen that in the *HOB-vín ehf* case the EFTA Court found the Icelandic provision in question in violation of the EEA Agreement. However, the rules examined by the EFTA Court in that case were not IP-related.

53 See, eg, *Directive 2008/95/EC of the European Parliament and of the Council of 22 October 2008 to Approximate the Laws of the Member States Relating to Trade Marks* [2008] OJ L 299/25, art 5(3); TRIPS Agreement art 16(1); *Directive 98/44/EC of the European Parliament and of the Council of 6 July 1998 on the Legal Protection of Biotechnological Inventions* [1998] OJ L 213/13, recital 14.

54 See also Mark Davison, 'The Legitimacy of Plain Packaging under International Intellectual Property Law: Why There is No Right to Use a Trademark under Either the Paris Convention or the TRIPS Agreement' in Voon et al, above n 7, 81, noting

that neither the TRIPS Agreement nor the *Paris Convention for the Protection of Industrial Property*, opened for signature 14 July 1967, 828 UNTS 306 (entered into force 26 April 1970), expressly provide for a right to use IP rights and in particular trademarks.

55   A ban on the use of tobacco advertising as a means of sponsorship of events, including Formula 1 races and other sporting events, came into force in the EU on 1 August 2005. See *Directive 2003/33/EC of the European Parliament and of the Council of 26 May 2003 on the Approximation of the Laws, Regulations and Administrative Provisions of the Member States Relating to the Advertising and Sponsorship of Tobacco Products* [2003] OJ L 152/16, art 5. See also Carlos Correa, *Trade Related Aspects of Intellectual Property Rights* (Oxford University Press, 2007) 200 n 30.

56   The fact that the TRIPS Agreement does not offer IP rights owners any positive right to use their protected assets rules out any conflict between that treaty and the WHO FCTC.

57   See Patrick Basham and John Luik, *Erasing Intellectual Property: 'Plain Packaging' for Consumer Products and the Implications for Trademark Rights* (Democracy Institute Washington Legal Foundation, 2011) 22–9. See also Daniel Gervais, *Analysis of the Compatibility of Certain Tobacco Product Packaging Rules with the TRIPS Agreement and the Paris Convention* (30 November 2010) Physicians for a Smoke-Free Canada <http://www.smoke-free.ca/trade-and-tobacco/Resources/Gervais.pdf> 11–12 (*'Gervais Report'*); Annette Kur, 'The Right to Use One's Own Trade Mark: A Self-evident Issue or a New Concept in German, European, and International Trade Mark Law?' (1996) 4 *European Intellectual Property Review* 203; Memorandum from Lalive to Philip Morris International Management SA, 23 July 2009 <http://www.smoke-free.ca/plain-packaging/documents/industry-responses/LALIVE_Analysis_23_July_2009.pdf>.

58   See, as far as trademarks are concerned, the *Gervais Report*, above n 57.

59   This is particularly true in the field of copyright. Indeed, in most jurisdictions copyright legislation offers rights owners exclusive rights from the date the work is created, regardless of any registration.

60   See Kur, above note 57, 199.

61   Panel Report, *European Communities – Protection of Trademarks and Geographical Indications for Agricultural Products and Foodstuffs, Complaint by Australia*, WTO Doc WT/DS290/R (adopted 20 April 2005) [7.602] (*'EC – Trademarks and Geographical Indications (Australia)'*).

62   See *R v Secretary of State for Health, ex parte British American Tobacco (Investments) Ltd and Imperial Tobacco Ltd (Advisory Opinion of Advocate-General Geelhoed)* (C-491/01) [2002] ECR I-11453; *Directive 2001/37/EC of the European Parliament and of the Council of 5 June 2001 on the Approximation of the Laws, Regulations and Administrative Provisions of the Member States Concerning the Manufacture, Presentation and Sale of Tobacco Products* [2001] OJ L 194/26.

63   *R v Secretary of State for Health, ex parte British American Tobacco (Investments) Ltd and Imperial Tobacco Ltd (Advisory Opinion of Advocate-General Geelhoed)* (C-491/01) [2002] ECR I-11453, [266]. Other courts have reached similar conclusions.

64   I refer in particular to the measures related to the presentation, advertising, supply and manufacturing of the products in question.

65   Panel Report, *EC – Trademarks and Geographical Indications (Australia)*.

66   Ibid [7.246]. See also Correa, above note 55, 182.

67   'The Big Picture', *The Economist* (London), 15 December 2012, 4.

68   Ibid.

69   Ibid.

70   Ibid.

71   TRIPS Agreement art 27(2); *Convention on the Grant of European Patents*, opened for signature 5 October 1973, 1065 UNTS 199 (entered into force 7 October 1977) art 53(a).

72   These suggestions build upon some observations made by the Californian IP lawyer Eric Lane in connection with green technologies: see Eric Lane, 'Building the Global Green Patent Highway: A Proposal for International Harmonization of Green

Technology Fast Track Programs' (2012) 27(3) *Berkeley Technology Law Journal* 1119, 1147–50; see also Eric Lane, *Clean Tech Intellectual Property: Eco-marks, Green Patents, and Green Innovation* (Oxford University Press, 2011) 218–26.

73 Emphasis added.

74 Emphasis added.

75 Panel Report, *Canada – Patent Protection of Pharmaceutical Products*, WTO Doc WT/DS114/R (adopted 7 April 2000) [7.92].

76 Ibid.

77 See Frederick Abbott, 'Compulsory Licensing for Public Health Needs: The TRIPS Agenda at the WTO after the Doha Declaration on Public Health' (Occasional Paper No 9, Friends World Committee for Consultation, February 2002) 49–50 <http://www.cptech.org/ip/health/cl/quno-op9.pdf>.

78 The first country to launch this program was the United Kingdom in May 2009 (see United Kingdom Intellectual Property Office, 'UK "Green" inventions to Get Fast-Tracked through Patent System' (Press Release, 12 May 2009).

79 Lane, above n 72, 1160–70.

80 Again these suggestions build upon some observations made by Eric Lane in connection with green technologies: Ibid 1138–45.

9 Constitutional Perspectives

United Kingdom and South Africa

Stephanie Palmer

1 Introduction

Over the last few decades, public and political perceptions about the dangers posed by non-communicable diseases ('NCDs') have shifted dramatically, leading to increased regulation of products that contribute to ill health. Such regulations have taken a number of different forms, but there are consistent public policy values underlying them: namely, an aim to reduce the consumption of these harmful products in order to protect health, with additional protection for minors. This aim has been achieved through a number of different mechanisms such as restrictions on the presentation and display of tobacco products, prohibition of advertising or indirect advertising through the promotion of sporting events, and supply limitation to minors through prohibiting sales to children and banning vending machines selling cigarettes, as well as the display of explicit health warnings of the danger posed by the consumption or use of the substance by consumers. Minimum unit pricing for alcohol and advice about the unit content on the label has been introduced in many countries.[1] Finally, controls imposed on the manufacture of products, such as a ban on trans fats in foodstuffs, are becoming increasingly common.

The European Parliament has recently voted on new rules concerning tobacco products. The size of health warnings on packets is to be greatly increased, and sweet and fruity flavourings in tobacco are to be banned, with a short reprieve for menthol. The catalyst behind these changes to the current European Union Directive is to make smoking less attractive to young people, the target audience of tobacco product corporations.[2] However, slim cigarettes, a successful marketing tool used by tobacco companies, are to remain in the European Union ('EU').[3]

A constitutional perspective of the regulation of tobacco, alcohol and unhealthy foodstuffs invites reflection on the nature of 'constitutionalism'. At its most basic, a constitution provides a framework for democratic government. As citizens in a democracy, we expect our elected governments to promote the public interest of the community in a manner consistent with constitutional values, including the rule of law, and with respect for fundamental human rights. While acting to protect the interests of the community, a government must balance broader social values with those of particular groups. Although uncontroversial, this perspective papers over constitutional developments as well as fundamental tensions within constitutional frameworks. Regulation in the area of public health provides a useful vehicle through which to examine these issues.

First, a striking change that has evolved in constitutional law concerns the influence of international and, in Europe, EU law. Whereas, traditionally, public health has been perceived as a policy issue for national governments, it has increasingly become a global issue and the concern of international law and law-making organisations such as the EU. A plethora of international instruments apply to protect and promote human health.[4] The *WHO Framework Convention on Tobacco Control* ('WHO FCTC')[5] has provided a catalyst for worldwide change. It has recently been reported that, due to legislation by many member states of the World Health Organization ('WHO'), about 2.3 billion people are now covered by at least one tobacco control measure.[6] Given the interest and influence of the wider global community, constitutional measures concerning public health can no longer be assessed solely by an examination of the laws of a sovereign state. There has thus been a major change to our understanding of 'constitutionalism' in the field of public health.

Second, the regulation of tobacco products, alcohol and unhealthy foods exposes a tension between the public interest and ownership of private property. From a constitutional law perspective, the 'right to property', including intellectual property rights, is a fundamental human right.[7] Such a direct clash between public and private legal interests will require the courts to determine the competing values using a proportionality test. Controls on advertising and presentation, limiting the commercial exploitation of products, may also infringe the rights of corporations to freedom of expression.

Finally, from a more philosophical perspective, it could be argued that too much regulation is an example of excessive intervention based upon a paternalistic view of the public interest and introduced at the expense of respect for individual autonomy and choice. Should some limits exist on the use of public interventions aimed at promoting behavioural change to individuals? Should the efficacy of a change be verifiable, or is the potential benefit of minimising risk sufficient to justify regulation of NCDs? Finally, is there a role in this debate for legally enforced social and economic rights? Should states be required to act positively to protect social interests such as public health? Such a contention exposes a further tension between such rights and a market-liberal ideology.

Non-communicable diseases and the regulatory approach to their common risk factors raise a myriad of questions of relevance to constitutional law. This chapter considers these questions through the prism of legal issues addressed in the United Kingdom ('UK') and South Africa.

2 NCD risk factors in the United Kingdom and South Africa

2.1 United Kingdom

NCDs have been identified as the leading cause of death in the UK.[8] As public awareness of these dangers has grown, so also has the regulatory burden placed on companies manufacturing and marketing these products. The liquor and tobacco corporations have traditionally been heavily regulated, but in recent years the amount of regulation has increased, limiting the commercial freedom of these corporations. Advertising and sponsorship of major sporting events, bans on smoking in public places, and limits on the display of tobacco products are some examples of new legal restrictions.[9] In 2013, the independent regulator and competition authority for the UK communications industries, Ofcom, requested the UK's advertising regulators to review the rules that limit the exposure of children to alcohol advertising on television.[10]

Unhealthy food marketing has also been the subject of regulation. In 2007, the UK was the first country to impose restrictions on food advertisements for children in some circumstances. The UK regulator, Ofcom, introduced regulations that banned advertisements of foods high in fat, salt and sugar on children's television channels. In addition, marketing of unhealthy food was banned on other channels during, before and after programs aimed at children aged between 4 and 15.[11] Concern about childhood obesity has led governments to apply stricter nutrient standards to food supplied at school.[12] Increased taxes on unhealthy foodstuffs have also been suggested as a mechanism to deter consumption. The Academy of Medical Royal Colleges Steering Group on Obesity has strongly suggested imposing an additional 20 per cent tax on soft drinks.[13] The Academy criticises attempts by governments to counter obesity as 'piecemeal and disappointingly ineffective', and woefully inadequate given the scale of the problem.[14] One in four adults in England is obese, and the figures are predicted to rise to 60 per cent of men, 50 per cent of women and 25 per cent of children by 2050.[15]

Changes or potential alterations to regulations concerning NCDs have been consistently challenged in the courts. Many constitutional lawyers, however, have even greater concerns about the indirect influence that large powerful business corporations may exert through political lobbying. Increased transparency has been a primary aim of public law reformers for many years.

In April 2012, the UK government introduced a consultation on the standardised packaging of tobacco products.[16] The UK-wide consultation sought views on plain packaging and whether it would: reduce the appeal of tobacco products to consumers; increase the effectiveness of health warnings on the packaging of tobacco products; reduce the ability of tobacco packaging to mislead consumers about the harmful effects of smoking; and have a positive effect on smoking-related attitudes, beliefs, intentions and behaviour, particularly among children and young people.

In July 2013, the Secretary of State for Health, Jeremy Hunt, concluded that the evidence of the efficacy of standardised packaging is not conclusive. According to him, there is no sound evidence indicating that the introduction of plain packaging would achieve the public health goal of reduced smoking. He proposed that the government wait on further studies from Australia before committing to such legislation in the UK. In the meantime, display bans on tobacco will be introduced and a 'further education' policy implemented.[17]

The response of tobacco companies to the UK government's consultation on the standardised packaging of tobacco products has been released due to a freedom of information request. The consultation led to active lobbying by tobacco companies of the Department of Health, as the transparency required by the *Freedom of Information Act 2000* (UK) has revealed.[18] The government found certain arguments of the tobacco companies persuasive, as these were cited as some of the reasons for not proceeding with standardised packaging. For example, BAT discussed with officials from the Department of Health their concern that 'standardised packs will lower barriers to entry for counterfeiters', and 'the Department of Health acknowledged the difficulty of evaluating the impact of standardised packaging on smoking rates in isolation from other tobacco control measures' such as the display ban.[19]

What is not known is whether any other business-led concerns of the tobacco industry, not specifically stated by the Minister or revealed through the freedom of information application, influenced the government's decision. The Department of Health noted that there could be costs to retail business, which could affect UK-based shareholders.[20] Mark Field, a Conservative Member of Parliament, was said to have welcomed the decision to postpone the decision on plain packaging, indicating that a move of this kind 'runs counter to our message that we are open for business'.[21] The relationship to government and the potential influence of large corporations in the marketplace should not be underestimated. Indeed, Dr Harpel Kumar, the Chief Executive of the charity Cancer Research UK, accused the government of putting 'profits of the tobacco industry' above public health.[22]

A few days after the announcement of the government that plain packaging of tobacco would not be introduced, the Prime Minister's Spokesperson ('PMS') was forced to respond to questions about the Prime Minister's relationship with Lynton Crosby, the political strategist who is coordinating the Conservative Party's 2015 general election campaign. In recent years, Mr Crosby's lobbying company has worked for the tobacco industry. In response to these allegations, the PMS stated that 'the Prime Minister has never been lobbied by Lynton Crosby on cigarette packaging … [and] that the important point to stress on this issue is that Lynton Crosby has had no involvement in the decision'.[23] Mr Crosby is employed by the Conservative Party and not as a UK civil servant. At no time, however, has the Prime Minister, Mr Cameron, denied that he has discussed the concerns of the tobacco industry with Mr Crosby.

The relationship between large powerful corporations and governments is often uncomfortable in a democracy.[24] Repeated questions addressed to the Prime Minister concerning the role of Lynton Crosby may have contributed to a recent UK government change of heart. On 28 November 2013, the Public Health Minister, Jane Ellison, announced that it was appropriate to study the emerging evidence on the issue of standardised tobacco packaging.[25] There will be a further independent review of cigarette packaging by Sir Cyril Chandler, who will report to the government in March 2014. The government has also tabled an amendment to the Children and Families Bill 2013 (UK), which 'would provide powers to bring forward regulations to bring in standardised packaging if the government decided to do so following Sir Cyril's review and consideration of the wider issues raised by this policy'.[26]

2.2 South Africa

During the 1990s, 'South Africa had one of the highest smoking rates in the world'.[27] In spite of this, the South African government did little to deal with this major health problem. A striking feature of this era in South Africa was the powerful tobacco industry, which acted as an obstacle to the development of a strategy to deal with tobacco consumption.[28] There were close ties between the apartheid National Party and the tobacco industry. The tobacco market was dominated by the Rembrandt Company, a politically powerful Afrikaner-owned multinational, with a long history of backing the National Party.[29] The two organisations had been founded in the same year (1948) and were powerful symbols of the Afrikaner community, with one dominating the tobacco industry and the other the political arena.[30] The National Party government had supported the tobacco industry through low excise taxes and with few restraints on advertising or sport sponsorships.[31]

During the last few years of apartheid, tobacco control emerged as an issue of political and national debate. In spite of strong resistance in the National Party Cabinet, the Minister of Health proposed a Bill introducing tobacco control.[32] The Tobacco Products Control Bill was passed by Parliament in 1993 and provided for the control of smoking in public places, the printing of health warnings and tar and nicotine levels on packaging, restrictions on advertising, and the prohibition of sales to minors.[33] Although a landmark Act, it did not meet international standards of prevention and control.

In 1994, South Africa held its first democratic elections, and President Mandela and the African National Congress ('ANC') came to power and apartheid was ended. The dramatic political changes transformed tobacco politics. The new government gave a prominent role to its health strategy and an aspect of this approach was tobacco control.[34] By 1997, new regulations for mandatory and explicit health warnings were implemented, and a new tax rate of 50 per cent on the retail sales of cigarettes was imposed.[35] In 1999, an amendment to the *Tobacco Products Control Act 1993* (South Africa) to prevent the display of tobacco company logos on television during sport matches was passed. The amendment banned all advertising and promotion of tobacco, including sponsorship and free distribution of tobacco products.[36] South Africa became a party to the WHO FCTC in 2005.[37]

The South African government has now identified alcohol as a health hazard needing further regulation. Relying on the success of reduced tobacco consumption after the banning of tobacco marketing, a Bill relating to marketing alcohol control has been opened for public discussion.[38] The Minister has stated:

> From a health perspective South Africa faces a quadruple burden of disease consisting of a maturing and generalised HIV and AIDS epidemic and high levels of Tuberculosis, high maternal and child morbidity and mortality;

non-communicable diseases and violence and injuries. In each of the major disease areas alcohol is either a critical primary risk factor and/or contributes negatively to the course of the disease/health predicament.

Alcohol is the third leading risk factor for death and disability in South Africa – after unsafe sex/STIs and interpersonal violence and injury. Alcohol is responsible for around 130 deaths every day.[39]

The Bill seeks to restrict the advertising of alcoholic beverages and prohibit sponsorship or promotion of alcohol. The unsuccessful constitutional challenge to the *Tobacco Products Control Act 1993* (South Africa) (discussed below) is likely to have given the government confidence that such public health regulations will not be found to be unconstitutional by the South African judiciary.

A recent and extensive health and nutrition study conducted by the Human Sciences Research Council and Medical Research Council reported that smoking and alcohol abuse remain a problem. The obesity levels in South Africa are also alarmingly high, with a growing number of young people prone to diabetes, high blood pressure and raised cholesterol levels.[40] The Minister of Health, Dr Aaron Motsoaledi, stated that the findings on NCDs backed many of the things that his department had been saying in recent years. He added that 'the department's non-communicable disease strategy would address some of these concerns, such as the smoking, alcohol and the high salt content in food'.[41]

3 Legal challenges to regulation

The courts have been used in both the UK and South Africa to test regulations imposing limits on the commercial interests of corporations supplying tobacco and alcohol. Challenges in the UK have been based on constitutional issues deriving from devolution, incompatibility with EU law, and fundamental rights guaranteed by the *Human Rights Act 1998* (UK). In South Africa, challenges have been based on the *Constitution of the Republic of South Africa Act 1996* (South Africa) ('South African Constitution').

3.1 Constitutional challenges on the basis of jurisdiction in the United Kingdom

In 1998, the UK government introduced a system of devolved government for certain regions in the UK. The *Scotland Act 1998* (UK) gave the new Scottish legislature considerable powers while reserving certain listed powers to the UK Parliament.[42] Two important cases from Scotland, based on challenges to changes in the alcohol and tobacco industry, have turned on the jurisdictional competence of the Scottish legislature.

The first concerned a challenge by tobacco companies to changes to the display and sale of tobacco products. The *Tobacco and Primary Medical Services (Scotland) Act 2010* (UK) prohibited the display of tobacco products in a place where tobacco products are offered for sale and also prohibited vending machines for the sale of tobacco products.[43] This was the first time that provisions of an Act of the Scottish Parliament had been challenged as falling outside its legislative competence on the ground that they relate to reserved matters – in this instance, consumer protection and product safety.[44] The challenge was unsuccessful. In the Supreme Court, Lord Hope stressed that the purpose of the legislation was not to protect consumers against unfair trade practices but to discourage the sale of tobacco. Similarly, the legislation was concerned not with safety but with promoting public health.[45]

The second constitutional challenge concerned fixing the unit price of cheap alcohol. In 2012, the *Alcohol (Minimum Pricing) (Scotland) Act 2012* (UK) introduced a minimum price per unit of alcohol as a means of reducing alcohol consumption and protecting health. The Scottish Ministers then proposed an order setting the minimum price at 50 pence. The Scotch Whisky Association sought judicial review to challenge the legality of the legislation and the proposed order on the basis that they fell outside the legislative competence of the Scottish Parliament.[46] The argument asserted that the measures were in breach of the *Acts of Union 1706 and 1707* and incompatible with EU law.[47] Lord Doherty, in the Court of Session, found no conflict between the *Acts of Union*, the proposed order and the minimum alcohol pricing legislation: setting a minimum price for alcohol did not affect trade between England and Scotland.[48] The court accepted that the Scottish measures would fall outside the legislative competence of the Scottish Parliament if found incompatible with EU law.[49] The petitioners asserted that the measures would be prohibited by art 34 of the *Treaty on the Functioning of the European Union* ('TFEU')[50] as hindering imports between member states.[51] According to the court, the legislation and the Scottish Ministers' proposed order could be justified under TFEU art 36 on grounds of 'the protection of health and life of humans'.[52] Lord Doherty identified the public interest in the reduction of alcohol consumption generally and, in particular, reduced consumption by harmful drinkers in the lowest income quintile of the population, who drank cheaper alcohol.[53] This public interest fell within the legitimate aims of art 36, and the measures were not disproportionate in addressing those aims.[54]

3.2 Challenges to tobacco advertising in the United Kingdom and South Africa

The UK introduced a ban on tobacco advertising in 2002.[55] According to the UK legislation, the Secretary of State could permit, subject to regulation, advertising at the point of sale. Thus, advertising could still be permitted at retail premises, on vending machines and on websites.[56] Regulations imposed various restrictions, including limits on the size of the advertisements and their place of display.[57] Tobacco manufacturers challenged the validity of the regulations, arguing that they restricted their freedom of expression.[58]

Article 10 of the *European Convention on Human Rights* ('ECHR')[59] (protecting freedom of expression) protects some commercial expression, but such expression receives less protection than does political or artistic speech.[60] In any event, art 10 does not provide an unqualified right, and safeguarding health is one of the listed aims in art 10(2), which may justify restrictions. The tobacco manufacturers' judicial review challenge was unsuccessful. Justice McCombe pointed out that as the primary legislation contemplated a comprehensive ban, the government was under no obligation to permit any advertising.[61] The restrictions imposed by the regulations could not be regarded as a disproportionate measure for achieving the legitimate aim of the protection of public health under art 10(2).[62] He stated:

> The protection of health is a far reaching social policy. The right to commercial free speech, while less fundamental than political or artistic free speech, is protected by the Convention and restrictions must be justified. However, it will be principally for the decision maker to resolve how best the aim can be achieved by restricting promotion of extremely harmful but historically lawful products. While the test of 'proportionality' cannot be escaped, the need for advertising restriction on tobacco products is not substantially in issue and we are dealing with a restriction on the very edge of a much wider restriction that is not challenged nor is capable of challenge.[63]

The judge also used a separation of powers argument to acknowledge that the legislator is in the best position to determine the balance between the lawful business of selling tobacco and the need to protect public health, subject to a proportionality test.[64] In any event, it is hard to justify protection for advertising based on free speech theories. Commercial advertising is not promoting a political message or a 'truth'; rather, it is trying to promote sales by persuading customers to purchase its product. This decision has stymied any attempt to challenge further regulations, such as the display ban, through free speech arguments.

In South Africa, the Supreme Court of Appeal has addressed a constitutional challenge to the blanket ban on the advertising and promotion of any tobacco products.[65] A tobacco manufacturer complained that these provisions in the amended *Tobacco Products Control Act 1993* (South Africa)[66] breached their right to engage in commercial expression and the tobacco consumers' rights to receive information. A second aspect of the argument concerned the inadequacy of the justifications put forward to legitimate the limitations on free expression.

The decision of the court turned on whether the limitation on expression was reasonable and justifiable. An interesting aspect of the decision was the analysis of legislative policy in assessing the justification. The appellants criticised the position of the Minister of Health for failing to provide specific data and relying on generalised policy arguments.[67] Deputy President Mthiyane viewed this as 'a classic example of a case in which matters of fact and policy are intertwined'.[68] His Honour acknowledged that legislation may seek to address a perceived mischief that is unsupported by empirical facts, or that the efficacy of a proposed policy cannot necessarily be proven in advance. If the concerns are of sufficient importance and there is an adequate connection between means and ends, this will not necessarily be fatal to the policy.[69]

Deputy President Mthiyane and the concurring judges had no hesitation in concluding that a compelling case had been made for justification.[70] The South

African Constitution requires judges to have regard to international law[71] when interpreting the Bill of Rights.[72] As South Africa is a party to the WHO FCTC, the court is obliged to give weight to that treaty when deciding whether an infringement of freedom of expression is justified.[73] Commercial speech is not absolute, and the hazards of smoking outweigh it.[74] Furthermore, smokers are not a 'monogenous group'.[75] Some smokers wish to quit, while former smokers may not want to return to the habit.[76]

In reaching its decision that a ban on promoting and advertising tobacco does not breach constitutional protections, the Supreme Court of Appeal referred to some of the social and economic rights enshrined in the South African Constitution. A reference to s 27(1), which provides that everyone has the right to health care services provided and paid for by the state, was used to justify the court's refusal to find that a less restrictive means existed to enforce the prohibition on advertising and promotion of tobacco products.[77] In addition, the court used the concept of a right to a healthy environment to find that the limitation imposed on commercial speech was reasonable.[78]

3.3　*The right to property in the United Kingdom and proportionality*

A further source of legal challenges to regulations of NCDs is through the protection of the right to property. Article 1 of the First Protocol to the ECHR ('First Protocol')[79] guarantees the right to property in the UK through the *Human Rights Act 1998* (UK). The First Protocol states:

(1) Every … natural or legal person is entitled to the peaceful enjoyment of his possessions. No one shall be deprived of his possession except in the public interest and subject to the conditions provided for by law and by the general principles of international law ….

(2) The preceding provisions shall not, however, in any way impair the right of a state to enforce such laws as it deems necessary to control the use of property in accordance with the general interest or to secure the payment of taxes or other contribution or penalties.[80]

The principle of proportionality plays a key role in assessing the lawfulness of an infringement of this right.

In *R (Sinclair Collis Ltd) v Secretary of State for Health*, the Court of Appeal of England and Wales analysed the fundamental question about the appropriate level of intensity of the proportionality test.[81] The owners and operators of tobacco vending machines ('TVMs') challenged a regulation that prohibited the sale of tobacco through vending machines.[82] The objective of the measure was to reduce the availability of cigarettes to, and their consumption by, young people under the age of 18.[83] The right to property as protected under art 1 of the First Protocol was engaged.[84] As TVMs are primarily imported from other EU member states, arts 34 and 36 of the TFEU were also relevant.[85] The appellants argued that the regulation was disproportionate, adducing evidence of their substantial economic loss. As stated by Laws LJ, 'the ban will wipe out the tobacco vending machine industry'.[86] The appellants argued that the Secretary of State should adopt a less dramatic policy alternative in order to achieve its aim. In particular, it was strongly contended that vending machines could be fitted with age restriction mechanisms and that a voluntary code, rather than a ban, would be equally effective.[87]

The legal issue turned on whether the measure taken was proportionate.[88] The Court of Appeal, by a majority (Laws LJ dissenting), held that the prohibition on TVMs was proportionate to the legitimate public health aim of reducing the sale of tobacco to young people. This justification was upheld in spite of the fact that it was not possible to prove empirically that the banning of TVMs would reduce under-age smoking.[89] The claimants had strongly contended that the end results would be minimal as young smokers would find other illicit sources of supply and that their suggested age restrictive measures would prove as efficacious.[90] The majority did not accept these arguments. According to Arden LJ and Neuberger MR, it was acceptable for the Minister to conclude that under-age smoking would be reduced, as one source of supply had been removed.[91]

There were some differences between the judges in their approach to the proportionality principle. Arden LJ stated that the '"core principle" of proportionality demands that the measure be "suitable and necessary"'.[92] The concept of 'necessary' also requires that 'where there is a choice of measures for achieving the legitimate aim, it must be shown that the least intrusive means of interfering with a fundamental freedom has been employed'.[93] Nevertheless, she concluded that 'different levels of scrutiny reflect the flexibility of the principles of proportionality'.[94] As this particular dispute involved important public health care issues, it would only be disproportionate if found to be 'manifestly inappropriate'.[95] Arguably this less intensive level of scrutiny is at odds with Arden LJ's earlier comments about the concept of 'necessary' and the adoption of a less restrictive means to achieve the legitimate aim. She explained:

> The 'manifestly inappropriate' test is not a licence to do things which are not rationally connected with their legitimate aim, or to do things in a manner which discriminates without justification. A member state cannot rely on the 'manifestly inappropriate' test if what it is doing, under the cloak of the proportionality test, actually amounts to achieving some quite different objective from its stated legitimate aim.[96]

In contrast, Laws LJ rejected the contention that different standards of proportionality ought to apply.[97] He concluded that even though the Secretary of State had a broad margin of appreciation, the failure to consider or adopt less restrictive options did not satisfy the requirements of the proportionality test.[98]

The Court of Appeal spent little time considering the aspect of the claim concerning art 1 of the First Protocol. Laws LJ was of the opinion that, as the ECHR protection of the right to property does not demand 'a more intrusive standard of review than article 36 TFEU, it is unnecessary to take time with such comparisons'.[99] According to Arden LJ, the application of a 'least intrusive means' test is not consistently applied in the Strasbourg jurisprudence (that is, the jurisprudence of the European Court of Human Rights).[100] However, she explained that:

> the comparison with Strasbourg jurisprudence should not be taken too far because for the Strasbourg court to use the 'least intrusive means' test in all circumstances would in any event be inconsistent with the ECHR system and the supervisory role of the Strasbourg court in the protection of human rights, whereas the role of the Court of Justice [of the European Union] is not purely supervisory.[101]

In Scotland, a subsequent case concerning the banning of TVMs arose and was considered by the Inner House of the Court of Session in 2012 in *Sinclair Collis Ltd v The Lord Advocate*.[102] Section 9 of the *Tobacco and Primary Medical Services (Scotland) Act 2010* made it an offence to operate a TVM. It was accepted that the legislation engaged art 1 of the First Protocol as it was a 'control of the use of vending machines'.[103] The petitioners argued that a fair balance had not been struck to justify limiting their fundamental rights.[104]

The court adopted a three part test.[105] First, permissible interferences with this fundamental right must have a legitimate aim.[106] The court decided that the objective of reducing smoking among young people was sufficiently important to justify the interference.[107] There is also a wide margin of appreciation available to the state in deciding social and economic policies, even where there is a cost to business. The courts will not interfere with this assessment unless it is shown to be 'manifestly without reasonable foundation'.[108] Secondly, the court assesses the 'fair balance' of the measure: is it rational, fair and not arbitrary? Finally, the court will consider whether the measure interferes to the minimum extent possible with the private economic interests of the petitioners. The court found that all three requirements were met and that the measure was not disproportionate.[109]

The court spent little time considering the First Protocol aspect of the claim. As the court had carefully analysed proportionality in connection with the EU challenge (art 34 TFEU), it found that the vending machine ban had not 'failed to strike a balance between the public interest in maintaining good public health and the petitioners' private economic interest … as required by the *Convention*'.[110]

According to the court, proportionality requires a measure to be both appropriate (or suitable) in securing the objective and necessary as a means of doing so.[111] The Scottish Court of Session referred to the prior Court of Appeal decision on TVMs.[112] While agreeing with Arden LJ's statement of the core principles of proportionality, Lord Carloway professed difficulty reconciling the low level of scrutiny applied in the English decision, namely 'manifestly inappropriate', with the requirement of necessity.[113] The court accepted that if a less restrictive measure is available, it cannot be considered 'necessary'.[114] The petitioners had proposed a procedure to check the age of purchasers of tobacco from vending machines. After examining the evidence produced by the respondent, the court concluded that:

the Government and Parliament were entitled to the view that such mechanisms were not effective to prevent sales to under eighteens and that only a complete prohibition would secure the legitimate objective of reducing sales by cutting off one source of supply.[115]

Although the court demanded a measure to be objectively justified, the government or Parliament was not 'required to conduct a series of empirical scientific experiments to establish the obvious'.[116] In this particular instance, the statistical material was sufficient to justify the ban, even though it was flawed in parts.[117]

The *Sinclair Collis* litigation in England and Scotland has exposed the uncertainty in the domestic courts when applying the principle of proportionality in EU law and when deciding the 'fair balance' of rights protected by the ECHR. To what extent should the court assess the 'least restrictive means' when considering the proportionality principle? Should judicial restraint be exercised when the subject matter of the case concerns policy issues relating to public health? How far should a court go in demanding and determining the evidential material necessary to decide on a less restrictive measure in the course of analysing the proportionality principle? Lady Justice Arden has recently suggested that these issues need resolution at the level of the Supreme Court of the United Kingdom.[118]

3.4 Plain packaging and fundamental rights: the future in the United Kingdom

Although regulations mandating 'plain' or standardised packaging of tobacco products may not be introduced into the EU or the UK immediately, it is highly probable that they will be implemented in the next few years.[119] Such regulations are likely to result in challenges on the basis of the fundamental right to property in art 1 of the First Protocol, freedom of expression and the *Charter of Fundamental Rights of the European Union* ('CFREU').[120]

Regulations on plain packaging would clearly fall within the right to property in art 1 of the First Protocol. Trademarks and intellectual property rights fall within the concept of 'possessions'.[121] Plain packaging would constitute an 'interference' with the right to property of the tobacco companies, as 'possessions' encompasses a right to use.[122] The inability of the tobacco companies to promote their brands or use logos on their cigarette packaging would be a major infringement of their commercial 'property' interests. However, the legal issue would turn on the legitimacy of the aim and whether a fair balance has been struck in the relevant regulations. The aim of promoting public health by deterring a target audience from taking up an addictive habit while also attempting to persuade existing smokers to abandon tobacco consumption is clearly a legitimate objective. Any court would also put weight on the democratically approved nature of the regulations.[123] Democratic claims play a critical role in legitimating the exercise of power, especially in circumstances where fundamental rights are affected. The extent of the debate in Parliament and other studies or reports by committees would also be of importance in considering the measure. As discussed above, there remains some uncertainty at the domestic level about the appropriate intensity of the proportionality test.

The thorny question of compensation to tobacco companies is an influential factor that may determine whether to proceed with plain packaging. The European Court of Human Rights has considered the issue of compensation[124] in relation to the ban on handguns introduced in the UK in 1997.[125] A compensation scheme covered the guns themselves but not the loss of business and goodwill.[126] The court found that 'possessions' includes 'goodwill' but not future income. In considering whether a fair balance had been achieved, the court took into account the important objective of gun control, the regulatory environment surrounding firearms and the fact that some compensation was paid.[127] The application was found to be inadmissible.[128] If plain packaging were introduced, it might not amount to a deprivation of property that would require compensation. As the tobacco companies would still be able to engage in the selling of tobacco, albeit without the advantage of all their trademarks, it may be possible for the government to proceed without compensation.

If plain packaging regulations were introduced into domestic law in the UK, the CFREU would be relevant. The CFREU became part of primary EU law in December 2009.[129] Plain packaging is likely to interfere with the free movement of goods pursuant to art 34 TFEU, which aims to protect trading inside the European internal market. The CFREU protects individuals and legal entities against actions by the EU institutions and domestic authorities that are not in conformity with fundamental rights. In these circumstances, the Court of Justice of the European Union ('CJEU') has the power to review the legality of the act. If a national authority violates the CFREU when implementing EU law, national judges, under the guidance of the CJEU, have the power to ensure that the CFREU is respected.[130]

Article 17 of the CFREU reads:

(1) Everyone has the right to own, *use*, dispose of and bequeath his or her lawfully acquired possessions. No one may be deprived of his or her possessions, except in the public interest and in the cases and under the conditions provided for by law, subject to fair compensation being paid in good time for their loss. The use of property may be regulated by law in so far as is necessary for the general interest.

(2) Intellectual property shall be protected.[131]

It is highly likely that the impact of plain packaging on the right to property could be justified on the grounds of public health, but a court would have to assess whether it is the 'least restrictive mechanism' to achieve the legitimate aim. As the CFREU has 'the same legal value' as the *Treaty on European Union*[132] and the TFEU, the stricter application of the proportionality test should apply.[133]

The issue of compensation would also need to be addressed if the EU or domestic courts decided to proceed with standardised packaging.[134] When viewed from a constitutional law perspective supporting the 'right' to property as a fundamental human right, there is a difficulty in reconciling the private property ownership and commercial interests with the wider 'public interest' objectives underlying regulation. Some further guidance is provided by the CFREU: art 35 provides for the protection of health and art 52 provides for the limitation of rights subject to proportionality.

Expression rights are also protected by the CFREU. Article 11(1) provides that '[e]veryone has the right to freedom of expression'. Pursuant to art 52(3), the right to expression protected in the CFREU and in art 10 ECHR have the same 'meaning and scope'. Restrictions on the design of cigarette packages, extended health warnings, and a prohibition on brand names and logos could constitute a prima facie violation of freedom of expression, but they are likely to be justified on the grounds of public health provided that they are a proportionate means to achieve the public health aim. Tobacco companies are likely to argue that less restrictive alternatives exist that would be equally effective in achieving the public health aim. Evidence of the efficacy of plain packaging in Australia will be a significant factor in this debate.[135]

The introduction of plain packaging does raise legal questions concerning the apparent infringement of the fundamental rights of tobacco manufacturers. Tobacco companies will use every available strategy to try to prevent the introduction of standardised packaging in the UK. Even if restrictions are found to be justified and proportionate, the issue of whether or not some compensation would have to be paid is unclear.

4 Conclusion

South Africa has a written constitution, whereas that of the UK, famously, is uncodified. Nevertheless, there are many similarities in the approach of these two states to NCDs and their courts' assessment of the general public interest and fundamental rights.

In South Africa, there is arguably a richer foundation for the courts to draw upon. The protection within the South African Constitution of social and economic rights can assist the court in determining the appropriate balance. For example, in *BAT Ltd v Minister of Health*, the court was able to rely upon the right to healthcare services and a healthy environment in reaching its conclusion. The courts are also directed to consider relevant international law and comparative constitutional law jurisprudence.

In the UK, constitutional changes over the last 20 years have led the courts to apply a more demanding level of scrutiny. Proportionality is a general principle of EU law and of the European Court of Human Rights. In these areas of the law, the courts are required to do more than assess the illegality, procedural impropriety or 'reasonableness' of a regulation.[136] The *Human Rights Act 1998* (UK), EU law and the new constitutional arrangements for Scotland, Wales and Northern Ireland have changed the nature of judicial review in the UK. A further consequence of these changes is the transformation of the nature of 'constitutionalism' in the UK and the role played by the courts.

A striking similarity between South Africa and the UK is the influence of international and, in the UK, European law. The field of public health has become multi-layered and globalised. The WHO FCTC has led to seminal changes in both jurisdictions. The democratic process has been able to implement change through legislation. Nevertheless, the power and wealth of corporations should not be underestimated. If plain packaging is introduced in either jurisdiction, issues surrounding intellectual property rights, as well as property and expression rights, are likely to be areas of legal contention.

The tension between the private property rights of corporations, engaged in lawful activities, and the public interest has been addressed in both jurisdictions through a proportionality test. The courts have carefully scrutinised the rationales behind legislation in order to ensure that the objective of the measure is a legitimate one. The courts have also examined the necessity and fair balance of any measure. As outlined above, there has been disagreement in the UK as to how the test should be implemented. The level of scrutiny that should apply when an impugned measure is directed at public health has not been agreed in the UK.

A further unresolved issue in the UK is the issue of risk assessment and the regulation of NCDs. The judiciary of South Africa and the UK have touched upon this matter when considering the legitimacy of a regulatory objective. What if the evidence forming the basis of the challenged measure is imperfect? In some circumstances the efficacy of a measure can be assessed only after it has been introduced. It is tempting to suspect that the demands for expert 'scientific' proof is used to hide the relationship between the government, its political interests and powerful corporate entities. A cautious approach tends to serve private interests over public ones and, while it may be appropriate in some circumstances, there is no debate that tobacco, for example, is a dangerous, lethal, habit forming drug. A deterrent policy that may be successful with some consumers, and potentially improve public health, could be worth trying.

Measures regulating alcohol and tobacco, major contributing factors to NCDs, have been unsuccessfully challenged in the courts of South Africa and the UK. The objectives based on public health have outweighed competing interests. The idea that the paternalistic state is acting to promote health at the expense of individual rights and 'lifestyle choice' has not gained credence in either jurisdiction. In neither jurisdiction has tobacco or alcohol been banned. Thus the 'choice' for individuals remains.

Notes

1 See, eg, United Kingdom, *The Government's Alcohol Strategy*, Cm 8336 (2012); *Alcohol (Minimum Pricing) (Scotland) Act* 2012 (Scot).
2 European Parliament, *Making Tobacco Less Attractive to Young People* (7 October 2013) <http://www.europarl.europa.eu/news/en/news-room/content/20131004 BKG21543/html/Making-tobacco-less-attractive-to-young-people>.
3 Ibid.
4 See, eg, WHO FCTC; *Political Declaration of the High-level Meeting of the General Assembly on the Prevention and Control of Non-communicable Diseases*, GA Res 66/2, UN GAOR, 66th

sess, 3rd plen mtg, UN Doc A/Res/66/2 (24 January 2012); World Health Assembly, *Global Strategy on Diet, Physical Activity and Health Diet: Report by the Secretariat*, WHA Res 57.17, 57th sess, 8th plen mtg, WHO Doc A57/2004/REC/1 (22 May 2004). See also *Convention for the Protection of Human Rights and Fundamental Freedoms*, opened for signature 4 November 1950, 213 UNTS 222 (entered into force 3 September 1953) ('ECHR') art 35.

5 *WHO Framework Convention on Tobacco Control*, opened for signature 16 June 2003, 2302 UNTS 166 (entered into force 27 February 2005) ('WHO FCTC').

6 World Health Organization, *WHO Report on the Global Tobacco Epidemic* (2013) <http://www.who.int/tobacco/global_report/2013/en/index.html>.

7 See, eg, *Protocol to the Convention for the Protection of Human Rights and Fundamental Freedoms*, opened for signature 20 March 1952, ETS No 9 (entered into force 18 May 1954) art 1; *Charter of Fundamental Rights of the European Union*, proclaimed 7 December 2000 [2012] C 326/391, art 17. See discussion below.

8 C3 Collaborating for Health, 'Non-communicable Diseases – An Introduction: A UK Briefing Paper' (February 2013) 3 <http://www.c3health.org/wp-content/uploads/2009/09/NCDs-briefing-paper-for-a-UK-audience-20130220.pdf>.

9 See, eg, *Tobacco Advertising and Promotion Act 2002* (UK); *Children and Young Persons (Protection from Tobacco) Act 1991* (UK).

10 Ofcom, *Ofcom Asks Advertising Bodies to Review Rules to Limit Children's Exposure to TV Alcohol Advertising* (24 May 2013) <http://media.ofcom.org.uk/2013/05/24/ofcom-asks-advertising-bodies-to-review-rules-to-limit-childrens-exposure-to-tv-alcohol-advertising/>.

11 Ofcom, *HFSS Advertising Restrictions – Final Review* (26 July 2010) <http://stakeholders.ofcom.org.uk/market-data-research/other/tv-research/hfss-final-review/>.

12 *Education (Nutritional Standards and Requirements for School Food) (England) (Amendment) Regulations 2011* (UK) SI 2011/1190. See also Department for Education, *School Food Standards* (10 September 2013) UK Government <http://www.education.gov.uk/schools/adminandfinance/schooladmin/a0012940/school-food-standards>.

13 Academy of Medical Royal Colleges, *Measuring Up: The Medical Profession's Prescription for the Nation's Obesity Crisis* (2013) 10.

14 Ibid.

15 Ibid.

16 Department of Health, *Standardised Packaging of Tobacco Products*, UK Government <http://consultations.dh.gov.uk/tobacco/standardised-packaging-of-tobacco-products/consult_view>.

17 Department of Health, *Consultation on Standardised Packaging of Tobacco Products: Summary Report* (July 2013) UK Government <https://www.gov.uk/government/uploads/system/uploads/attachment_data/file/212074/Summary_of_responses_to_consultation_-_standardised_packaging_tobacco.pdf>.

18 The Department of Health website provides details and dates of meetings: Department of Health, *Proposals to Introduce Standardised Tobacco Packaging* (17 May 2013) UK Government <https://www.gov.uk/government/publications/proposals-to-introduce-standardised-tobacco-packaging-de775233>. See also Department of Health, *DH FOI Release: Correspondence between DH and Tobacco Manufacturers and Tobacco Trade Bodies* (14 December 2012) UK Government <https://www.gov.uk/government/publications/dh-foi-release-correspondence-between-dh-and-tobacco-manufacturers-and-tobacco-trade-bodies>.

19 Department of Health, *Note of Meeting – British American Tobacco (BAT) and Department of Health (DH)* (25 January 2013) UK Government <https://www.gov.uk/government/uploads/system/uploads/attachment_data/file/200230/DE775233_Attchment1.pdf>.

20 Ibid.

21 Andrew Sparrow, 'UK Plans for Plain Cigarette Packaging to be Shelved', *Guardian* (online), 12 July 2013 <http://www.theguardian.com/society/2013/jul/12/plans-plain-cigarette-packaging-shelved>.

22 Ibid.

23 Prime Minister's Office, 'Press Briefing: Morning 12 July 2013' (Press Release, 17 July 2013) <https://www.gov.uk/government/news/press-briefing-morning-12-july-2013>.

24 There is also evidence of tobacco corporations lobbying the EU.

25 United Kingdom, *Parliamentary Debates*, House of Commons, 28 November 2013, col 25WS (Jane Ellison).

26 Department of Health, 'Independent Review of Standardised Packaging for Tobacco' (Press Release, 28 November 2013) <https://www.gov.uk/government/news/independent-review-of-standardised-packaging-for-tobacco>.

27 Huan-Ying Lin and Michael Reich, *Case: Tobacco Control Policy in South Africa* (2012) Ministerial Leadership in Health <http://www.ministerialleadershipinhealth.org/political-change-in-south-africa-new-tobacco-control-and-public-health-policies/>.

28 Mia Malan and Rosemary Leaver, 'Political Change in South Africa: New Tobacco Control and Public Health Policies' in Joy de Beyer and Linda Waverley (eds), *Tobacco Control Policies: Strategies, Successes and Setbacks* (RITC and World Bank, 2003) 121, 122.

29 Frederick Appah, *The Politics of Health Promotion: Analyzing Healthy Public Policy's Impact on Tobacco Control in United States and South Africa* (PhD Thesis, West Virginia University, 2007); Derek Yach, Di McIntyre and Yusuf Saloojee, 'Smoking in South Africa: The Health and Economic Impact' (1992) 1 *Tobacco Control* 272. See also Lin and Reich, above n 27. I have drawn on this case study in the following paragraphs.

30 Malan and Leaver, above n 28, 123.

31 Ibid 131.

32 Ibid.

33 Ibid 136.

34 Ibid 140.

35 Ibid 141.

36 *Tobacco Products Amendment Act 1999* (South Africa). See also *Tobacco Products Control Act 1993* (South Africa); *Tobacco Products Control Amendment Act 2008* (South Africa). These various amendments were introduced to strengthen the existing legislation.

37 *Parties to the WHO Framework Convention on Tobacco Control*, WHO FCTC (27 November 2013) <http://www.who.int/fctc/signatories_parties/>.

38 Control of Marketing of Alcohol Beverages Bill 2013 (South Africa).

39 Bathabile Dlamini, *Statement by the Minister of Social Development, Ms Bathabile Dlamini during a Media Briefing on the Control of Marketing of Alcohol Beverages Bill*, South Africa Government Online (20 September 2013) <http://www.gov.za/speeches/view.php?sid=39918>.

40 O Shisana et al, *South African National Health and Nutrition Examination Survey (SANHANES-1)* (HSRC Press, 2013) 40 <http://www.hsrc.ac.za/uploads/pageNews/72/SANHANES-launch%20edition%20(online%20version).pdf>.

41 *Obesity in Women at Alarming Proportions – HSRC Survey*, South African Government News Agency (6 August 2013) <http://www.sanews.gov.za/south-africa/obesity-women-alarming-proportions-%E2%80%93-hsrc-survey>.

42 See *Scotland Act 1998* (UK), sch 5 pt II.

43 Sections 1 and 9.

44 *Imperial Tobacco Ltd v Lord Advocate (Scotland)* [2012] UKSC 61 (12 December 2012) [6].

45 Ibid [42]–[43].

46 *Scotch Whisky Association v Lord Advocate (Scotland)* [2013] SLT 776.

47 Ibid [6].

48 Ibid [21]–[22].

49 The *European Communities Act 1972* (UK) establishes that EU law prevails over any provision of domestic law inconsistent with it. This is the legal position even if the inconsistent domestic provision is contained in primary legislation. See *R v Secretary of State for Transport, Ex parte Factortame Ltd (No 2)* [1991] 1 AC 603.

50 *Treaty on the Functioning of the European Union*, opened for signature 7 February 1992 [2012] OJ C 326/47 (entered into force 1 November 1993) ('TFEU') art 34: 'Quantitative restrictions on imports and all measures having equivalent effect shall be prohibited between Member States'.

51 *Scotch Whisky Association v Lord Advocate (Scotland)* [2013] SLT 776, [28].

52 TFEU art 36.

53 *Scotch Whisky Association v Lord Advocate (Scotland)* [2013] SLT 776, [53].

54 Ibid [55]–[60], [79]-[81].

55 *Tobacco Advertising and Promotion Act 2002* (UK).

56 Ibid s 4.

57 *Tobacco Advertising and Promotion (Point of Sale) Regulations 2004* (UK) regs 3, 4, 6.

58 *R (British American Tobacco UK Ltd) v Secretary of State for Health* [2004] EWHC 2493 (Admin).

59 See above n 4.

60 *R (British American Tobacco UK Ltd) v Secretary of State for Health* [2004] EWHC 2493 (Admin) [28]. See also Eric Barendt, *Freedom of Speech* (Oxford University Press, 2nd ed, 2005) 393.

61 *R (British American Tobacco UK Ltd) v Secretary of State for Health* [2004] EWHC 2493 (Admin) [24].

62 Ibid [51]–[54].

63 Ibid [37].

64 Ibid.

65 *British American Tobacco South Africa (Pty) Ltd v Minister of Health* [2012] 3 All SA 593 (Supreme Court of Appeal) ('*BAT v Minister of Health*').

66 Section 3(1).

67 *BAT v Minister of Health* [2012] 3 All SA 593, [19].

68 Ibid [22].

69 Ibid [21], quoting *Minister of Home Affairs v National Institute for Crime Prevention and the Re integration of Offenders* [2005] 3 SA 280, [35] (Chaskalson CJ) (Constitutional Court).

70 *BAT v Minister of Health* [2012] 3 All SA 593, [28].

71 Ibid [22].

72 *Constitution of the Republic of South Africa Act 1996*, ch 2, 'Bill of Rights'.

73 *BAT v Minister of Health* [2012] 3 All SA 593, [23].

74 Ibid [25],

75 Ibid.

76 Ibid [26].

77 Ibid.

78 Ibid [28].

79 *Protocol to the Convention for the Protection of Human Rights and Fundamental Freedoms*, opened for signature 20 March 1952, ETS No 9 (entered into force 18 May 1954) ('First Protocol').

80 Ibid art 1.

81 *R (on the application of Sinclair Collis Ltd) v Secretary of State for Health* [2011] EWCA Civ 437. The court also considered arts 34 and 36 of the TFEU (intra-EU trade) in this decision.

82 The ban had been imposed through secondary legislation. Section 3A of the *Children and Young Persons (Protection from Tobacco) Act 1991* (UK), as amended by the *Health Act 2009* (UK), empowered the Secretary of State to make regulations prohibiting the sale of tobacco through vending machines. The Secretary of State exercised this power

through the *Protection from Tobacco (Sales from Vending Machines) (England) Regulations 2010*. Regulation 2(1) provides that 'the sale of tobacco from an automatic machine is prohibited'.

83 See the explanatory memorandum accompanying r 2(1) of the *Protection from Tobacco (Sales from Vending Machines) (England) Regulations 2010*. See also *R (on the application of Sinclair Collis Ltd) v Secretary of State for Health* [2011] EWCA Civ 437, [91]–[92].

84 *R (on the application of Sinclair Collis Ltd) v Secretary of State for Health* [2011] EWCA Civ 437, [19], [184].

85 Ibid [192].

86 Ibid [6].

87 Ibid [226].

88 Ibid [215]–[229].

89 Ibid [141]–[142].

90 Ibid [66].

91 Ibid [251]–[254].

92 Ibid [115].

93 Ibid.

94 Ibid [127].

95 Ibid [127], [164].

96 Ibid [124].

97 Ibid [47].

98 Ibid [80].

99 Ibid [54].

100 Ibid [146].

101 Ibid [147].

102 *Sinclair Collis Ltd v The Lord Advocate* [2012] CSIH 80.

103 Ibid [64].

104 Ibid. See also *R v Secretary of State for Health; Ex parte Eastside Cheese Co* [1999] 3 CMLR 12.

105 *Sinclair Collis Ltd v The Lord Advocate* [2012] CSIH 80, [65].

106 Ibid.

107 Ibid [56].

108 Ibid [65], citing *JA Pye (Oxford) Ltd v UK* (2008) 46 EHRR 45, [75] and *James v UK* (1986) 8 EHRR 123, [46].

109 *Sinclair Collis Ltd v The Lord Advocate* [2012] CSIH 80, [66].

110 Ibid [66].

111 Ibid [57].

112 *R (on the application of Sinclair Collis Ltd) v Secretary of State for Health* [2011] EWCA Civ 437.

113 *Sinclair Collis Ltd v Lord Advocate* [2012] CSIH 80, [57].

114 Ibid [58].

115 Ibid [46].

116 Ibid [61].

117 Ibid [66].

118 The Right Honourable Lady Justice Arden, 'Proportionality: The Way Ahead?' [2013] *Public Law* 489, 513.

119 Ireland has announced that it intends to implement such legislation. See Department of Health, 'Ireland set to become second country in the world to introduce plain pack cigarettes' (Press Release, 28 May 2013) <http://www.dohc.ie/press/releases/2013/20130528.html>. See also Chapter 13 of this volume.

120 *Charter of Fundamental Rights of the European Union*, proclaimed 7 December 2000 [2012] C326/391 ('CFREU'). Although the European Court of Justice has referred to the CFREU as a persuasive authority since its proclamation in 2000, the CFREU did not

have binding legal effect before the entry into force of the *Treaty of Lisbon*, signed 13 December 2007, [2007] OJ C 306/01 (entered into force 1 December 2009). Article 6(1) of the *Treaty on European Union*, opened for signature 7 February 1992, [2012] OJ C 326/01 (entered into force 1 November 1993), as amended by the *Treaty of Lisbon*, now states that the CFREU has 'the same legal value' as the *Treaty on European Union* and the TFEU.

121 *Anheuser-Busch Inc v Portugal* (European Court of Human Rights, Grand Chamber, Application No 73049/01, 11 January 2005); *Dima v Romania* (European Court of Human Rights, First Section, Application No 58472/00, 26 May 2005); *Donald v France* (European Court of Human Rights, Fifth Section, Application No 36769/08, 10 January 2013).

122 *Pinnacle Meat Processors Co v United Kingdom* (European Court of Human Rights, First Section, Application No 33298/96, 21 October 1998).

123 *Friend v United Kingdom* (European Court of Human Rights, Fourth Section, Application Nos 16072/06 and 27809/08, 24 November 2009).

124 *Ian Edgar (Liverpool) Ltd v United Kingdom* (European Court of Human Rights, Third Section, Application No 37683/97, 25 January 2000).

125 *Firearms (Amendment) Act 1997* (UK); *Firearms (Amendment) (No 2) Act 1997* (UK).

126 *Ian Edgar (Liverpool) Ltd v United Kingdom* (European Court of Human Rights, Third Section, Application No 37683/97, 25 January 2000) [1]. The court considered that this was a 'control of use' rather than a de facto 'deprivation of possessions': [1]. See also *Pinnacle Meat Processors Company v United Kingdom* (European Court of Human Rights, First Section, Application No 33298/96, 21 October 1998).

127 *Ian Edgar (Liverpool) Ltd v United Kingdom* (European Court of Human Rights, Third Section, Application No 37683/97, 25 January 2000) [1].

128 Ibid. The claim that there was a violation of art 13 of the ECHR as there was no remedy to claim compensation in the domestic courts was also found to be 'manifestly ill-founded': [13].

129 See above n 120.

130 See, eg, *Janah v Libya* [2013] All ER (D) 190. Primary legislation (in this case, the *State Immunity Act 1978* (UK)) is to be 'disapplied' in a dispute between two private parties where its application would breach a party's rights under the ECHR: [43]–[70].

131 Emphasis added.

132 Opened for signature 7 February 1992, [2012] OJ C 326/01 (entered into force 1 November 1993).

133 See above n 120.

134 See Tanguy de Haan, 'Plain Packaging: Expropriation and Disproportion' (2013) 35 *European Intellectual Property Review* 497.

135 See, eg, Melanie Wakefield et al, 'Introduction Effects of the Australian Plain Packaging Policy on Adult Smokers: A Cross-sectional Study' (2013) 3 *BMJ Open* e003175.

136 *Associated Picture Houses Ltd v Wednesbury Corp* [1948] 1 KB 223, Lord Greene MR 229–30 (Lord Greene MR). The *Wednesbury* test continues to be applied as the usual test in 'non-rights' cases.

Part III

National and Regional Perspectives of NCD Risk Regulation

10 United States

*Stephen D Sugarman**

1 Introduction

In furtherance of public health goals, multiple levels of government in the United States ('US') have sought to reduce the incidence of non-communicable diseases ('NCDs') by influencing the conduct of enterprises involved in the tobacco, alcohol and unhealthy food businesses. In this chapter, I first explain the implications of the complex nature of the US government for regulation in this field, before providing examples of recent public health measures targeted at these three risk factors for NCDs. The balance of the chapter explores a range of legal attacks brought by the relevant industries on public health measures in this field. The chapter demonstrates the difficulties arising for public health regulation as a result of the litigious nature of US society and the propensity of the courts to be wary of interference with business interests.

2 The complex nature of US government: federal, state and local health measures

Some of the regulatory action in addressing NCD risk factors in the US has been at the federal (or national) level through legislation enacted by the US Congress and regulations adopted by administrative agencies (such as the Food and Drug Administration ('FDA')). It is critical to appreciate at the outset that because the US does not have a parliamentary form of government, the President is in a very different position from that of the typical Prime Minister, who can ordinarily get the Parliament to enact the laws put forward by the government currently in power. In the US, the legislature (the US Congress) is comprised of two houses – the Senate and the House of Representatives – and either or both may well be under the control of a political party other than the President's. Either of those branches of Congress can block the adoption of what the President proposes. Moreover, even if the Senate, say, is controlled by the party in the White House, still the chair of the specific committee through which any proposed legislation must go has the power to block a proposed law, and committee chairs often do this even when they and the President belong to the same party. Hence, industry opponents of proposed legislation have many points at which they can battle to defeat it. Executive departments like the FDA are somewhat more under the President's control. But independent administrative agencies such as the Federal Trade Commission are another matter. Although those sorts of agencies are typically run by a five-member board in which there is a 3–2 majority (including the key chair position) who are Presidential appointees from the President's party, nonetheless, once in office, agency chairs (and members) have substantial freedom to pursue their own agendas.

At the state level, the story is much the same. Legislatures and executive departments under the control of the state's Governor can also seek to regulate companies involved with alcohol, tobacco and unhealthy foods. Indeed, the US is a nation ideologically rooted in 'federalism', which means for these purposes that 'public health' is normally viewed as primarily a problem for state (and local) government to deal with, rather than the national (federal) government. Of course, in today's world, the reality is that the federal government has more powerful taxing and other powers than do states, and many problems transcend state (and even national) boundaries. Still, public health legislation in the US remains primarily state legislation, and among other things this means that the law can vary considerably from state to state. To give one brief illustration, although national tobacco control policy is quite weak in the US,[1] in the state of Washington it is reasonably strong (and smoking prevalence rates are relatively low, about 17 per cent of adults); by contrast, the state of Kentucky has a very weak tobacco control program (and smoking rates there are very high, about 29 per cent of adults).[2]

Finally, many key public health measures are initiated at the local level. These turn out to be extremely important (albeit again raising the problem of uneven policy from place to place). Local government is complex in the US, but most important here are cities and counties, in addition to local boards of health (or similarly named bodies). Cities are usually contained within the borders of counties (although San Francisco, for example, is a somewhat unusual exception, being both a city and a county). In some places, cities take the lead on local public health matters and counties, if they act at all, focus primarily on geographic areas within counties that are not organised into cities (often this means somewhat less populated suburban or rural areas). But elsewhere county government takes the lead adopting policies applicable to (or quickly adopted by) cities within their territories. The legal powers of cities, counties and local boards of health vary significantly from place to place. And, of course, while city and county legislators sometimes lead the way, at other times they follow the lead of their elected chief executives (like mayors or chairs of boards of supervisors).

One reason that public health advocacy groups will seek reform through local governmental action is that they believe their political leverage is strongest there. Local citizens can more easily lobby local political actors; those actors may more directly feel accountable to local political opinion; and those in the alcohol, tobacco and unhealthy food industries might be less able to fight back, especially if many localities are simultaneously considering similar measures and these businesses are seen as outsiders who don't have local health values on their side. Hence, it is common for public health advocates to seek early adoption of new ideas in places like San Francisco and New York City with the hope that from there they and colleagues around the country can promote diffusion to ever more places.[3]

While it is possible, of course, to impact the nation as a whole all at once via the US Congress, that is precisely where public health advocates often feel that industry has the most clout. This potential difference in political strength at different levels of government has resulted in the alcohol, tobacco and unhealthy food industries adopting a 'pre-emption' strategy, as discussed in more detail below. For example, these industries seek to get weak state laws adopted that (either expressly, or, with the cleverness of their lawyers later on, impliedly) preclude stronger laws from being put into place at the local level; or similarly, they seek a weak federal regime to occupy the field thereby blocking what might be stronger state or local laws.

3 Examples of recent public health measures aimed at tobacco, alcohol and unhealthy foods

Public health laws and regulations proposed and adopted in the US with respect to tobacco, alcohol and unhealthy foods may be grouped in various ways. Below is one way of grouping them:

1) Excise (or similar) taxes that seek to discourage demand for socially undesirable products such as cigarettes, alcoholic beverages and sugar-sweetened sodas by forcing a price increase that it is assumed the tax will generate.
2) Bans on the sale or use of certain products (or ingredients in products), such as trans fats.
3) Partial bans such as: making illegal the sale to minors of certain products such as tobacco and alcohol; imposing portion size limits on, say, sweetened carbonated drinks; forbidding businesses from combining the sale of unhealthy children's meals with toy giveaways; enacting neighbourhood density limits, such as allowing a limited number of stores to sell alcoholic beverages in an area, or blocking new business permits for undesirable retailers such as fast food outlets; requiring apartment complexes or some parts of them to be smoke free; precluding the sale of cigarettes in less than a full pack or at a discount price; forbidding pharmacies to sell unhealthy items such as cigarettes.
4) Marketing restrictions such as: forbidding television advertising for tobacco products and beverages with high alcohol content; banning particular advertisements from being shown on certain sorts of television programs or at certain times, eg excluding unhealthy food advertising on television programs aimed at children; restricting billboard use, such as preventing posters for tobacco products to appear near schools or day care centres; limiting where products may be placed in stores, such as forcing alcohol products to be under lock and key or otherwise unavailable for customer self-service, or requiring food store check-out aisles to be free of certain unhealthy food that might otherwise prompt impulse purchases or pressure by children to have parents buy them.

5)   Required warnings and disclosures such as: demanding that calorie counts appear on restaurant menu labels; having processed foods list their sugar, salt and fat quantities on product package labels; insisting that risk-of-harm warnings be included in advertisements of products such as cigarettes and alcoholic spirits.

4 Industry legal attacks on public health measures

4.1 Types of legal attack

When laws, regulations and other initiatives of the sort just described are launched (or about to be launched) that the impacted industry does not favour, but has exhausted its many opportunities to block in conventional political fora, the typical next move is for the industry to consider attacking these measures in court. This chapter is primarily organised around these legal attacks.

Put simply, federal initiatives on behalf of public health will typically be attacked in court as either violating the *United States Constitution* or as illegal behaviour by the adopter of the measure at issue (eg it is beyond the legal power of the agency to regulate in the way it proposes, or the agency has illegally failed to follow the proper procedure in adopting the regulations). For measures pursued at the state level, industry legal attacks can include claims that the measures they are complaining about violate the *United States Constitution* and/or the relevant state constitution or are pre-empted by federal legislation, or that the state agency promulgating them either does not have the legal power to do so or did so in an illegal manner. A similar set of legal challenges is available to attack local measures, with both federal and state pre-emption potentially looming over them. This sort of litigation may be brought by industry in a state or federal court, depending on the issue at stake (although sometimes the industry has a choice about where to sue).

This does not of course mean that industry attacks everything, or that industry wins all of the legal attacks it launches. But business has won what might be thought a surprising number of important cases (as detailed below), and even when industry does not win, its lawyers are often able to use the litigation strategy to impose a substantial delay on the implementation of public health measures.

4.2 Statutory claims: pre-emption case examples

As noted above, pre-emption cases centre on legal arguments that actions of higher levels of government have precluded the targeted (typically stronger) actions of lower levels. The pre-emption claim has been an especially powerful legal tool for the tobacco industry.

Since the 1950s, tobacco companies have been the object of civil actions (tort claims) for money damages by smokers (or their heirs).[4] For years, the tobacco industry mounted vigorous and universally successful defences against these claims.[5] In the 1980s and early 1990s, however, when considerable unflattering information became increasingly available to the public about what the tobacco industry had long known about the dangers of its products,[6] a new round of lawsuits was filed, and some thought these were far more promising.[7] To be sure, going back to 1969, cigarette packages and advertisements contained the nationally required statement: 'Warning: The US Surgeon General Has Determined that Cigarette Smoking Is Dangerous to Your Health'.[8] But a lawsuit filed in New Jersey in 1983 claimed, among other things, that a stronger warning should have been provided, and a jury eventually awarded money damages to the surviving husband of the deceased smoker.[9] When this *Cipollone* case[10] was finally resolved in 1992, however, a divided US Supreme Court decided that state 'failure to warn' tort claims were pre-empted by s 5(b) of the federal cigarette labelling law, which provides: 'No requirement or prohibition based on smoking and health shall be imposed under State law with respect to the advertising or promotion of any cigarettes the packages of which are labeled in conformity with the provisions of this Act'.[11] The court determined that awarding money damages via tort law for the failure to provide a stronger warning amounted to a precluded 'requirement ... based on smoking and health'.

Since then, tobacco companies have invoked this pre-emption language in the *Federal Cigarette Labeling and Advertising Act* ('FCLAA')[12] in a variety of settings. For example, in 1999, the Attorney General of the State of Massachusetts adopted rules that precluded tobacco advertising on billboards located within 1000 feet (about 300 meters) from schools and playgrounds.[13] The purpose of these rules was to protect children from being assaulted by appealing cigarette advertisements when leaving their school grounds, especially when the sale of tobacco products to minors has long been illegal. The tobacco industry challenged these rules, and with respect to cigarette advertising the industry won once again on the ground that this state regulation was pre-empted by the federal law. Specifically, in the 2001 *Lorillard* case, a divided US Supreme Court held that the pre-emption provision applied not merely to advertising *content* restrictions (as Massachusetts had argued) but also to *locational* restrictions, and since the billboard ban was based on concerns about smoking and health (and not just about preventing crime, as Massachusetts had argued), the state rules were struck down.[14]

In 2009, however, Congress enacted an exception to the pre-emption provision that permits some restrictions on promotional activity.[15] This exception states that 'a State or locality may enact statutes and promulgate regulations, based on smoking and health ... imposing specific bans or restrictions on the time, place, and manner, but not content, of the advertising or promotion of any cigarettes'. It was clearly understood that this amendment was meant to overturn this aspect of the *Lorillard* decision.

At that same time, New York City's Board of Health adopted rules that required merchants to place signs in retail stores where tobacco is sold.[16] The signs were to contain one of three vivid graphic warnings about the use of tobacco products, as well as a smoking quit-line phone number. New York City argued that this was a valid restriction on the *sale* of cigarettes, but in 2012 the federal Court of Appeals found that these new signs amounted to the imposition of additional content to the nationally mandated uniform warning. As a result, this regime was said to have added a forbidden additional 'requirement' with respect to the promotion of cigarettes that did not qualify under the recent amendment and therefore was still pre-empted by the FCLAA.[17]

By contrast, the city of Providence, Rhode Island, was recently successful in fending off a pre-emption claim. Hoping to reduce the sale of tobacco use by young people, the city adopted two ordinances that (i) restrict the city's tobacco and cigarette retailers from reducing prices on tobacco products by means of coupons and certain multi-pack discounts and (ii) restrict the sale of certain flavoured tobacco products other than cigarettes.[18] Late in 2013, the federal Court of Appeals upheld these ordinances, concluding that they impose limitations primarily on prices and product features rather than on advertising and promotion.[19]

Turning to the area of unhealthy foods, when New York City sought to require chain restaurants to post on their menus (and menu boards) the number of calories in the meals they offered, this initiative initially also ran into pre-emption problems. The first version of the law applied only to those chains that had already voluntarily made calorie information available (albeit usually not in the prominent way required by the new law).[20] This version was invalidated in 2007 by a federal trial judge[21] on the ground that it was pre-empted by the federal *Nutrition Labeling and Education Act*.[22] The judge's ruling was very technical and perhaps motivated by a sense that the city had unfairly leaned on those firms that had already been more forthcoming with calorie data. He explained how New York City could come into compliance with the federal regime, and it did so by adjusting the menu labelling requirement to apply to all chains with 15 or more stores.[23] This revised version was upheld against a renewed pre-emption challenge by both the original trial judge[24] and, in 2009, the federal Court of Appeals.[25]

The important message here is that federal courts in the US are regularly called upon to interpret somewhat opaque federal legislation and apply its provisions to state and local exercises of their ordinary powers in order to decide whether Congress meant to pre-empt such laws. Although the US Supreme Court often speaks of a 'presumption against pre-emption',[26] lawyers representing industry have been able to convince the courts that a number of important measures that otherwise would be valid are no longer available to lower levels of government. We have also seen that it is at least possible for a higher level of government (namely Congress) to respond to a judicial pre-emption ruling by providing that, regardless of whether or not the courts had interpreted the existing statute correctly, for the future the rules are clearly changed and states and localities can proceed to enact certain sorts of measures if they wish.[27] This sort of 'corrective' change may be made in the field of pre-emption because the legal question is a matter of whether the higher level of government wants to control public health policy concerning the issue. A very different situation applies to objections that industry makes to legislation on the basis of the *United States Constitution*, to which I now turn.

4.3 Constitutional claims: commercial free speech examples

4.3.1 Commercial vs political or artistic speech

In 1976, the US Supreme Court abandoned its prior position (established in *Valentine* in 1942)[28] that the 'free speech' clause of the First Amendment to the *United States Constitution*[29] did not apply to 'pure commercial advertising'. Specifically, in *Virginia Pharmacy*, the court concluded that the First Amendment protected not only individual political speech and artistic speech, but also 'commercial' speech;[30] the court accordingly invalidated a law that prohibited advertising the prices of prescription drugs.[31] In effect, the court used the First Amendment to deal with what is perhaps best seen as a problem of unfair competition (better handled perhaps by changes in antitrust/competition laws). Paving the way for chain pharmacies especially to promote their lower prices, the court concluded that, because listeners have a right to receive information about product prices, price advertisements must be given free speech protection.

To be sure, just as defamatory speech and obscene speech are not protected by the First Amendment, neither is false and misleading advertising. But truthful advertisements, informing consumers about where to buy certain products and for how much money, were brought by the court in *Virginia Pharmacy* within the First Amendment. This sort of speech was not given as complete protection as is given, say, to political speech (as the court later clarified in *Central Hudson* in 1980).[32] Nonetheless, in the years to follow the court has struck down many advertising restrictions as inconsistent with the 'free speech' clause.[33]

4.3.2 Tobacco and alcohol advertising

One important example concerns the effort of the State of Rhode Island to preclude advertisements promoting low-priced alcoholic beverages.[34] Although plausibly justified as a public health measure designed to reduce alcohol consumption, as a practical matter this law was best viewed as a politically successful effort by small local alcohol sellers to ward off competition by large, price-cutting competitors,[35] again something perhaps better dealt with by antitrust laws. But in *44 Liquormart*,[36] this advertising restriction was seen as a free speech issue, and despite a specific provision in the *United States Constitution* giving states special authority to regulate the sale of alcohol,[37] the Rhode Island restriction was invalidated just as other advertising bans had been.

Tobacco advertising on billboards has also been given First Amendment protection. As noted above, in the *Lorillard* case, cigarette advertisers successfully blocked Massachusetts' restrictions on the proximity to schools of tobacco advertising on the ground that such restrictions were pre-empted by the FCLAA. In addition, in the same opinion, the US Supreme Court concluded that tobacco companies also had First Amendment rights to advertise, again focusing on the rights of adults to receive information via billboards about tobacco products.[38] This part of the court's opinion had the effect of invalidating rules that would otherwise have done away with billboard advertisements for cigars, chewing tobacco and other non-cigarette tobacco products in most of the State[39] (since state regulation of those tobacco products was not pre-empted by the national cigarette labelling law).[40] The court noted that, in urban areas, the 1000 foot from school restriction almost entirely precluded billboard advertising, and in light of that interference in the right of adults to receive tobacco advertising, the restriction was too sweeping and hence invalid.[41]

In the same opinion, the court upheld Massachusetts' requirements that cigarettes may not be placed on open shelves for self-service by customers but rather had to be physically obtained from store clerks.[42] The court viewed these measures as largely about the regulation of sales rather than of speech or advertising and promotion and hence not precluded by either the First Amendment or the FCLAA.[43]

4.3.3 Textual and graphic warnings on tobacco products

Seeing the success of First Amendment claims in a variety of contexts, industry lawyers have been quick to make even more aggressive arguments against various government actions, perhaps sensing that the US Supreme Court's conservative justices (or at least some of them) now view the commercial free speech doctrine as a tool for pushing back against all sorts of public regulation – in line with the wider deregulation agenda of their ideological bedfellows in the political process.

For example, in 2009, the US Congress passed a statute calling for nine stronger rotating text warnings to be placed on cigarette packages and ordered the Food and Drug Administration to select graphic images that illustrate those warnings that cigarette companies would also have to display on the packs.[44] This is a strategy that has been used in many other nations including, for example, Australia and Canada.[45] The FDA also interpreted the statute to require that tobacco companies limit themselves to black-and-white text and no colour advertising in their advertisements in most media (sometimes called 'tombstone advertising' provisions),[46] a variation on the 'plain packaging' strategy already employed in Australia.[47] The industry launched legal attacks on both the limits on what it could display in its advertisements and the required graphic images. In line with the earlier decisions noted above, the tombstone advertising limit has been struck down by a federal Court of Appeals as violating the industry's affirmative right to free speech.[48] Moreover, the industry has made at least some headway with its claim that the graphic image requirement violates the so-called 'compelled speech' feature of the First Amendment, as I explain further below.

By way of background, during World War II, some schoolchildren and their parents objected to the requirement that during the school day they had to recite the Pledge of Allegiance to the US government, a pledge that was (and in some places still is) routinely recited in government (public) schools. The text of what children recite technically pledges allegiance to the US flag as a representation of the republican government and ideals for which it stands. Although the objecting families centrally had religious objections to the pledge, the case was presented as a free speech claim. In the resulting *Barnette* case, the US Supreme Court agreed that forcing someone to speak can violate the First Amendment just as a prohibition on speaking can.[49] This, of course, was an example of requiring individual children to recite a political statement with which they did not agree. The compelled speech doctrine was later applied, for example, to a law in the state of Florida that required newspapers to provide free space in the paper for politicians they attack in editorials[50] (a provision purportedly justified on the ground that the press was becoming too powerful in determining which candidates were being elected).[51] In effect, the 'right of reply' law mandated the carrying of a substantial 'letter-to-the-editor' from a political figure the paper had criticised. The US Supreme Court also held this to be unconstitutional compelled speech.[52] Again, this case involved political speech, and the court feared that the Florida requirement would chill the willingness of the press to take political stands in the first place.

Seeing that the commercial speech doctrine could be used to attack bans on advertising, tobacco companies have now attacked, as unconstitutional compelled speech, the requirement that they include the FDA's selection of graphic images.

It appears that nearly everyone in the business sector concedes that government can require product sellers to print government mandated disclosures of facts. Indeed, for this reason tobacco companies have not attacked, and are not likely to attack, the new text warnings that Congress now requires.[53]

Yet, it should be noted that, in other contexts, where the 'facts' are claimed to be controversial, just this sort of attack has been successfully made. For example, in the 1990s, the State of Vermont, in effect, required food retailers to post a notice disclosing which, if any, of the milk it offered for sale came from cows that were treated with a synthetic growth hormone ('rBST'). The FDA at the time had concluded that the milk from cows treated with rBST was no different from traditional milk,[54] but there had been considerable public concern about the use of this new technology, and surveys of Vermont citizens suggested that a good share of the public wished to know whether the milk it was being offered came from cows that were so treated.[55] Yet a divided federal Court of Appeals enjoined the operation of the Vermont law on the ground that consumer curiosity was an insufficient basis for compelling a disclosure that dairy farmers using the treatment did not want retailers to make.[56]

So, too, in 2010, the city of San Francisco adopted an ordinance requiring labels on mobile telephones to disclose the specific amount of electronic radiation they emit, and then later amended the law requiring instead that cell phone sellers generally inform consumers that there may be a risk of harm from cell phone emissions and what consumers might do to reduce that possible risk.[57] But even if citizens might wish to know about this potential danger, since any actual danger is thought to be speculative at this point, both the initial and amended versions were attacked in court, and, after a temporary injunction was granted,[58] the city decided to abandon the litigation and agreed not to enforce the ordinance.[59] Again, industry was successful in using the compelled speech doctrine.

On the other hand, the First Amendment attack on New York City's menu labelling requirement (discussed above),[60] which also raised 'compelled speech' claims, failed when the Court of Appeals concluded that calorie counts were facts that the government clearly had the right to demand that food sellers disclose with their products.[61]

The Vermont and San Francisco decisions seem ironically inconsistent with the original idea underlying the application of the First Amendment's free speech clause to commercial speech: that consumers have a right to receive information. In these decisions, where state or local government is responding to public demand, courts, in effect, are stepping in and effectively precluding consumers from receiving information that many would like to have. Although it is commonly said that the best way to deal with speech you disagree with is to encourage more speech, the judiciary here is behaving paternalistically (or, some might say, it is simply being hostile to regulation): sellers cannot be required to convey information when the alarm raised is of scientific dubiousness and where, as a result, in the court's view, a different branch of government might be misleading the public. Of course, Vermont and San Francisco could rent billboard space or mail flyers to voters expressing the very concerns that motivated the invalidated laws, and that would surely be legal. But it probably makes a substantial difference if government is unable to put the information right in front of consumers just as they are making product purchase decisions.

Returning then to the graphic images the FDA selected to be placed on cigarette packages, the industry complained that these images (unlike the text) do not convey 'facts' but rather are emotional appeals intentionally designed to get people not to smoke (that is, to quit, or not to start, or not to relapse after having previously quit).[62] And while one US Court of Appeals upheld the general power of Congress and the FDA to require graphic images,[63] in 2012 the Court of Appeals for the District of Columbia (by a divided 2–1 vote) later held the specific images selected by the FDA to be unconstitutional compelled speech.[64]

At one point, the majority of the District of Columbia Court says of the graphic images: 'They are unabashed attempts to evoke emotion (and perhaps embarrassment) and browbeat consumers into quitting'.[65] This seems a not unfair appraisal. Yet, later in the opinion, the majority finds that despite the widespread requirement in nations throughout the world that cigarette packs carry such warnings, there is no persuasive evidence that they actually make any significant difference in reducing smoking prevalence rates.[66] And, as a result of that finding, the court concluded that the government could not force tobacco companies to carry messages designed to reduce the sale of its products even if the companies probably had little to worry about in terms of lost sales.[67] (Of course, the companies surely do worry about lost sales, and there is a certain irony here that had the images been shown clearly to work elsewhere in driving down smoking rates, they might well have been upheld.)[68] The FDA so far has chosen not to appeal the matter to the US Supreme Court and instead is currently reconsidering whether there are other graphic images it might require that the Court of Appeals would approve.[69]

There is some reason to doubt the sensibility of this decision on a number of grounds. First, just how do you illustrate graphically the fact that 'cigarettes cause lung cancer' without showing an unattractive picture of a diseased lung next to a healthy one, or that 'cigarettes can kill you' without showing a clearly dead (not sleeping) body, and so on? That such photos appeal to the emotions of the viewers fails to counter the argument that the photos are illustrating facts. Second, in any event, it is ludicrous to say that the text warnings themselves are merely designed to create informed consumers who are to decide for themselves whether or not to smoke. These warnings are required to be placed on the packs and on cigarette advertisements because the public, through government, has decided that smoking is bad and wants to discourage it (without making it formally illegal, other than with respect to sales to teens, given past experience with alcohol prohibition and current experience with marijuana prohibition). Therefore, the fact-emotion distinction seems the wrong way to analyse these issues.

I believe that there is a better way to look at these new text warnings and required graphic images (as well as the disclosures challenged in the Vermont and San Francisco cases discussed above). They should be treated as instances of government requiring business owners to carry a *government* message on their product packaging as a condition of being allowed to sell the product. That is, what is being compelled is the carrying of government speech, and that should be made quite clear if need be (eg 'the US Surgeon General wants you to know that cigarettes cause strokes and heart disease'). Cigarette companies are not compelled to say they believe the message (as were the schoolchildren in the pledge case), and surely no viewer of the package would take the photos at stake in the *RJ Reynolds* case to be messages from the tobacco companies.

The government clearly has the right to convey this view, for example, on billboards, on television, in schools and the like. To be clear, we, through our elected leaders, have the right to say that we want people not to smoke (just as government has the right to tell the public that some people are concerned about rBST in milk and mobile telephone emissions, just as government has the right to encourage people to take public transport instead of driving automobiles and so on).

The legal issue then is to what extent may the public place its view on the products in question? As I see it, this sort of regulatory restriction does not involve the First Amendment so long as it does not preclude the tobacco sellers from also conveying their message (which the graphic image requirement surely does not). To be sure, at the extreme, using up too much of a product's packaging could amount to a 'taking' of property without compensation under the Fifth Amendment of the *United States Constitution*. Indeed, sometimes courts and commentators talk about these matters as government using what might otherwise be viewed as people's private property to serve as a billboard for the government's message. But the legal doctrine in that area of constitutional law (the Fifth Amendment, not the First Amendment) would seem to readily allow the government to claim a substantial portion of one side of the cigarette package for its message without that amounting to a regulatory taking.[70] Whether this view of how to think about the so-called 'compelled commercial speech' cases will ultimately carry the day remains to be seen.[71]

4.3.4 Prohibition on tobacco sales in pharmacies

Turning now to a matter raising a variety of complex constitutional law issues, the city of San Francisco recently adopted an ordinance banning the sale of tobacco in pharmacies.[72] The idea behind the law is that pharmacies are supposed to reflect and promote health, and selling cigarettes is the opposite of that. Philip Morris attacked the law as violating its free speech rights, saying in effect that by offering its products for sale via pharmacies it was engaging in advertising (through the product packs) that is legally protected. This argument was roundly rejected on the ground that the law banned the sale of a product, not advertising.[73]

The San Francisco law initially applied only to stores that were primarily pharmacies[74] and thereby exempted from its reach 'big box' stores such as WalMart, Safeway and the like that included a pharmacy within their premises but where the pharmacy business accounted for only a small share of their revenues. Because of this exemption, the San Francisco law was next challenged by Walgreen, a large pharmacy chain, which protested that it was singled out for regulation when its competitors (or at least some of them) were not. This complaint rested on the Equal Protection clause of the *United States Constitution*. Normally, courts apply only a 'rational basis' test to challenged laws like this,[75] and almost always some rational basis is found for distinctions that are made – after all, Walgreen centrally presents itself as a pharmacy, and WalMart does not. But, surprisingly, a California appeals court at least preliminarily sided with Walgreen.[76] Instead of appealing the legal ruling, San Francisco amended its law to eliminate the big box exception,[77] thereby removing Walgreen's objection.

This caused Safeway then to sue, claiming now that it was penalised in ways that did not apply to other grocery chains that sold cigarettes but did not operate pharmacies within their facilities. While one readily sees the delicate policy choice that San Francisco had to make, one can also see why retailers of tobacco products such as Safeway were unhappy that they could no longer sell cigarettes when some of their competitors could. This time, however, a federal district court applied the normal rational basis test and upheld the distinction between Safeway and other grocery chains in the face of an equal protection challenge.[78] Hence, the measure went into effect, leaving big box stores in San Francisco with the option of either removing tobacco sales or removing pharmacies from their premises.

What seems clear for now is that tobacco, alcohol and unhealthy food companies will be quick to invoke their 'free speech' (and other constitutional) rights whenever they can fashion even a plausible legal challenge to public health regulation; and their position has gained considerable support from the federal courts, not only where government tries to limit anything that could be termed an advertisement, but also when government seeks to have product sellers provide information to would-be buyers. Of course, government, if sufficiently stymied by lawsuits, could, for example, impose ever higher taxes on these products without a serious fear of unconstitutionality. Yet, not only are such taxes politically more difficult to adopt, at least sometimes they are not as carefully targeted in ways that other public health measures might be, albeit measures that are more vulnerable to legal defeat.

4.4 Attacking the scope of legal authority: ultra vires examples

4.4.1 New York City Board of Health: limiting soda sizes

Former New York City Mayor Michael Bloomberg devoted considerable attention during his time in office to promoting a range of public health initiatives, including controls on second hand smoke,[79] eliminating trans fats from restaurant food[80] and requiring calorie counts to be posted on chain restaurant menus.[81] One ongoing target of his has been what he views as, and public health leaders agree is, the American over-consumption of sweetened beverages.[82] He supported ideas such as significantly taxing the purchase of these sodas,[83] and preventing those low income Americans who are given food stamps from using those stamps to buy sugar-sweetened beverages.[84] Neither of these was adopted. Instead, the New York City Board of Health adopted perhaps his most controversial proposal: limiting the portion size of the sale of these beverages by restaurants to 16 ounces (about 500 millilitres).[85] People could buy additional servings and in effect consume as much as they like. But the cup or glass size had to be limited on the theory that most people would not pursue a second serving, and this would in turn reduce consumption in places where the default standard serving absent the law was more than 16 ounces, or often even as much as twice that amount.[86]

Before this measure went into effect, it was attacked on a range of grounds by soda retailers, and as of this writing those attacks have been successful. The trial judge held that this rule was 'arbitrary and capricious' (eg because it applies only to some sweetened beverages and only to some establishments that sell such beverages, while failing to ban 'refills') and therefore is unconstitutional.[87] It is questionable whether a judge should override a justifiable public health measure such as this because of the way the drafters resolved certain policy details. Governments regularly adopt all sorts of arguably right but in the end wrong or meaningless or ineffective laws, and the remedy for this is supposed to be repeal in the political process, not invalidation by the judge.

In addition, the trial judge found that the Board of Health did not have the legal authority to adopt such a rule, in effect concluding (after extensive review of the history of the Board's delegated powers) that it could regulate only with respect to communicable diseases and not NCDs.[88] Such a broad holding threatens not only this policy but other policies that the Board adopted under Mayor Bloomberg's time in office.

The city appealed, and the appeals court, on a narrower basis, affirmed the trial judge's conclusion that because of the way this particular measure was drafted, presented and decided, the 'Board of Health overstepped the boundaries of its lawfully delegated authority'.[89] The city then further appealed the case to New York's highest court, which in October 2013 agreed to decide the matter.[90]

It seems clear that had the City Council adopted the portion size limit, that would have been well within its legal authority. But apparently the Mayor did not have the votes for that, which explains why he instead sought approval and obtained it through the Board of Health, a very special institution in New York City. Hence, while this legal battle, as it now stands, represents an example of a so far successful challenge to an action being beyond the legal power of the enacting body, it is perhaps a special case.

4.4.2 *Food and Drug Administration: regulating tobacco*

The legal strategy used by industry of attacking the scope of legal authority of a regulating body might be better illustrated by tobacco's attack on an effort in the 1990s by the FDA.[91] Prior to that time, it had been largely taken for granted that the FDA did not have jurisdiction over tobacco products.[92] Yet, FDA head Dr David Kessler (who is both a physician and lawyer) finally concluded that it was socially intolerable that the product causing the greatest number of preventable deaths in the nation each year – cigarettes (and related tobacco products) – would remain essentially unregulated by the federal government.[93] Existing federal jurisdiction had been effectively exercised only with respect to cigarette smuggling (and contraband trafficking)[94] and the collection (and evasion) of tobacco taxes.[95]

When Kessler and his lawyers proposed to assert FDA jurisdiction, they first focused on the idea that even if the FDA could not regulate cigarettes directly, it had the right to regulate the nicotine they contained, since nicotine seemed to meet the statutory definition of a 'drug'.[96] Agency officials gathered evidence showing how carefully the tobacco companies mixed the types of tobacco leaves they utilised so as to achieve a targeted level of addictive nicotine in their products. One serious legal hurdle, however, was that if nicotine-carrying cigarettes were viewed as a new product coming onto the 1990s market as a 'drug', they would surely be banned. They clearly are not 'safe' and obviously could not be shown to be so 'effective' in curing some health problem as to be permitted with warnings about their lethal quality.[97] But Kessler did not propose to make future sales illegal. So, he and his lawyers adjusted their legal focus and further claimed that cigarettes were drug-delivery devices, and as 'medical devices' the agency not only had jurisdiction over them but also had more flexibility as to how to regulate them.[98] In 1995, Kessler proposed a medley of regulatory measures through which he hoped the agency could achieve a substantial reduction in smoking rates, especially among youths.[99] Having lost in battle against the FDA in the regulatory process, the tobacco industry attacked this effort in court, and in due course the US Supreme Court sided with industry, as I now explain.

In 2000, in the *Brown and Willliamson* case,[100] the Supreme Court concluded (in a 5–4 vote) that Congress had deliberately intended tobacco products to fall outside the jurisdiction of the FDA,[101] so that this effort by the agency amounted to an illegal overreach and was not entitled to the judicial deference that is frequently given to an agency's interpretation of its authority.[102] Taking a big picture overview of drug and device regulation, the court majority concluded that, if tobacco products were to be regulated under the then existing legal structure, the regulatory solution would be to ban them from the marketplace,[103] something that the FDA had no intention of doing. The court also viewed other statutory measures regulating tobacco, such as the FCLAA, as having been enacted with the understanding that it was Congress, and not the FDA, that was to make tobacco policy for the nation.[104]

Interestingly enough, this regulatory initiative did not go away, and in due course a substantial share of what Kessler proposed was actually adopted by Congress. In 2009, it enacted the *Family Smoking Prevention and Tobacco Control Act* (discussed above), with the result that at least certain sorts of FDA oversight of tobacco products is now the law, but with the proviso that the FDA has no authority to ban them as unsafe.[105]

These two examples – the New York City portion-size limit law and the attempt by the FDA to seize regulatory control of tobacco products – show how the impacted industries will by no means accept new innovative public health initiatives advanced by government, and will vigorously pursue legal avenues to rein in measures that they can convince judges are beyond the existing authority of those adopting them. This experience also shows that legislation by core legislative bodies – Congress, state legislatures and city councils – will not be vulnerable to such challenges in the way that actions by public health bodies such as the FDA and the New York City Board of Health are.

5 Conclusion

This chapter illustrates that various sorts of public health measures aimed at tobacco, alcohol or unhealthy foods that seem quite sensible to the governmental body adopting them may turn out in the US to be invalid. That there is more 'adversarial legalism' in the US than elsewhere is well known.[106] That the big tobacco, alcohol and unhealthy food companies would vigorously fight to protect their interests is hardly a surprise. But this chapter shows what might well be surprising elsewhere – how effective those industries have been, using a variety of legal arguments, in convincing often badly divided courts to come out their way. Many of these outcomes, especially the First Amendment constitutional rights cases, would probably be different in other nations. Yet not only is the US especially wedded to 21st century capitalism, in turn our courts, which seem to some to be increasingly politicised, appear to be generally leery of public health measures that regulate business. Perhaps this is not surprising if many judges start with a strong ideological commitment to the private market, for then public health measures that seek to have widespread population effects that may be characterised as undermining the current preferences of individual consumers immediately become suspect.

Notes

* Many thanks to Aram Boghosian for research assistance.

1 See generally Robert Rabin and Stephen Sugarman (eds), *Regulating Tobacco* (Oxford University Press, 2001).

2 American Lung Association, *State Rankings* (2013) <http://www.stateoftobaccocontrol.org/state-grades/state-rankings/>; Meg Riordan, *Key State-specific Tobacco-related Data & Rankings* (30 July 2013) Campaign for Tobacco-Free Kids <http://www.tobaccofreekids.org/research/factsheets/pdf/0176.pdf>.

3 See, eg, Mark Wolfson, *The Fight Against Big Tobacco: The Movement, the State, and the Public's Health* (Aldine De Gruyter, 2001).

4 Robert Rabin, 'Institutional and Historical Perspectives on Tobacco Tort Liability' in Robert Rabin and Stephen Sugarman (eds), *Smoking Policy: Law, Politics and Culture* (Oxford University Press, 1993) 110, 111.

5 Ibid 111–18.

6 Ibid 118–25.

7 Robert Rabin, 'The Third Wave of Tobacco Tort Litigation' in Rabin and Sugarman, *Regulating Tobacco*, above n 1, 176, 179–85.

8 *The Federal Cigarette Labeling and Advertising Act* ('FCLAA'), enacted in 1965, as amended by the *Public Health Cigarette Smoking Act of 1969*, 15 USC §§ 1331–40 (2012). In 1984, Congress again amended the FCLAA in the *Comprehensive Smoking Education Act*, Pub L No 98-474 (1984), which introduced a scheme of four rotating warnings. More recent amendments are discussed below.

9 *Cipollone v Liggett Group Inc*, 505 US 504, 512 (1992).

10 *Cipollone v Liggett Group Inc*, 505 US 504 (1992).

11 FCLAA § 5(b).

12 See above n 8.

13 940 Code of Mass Regs § 21.01 (2000).

14 *Lorillard v Reilly*, 533 US 525, 551 (2001).

15 *Family Smoking Prevention and Tobacco Control Act*, Pub L No 111-31, § 203 (2009), codified at 15 USC § 1334(c) (2012).

16 NY City Health Code § 181.19.

17 *23-34 94th Grocery Corp v New York City Board of Health*, 685 F 3d 174 (2nd Cir, 2012).

18 Providence, Rhode Island Code of Ordinances §§ 14-303, 14-309.

19 *National Association of Tobacco Outlets Inc v City of Providence Rhode Island*, F 3d (1st Cir, 2013) <http://media.ca1.uscourts.gov/cgi-bin/getopn.pl?OPINION=13-1053P.01A>.

20 Original Regulation 81.50.

21 *New York State Restaurant Association v New York City Board of Health (NYSRA I)*, 509 F Supp 2d 351 (SD NY, 2007).

22 21 USC 343 (q), (r), 343–1 (a) (4), (5).

23 Amended Regulation 81.50.

24 *New York State Restaurant Association v New York City Board of Health (NYSRA II)*, 2008 WL 1752455 (SD NY, 2008).

25 *New York State Restaurant Association v New York City Board of Health*, 556 F 3d 114, 135 (2nd Cir, 2009). For the story of the New York experience and surrounding litigation, see Thomas Farley et al, 'New York City's Fight over Calorie Labeling' (2009) 28 *Health Affairs* 1098.

26 See, eg, *Medtronic Inc v Lohr*, 518 US 470, 485 (1996).

27 See above n 15 and corresponding text.

28 *Valentine v Chrestensen*, 316 US 52 (1942).

29 Government 'shall make no law … abridging the freedom of speech …'.

30 *Virginia State Board of Pharmacy v Virginia Citizens Consumer Council Inc*, 425 US 748 (1976).

31 Va Code Ann § 54-524.35 (1974).

32 *Central Hudson Gas & Electric Corp v Public Service Commission of New York*, 447 US 557 (1980). (Restrictions on commercial speech must be carefully tailored to serve and in fact further very important governmental interests.)

33 For example, the right of lawyers to advertise was upheld in *Bates v State Bar of Arizona*, 433 US 350 (1977).

34 Rhode Island Gen Laws §3-8-7 (1987).

35 In her dissent in *Rhode Island Liquor Stores Assn v Evening Call*, Pub Co, 497 A 2d 331, 342, n 10 (RI 1985), Justice Murray suggested that the advertising ban was motivated, at least in part, by an interest in protecting small retailers from price competition.

36 *44 Liquormart Inc v Rhode Island*, 517 US 484 (1996).

37 *United States Constitution* amend XXI, § 2. This amendment was adopted in 1933 and repealed amend XVIII, which had been ratified in 1919 and, during the interim 14 years, had imposed alcohol prohibition in the US.

38 *Lorillard v Reilly*, 533 US 525, 566 (2001).

39 Ibid 562–3.

40 Ibid 553.

41 Ibid 565.

42 940 Code of Mass Regs §§ 21.04(2)(c)–(d), 22.06(2)(c)–(d) (2000).

43 *Lorillard v Reilly*, 533 US 525, 567–70 (2001).

44 *Family Smoking Prevention and Tobacco Control Act*, Pub L No 111-31, § 2 (2009).

45 See Chapters 16 and 11 of this volume respectively.

46 21 CFR § 1140.32(a).

47 *Tobacco Plain Packaging Act 2011* (Cth). See also Chapter 17 of this volume.

48 *Discount Tobacco City & Lottery Inc v US*, 674 F 3d 509 (6th Cir, 2012).

49 *West Virginia State Board of Education v Barnette*, 319 US 624 (1943).

50 Florida Statute s 104.38 (1973).

51 *Miami Herald Publishing Co v Tornillo*, 418 US 241, 249–50 (1974).

52 *Miami Herald Publishing Co v Tornillo*, 418 US 241 (1974).

53 *Family Smoking Prevention and Tobacco Control Act*, Pub L No 111-31, § 203, amending 15 USC 1333, s 4 (a)(1).

54 *International Dairy Foods Association v Amestoy*, 92 F 3d 67, 69 (1st Cir, 1996).

55 Vt Stat Ann tit 6 § 2754.

56 *International Dairy Foods Association v Amestoy*, 92 F 3d 67 (1st Cir, 1996). In an interesting variation on this theme, 14 years later, a different federal Court of Appeals enjoined the State of Ohio's regulations that sought to restrict voluntary efforts by milk producers to identify their products as being free from rBST, also relying on the First Amendment: *International Dairy Foods Association v Boggs*, 622 F 3d 628 (6th Cir, 2010). In light of more recent research findings, this court panel thought that wanting to know whether your milk came from cows treated with rBST was considerably more than a matter of consumer curiosity. Together, these two milk hormone cases show the courts being quite supportive of private enterprise being able to speak or not speak as it wishes, while being hostile to government interference with those preferences, regardless of whether government seems motivated by a desire to be sure consumers are told about rBST or to dissuade consumers from thinking there is a difference between the two types of milk.

57 On the initial law, see Jesse McKinley, 'San Francisco Passes Cellphone Radiation Law', *New York Times* (online), 15 June 2010 <http://www.nytimes.com/2010/06/16/us/16cell.html>. On the amended law, see Amy Gahran, 'San Francisco Passes Cell Phone Radiation Law, but What's the Risk?' *CNN* (online), 28 July 2011 <http://www.cnn.com/2011/TECH/mobile/07/28/san.francisco.cellphone.law/>.

58 *CTIA – The Wireless Assn v City & Cnty of San Francisco*, 827 F Supp 2d 1054 (ND Cal 2011).

59 For a report on the San Francisco case and the settlement, see Chloe Albanesius, *San Francisco Drops Fight for Cell Phone Radiation Labeling Law* (8 May 2013) PCMag.com <http://www.pcmag.com/article2/0,2817,2418719,00.asp>.

60 See above n 25 and corresponding text.

61 *New York State Restaurant Association v New York City Board of Health*, 556 F 3d 114, 135 (2nd Cir, 2009).

62 *Required Warnings for Cigarette Packages and Advertisements*, 76 Fed Reg 36,628 (22 June 2011) contains objections that the cigarette companies made to the proposed images.

63 *Discount Tobacco City & Lottery Inc v US*, 674 F 3d 509 (6th Cir, 2012).

64 *RJ Reynolds Tobacco Co v Food and Drug Administration*, 696 F 3d 1205 (DC Cir, 2012).

65 Ibid slip op 20 <http://www.cadc.uscourts.gov/internet/opinions.nsf/4C0311C78E B11C5785257A64004EBFB5/$file/11-5332-1391191.pdf>.

66 'FDA has not provided a shred of evidence – much less the "substantial evidence" required by the APA – showing that the graphic warnings will "directly advance" its interest in reducing the number of Americans who smoke': Ibid slip op 25.

67 Ibid slip op 30.

68 Moreover, more recent research has found that the graphic warnings in Canada have had a very substantial impact in lowering smoking rates: Jidong Huang, Frank Chaloupka and Geoffrey Fong, 'Cigarette Graphic Warning Labels and Smoking Prevalence in Canada: A Critical Examination and Reformulation of the FDA Regulatory Impact Analysis' (2013) *Tobacco Control*, published online first 11 November 2013 doi:10.1136/tobaccocontrol-2013-051170.

69 'FDA's Graphic Cigarette Labels Rule Goes Up in Smoke after US Abandons Appeal', *CBSNews* (online), 19 March 2013 <http://www.cbsnews.com/news/fdas-graphic-cigarette-labels-rule-goes-up-in-smoke-after-us-abandons-appeal/>.

70 The US law on 'regulatory takings' is well captured by *Penn Central Transportation Co v City of New York*, 438 US 104 (1978) and *Lingle v Chevron USA Inc*, 544 US 528 (2005).

71 Note that my argument concerning how to deal with government speech applied in the commercial setting would not apply to the Florida 'right of reply' case because, among other things, the message required there is not the government's message (moreover, a newspaper is a special sort of commercial party because the core of its identity is bound up with free speech). Nor would it apply to the 'pledge of allegiance' case, as there the whole point of the school exercise was to require the pupils personally to take the pledge.

72 SF Health Code § 1009.92.

73 *Philip Morris USA v City and County of San Francisco*, 2009 WL 2873765 (Cal, 2009).

74 SF Health Code § 1009.93.

75 See, eg, *People v Hofsheier* (2006) 37 Cal 4th 1185, 1200 [39 Cal Rptr 3d 821, 129 P 3d 29].

76 *Walgreen Co v City and County of San Francisco*, 185 Cal App 4th 424 (Ct App, 2010).

77 In September 2010, the exception contained in the SF Health Code § 1009.93 was repealed.

78 *Safeway Inc v City and County of San Francisco* (ND Cal, No 11-00761 CW, 15 July 2011) <http://www.courthousenews.com/2011/07/19/safeway.pdf>.

79 For information on the *Smoke-Free Air Act of 2002* (NY), see *Smoke-Free Air Act of 2002*, NYC Health <http://www.nyc.gov/html/doh/html/environmental/smoke-free-act.shtml>.

80 NY City Health Code, § 81.08 (2006).

81 Ibid § 81.50.

82 See, eg, Robert Lustig, 'Sugar: The Bitter Truth' (speech delivered for *Current Controversies in Nutrition: Letting Science Be the Guide – Mini Medical School for the Public* presented by UCSF Osher Center for Integrative Medicine, 27 July 2009), University of California Television <http://www.uctv.tv/shows/Sugar-The-Bitter-Truth-16717>.

83 AG Sulzberger, 'Bloomberg Says a Soda Tax "Makes Sense"', *New York Times* (online), 7 March 2010 <http://www.nytimes.com/2010/03/08/nyregion/08soda.html>.

84 Robert Pear, 'Soft Drink Industry Fights Proposed Food Stamps Ban', *New York Times* (online), 29 April 2011 <http://www.nytimes.com/2011/04/30/us/politics/30food.html>.

85 NY City Health Code § 81.63.

86 For the evidence collected and presented by the Department of Health on behalf of the portion size limit, see Susan Kansagra, 'Maximum Size for Sugary Drinks: Proposed Amendment of Article 81 Response to Comments' (13 September 2012) <http://www.nyc.gov/html/doh/downloads/pdf/boh/article81-response-to-comments-ppt.pdf>.

87 *New York Statewide Coalition v New York City Department of Health and Mental Hygiene* (NY Sup Ct, No 653584/12, 11 March 2013) slip op 27 <http://online.wsj.com/public/resources/documents/sodaruling0311.pdf>.

88 Ibid 28.

89 *New York Statewide Coalition of Hispanic Chambers of Commerce v New York City Department of Health and Mental Hygiene* 110 AD 3d 1, 10 (NY Sup Ct, App Div, 30 July 2013) <http://www.nycourts.gov/reporter/3dseries/2013/2013_05505.htm>. The appeals court did not reach the question of whether the Board's action was arbitrary and capricious.

90 'Top NY Court Agrees to Hear Bloomberg's Large Soda Ban Appeal', *Channel 4 New York* (online), 17 October 2013 <http://www.nbcnewyork.com/news/local/Soda-Ban-Sugar-Drink-Mayor-Bloomberg-New-York-City-Ban-Appeal-Court-Judge-228194631.html>.

91 For the story of this battle, see Theodore Ruger, 'FDA v Brown & Williamson and the Norm of Agency Continuity' in William Eskridge, Elizabeth Garrett and Philip Frickey (eds), *Statutory Interpretation Stories* (Foundation Press, 2010) 334.

92 See, eg, *Cigarette Labeling and Advertising – 1965: Hearings on HR 2248 before the House Committee on Interstate and Foreign Commerce*, 89th Cong, 1st sess, 193: '[t]he Food and Drug Administration has no jurisdiction under the Food, Drug, and Cosmetic Act over tobacco, unless it bears drug claims': FDA Deputy Commissioner Rankin.

93 David Kessler, *A Question of Intent: A Great American Battle with a Deadly Industry* (Public Affairs, 2001) 27.

94 For information about current efforts to deal with these issues by the Bureau of Alcohol, Tobacco, Firearms and Explosives, see *Alcohol & Tobacco*, United States Department of Justice <http://www.atf.gov/content/alcohol-and-tobacco>.

95 For information about the collection of tobacco taxes now the responsibility of the Alcohol and Tobacco Tax and Trade Bureau, see *Tobacco Industry*, United States Department of the Treasury <http://www.ttb.gov/tobacco/index.shtml>.

96 Kessler, above n 93, 62–3.

97 21 USC § 393(b)(2) (drugs); 21 USC §§ 360c(a)(1)(A)(i), (B), (C) (devices).

98 *Regulations Restricting the Sale and Distribution of Cigarettes and Smokeless Tobacco Products To Protect Children and Adolescents*, 60 Fed Reg 41314, 41314 (11 August 1995).

99 Ibid.

100 *FDA v Brown and Williamson*, 529 US 120 (2000).

101 Ibid 131–61.

102 See, eg, *Chevron USA Inc v Natural Resources Defense Council Inc*, 467 US 837 (1984).

103 *FDA v Brown and Williamson*, 529 US 120, 131–3 (2000).

104 Ibid 143–59.

105 *Family Smoking Prevention and Tobacco Control Act*, Pub L No 111-31, § 901 (2009).

106 Robert Kagan, *Adversarial Legalism: The American Way of Law* (Harvard University Press, 2001).

11 Canada

Barbara von Tigerstrom

1 Introduction

As in many countries, chronic diseases are leading causes of disability and death in Canada.[1] A significant proportion of this morbidity and mortality can be attributed to the consumption of tobacco, alcohol and unhealthy foods. For example, approximately 17 per cent and 4 per cent of deaths in Canada are attributable to tobacco and alcohol, respectively.[2] Smoking prevalence is gradually decreasing in Canada, but remains at approximately 17 per cent (among those aged 15 years and older).[3] Over the last few decades, Canada has seen increases in total alcohol consumption, rates of high-risk drinking and rates of mortality attributable to alcohol.[4] Meanwhile, more than half of the Canadian population is overweight or obese,[5] putting them at increased risk for diabetes, cardiovascular disease, some cancers and osteoarthritis.[6] Few Canadians meet national recommendations for physical activity or follow nutrition guidelines.[7] The average Canadian consumes 50 per cent more than the recommended daily upper limit of sodium,[8] and 110 grams of sugar daily (about 26 teaspoons), which accounts for more than 20 per cent of daily calories.[9]

2 Overview of the legal framework

The legal framework governing tobacco, alcohol and food products in Canada is shaped by the country's constitutional structure, including the federal/provincial division of powers and constitutionally entrenched rights and freedoms. The *Constitution Act 1867* assigns jurisdiction over listed matters to either the federal government or the ten provincial governments.[10] Federal powers relevant to public health include trade and commerce, quarantine and criminal law; the federal government also has jurisdiction to legislate for the 'Peace, Order and good Government of Canada' in matters not assigned to provincial jurisdiction.[11] The provincial governments have powers over: hospitals; municipal institutions (to which they also delegate powers); 'Shop, Saloon, Tavern… and other Licences'; 'Property and Civil Rights in the Province'; and 'Generally all Matters of a merely local or private Nature in the Province'.[12] In addition to the ten provinces, there are three territories (Yukon, Northwest Territories and Nunavut), which exercise powers delegated by the federal government that are generally equivalent to those of the provinces, though unlike the provinces, they are given specific authority over 'intoxicants'.[13]

The *Canadian Charter of Rights and Freedoms* ('*Charter*'), enshrined in the *Constitution Act 1982*, sets out constitutionally protected rights and freedoms.[14] All of these are subject to 'such reasonable limits prescribed by law as can be demonstrably justified in a free and democratic society'.[15] The *Charter* applies to all levels and parts of government in Canada, and laws that are inconsistent with it are of no force and effect.[16] The *Constitution Act 1982* also recognises and affirms 'existing aboriginal and treaty rights of the aboriginal peoples of Canada'.[17]

2.1 Tobacco

Tobacco legislation exists at all three levels of government in Canada: federal, provincial/territorial and municipal. The federal *Tobacco Act* and its regulations deal with product standards and information, sale of tobacco products, labelling and packaging and restrictions on advertising and promotion.[18] This Act was amended in 2009 to prohibit the use of additives, including flavours, in the manufacture of tobacco products, with some exceptions, including menthol.[19] The *Non-Smokers' Health Act* bans smoking in federally regulated workplaces,[20] and provincial laws typically now ban smoking in workplaces and most public places.[21] In some cities, municipal smoking bans also apply and in some cases are stricter than provincial laws.[22] Provincial and territorial laws also deal with many of the same matters as federal legislation, including marketing and sales to minors. Most jurisdictions within Canada also prohibit the sale of tobacco products in certain locations, such as schools, health care and child care facilities and pharmacies.[23]

Both federal and provincial/territorial legislation affects the price of tobacco products. Federal excise legislation provides for taxes and customs duties,[24] and provincial/territorial legislation imposes additional taxes.[25] In some parts of Canada, dealers are specifically prohibited from advertising or otherwise stating that they will absorb or refund the tax payable.[26]

2.2 Alcohol

The regulation of alcohol has a long and complex history in Canada, influenced by the country's constitutional structure as well as social and political forces. Like some other countries, Canada moved from a period of minimal regulation to increasing restrictions, including periods of prohibition at the local, provincial and national level.[27] By the 1920s, however, prohibition had been repealed in most parts of the country;[28] the only remaining nationwide prohibition was on the sale of alcohol to 'Indians' (Aboriginal people), which survived until 1951.[29] Prohibition was replaced by a model of government control, which included a governmental monopoly on retail sales and strict controls on drinking establishments, all administered by a provincial administrative body aimed at encouraging moderation in the consumption of alcohol.[30] Though restrictions have been loosened considerably, the key elements of the government control model can still be seen in the current law.

Federal and provincial statutes work together to give provincial governments a monopoly on the sale of liquor (including beer, wine and spirits). A federal statute prohibits the importation of liquor into a province unless it is purchased on behalf of and consigned to the government of the province.[31] Provincial liquor control legislation then defines the powers of the relevant government body (eg board, commission or corporation), including the authority to sell and control the sale of liquor and to establish and operate government stores for the sale of liquor to the public.[32] They also prohibit any other person from selling liquor except under licence.[33] Through licensing, provincial governments are able to control matters such as entertainment or activities in licensed establishments[34] and hours of sale.[35] Provincial governments also establish the legal drinking age for the province[36] and prohibitions on consumption in specific places (eg in a public place[37] or vehicle[38]). As will be discussed further below, alcohol advertising is affected by both federal and provincial legislation.

There are three main legislative mechanisms that influence the price of alcoholic beverages in Canada: taxes, minimum prices and price markups. Taxes are imposed by both the federal government, in the form of excise taxes and customs duties,[39] and provincial governments, in the form of a consumption or sales tax.[40] In addition, the government monopoly allows the liquor boards to set the 'markup' at which alcoholic beverage products will be sold to licensed establishments or retailers and the minimum prices at which alcohol will be sold by government liquor stores, retailers or licensed establishments.[41] Canada has considerable experience with minimum price policies,[42] and thus can serve as a useful example for other jurisdictions considering such policies.

2.3 Food

The legal landscape with respect to food is largely dominated by federal legislation. The *Food and Drugs Act* and its regulations deal with food safety, standards, labelling and advertising.[43] The federal *Consumer Packaging and Labelling Act* also applies to food.[44] Oversight of these regulations is the responsibility of Health Canada and the Canadian Food Inspection Agency.

The federal and provincial governments share concurrent jurisdiction over agriculture,[45] under which they administer schemes relating to the production and marketing of agricultural products. There are also some examples of provincial legislation relevant to unhealthy foods. For example, the province of British Columbia adopted regulations in 2009 that limit the amount of trans fat in foods sold in food service establishments,[46] and a few other provinces impose similar restrictions for foods provided or sold in schools.[47] Several groups have called for the federal government to regulate trans fat and sodium content,[48] but to date the government has preferred a voluntary approach.[49]

As this brief summary shows, many of the same strategies have been applied to tobacco, alcohol and food, respectively, adapted to take account of the particular characteristics of each type of product. The remainder of this chapter will explore in greater detail restrictions on labelling and marketing of these three product types. The debate and litigation surrounding these laws illustrate some of the key issues involved in legal strategies targeting risk factors for chronic disease.

3 Regulation of labelling and marketing

Among the regulatory strategies that can be used to discourage consumption of unhealthy products are restricting the marketing of those products and requiring labels that provide consumers with accurate information and influence their choices. Federal and provincial legislation in Canada implements these strategies in relation to all three categories of products (tobacco, alcohol and food), though not to the same extent. The industries affected by these laws have resisted and challenged them, often on constitutional grounds. These challenges, and governments' responses to and anticipation of them, have played a significant role in shaping the current framework, and at the same time, have highlighted some important issues in public health regulation.

3.1 Tobacco

The labelling and marketing of tobacco products are regulated by both federal and provincial law. Canada was the first country to require large, graphic warning labels on cigarette packages, now covering 75 per cent of the principal display surface of cigarette packages.[50] Federal regulations ban the use of the terms 'light' and 'mild', and variations thereof, on packaging or in promotion of tobacco products.[51] Canada has yet to introduce plain packaging legislation, despite renewed calls from public health advocates.[52]

The federal *Tobacco Act*[53] sets out restrictions on promotion. Its predecessor, the *Tobacco Products Control Act*,[54] contained a broad prohibition on marketing of tobacco products, which was held by a 1995 decision of the Supreme Court of Canada (discussed below) to be an unjustified infringement of freedom of expression.[55] The current legislation allows limited exceptions, for example for information or brand preference advertising to adults.[56] Any advertising 'that could be construed on reasonable grounds to be appealing to young persons' or 'lifestyle advertising' is prohibited.[57] 'Lifestyle advertising' is defined as 'advertising that associates a product with, or evokes a positive or negative emotion about or image of, a way of life such as one that includes glamour, recreation, excitement, vitality, risk or daring'.[58] Specific types of promotions, such as endorsements, sponsorships, use of tobacco brand or manufacturer names on sporting or cultural facilities, and sales promotions including gifts or contests, are also prohibited.[59] Finally, the Act prohibits promotion by any means that are 'false, misleading or deceptive or that are likely to create a false impression about the characteristics, health effects or health hazards of the tobacco product or its emissions'.[60] This legislation was the subject of a new constitutional challenge but was upheld in a 2007 decision of the Supreme Court of Canada (also discussed below).[61]

Provincial laws supplement the federal legislation; these laws generally duplicate the federal prohibitions, but in some respects are more restrictive. For example, retail displays of tobacco products are permitted under the federal *Tobacco Act*,[62] but are prohibited or restricted by the statutes of most provinces and territories.[63]

3.2 *Alcohol*

There are some federal regulations that govern the labelling of alcoholic beverages. For example, the *Food and Drug Regulations* set out product standards for various types of alcoholic beverages, which must be met in order for the name (eg, 'Irish Whisky' or 'Brandy') to be used.[64] The regulations also require any beverage containing more than 1.1 per cent alcohol by volume to show the percentage of alcohol on the label.[65] However, unlike tobacco products, alcoholic beverages are not required by Canadian federal law to carry warning labels, even though many other countries have this requirement, and it has been repeatedly recommended in Canada.[66] Federal bills to require warning labels have been introduced a number of times, but none has ever passed. Two northern territories (Yukon and the Northwest Territories) place labels on alcoholic beverage containers warning of the risks of drinking alcohol during pregnancy, but there is no specific territorial legislation requiring this.[67] Some provinces have legislation that requires a warning sign to be posted in liquor stores or establishments that serve alcohol.[68]

The post-prohibition era of government control included bans or restrictions on advertising of alcoholic beverages,[69] and marketing of alcohol is still regulated by both federal and provincial governments, though not as strictly as for tobacco. Federal radio and television broadcasting legislation prohibits licensees from broadcasting advertisements that are 'designed to promote the general consumption of alcoholic beverages'[70] but allows 'industry, public service or brand preference advertising'.[71] The regulations previously included a restriction on who can sponsor alcoholic beverage advertisements (only producers), but this was removed in 1997,[72] despite concerns that this might increase the total amount of alcohol advertising, but noting that the restriction might be successfully challenged under the *Charter of Rights and Freedoms* as a violation of freedom of expression.[73]

Federal regulations also require compliance with the Code for Broadcast Advertising of Alcoholic Beverages, adopted by the Canadian Radio-television and Telecommunications Commission ('CRTC'), a federal administrative agency. The Code's provisions show a specific concern with preventing encouragement of youth or under-age drinking. For example, advertisements are not permitted to be directed to persons under the legal drinking age or to encourage them to drink or purchase alcoholic beverages. They are also prohibited from associating alcoholic beverages with symbols or activities that would be attractive to persons under the legal drinking age or persons, characters or groups that would be seen as role models for minors. The Code also contains provisions directed at high-risk drinking, by prohibiting the encouragement of or association with compulsive or abusive drinking, or drinking in the context of dangerous activities.

Although federal regulations prohibit licensed broadcasters from broadcasting advertisements that do not comply with the Code,[74] the CRTC does not directly enforce compliance. Any public complaints about advertising are directed to Advertising Standards Canada ('ASC'), an industry self-regulatory body.[75] Mandatory preclearance by the CRTC was required until 1996,[76] but the ASC now conducts voluntary preclearance of alcoholic beverage advertisements under the CRTC Code and some provincial regulations.[77]

Some provincial and territorial governments adopt the federal Code,[78] while others have their own regulations,[79] policies[80] or requirements for board approval.[81] Many of the restrictions are similar to each other and to the federal Code, including prohibitions on advertisements depicting, directed at or appealing to young people; encouraging excessive or dangerous consumption; or suggesting that consumption of alcohol is needed or desirable for personal or social success, or to resolve social, physical or personal problems.

Unfortunately, none of the domestic attempts to regulate advertising, whether at the federal or provincial/territorial level, have any effect on content originating in other countries, particularly the United States. Enforcement of advertising restrictions has long been a problem, due to the prevalence of broadcast and print material from the United States in the Canadian market.[82] Widespread access to the internet and international satellite television has only exacerbated this problem.

3.3 Food

Food labelling is regulated in several respects by federal legislation. Nutrition labelling is mandatory for packaged foods,[83] and federal regulations set conditions for the use of nutrient content and health claims.[84] The *Food and Drugs Act* prohibits representing any food, in an advertisement or label, as a 'treatment, preventative or cure for any of the diseases, disorders or abnormal physical states referred to in Schedule A', which include obesity, diabetes and heart disease.[85]

It has been suggested that some form of nutrition disclosure should be extended to restaurant and other non-packaged foods, along the lines of the menu labelling legislation now in place in the United States.[86] Several bills to this effect have been introduced in Canada, but none has yet been passed.[87] The Canadian Restaurant and Foodservices Association promotes a voluntary nutrition information program.[88] There is also some support for the introduction of a consistent front-of-package labelling framework that would be easier for consumers to use and reduce confusion from the multiplicity of industry labelling schemes.[89] To date no regulations to implement this recommendation have been developed, though it is possible that recent consideration of front-of-package labelling schemes in the United States might have some influence in Canada.[90] Recently, the Ontario Medical Association called for graphic warning labels, similar to those on cigarette packages, to be placed on soft drinks and 'other high calorie foods with little to no nutritional value'.[91]

There are no specific advertising restrictions for food products that parallel those for tobacco and alcohol. Food and beverage advertising is subject to general prohibitions on false, misleading or deceptive promotion, as well as regulations on use of names and health and nutrient content claims that also apply to labelling.[92] ASC does preclearance review for food and non-alcoholic beverage advertising to check for compliance with federal regulations; as for alcohol, responsibility for preclearance was transferred from the government to ASC in the 1990s.[93]

In Canada, as in other countries, marketing of unhealthy foods and beverages to children and young people is a significant concern. The province of Quebec is unique in having a legislative prohibition against commercial advertising directed at children under the age of 13, subject to some limited exceptions.[94] Even exempt advertisements may not 'directly incite a child to buy or urge another person to buy' a product, use animated cartoons or suggest that the product will give the child 'a physical, social or psychological advantage'.[95] Though this legislation applies to all commercial advertising, it is of special interest in the context of food and beverage advertising given concerns about the impact of marketing unhealthy products to children. The law was challenged as an infringement on freedom of expression, but the Supreme Court of Canada held the infringement was justified.[96]

In the rest of Canada, there is no specific legislation that restricts advertising directed at children, though some bills to that effect have been introduced.[97] Industry codes, such as the general Code of Advertising Standards and a specific Broadcast Code for Advertising to Children, set out guidelines that are similar in some respects to the restrictions in the Quebec law.[98] The Canadian Children's Food & Beverage Advertising Initiative is a voluntary industry initiative that was developed in 2007 and is overseen by Advertising Standards Canada.[99] Participants in the initiative make commitments based on five core principles relating to the type of products advertised and marketing methods.[100] Many large food and beverage companies, including Coca-Cola, PepsiCo, Kraft Canada, McDonald's and Nestle, are part of this initiative.[101] As a voluntary initiative, it has no enforcement authority or mechanism, but Advertising Standards Canada monitors compliance and publishes annual reports.[102]

4 Discussion

Two main themes emerge from this review of the Canadian legal framework and in particular the laws and policies on labelling and marketing: the interplay between regulatory and voluntary or self-regulatory approaches, and the impact of the Constitution on legislative options. These dynamics play out somewhat differently in relation to tobacco, alcohol and unhealthy food.

4.1 Government regulation or voluntary industry initiatives

The choice between mandatory regulations and voluntary measures is a common theme in discussions of strategies to prevent non-communicable diseases.[103] Debates about regulatory or voluntary approaches have been prominent in the context of food product regulation in Canada (for example in relation to trans fats or sodium, as mentioned above),[104] as well as in the marketing context. In the case of tobacco, violations of the labelling requirements or marketing restrictions are defined as offences, punishable by fines or even terms of imprisonment.[105] However, in the case of alcohol or food and beverage advertising, both mandatory and voluntary restrictions are now monitored primarily by an industry self-regulatory body, ASC, which has no enforcement authority. The regulations concerning advertising of alcoholic beverages are indirectly enforceable in the sense that compliance by broadcasters could affect their licensing, but in practice, the CRTC has stepped away from its enforcement role and leaves monitoring to ASC. The lack of mandatory pre-screening and weak monitoring mechanisms have been criticised as deficiencies in this framework.[106] The existence of overlapping provincial and territorial regulations may mitigate some of these concerns, to a degree: some require board approval,[107] which could act as a mandatory pre-screening mechanism. However, these are not consistent across the country and it is unclear how effective any of the enforcement mechanisms are.

The role of industry self-regulation is even more prominent in relation to food and beverage marketing, where the scope of restrictions that are enforceable even in theory is much narrower. With the exception of the restrictions on advertising to children in Quebec, the landscape is dominated by industry-led initiatives, including voluntary programs on restaurant nutrition disclosure, manufacturers' front-of-package labelling schemes and voluntary advertising guidelines. Most controversially, each of these allows food and beverage manufacturers to define the standards and criteria that will be applied in these initiatives. For example, when a company pledges to advertise only 'better-for-you' products to children as part of the Canadian Children's Food and Beverage Advertising Initiative, that company can determine what it considers a 'better-for-you' product.[108] Since the companies themselves are setting the terms of their own commitments, it is not clear whether 'excellent'[109] compliance actually represents meaningful progress. The latest report on this initiative notes that participants are exploring the possibility of 'developing uniform nutrition criteria for the program';[110] this would be a step in the right direction, but food and beverage companies would still be setting the criteria.

4.2 Constitutional issues

Where governments in Canada establish mandatory regulations on tobacco, alcohol and food marketing, these efforts must respect constitutional constraints relating to both jurisdiction and protection of fundamental rights and freedoms. The coexistence of federal and provincial legislation regarding tobacco and alcohol has given rise to a series of legal challenges contesting either level of government's jurisdiction to enact various measures. Indeed, alcohol regulation was central to many important early decisions interpreting the division of powers in Canada's federal system.[111] More recently, challenges to legislation on tobacco and food have come before the courts.

4.2.1 Division of powers

As explained above, the Canadian constitution does not specifically allocate juris-diction over health to either level of government. The federal government has often relied on its criminal law power to legislate with respect to potential health threats. The criminal law power is broad, but two essential conditions must be met for its use: the law must take the form of a prohibition (backed by a penalty) and it must have a valid criminal law purpose, which has long been interpreted to include the protection of health.[112] Cases challenging tobacco and food laws have illuminated the boundaries of these requirements.

For example, in *RJR-MacDonald*, the tobacco companies had successfully argued in a lower court that the federal tobacco legislation fell outside the federal govern-ment's competence because 'it was not addressed directly to the "evil" against which it was purportedly aimed', but rather sought to regulate advertising and promotion.[113] The Supreme Court of Canada rejected this line of argument and found that the purpose of the legislation was clearly the protection of Canadians' health from the effects of tobacco consumption.[114] Given the extensive evidence of serious harm caused by tobacco consumption, there was no question that this was a valid use of the criminal law power.[115] The law was structured as a series of prohibitions with penal sanctions and the reason that it prohibited advertising and promotion of tobacco products rather than their consumption was simply that the latter was not a practical policy option.[116] This was a difference in form, rather than substance, which did not invalidate the legislation.[117] Furthermore, legislation could be valid as an exercise of the criminal law power even if it allowed exemptions from some prohibitions.[118] The decision provided important confirmation that under the criminal law power, 'Parliament may use indirect or intermediate forms of regulation to address public health hazards where more direct or drastic measures are not feasible'.[119]

By contrast, in an earlier case, federal provisions on the labelling of beer were held to be outside the jurisdiction of the federal government, because they lacked a legitimate public health purpose.[120] The legislation prescribed a standard for 'light' beer (beer with an alcohol content between 1.2 and 2.6 per cent) and pro-hibited products from being labelled or advertised in a way that they would be likely to be mistaken for light beer unless they met that standard.[121] The appellant company marketed a brand of beer called 'Special Lite' with an alcohol content of 4 per cent. The majority of the Supreme Court of Canada found that this would violate the legislation, but that the regulation prescribing the standard for light beer was outside the federal government's criminal law jurisdiction.[122] Preventing deception could be a valid criminal law purpose, so the prohibition on mislabel-ling itself was not problematic, but this purpose did not extend to setting detailed standards for particular classes of product.[123] In the view of the majority, there was no legitimate health purpose – unlike in some of the regulation's provisions dealing with adulteration of food and beverage products – because the products (beer and malt liquors) were not hazardous to health.[124]

The approach taken by the majority in this case casts some doubt on the federal government's ability to regulate food and beverage products and their labelling, apart from food safety in a narrow sense (freedom from disease and contamination).[125] More than three decades later, one might hope the court would not dismiss so quickly the idea that alcoholic beverages are hazardous to health. However, it is still not obvious that setting standards for products and specifying how they are to be labelled are necessarily directed at protecting health rather than regulating the food and beverage industry more generally, which is beyond federal competence. One might even ask whether nutrition labelling, which might better be characterised as promoting healthy choices than preventing health hazards per se, could be upheld under the federal criminal law power if challenged.[126] The *RJR-MacDonald* decision shows that the court is willing to support use of the criminal law power to discourage consumption of products like tobacco that are clearly hazardous, but where the risks are more relative it is less clear how far the scope of jurisdiction will extend.

Another important aspect of the federal system is the way in which the courts define the relationship between overlapping federal and provincial legislation. For example, the provision prohibiting tobacco retail displays in the province of Saskatchewan[127] was challenged on the basis that it conflicted with federal legislation, which expressly permits retail displays, and was therefore invalid under the constitutional doctrine of federal paramountcy. The Supreme Court of Canada held, however, that a true conflict – which is a prerequisite for the application of the paramountcy doctrine – did not exist in this case, since it was possible to comply with both laws by respecting the stricter of the two statutes.[128] This approach to federal paramountcy is helpful to public health laws because it allows stricter local laws to coexist with federal legislation, increasing the level of protection for at least part of the population,[129] and contributing to the progressive development of public health regulatory strategies.

4.2.2 Canadian Charter of Rights and Freedoms

Among the legal strategies targeting tobacco, alcohol and food as risk factors for non-communicable diseases, labelling and marketing regulation is most likely to raise *Charter* issues because it involves potential interference with freedom of expression, which is protected by s 2(b) of the *Charter*. Several of the laws discussed above have been challenged as violations of freedom of expression, and even the possibility of a challenge has had a chilling effect in other cases, for example in relation to restrictions on alcohol advertising.[130]

Corporations can claim the benefit of freedom of expression under the *Charter*, and commercial speech is protected as a form of expression.[131] Unlike in American jurisprudence,[132] there is no distinct test to be applied to limits on commercial expression, but the nature of the expression and its value may affect a court's judgment as to what is a reasonable limit under s 1 of the *Charter*.[133] Any law that has the purpose or effect of restricting commercial expression such as advertising will infringe s 2(b).[134] The right to freedom of expression includes 'the right to say nothing or the right not to say certain things'.[135] Compelled speech, including mandatory labelling, may infringe freedom of expression if the speaker would be publicly identified with the message and has no opportunity to disavow its content.[136] Thus, the majority in *RJR-MacDonald* held that s 2(b) was infringed by the federal law requiring unattributed health warnings on tobacco product packages while also restricting other information that could be printed on packages.[137] When the new law requiring larger warnings but allowing them to be attributed to Health Canada came before the Supreme Court in *JTI-Macdonald*, it was less obvious that a s 2(b) infringement would be found, since the attribution could allow manufacturers to distance themselves from the messages, and they were less restricted in what they could print on the rest of the package.[138] However, the court concluded that freedom of expression was infringed, noting the broad scope usually given to its interpretation and the fact that the size of the mandatory warnings (then 50 per cent of the package surface) 'arguably rises to the level of interfering with how [the manufacturers] choose to express themselves'.[139] These cases suggest that mandatory warning labels on their own might or might not be considered infringements of s 2(b), depending on their size, content and attribution, while any direct restrictions on a company's ability to express its own messages through labelling or advertising will almost certainly infringe.

The crux of the matter then becomes – as it does in most freedom of expression cases – whether the infringement can be justified as a reasonable limit under s 1 of the *Charter*. The government bears the burden of proving, on a civil standard, that the infringement is justified according to the established test.[140] This test first examines whether the infringing law has a pressing and substantial objective.[141] Public health and consumer protection have generally been uncontroversial as pressing and substantial objectives.[142]

The second question in the test for s 1 justification is whether the infringement is proportionate to the law's objective. This proportionality analysis itself has three parts, requiring the court to consider whether there is a rational connection between the impugned provisions and their objective, whether the law minimally impairs the right, and whether the deleterious effects of the law outweigh its beneficial effects.[143] It can be difficult for a government to bring sufficient evidence to satisfy this test, particularly given the challenges associated with measuring the effectiveness of public health interventions.[144] The minimal impairment analysis, which requires the government to demonstrate that the law infringes rights as little as reasonably possible compared to available alternatives, can be especially problematic. In *RJR-MacDonald*, the judges of the Supreme Court of Canada recognised these difficulties, and accepted that conclusive scientific evidence should not necessarily be required.[145] Having said that, the majority and dissenting judgments seem to reflect different perceptions of what evidence would be sufficient to justify the tobacco marketing ban. The dissenting judgment, which would have upheld the law, asked whether there was a rational basis for Parliament's choice, and reviewed a substantial body of evidence, including industry documents and expert reports, that supported the government's position. The majority, however, criticised the government for submitting insufficient evidence to satisfy its burden under s 1. The majority seems to have drawn an adverse inference against the government based on its decision to invoke Cabinet privilege and not disclose documents regarding the consideration of alternatives to an advertising ban.[146]

The contrast between this decision and the later challenge to federal tobacco legislation in *JTI-Macdonald* is striking. Whereas *RJR-MacDonald* was a long and divided decision, *JTI-Macdonald* was unanimous and relatively brief; the scepticism that seemed to be directed towards the government's arguments in the earlier case was later turned on the tobacco manufacturers' position. In a noteworthy example of the dialogue between Parliament and the courts, the Supreme Court rejected an argument by the tobacco companies that the new federal law should again be struck down because it did not 'comply' with the court's decision in *RJR-MacDonald*. Instead, the court accepted the contrary argument that changes in context and evidence should be considered in evaluating the justification for the new, comprehensive advertising restrictions.[147] These changes included a better understanding of the impact of tobacco and tobacco marketing strategies and the adoption and ratification of the *WHO Framework Convention on Tobacco Control*,[148] which calls for a comprehensive ban on promotion.[149]

The new federal tobacco legislation was described by the court as 'more restrained and nuanced than its predecessor ... a genuine attempt by Parliament to craft controls on advertising and promotion that would meet its objectives as well as the concerns expressed by the majority of this court in *RJR*'.[150] Just as important as the change in the law, though, was the evidentiary record in *JTI* and the court's response to it.[151] The judgment refers to 'detailed and copious evidence' brought by government in support of the legislation.[152] Information about tobacco marketing strategies undermined the tobacco companies' position and supported the government's argument that more comprehensive restrictions were indeed necessary. Discussing the ban on tobacco advertising that could be appealing to young people, for example, the judgment states:

> Given the sophistication and subtlety of tobacco advertising practices in the past, as demonstrated by the record in this case, Parliament cannot be said to have gone farther than necessary in blocking advertising that might influence young persons to start smoking.[153]

The *JTI* decision was clearly an important victory for government regulation of tobacco marketing, though not an unqualified one, since some sections were upheld only based on narrower readings of them than would be ideal from a public health perspective.[154] Furthermore, it is not necessarily a reliable indicator of how courts might respond in future cases where such extensive and overwhelming evidence of the negative health impacts and manipulative industry conduct may not be available. Where it is less obvious that drastic measures are called for, the government will need to bring forward evidence to prove minimal impairment, including evidence of the relative effectiveness of different potential strategies. This will be particularly challenging when the harms associated with the product (eg, certain food or beverage products) or the impact of various policy options (eg, nutrition labelling, warning labels or advertising restrictions) are less clear.

5 Conclusion

The issues raised in the context of advertising and labelling regulation provide useful illustrations of the recurring questions that arise in chronic disease prevention about the role and limits of government intervention. Constitutional rights and more nebulous – but nonetheless important – ideas about consumer autonomy and free markets come into play when government intervention to curb consumption of unhealthy products is proposed. The limits on government action are often as much political (eg, a preference for industry self-regulation) as legal (eg, limits on jurisdiction). As has been observed in the context of alcohol policy, 'policies with the least evidence of effectiveness (eg, public awareness campaigns, alcohol education in schools) attract the greatest public support'[155] while other more effective policies are less popular. At the same time, evidence of effectiveness clearly *is* important in legal debates, for example when a court is required to determine whether a regulation is a reasonable limit on a constitutionally protected right. The complexities of assessing the potential public health impact of policies targeting unhealthy products will be an increasing challenge for legislators and judges alike, mirrored by the challenge for public health researchers to generate, analyse and explain the evidence to be used in these assessments.

It is difficult to draw clear conclusions from comparing the laws on product types that are very different in some respects. However, there are clear parallels between the strategies that have been used to discourage consumption of tobacco, alcohol and unhealthy foods, and comparing the legal frameworks for each reveals some gaps and opportunities to strengthen Canada's efforts to address these risk factors. Since foods and (non-alcoholic) beverages are the most diverse category, regulating them in a way that will encourage healthier consumer habits is particularly challenging. Some important opportunities include stronger labelling regulations and mandatory, enforceable restrictions on advertising, especially to children. Industry resistance and an apparent preference by the current federal government for voluntary approaches are among the barriers to further development of these strategies, however. With alcohol consumption, high-risk drinking and mortality associated with alcohol consumption all on the rise in Canada, the relative weakness of some branches of alcohol policy is a particular concern. In most respects, the regulations on alcohol are weaker than those on tobacco, and seem to be lagging behind other jurisdictions. Key areas to target would be warning labels and stronger enforcement of advertising restrictions. Existing *Charter* jurisprudence indicates that Canadian governments have not taken full advantage of the regulatory space available to them in relation to food and alcohol. Finally, although tobacco regulation is already the strictest and most comprehensive of the three areas and in many respects serves as a model, with smoking prevalence rates still at almost one in five Canadians, there is a pressing need to develop new strategies for tobacco control or ways of making existing strategies more effective.[156] All of these efforts will best be undertaken together with other jurisdictions, learning from others' initiatives and collaborating to address global enforcement challenges.

Notes

1 Statistics Canada, *Leading Causes of Death in Canada, 2009: Highlights* (2012) <http://www.statcan.gc.ca/pub/84-215-x/2012001/hl-fs-eng.htm>.
2 Jayadeep Patra et al, 'Substance-attributable Morbidity and Mortality Changes to Canada's Epidemiological Profile' (2007) 98 *Canadian Journal of Public Health* 228, 232.
3 Health Canada, *Canadian Tobacco Use Monitoring Survey (CTUMS) 2011* (17 September 2012) <http://www.hc-sc.gc.ca/hc-ps/tobac-tabac/research-recherche/stat/ctums-esutc_2011-eng.php>.
4 Catherine Paradis, Andrée Demers and Elyse Picard, 'Alcohol Consumption: A Different Kind of Canadian Mosaic' (2010) 101 *Canadian Journal of Public Health* 275, 275; Patra et al, above n 2, 231.
5 Public Health Agency of Canada and Canadian Institute for Health Information, *Obesity in Canada* (Public Health Agency of Canada and Canadian Institute for Health Information, 2011), 4 <http://www.phac-aspc.gc.ca/hp-ps/hl-mvs/oic-oac/assets/pdf/oic-oac-eng.pdf>.
6 AH Anis et al, 'Obesity and Overweight in Canada: An Updated Cost-of-illness Study' (2010) 11(1) *Obesity Reviews* 31.
7 Rachel Colley et al, 'Physical Activity of Canadian Children and Youth: Accelerometer Results from the 2007 to 2009 Canadian Health Measures Survey' (2011) 22(1) *Health Reports* 15; Didier Garriguet, 'Canadians' Eating Habits' (2007) 18(2) *Health Reports* 17.
8 Health Canada, *Sodium* (June 2012) <http://www.hc-sc.gc.ca/hl-vs/alt_formats/pdf/iyh-vsv/food-aliment/sodium-eng.pdf>.
9 Kellie Langlois and Didier Garriguet, 'Sugar Consumption among Canadians of All Ages' (2011) 22(3) *Health Reports* 1, 1, 3.
10 *Constitution Act 1867* (Imp), 30 & 31 Vict, c 3, ss 91, 92 ('*Constitution Act 1867*').
11 Ibid s 91.
12 Ibid s 92.
13 See *Northwest Territories Act*, RSC 1985, c N-27, s 16(p); *Nunavut Act*, SC 1993, c 28, 23(p); *Yukon Act*, SC 2002, c 7, s 18(r).
14 *Canada Act 1982* (UK) c 11, sch B pt I ('*Canadian Charter of Rights and Freedoms*').
15 Ibid s 1.
16 Ibid ss 32, 52.
17 *Canada Act 1982* (UK) c 11, sch B pt II, s 35.
18 *Tobacco Act*, SC 1997, c 13; *Tobacco (Access) Regulations*, SOR/99-93; *Tobacco Products Information Regulation*, SOR/2000-272, s 5(2); *Tobacco Products Labelling Regulation (Cigarettes and Little Cigars)*, SOR/2011-177; *Promotion of Tobacco Products and Accessories Regulations (Prohibited Terms)*, SOR/2011-178.
19 *Cracking Down on Tobacco Marketing Aimed at Youth*, SC 2009, c 27; *Tobacco Act*, SC 1997, c 13, s 5.1, Schedule. The recent decision in the WTO finding that a similar law in the United States violates the Agreement on Technical Barriers to Trade has clear implications for this Canadian regulation, but as of the time of writing it remains in place: Appellate Body Report, *United States – Measures Affecting the Production and Sale of Clove Cigarettes*, WTO Doc WT/DS406/AB/R (adopted 24 April 2012).
20 *Non-Smokers' Health Act*, RSC 1985, c 15.
21 See, eg, *Tobacco Control Act*, RSBC 1996, c 451; *Tobacco Reduction Act*, SA 2005, c T-3.8; *The Non-Smokers Health Protection Act*, CCSM c N92; *Smoke-Free Ontario Act*, SO 1994, c 10; *Tobacco Act*, RSQ c T-0.01; *Smoke-free Places Act*, SNS 2002, c 12; *Tobacco Control Act*, SNu 2003, c 13; *Smoke-Free Places Act*, SY 2008, c 8.
22 See Non-Smokers' Rights Association, *Compendium of Smoke-Free Workplace and Public Place Bylaws* (Spring 2012) <http://www.nsra-adnf.ca/cms/file/files/Compendium_Spring_2012.pdf>.

23 See, eg, *Tobacco Control Act*, SS 2001, c T-14.1 s 8; *Smoke-Free Ontario Act*, SO 1994, c 10, s 4; *Tobacco Act*, RSQ c T-0.01 ss 17, 17.1, 18; *Tobacco Sales Act*, SNB 1993, c T-6.1, s 6.1; *Tobacco Control Act*, SNL 1993, c T-4.1, s 4.1; *Tobacco Control Act*, SNu 2003, c 13 s 9; *Tobacco Control Act*, SNWT 2006, c 9, s 7.

24 *Excise Act*, RSC 1985, c E-14, s 200; *Excise Act, 2001*, SC 2002, c 22, s 42.

25 See, eg, *Tobacco Tax Act*, RSBC 1996, c 452; *Tobacco Tax Act*, RSA 2000, c T-4; *Tobacco Tax Act*, RSO 1990, c T.10.

26 See, eg, *Tobacco Tax Act*, RSBC 1996, c 452, s 4; *Tobacco Tax Act*, RSO 1990, c T.10, s 15; *Tobacco Tax Act*, RSY 2002, c 219, s 4.

27 Craig Heron, *Booze: A Distilled History* (Between the Lines, 2003) 180, 377.

28 Ibid 270. Local option provisions, allowing municipalities to vote to allow or prohibit the sale of liquor within their boundaries, still exist in some provincial statutes: see, eg, *Liquor Licence Act*, RSO 1990, c L.19, ss 53–4.

29 Heron, above n 27, 135.

30 Ibid 269–81.

31 *Importation of Intoxicating Liquors Act*, R.S.C. 1985, c I–3, s 3. There are some exceptions provided for in this section, for example licensed distillers who are importing liquor to be packaged, or importation of wine by individuals as permitted by the provincial government. Provincial legislation also allows some importation by individuals, for example of limited quantities of wine or other liquor from other provinces or countries: see, eg, *Gaming and Liquor Regulation*, Alta Reg 143/1996, ss 89–90.

32 See, eg, *Liquor Control Act*, RSO 1990, c L.18, s 3; *Liquor Distribution Act*, RSBC 1996, c 268, ss 8, 10, 18; *Gaming and Liquor Act*, RSA 2000, c G-1, ss 76, 80; *Alcohol and Gaming Regulation Act*, SS 1997, c A-18.011, s 14; *Liquor Control Act*, RSNS 1989, c 260, s 12.

33 See, eg, *Liquor Licence Act*, RSO 1990, c L.19, s 5; *Liquor Control and Licensing Act*, RSBC 1996, c 267, s 38; *Gaming and Liquor Act*, RSA 2000, c G-1, s 50.

34 See, eg, *Liquor Control and Licensing Act*, RSBC 1996, c 267, s 12(3)(e); *Gaming and Liquor Act*, RSA 2000, c G-1, s 69.

35 See, eg, *Liquor Control Act*, RSNB 1973, c L-10, s 40; *Liquor Control and Licensing Act*, RSBC 1996, c 267, s 12(3)(c); *Gaming and Liquor Act*, RSA 2000, c G-1, s 68(1)(b).

36 See, eg, *Alcohol and Gaming Regulation Act*, SS 1997, c A-18.011, s 110; *Liquor Control Act*, RSNS 1989, c 260, s 89; *Liquor Licence Act*, RSO 1990, c L.19, s 30.

37 *Gaming and Liquor Act*, RSA 2000, c G-1, s 89; *Alcohol and Gaming Regulation Act*, SS 1997, c A-18.011, s 107; *Liquor Licence Act*, RSO 1990, c L.19, s 31.

38 *Gaming and Liquor Act*, RSA 2000, c G-1, s 84; *Alcohol and Gaming Regulation Act*, SS 1997, c A-18.011, s 109; *Liquor Licence Act*, RSO 1990, c L.19, s 32.

39 *Excise Act, 2001*, SC 2002, c 22, Schedules 4–6; *Excise Act*, RSC 1985, c E-14, ss 135, 170; *Customs Tariff*, SC 1997, c 36, ss 21.1–21.3.

40 *Liquor Consumption Tax Act*, SS 1979, c L-19.1; *Retail Sales Act*, RSQ, c I-1, s 20.9.3–20.9.5; *Liquor Tax Act*, RSY 2002, c 141; *Liquor Control Act*, RSNL 1990, c L-18, s 56.1; *Liquor Control Act*, RSNB 1973, c L-10, s 131.3; *Health Tax Act*, RSPEI 1988, c H-3, s 21.

41 For a recent review of these provisions, see Gerald Thomas, *Price Policies to Reduce Alcohol-related Harm in Canada* (Canadian Centre on Substance Abuse, 2012) <http://www.ccsa.ca/2012%20CCSA%20Documents/CCSA-Price-Policies-Reduce-Alcohol-Harm-Canada-2012-en.pdf>.

42 Tim Stockwell et al, 'Does Minimum Pricing Reduce Alcohol Consumption? The Experience of a Canadian Province' (2011) 107 *Addiction* 912, 912.

43 *Food and Drugs Act*, SC 1985, c F-27 ('*F&D Act*'); *Food and Drug Regulations*, CRC c 870 ('*F&D Regulations*').

44 *Consumer Packaging and Labelling Act*, RSC 1985, c C-38.

45 *Constitution Act 1867*, s 95.

46 *Public Health Impediments Regulation*, BC Reg 50/09.

47 *The Public Schools Act*, CCSM c P250, s 47.2; *Trans Fat Standards*, OReg 200/08.

48 Health Canada, *TRANSforming the Food Supply: Report of the Trans Fat Task Force* (2006) <http://www.hc-sc.gc.ca/fn-an/alt_formats/hpfb-dgpsa/pdf/nutrition/tf-gt_rep-rap-eng.pdf>; Center for Science in the Public Interest, *Joint Statement of Canadian Health and Citizens' Groups in Support of Bill C-460, Sodium Reduction Strategy for Canada Act* (2013) <http://cspinet.org/canada/pdf/jan30-2013.c-460.jointstatement.pdf>.

49 Health Canada initially said it would regulate trans fat content if the industry did not meet recommended targets within a two-year period: Health Canada, *Trans Fats: It's Your Health* (December 2007) 2 <http://www.hc-sc.gc.ca/hl-vs/alt_formats/pacrb-dgapcr/pdf/iyh-vsv/food-aliment/trans-eng.pdf>. However, it subsequently stated that it would rely on nutrition labelling to encourage changes in behaviour by consumers and manufacturers: Health Canada, *Fats: The Good the Bad and the Ugly* (2012) 2 <http://www.hc-sc.gc.ca/hl-vs/alt_formats/pdf/iyh-vsv/med/fats-gras-eng.pdf>. Its approach to sodium includes awareness and education, support for research, and guidance to industry on reducing sodium content in processed foods: Health Canada, *Sodium in Canada* (2012) <http://www.hc-sc.gc.ca/fn-an/nutrition/sodium/index-eng.php>.

50 *Tobacco Products Labelling Regulation (Cigarettes and Little Cigars)*, SOR/2011-177, ss 12–13. Written warnings covering a minimum of 50 per cent of the package surface are required for other tobacco products, such as chewing tobacco or snuff: *Tobacco Products Information Regulation*, SOR/2000-272, s 5.

51 *Promotion of Tobacco Products and Accessories Regulations (Prohibited Terms)*, SOR/2011-178.

52 Canadian Cancer Society, 'Canada Ranks 4th in International Cigarette Health Warnings Report, with Australia in the Lead' (14 November 2012) <https://www.cancer.ca/Canada-wide/About%20us/Media%20centre/CW-Media%20releases/CW-2012/International%20Warnings%20report.aspx?sc_lang=EN>.

53 *Tobacco Act*, SC 1997, c 13.

54 *Tobacco Products Control Act*, RSC 1985, c 14.

55 *RJR-MacDonald Inc v Canada (Attorney General)*, [1995] 3 SCR 199 ('*RJR-MacDonald*').

56 *Tobacco Act*, SC 1997, c 13, s 22(2).

57 Ibid s 22(3).

58 Ibid s 22(4).

59 Ibid ss 21, 24, 25, 29.

60 Ibid s 20.

61 *Canada (Attorney General) v JTI-Macdonald Corp*, [2007] 2 SCR 610 ('*JTI-Macdonald*').

62 *Tobacco Act*, SC 1997, c 13, s 30.

63 *Tobacco Reduction Act*, SA 2005, c T-3.8, s 7.1; *Tobacco Control Act*, SS 2001, c T-14.1, s 6; *Non-Smokers Health Protection Act*, CCSM c N92, s 7.2; *Smoke-Free Ontario Act*, SO 1994, c 10, s 3.1; *Tobacco Sales Act*, SNB 1993, c T-6.1, s 6.4; *Tobacco Access Act*, SNS 1993, c 14, s 9A; *Tobacco Act*, RSQ c T-0.01, s 20.2; *Tobacco Control Act*, SNu 2003, c 13, s 8; *Smoke-Free Places Act*, SY 2008, c 8, s 8; *Tobacco Control Act*, SNWT 2006, c 9, s 5.

64 *FCD Regulations*, pt B, div 2. See, however, the decision in *Labatt Brewing Co v Canada*, [1980] 1 SCR 914, below n 120, which casts doubt on the constitutionality of some of these provisions.

65 Ibid s B.02.003.

66 Mia Rabson, 'Warning Label "Such a Simple Thing"', *Winnipeg Free Press* (online), 18 June 2011 <http://www.winnipegfreepress.com/opinion/fyi/warning-label-such-a-simple-thing-124123739.html>.

67 Yukon Liquor Corporation, 'Alcohol Warning Labels' (2013) <www.ylc.yk.ca/pdf/warning_label_initiative.pdf>; Northwest Territories Liquor Commission, 'Social Responsibility' (2012) <http://www.fin.gov.nt.ca/liquor/social-responsibility/index.htm>.

68 *Public Education About Fetal Alcohol Syndrome Regulations*, NS Reg 181/2005, s 2; *Liquor Licence Act*, RSO 1990, c L.19, s 30.1.

69 Heron, above n 27, 279, 318–19.

70 *Radio Regulations*, 1986, SOR/86-982, s 4(1)(b); *Television Broadcasting Regulations*, 1987, SOR/87-49, s 6(1)(b).

71 *Radio Regulations*, 1986, SOR/86-982, s 4(2); *Television Broadcasting Regulations*, 1987, SOR/87-49, s 6(2).

72 Canadian Radio-television and Telecommunications Commission, 'Amendments to the Radio, Television and Speciality Services Regulations Respecting the Broadcast of Alcoholic Beverage Advertising' (Public Notice CRTC 1997-12, 31 January 1997) <http://www.crtc.gc.ca/eng/archive/1997/PB97-12.HTM> ('*Public Notice CRTC 1997-12*').

73 Canadian Radio-television and Telecommunications Commission, 'New Regulatory Framework Governing the Broadcast of Alcoholic Beverage Advertising' (Public Notice CRTC 1996-108, 1 August 1996) <http://www.crtc.gc.ca/eng/archive/1996/PB96-108.HTM>.

74 *Radio Regulations*, 1986, SOR/86-982, s 4(1)(c); *Television Broadcasting Regulations*, 1987, SOR/87-49, s 6(1)(c).

75 Advertising Standards Canada, *Fostering Community Confidence in Canadian Advertising* (2012) <http://www.adstandards.com/en/AboutASC/aboutASC.aspx>.

76 Canadian Radio-television and Telecommunications Commission, *Public Notice CRTC 1997-12*, above n 72.

77 Advertising Standards Canada, *Alcoholic Beverages Advertising Clearance Services* (2012) <http://www.adstandards.com/en/AdvertisingPreclearance/alcoholicBeverages.aspx>.

78 *Liquor Control and Licensing Regulation*, BC Reg 244/2002, s 57(4)(a); *Nova Scotia Liquor Corporation Regulations*, NS Reg 22/91, s 10; *Liquor Regulations*, NWT Reg 069/2008, s 72(1).

79 *Nova Scotia Liquor Corporation Regulations*, NS Reg 22/91, ss 3–11; *Liquor Advertising Rules of Conduct Regulation*, Man Reg 125/95; *Manufacturers' Licences*, RRO 1990, Reg 720, s 5; *Licences to Sell Liquor*, RRO 1990, Reg 719, s 87; *Special Occasion Permits*, O Reg 389/91, s 7; *Regulation respecting promotion, advertising and educational programs relating to alcoholic beverages*, RRQ, c P-9.1, r 6; *Advertising of Liquor Regulation*, NB Reg 90-10; *Liquor Control Act*, RSPEI 1988, c L-14, s 50; *General Regulations*, PEI Reg EC704/75, s 96.

80 Alberta Gaming and Liquor Commission, *Liquor Agency Handbook* (2013), c 4; Saskatchewan Liquor and Gaming Authority, *Commercial Liquor Permittee Policy Manual* (2009), c X. Compliance with these is required by legislation: *Gaming and Liquor Act*, RSA 2000, c G-1, s 67(2); *Alcohol and Gaming Regulation Act, 1997*, SS 1997, c A-18.011, s 134(1).

81 See, eg, *Liquor Regulations*, YCO 1977/37, ss 9(1)(e), 40(1); *Liquor Regulations*, RRNWT (Nu) 1990, c L-34, s 117.

82 Heron, above n 27, 319; Carly Heung, Benjamin Rempel and Marvin Krank, 'Strengthening the Canadian Alcohol Advertising System' (2012) 103 *Canadian Journal of Public Health* 263, 264.

83 *F&D Regulations*, s B.01.401.

84 Ibid ss B.01.500–513, B.01.600–03.

85 *F&D Act*, s 3(1).

86 See, eg, Ontario Medical Association, 'Ontario's Doctors Call for Urgent Action to Combat Obesity Epidemic' (23 October 2012) <https://www.oma.org/Mediaroom/PressReleases/Pages/ActiontoCombatObesityEpidemic.aspx>; Centre for Science in the Public Interest (Canada), *Writing on the Wall: Time to Put Nutrition Information on Restaurant Menus* (2012) <http://cspinet.org/canada/pdf/writing-on-the-wall.

complete-report.pdf>. For discussion, see Barbara von Tigerstrom, 'Mandatory Nutrition Disclosure for Restaurants: Is Menu Labelling Coming to Canada?' (2010) 28 *Windsor Review of Legal & Social Issues* 139.

87 Bill C-283, *An Act to Amend the Food and Drugs Act (Food Labelling)*, 1st Sess, 39th Parl, (negatived 8 November 2006); Bill 156, *Healthy Decisions for Healthy Eating Act*, 1st Sess, 39th Leg, Ontario, 2009; Bill 90, *Healthy Decisions for Healthy Eating Act, 2010*, 2nd Sess, 39th Leg, Ontario, 2010; Bill 126, *An Act to enact the Skin Cancer Prevention Act, 2012 and to amend various statutes with respect to health matters*, 2012, 1st Sess, 40th Leg, Ontario.

88 Canadian Restaurant and Foodservices Association, *Informed Dining is Coming to Restaurants across Canada!* (12 December 2012) <http://www.crfa.ca/news/2012/informed_dining_is_coming_to_restaurant_chains_across_canada.asp>.

89 See, eg, Canada, House of Commons, Standing Committee on Health, *Healthy Weights for Healthy Kids*, 39th Parl, 1st Sess (March 2007) (Chair: Rob Merrifield), 22.

90 See, eg, Institute of Medicine, *Examination of Front-of-package Nutrition Rating Systems and Symbols: Phase I Report* (National Academies Press, 2010); Institute of Medicine, *Front-of-package Nutrition Rating Systems and Symbols: Promoting Healthier Choices* (National Academies Press, 2012).

91 Ontario Medical Association, above n 86. Examples of the proposed warning labels can be found at: <https://www.oma.org/HealthPromotion/Obesity/Pages/default.aspx>.

92 The relevant federal regulations are explained and interpreted in: Canadian Food Inspection Agency, *Guide to Food Labelling and Advertising* (revised 2012) <http://www.inspection.gc.ca/food/labelling/guide-to-food-labelling-and-advertising/eng/1300118951990/1300118996556>.

93 Advertising Standards Canada, 'Food and Non-alcoholic Beverage Advertising Clearance' (2012) <http://www.adstandards.com/en/clearance/FoodAndNonAlcoholicBeverages/foodAndNonAlcoholicBeverages.asp>.

94 *Consumer Protection Act*, RSQ c P-40.1, s 248. This section creates a general prohibition, which is subject to some exemptions appearing in the *Regulation respecting the application of the Consumer Protection Act*, RRQ, c P-40.1, r 3, ss 87–91.

95 *Regulation respecting the application of the Consumer Protection Act*, RRQ, c P-40.1, r 3, s 91.

96 *Irwin Toy v Québec (Attorney General)*, [1989] 1 SCR 927 ('*Irwin Toy*').

97 See, eg, Bill C-430, *An Act to amend the Competition Act and the Food and Drugs Act (child protection against advertising exploitation)*, 41st Parl, 1st Sess.

98 Advertising Standards Canada, *Canadian Code of Advertising Standards* (revised February 2013)<http://www.adstandards.com/en/Standards/canCodeOfAdStandards.aspx> para 12; Advertising Standards Canada, *Broadcast Code for Advertising to Children* (revised 1993, last update 2010), <http://www.adstandards.com/en/clearance/childrens/broadcastCodeForAdvertisingToChildren.aspx>.

99 Advertising Standards Canada, *Canadian Children's Food & Beverage Advertising Initiative* (2010), <http://www.adstandards.com/en/childrensinitiative/CCFBAI_EN.pdf> ('CCFBAI').

100 Ibid 2–3.

101 Advertising Standards Canada, *Children's Advertising Initiative Participant Commitments* <http://www.adstandards.com/en/childrensinitiative/participantCommitments.html>.

102 CCFBAI, above n 99, 3.

103 Nola Ries and Barbara von Tigerstrom, 'Legal Interventions to Address Obesity: Assessing the State of the Law in Canada' (2011) 43 *UBC Law Review* 401–04.

104 See above n 49 and accompanying text.

105 See, eg, *Tobacco Act*, SC 1997, c 13, ss 43–48; *Tobacco Control Act*, RSBC 1996, c 451, s 12; *Smoke-Free Ontario Act*, SO 1994, c 10, s 15.

106 Heung, Rempel and Krank, above n 82, 264.

107   See, eg, *Nova Scotia Liquor Corporation Regulations*, NS Reg, 22/91, s 3; *Liquor Regulations*, YCO 1977/37, s 40(1).
108   The document does give some examples of how standards should be defined, for example by reference to federal government guidance and regulations, but these are not mandatory and are open to interpretation by each company: CCFBAI, above n 99, 2.
109   Advertising Standards Canada, *The Canadian Children's Food and Beverage Advertising Initiative: 2011 Compliance Report* (2012) <http://www.adstandards.com/en/childrensi nitiative/2011ComplianceReport.pdf> 8.
110   Ibid ii.
111   Morris Fish, 'The Effect of Alcohol on the Canadian Constitution … Seriously' (2011) 57 *McGill Law Journal* 189.
112   *Reference re Validity of Section 5(a) of the Dairy Industry Act*, [1949] SCR 1.
113   *RJR-MacDonald*, [1995] 3 SCR 199, [14].
114   Ibid [30].
115   Ibid [32].
116   Ibid [33]–[34].
117   Ibid [44].
118   Ibid [53]–[56].
119   Barbara von Tigerstrom, 'Healthy Communities: Public Health Law at the Supreme Court of Canada' in Jocelyn Downie and Elaine Gibson (eds), *Health Law at the Supreme Court of Canada* (Irwin Law, 2007) 81, 89.
120   *Labatt Brewing Co v Canada*, [1980] 1 SCR 914.
121   *F&D Act*, s 6; *F&D Regulations*, s B.02.134 (later repealed).
122   The majority also rejected the trade and commerce power and the 'peace, order, and good government' power as possible bases for the regulation.
123   *Labatt Brewing Co v Canada*, [1980] 1 SCR 914, 933–94.
124   *Labatt Brewing Co v Canada*, [1980] 1 SCR 914, 934.
125   Food safety regulations were upheld in *Standard Sausage Co v Lee*, [1933] 4 DLR 501. See also *R v Wetmore (County Court Judge)*, [1983] 2 SCR 284.
126   There are other possible heads of power that could be invoked in support of nutrition labelling regulations (notably the trade and commerce power), but they also have limitations.
127   *Tobacco Control Act*, SS 2001, c T-14.1, s 6(3), (4).
128   *Rothmans, Benson & Hedges Inc v Saskatchewan*, [2005] 1 SCR 188.
129   von Tigerstrom, 'Healthy Communities', above n 119, 97, 109.
130   See above n 73 and accompanying text.
131   *Ford v Quebec (Attorney General)*, [1988] 2 SCR 712; *Irwin Toy*, [1989] 1 SCR 927.
132   *Central Hudson Gas & Electric Corp v Public Service Commission of New York*, 447 US 557 (1980).
133   *Rocket v Royal College of Dental Surgeons of Ontario*, [1990] 2 SCR 232, [15]. There are notable similarities, however, between the United States' test from *Central Hudson*, Ibid and the Canadian courts' approach to s 1 analysis: *Ford v Quebec (Attorney General)*, [1988] 2 SCR 712, [48].
134   *Irwin Toy*, [1989] 1 SCR 927, [47].
135   *Slaight Communications v Davidson*, [1989] 1 SCR 1038, [92].
136   *Lavigne v Ontario Public Service Employees Union*, [1991] 2 SCR 211, [128]–[131].
137   *RJR-MacDonald*, [1995] 3 SCR 199, [124]. The dissenting judgment on this point doubted that the public would identify the tobacco manufacturers with health warnings ([115] (La Forest J)).
138   *JTI-Macdonald*, [2007] 2 SCR 610, [131].
139   Ibid [132].
140   *R v Oakes*, [1986] 1 SCR 103.

141 Ibid [69].

142 See, eg, *RJR-MacDonald*, [1995] 3 SCR 199, where the appellant tobacco companies conceded that 'protecting Canadians from the health risks associated with tobacco use' was a pressing and substantial objective: [61]. See also *JTI-Macdonald*, [2007] 2 SCR 610, [65]; *Ontario Restaurant Hotel & Motel Assn v Toronto (City)* (2005), 258 DLR (4th) 447.

143 *R v Oakes*, [1986] 1 SCR 103, 139–40 [70]–[71].

144 von Tigerstrom, 'Healthy Communities', above n 119, 103; Barbara von Tigerstrom, 'Law and Policy Interventions to Prevent Chronic Disease: The Challenges of Evidence-based Public Health' in Robert Kouri and Catherine Régis (eds), *Les grands défis en droit et politiques de la santé* [*Grand Challenges in Health Law and Policy*] (Editions Yvon Blais, 2009) 323.

145 *RJR-MacDonald*, [1995] 3 SCR 199, [67], [127], [137], 184].

146 For critical discussion on this point, see Robin Basu, 'The RJR-JTI Saga – Lessons Learned and Unresolved Issues' (2007) 23 *National Journal of Constitutional Law* 107, 123–5.

147 This was the position argued by the government and interveners: see ibid 109–12.

148 Opened for signature 16 June 2003, 2302 UNTS 166 (entered into force 27 February 2005). See the detailed discussion in Chapter 2 of this volume.

149 *JTI-Macdonald*, [2007] 2 SCR 610, [10].

150 Ibid [7].

151 Basu, above n 146, 109.

152 *JTI-Macdonald*, [2007] 2 SCR 610, [8].

153 Ibid [93].

154 *JTI-Macdonald*, [2007] 2 SCR 610, [52]–[57] (interpretation of the prohibition on publication of scientific work sponsored by tobacco companies), [87]–[89] (interpretation of the prohibition on advertisements appealing to young persons).

155 Tim Stockwell et al, 'The Raising of Minimum Alcohol Prices in Saskatchewan, Canada: Impacts on Consumption and Implications for Public Health' (2012) 102 *American Journal of Public Health* e103, e103.

156 See, eg, Health Canada, *Looking Forward: The Future of Federal Tobacco Control* (12 September 2011) <http://www.hc-sc.gc.ca/hc-ps/alt_formats/pdf/consult/2011/foward-avenir/foward-avenir-eng.pdf>; Richard Bonnie, Kathleen Stratton and Robert Wallace (eds), *Ending the Tobacco Problem: A Blueprint for the Nation* (National Academies Press, 2007); Ronald Davis, 'Moving Tobacco Control Past the "Tipping Point"' (2000) 321 *British Medical Journal* 309; Jonathan Samet and Heather Wipfli, 'Unfinished Business in Tobacco Control' (2009) 302 *Journal of the American Medical Association* 681.

12 Latin America

Fernanda Alonso and Alejandro Madrazo

1 Introduction

Latin America is currently at a crossroads regarding non-communicable diseases ('NCDs'); millions of deaths are caused by tobacco, alcohol consumption and poor diet, the three factors most closely related to NCDs. In Mexico, in 2010 alone, there were more than 25,000 deaths related to alcohol, over 53,000 attributable to tobacco and over 80,000 due to obesity and diabetes.[1] These growing epidemics are generating important health regulation transformations in Latin America. The epidemiological transition from infectious diseases to NCDs requires the regulation of behaviour and consumption patterns that result in chronic diseases. Although alcohol regulation has existed for a long time and, more recently, demands for food and diet regulation are growing, the pioneer in NCD regulation in Latin America has been tobacco control.

This chapter will focus on tobacco control in Latin America, mainly because it has been the primary area of focus in Latin America in the last decade and the object of the most advanced regulation. Many of aspects related to tobacco control are also applicable to the other two areas, and most of the lessons learned from tobacco will be crucial in advancing the regulation of alcohol and food. Before addressing the details of tobacco control regulation in Latin America we examine the problems of food and alcohol in the region and the limited regulation that has been undertaken so far.

2 Food

2.1 Overview

According to the World Health Organization, at least 2.8 million people die each year as a result of being overweight or obese.[2] Between 1980 and 2008, the worldwide prevalence of obesity almost doubled, and the highest prevalence was found in the Americas, with 62 per cent of the population being considered overweight and 26 per cent obese. Of the countries in the region, Mexico has the highest prevalence of both obesity and overweight. In 2009, Mexico reached 30 per cent obesity rates.[3] Rates for children aged 5–17 are also alarmingly high, with 29 per cent of children in Mexico now overweight.[4] Today, only North America rivals South America in terms of obesity and overweight,[5] and even in poorer countries in the region historically associated with malnutrition, especially in Central America, obesity levels are rising.[6]

Although this problem has been developing since the early 1970s,[7] the necessary preventive measures are yet to be adopted in the region. Most of the direct causes of obesity are attributable to poor diet, yet evidence now points to a wider range of factors – social, economic, cultural – as well as existing infrastructure.[8] In mid- or high-income countries, individuals in the lowest socioeconomic strata typically suffer the most from obesity. In the case of Latin America, a different phenomenon is observed: obesity is slightly lower in populations with lower incomes.[9] People of all income levels suffer from a high proportion of obesity,[10] and obesity rates in Latin America exceed those in many developed countries.[11]

In Latin America, the decrease in prices of certain foods has been of great importance, giving incentives for the replacement of traditional, more balanced diets, by those based on and dependent on highly processed, industrialised goods. The more widespread availability of certain products and the increase in their energetic density, increasing industrialisation and urbanisation, and more sedentary work environments and recreational activities all contribute to the problem.[12] One of the most crucial problems in the region regarding diet is the growing link between poverty, obesity and malnutrition, as the Mexican case will illustrate in the next section.

Although the problem is growing, few countries in the region have addressed the problem directly. One of the few has been Chile, which passed a law on 6 July 2012 requiring that high-salt and high-calorie foods be labelled accordingly. The law also prohibits samples of these foods being given to children, being sold at schools or even being advertised.[13] Recommendations for an increase in physical activities and sports have also been put in place. Chile and Mexico, as well as (to a lesser extent) Brazil, are among the only countries taking up these possibilities.[14] Important in the equation is the power and interference of the food industry in the region.[15]

2.2 Case study: food security in Mexico – the link between obesity, malnutrition and poverty

Being overweight or obese can lead to harmful metabolic effects on blood pressure and cholesterol levels and can result in diabetes. This in turn increases the risks of coronary heart disease, strokes and cancer.[16] Because of the rise in obesity and its adverse effects, it is not surprising that in Mexico the leading cause of death since 2000 has been diabetes, followed closely by coronary heart disease (a condition also closely linked to obesity). In 2008, 14 per cent of deaths in Mexico were attributable to diabetes, a number that has been increasing since 2000 when it was 10.7 per cent.[17]

Another worrisome fact is that, simultaneously, another cause of death related to food and nutrition is also a relevant health problem. Protein-energy malnutrition was the twelfth leading cause of death among the general population in 2008, ninth among children aged 5 to 14, and the fifth leading cause in children aged 1 to 4.[18] While intuitively this would appear to be a separate problem, in Mexico's case there appears to be an underlying factor linking obesity and under-nutrition.

Between 2006 and 2008, the number of people living in conditions of food poverty in Mexico rose from 13.8 per cent to 18.2 per cent.[19] Food poverty is defined as the percentage of the population that has insufficient income per capita to acquire healthy and nutritious food.[20] While obesity is normally seen as a problem in developed countries, and hunger and malnutrition as problems in developing countries, in Mexico there is a close relationship between the two: there is an overlap in the population living in poverty and those suffering from overweight or obesity. The five states with the highest levels of food poverty also have similar percentages of the population with excessive fat intakes and weight problems.[21] This link shows the necessity of addressing all aspects of food security.[22]

The United Nations' Food and Agriculture Organization has defined food security as existing not only in terms of whether people have physical and economic access to food but also whether this is sufficient, safe and adequately *nutritious* to meet their dietary needs.[23] In Mexico, the evidence indicates that when faced with insufficient resources to acquire items in the basic food basket, people consume food with a high calorie count and high in fats and sugars but low in vitamins, minerals and nutrients.[24] The price of foods as well as its availability can play an important role in what those in the lower economic strata consume. Malnutrition can result in conditions such as physical and mental stunting that lead to irreversible harm and difficulty in development.[25] Children are now more vulnerable, receiving inadequate nutrition while suffering from sharp increases in obesity.[26]

Access to food may no longer be the primary concern for policy makers or government initiatives. The question is, what type of food can people access? Large corporations have ensured access to soft drinks, fatty snacks and fast food, making them easily available and affordable in the most remote corners of the country. A change in regulation is needed in order for the state to ensure not only the distribution, availability and accessibility of food but, specifically, the quality of the food. Put another way, access to nutrition, not merely access to (any type of) food, should be ensured. Food security in Mexico now requires an integrated approach that includes the support of local agriculture, education and research and the creation of a detailed legal framework.

In President Calderon's administration, the government put in place the *Acuerdo Nacional de Salud Alimentaria* [The National Agreement for Food Health and Safety ('Agreement')].[27] The Agreement, based on scientific evidence and social determinants, included ten objectives that had to be carried out by different sectors of the government. The result was that Mexico became one of the few countries to have an agreement that encompasses all actions in a single public policy. Although in theory it was a great stepping-stone for food regulation in Mexico, it was weakened in practice, and the majority of the established objectives were not met.[28] One of the main points in the Agreement sought to regulate food in elementary schools through the prohibition of the sale of fatty foods and soft drinks (*Programa de Acción en el Contexto Escolar* and the *Lineamientos Generales para el Expendio de los Planteles de Educación Básica*), which largely failed.[29] Importantly, compliance was voluntary, without evaluation mechanisms or accountability.

Government action through the Agreement had limited effects, obliging the government to take other measures. An example of this is the anti-obesity campaign 'Wrestling Against Obesity'[30] put in place by the *Lucha Libre* in partnership with the Health Ministry, which includes informational videos (exercise routines and healthy eating habits) and aims to motivate wrestling fans to have an active lifestyle, through a physical activity of great importance to the Mexican population. Although it is too early in the program to see results, it does allow us to consider a wider array of actions.

3 Alcohol

3.1 Overview

Alcohol consumption is the world's third largest risk factor for disease and disability: a causal factor in 60 types of diseases and injury, with almost 4 per cent of deaths worldwide attributed to alcohol.[31] Although many of the health, safety and socioeconomic problems related to alcohol can be effectively reduced, few countries have put effective measures into place. Since 1999, when the World Health Organization ('WHO') first began to take into account alcohol policies, 34 countries have adopted some type of formal policy, but in general there are no clear trends.[32] This is certainly the case in Latin America, where weak policies that do not effectively protect health are in place.

The average worldwide per capita consumption of alcoholic beverages in 2005 was 6.13 litres of pure alcohol. The majority of Latin America had medium consumption levels, except for Argentina, which was in the high consumption group. In any case, the region is above the global average, at around 6.7 litres.[33] Since the 1990s, when there was an initial decline, levels have been maintained. More problematic in the region is the high level of heavy episodic drinking, one of the most important indicators for acute consequences of alcohol use, as can be seen through injuries. Heavy episodic drinking is common in countries in the region such as Brazil.[34] Brazil also suffers from a high proportion of alcohol-attributable mortality. Although not as high, the rest of the region also suffers from above average levels of alcohol-attributable mortality.[35] According to Maristela Monteiro, principal advisor of the Pan American Health Organization ('PAHO') with respect to alcohol and substance abuse, alcohol has a disproportionate effect on the younger sectors of the American continent; it is the primary cause of death for people between the ages of 15 and 39.[36]

Deaths attributable to alcohol can include injury, cancer, cardiovascular disease and liver cirrhosis. In Mexico in 2008, for example, several of the top ten causes of death were alcohol-related. Cardiovascular disease was number two with 11.1 per cent, cirrhosis and other chronic diseases of the liver were fourth on the list at 5.3 per cent, and motor vehicle accidents was number six with 3.1 per cent.[37]

There have been different types of policies to control problematic alcohol consumption including warnings, alcoholometry and taxes. The most common type in Latin America is warnings on alcoholic beverage containers or in alcohol advertisements. Examples include: 'Consuming alcohol produces damage to health' in Panama, 'Drinking alcohol in excess is harmful' in Peru and other focused warnings about specific problems such as 'Alcohol consumption is dangerous for your health and affects the family' in Ecuador.[38]

Several Latin American countries have taken certain measures to control the increase in problematic drinking. In Venezuela, taxes on all alcoholic beverages have increased; in Costa Rica, the government controls all alcoholic beverage advertising; in Chile, El Salvador and Peru, plans and integrated policies are being enacted to reduce the excessive consumption of alcohol; Mexico has started preventative measures to detect and give help to those people who are at risk of dangerous alcohol consumption; and Brazil has adopted a zero tolerance law for drinking and driving while carrying out a strong media campaign.[39] PAHO is currently elaborating a regional plan of action to promote similar measures in all member states throughout the Americas. Many countries in the region have put in place the following types of measures: taxes,[40] restrictions on on/off premise sales of alcoholic beverages,[41] legally binding regulations on alcohol advertising,[42] product placement restrictions,[43] sponsorship[44] and promotion[45] restrictions, and drinking and driving regulations.[46]

3.2 *Case study: alcoholometry in Brazil and Mexico*

Laws that have had positive results with regard to both drinking and driving have been passed in a few countries in the region including Brazil and Mexico. In the case of Brazil, the *Lei Seca* was passed on 19 June 2008.[47] This law indicates that anyone caught drinking and driving with a blood alcohol concentration ('BAC') of 0.2 g/L can be arrested and criminally charged. The punishment can include up to three years in prison, a hefty fine and suspension of the offender's driving licence for one year. This law also prohibits the sale of alcoholic drinks at businesses along the rural stretches of federal roads. Police across Brazil test the BAC levels of suspected offenders on the spot using breathalysers.[48] As a result of this law, levels of road accidents have decreased.[49]

In Mexico similar measures – which make use of administrative, as opposed to criminal, law – were put in place in 2009. The National Center for the Prevention of Accidents, in coordination with the State Councils for the Prevention of Accidents, established the National Alcoholometry program in the municipalities with the largest number of traffic accident mortality throughout the 32 federal entities. The program imposes alcohol limits for drivers of public transport and people under the age of 21 at 0.00 mg/L (milligrams of alcohol in 1 litre of breath taken in, approximately the same as BAC levels of 0.1 g/L). Maximum levels for the rest of the driving population were set at 0.4 mg/L.[50] Those above the limit can be punished with an administrative fine and up to 36 hours in prison.[51] According to the Ministry of Public Security in Mexico City ('SSPDF'), results for this program have been very positive. Since the program was put in place it has helped reduce fatal accidents associated with the consumption of alcohol by 30 per cent, especially among younger drivers, and the SSPDF is being asked to help replicate the model in other federal entities.[52]

4 Tobacco control in Latin America

4.1 Overview

Latin America has been classified as being at Stage 2 of the tobacco epidemic with over 120 million smokers.[53] This means an increasing prevalence of tobacco consumption among men and a rapid increase in the prevalence of smoking among women, and the tobacco-attributable mortality rate among men has not yet reached its peak.[54]

In the midst of this epidemic, the 21 countries of the region[55] have adopted some important control policies. At the end of 2012, 18 of the 21 countries[56] had ratified the *WHO Framework Convention on Tobacco Control* ('WHO FCTC'),[57] spurring the adoption of domestic legislation at national, local and municipal levels. Uruguay adopted landmark regulations in 2006 (as described further below), with other countries closely following suit. Today, only Bolivia has not adopted any smoke-free measures. These changes have resulted from close collaboration between governments and civil society.

Because Latin America is simultaneously at a critical point in the development of the tobacco epidemic and at a crucial juncture in its effort to establish and implement policies, the region has become a key battleground for both the tobacco control movement and the tobacco industry and its allies. Thus, it is particularly important to understand and follow the adoption and implementation of tobacco control policies in the region, assessing their impact. With relevant exceptions – such as Mexico – the main thrust of tobacco control efforts in the region has been in smoke-free measures and confronting industry interference in tobacco control policy, while only later shifting focus to matters such as advertising, promotion and sponsorship ('APS') or product packaging and labelling. As elaborated further below, the tobacco industry has had to move quickly, coming up with new and innovative ways to intervene and new strategies that represent challenges for policy makers and tobacco control advocates.

A key issue today is the application (or rather misapplication) of adopted measures, and the evaluation of their effects. Following initial success in adopting legislation, a systematic weakening of the application of legislation has followed, due in part to the influence of the tobacco industry and its allies, including some governmental agents, and the endemic weakness of many countries' enforcement mechanisms.[58] The judiciary, as described further below, has also been involved in establishing important tobacco control precedents.

Below we examine the laws and institutions of different countries, the persistent problem of tobacco industry interference in the region, and the region's tobacco control litigation. A more detailed breakdown of these different areas will be made for Mexico for two main reasons. First, it is the country we have studied in most detail and about which we can write with the most authority; second, because the problems, advancements and other dynamics that are present across the region seem to be playing out in Mexico particularly vigorously.

4.2 The WHO FCTC in Latin America

Originally, support for a strong convention in the region was notoriously weak. This, however, changed through the leadership of Brazil, Panama and Paraguay.[59]

As can be seen in Table 12.1, Brazil and Paraguay were the first Latin American countries to *sign*, followed closely by nine others. The rest followed suit in 2004. The only two exceptions were Guyana and Colombia, who joined the treaty through accession in 2005 and 2008 respectively. Support from the region carried on to the *ratification* phase of the Convention in 2004. Three countries were among the 40 required for the WHO FCTC to enter into force: Mexico, Panama and Uruguay.[60] In 2009, Suriname was the last country for which the WHO FCTC entered into force. Except for Argentina, Cuba and El Salvador, which have yet to ratify it, all countries in the region were party to the treaty by the end of 2008.

Table 12.1 Signature and ratification of the WHO FCTC by Latin American countries.

Country	Signature date	Ratification / Accession (a)	Entry into force
Argentina	25/09/2003		
Belize	26/09/2003	15/12/2005	15/03/2006
Bolivia	27/02/2004	15/09/2005	14/12/2005
Brazil	16/06/2003	03/11/2005	01/02/2006
Chile	25/09/2003	13/06/2005	11/09/2005
Colombia		10/04/2008a	09/07/2008
Costa Rica	03/07/2003	21/08/2008	19/11/2008
Cuba	25/06/2004		
Ecuador	22/03/2004	25/07/2006	23/10/2006
El Salvador	18/03/2004		
Guatemala	25/09/2003	16/11/2005	14/02/2006
Guyana		15/09/2005a	14/12/2005
Honduras	18/06/2004	16/02/2005	17/05/2005
Mexico	12/08/2003	28/05/2004	27/02/2005
Nicaragua	07/06/2004	09/04/2008	08/07/2008
Panama	26/09/2003	16/08/2004	27/02/2005
Paraguay	16/06/2003	26/09/2006	25/12/2006
Peru	21/04/2004	30/11/2004	28/02/2005
Suriname	24/06/2004	16/12/2008	16/03/2009
Uruguay	19/06/2003	09/09/2004	27/02/2005
Venezuela	22/09/2003	27/06/2006	25/09/2006

Source Data compiled from: *Parties to the WHO Framework Convention on Tobacco Control* (2013) WHO Framework Convention on Tobacco Control <http://www.who.int/fctc/signatories_parties/en/>

Before the establishment of the WHO FCTC, only Brazil had strong tobacco control measures in place through law. Other countries had adopted relevant measures – such as Mexico's banning of advertising through electronic media in the early 2000s[61] – through administrative or other non-legislative means.[62] In Brazil in 1996, a law required the use of warnings on cigarette packages and restricted advertising.[63] The law did not include sanctions for violations and did not clearly define the rules for where smoking was allowed, giving the tobacco industry the opportunity to design strategies where law enforcement was close to impossible. In December 2000, federal law number 10,167 put in place a comprehensive advertising ban[64] and established strong graphic health warnings among other measures, making Brazil a pioneer in tobacco control. As mentioned above, it was after signature and ratification of the WHO FCTC that most other countries moved to adopt strong measures.

4.3 Tobacco control legislation by country

4.3.1 Argentina

Although Argentina has signed the WHO FCTC, it has not yet ratified the treaty. It has, however, passed tobacco control legislation. The primary legal tobacco control instrument[65] includes: regulation regarding tobacco APS; smoking in public places; product packaging and labelling; sale and distribution; tobacco product composition; and programs for prevention and education. In respect of smoke-free spaces, it establishes basic regulations, but allows for relevant exceptions. Smoking is prohibited in indoor workplaces and indoor public places and on public transport, but allowed in: (i) enclosed private office spaces that are not shared or visited by other workers and are not used for public services; (ii) smoking clubs and tobacco shops with designated areas; and (iii) patios, terraces, balconies or other open spaces, except for those healthcare or educational facilities (eg open space smoking university level). Sub-national jurisdictions can enact smoke-free laws that are stricter than the national law.[66] Since 2006, 12 out of 23 provinces[67] have passed smoke-free legislation that is stricter than at the national level. The Mendoza province, for example, prohibits smoking in all enclosed public spaces with public access, with the exception of penitentiary and mental health institutions.[68]

In Argentina, most forms of tobacco advertising and promotion are prohibited. However, point-of-sale advertising (as long as it includes health warnings) and advertising and promotion through direct communication to persons over 18 (subject to certain requirements, such as obtaining previous consent and verifying age) are allowed. In respect of sponsorship, cases that promote a tobacco product are prohibited, but not those that promote a brand name. In respect of packaging and labelling, health warnings and pictograms are required on all tobacco products (text warnings must appear on the lower 50 per cent of one principal display area and pictograms on the lower 50 per cent of the other principal display area). Misleading terms and descriptors such as 'light' or 'mild' are prohibited.[69]

4.3.2 Brazil

In Brazil, federal regulation of smoking in public places, APS, and packaging and labelling have been established through many different laws and regulations. Under the main instrument regulating tobacco APS and packaging and labelling of tobacco products, smoking is prohibited in all enclosed public places, and the majority of enclosed workplaces (excluding workplaces with only one worker such as housekeepers in private homes).[70] In terms of APS, direct advertising through most forms of mass media is prohibited, as are forms of promotion (except for the display of the products at points of sale). All sponsorship for cultural or sporting activities is prohibited. Regarding packaging and labelling, tobacco products must carry warning pictograms covering 100 per cent of the back and one side of the packages.[71] In January 2016, an additional text warning will have to cover 30 per cent of the lower part of the front of the packages.[72] Brazil was the first country in the world to ban misleading terms such as 'light', 'mild' and 'low-tar'[73] and is one of the countries with the strongest health warning measures worldwide.

4.3.3 Colombia

The main tobacco control instrument in Colombia[74] regulates smoking in public places, tobacco APS and tobacco packaging and labelling. Smoking is prohibited on public transport, in enclosed public places and enclosed workplaces. Colombia has one of the most complete smoke-free laws, with no exceptions to the smoking ban. Tobacco advertising is also prohibited in all forms of media as well as promotion. Importantly, the law itself does not define 'promotion', so the Constitutional Court found that 'promotion' should be understood as 'tobacco advertising and promotion' in the WHO FCTC.[75] The law prohibits certain sponsorship of events such as cultural or sporting but not other activities including 'corporate social responsibility' or youth smoking prevention programs. Concerning packaging and labelling, a warning text and image must occupy at least 30 per cent of the two principal display areas.

4.3.4 Ecuador

The Organic Law for the Regulation and Control of Tobacco[76] is the main instrument for tobacco control, regulating smoke-free places, tobacco APS and tobacco packaging and labelling. In Ecuador, smoking is prohibited in indoor workplaces, indoor public places, all health and educational facilities (excluding universities) and on public transport. The only exemption to this rule allows hotels to identify 10 per cent of rooms as smoking rooms. Subnational jurisdictions must adopt regulations and ordinances in accordance with or stricter than the national law. Tobacco APS are generally prohibited but permitted inside places that may be accessed only by adults (18+ years) as well as through direct communication online or regular mail (as long as previous written consent exists and age is verified). Sponsorship is completely prohibited, explicitly specifying that corporate social responsibility programs and youth prevention programs are included in the ban. In terms of packaging and labelling, text and image health warnings must cover 60 per cent of both the front and back of the pack.

4.3.5 Guatemala

The main health legislation in Guatemala regulates, among many other matters pertaining to health, tobacco APS, tobacco packaging and labelling, and restrictions on smoking places.[77] Other decrees and agreements[78] touch upon aspects of the regulation. Smoking is prohibited in any workplace, including outdoor areas of workplaces, as well as in any closed public places and on all public transport. The only exception to this comprehensive ban is for hotel and motel guest-rooms. Unlike other countries, sub-national jurisdictions cannot enact smoke-free laws that are stricter than this national law. Tobacco APS is generally allowed, with only a few restrictions on some forms of tobacco advertising (such as hours of advertising on television and radio intended for youth). All advertising must have the prior approval of a special Commission set up by the Ministry of Health ('MoH') to oversee tobacco advertising. Although tobacco advertising is allowed, it must always be accompanied by health warnings. In terms of packaging and labelling, the law is also weak. Health warnings must occupy only 25 per cent of the front of the pack, and the law does not ban the use of misleading terms, descriptors, trademarks or other signs on tobacco products.

4.3.6 Honduras

The *Special Tobacco Control Law*[79] (effective February 2011) was the first comprehensive tobacco control law to be passed in Honduras. It regulates smoke-free places, tobacco APS and packaging and labelling as well as other aspects of tobacco regulation such as sale and distribution of tobacco products and programs for tobacco prevention and education. The law prohibits the consumption of all tobacco-derived products, rather than just cigars and cigarettes (including smokeless tobacco products and e-cigarettes), in all workplaces, public places and on all means of public transport (including terminals and stations). The law contains two limited exceptions to this comprehensive ban: consumption of tobacco-derived products in cigar factories (in specially designated smoking cabins) and in spaces where 'tobacco tasting' takes place. In terms of APS, all tobacco advertising and promotion by mass media as well as internet sales are prohibited. The same goes for sponsorship of any events where minors can attend. In terms of packaging and labelling, all tobacco-derived products must have text and image warnings on both the front and back of packages (minimum of 50 per cent on each side). Additionally, the use of misleading terms, descriptors and other symbols is banned.

4.3.7 Mexico

The *General Law on Tobacco Control*[80] ('GLTC') is the main instrument governing tobacco control in Mexico. The law covers many aspects of tobacco control, including smoke-free policies, APS, packaging and labelling and enforcement. The Bylaws of the GLTC were established by the Federal Executive in 2009 and fill in the details of broad regulation set out by the GLTC on subjects such as: health licensing; packaging and labelling; APS; restrictions on public smoking; and enforcement authorities and sanctions. In December 2009, the MoH issued an administrative provision (*Acuerdo*) regulating health warnings, pictograms and information contained on packaging. Notwithstanding WHO FCTC art 5.3, these provisions resulted from an agreement between the MoH and the tobacco industry.

In Mexico, indoor smoking is completely prohibited only in primary and secondary schools and in government facilities. In all other public places (referred to in the law as 'places with public access') and workplaces ('interior public or private work areas'), isolated indoor areas exclusively for smoking may be provided.[81] Sub-national jurisdictions can enact smoke-free laws that are stricter than the national law. We will address some examples below.

Mexican law bans most means of tobacco advertising and promotion but provides an exemption for advertising and promotion aimed only at adults through adult publications (although there is no clear definition of what an 'adult' publication is, and the clause has been interpreted liberally by the publishers) and personal communication by mail or within establishments that restrict access to adults. Any form of sponsorship as a means of placing the elements of any brand of tobacco products or that promotes the purchase and use of tobacco products by the population is prohibited, but this prohibition has often not been strictly enforced.[82] Tobacco industry contributions to 'socially responsible' causes are common practice in Mexico. A comprehensive tobacco APS ban is thought to be constitutionally permissible,[83] given that in Mexico protection of free speech does not normally extend to commercial speech.[84]

In terms of packaging and labelling, rotating pictorial and text health warnings are required to cover at least 30 per cent of the front, 100 per cent of the back and 100 per cent of one side of smoked tobacco products packages. The law also prohibits misleading tobacco product packaging and labelling and requires the qualitative (descriptive) disclosure of constituents and emissions.

Important legislation has been passed at the state level.[85] One of the strongest and most comprehensive bans regarding smoke-free spaces is that of Mexico City. The *Law for the Protection of Non-Smokers in Mexico City*[86] was originally passed in 2004; however, a comprehensive ban ensuring smoke-free places was not passed until years later. In 2007, the first reform took place, prohibiting smoking outside expressly authorised and properly adapted smoking areas, enclosed premises, establishments and industries, as well as in other public and private establishments that offer services to the public, educational and health facilities, theatres and on public transport.[87] On 4 March 2008, a new reform was published, which banned smoking in all enclosed public and workplaces, including restaurants and bars, elevators and indoor stairways in any building; establishments where direct attention or services to the public are given (such as banks), government offices or spaces, health and educational facilities, auditoriums, libraries, museums and sport facilities; and on any form of public transport.[88] This was of enormous importance and a great achievement, making the most populated city in the world 100 per cent smoke free in all enclosed public spaces.

Because some of the local laws have been in effect for over five years it is possible to partially measure their impact. In the case of Mexico City, for example, the National Institute of Public Health pointed out in 2009 that since the Law for the Protection of Health of Non-smokers in Mexico City was passed, hospitalisations due to acute myocardial heart attacks had reduced by 19.8 per cent and deaths by 10.6 per cent.[89] Apart from the health benefits, during the time analysed, the state had been able to save up to 717,000 pesos monthly, being funds previously allocated to the care and hospitalisation of the population suffering from acute myocardial heart attacks.

4.3.8 Panama

On 13 January 2008, Panama passed *Law No 13*,[90] which required that the executive branch issue regulations in regard to tobacco control. Pursuant to this law, the MoH issued several executive orders and resolutions,[91] which comprehensively regulated smoke-free places, APS and packaging and labelling. The result is that smoking is prohibited in all indoor public places and indoor workplaces, on public transport and at outdoor sports venues. Apart from this very complete ban, there is also a ban on all types of APS. In terms of packaging and labelling, tobacco product packaging must display text and pictorial warnings on 50 per cent of all the principal display areas, as well as a warning on the lateral sides of the package.

4.3.9 Peru

Peru's primary law on tobacco control was passed in 2006[92] and amended by law in 2010[93] and by Supreme Court decrees[94] in the following years. The initial law and subsequent amendments regulate smoke-free environments, tobacco APS and tobacco packaging and labelling. With the 2010 amendments, all indoor workplaces, public transport and indoor public places became 100 per cent smoke free. There is no comprehensive ban of APS, but some restrictions are in place: media targeted towards minors and advertisements near education facilities or public offices are prohibited. Health text and image warnings are required on at least 50 per cent of both principal display areas of tobacco product packaging. Misleading descriptors are also prohibited. As in Guatemala, sub-national jurisdictions may not enact stricter smoke-free laws.

4.3.10 Uruguay

In 2006, Uruguay was one of the first countries to initiate a series of comprehensive smoke-free area measures. The main instrument regulating tobacco control policy was passed in 2008.[95] Apart from this law, the MoH has enhanced tobacco control through decrees and ordinances so that Uruguayan law now regulates smoke-free places, tobacco APS and packaging and labelling of tobacco products, including provisions on enforcement and sanctions. Smoking is prohibited in all enclosed public places and enclosed workplaces, on public transportation as well as in all areas (including outdoors) of health and educational institutions. Additionally, all forms of tobacco APS are banned (except at points of sale). Uruguay has one of the strongest packaging and labelling policies worldwide: warnings and pictograms must cover 80 per cent of the two principal display areas. Each tobacco brand may use only a single form of presentation, such that misleading tobacco brand variants (including colour-coded gradations) are prohibited.

Uruguay's campaign has been praised as leading to a substantial decrease in tobacco use in the country. In the period 2005–11, per person consumption of cigarettes in Uruguay decreased by 4.3 per cent per year, and the 30-day prevalence of tobacco use in Uruguayan students ages 13, 15 and 17 decreased an average of 8 per cent per year. Overall the prevalence of tobacco use has decreased annually by an estimated 3.3 per cent.[96]

The positive effect of these measures has prompted action by tobacco manufacturers. In 2010, Philip Morris International took legal action against Uruguay, arguing that the single presentation rule for each brand as well as the 80 per cent health warnings violate the country's bilateral investment treaty with Switzerland. The results of this case are pending.[97]

4.4 Tobacco industry interference in the region

4.4.1 Introduction

Latin America has been facing fierce industry interference in the last decade. Although the most visible case is the challenge by Philip Morris International to Uruguay's strong measures, it is certainly not the only one. Other examples can be found in Brazil and Paraguay. After being one of the strongest players through its signing of the WHO FCTC in 2003, Brazil had problems ratifying the treaty due to the interference of the tobacco industry via the country's tobacco growers. More recently, in 2011, Brazil's Congress passed a national smoke-free law, but the President has not yet endorsed it due to interference from tobacco growers and the tobacco industry.[98] When Paraguay was close to signing a smoke-free law, the tobacco industry interfered, halting the initiative.[99] The most recent example was the fifth session of the Conference of the Parties to the WHO FCTC in November 2012, where Honduras and Nicaragua sent official delegations with the objective of fighting Australia's plain packaging laws.[100] Although most of the region has passed laws regarding smoke-free areas, APS and packaging and labelling lag behind. Enforcement of WHO FCTC art 5.3 is also problematic.

Apart from having a large market in Latin America, tobacco companies have many other reasons for interfering in the region. Brazil is the greatest producer of tobacco in the region (second worldwide), followed by Argentina (eighth worldwide).[101] In both countries, the area cultivated has grown significantly since 2000. Latin America also plays an important role in production. Souza Cruz's factory in Brazil is the largest in the region, and in 2009 it was responsible for 30 per cent of the production of British American Tobacco in the region. Countries like Argentina, Chile, Mexico, Paraguay and Venezuela also play a strong role in the production of cigarettes, with a large number of factories mainly supplying British American Tobacco and Philip Morris International.[102]

Tobacco interference in Latin America has targeted both the adoption and implementation of tobacco control policies and has included a range of strategies such as lobbying (eg interference in the decision making process, dissemination of favourable legislative models, amendment proposals for laws and the promotion of useless regulation), mechanisms for political pressure (eg financing electoral campaigns), the hiring of scientific consulting firms to disseminate biased research, information manipulation, using allies and front groups that defend the industry's interests, litigation, intimidation, corporate social responsibility ('CSR') (for instance, using CSR to improve the industry's corporate image with the public, government officials and media outlets and to decrease negative media coverage), contraband and smuggling, and simply violating legislative norms and encouraging the violation of such norms through disinformation or direct intervention.[103]

The following are more detailed examples of industry interference in the region.

4.4.2 Case study: Mexico

Although Mexico has made progress in implementing tobacco control policies, the tobacco industry has designed and implemented various strategies to constrain the adoption of public health policies established by the WHO FCTC. The tobacco industry interference has intensified since the signing of the WHO FCTC. Four key moments for tobacco control in Mexico took place between 2004 and 2010, each entailing formal and informal intervention by institutions, individuals and other actors.[104] These four moments are: (i) the WHO FCTC signing in 2003;[105] (ii) the agreement between the executive branch of the federal government and the tobacco industry concerning the tobacco commonly known as 'peso por cajetilla', implemented in 2004;[106] (iii) the enactment of the *General Law for Tobacco Control* in 2008 and its aftermath, including litigation against the more stringent local Mexico City law;[107] and (iv) the approval of a scheme of gradual increase of tax provisions of the *Law for the Special Tax on Production and Services* in 2009.[108] Formal tobacco industry strategies for intervening in these different events included reaching mutual agreements with different government officials, undertaking corporate social responsibility efforts, such as British American Tobacco Mexico's volunteer program winning Best Socially Responsible Practice Award from the Mexican Centre for Philanthropy in 2006,[109] and image promotion of the brand through participation of the brand in cultural and educational events in Mexico. Informal strategies included obstructing the legislative process (for instance, multiplying the number of legislative commissions involved in tobacco legislation), lobbying, economic and political benefits through bribes and corruption, high profile hiring, and donations to the state.[110]

The annual and biennial reports of major tobacco companies operating in Latin America, British American Tobacco and Philip Morris International,[111] reveal the priority areas for tobacco control, and can be grouped into the following categories in descending order of importance: taxation, free trade, 100 per cent smoke-free areas, health warnings, advertising and public relations. Within each of these areas, the industry consistently pursues certain objectives: first, to avoid the adoption of tobacco control policies; second, to encourage the adoption of policies that minimise tobacco control impact; finally to obstruct proper implementation of adopted policies.[112]

The internal documents of the tobacco industry show that they are faced with the same issues around the world. The priority for the tobacco industry is taxation, aiming for the lowest possible level as a percentage of final consumer price or, failing that, slow gradual increases more easily absorbed by consumers.[113] More generally, the tobacco industry systematically seeks to prevent or delay the entry into force of tobacco control policies.[114] In Mexico, the tobacco industry has aggressively targeted tax laws. From 2000 to 2009, the tobacco industry was successful in Mexico in restricting the annual average increase in final price to less than 1 per cent.[115] In 2009, the Mexican Congress approved an increase of two Mexican pesos for every cigarette pack, to be implemented gradually between 2010 and 2013.[116] Civil society argued through a strong media campaign that this increase would be insignificant in the long run and would not aid in reducing demand for tobacco products.[117] In October 2010, after previous failures, legislators and civil society involved in the tobacco control movement acted together and pushed through a 25 per cent increase in the final price.[118] With this increase, taxes for tobacco products now represent 68.8 per cent of the sales price.[119]

The tobacco industry reacted quickly to this accomplishment. In 2011, with the fear of yet another increase, the tobacco industry created new obstacles with their own intense media campaign against the tax reform of 2010. This campaign tried to discredit the fiscal policy in the eyes of the public and at the same time pressured political figures not to increase taxes even more.[120] Civil society has played a crucial role in countering the tobacco industry's arguments.

Other actions of the tobacco industry were seen in the legislative process of the *General Law for Tobacco Control*. Not only were there last minute changes in the legislative process,[121] but there was also, by some accounts, direct tobacco industry involvement in the drafting of the law.[122] Once approved, the tobacco industry managed to delay the publication for months and the publication of its bylaws for over a year.[123] On 31 August 2007, the law initiative for the *General Law for Tobacco Control* was filed before Congress. Its main proposal included establishing a comprehensive ban on smoking in enclosed public places, limiting advertising to adult magazines and publications, including pictograms and health warnings on at least 50 per cent of the front part of the display, and prohibiting cigarette sale by the unit. The law passed a complex legislative process that was delayed by members of Congress. Even the Health Commission modified the law, making it more permissive and excluding certain sectors of the tobacco industry from its prohibitions. On 30 May 2008, the law was finally published, with many modifications to the original proposal that substantively weakened it. The new law allowed for more types of advertising than those originally contemplated, established an *obligation* to create smoking areas in closed spaces where smoking was banned and reduced to 30 per cent the display areas for the warning pictograms. After the law was passed, again tobacco industry intervention weakened and delayed the approval of bylaws at every opportunity. The bylaws were published with a six month delay after publication of the law – which itself was published over three months after its approval, contrary to constitutional mandate, which gives the Executive a few days for publication – and the warning and pictogram bylaws a full year after that.[124] In all, regulations approved by Congress in mid-2008 were fully in force by 30 June 2009, with no reasonable explanation except tobacco industry interference. They were much more permissible and flexible than originally sought.

Importantly, tobacco industry interference managed to challenge Mexico City's tobacco control law – much more stringent and rapidly put in place by local government – twice before the Supreme Court. The first challenge, an *Acción de Inconstitucionalidad 167/2007* (unconstitutionality claim), was presented by the Federal Executive on 3 December 2007 against a local congressional law approved in October 2007 for restricting tobacco promotion, arguing that promotion was a form of advertising and that this was federal jurisdiction.[125] The challenge put pressure on Mexico City's local congress throughout the latter part of 2007, in the process of amending its local law to adopt more stringent smoke-free regulations. In the end, the local ban on promotion was removed from the law in exchange for the federal Executive party's local support for more stringent smoke-free regulations in the January 2008 amendment to the law. Later, a minority of local congress – among whom were several congressmen who had previously supported the tobacco control measures that they were now questioning – unsuccessfully challenged the legislation as whole before the Supreme Court, reportedly with tobacco industry backing, as discussed further below.

Other strategies included blatant disregard of the law, such as the launching of a series of concerts – Marlborough MX Beat – openly promoted by (and advertising) tobacco products, testing if authorities would respond. No sanction was applied for such activities.

4.4.3 Case study: Brazil

When Brazil passed a law prohibiting the advertising of tobacco products (with the exception of inside point of sale) in 2000, the tobacco companies quickly came up with new strategies to trump the law. Since advertising could now be found at points of sale, the industry provided support for the number and types of points of sales to grow considerably. Supermarkets, bakeries, newspaper stands and other traditional places acting as points of sale were used for advertising, and even events such as concerts and parties were becoming temporary points of sale allowing advertising to reach a large number of people.[126] The problem with industry interference is that it dedicates a large amount of resources to exploiting exceptions in regulation. Because of this, points of sale started popping up with new and innovative designs and promotions.[127] In most cases, these new bold and flash displays were directed at children.[128]

Additionally, tobacco companies started addressing many campaigns towards youth, with sponsorship and branding.[129] What the Brazilian case shows is that leaving legislative gaps or allowing for exceptions enables the realignment of the tobacco industry's strategies from one site to another.

4.4.4 Case study: Colombia

Colombia has one of the most comprehensive sets of tobacco control legislation in the region. On 21 July 2011, a full ban on advertising, promotion and sponsorship came into effect, one of the first in the region. The tobacco industry focused their resources and efforts on the point-of-sale exhibits creating new and flashy dispensaries and on creating a bond with the private sector such as store-owners, supermarket administrators and other establishments that sell cigarettes. Tobacco companies looked to use the weaker or unclear parts of the legislation or to simply violate the law. Parallel to these changes, the tobacco industry took on a strong role in corporate social responsibility in order to assure the continuity of positive public visibility and lower support for the Colombian legislation. The tobacco industry tried to weaken the law in stages. First, the industry tried to have the law declared unconstitutional, by arguing that *Law No 1335* went against the freedom of commerce and the freedom of expression. Having failed at that, they sought out ways to undermine the law by taking advantage of the fact that all legislation is subject to interpretation and in this way sought to exploit the grey areas. For example, tobacco companies sought to strengthen ties with storekeepers by implementing promotions, contests, discounts and prices to promote the sale of particular brands, a strategy that was not directly prohibited by the law.[130] At the beginning of 2012, in order to tighten some of the areas of ambiguity in the legislation, the government passed bylaws[131] to regulate the display of tobacco products at point of sale, establishing for example that only one packet could be displayed, that the warnings could not be hidden and that tobacco products could not be visible to the public but rather only revealed upon request through the salesperson.[132] By clarifying the law, however, leeway was given to the tobacco industry by allowing the display of a single packet of tobacco products.

4.5 The region's tobacco litigation

4.5.1 Introduction

Litigation has been used to both obstruct and further tobacco control. The tobacco industry has put forth legal challenges with arguments similar to those deployed in other regions and invoking fundamental rights such as free speech, the right to economic freedom, property rights, anti-discrimination principles, the right to work and the freedom of commerce. As so many countries in the region have passed effective laws at the national and local level, the tobacco industry's strategy has often focused on the courts. In an increasing number of cases, the tobacco industry or their representatives challenge tobacco control policies, both through tort claims and constitutional challenges.

In Brazil, for example, where Souza Cruz, a local tobacco company, had in the past been a defendant, the company turned plaintiff. In *Souza Cruz v ACT Brazil*, Souza Cruz sought to prevent ACT Brazil, a public health non-governmental organisation, from publishing a video criticising the placement of tobacco products near candies, gum and other products popular with children. Souza Cruz argued that the video suggested the company was encouraging the criminal act of selling cigarettes to minors. The court ruled that the video did not target the company specifically but was instead generally advocating for greater restrictions on point of sale placement of tobacco products. The court found there was no injury to the company sufficient to justify a restriction of ACT Brazil's freedom of expression.[133]

Other cases are brought by legislative minorities arguing either that tobacco control legislation is too strong or in some cases not effective or not in accordance with WHO FCTC guidelines. In Costa Rica, for example, in a case of Legislative Consultation with the Constitutional Division of the Supreme Court,[134] part of the legislative assembly claimed before the Supreme Court that the restrictions regarding advertising, promotion and sponsorship; price and tax measures; smoke-free measures; contents and disclosure measures; illicit trade; and other such measures were disproportionate and unreasonable. The court declared the law constitutional and explained that the country has the power to place effective restrictions on tobacco, with the goal of protecting public health.

From the tobacco control camps we can identify two types of litigation: litigation on the 'defensive' and litigation on the 'offensive'. In defensive litigation, the government or a group of individuals is looking to protect tobacco control regulations against industry attacks.[135] Litigation on the offensive includes lawsuits against the state for failing to comply with the duty to protect and regulate its citizens. In other words, these types of cases are where individuals argue that the minimum standards for the protection of the right to health are not met. The following three cases are emblematic of litigation in the region, providing relevant precedents.

A very important precedent, also coming from the judiciary, but not through adjudication, is the consideration of the WHO FCTC as a human rights treaty by Mexico's Supreme Court. In the summer of 2011, a constitutional amendment recognising the principle of progressive realisation of human rights and granting constitutional hierarchy to human rights established in international treaties was adopted in Mexico.[136] In response, the Mexican Supreme Court deemed those international treaties signed and ratified by the government to be incorporated in that 'constitutional block'. The WHO FCTC was included as developing the right to health.[137] Thus, the WHO FCTC has been explicitly identified as a human rights treaty by a Supreme Court, which should be considered by the tobacco control movement as a signal regarding the potential use of human rights law in advancing tobacco control.[138]

4.5.2 Mexico City's local tobacco control legislation

Unlike countries such as Argentina and Guatemala, Mexico did not determine explicitly in its national legislation whether local and state measures could be stricter than the federal law. Following Mexico City's enactment of stringent tobacco control measures, a legislative minority claimed that Mexico City's tobacco control law was unconstitutional insofar as it did not conform to the federal law and established more stringent smoke-free measures. The Mexican Supreme Court ruled that as long as local congress enhanced the right to health, it could establish divergent measures.[139] This was the first major precedent in Mexico, establishing tobacco control as a question that needed to be decided, fundamentally, from the perspective of a basic right to health.

4.5.3 Balderas Woolrich Amparo

The Balderas Woolrich Amparo[140] case involved a challenge to Mexico's federal tobacco control law on the grounds that it does not sufficiently protect the constitutional right to health by not complying with the minimum level of protection recognised by the Mexican government upon ratification of the WHO FCTC. The plaintiff was a social smoker who argued that portions of the GLTC – specifically those authorising certain types of publicity and allowing for smoking areas indoors – and the corresponding amendments to the *General Health Law*, which deregulated the content of tobacco publicity, actually diminished protection of the constitutional right to health against the tobacco epidemic. The court only heard the challenge against the authorisation of publicity and advertising, for changes to the wording of the clauses regarding smoking areas (see above) rendered the challenge of that portion procedurally moot. The ground for the challenge was the constitutional right to health, with the WHO FCTC serving mostly as *evidence* that the government acknowledged the legislation it passed as too weak to protect health effectively. The WHO FCTC served mainly as the minimum standard, but was also held up as binding under domestic law. The Supreme Court ruled that the case was justifiable on right to health grounds, but refused to decide on the merits of the case because an explicit constitutional clause at the time banned remedies with 'general effects' for constitutional challenges brought forth by citizens, and the restriction of publicity would have required that the case have general effects.[141] Thus, the case was dismissed on procedural grounds, but a precedent was set establishing tobacco control legislation as a right to health matter, which would be later reflected in the court's decision to include the WHO FCTC in the list of human rights instruments that were to become binding following a constitutional amendment in 2010.[142]

4.5.4 *Decision C-830/10 Colombia*

The plaintiff in this case[143] argued that a law banning advertising, the promotion of tobacco products and the sponsorship of sporting events by tobacco companies is unconstitutional because it impinges economic freedom and the freedom of commerce, while being a 'disproportionate and unreasonable' restriction to the exercise of the right to free private initiative and an impediment to the right of consumers to information. The court held that the law is not unconstitutional because, although free enterprise and freedom of expression are constitutional guarantees, they are not absolute and therefore they accept restrictions and legitimate interventions. Additionally, commercial advertising is a mode of discourse that does not have the same degree of protection as other manifestations of ideas covered by freedom of expression: its purpose is to facilitate economic transactions and not to encourage participation and democratic deliberation. The legislature may impose restrictions, even strict restrictions, in commercial advertising, so this is not part of freedom of expression.

Furthermore, the court stated that the legality of an action per se did not make its promotion a fundamental right, and that the state could restrict promotion because of its harmful effects to public health.

4.5.5 *5000 Citizens v Article 3 of Law No 28705*

In this case,[144] 5000 Peruvian citizens brought direct action before the Constitutional Court challenging the constitutionality of an article of the tobacco control law that completely prohibits smoking in certain public places, including outdoor areas of educational facilities. They argued that these limits impinged the right to personal autonomy, the right to commerce and the right to economic freedom, and that smoking should be allowed in outdoor areas of institutions for higher learning for adults and in special smoking areas. The court dismissed the plaintiffs' suit and confirmed the constitutionality of the law. The court held that the law was strictly proportional, placing the right to health above the alleged violated rights, and that the smoking ban was the ideal means to comply with provisions of the WHO FCTC that require protection from exposure to tobacco smoke.

5 Conclusions

Understanding and coming to terms with an epidemiological transition by which Latin America is shifting away from infectious diseases towards chronic NCDs may be the key health challenge facing the region. This will require a major shift in the role governments are expected to play. In addition to the provision of basic health services, governments need to revise their role as regulator. If NCDs are raising the greatest threat to health in the region, then it is prevention, not provision (of services), that needs to take centre stage. If consumption patterns are a key element in prevention, regulation of markets and products are probably the key intervention that governments need to undertake. This is actually an opportunity: most often it is cheaper to regulate a market than to provide health services. It is also a broader intervention which benefits – or should benefit – the population at large and not just those lucky enough to gain access to health services. Finally, because it demands proper regulation and not specific investments of budget that are difficult to direct from outside government bureaucracies, it is a type of intervention particularly vulnerable to legal action, whether through the international establishment of framework conventions, or by being justiciable through courts. In any case, tobacco control seems to be the wedge that is opening the way for health regulation in the region, so special attention needs to be paid to enforcing tobacco regulation, and documenting the effects of good (and not-so-good) enforcement.

Tobacco control has come a long way in a short time in Latin America. Its importance as both a market for tobacco products and a laboratory for tobacco control ensures that it will continue to be a key battleground for both the tobacco industry and the tobacco control movement. It is difficult to draw general conclusions for the whole region, for even a rapid overview of policies throughout the region, when put together with a more nuanced understanding of the differences between countries, tells us of the risk of so-called 'one-size-fits-all' solutions. There are, however, several lessons to be learned and common elements to observe. First, the fact that taxes have not been the central thrust of tobacco control policies in the region is significant. This is surely the result, at least in part, of the more complex nature of taxes, involving all areas of government and not mainly health. If we take into consideration that the first priority of the tobacco industry is to obstruct taxes, then the failure to establish taxes might also suggest that the industry's key objectives are being achieved, even while tobacco control policies advance.

Second, a general claim might be made that carving out exceptions to general rules – such as a ban on advertising or a ban on indoor smoking – can potentially undermine tobacco control policies by making enforcement of the general rule more difficult. That is: concessions made to the tobacco industry by carving out general protective rules are not only a defeat of the specific issue at hand, but also risk becoming a platform from which the tobacco industry and its allies will undermine broader tobacco control efforts.

This brings us to our key finding: the challenge in Latin America today is not so much setting up tobacco control policies but ensuring their enforcement. Particular attention needs to be paid to the disconnect between law in theory and law in practice. It is paramount for authorities and tobacco control advocates to gather the information necessary to properly assess how much and in what respects tobacco control policies are being undermined in their application, and to reflect upon what needs to be done to assure enforcement before the tobacco industry undermines tobacco control efforts by wedging in exceptions and then promoting non-compliance. The task remains considerable.

Notes

1 Sistema Nacional de Información en Salud, *Base de Datos Sobre Defunciones* [Mortality Database] (21 December 2010) <http://www.sinais.salud.gob.mx/basesdedatos/std_defunciones.html>.
2 'Obesity and Overweight' (Fact sheet No 311, World Health Organization, May 2012) <http://www.who.int/mediacentre/factsheets/fs311/en/>.
3 Franco Sassi, *Obesity and the Economics of Prevention: Fit Not Fat* (OECD, 2010) 60 <http://www.oecd.org/health/health-systems/obesityandtheeconomicsofprevention fitnotfat.htm>.
4 Ibid 108.
5 Steven Bodzin, 'Obesity Weighing on America – Latin America, That Is', *The Christian Science Monitor* (online), 4 September 2012 <http://www.csmonitor.com/World/Americas/2012/0904/Obesity-weighing-on-America-Latin-America-that-is>.
6 Ibid.
7 Sofía Charvel, Martin Lajous and Hernández Mauricio, *Obesidad, la Epidemia* (1 March 2013) Nexos [2] <http://www.nexos.com.mx/?P=leerarticulo&Article=2103173>.
8 Ibid [3].
9 Ibid [16].
10 Ibid [16].
11 Ibid [18].
12 Ibid [10].
13 Bodzin, above n 5.
14 Ibid.
15 Ibid.
16 'Obesity and Overweight', above n 2.
17 Secretaría de Salud, 'Principales causas de mortalidad general 2000–2008' (Sistema Nacional de Información en Salud, 2010).
18 Ibid.
19 Consejo Nacional de Evaluación de la Política de Desarrollo Social (CONEVAL), Comunicado de prensa 006/09, Distrito Federal (18 July 2009).
20 Consejo Nacional de Evaluación de la Política de Desarrollo Social, *Pobreza por ingresos y alimentación* (12 February 2013) <http://www.coneval.gob.mx/rw/resource/coneval/med_pobreza/3489.pdf>.
21 *Acuerdo Nacional para la Salud Alimentaria, estrategia contra el sobrepeso y la obesidad*, Secretaría de Salud Pública, primera edición, January 2010.
22 This link was developed by Daniel Mirand Terrés as part of an investigation regarding food security for the Substance Control Area in the Right to Health Program at the Center for Economic Research and Teaching, Mexico ('CIDE').
23 World Food Summit, *Report of the World Food Summit*, FAO Doc WFS 96/REP (13–17 November 1996) <http://www.fao.org/docrep/003/w3548s/w3548s00.htm>.
24 Centro de Investigación e Inteligencia Económica, 'El índice de paridad poder de compra nutricional (Nut3-Cio) ¿En qué ciudad de México es más barato ser obeso?' (November 2010) *Boletín Económico*, 4 <http://pcwww.liv.ac.uk/~kitamend/ciie/Boletin7merged.pdf>.
25 Kate Kelland, 'Malnutrition Condemns Millions to Stunted Lives: UNICEF', *Reuters* (online), 7 June 2013 <http://www.reuters.com/article/2013/06/07/us-nutrition-idUSBRE9560DL20130607>.
26 Ibid.

27 Secretaría de Salud, *Acuerdo Nacional para la Salud Alimentaria* (January 2010) <http://www.promocion.salud.gob.mx/dgps/descargas1/programas/Acuerdo%20Original%20con%20creditos%2015%20feb%2010.pdf>.

28 Charvel, Lajous and Mauricio, above n 7.

29 Ibid.

30 'Lucha Libre Wrestlers Help Promote Healthy Eating in México', *BBC News* (online), 14 August 2012 <http://www.bbc.co.uk/news/world-latin-america-19262516>.

31 World Health Organization, *Global Status Report on Alcohol and Health* (WHO, 2011) 20.

32 Ibid 42.

33 Ibid 8.

34 Ibid 17.

35 Ibid 17, 31.

36 *Informe de la OMS insta a tomar medidas para reducir el consumo nocivo de alcohol*, Oficina Regional de la Organización Mundial de la Salud, Organización Panamericana de la Salud (14 February 2011) <http://new.paho.org/arg/index.php?option=com_content&view=article&id=662&catid=724 per cent3A----alcoholismo-y-consumo-de-otras-sustancias-psic&Itemid=1> ('*Informe de la OMS*').

37 Secretaría de Salud, above n 17.

38 World Health Organization, above n 31, 52.

39 *Informe de la OMS*, above n 36.

40 Bolivia, Brazil, Chile, Colombia, Costa Rica, Ecuador, El Salvador, Guyana, Honduras, Mexico, Nicaragua, Panama, Suriname, Uruguay and Venezuela.

41 Argentina, Bolivia, Brazil, Colombia, Costa Rica, Ecuador, El Salvador, Guatemala, Guyana, Honduras, Mexico, Nicaragua, Panama, Paraguay, Peru, Suriname, Uruguay and Venezuela.

42 Brazil, Colombia, Costa Rica, Ecuador, Honduras, Mexico, Panama and Venezuela.

43 Brazil, Ecuador, Honduras, Mexico, Panama and Venezuela.

44 Bolivia, Costa Rica, Ecuador, Honduras, Mexico, Paraguay and Venezuela.

45 Bolivia, Costa Rica, Honduras and Mexico.

46 Argentina, Belize, Brazil, Chile, Colombia, Costa Rica, Ecuador, El Salvador, Honduras, Mexico, Nicaragua, Panama, Peru, Suriname, Uruguay and Venezuela: World Health Organization, above n 31.

47 [Dry Law] (Brazil), Federal Law No 11.705, 19 June 2008.

48 World Health Organization, above n 31, 47.

49 Ibid 47.

50 *Manual de Alcoholimetría*, Centro Nacional para la Prevención de Accidentes (CENAPRA) y Secretaría de Salud (2009).

51 Secretaría de Segurdad Pública del DF, *Conduce sin alcohol. Alcoholimetro* (19 August 2013) <http://www.ssp.df.gob.mx/PartCiudadana/Pages/Alcoholimetro.aspx>.

52 Ibid.

53 'Tobacco Industry Strategy in Latin American Courts: A Litigation Guide' (O'Neill Institute for National and Global Health Law, February 2012) 12.

54 Ibid.

55 Although there are different expert opinions about what constitutes Latin America, for practical reasons in this chapter we will use the following list of countries: Argentina, Belize, Bolivia, Brazil, Chile, Colombia, Costa Rica, Cuba, Ecuador, El Salvador, Guatemala, Guyana, Honduras, Mexico, Nicaragua, Panama, Paraguay, Peru, Suriname, Uruguay and Venezuela.

56 Almost all the countries in the region have ratified the WHO FCTC. The only countries in the region that have not done so are Argentina, Cuba and El Salvador. See World Health Organization, *Parties to the WHO Framework Convention on Tobacco Control* (2013) Framework Convention on Tobacco Control <http://www.who.int/fctc/signatories_parties/en/>.

57 *Framework Convention on Tobacco Control* opened for signature 16 June 2003, 2302 UNTS 166 (entered into force 27 February 2005) ('WHO FCTC').

58 Eduardo Bianco, 'Tobacco Control in Latin America: Past, Present and Future' (The Framework Convention Alliance for Tobacco Control, 2012) <http://www.fctc.org/index.php?option=com_content&view=article&id=947:tobacco-control-in-latin-america-past-present-and-future&catid=257:opinion-pieces&Itemid=263>.

59 Ibid.

60 Ibid.

61 On 4 May 2000, the bylaw of the *Ley General de Salud en materia de publicidad* [General Health Law in Regard to Advertising] (Mexico) was passed establishing certain prohibitions on tobacco advertising. Tobacco advertisements and gifts with trademarks or brands cannot be directed towards minors; advertisements can be transmitted via television and radio only after 10:00pm, via cinemas only in films rated R or X and via the internet only in websites targeting adults.

62 The 1988 Brazilian Constitution in its art 220 gave competence to the federal sphere to impose restrictions on cigarette, alcoholic beverage and medication advertisements and to require the inclusion of health warnings.

63 *Lei No 9.294: Dispõe sobre as restrições ao uso e à propaganda de produtos fumígeros, bebidas alcoólicas, medicamentos, terapias e defensivos agrícolas, nos termos do § 4° do art 220 da Constituição Federal* (Brazil) 15 July 1996 ('*Lei No 9.294*'); Luiz Antonio Teixeira and Tiago Alves Jaques, 'Legislation and Tobacco Control in Brazil' (2011) 57(3) *Brazilian Journal of Cancerology* 295.

64 Commercial tobacco advertisements were restricted to internal areas at points of sale. Advertisements cannot associate the product with sports, children or adolescents. Tobacco product publicity was banned from radio, television, cinema, newspapers, magazines, printouts and billboards, as well as advertisements on the internet. Sponsorship of cultural and international sports activities by tobacco companies was banned with effect from 2005: Teixeira and Jaques, above n 63.

65 *Ley 26.687: Regulación de la publicidad, promoción y consumo de los productos elaborados con tabaco.* (Argentina) 14 July 2011.

66 Campaign for Tobacco-Free Kids, *Tobacco Control Laws: Country Details for Argentina* (15 October 2013) <http://www.tobaccocontrollaws.org/legislation/country/argentina/summary>.

67 Buenos Aires, Cordoba, Entre Rios, La Rioja, Mendoza, Neuquen, San Juan, Santa Fe and Tucuman.

68 The Mendoza province law that prohibits smoking in enclosed places is Law 7.790.

69 'Tucuman se despide del cigarillo', *La nación* (online), 29 June 2006 <http://www.lanacion.com.ar/818978-tucuman-se-despide-del-cigarrillo>; Campaign for Tobacco-Free Kids, above n 66.

70 *Lei No 9.294* (Brazil), above n 63.

71 Ibid.

72 Ibid.

73 Campaign for Tobacco-Free Kids, *Tobacco Control Laws: Country Details for Brazil* <http://www.tobaccocontrollaws.org/legislation/country/brazil/summary>.

74 *Ley No. 1335: Disposiciones por medio de las cuales se previenen daños a la salud de los menores de edad, la población no fumadora y se estipulan políticas públicas para la prevención del consumo del tabaco y el abandono de la dependencia del tabaco del fumador y sus derivados en la población colombiana* (Colombia), 21 July 2009.

75 *Demanda de inconstitucionalidad contra los artículos 14, 15, 16 y 17 de la Ley 1335 de 2009* [Colombian Constitutional Court], Sentencia C-830/10, 20 October 2010.

76 *Ley Orgánica para la Regulación y Control del Tabaco* (Ecuador), 22 July 2011.

77 *Decreto Número 90–97* (Guatemala), *Diario de Centroamérica* (7 November 2000).

78 *Government Agreement No 426-2001 (Bylaws for the Regulation, Approval and Advertising and Places of Use for Tobacco-Related Products)* (Guatemala); *Decree No 74-2008 (Law Creating Tobacco Smoke Free Environments)* (Guatemala); *Government Agreement No 137-2009 (Bylaws of Decree No 74-2008)* (Guatemala).

79 *Decreto 92-2010: Ley Especial para el Control de Tabaco* (Honduras), *La Gaceta, Diario Oficial de la República de Honduras* (21 August 2010).

80 *Ley General para el Control del Tabaco* (Mexico), *Diario Oficial de la Federación* (30 May 2008).

81 Importantly, the original text of the law approved in 2008 spoke of an obligation to establish smoking areas indoors (art 27: 'En lugares con acceso al público, o en áreas interiores de trabajo, públicas o privadas, incluidas las universidades e instituciones de educación superior, *deberán* existir zonas exclusivamente para fumar, las cuales deberán de conformidad con las disposiciones reglamentarias'), as a result of a number of last minute changes that the tobacco industry managed to introduce into the bill immediately before it was submitted to a vote. Civil society managed to overturn that wording and eliminate the 'obligatory' character of such spaces in a subsequent amendment in January 2010.

82 In 2008 and 2009, for example, Philip Morris sponsored a large music festival in Mexico City named the Marlboro MX Beat without any reprimands.

83 *Amparo en Revisión 7/2009* [Supreme Court of Justice of the Nation, Mexico], June 2011.

84 Ibid.

85 Apart from Mexico City, other states have passed laws that make all enclosed spaces 100 per cent smoke free. These include Tabasco (2011), Zacatecas (2011), Morelos (2012), Veracruz (2012) and Jalisco (2013). Other states such as Aguascalientes (October 2006) passed smoke-free laws (with exceptions) before the passing of the GLTC. The Law for the Protection of Non-smokers in Aguascalientes is not as comprehensive as that of Mexico City or the other states mentioned above.

86 *Decreto de la ley de Protección a la Salud de los no Fumadores en el Distrito Federal* (Mexico), *Gaceta Oficial del Distrito Federal* (29 January 2004).

87 *Decreto de la ley de Protección a la Salud de los no Fumadores en el Distrito Federal* (Mexico), *Gaceta Oficial del Distrito Federal* (1 November 2007).

88 *Decreto de la ley de Protección a la Salud de los no Fumadores en el Distrito Federal* (Mexico), *Gaceta Oficial del Distrito Federal* (4 March 2008).

89 Edith Martínez, 'Ley antihumo disminuyó 20 per cent infartos dice Salud', *El Universal* (online), 30 May 2009 <http://www.eluniversal.com.mx/ciudad/95615.html>. According to an article by the newspaper *El Universal*, this study was obtained by the National Institute of Public Health from an analysis of the first 14 months after the law was put into effect in April 2008, allowing many establishments in Mexico City to become smoke free. This article presents an interview with the Chief of the Department of Investigation on Tobacco (of this same institute), Luz Myriam Reynales, where she maintains that smoke-free spaces have benefited the physical state of all Mexican citizens and have reduced medical costs.

90 *Ley No 13 Que adopta medidas para el control del tabaco y sus efectos nocivos en la salud* (Panama), *Gaceta Oficial Digital* (25 January 2008).

91 Ministry of Health Executive Order No 230; Ministry of Health, Office of Public Health, Resolution No 809; Ministry of Health, Office of Public Health, Images for Resolution No 809; Ministry of Health, Office of Public Health, Resolution No 868; Ministry of Health, Office of Public Health, Resolution No 153; Ministry of Health Executive Decree No 611; Ministry of Health, Office of Public Health, Resolution No 0968.

92 *Law No 28705: Ley General para la Prevención y Control de los Riesgos del Consumo del Tabaco* (Peru), *Gaceta Jurídica* (13 March 2006).

93 *Law No 29517: Ley que modifica la Ley Núm. 28705, Ley General para la Prevención y Control de los Riesgos del Consumo del Tabaco* (Peru), *Gaceta Jurídica* (1 April 2010).
94 Supreme Decrees No 015-2008 and 001-2010.
95 *Ley No 18.256: Control del Tabaquismo* (Uruguay) *Diario Oficial* (10 March 2008).
96 Winston Abascal, et al, 'Tobacco Control Campaign in Uruguay: A Population-based Trend Analysis', *The Lancet*, 14 September 2012 <http://dx.doi.org/10.1016/S0140-6736(12)60826-5>.
97 Ibid.
98 Bianco, above n 58.
99 Ibid.
100 Ibid.
101 *La salud no se negocia: La sociedad civil frente a las estrategias de la industria tabacalera en América Latina. Casos de estudio 2010–2012*, Fundación InterAmericana del Corazón – Argentina, Fundación InterAmericana del Corazón – México (Corporate Accountability International and Aliança de Controle do Tabagismo, 2012) 13 ('*La salud no se negocia*').
102 Ibid 15.
103 Ibid 11–12.
104 Alejandro Madrazo et al, *Identificación de las estrategias de la industria tabacalera en México* (Documentos de Trabajo No 53, CIDE, 2011) 6–9.
105 FCTC, *Parties to the WHO Framework Convention on Tobacco Control* (25 June 2013) <http://www.who.int/fctc/signatories_parties/en/>.
106 Secretaría de Salud, *Convenio para ampliar la regulación y normatividad relativos a cigarros y otros productos* (18 June 2004) <http://www.salud.gob.mx/unidades/ cdi/ressisi/0001200020306_055.pdf>.
107 *Ley General para el Control del Tabaco* (Mexico), 30 May 2008; *Acción de Inconstitucionalidad 119/2008* [Supreme Court of Justice of the Nation, Mexico], 3 September 2009.
108 Cámara de Diputados, *Boletín de Información No 0361* (October 2009) <http://www3.diputados.gob.mx/camara/005_comunicacion/a_boletines/2009_2009/010_octubre/31_31/0361_rechazan_diputados_modificacion_del_senado_sobre_impuesto_especial_al_tabaco>.
109 British American Tobacco, *Corporate Citizenship – Local Recognition* (19 August 2013) <http://www.bat.com/group/sites/uk__3mnfen.nsf/vwPagesWebLive/DO6ZKMPT?opendocument&SKN=1>.
110 Madrazo et al, above n 104, 26–36.
111 Ibid 13–19.
112 Ibid 13.
113 Ibid 13–14.
114 Ibid 1–19.
115 Ibid 64.
116 *La salud no se negocia*, above n 101, 19.
117 Ibid 19.
118 Ibid 19–21.
119 Ibid 21–2.
120 Ibid.
121 Madrazo et al, above n 104, 2, 64.
122 Ibid 76–9.
123 Ibid 78–9.
124 The complete bylaws (*Reglamento de la Ley General de Control del Tabaco*) were published on 31 May 2009.
125 *Acción de Inconstitucionalidad 167/2007* [Supreme Court of Justice of the Nation, Mexico], 9 April 2008.
126 *La salud no se negocia*, above n 101, 46.

127   Ibid 47.
128   Ibid.
129   Ibid.
130   Ibid 29.
131   *Circulares 05 and 11.*
132   *La salud no se negocia,* above n 101, 30.
133   *Souza Cruz v ACT Brazil,* Sixth Civil Chamber, Court of Appeals, State of Rio de Janeiro, Brazil (28 September 2012).
134   Costa Rica, Legislative Consultation, Constitutional Division of the Supreme Court, No 2012-003918 (2012).
135   Oscar Cabrera (O'Neill Institute for National and Global Health Law), 'Global Context in Tobacco Control' (Paper presented at the Campaign for Tobacco-Free Kids Legal Seminar Workshop, Washington DC, December 2012).
136   Article 1 of the Mexican Constitution was changed to include: 'In the United Mexican States, all people will enjoy the human rights granted by this Constitution and the international treaties of which Mexico is a part of ...'.
137   For the full list of international treaties protected by the Mexican government due to the recognition of human rights see: Suprema Corte de Justicia de la Nación, *Reformas Constitucionales en material de Amparo y Derechos Humanos publciadas en junio de 2011* (19 August 2013) <http://www2.scjn.gob.mx/red/constitucion/TI.html>.
138   For a more nuanced exploration of the potential of human rights law in tobacco control see Oscar Cabrera and Alejandro Madrazo, 'Human Rights as a Tool for Tobacco Control in Latin America' (2010) 52(2) *Salud Pública de México* 288. In that article it is argued that considering the WHO FCTC itself as a human rights instrument was problematic from a doctrinal point of view. The decision of the Mexican Supreme Court, if accompanied by similar positioning, could well change that.
139   *Acción de Inconstitucionalidad 119/2007* [Supreme Court of Justice of the Nation, Mexico] 3 December 2007.
140   The Balderas Woolrich case was part of a larger strategy put in place by the Mexican tobacco control movement with the support of the international movement. It was one of 48 cases presented to Mexican courts, showing the importance and the participation of the civil society in the tobacco control movement: *Amparo en Revisión 315/2010* [Supreme Court of Justice of the Nation, Mexico], 28 March 2011.
141   The Mexican Constitution signals in art 107:

>   Todas las controversias de que habla el Artículo 103 se sujetarán a los procedimientos y formas del orden jurídico que determine la ley, de acuerdo a las bases siguientes: ... II. La sentencia será siempre tal, que sólo se ocupe de individuos particulares, limitándose a ampararlos y protegerlos en el caso especial sobre el que verse la queja, sin hacer una declaración general respecto de la ley o acto que la motivare. In other words, it follows the doctrine that a court ruling deeming a law unconstitutional should only benefit the plaintiff in the specific case brought before the court, without making a general declaration, or else it would mean the usurpation of legislative functions by the judiciary.

142   The case is currently before the Inter-American Court of Human Rights as a case related to the right to health and access to justice (given that the claim was denied due to the lack of a remedy).
143   *Demanda de Inconstitucionalidad Contra los Artículos 14, 15, 16 y 17 de la Ley 1335 de 2009* [Colombian Constitutional Court], Sentencia C-830/10, 20 October 2010.
144   *5000 Citizens v Article 3 of Law No 28705* [Constitutional Court of Peru], 19 July 2011.

13 European Union

Alberto Alemanno and Amandine Garde

1 Introduction

According to World Health Organization ('WHO') data, non-communicable diseases ('NCDs') account for nearly 86 per cent of deaths and 77 per cent of the disease burden in Europe.[1] These alarming rates have led the European Union ('EU') to progressively acknowledge the impact of NCDs on the EU's economy and the well-being of its citizens. Thus, despite its limited competence in public health, the EU has expressed its commitment to 'accelerate progress on combating unhealthy lifestyle behaviours'.[2]

There is a clear consensus that effective NCD prevention and control strategies must be 'multi-sectoral', 'multi-stakeholder' and 'multi-level'. However, unlike most other jurisdictions engaged in NCD prevention policies, the EU has only limited powers in public health matters.[3] In particular, EU health prevention policies have historically been based on the competence to establish and regulate a European internal market.[4] As a result, most NCD prevention measures, such as maximum tar yields and health warnings on tobacco products or health claims on food products, despite their manifest public health objective, are introduced with the express objective of promoting cross-border trade in these products. Although pursuing a public health goal by promoting – rather than restricting – the free movement of cigarettes, alcohol and food products in Europe might appear somehow contradictory, this is the legal logic that has dominated and continues to dominate the EU's NCD regulatory approach. Hence the need felt by the EU to experiment also with other forms of policy interventions, such as the exchange of best practice and self-regulation. As a result of these dynamics, the NCD prevention policy, which is emerging in Europe, is the result of a combination of both regulatory and self-regulatory measures adopted at either EU or national levels.[5] The resulting regulatory landscape is therefore particularly complex.

After discussing how the EU has engaged with the NCD prevention and control agenda (Part 2), this chapter will focus on the key constitutional principles constraining EU powers and their exercise in this field (Part 3).

2 The genesis and evolution of the EU's NCD policy

The EU's involvement in NCD prevention is relatively recent. While some measures aimed at regulating lifestyle choices vis-à-vis tobacco, alcohol and unhealthy food were adopted in the early days of the European Community,[6] these measures were not intended to promote systematically healthy lifestyles: they were incremental and, as such, only by-products of the internal market.

It is only in the 1990s that the EU started to address lifestyle risks at EU level. The momentum stemmed not only from the pressing warnings of the international and the scientific communities, but also from the increased recognition that the EU had a role to play in the area of public health. Following the introduction of a chapter on public health in the EU treaties, the EU has been under a legal obligation to ensure a high level of public health in all policy areas.[7] This change subsequently led to the adoption of two programs of EU action in the field of public health for the periods of 2003–8[8] and 2008–13.[9] One of their main common objectives is 'to promote health and prevent disease through addressing health determinants across all policies and activities',[10] not least 'by preparing and implementing strategies and measures, including those related to public awareness, on lifestyle related health determinants, such as nutrition, physical activity, tobacco, alcohol, drugs and other substances and on mental health'[11] and 'by tackling health determinants …, creating supportive environments for healthy lifestyles and preventing disease'.[12]

After several calls from the Council of the European Union ('Council') for EU action on NCDs,[13] the EU adopted three separate strategies intended to tackle the major NCD risk factors more comprehensively and support its citizens in improving their lifestyles: the EU Alcohol Strategy (2006),[14] the Obesity Prevention White Paper (2007)[15] and a *Council Recommendation on Smoke-free Environments* (2009),[16] which complements the adoption of the 2001 *Tobacco Products Directive*[17] and the 2003 *Tobacco Advertising Directive*.[18]

2.1 Tobacco versus alcohol versus diets

These three areas of EU intervention have several features in common: they acknowledge the paramount role of prevention and recognise that NCDs often share common determinants that are influenced by multi-sectoral policies. Moreover, they emphasise that only a multi-level approach, with mechanisms ensuring the effective coordination between the different levels of intervention, can durably reverse current NCD trends. Finally, they call for the involvement of a wide range of stakeholders in the NCD debates, including public authorities, civil society representatives, not least consumer and public health organisations, and, where appropriate, private actors from the relevant industries.

However, despite common themes, the involvement of the EU has varied significantly in nature, scope and intensity according to the risk factor at stake. If its regulatory intervention has been significant in relation to tobacco control, it has been minimal in relation to alcohol control; the EU nutrition and obesity prevention policy falls somewhere between the two.

2.2 Tobacco

EU tobacco control has been at the forefront of a 'federal' experimentation, help-ing delineate the limits of EU competences and the relevance of the principles of subsidiarity and proportionality for EU law and policy-making.[19] It is marked by a strong EU regulatory involvement, coupled with recommendations to member states and EU-wide anti-smoking campaigns. In this field, the EU has frequently invoked its duty to mainstream public health into all EU policies to justify the EU agenda, as illustrated by the on-going debates surrounding the revision of the *Tobacco Products Directive*.[20] The EU has also signed and acceded to the *WHO Framework Convention on Tobacco Control* ('WHO FCTC'),[21] thus becoming an actor alongside its member states on the global public health scene. The EU has also recently undertaken to sign, ratify and implement the Protocol of the WHO FCTC[22] at EU level, and to ensure compliance with its provisions as far as matters falling within EU competences are concerned.[23]

2.3 Alcohol

By contrast, the EU Alcohol Strategy entrusts member states (and not the EU) with the adoption of comprehensive multi-sectoral strategies. Thus, very few har-monising rules have been adopted to date at EU level to combat alcohol-related harm. The *Audiovisual Media Services Directive* constitutes an exception in that it lays down rules on the content of alcohol promotions in audiovisual media services.[24] These provisions are nonetheless extremely weak, and most member states have relied on the minimum harmonisation clause contained in the Directive to adopt stricter measures to better protect the health of their citizens – leading in turn to a high degree of fragmentation of the internal market.[25] Notwithstanding the fact that an effective multi-sectoral, multi-level strategy calls for EU intervention when policies have clear cross-border implications, the EU has responded to the calls for more robust EU intervention by reiterating that the primary responsibility for health matters lie with member states – a response very much at odds with the approach the European Commission has adopted in the field of tobacco control.[26]

The EU has been much more willing to facilitate the exchange of best practice and the adoption of self-regulatory standards. In 2007, it set up the European Alcohol and Health Forum, which includes a broad range of members, from industry operators to consumer, youth and public health organisations. The Forum is innovative in that it requires that each of its now 71 members adopts at least one specific, concrete commitment to help fight alcohol-related harm. These commitments are published on a dedicated database.[27]

2.4 Diets

In the area of nutrition, the EU has adopted a combination of regulation and self-regulation. The Obesity Prevention White Paper laid down an integrated EU approach in order to reduce ill health resulting from poor nutrition, overweight and obesity. In contrast to the EU Alcohol Strategy, it is much more forthcoming in identifying the policies in which the EU has a role to play, including if necessary through the adoption of binding rules. Thus, it lists specifically the EU policies relevant to obesity prevention, which in itself suggests that the Commission envisages a stronger EU involvement in relation to nutrition and physical activity than in relation to alcoholic beverages.[28]

Besides these traditional forms of regulatory intervention, a significant part of EU activity in the field of nutrition has occurred via the EU Platform on Diet, Physical Activity and Health. The Platform, set up in 2005, served as a model for the EU Forum on Alcohol and Health. Its functioning is therefore identical: it is a multi-stakeholder forum that requires that each of its 34 members adopt at least one commitment to participate in the Platform's activities.[29] To facilitate the exchange of best practice between the EU and its member states, the Commission also coordinates a high level group on nutrition gathering representatives of the 28 EU member states as well as Norway and Switzerland.[30]

3 The legality of the EU NCD policy

This part discusses the legal framework governing the adoption of EU NCD regulatory measures. Article 5(1) of the *Treaty on European Union*[31] ('TEU') is the starting point of the enquiry: 'the limits of Union competences are governed by the principle of conferral. The use of Union competences is governed by the principles of subsidiarity and proportionality'. Consequently, it requires that the European Commission ask itself a series of questions before proposing any legislative measure:

- Could the EU act? The EU must first have the required powers to adopt the proposed measure (principle of conferral) (1).
- Should the EU act? If the EU has the powers to adopt a given measure, the question then arises whether it should exercise its powers (principle of subsidiarity) (2).
- How should the EU act? Finally, if it is agreed that action at EU level is preferable to action at national level, the EU is under an obligation to ensure that its intervention is proportionate (principle of proportionality) (3) and compatible with fundamental rights (4).

3.1 The principle of conferral: does the EU have the required competence to act?

According to the principle of conferral, the EU may act only insofar as it has been granted the competence to do so. Otherwise, the responsibility remains with member states. Delineating what falls within the scope of EU powers and what does not has proven extremely complex in practice.

Although the EU is under a duty to take as a base a high level of public health protection in the definition and implementation of all its policies or activities,[32] art

168(5) of the *Treaty on the Functioning of the European Union* ('TFEU') explicitly excludes the possibility of the EU harmonising the laws and regulations of the member states under this provision. While this provision was amended to allow the EU to adopt

> incentive measures designed to protect and improve human health and in particular to combat the major cross-border health scourges … and *measures which have as their direct objective the protection of public health regarding tobacco* and *the abuse of alcohol*

it still excludes 'any harmonization of the laws and regulations of the Member States'.[33] Despite the fact that this provision is the first express reference to tobacco and alcohol ever made in the EU treaties, it does not provide a new legal basis for the adoption of binding measures.[34]

Nevertheless, even though the scope of EU regulatory action is limited, one should not underestimate the role the EU can play in health matters. Under the revised version of the EU treaties, art 3 of the TEU requires that the Union promote not only 'peace and its values' but also 'the well-being of its peoples'. Moreover, art 168(1) of the TFEU mandates that 'a high level of human health protection shall be ensured in the definition and implementation of all Union policies and activities'. According to this horizontal ('mainstreaming') obligation, health protection must be considered in all fields of Union action, and health interests taken into account when pursuing potentially competing goals in other policy areas, some of which will grant them the power to adopt binding rules.[35] Relevant legal bases allowing for the adoption of binding EU measures include: arts 38 (agriculture), 91 (transport), 113 (taxation), 114 and 59 (internal market), 153 (worker's protection), 169 (consumer protection) and 207 (commercial policy) of the TFEU.[36]

To date, most EU NCD prevention rules have been adopted on the internal market legal basis: art 114 of the TFEU. This provision empowers the EU to harmonise national rules by qualified majority voting for the establishment and the functioning of the internal market.[37] Under established case law, the EU legislature 'cannot be prevented from relying on that legal basis on the ground that public health protection is a decisive factor in the choices to be made'.[38] Consequently, 'it is perfectly legitimate for the Community legislator to pursue simultaneously internal market and public health objectives'.[39] However, certain conditions must be met for art 114 to be successfully relied on: (i) there must be an 'internal market barrier' resulting from the disparities in the legal systems of the member states' measures 'such as to obstruct the fundamental freedoms' or create 'distortions of competition' within the internal market; and (ii) the intended harmonisation should 'genuinely have as its object the improvement of the conditions for the establishment and functioning of the internal market'.[40]

The existence of barriers to trade depends on the overall level of EU harmonisation in a given area. The less an aspect is regulated, the higher the potential for the existence of obstacles to trade. In the absence of common harmonising rules, member states remain competent to adopt national measures regulating, for instance, information schemes, sales conditions and product requirements in order to fulfil public health objectives.[41] Thus, the rules governing the information, sale conditions and product requirements of tobacco, alcohol and food products may differ from one member state to another. For instance, some member states have introduced rules banning the display of tobacco at points of sale, whilst others have not. Would this be enough to enable the EU to step in? According to well-established case law, 'a mere finding of disparities between national rules is not sufficient to have recourse' to art 114 of the TFEU.[42] One must consider the effects of such disparities: the differences must be 'such as to obstruct the fundamental freedoms or to create distortions of competition' and thus have a direct effect on the functioning of the internal market.[43] While 'national rules laying down the requirements to be met by products – in particular those relating to their designa-tion, composition or packaging – are in themselves liable, in the absence of harmo-nization throughout the Community, to constitute obstacles to the free movement of goods',[44] it is disputable that other requirements, such as those dealing with the way in which products are sold, may be considered per se as barriers to trade. The *Philip Morris* judgment[45] delivered in September 2011 by the European Free Trade Association ('EFTA') Court[46] provides some guidance on this point.[47] The EFTA Court held that 'by its nature' a visual display ban of tobacco products is not only liable to favour domestic products over imported ones – as consumers tend to be more familiar with the former,[48] but also that such a discriminatory effect would be particularly significant with regard to the market penetration of new products.[49] Thus, one approach for relying on art 114 of the TFEU as a legal basis for an EU-wide lifestyle regulatory intervention would be to establish that, due to the progressive emergence of national restrictions, there exists a risk of obstacles to trade such as to obstruct the free movement of goods or create distortions of competition on the relevant market, especially vis-à-vis new products.[50]

This interpretation is further supported by the one given to the other require-ments justifying reliance on art 114 of the TFEU: even though an identified obstacle to trade is merely prospective it could still be adopted under this provision insofar as: (i) the emergence of such obstacles is 'likely'; and (ii) the measure in question is 'designed to prevent them'.[51] As stated by the EFTA Court:

> In that context, having regard to the fact that the public is increasingly conscious of the dangers to health posed by consuming tobacco products, it is likely that obstacles to the free movement of those products would arise by reason of the adoption by the Member States of new rules reflecting that development and intended more effectively to discourage consumption of those products by means of warnings and information appearing on their packaging or to reduce the harmful effects of tobacco products by introducing new rules governing their composition.[52]

As a result, it is arguable that a competence to harmonise national rules that did not exist in the past may come into being where public pressure for national regulation increases.[53]

3.2 *The principle of subsidiarity: should the EU exercise its powers?*

Once it is established that the EU has the required competence to adopt regulatory measures as part of its NCD prevention and control agenda, the question arises whether it should exercise its powers and, if so, how it should act in light of its obligation to comply with the principle of subsidiarity, the principle of proportionality and fundamental rights.

The principle of subsidiarity constrains EU action by requiring that EU intervention can be triggered only where it adds value to action at national or local level.[54] For each measure envisaged as part of the EU NCD policy, the question therefore arises whether the EU can better achieve the objectives of a proposed measure than the member states.

Traditionally, EU institutions have tended to pay lip service to the principle of subsidiarity, due probably to 'its lack of conceptual contours'.[55] In particular, the Court of Justice has often been criticised for failing to engage meaningfully with the question of whether the EU legislature has complied with its requirements.[56] One may wonder whether the *Vodafone* decision, which upholds the establishment of maximum roaming charges within the EU, could be interpreted as signalling a change in the court's approach.[57] On the one hand, the court referred explicitly and for the first time to the *Protocol on Subsidiarity and Proportionality* ('*Protocol*'), which requires that the EU legislate only to the extent necessary and that EU measures leave as much scope for national decisions as possible, consistent however with securing the aim of the measure and observing the requirements of the EU treaties.[58] On the other hand, the court's reference to the *Protocol* did not trigger a thorough subsidiarity review of EU action.[59] It did not engage in any detail with the substantive aspects of subsidiarity to conclude that the EU legislature had not infringed the principle of subsidiarity.[60] Rather, it simply recognised the existence of economic interdependence between retail and wholesale charges for roaming services.[61] This is perhaps all the more surprising, as Advocate General Maduro had explicitly invited the court to carry out a more thorough subsidiarity review. In light of the inherently cross-border nature of roaming services, he concluded that the EU would be both more willing to address the problem of high prices than member states individually and in a better position to balance the costs and benefits of the intended action for the internal market, and that the roaming regulation therefore complied with the principle of subsidiarity.[62]

By analogy with the *Vodafone* decision, one can argue that services with significant cross-border implications (for example internet advertising) are such that EU action provides by nature a far more effective intervention than action by member states at national level.[63] Similarly, the EU tends to be in a better position than member states to regulate the composition, labelling and presentation of products such as tobacco, food and alcoholic beverages that are traded extensively across borders within the EU (and beyond). The EU has therefore adopted a wide range of measures on the content, labelling or packaging of tobacco and food products. The EU could envisage the adoption, on the basis of art 114 of the TFEU, of further harmonising measures to regulate the labelling of alcoholic beverages, to mandate the plain packaging of tobacco products or to ban the use of trans-fats in foods.[64]

3.3 The principle of proportionality

Any EU measure must also comply with the principle of proportionality, which requires that the content and form of Union action not exceed what is necessary to achieve the objectives of the EU treaties.[65] According to settled case law, an EU act is proportionate when it is suitable and necessary to achieve its declared goal.[66] In particular, the principle of proportionality requires that (i) measures adopted by EU institutions not exceed the limits of what is suitable or appropriate in order to attain the legitimate objective pursued by the legislation in question (suitability); and (ii) where there is a choice between several appropriate measures, the least onerous method be used (necessity).[67]

3.3.1 Suitability

Under the suitability limb of the proportionality test, it is necessary to determine whether a given NCD prevention intervention is capable of attaining its internal market and public health objectives. As previously discussed, any EU-wide scheme harmonising domestic rules should be capable of overcoming the disparities between national schemes. Yet the question remains whether the chosen EU-wide scheme is appropriate to contribute to the attainment of its other declared objective: ensuring a high level of public health protection. This inquiry shifts the focus of the suitability analysis from the harmonisation to the public health objective of the measure. It inevitably requires the court to open the Pandora's box of the effectiveness of the measure in achieving a high level of human health protection through the reduction of the morbidity and the mortality induced by the consumption of tobacco products, alcoholic beverages and unhealthy diets.

Scrutinising the suitability of a lifestyle measure in attaining a high level of public health protection raises several difficulties, which largely derive from the inherent scientific uncertainty surrounding the adoption of regulatory measures as part of the NCD prevention and control agenda and from the difficulty in establishing a causal link between these measures and their expected outcome. The difficulties are further compounded by the fact that lifestyles cannot be improved by individual measures taken in isolation. There is no 'magic bullet': only a multi-sectoral policy will lead to healthier lifestyles, which makes the effectiveness of a specific intervention all the more difficult – if not impossible – to quantify.[68] Moreover, it is well known that the effect of any form of lifestyle intervention tends to appear gradually and over time. More critically, the specific effects of lifestyle control policy are difficult to discern from those stemming from the overall policy. In these circumstances, it is to be welcomed that the court is prepared to grant a broad margin of discretion to the EU legislature to determine which policy tools are likely to achieve public health objectives.[69]

3.3.2 *Necessity*

The necessity limb requires verification of whether a less restrictive measure could achieve the declared goal of ensuring a high level of public health protection.[70] Among alternative, equally effective policy options, the EU legislature is bound to choose the least intrusive. Such assessment inevitably requires a comparative analysis between the measure under review and other policy options. In an area such as NCD prevention and control, this analysis is extremely difficult to carry out as a result of the multi-sectoral approach required from competent authorities. Which policy options should be considered? How should they be measured and compared, and with reference to what benchmark?

The current practice of carrying out an impact assessment for all major Commission initiatives may lead EU courts to refer to such preparatory works before reaching their conclusions. Thus, as the *Impact Assessment Guidelines* require the Commission to establish 'which policy options and delivery mechanisms are most likely to achieve' the objectives pursued by the underlying initiative,[71] they may take this assessment into account when determining whether the final measure is necessary and therefore compatible with the principle of proportionality.[72]

3.4 Fundamental rights

Finally, EU measures promoting healthier lifestyles must comply with fundamental rights recognised in the EU.[73]

In their challenges to EU NCD prevention and control measures, industry operators have often argued that these measures infringe several of the fundamental rights they derive from EU law:[74] the freedom of expression and information, the freedom to choose an occupation and the right to engage in work, the freedom to conduct a business, and the right to property.[75] Nevertheless, whilst these rights are protected by the EU legal order, none of them is absolute: they may all be restricted on grounds of public health protection.[76] The Court of Justice has never annulled any EU measures intended to promote healthier lifestyles on the ground that it violated EU fundamental rights. Rather, when assessing the proportionality of the restrictions imposed on the rights invoked by industry operators for public health reasons, the court has granted a particularly broad margin of discretion to the EU legislature. For example, it rejected any suggestion that the EU had unlawfully interfered with the right to property of tobacco manufacturers and their freedom to pursue a trade or profession by adopting the *Tobacco Products Directive*:

> As regards the validity of the Directive in respect of the right to property … the only effect produced by Article 5 of the Directive is to restrict the right of manufacturers of tobacco products to use the space on some sides of cigarette packets to show their trademarks without prejudicing the substance of their trade mark rights, the purpose being to ensure a high level of health protection when the obstacles created by national laws on labelling are eliminated.[77]

One could argue on the basis of the court's settled case law that if the EU were to impose further measures such as plain packaging of tobacco products across the EU, preventing the use of brands on tobacco (or other products) packs – a step that it has not yet proposed to take – then the very substance of the right to property and the freedom to trade would not be affected and the measure would therefore be compatible with the right to property and the freedom to conduct a business.[78]

Similarly, when called upon to assess the validity of the *Tobacco Advertising Directive*, the court rejected the claim that the EU-wide ban on all forms of cross-border advertising and sponsorship for tobacco products violated the freedom of expression of tobacco manufacturers.[79] This is compatible with the EU's obligations under the WHO FCTC, which has called on its parties to introduce comprehensive bans on tobacco advertising, promotion and sponsorship as part of their tobacco control efforts.[80] It is therefore legitimate for the EU and its member states as parties to the WHO FCTC to limit the freedom of industry operators to promote cigarettes and other tobacco products whose consumption is inherently harmful to health.

It is highly commendable that, in all these cases, the court has not substituted its assessment for that of the legislature. Lifestyle risk regulation involves complex assessments, which result not only from the scientific understanding of specific health risks but also from the social and political evaluation of those risks. [81] EU political institutions are better equipped than the court to determine how competing interests should be balanced against each other. This does not mean, however, that the EU legislature enjoys a *carte blanche*: it bears the burden of proving that the measures it has adopted are suitable and necessary to achieve their objective of reducing the burden of NCDs in the EU. Discretion does not mean arbitrariness.[82]

In any event, the fundamental rights narrative that the industry has developed is far too incomplete to be convincing.[83] Any EU law discourse that has developed to defend tobacco control measures has been framed in proportionality terms to address the arguments they have put forward and has been, as such, necessarily reactive. Nevertheless, the law can be used as a tool to promote the right to health and several other fundamental rights protected by the EU legal order, including the right to life, the right to a clean environment and the right to information, as mentioned above, but also the right to (nutritious) food,[84] the right to education and the principle that all actions concerning children shall be taken in their best interest.[85] Thus, in its recent decision in the *Deutsches Weintor* case,[86] the court explicitly invoked art 35 of the *EU Charter* – which requires that 'a high level of human health protection be ensured in the definition and the implementation of all Union policies and activities' – to dismiss the argument of alcoholic beverages operators that the EU legislature had unduly restricted their fundamental rights by banning the use of health claims on all beverages containing more than 1.2 per cent by volume of alcohol.[87]

4 Conclusion

Our analysis discusses the emergence of an embryonic EU NCD prevention policy addressing the three main risk factors: tobacco consumption, the harmful use of alcohol and unhealthy diets. As demonstrated, besides the inherent complexity of this emerging policy resulting from the multi-factorial character of this set of risk factors, the very nature of the EU gives rise to additional issues surrounding the respective roles of the EU and its member states. In particular, the constitutional structure of the EU as a union of member states adds a further level of complexity to the already difficult process of translating research into effective policies.

In the last few years, the EU has started to experiment by adopting a diversity of measures, though it has admittedly used its 'regulatory tool-box' to different degrees depending on the risk factor at stake, preferring at times to promote the exchange of best practice and the adoption of commitments by industry operators over the adoption of legally binding rules. It is not surprising that it is in the field of tobacco control that the validity of EU rules has systematically been challenged before courts in judicial review actions:[88] in no other field has the EU been so active in adopting binding measures to reduce smoking rates across all its member states. The EU and the public health community must learn from the tobacco litigation experience in order to develop regulatory strategies able to contribute effectively to the developing NCD agenda at global, regional and national levels, whilst being able to withstand judicial review challenges from tobacco, food and alcoholic beverages operators.

This chapter has attempted to systematise the constraints that EU law poses to the emergence of the EU's NCD prevention and control policy in order to highlight the importance of designing litigation-proof strategies. This should not be interpreted as suggesting that EU law should not play an important part in the NCD agenda. Quite the opposite: even though law is not a panacea, it has an important role to play in ensuring that healthy choices are facilitated across the EU. As the fight against NCDs has become a strategic priority worldwide at national, regional and global level, especially in the aftermath of the WHO 2013 global action plan for NCDs,[89] the EU must embrace – in light of both its constitutional principles and its international obligations – the challenges that it poses.

Notes

1 WHO Regional Office for Europe, *Action Plan for Implementation of the European Strategy for the Prevention and Control of Non-Communicable Diseases 2012–2016* (2012) 1 <http://www.euro.who.int/en/what-we-publish/abstracts/action-plan-for-implementation-of-the-european-strategy-for-the-prevention-and-control-of-noncommunicable-diseases 20122016>.

2 *Council Conclusions on Closing Health Gaps Within the EU Through Concerted Action to Promote Healthy Lifestyle Behaviours* [2011] OJ C 359/5.

3 The only sector-specific treaty provision dealing with public health expressly excludes harmonising measures in this area. See *Treaty on the Functioning of the European Union*, opened for signature 7 February 1992, [2009] OJ C 115/199 (entered into force 1 November 1993) art 168 ('TFEU').

4 TFEU art 26.
5 For a first study of the emerging EU NCD policy, see Alberto Alemanno and Amandine Garde (eds), *Regulating Lifestyle Risks: Europe, Alcohol, Tobacco and Unhealthy Diets* (Cambridge University Press, forthcoming).
6 These measures included food labelling rules and excise duties on tobacco products and alcoholic beverages.
7 The mainstreaming obligation laid down in art 168(1) of the TFEU has been strengthened by the *Lisbon Treaty* with the introduction of TFEU art 9: see *Treaty of Lisbon Amending the Treaty on European Union and the Treaty Establishing the European Community*, opened for signature 13 December 2007, [2007] OJ C 306/1 (entered into force 1 December 2009).
8 *Decision 1786/2002 of the European Parliament and the Council of 23 September 2002 Adopting a Programme of Community Action in the Field of Public Health (2003–2008)* [2002] OJ L 271/1.
9 *Decision 1350/2007 of the European Parliament and the Council of 23 October 2007 Establishing a Second Programme of Community Action in the Field of Health (2008–2013)* [2007] OJ L 301/3.
10 *Decision 1786/2002 of the European Parliament and the Council of 23 September 2002 Adopting a Programme of Community Action in the Field of Public Health (2003–2008)* [2002] OJ L 271/1, art 2(2)(c).
11 Ibid annex [3(1)].
12 *Decision 1350/2007 of the European Parliament and the Council of 23 October 2007 Establishing a Second Programme of Community Action in the Field of Health (2008–2013)* [2007] OJ L 301/3, art 2(2), annex, 2.2. See also European Commission, 'Together for Health: A Strategic Approach for the EU 2008–2013' (White Paper No COM(2007) 630 final, 23 October 2007) <http://eur-lex.europa.eu/LexUriServ/site/en/com/2007/com2007_0630en01.pdf>. The Lisbon Agenda on Growth and Competitiveness further strengthened the economic and social case for EU intervention by stressing that, in addition to good health being a valuable goal in itself, it also leads to better economic results, increased social cohesion and consequently makes the European economy more competitive: see European Council, *Lisbon European Council 23 and 24 March 2000: Presidency Conclusions* (2000) European Parliament <http://www.europarl.europa.eu/summits/lis1_en.htm>.
13 Some of these calls have focused specifically on one risk factor, whilst others have tended to be more horizontal in nature. Examples of the latter type include: *Council Conclusions of December 2003 on Healthy Lifestyles: Education, Information and Communication* [2004] OJ C 22/1; Council of the European Union, *Proposal for Draft Council Conclusions on Promoting Heart Health* (18 May 2004) Consilium: Public Register of Council Documents <http://register.consilium.europa.eu/pdf/en/04/st09/st09627.en04.pdf> (adopted 14 July 2004, see Council of the European Union, *Draft Minutes: 2586th Meeting of the Council of the European Union* (14 July 2004) Consilium: Public Register of Council Documents http://register.consilium.europa.eu/pdf/en/04/st10/st10014.en04.pdf); Council of the European Union, *Council Conclusions on the Promotion of Healthy Lifestyles and Prevention of Type 2 Diabetes* (2 June 2006) Presidency of the European Union Autriche 2006 <http://www.eu2006.at/en/News/Council_Conclusions/0106HealthyLife.pdf>).
14 European Commission, 'Communication from the Commission to the Council, the European Parliament, the European Economic and Social Committee and the Committee of the Regions: An EU Strategy to Support Member States in Reducing Alcohol Related Harm' (COM(2006) 625 final, 24 October 2006) <http://eur-lex.europa.eu/LexUriServ/site/en/com/2006/com2006_0625en01.pdf>.
15 European Commission, 'A Strategy for Europe on Nutrition, Overweight and Obesity Related Health Issues' (White Paper No COM(2007) 279 final, 30 May 2007). On the EU's obesity prevention strategy, see Amandine Garde, *EU Law and Obesity Prevention* (Kluwer Law International, 2010).

16 *Council Recommendation on Smoke-free Environments* [2009] OJ C 296/4.
17 *Directive 2001/37 of the European Parliament and of the Council of 5 June 2001 on the Approximation of the Laws, Regulations and Administrative Provisions of the Member States Concerning the Manufacture, Presentation and Sale of Tobacco Products* [2001] OJ L 194/26 ('*Tobacco Products Directive*').
18 *Directive 2003/33 of the European Parliament and of the Council of 26 May 2003 on the Approximation of the Laws, Regulations and Administrative Provisions of the Member States Relating to the Advertising and Sponsorship of Tobacco Products* [2003] OJ L 152/16 ('*Tobacco Advertising Directive*').
19 This is discussed more fully below. See Geraint Howells, *The Tobacco Challenge* (Ashgate Publishing, 2011); Alberto Alemanno, 'Out of Sight Out of Mind: Towards a New European Tobacco Products Directive' (2012) 18 *Columbia Journal of European Law* 197; Garde, above n 15, ch. 3.
20 *Directive 2014/40/EU of the European Parliament and of the Council of 3 April 2014 on the Approximation of the Laws, Regulations and Administrative Provisions of the Member States Concerning the Manufacture, Presentation and Sale of Tobacco and Related Products and Repealing Directive 2001/37/EC* [2014] OJ L 127/1. TEU Member States are expected to bring into force the laws, regulations and administrative provisions necessary to comply with this Directive by 20 May 2016.
21 *WHO Framework Convention on Tobacco Control,* opened for signature 16 June 2003, 2302 UNTS 166 (entered into force 27 February 2005) ('WHO FCTC').
22 The WHO FCTC *Protocol to Eliminate Illicit Trade in Tobacco Products* was opened for signature on 10 January 2013: <http://www.who.int/fctc/protocol/about/en/>.
23 European Commission, 'Communication from the Commission to the Council and the European Parliament: Stepping up the fight against cigarette smuggling and other forms of illicit trade in tobacco products – A comprehensive EU Strategy' (COM(2013) 324 final, 6 June 2013) 15 <http://ec.europa.eu/anti_fraud/documents/2013-cigarette-communication/1_en_act_part1_v9_en.pdf>.
24 *Directive 2010/13 of the European Parliament and of the Council of 10 March 2010 on the Coordination of Certain Provisions Laid Down by Law, Regulation or Administrative Action in Member States Concerning the Provision of Audiovisual Media Services (Audiovisual Media Services Directive)* [2010] OJ L 95/17, arts 9(1)(e) and 22.
25 Oliver Bartlett and Amandine Garde, 'Time to Seize the (Red) Bull by the Horns: The EU's Failure to Protect Children from Alcohol and Unhealthy Food Marketing' (2013) 38 *European Law Review* 498.
26 In its first implementation report, published in September 2009, the Commission praised the EU Alcohol and Health Forum: Directorate-General for Health & Consumers, *First Progress Report on the Implementation of the EU Alcohol Strategy* (September 2009) European Commission <http://ec.europa.eu/health/archive/ph_determinants/life_style/alcohol/documents/alcohol_progress.pdf>.
27 See *EU Alcohol and Health Forum* <http://ec.europa.eu/health/alcohol/forum/index_en.htm>.
28 The range of food information rules it has adopted over the years confirms this interpretation: see especially *Regulation 1169/2011 of the European Parliament and of the Council of 25 October 2011 on the Provision of Food Information to Consumers* [2011] OJ L 304/18; *Regulation 1924/2006 of the European Parliament and of the Council of 20 December 2006 on Nutrition and Health Claims Made on Foods* [2006] OJ L 404/9, as amended by *Commission Regulation (EU) No 116/2010 of 9 February 2010 Amending Regulation (EC) No 1924/2006 of the European Parliament and of the Council with Regard to the List of Nutrition Claims* [2010] OJ L 37/16.
29 European Commission, *EU Platform for Action on Diet, Physical Activity and Health* <http://ec.europa.eu/health/nutrition_physical_activity/platform/index_en.htm>.

30 European Commission, *High Level Group on Nutrition and Physical Activity* <http://ec.europa.eu/health/nutrition_physical_activity/high_level_group/index_en.htm>. The high level group and the Platform meet together regularly to improve the coordination of their activities.

31 *Treaty on European Union*, opened for signature 7 February 1992, [2009] OJ C 115/13 ('TEU').

32 Ibid arts 9 and 168(1).

33 Ibid art 168(5) (emphasis added).

34 See, eg, Paul Craig, *The Lisbon Treaty – Law, Politics and Treaty Reform* (Oxford University Press, 2010) 325; Jean-Claude Piris, *The Lisbon Treaty – A Legal and Political Analysis* (Cambridge University Press, 2010) 320–1.

35 This is echoed in arts 9 and 114(3) of the TEU.

36 For a more detailed typology of EU regulatory intervention to prevent and control NCDs, see Alberto Alemanno and Amandine Garde, 'The Emergence of an EU Lifestyle Policy: The Case of Alcohol, Tobacco and Unhealthy Diets' (2013) 50 *Common Market Law Review* 1745.

37 Nicolas de Sadeleer, 'Procedures for Derogations from the Principle of Approximation of Laws under Art. 95 EC' (2003) 40 *Common Market Law Review* 889.

38 *Germany v European Parliament* (C-376/98) [2000] ECR 1-8419, [88] ('*Tobacco Advertising I*'); *Germany v European Parliament* (C-380/03) [2006] ECR I-11573, [39] ('*Tobacco Advertising II*'); *R (on the application of Alliance for Natural Health) v Secretary of State for Health* (C-154 and 155/04) [2005] ECR I-6451, [30]. See also Bruno De Witte, 'Non-market Values in Internal Market Legislation', in Niamh Nic Shuibhne (ed), *Regulating the Internal Market* (Edward Elgar Publishing, 2006) 61.

39 *Tobacco Advertising I* (C-376/98) [2000] ECR 1-8419, [149] (AG Fennelly).

40 See *R (on the application of Vodafone Ltd) v Secretary of State for Business, Enterprise and Regulatory Reform* (C-58/08) [2010] ECR I-4999, [32] ('*Vodafone*').

41 For an overview of member states' regulatory autonomy in the EU, see Isidora Maletic, *The Law and Policy of Harmonisation in Europe's Internal Market* (Edward Elgar Publishing, 2013).

42 See, lastly, *Ireland v European Parliament* (C-301/06) [2009] ECR I-0593, [63]–[64].

43 See, eg, *Tobacco Advertising II* (C-380/03) [2006] ECR I-11573, [37], [51]; *Tobacco Advertising I* (C-376/98) [2000] ECR 1-8419, [90].

44 *R v Secretary of State for Health* (C-491/01) [2002] ECR I-11453, [64]. See also *Criminal Proceedings against Bernard Keck and Daniel Mithouard* (C-267/91 and C-268/91) [1993] ECR I-06097, [15]; *Tobacco Advertising I* (C-376/98) [2000] ECR 1-841, [64].

45 *Philip Morris Norway AS v Ministry of Health and Care Services* (E-16/10) [2011] EFTA (12 September 2011) ('*Philip Morris Norway*').

46 The EFTA Court has jurisdiction with regard to EFTA states that are parties to the *Agreement on the European Economic Area* [1994] OJ L 1/3 (at present Iceland, Liechtenstein and Norway). See *Agreement between the EFTA States on the Establishment of a Surveillance Authority and a Court of Justice* [2012] OJ L 344/3. Even though the Court of Justice is not bound to the EFTA Court's case law, it has sometimes followed its sister court especially in those instances in which the EFTA Court has been called upon to answer legal questions that had not been fully decided by the Court of Justice.

47 *Philip Morris Norway* (E-16/10) [2011] EFTA (12 September 2011), [84]. For a review of this judgment, Alberto Alemanno, 'The Legality, Rationale and Science of Tobacco Display Bans after the Philip Morris Judgment' (2011) (4) *European Journal of Risk Regulation* 591.

48 *Philip Morris Norway* (E-16/10) [2011] EFTA (12 September 2011), [48], referring to *Konsumentombudsmannen v Gourmet International Products AB* (C-405/98) [2001] ECR I-1795, [21].

49 *Philip Morris Norway* (E-16/10) [2011] EFTA (12 September 2011), [49].

50 See, eg, *Tobacco Advertising II* (C-380/03) [2006] ECR I-11573, [37], [51]; *Tobacco Advertising I* (C-76/98) [2000] ECR 1-8419, [90].

51 See *Tobacco Advertising I* (C-376/98) [2000] ECR 1-8419, [86]; *R v Secretary of State for Health* (C-491/01) [2002] ECR I-11453, [61]; *Tobacco Advertising II* (C-380/03) [2006] ECR I-11573, [38]; *Vodafone* (C-491/01) [2010] ECR I-4999, [33].

52 *R v Secretary of State for Health* (C-491/01) [2002] ECR I-11453, [67].

53 See *Swedish Match AB v Secretary of State for Health* (C-210/03) [2004] ECR I-11893, [38].

54 TEU art 5(3).

55 For a criticism of the wording of art 5(3) of the TFEU, see Robert Schütze, *European Constitutional Law* (Cambridge University Press, 2012) 178.

56 See in particular Alan Dashwood, 'The Relationship between the Member States and the European Union/European Community' (2004) 41 *Common Market Law Review* 2. This is not to suggest, however, that if the court had reviewed the EU's compliance with the principle of subsidiarity it would necessarily have concluded that the measures under review did not comply with this principle: Paul Craig, 'Subsidiarity: A Political and Legal Analysis' (2012) 50 *Journal of Common Market Studies* 72, 81.

57 *Vodafone* (C-58/08) [2010] ECR I-4999.

58 *Protocol (No 2) on the Application of the Principles of Subsidiarity and Proportionality* [2010] OJ C 83/206.

59 *Vodafone* (C-58/08) [2010] ECR I-4999, [77]–[79]. One could also note that the court did not refer to paragraph 5 of the *Protocol*, which requires that: draft legislative acts shall be justified with regard to the principles of subsidiarity and proportionality. Any draft legislative act should contain a detailed statement making it possible to appraise compliance with the principles of subsidiarity and proportionality. ... The reasons for concluding that a Union objective can be better achieved at Union level shall be substantiated by qualitative and, wherever possible, quantitative indicators. (*Protocol (No 2) on the Application of the Principles of Subsidiarity and Proportionality* [2010] OJ C 83/206)

60 Martin Brenncke, 'Case Law' (2010) 47 *Common Market Law Review* 1793, 1812. In a similar vein, see Andrea Biondi, 'Subsidiarity in the Courtroom', in Andrea Biondi and Piet Eeckhout (eds), *EU Law After Lisbon* (Oxford University Press, 2012) ch 10, 213–27.

61 *Vodafone* (C-58/08) [2010] ECR I-4999, [78], [79].

62 Ibid [30]–[34] (AG Maduro).

63 The role of advertising in EU market integration has been most vividly described by Advocate General Jacobs in his Opinion in *Société d'Importation Edouard Leclerc-Siplec v TF1 Publicité SA* (C-412/93) [1995] ECR I-179, [21]: 'Without advertising it would be extremely difficult for a manufacturer located in one Member State to penetrate the market in another Member State where his products have not previously been sold and so enjoy no reputation among consumers'.

64 However, in the absence of legislative harmonising measures on these issues, member states retain their freedom to regulate these areas, on the condition that they comply with the general treaty provisions, not least those on the free movement of goods and services. For a more thorough discussion of the role of the principle of subsidiarity in relation to the EU NCD policy, see Alemanno and Garde, above n 36; Isidora Maletic, 'The Role of the Principle of Subsidiarity in the EU Lifestyle Risk Policy' in Alemanno and Garde, above n 5.

65 TFEU art 5(4).

66 *Internationale Handelsgesellschaft mbH v Einfuhr* (C-11/70) [1970] ECR 1125.

67 See, to that effect, *Tempelman v Directeur van de Rijksdienst voor de keuring van Vee en Vlees* (C-96/03 and C-97/03) [2005] ECR I-1895, [48]; *Greece v Commission of the European Communities* (C-86/03) [2005] ECR I-10979, [96]; *Agrarproduktion Staebelow GmbH v Landrat des Landkreises Bad Doberan* (C-504/04) [2006] ECR I-679, [37]; *Pfizer Animal Health SA v Council of the European Union* (T-13/99) [2002] ECR II-3305, [411] as well

as the parallel case *Alpharma Inc v Council of the European Union* (T-70/99) [2002] ECR II-3495. See more recently, *Vodafone* (Case C-58/08) [2010] ECR I-4999, [53].

68   Amandine Garde, 'Freedom of Commercial Expression and Public Health Protection: The Principle of Proportionality as a Tool to Strike the Balance' in Laurence Gormley and Niamh Nic Shuibhne (eds), *From Single Market to Economic Union – Essays in Honour of John Usher* (Oxford University Press, 2012), 117.

69   *Philip Morris Norway* (E-16/10) [2011] EFTA (12 September 2011).

70   See, eg, *Maizena Gesellschaft mbH v Bundesanstalt für landwirtschaftliche Marktordnung* (C-137/85) [1987] ECR 4587, [15]; *ADM Ölmühlen GmbH v Bundesanstalt für landwirtschaftliche Marktordnung* (C-339/92) [1993] ECR I-6473, [15]; *Käserei Champignon Hofmeister GmbH & Co KG v Hauptzollamt Hamburg-Jonas* (C-210/00) [2002] ECR I-6453, [59].

71   European Commission, *Impact Assessment Guidelines* (15 January 2009) <http://ec.europa.eu/governance/impact/commission_guidelines/docs/iag_2009_en.pdf>, 28.

72   Alberto Alemanno, 'The Better Regulation Initiative at the Judicial Gate: A Trojan Horse within the Commission's Walls or the Way Forward?' (2009) 15(3) *European Law Journal* 382; Alberto Alemanno, 'A Meeting of Minds on Impact Assessment: When Ex Ante Evaluation Meets Ex Post Judicial Control' (2011) 17(3) *European Public Law* 485.

73   The EU is 'founded on the values of respect for human dignity, freedom, democracy, equality, the rule of law and respect for human rights': TFEU art 2(1); see also *Parti écologiste 'Les Verts' v European Parliament* (C-294/83) [1986] ECR 1339.

74   The three main sources of EU fundamental rights are the *Charter of Fundamental Rights of the European Union* [2000] OJ C 364/01 ('the *EU Charter*'), the *Convention for the Protection of Human Rights and Fundamental Freedoms*, opened for signature 4 November 1950, 213 UNTS 221 (entered into force 3 September 1953), and the general principles of EU law resulting from the constitutional traditions common to the member states: TFEU art 6.

75   See, in particular, *Tobacco Advertising I* (C-376/98) [2000] ECR 1-8419; *R v Secretary of State for Health* (C-491/01) [2002] ECR I-11453; *RJ Reynolds Tobacco Holdings, Inc v Commission of the European Communities* (C-131/03) [2006] ECR I-7795; *Tobacco Advertising II* (C-380/03) [2006] ECR I-11573; *Ireland v European Parliament* (C-301/06) [2009] ECR I-0593.

76   Human rights are 'far from constituting unfettered prerogatives': see in this respect *J Nold und Baustoffgroßhandlung v Commission of the European Communities* (4/73) [1974] ECR I-491, [14].

77   *R v Secretary of State for Health* (C-491/01) [2002] ECR I-11453, [149], [150]. For other cases in which the court discussed the right to property and the freedom to conduct a business – often invoked in tandem – see in particular *Hauer v Land Rheinland-Pfalz* (44/79) [1979] ECR 3727; *Werner Faust v Commission of the European Communities* (52/81) [1982] ECR 3745; *Hermann Schräder HS Kraftfutter GmbH & Co KG v Hauptzollamt Gronau* (265/87) [1989] ECR 2237; *Wachauf v Bundesamt für Ernährung und Forstwirtschaft* (5/88) [1989] ECR 2609; *Germany v Council of the European Union* (C-280/93) [1994] ECR I-4973; *R v Secretary of State for the Environment* (C-293/97) [1999] ECR I-2603; *Sky Österreich GmbH v Österreichischer Rundfunk* (Court of Justice of the European Communities, C-283/11, 22 January 2013).

78   Article 52(1) of the *EU Charter* provides that 'any limitation on the exercise of the rights and freedoms recognised by this Charter must be provided for by law and respect the essence of those rights and freedoms', thus recognising that there are 'limitations on limitations' to fundamental rights and freedoms under the 'essential core' doctrine: limitations on fundamental rights – even if proportionate – must never undermine the 'very substance' of a fundamental right. This sets an absolute limit on all governmental power by identifying an 'untouchable' core within a right (though the role of this doctrine remains unclear in EU law: see Robert Schütze, above n 55, 419.

79 *Tobacco Advertising II* (C-380/03) [2006] ECR I-11573.

80 WHO FCTC art 13.

81 See *R v Secretary of State for Health* (C-491/01) [2002] ECR I-11453, [120] (AG Geelhoed).

82 For a more in-depth discussion of the relationship between freedom of expression and public health, see Amandine Garde, 'Freedom of Commercial Expression and the Protection of Public Health in Europe' (2010) 12 *Cambridge Yearbook of European Legal Studies* 225.

83 On the relationship between tobacco control and fundamental rights, see Oscar Cabrera and Larry Gostin, 'Human Rights and the Framework Convention on Tobacco Control: Mutually Reinforcing Systems' (2011) *International Journal of Law in Context* 285; Carolyn Dresler and Stephen Marks, 'The Emerging Human Right to Tobacco Control' (2006) 28 *Human Rights Quarterly* 599; Melissa Crow, 'Smokescreen and State Responsibility Using Human Rights Strategies to Promote Global Tobacco Control' (2004) 29 *Yale Journal of International Law* 209.

84 The UN Special Rapporteur to the right to food, Olivier de Schutter, has interpreted this right so as to include the right to nutritious food: see Human Rights Council, *Report Submitted by the Special Rapporteur on the Right to Food*, 19th sess, Agenda Item 3, UN Doc A/HRC/1/9/59 (26 December 2011). This, in turn, has led him to argue forcefully in favour of the adoption of regulatory (as opposed to self-regulatory) measures restricting the marketing of unhealthy food to children.

85 On the EU children's rights strategy, see Helen Stalford, *Children and the European Union – Rights, Welfare and Accountability* (Hart Publishing, 2012). On the failure of the EU to uphold the best interests of the child in its consumer and public health policies more specifically, see Amandine Garde, 'Advertising Regulation and the Protection of Children-Consumers in the European Union: In the Best Interest of … Commercial Operators?' (2011) 19 *International Journal of Children's Rights* 523.

86 *Deutsches Weintor eG v Land Rheinland-Pfalz* (Case C-544/10), judgment of 6 September 2012.

87 *Regulation 1924/2006 of the European Parliament and of the Council of 20 December 2006 on Nutrition and Health Claims Made on Foods* [2006] OJ L404/9, art 4(3), as amended by Commission Regulation 116/2010 of 9 February 2010, [2010] OJ L37/16.

88 See, eg, *Tobacco Advertising I* (C-376/98) [2000] ECR 1-8419; *R v Secretary of State for Health* (C-491/01) [2002] ECR I-11453; *RJ Reynolds Tobacco Holdings, Inc v Commission of the European Communities* (C-131/03) [2006] ECR I-7795; *Swedish Match AB v Secretary of State for Health* (C-210/03) [2004] ECR I-11893; *Tobacco Advertising II* (C-380/03) [2006] ECR I-11573; *Ireland v European Parliament* (C-301/06) [2009] ECR I-0593.

89 World Health Assembly, *Follow-up to the Political Declaration of the High-level Meeting of the General Assembly on the Prevention and Control of Non-communicable Diseases*, WHA Res WHA66.10, 66th sess, 9th plen mtg, Agenda Items 13.1 and 13.2 (27 May 2013) annex, *Global Action Plan for the Prevention and Control of Noncommunicable Diseases 2013–2020*.

14 Africa

*Rachel Kitonyo-Devotsu**

1 Introduction

Among the four preventable risk factors for non-communicable diseases ('NCD') of tobacco use, alcohol abuse, unhealthy diet and lack of physical exercise, tobacco regulation is the most advanced in Africa in terms of the adoption and implementation of policy measures. This is largely due to the process of adoption and implementation of the *WHO Framework Convention on Tobacco Control* ('WHO FCTC'),[1] which provides legally binding obligations and also requires countries to report back on implementation. The process of adoption also created technical and advocacy capacity within government and civil society in Africa, which have been critical in securing political will to take action. Tobacco control therefore provides specific examples of the challenges faced in adoption and implementation of policies to counter the NCD epidemic and also offers lessons for dealing with the other risk factors.

Forty-one of the 47 countries in the World Health Organization's ('WHO') African region are party to the WHO FCTC and an increasing number of countries are enacting domestic legislation to implement the treaty. This chapter will briefly discuss the current state of the regulation of tobacco in Africa and then use examples from three African countries (Kenya, Mauritius and Chad) to highlight areas in tobacco control in which progress is being made. Case studies from these countries are used to illustrate best practice and the legal and political battles being faced in the pursuit of regulation in Africa, including what strategies the tobacco industry has employed and how the governments concerned have responded.

Common success factors identified from the case studies include the presence of political will and champions for given causes, the presence of strong civil society organisations to carry out advocacy, the availability of funds for advocacy and the availability of relevant research to influence policy decisions. The case studies also show common challenges facing tobacco control in Africa including tobacco industry interference, low priority accorded to tobacco control within health and broader development agendas, and inadequate resourcing of tobacco control programs within government budgets. These problems need to be addressed for more progress in tobacco control in Africa to be realised.

2 Current state of regulating tobacco in Africa

According to the WHO:[2]

- With regard to measures to ban smoking in public under art 8 of the WHO FCTC, only four countries in Africa (Namibia, Chad, Burkina Faso and Tunisia) have a complete ban on smoking in all public places (ie no provision for designated smoking areas), while the rest have varying numbers of places covered by smoke-free legislation ranging from 6–7 public places to 2–3 public places.
- With regard to art 11 of the WHO FCTC, which deals with packaging and labelling of tobacco products, 18 countries have banned false and misleading descriptors, 19 have some form of health warning on tobacco packaging, 13 have rotated warnings, 16 have warnings on no less than 30 per cent of the pack and 13 have warnings covering 50 per cent or more of the pack, while only 8 have pictorial health warnings.
- With regard to art 13 of the WHO FCTC, which deals with tobacco advertising, promotion and sponsorship, only 6 countries – Kenya, Mauritius, Chad, Sudan, Eritrea and Djibouti – have a comprehensive ban, meaning all forms of direct and indirect advertising are prohibited; 18 countries have banned advertising promotion and sponsorship on national radio, television and print media including some forms of direct and indirect advertising; and 15 countries have no ban at all.
- With regard to tobacco taxation measures under art 6 of the WHO FCTC, only one country (Mauritius) has taxes greater than 75 per cent of retail price; 12 countries have tobacco taxes that are 51–75 per cent of retail price; 20 countries have taxes that are 26–50 per cent of retail price; and 9 countries have taxes below 25 per cent of retail price.

3 Experiences with tobacco taxation: a case study of Kenya

3.1 Enactment of the Tobacco Control Act 2007

Kenya signed and ratified the WHO FCTC on 25 June 2004. This made it the second country, after Norway, to sign and ratify the treaty on the same day. Kenya was among the first 40 parties of the WHO FCTC.[3] However, despite this indication of political will and commitment to tobacco control, it took three more years for Kenya to adopt and enact comprehensive tobacco control legislation. Initial efforts to adopt tobacco control legislation began before the advent of the WHO FCTC. The government first introduced a bill into parliament in 1998. The bill was weak and highly influenced by the tobacco industry, as some government agencies had invested in the industry, such as the national, state-run pension service, the National Social Security Fund ('NSSF').

In 2004, after ratification of the WHO FCTC, the Ministry of Health again introduced a weak tobacco control bill. Attempts by tobacco control advocates to strengthen the provisions proved unsuccessful, and in 2005 the advocates changed tactics and identified a private member, the Hon Eric Gor Sungu, to move a private member's bill. In 2006, both the government legislation and the private member's bill came before the parliament for debate, and the Speaker of the House ordered that the two bills be consolidated. Between 2006 and 2007, the Ministry of Health, the private member and civil society worked together to push for adoption of the legislation. The *Tobacco Control Act 2007* (Kenya) ('TCA') was adopted by parliament on 9 August 2007 and came into force on 8 July 2008. In total the legislation took close to 10 years to enact.

The Act is comprehensive, covering the major supply and demand reduction strategies recommended in the WHO FCTC such as providing for: the setting up of a Tobacco Control Board and Fund; public education and awareness by both government and civil society; smoke-free public places; comprehensive bans on advertising, promotion and sponsorship; larger warning labels on tobacco products; increased taxation of tobacco products; alternative economic livelihoods; and smuggling.

In terms of strengths, Kenya has one of the most comprehensive tobacco advertising and promotion bans in Africa,[4] although it is yet to ban advertising at the point of sale. A major weakness in Kenya's smoke-free provisions is that, like many other African countries that have banned smoking in public, the ban is not complete, as it provides for designated smoking areas.[5]

3.2 Reforming tobacco taxation in Kenya

Good tobacco tax policies have enormous potential to encourage quitting amongst tobacco users, prevent young people from starting and simultaneously generate considerable tax revenue. The WHO recognises tax and price policies as one of the most effective strategies for combating the tobacco epidemic by reducing demand for tobacco and tobacco products.[6] Yet few African countries are utilising tobacco taxation for not only revenue generation but also public health benefits. Kenya has made considerable progress in the last two years on tobacco taxation and shall be used as a case study to illustrate best practice and challenges.

Section 12 of the TCA provides that the Minister of Finance shall 'implement tax and price policies on tobacco and tobacco products so as to contribute to the objects of the Act'. In Kenya, tax increases at the rate of 10 per cent per annum were implemented in the financial years 2005/6, 2006/7, 2007/8 and 2008/9. However, no evaluation was undertaken to ascertain whether these tax increases had the effect of reducing consumption or whether more substantial increases were needed. In the 2009/10 financial year, no increase in taxation of tobacco products took place, despite the enabling provision in the law and lobbying by Ministry of Health and tobacco control non-governmental organisations ('NGOs') for the same. Section 7 of the TCA also sets up a Tobacco Control Fund, whose main source of funding is public budget allocations. However, in the financial year 2009/10, the Tobacco Control Fund received no budgetary allocation, leading to difficulty within the Ministry of Health in implementing tobacco control programs. Eventually tobacco control advocates realised that for the relevant decision makers to raise the taxes so as to achieve the desired public health goals, the decision makers needed evidence of the feasibility of tobacco taxation increases.

Thus, the International Institute for Legislative Affairs, a Kenyan non-governmental organisation carrying out advocacy for policy change, through funding from the Campaign for Tobacco Free Kids, conducted research on the 'Economics of Tobacco Taxation in Kenya' in 2011.[7] The specific objectives of the study were: to review the trends in the prices of tobacco products, their tax structure and total revenue accrued to the government; to determine the responsiveness of tobacco consumption to changes in prices and taxation; and to review the global approaches to the tobacco epidemic through tax policies (compared to Kenya's experience), outlining challenges, lessons and successes to date. Finally, the study sought to make recommendations on how tobacco tax could be used to reduce tobacco use and raise much needed revenue.

Though tobacco products in Kenya are subject to excise duty, value added tax and import duty, the study focused on excise taxes, since it is this tax that inflates the prices of tobacco relative to other consumer products, providing the dual benefits of additional revenue and reduced consumption. Cigarette taxes account for 30 per cent of all excise tax revenue in Kenya (approximately Ksh 7 billion in 2008).[8] The structure of the tobacco excise tax in Kenya has changed multiple times over the last decade, switching from specific rates to *ad valorem* rates, back to specific rates, and then, for some product classes, a mixture of *ad valorem* and specific rates.[9] Before the commencement of the Tax Modernization Programme in 1986, the tobacco excise tax regime in Kenya was specific, but this changed to an *ad valorem* regime in 1991/2.[10] Unfortunately, the elimination of price controls in 1993 and the conversion of excise tax from specific to *ad valorem* created a loophole for tax leakage. Manufacturers would cheat on valuation by excluding certain cost elements such as distribution costs in order to evade some portion of tax.[11] The Ministry of Finance responded to this by providing a more elaborate definition of value for excise duty purposes that included all the direct costs such as packaging, advertising and distribution.[12]

These definitional changes failed to meet the tax simplicity principle, which was one of the primary objectives of tax reform.[13] Specifically, cigarette taxes in the country continued to be complex due to multiple tax rates. For example, prior to 1993/4, cigarettes were subject to three different price-based excise duty brackets. However, in 1993/4, this was changed and linked to two length-based bands. Then in 1997/8 the excise duty on cigarettes was rationalised to a uniform rate of 135 per cent, before further changes in 2008 that subjected cigarettes to four different price-based excise duty brackets.[14] The frequent changes to the taxation regime failed to produce predictable impacts on consumption and revenue, and various studies suggested that the design and administration of excise duty was problematic.

For example, a study carried out by the International Monetary Fund (IMF) in 2010 found that the structure for tobacco products was too complex and lacking in policy rationale.[15] The system made it difficult for the government to reduce consumption, predict revenue and control illicit trade. Official tobacco sales figures and government revenues also showed considerable variation over time, suggesting that the availability of non-duty paid cigarettes was impacting formal sales and tax collection. It was estimated that approximately 20 per cent of the cigarette market is non-duty paid.[16] This highlighted the critical importance of developing a tax structure that is simple to administer and reduces tax evasion. The study by the International Institute for Legislative Affairs further found that the trend in cigarette tax revenue (nominal) was not in line with the trend in cigarette consumption.[17] Ideally, the two trends should be positively correlated so that periods with high cigarette consumption are matched with a higher yield in taxes. The contrary finding suggested that tax evasion, smuggling and sales of non-duty paid products was occurring and that inflation was reducing the real value of the taxes. The International Institute for Legislative Affairs study made the following recommendations:

- the excise tax system should be simplified to enable better tax administration, and price categories should be eliminated;
- the system should be changed to a specific tax system, to allow the government to better predict revenue;
- regular adjustments for inflation and income growth should be established;
- tobacco taxes should be increased to at least 70 per cent of the retail price to ensure consumption declines; and
- all tobacco products should be taxed equally to prevent users from switching brands and types due to price differences.[18]

The advocacy that followed, based on the study's findings, had some success. The *Finance Act 2012* (Kenya) was adopted, changing the structure of tobacco taxation by collapsing the four tax bands (which were based on the retail selling price) into one. Under that legislation, the excise tax on cigarettes is now charged at a rate of Ksh 1200 per thousand or 35 per cent of the retail selling price – whichever is higher – irrespective of the brand, type or price.[19] The effect is as follows:

- The tax rate for the lower end cigarettes (previously described as 'plain' cigarettes and categorised under Tier A) rose by 71.4 per cent. The rate for the second tier, which was effectively the rate for all soft cap cigarettes, rose by 20 per cent. Even though the rate for the up-market brands may fall to an average of Ksh 1600 per thousand, the general effect is an increase of Ksh 2 billion, representing a 25 per cent rise in tobacco taxes.
- The chances of substitution between brands has been minimised based on the reasoning that all forms and brands of cigarettes have the same negative health impact on the consumer.

Advocacy for implementation of the other recommendations of the International Institute for Legislative Affairs is ongoing.

3.3 Lessons from the adoption of the legislation and subsequent taxation changes

The following factors facilitated the adoption of the Kenyan legislation and tobacco advocacy for subsequent taxation changes:

- The obligation of Kenya as a party to the WHO FCTC to adopt effective tobacco control measures. Only after ratification of the WHO FCTC did advocacy for the adoption of tobacco control measures pick up and begin bearing fruit.
- The availability of information and evidence from research to support the advocacy. In 2007, an opinion poll was carried out to demonstrate public support for the proposed legislation, data was available on the health and economic impacts of tobacco use in Kenya, and research in support of tobacco taxation was also available.[20]
- The availability of champions within the Ministry of Health and members of parliament, who mobilised the required political support for the legislation.
- The partnership between government and civil society. Technical and political leadership came from the Ministry of Health, and civil society played a major role in resource mobilisation, providing technical support in drafting legislation, defending legal challenges, and facilitating research on taxation. This partnership saw a common strategy, including identification of a private member to ensure political visibility of the need for legislation. The partnership ensured that the required research was conducted and public support for the legislation was secured.
- The involvement of the Ministry of Finance officials from the Kenyan Revenue Authority during negotiations for the *Protocol to Eliminate Illicit Trade in Tobacco Products*,[21] which sensitised them to the benefits of tobacco taxation for public health, made them partners in tobacco control and provided useful contacts that facilitated public health advocacy regarding taxation reform.

Kenya faced the following challenges in the implementation of the TCA and the proposed tax changes:

- The lack of coordination in the implementation of the TCA. There is a perception that tobacco control is the sole domain of the Ministry of Health, yet it is clear from the WHO FCTC that a multi-sectoral approach is necessary to achieve results.[22] The tobacco industry has utilised this lack of ministerial coordination to play off one government ministry against another, as detailed further below.
- A lack of funds within the Ministry of Health budget for tobacco control. As foreshadowed above, although the TCA provides for a Tobacco Control Fund, no allocations have been made to it since 2007. This failure has compromised the Ministry's ability to carry out public education and awareness campaigns, build capacity of enforcement officers and other government

agencies responsible for tobacco control, and run an effective tobacco control program.

- The country is a manufacturing hub for tobacco products for East and Central Africa, and the tobacco industry wields immense influence as a result. The industry uses arguments about losses to employment and smuggling to object to tobacco taxation increases.
- Inadequate access by the government to information on tobacco taxation. This delayed the necessary research, with advocates having to build relationships with relevant individuals within government departments to obtain the required information.
- Limited information among policy makers on the use of fiscal policies to reduce tobacco use and its harms. Contrary to the TCA[23] and WHO FCTC,[24] the prevailing approach was simply to obtain revenue. Advocates organised several sensitisation meetings and disseminated research findings to overcome this difficulty.

4 Experiences with pictorial health warnings: a case study of Mauritius

4.1 Introduction of pictorial health warning regulations

Mauritius ratified the WHO FCTC on 17 May 2004, and the WHO FCTC came into force on 27 February 2005. Like Kenya, Mauritius was among the first 40 parties of the WHO FCTC.[25] Mauritius had adopted legislation in 1999 that did not now comply with the WHO FCTC. Soon after the WHO FCTC came into force for Mauritius, the Ministry of Health and Quality of Life started working on WHO FCTC-compliant draft legislation, which took the form of regulations under the *Public Health Act 1925* (Mauritius). The *Public Health (Restrictions on Tobacco Products) Regulations 2008* (Mauritius) were adopted in November 2008 and implemented in two phases:

- Phase One, which came into force on 1 March 2009, included: a ban on smoking in public indoor and outdoor areas, hospitality venues, recreational venues and private vehicles carrying passengers; smoking restrictions in workplaces with provision for designated smoking areas; a ban on the sale of tobacco to and by minors; a ban on the advertising, promotion and sponsorship of tobacco products (with the exception of internet advertising), including a ban on display of tobacco products at the point of sale except at duty free shops at airports; measures to reduce the illicit trade in cigarettes; and an increase in the penalties for failure to adhere to the tobacco control regulations.[26]
- Phase Two, which was implemented on 1 June 2009, focused on cigarette packaging and included:
  - pictorial health warnings ('PHWs');
  - a ban on descriptors such as 'light', 'mild' or 'low tar' on packages;

- a ban on the display of tar and nicotine content or carbon monoxide yield on packs; and
- a ban on the sale of single cigarettes or loose cigarettes and packages of less than 20 cigarettes.[27]

Mauritius was the first country in Africa to implement PHWs. These pictorial health warnings were the largest in the world at the time of their introduction and consisted of a set of eight rotating PHWs on addiction, second-hand smoke, impotence, disease conditions (cancer of the mouth, cancer of the lungs, slow death), stroke and heart problems. The warnings covered an average of 65 per cent of the principal surface areas (60 per cent on the front and 70 per cent on the back), while the sides carried a text warning covering 65 per cent of the total surface area.[28]

4.2 *Lessons from the adoption of regulations and pictorial health warnings*

The following factors enabled the enactment of new tobacco control regulations in Mauritius:

- the ratification of the WHO FCTC and the legal obligation as a party to comply with the Convention;
- the participation of the then Minister of Health and Quality of Life in the ratification process;
- political will and support from the Ministry of Health and the Office of the Prime Minister;
- the support of all stakeholders through the National Tobacco Control Steering Committee;
- the existence of a strong civil society organisation (Association ViSa) to carry out advocacy.[29]

More specifically, the following factors facilitated the adoption of PHWs in Mauritius:

- the low cost involved (around US$3000);
- the expertise available within the Ministry of Health and Quality of Life and the Mauritius Institute of Health to undertake the development of the PHWs, including technical and administrative support from senior officials; and
- the support from stakeholders including civil society.

Mauritius also faced the following challenges when trying to secure PHWs:

- Difficulty in obtaining a suitable picture depicting mouth cancer for one of the PHWs. A global search finally traced the picture that was required from pictures used in PHWs in Taiwan, and the Taiwanese government graciously provided copyright permission.

- Garnering support for adoption of the biggest PHWs in the world, which was attained through strong advocacy with senior officials of the Ministry of Health and Quality of Life and eventually with the Minister.
- Selecting the eight priority topics addressed in the PHWs, which was achieved through a review of survey findings and existing data.
- Working with an advertising agency that was not used to developing health messages to capture the needs of the health sector and develop PHWs that conformed to the relevant requirements, which entailed close collaboration with and technical guidance to the graphic design team.

4.3 The role of research in the adoption and implementation of tobacco control policies in Mauritius

Two major pieces of research have influenced the adoption and implementation of tobacco control policy in Mauritius. First, the Global Youth Tobacco Survey ('GYTS') carried out by the WHO and the Centers for Disease Control and Prevention contained important findings. In 2003 the GYTS indicated that the accessibility of cigarettes among youth was increased by the sale of single/loose cigarettes and packets of 10 sticks.[30] Advocates relied on this finding, as well as WHO FCTC art 16, to successfully advocate for a ban on the sale of single cigarettes and packets of less than 20 sticks.[31] In 2003 and 2008 the GYTS indicated high exposure to second-hand smoke among youth.[32] Advocates again used this finding to advocate for an extensive ban on smoking in public places in the 2008 tobacco legislation.[33] The GYTS also revealed that the majority of youth currently smoking desired to quit,[34] leading to the provision of cessation services to young people under the age of 18 in the public health sector, provided that they are accompanied by one of their parents.

Second, the Mauritius Institute of Health and University of Waterloo carried out the International Tobacco Control Policy Evaluation Project ('ITC Project'), which systematically evaluates key policies of the WHO FCTC at the population level through longitudinal cohort studies. Mauritius was the first African country to participate in the ITC Project survey and one of only a few African countries other than South Africa to have invested in monitoring and evaluating the impact of tobacco control policies. So far, three waves of the survey have been carried out (April–May 2009, August–October 2010 and June–July 2011).

The first wave of the ITC Project survey,[35] which was carried out approximately two months after the implementation of Phase One of the newly adopted tobacco control regulations, indicated the following:

- Strong support by the Mauritian public for comprehensive smoke-free policies in all public places, including workplaces. Smokers most strongly supported bans on smoking in cars (90 per cent), followed by restaurants/tea rooms (86 per cent), workplaces (84 per cent) and bars/pubs (74 per cent). Support for these measures was even higher among non-smokers (93 per cent, 94 per cent, 92 per cent and 92 per cent, respectively).[36] This finding is being used by Ministry of Health and Quality of Life and civil society to lobby the Ministry of Labour to abolish designated smoking areas at workplaces.

- Three-quarters of Mauritian smokers wanted to quit, wanted the government to do more to help them to quit and were willing to access services at smoking cessation clinics.[37] The Ministry of Health and Quality of Life set up smoking cessation services in 2010, which provide both behavioural and drug therapies.[38]
- Smoking in restaurants and tea rooms had decreased dramatically two to three months after the ban. Before the smoking ban, 61 per cent of smokers noticed people smoking in restaurants or tea rooms, and 88 per cent of smokers noticed people smoking in pubs and bars. Two to three months after the smoking bans, among those who visited these venues after the bans (42 per cent of smokers who visited a restaurant or tea room and 26 per cent of smokers who visited a bar or pub), 18 per cent reported that people were smoking inside a restaurant and 40 per cent reported the presence of smoking in bars/pubs.[39]
- Mauritian smokers were ready for pictorial warnings. Two-thirds of smokers and 87 per cent of non-smokers agreed that there should be more information on Mauritian health warnings.[40]
- Cigarettes were easily affordable in Mauritius despite taxes representing more than 70 per cent of the retail price.[41] Based on this finding, advocates are currently lobbying national authorities for an increase in taxes of tobacco products.

The second wave of the ITC Project survey[42] was conducted between 30 August and 2 October 2010, approximately 14 to 15 months after the Phase Two regulations were implemented, strengthening regulations on packaging, including the new requirement for pictorial warnings. The survey findings indicated that the pictorial health warnings were highly effective when compared to the previous text warnings. The new warning labels had successfully increased label awareness, smokers' awareness of the health risks of smoking, and smokers' consideration of quitting, compared to the text-only labels that were assessed in the first wave. However, Mauritians still wanted more information about the health risks of smoking to appear on cigarette warning labels.[43]

The third wave of the ITC Project survey[44] was conducted between 20 June and 11 July 2011 and continued to measure the effectiveness and strength of both the Phase One and Two regulations that were implemented in 2009. The survey assessed smoking and quitting behaviour, public support for and use of cessation services, effectiveness of smoking bans in public places and workplaces, and effectiveness of pictorial warnings. In addition, the third wave evaluated a mass media campaign (an adaptation of the World Lung Foundation 'Sponge Campaign' carried out in Mauritius between 30 May and 19 June 2011),[45] which was designed to increase awareness of the harms of tobacco smoke for smokers and non-smokers.

The survey findings indicated:

- Smoke-free laws and pictorial health warnings had been successful in encouraging smokers to think about the health risks of smoking, and to think about quitting.[46]
- The majority of smokers who visited a doctor or health care professional were not receiving advice to quit or referrals to cessation services.[47]
- Strong support among smokers and non-smokers for comprehensive smoke-free policies in all public places.[48] Since the implementation of the 2009 smoke-free regulations in Mauritius, complete smoking bans had become prevalent in restaurants, bars and public transportation. However, further effort is needed to increase the prevalence of complete smoking bans in workplaces and to strengthen enforcement and improve compliance with smoking bans in bars.[49]
- The implementation of smoke-free laws in indoor workplaces and public places had increased the prevalence of smoke-free homes in Mauritius.[50]
- The set of eight PHWs appeared to be having less impact on smoking behaviour at 20 to 21 months post-implementation. There was also evidence of wear-out (decline in effectiveness) – the majority of warning label effectiveness indicators showed either a decline or no further improvement from the second wave in 2010.[51] This suggested a need to revise and strengthen the PHWs to prevent further declines in label effectiveness. This finding has prompted national authorities to develop a second set of PHWs.

5 Raising the priority of tobacco control within national health and development agendas: experiences from Chad

5.1 Enactment of legislation

Chad ratified the WHO FCTC on 30 January 2006, and the WHO FCTC came into force for Chad on 30 April 2006.[52] Chad's tobacco control legislation was adopted in 2010. The content of the *Tobacco Act 2010* (Chad) focuses on four articles of the WHO FCTC, namely arts 8, 11, 13 and 16. The legislation contains:

- A total ban on smoking in public places, places of public transport and workplaces including homes if a domestic worker works there.[53] Chad is one of the few African countries to have avoided designated smoking areas.
- A total ban on tobacco advertising, promotion and sponsorship in all its forms, including in retail outlets.[54]
- Provision for health warnings on tobacco packages. The law provides for warnings of at least 50 per cent.[55] An application decree that has been validated by stakeholders and is awaiting adoption by the Ministerial Council proposes to increase this figure to 65 per cent with PHWs.
- Provisions under which tobacco products may be sold, including banning sales to minors.
- Provisions on sanctions and enforcement.[56]

However, the legislation does not cover WHO FCTC art 5.3 (which deals with tobacco industry interference), tobacco taxation or financing for tobacco control, all of which are areas in which tobacco control advocates are currently facing challenges.

5.2 Lessons from adoption and implementation of tobacco control legislation

The factors that facilitated successful adoption of tobacco control legislation in Chad include funding and technical support from the Bloomberg Initiative, which enabled an advocacy campaign focusing on sensitisation of decision makers and the public to the harms of tobacco use and the need for regulation. Advocates also relied on local data on youth smoking prevalence collected in 2005 and 2006 by the Observatoire du Tabac en Afrique Francophone ('OTAF'), a regional alliance of tobacco control organisations in francophone African countries, as well as the GYTS 2008, to convince policy makers to take action.[57]

The tobacco control community in Chad faced three major challenges during advocacy for the legislation: (i) political instability in the form of frequent changes of Minister and senior Ministry of Health officials; (ii) lack of information by decision makers on the health and economic impacts of tobacco use in Chad; and (iii) tobacco industry interference. Advocates overcame these challenges through intensive sensitisation campaigns among journalists, the media, religious leaders, representatives of civil society, parliamentarians and the public.

The major challenge facing implementation of tobacco control legislation in Chad is the low priority given to tobacco control within the health and development agenda in Chad. This prioritisation is exemplified by frequent replacement of the tobacco control focal point within the Ministry of Health, inadequate resources dedicated to sensitising the public and enforcement agencies to the legislation and their responsibilities thereunder, leading to poor enforcement and lack of resources to run an effective tobacco control program. The Ministry of Health has tended to rely on resources raised by civil society instead of dedicating its own budget to tobacco control.

5.3 The campaign to raise the priority of tobacco control in Chad

Once tobacco control advocates realised that tobacco control was not a priority for the Ministry of Health or the broader government, they embarked on a campaign to remedy the problem. Chad is part of a three country initiative (Chad, Burkina Faso and Niger) funded by the Bloomberg Initiative to reduce tobacco use.[58] The project seeks to raise the priority of tobacco control within the development agendas of the three countries and includes studies on how domestic resources can be mobilised for tobacco control. These studies enabled tobacco control advocates in Chad to understand the mechanisms and processes of government funding and identify opportunities for sourcing funds for tobacco control within the government budget.

The advocates promoted the integration of tobacco control into the national development planning documents that highlight the country's priorities. They succeeded in having the WHO FCTC identified as one of the priorities in the Chad Draft National Development Plan (2013–15).[59] As part of campaigns to increase tobacco taxes in Chad, advocates lobbied members of the National Assembly, several of whom are now committed to dedicating funds to tobacco control within the 2014 budget.

In Burkina Faso, the advocacy campaign resulted in an allocation of CFA franc100 million per annum to the Ministry of Health from 2012/13 for tobacco control. In Niger, the advocacy resulted in the development of the National Strategic Plan against Non-communicable Diseases,[60] which includes tobacco control.

6 Tobacco industry interference in Africa

As noted from the three case studies above, tobacco industry interference with the adoption and enactment of tobacco control policy is a major obstacle faced in the pursuit of regulation of tobacco in Africa. This interference takes many forms.

6.1 Drafting weak legislative text

In Kenya, in 2004, British American Tobacco ('BAT') came up with weak draft legislative text and attempted to bribe Members of Parliament to adopt the text by taking them to an expensive seaside resort for a lobbying meeting.[61]

6.2 Playing off government departments

In many African countries, tobacco control is seen as the domain of the Ministry of Health. The tobacco industry has been quick to exploit this perception, mounting attacks against Ministry of Health attempts to secure and implement tobacco control policy through such ministries as trade, agriculture and finance. In Kenya, for example, the tobacco industry attempted to halt implementation of a ban on smoking in public imposed by various city council bylaws adopted prior to the enactment of the comprehensive national legislation by persuading the Office of the Deputy Prime Minister and Ministry of Local Government to purchase advertisements in the national media advising the public that there were 'inconsistencies' in the definition of a public place contained in the national legislation and the bylaws. This was intended to portray confusion within government ministries and also to indicate that the Office of the Deputy Prime Minister, which sits about the Ministry of Health, did not support the relevant tobacco control measures.[62]

During negotiations on the draft guidelines to art 6 of the WHO FCTC on tobacco taxation at the Fifth Conference of the Parties ('COP') held in Seoul, South Korea from 12–17 November 2012, the tobacco industry attempted to intimidate members of the Kenyan delegation to prevent them from supporting proposals to set a minimum rate of 70 per cent of excise tax on the recommended sale price of tobacco products. The industry wrote to the Permanent Secretary, Ministry of Foreign Affairs, complaining that the Kenyan delegation was deviating from agreed upon positions taken in Kenya at a 'stakeholder' meeting convened by the Kenya Association of Manufacturers.[63]

Prior to the COP, the tobacco industry had attempted to influence the positions to be taken at the COP by the Kenyan delegation by paying a 'stakeholder' visit to the Ministry of Agriculture on 2 February 2012 and asking the Ministry of Agriculture to intervene with the Ministry of Health over areas of concern to the tobacco industry, including the guidelines on art 6, the ban on corporate social responsibility by the tobacco industry, and the ban on smoking in public among others.[64] Following this meeting the Ministry of Agriculture wrote to the Ministry of Health seeking dialogue between the Ministry and the 'concerned stakeholders', as well as a formal response to the issues raised. The Ministry of Health declined to convene or attend any such meetings but delivered a written response.

6.3 Seeking to delay implementation

In Mauritius, the tobacco industry attempted to delay implementation of the pictorial health warnings. A high level delegation from BAT visited Mauritius from the regional BAT office in Nairobi to lobby for changes. The delegation proposed smaller PHWs (30 per cent on front and back of packets, rather than 65 per cent as prescribed), claiming that bigger warnings would be a violation of Mauritius' obligations under the World Trade Organization's ('WTO') *Agreement on Trade-Related Aspects of Intellectual Property* ('TRIPS').[65] The BAT delegation also proposed a transition period of 12–18 months, instead of 6 months as prescribed in the draft regulations. Due to strong political support by the Minister for Health, these objections were overcome, and the warnings came into effect. However, the law did not prescribe the time period for removal from shelves of old packets without the necessary warnings. Before entry into force of the regulations, the tobacco industry therefore imported large quantities of the old packs, which remained on the shelves long after the warnings came into effect.

6.4 Constitutional challenges to adopted legislation

In Kenya, the tobacco industry has filed two suits against the government. The first was in 2006, when the Ministry of Health issued the *Public Health ('Tobacco Products Control) Rules 2006* (Kenya), which provided for smoke-free legislation and health warnings consistent with the WHO FCTC. BAT and Mastermind Tobacco (K) Ltd filed two suits claiming that they were not consulted and faced massive losses if the rules were applied.[66] The tobacco companies managed to have an interim injunction issued, suspending the measures and ordering the Ministry of Health to consult with the tobacco industry.[67] These two cases were later overtaken by events when the *Tobacco Control Act 2007* (Kenya) came into force, superseding the challenged regulations.

In 2008, following the adoption of the 2007 tobacco control law, the tobacco industry filed another suit[68] under s 84 of the original *Constitution of Kenya*[69] alleging that: provisions prohibiting sales of tobacco products in packs of fewer than 10 and requiring taxation to achieve public health goals were discriminatory; the ban on tobacco advertising, promotion and sponsorship violated their right to freedom of expression and assembly; and provisions of the TCA criminalised an otherwise legitimate trade.[70] Tobacco control advocates gave technical assistance to the Ministry of Health and the Attorney-General's Department in drafting the government's response and also joined the suit as amicus curiae.[71] The tobacco industry then attempted to delay the case by seeking numerous adjournments and leave to file further affidavits. The case was finally dismissed for want of prosecution in December 2012.[72]

In South Africa, the tobacco industry has also filed three suits against the government. In 2009, BAT South Africa filed a claim[73] challenging s 3(1)(a) of the *Tobacco Products Control Act 1993* (South Africa), which prohibits advertising or promotion of tobacco products through direct or indirect means.[74] The company alleged that this provision does not apply to one-to-one communications with consenting adult tobacco users or, in the alternative, is unconstitutional.[75] Emphasising that one of the purposes of the law is to encourage existing smokers to stop smoking, the High Court held that the law must be interpreted as prohibiting one-to-one communication.[76] The court also upheld the constitutionality of the law, reasoning that limiting the right to freedom to receive or impart information to consenting adult tobacco consumers is reasonable and justifiable given the objective of protection of public health.[77]

BAT then appealed.[78] To determine if the limitation on speech was justified, the Appeals Court balanced the right of smokers to receive information concerning tobacco products against the government's obligation to take steps to protect its citizens from the dangers of tobacco. The court found that the hazards of smoking far outweigh the interests of the smokers as a group, so the limitation was justified.[79] Further, the court stated that South Africa is a party to the WHO FCTC, and is therefore obliged to have regard to the requirements of that treaty, specifically art 13, which requires that parties ban all tobacco advertising, promotion and sponsorship.[80] For these reasons, the lower court's decision was affirmed.[81]

BAT then sought leave to appeal to the Constitutional Court, which denied leave because the company had no prospects of success.[82]

6.5 Agreements between industry and government

In order to defeat advocacy by civil society for increased tobacco taxes in Chad, Imperial Tobacco sought to renew a memorandum of understanding with the Ministries of Commerce and Finance that would have a lower rate of taxes applied to tobacco products. In February 2013, the Africa Director of Imperial Tobacco was received personally by Chadian President Deby, who indicated he would need to consider the request to renew the agreement taking into account the changing international environment and Chad's health goals. Imperial Tobacco then launched a mass media campaign in April 2013 to showcase its corporate social responsibility programs aimed at assisting tobacco growers to switch from growing tobacco to growing groundnuts.[83]

6.6 Reliance on international trade law arguments

Prior to the fourth session of the COP of the WHO FCTC, which was held in Uruguay from 15 to 20 November 2010, the International Tobacco Growers Association ('ITGA') mounted attacks against the adoption of partial guidelines on arts 9 and 10, which sought to restrict or ban the use of flavourings and other additives used in tobacco products to increase their palatability or attractiveness.[84] Under the guise of protecting farmers' livelihoods, the ITGA peddled misconceptions about the guidelines, claiming that they would result in a ban contrary to WTO law on certain types of tobacco, particularly burley tobacco, which is the major type of tobacco grown in Africa.[85] The ITGA convinced the Secretariat and 18 member states of the Common Market for Eastern and Southern Africa ('COMESA') that these guidelines would adversely affect the livelihoods of farmers in Malawi, Zambia, Tanzania, Zimbabwe and Mozambique (the five biggest producers of tobacco in Africa), as well as to a smaller extent Uganda and Kenya, which also have tobacco farmers. Though the remaining member states of COMESA have no significant numbers of tobacco farmers, they rallied in support of the seven countries, and several statements were issued calling for the member states to oppose the guidelines at the COP.[86] For the first time, a region that had always unanimously supported effective tobacco control policies was split, with some opposing the proposed guidelines. Following concerted advocacy by civil society organisations in Malawi, Zambia, Tanzania, Kenya and Uganda, both at home and with their delegations at the COP, the threat was overcome, and eventually the African region voted in support of the guidelines.

7 Conclusion

Tobacco control in Africa has made some progress, as evinced by increasing numbers of countries adopting tobacco control measures. Common factors required for success based on the case studies profiled include political will and leadership from the Ministry of Health and other political champions, availability and use of research data to back policy recommendations, strong civil society organisations to carry out advocacy, availability of funding for advocacy, and research and availability of technical capacity within the Ministry of Health and civil society. If these factors can be replicated in other countries, similar progress can be achieved.

However, tobacco control faces three significant challenges in Africa: (i) low priority accorded to tobacco control as manifested by the lack of funding allocated to it within government budgets; (ii) tobacco industry interference in the adoption and implementation of tobacco control policies; and (iii) securing multi-sectoral government cooperation to tackle the problems of tobacco use. Further campaigns to promote implementation of art 5.3 of the WHO FCTC, to link tobacco control to broader health and development agendas, are therefore needed, as well as more outreach to other government ministries such as finance, trade and industry so as to secure a whole of government approach to tobacco control.

Similar difficulties and challenges can be expected to be faced in increasing regulation of alcohol (and, potentially, poor diet) in Africa. The achievements to date in the area of tobacco control nevertheless offer hope for positive movement in these other fields, and the identification of challenges faced in tobacco control may enable those same challenges to be avoided or at least mitigated when it comes to facing the alcohol and unhealthy food industries.

Notes

* Some statements in this chapter are not attributed as they are based on my own personal and professional experiences or informal discussions with individuals from relevant governmental, non-governmental and intergovernmental organisations.

1 *Convention on Tobacco Control*, opened for signature 16 June 2003, 2302 UNTS 166 (entered into force 27 February 2005) ('WHO FCTC'). As at November 2013, the six countries within the WHO Afro region that are not party to the WHO FCTC are Ethiopia, Eritrea, Malawi, Mozambique, South Sudan and Zimbabwe.

2 World Health Organization, *Tobacco Free Initiative (TFI): Tobacco Control Country Profiles* (2013)<http://www.who.int/tobacco/surveillance/policy/country_profile/en/index.html>.

3 *Parties to the WHO Framework Convention on Tobacco Control* (27 November 2013) WHO FCTC <http://www.who.int/fctc/signatories_parties/en/index.html>.

4 *Tobacco Control Act 2007* (Kenya) ('TCA'). Part V of the Act – dealing with tobacco advertising, promotion and sponsorship – bans both direct and indirect advertising including: the use of false, misleading or deceptive advertising (s 23); the use of testimonials or endorsements (s 24); advertising in any print or electronic media (s 25); promotion of tobacco at sporting, cultural or entertainment events (s 26); the use of manufacturers' names or brand names on facilities other than those owned or leased by the manufacturers (s 27); the manufacture, distribution or sale of accessories that display manufacturer or brand names (s 28); the display of tobacco brand elements on non-tobacco products (s 29); free giveaways of tobacco products or tobacco accessories (s 30); and cross-border advertising (s 31).

5 Ibid s 32(2), which bans smoking in public places but provides an exception for designated smoking areas.

6 WHO FCTC art 16; WHO, *WHO Technical Manual on Tobacco Tax Administration* (WHO, 2010) 9 (foreword).

7 International Institute for Legislative Affairs, *Economics of Tobacco Taxation in Kenya* (2011) <http://ilakenya.org/wp-content/uploads/2012/12/Taxrprt.pdf>.

8 Computations using government of Kenya data from the statistical abstracts, as cited in International Institute for Legislative Affairs, above n 7.

9 P Gerson, M Grote and E Hutton, *Kenya: Tax Policy Reform* (International Monetary Fund, 2010).

10 International Institute for Legislative Affairs, above n 7.

11 Ibid.

12 Ibid.

13 Stephen Njuguna Karingi and Bernadette Wanjala, 'The Tax Reform Experience of Kenya' (Research Paper No 2005/67, United Nations University and World Institute for Development Economics Research, December 2005).

14 *Finance Act 1993* (Kenya); *Finance Act 1997* (Kenya); *Finance Act 2008* (Kenya).

15 Gerson, Grote and Hutton, above n 9.

16 Ibid.

17 International Institute for Legislative Affairs, above n 7.

18 Ibid.

19 *Finance Act 2012* (Kenya) sch 1.

20 International Institute for Legislative Affairs and Ministry of Health, *National Opinion Poll on Tobacco Control, Kenya* (May 2007).

21 *Protocol to Eliminate Illicit Trade in Tobacco Products*, opened for signature 10 January 2013 (not yet in force).

22 WHO FCTC art 4.2 ('[s]trong political commitment is necessary to develop and support, at the national, regional and international levels, comprehensive multisectoral measures and coordinated responses'), art 5.1 (calling for parties to 'develop, implement, periodically update and review comprehensive multisectoral national tobacco control strategies, plans and programmes in accordance with this Convention and the protocols to which it is a Party').

23 TCA s 12(a) stipulates that the Minister for the time being in charge of finance shall implement tax policies and, where appropriate, price policies on tobacco and tobacco products so as to contribute to the objectives of the TCA.

24 WHO FCTC art 6(2): 'Without prejudice to the sovereign right of the Parties to determine and establish their taxation policies, each Party should take account of its national health objectives concerning tobacco control and adopt or maintain, as appropriate, measures which may include: (a) implementing tax policies and, where appropriate, price policies, on tobacco products so as to contribute to the health objectives aimed at reducing tobacco consumption'.

25 *Parties to the WHO Framework Convention on Tobacco Control* (27 November 2013) WHO FCTC <http://www.who.int/fctc/signatories_parties/en/index.html>.

26 *Public Health (Restrictions on Tobacco Products) Regulations 2008* (Mauritius) ss 3, 4(a), 5.

27 Ibid ss 4(a), 4(d); sch 3, 4.

28 Ibid sch 3, 4.

29 *ITC Mauritius National Report* (University of Waterloo and Mauritius Institute of Health, May 2010) 10 (message from Minister for Health, Mauritius).

30 Deowan Mohee, *Mauritius Global Youth Tobacco Survey Fact Sheet* (2003) World Health Organization <http://www.afro.who.int/index.php?option=com_docman&task=doc_download&gid=1860>.

31 *Public Health (Restrictions on Tobacco Products) Regulations 2008* (Mauritius) s 4(a)(i), enacted under the *Public Health Act 1925* (Mauritius), prohibits sale or distribution of cigarettes other than in a package containing 20 cigarettes.

32 *Mauritius Global Youth Tobacco Survey Fact Sheet* (2003), above n 30; Deowan Mohee, *Mauritius Global Youth Tobacco Survey Fact Sheet* (2008) <http://nccd.cdc.gov/gtssdata/Ancillary/DownloadAttachment.aspx?ID=315>.

33 *Public Health (Restrictions on Tobacco Products) Regulations 2008* (Mauritius) s 3.

34 *Mauritius Global Youth Tobacco Survey Fact Sheet* (2003), above n 30; *Mauritius Global Youth Tobacco Survey Fact Sheet* (2008), above n 32.

35 International Tobacco Control Policy Evaluation Project, *ITC Mauritius National Report* (May 2010) <http://www.itcproject.org/documents/keyfindings/itcmauritiusnationalreport_webpdf>.

36 Ibid 26.

37 Ibid.

38 Ibid.

39 Ibid.

40 Ibid 27.

41 Ibid.

42 International Tobacco Control Policy Evaluation Project, *ITC Mauritius National Report: Results of the Wave 2 Survey* (May 2011) <http://www.itcproject.org/documents/keyfindings/itcmauritiusnationalreport_finalmay2011webpdf>.

43 Ibid 26.

44 International Tobacco Control Policy Evaluation Project, *ITC Mauritius National Report: Results of the Wave 3 Survey* (May 2012) <http://www.itcproject.org/documents/keyfindings/itc-mauritius-nr_w3may-25v25webpdf>.

45 Ibid 23.

46 Ibid 26.

47 Ibid.

48 Ibid.

49 Ibid.

50 Ibid.

51 Ibid.

52 *Parties to the WHO Framework Convention on Tobacco Control* (27 November 2013) WHO FCTC <http://www.who.int/fctc/signatories_parties/en/index.html>.

53 *Tobacco Act 2010* (Chad) art 4.

54 Ibid arts 14–17.

55 Ibid art 13.

56 *Tobacco Act 2010* (Chad) ch VII, arts 18–40.

57 Nganguenon Gode Donbe, *GYTS Tchad 2008 Fact Sheet* (2008) <http://nccd.cdc.gov/gtssdata/Ancillary/DownloadAttachment.aspx?ID=496>.

58 *Bloomberg Initiative to Reduce Tobacco Use Grants Program* <http://www.tobaccocontrolgrants.org/Pages/40/What-we-fund>.

59 Government of Chad, *Draft National Development Plan* (2013).

60 Government of Niger, *Politique nationale de lutte contre les maladies nontransmissibles* (May 2013).

61 Ngumbao Kithi, 'MPs Mix Tobacco Bill Talks with Pleasure', *Daily Nation* (Nairobi), 22 November 2004.

62 Sammy Kirui (Permanent Secretary, Ministry of Local Government, Kenya), 'Tobacco Control Act 2007: Notice of Clarification', *Daily Nation* and *East African Standard* (Nairobi), 24 October 2008.

63 Letter from British American Tobacco (K) Ltd, Mastermind Tobacco (K) Ltd, Alliance One (Ltd) and Kenya Tobacco Farmers Association (KETOFA) to Mr Thuita Mwangi, Permanent Secretary, Ministry of Foreign Affairs, 14 November 2012.

64 *Minutes of the Meeting between the Secretary of Agriculture, Ministry of Agriculture (Kenya) and Representatives of British American Tobacco (K), Alliance One Ltd, and Philip Morris (K) Ltd*, (Kilimo House, Ministry of Agriculture), 2 February 2012.

65 *Marrakesh Agreement Establishing the World Trade Organization*, opened for signature 15 April 1994, 1867 UNTS 3 (entered into force 1 January 1995) annex 1C ('*Agreement on Trade-Related Aspects of Intellectual Property Rights*').

66 See *R v Minister of Health ex parte Mastermind Tobacco (K) Ltd*, Civil Case No 278/2006 (Nairobi High Court); *R v Minister of Health ex parte British American Tobacco Ltd*, Civil Case No 279/2006 (Nairobi High Court).

67 Ibid.

68 *Mastermind Tobacco (K) Ltd v Attorney-General*, Case No 416/2008 (Nairobi High Court).

69 The original constitution was adopted at independence in 1963; subsequently a new constitution was adopted in 2012, making changes to the Bill of Rights under which the court cases previously mentioned were filed.

70 *Mastermind Tobacco (K) Ltd v Attorney-General*, Case No 416/2008 (Nairobi High Court) petition B[3], C[3], C[5], D[6].

71 Order, 13 August 2008 (Okwengu J).

72 *Mastermind Tobacco (K) Ltd v Attorney-General*, Case No 416/2008 (Nairobi High Court).

73 *British American Tobacco South Africa (Pty) Ltd v Minister of Health*, Case No 60230/2009 (High Court of South Africa).

74 The *Tobacco Products Control Act 1993* (South Africa) is the primary tobacco control law of South Africa. It contains, among other things, smoking restrictions, a ban on tobacco advertising, promotion and sponsorship and provisions on packaging and labelling.

75 *British American Tobacco South Africa (Pty) Ltd v Minister of Health*, Case No 60230/2009 (Judgment, 19 May 2011, High Court of South Africa) [1]–[2] <http://www.tobacco controllaws.org/litigation/advancedsearch/?country=South%20Africa>.

76 Ibid [23].

77 Ibid [32]–[40].

78 *British American Tobacco South Africa (Pty) Ltd v Minister of Health*, Case No 463/2011 [2012] ZASCA 107 (Judgment, 20 June 2012, Supreme Court of Appeal).

79 Ibid [25].

80 Ibid [23].

81 Ibid [29].

82 *British American Tobacco South Africa (Pty) Ltd v Minister of Health*, Case No CCT 65/12, Order, 6 August 2012 (Constitutional Court of South Africa).

83 Observatoire du Tabac en Afrique Francophone, *Tchad – La Stratégie de reconversion des anciens tabaculteurs proposée par Imperial Tobacco est un leurre* (13 April 2013) <http://www.otaf.info/node/20>.

84 WHO FCTC Conference of the Parties, *Partial Guidelines for Implementation of Articles 9 and 10 of the WHO Framework Convention on Tobacco Control*, WHO Doc FCTC/COP4(10) (20 November 2010), as adopted in 2012: <http://www.who.int/entity/fctc/guide lines/Guideliness_Articles_9_10_rev_240613.pdf>.

85 International Tobacco Growers' Association, 'International Tobacco Growers' Association Exposes the Likely Loss of Millions of Jobs Due to WHO Proposal on Tobacco Ingredients' (Press Release, 25 May 2010) <http://www.businesswire.com/news/home/20100525005846/en/International-Tobacco-Growers-Association-Exposes-Loss-Millions#.UsVuGfR5OSo>.

86 Common Market for Eastern and Southern Africa, *Final Communiqué of the Fourteenth Summit of the Authority of the Common Market for Eastern and Southern Africa*, COMESA Doc COM/AUTH/FC/XIV/2 (1 September 2010) 8.

15 New Zealand

Regulation of Tobacco, Alcohol and Unhealthy Food in New Zealand and Coordinating the Trans-Tasman Relationship

Susy Frankel*

1 Introduction

This chapter discusses New Zealand's approach to regulating tobacco, alcohol and unhealthy foods and compares some of the drivers and frameworks of the relevant regulations. Tobacco is regulated in several ways including: sales permitted only to persons of a certain age, point of sale restrictions, packaging requirements, price controls, tax measures, advertising prevention and areas where smoking is not permitted. Alcohol is also regulated in a variety of ways including: sales permitted only to persons of a certain age, licences required to sell alcohol, hour restrictions on sales, advertising limitations and taxation. Overall, alcohol is less regulated than tobacco, and unhealthy foods are even less regulated. Unhealthy foods are subject to some labelling regulation and light-handed advertising codes. This pattern of degrees of regulation is found in many jurisdictions. It broadly reflects the degrees of harm that successive governments have felt compelled to address through regulation. The approach to regulation in New Zealand also reveals that in some instances regulatory policy is triggered by offshore (including Australian) regulatory developments. Although the trigger for regulation may come from offshore, the driver of that regulation can easily become local health and social concerns.

After providing an overview of the New Zealand regulations, in all three areas, this chapter uses examples from the regulation of tobacco, alcohol and unhealthy foods to discuss regulatory coordination issues and the trading relationship between New Zealand and Australia. There are similarities between the countries' overall approaches to regulation in these areas. The most coordination arises in the trans-Tasman product labelling and mutual recognition laws, which have developed from the Closer Economic Relationship ('CER') agreements.[1] The chapter concludes with a discussion about the incentives and sometimes problems of adopting regulations designed for other countries. Greater and earlier coordination in regulation could have a better outcome for both sides of the Tasman going forward, particularly in relation to the relatively unchartered area of regulation of unhealthy foods.

2 Tobacco regulation

This part provides an overview of the diverse measures that regulate tobacco in New Zealand. The pattern of regulation shows a gradual reduction towards a complete (or almost complete)[2] ban on tobacco advertising. The goals of the various regulatory measures (ranging from revenue gathering exercises to health concerns) have not always been well targeted. The last decade, however, has seen an increased focus on regulating to address health concerns and explicit goals of targeting reductions in youth smoking and smoking rates in Māori and Pacific Island communities.[3]

2.1 Age restrictions

New Zealand's first tobacco regulation dates back to 1903, when it was made illegal to sell cigarettes to anyone under the age of 16. It was also illegal for minors to smoke.[4] In 1988, this law was replaced with a measure that classified tobacco as a toxic substance, which was banned for sale to those under 16.[5] This ban was replaced with the enactment of the *Smoke-free Environments Act 1990* (NZ) ('1990 Act'), which prohibited the sale of all tobacco products to people under the age of 16.[6] At this time, the Ministry of Health was funded to send under-age people into shops to see if that shop would sell them tobacco products.[7]

In 1997, the purchase age of tobacco products was increased to 18.[8] In 2003, further prohibitions were made against supply to under-18 year olds of cigarettes, and a prohibition on the sale of toy cigarettes and herbal smoking products to under-18s was introduced.[9] In 2003, the law was strengthened by banning offenders from making sales for 18 months.[10] In 2011, Smoke-free Enforcement Officers were empowered to issue instant infringement fines to those selling tobacco products to under-18s.[11]

2.2 Signage at point of sale, advertising and event promotion

All tobacco company product signs were banned in retail stores from 1995.[12] The *Smoke-free Environments Amendment Act 1997* (NZ) enforced a number of restrictions on point of sale promotion, including banning incentives for retailers to promote tobacco products, reducing the size of in-shop tobacco advertising, and banning free-giveaways of tobacco. In 2003, more restrictions were placed on the retail display of tobacco products, and a 'smoking kills' sign was required near any display.[13] No counter displays, no co-packaging with other products and no displays near children's products were permitted. Restrictions were also placed on automatic vending machines for cigarettes. Tobacco retail displays were completely prohibited from July 2012.[14]

A 2011 amending Act created stringent internet sale controls. Internet sellers must not show images of packs or brands and must show the mandatory health warnings on packages.[15]

In 1962, the government and the tobacco industry entered into an agreement that the industry would not target youth with advertising. The Cancer Council says this agreement was not observed, as the tobacco industry found subtle ways of targeting youth.[16] In 1963, the then broadcasting authority banned cigarette advertising on New Zealand television and radio stations.[17] In 1973, the tobacco industry agreed to a ban of billboard and cinema advertising. Newspaper and magazine advertising was banned in 1990.[18]

The 1990 Act provided for the regulation of marketing, advertising and promotion of tobacco products, and the phasing out of sponsorship by tobacco companies of products, services and events. The incoming 1991 National government did not support a ban on tobacco sponsorship, and in 1993 the law was amended to allow existing tobacco sponsorship to continue until 1995, to allow some sporting events to continue.[19] The ban was extended from sport to other events, such as fashion and music shows.[20]

2.3 Smoke-free places

By 1988, domestic airlines became smoke-free.[21] The 1990 Act restricted smoking in many indoor workplaces and required all workplaces to have a smoking policy. There were also smoking bans on public transport, and restrictions in cafes and restaurants.[22] From January 2004, all buildings, school grounds and early childhood centres became smoke free. All licensed premises (bars, restaurants, cafes, sports clubs and casinos) and all other workplaces (offices, factories, warehouses and work canteens) became smoke free in 2004. The surrounding areas outside of many buildings, such as Victoria University of Wellington, are now also smoke free.

2.4 Taxes

Tobacco has been the subject of an excise tax since 1839. The tax was primarily a revenue gathering mechanism. Perhaps most significantly, the excise tax is not dedicated to spending on tobacco control, such as the Ministry of Health campaigns discussed below. The excise tax is indexed to the Consumer Price Index ('CPI') and adjusted annually to ensure that as the price of other foods and services rises, so does the price of tobacco.[23]

2.5 Health warnings and packaging

In 1973, the government and tobacco industry entered into an agreement whereby the tobacco industry would print warnings and tar levels on the packaging of cigarette products.[24] By 1997, the requirement was for both the front and back of cigarette packets to display health warnings linking smoking to heart and lung disease.[25] Packaging laws could not be avoided by selling single cigarettes in less than quantities of 20.[26]

A 2003 amending Act forecast the potential of stronger packaging regulation.[27] In 2008, regulations mandated that graphic pictorial health warnings cover 30 per cent of the front and 90 per cent of the back of tobacco packages manufactured in or imported to New Zealand.[28] New Zealand now proposes to adopt a plain packaging approach analogous to that in Australia.[29] Its regulatory management strategy has been to 'wait to see'[30] what happens in the World Trade Organization ('WTO') and investment treaty disputes over Australia's measures before making legislative changes.[31] More recently, Tariana Turia, on behalf of the New Zealand government, has stated:[32]

> Further research and evaluation of the impact of plain packaging is underway, and we can expect to start to see the results next year. I am confident this will confirm that plain packaging works and that it is the right thing to do ...

Ms Turia stated that the government would introduce legislation by the end of 2013 and that:[33]

> our Government is committed to introducing plain packaging as part of our drive to Smokefree 2025, and we are continuing to progress the legislation and regulations to make this a reality.

2.6 *Government funded campaigns*

Despite this compendious regulation,[34] youthful and other New Zealanders still smoke. Alongside regulation there have been government funded campaigns. In 1948, the Department of Health launched posters linking smoking with cancer. In 1970, the Department, in collaboration with the Cancer Society, the National Heart Foundation and the Tuberculosis and Chest Disease Society, launched a national anti-smoking campaign. In 1979 and 1980, the Department launched a mass media campaign to urge teenagers to remain smoke free. In 1985, the Minister of Health initiated a 'comprehensive policy to promote non-smoking', which asked the government to invest in a tobacco control program including better health education, the establishment of a quit clinic, further restrictions on tobacco access for adolescents, increased taxation, regulation of tar in cigarettes, health warnings and smoke-free environments.[35]

The government established the Health Sponsorship Council under the 1990 Act. It introduced the 'smoke-free' brand, which would provide sponsorship in place of the tobacco industry. In 1991 it commenced a smoke-free campaign characterising smoking as abnormal behaviour and promoting healthy lifestyle choices. A youth targeted media campaign entitled 'Why Start?' ran from 1996 to 1999.[36] 1999 saw the launch of the national Quitline and Quit/Me Mutu campaign at the Public Health Association Conference. From November 2000, subsidised nicotine patches and gum were made available through the Quitline via authorised community providers.[37]

But still New Zealanders smoke. Of particular concern is the number of smokers among the young population in general and among Māori youth and Māori adults.[38] The government has stated that it aims to achieve a smoke-free New Zealand by 2025.[39]

3 Alcohol regulation

3.1 Purchase age and licensing

The legal age at which New Zealanders can purchase alcohol was lowered from 21 to 20 in 1969,[40] and from 20 to 18 in 1999.[41]

Between 1890 and 1950, alcohol was predominantly regulated by hindering sales and purchases. The regulations relating to licensing and sales are detailed. An overview is given in the next few paragraphs to give the flavour of the complexities of the regime.[42] The goals of these complex regulations have been unclear and poorly articulated. There is, therefore, little against which to measure their success.[43] However, if the goal was to reduce the harmful effects of excess consumption of alcohol, it would seem that the complex licensing regimes have not been successful.

The *Alcoholic Liquor Sales Control Act 1893* (NZ) disposed of the existing licensing districts and created new districts matching electoral boundaries. From 1895, a district could vote itself 'dry' in a local poll held in conjunction with each general election.[44] It took until 1999 for the last dry areas to disappear, and then licensing became the norm.[45]

Because obtaining a licence was difficult, substandard premises became common, which led in 1948 to a national body to police standards and redistribute licences, the Licensing Control Commission ('LCC').[46] New outlets had to satisfy a test assessing the need to respond to public demand for liquor facilities, the effect of granting the licence on existing businesses, and the impact on the provision of accommodation for the travelling public.[47] In 1962 the government divided hotel licences into two classes: tavern and hotel licences. Although taverns no longer had to provide accommodation facilities, they had to pay a levy of 3 per cent.[48]

In 1976, two legislative changes led to big increases in outlet numbers. Sports clubs could obtain an ancillary licence (now known as a club licence), and restaurants could obtain bring your own ('BYO') permits.[49]

The *Sale of Liquor Act 1989* (NZ) introduced a system of sales and supply control with the goal of reducing alcohol abuse. The Act moved away from the approach focused on availability or need towards granting licences based on the suitability of the applicants and the nature of the business to be conducted.[50] Supermarkets and grocery stores could now obtain off-licences for wine sales, and this was extended to beer in 1999.[51] The number of licences has doubled since 1990.[52]

The *Sale and Supply of Alcohol Act 2012* (NZ) set up the Alcohol and Licensing Authority. The Act also expands the criteria for the granting of licences to include whether granting a licence will increase alcohol related harm or negatively impact on the community and neighbourhood.[53] On-licences now have to supply water, low alcohol beverages, food and information about safe transport.[54]

3.2 Trading times

The *Licensing Act 1881* (NZ) imposed nationwide Sunday closing for taverns, hotels and off-licences, but not restaurants. The 1881 Act also prevented bars from remaining open past 10:00pm unless they had a special midnight closing permit. Those permits were abolished in 1910.[55] In 1917, the *Sale of Liquor Restriction Act 1917* (NZ) came into force, prohibiting sales after 6:00pm on a national basis.[56] The era of 6:00pm closing ended in October 1967 after a nationwide referendum.[57]

The *Sale of Liquor Act 1962* (NZ) set specific times within which most on-licences had to trade. From 1990 onwards, the hours of sale for on-licences were determined by local licensing authorities and closing times of 3:00am or later were common.[58] From 18 December 2013, the *Sale and Supply of Alcohol Act 2012* (NZ) will impose maximum trading hours. On-licences can be open between 8:00am and 4:00am. Off-licences can be open between 7:00am and 11:00pm.[59]

3.3 Advertising

Unlike tobacco advertising, alcohol advertising is permitted within a light-handed regulatory framework, which has liberalised over time. Before 1980, all alcohol advertising on television and radio was regulated. In 1973, a Royal Commission on the Sale of Alcohol recommended the establishment of a voluntary code for advertising alcohol.[60] The code was implemented in 1980 and is administered by the New Zealand Broadcasting Corporation ('NZBC').[61] In 1981, the NZBC dropped the rule prohibiting advertisements that are designed to encourage alcohol consumption.[62] Over the period 1980 to 1987, responsibility for administering the advertising standards was shared between the Advertising Standards Authority ('ASA') (a voluntary industry body established by the *Broadcasting Act 1989* (NZ))[63] and the NZBC. In 1987, the major breweries began producing television commercials advertising the corporate body, not the products themselves. In 1992, Cabinet approved a proposal for the advertising industry to become self-regulating, and by 1993 ASA had gained sole jurisdiction over the content of advertising.[64]

The ASA administers a voluntary system of pre-vetting all liquor advertisements, the Liquor Advertising Pre-vetting System ('LAPS'). In 1989, the Commercial Approvals Bureau ('CAB') was set up to vet and approve the content of all television commercials before they are broadcast on television in New Zealand. Most alcohol advertisements will have to receive both LAPS and CAB approval before broadcast.[65]

The code for advertising alcohol has six principles:

> **Principle 1** – Liquor advertisements shall neither conflict with nor detract from the need for responsibility and moderation in liquor consumption. …
> **Principle 2** – Liquor advertisements shall observe a high standard of social responsibility. …

Principle 3

1. Liquor advertisements shall not depict or imply the consumption of liquor in potentially hazardous situations or include any unsafe practices.
2. Liquor advertisements shall not offer motor vehicles or boats as prizes in any competition. …

Principle 4

1. Liquor advertisements shall be directed to adult audiences. Liquor advertisements shall not be directed at minors nor have strong or evident appeal to minors in particular. …

Principle 5 – Sponsorship advertisements and sponsorship credits shall clearly and primarily promote the sponsored activity, team or individual. The sponsor, the sponsorship and items incidental to them may be featured only in a subordinate manner. …

Principle 6 – Liquor advertisements shall not by any means, directly or by innuendo, contain any misleading description, claim or comparison about the product advertised, or about any other product, or suggest some special quality which cannot be sustained.[66]

The *Sale and Supply of Alcohol Act 2012* (NZ) creates a number of offences for irresponsible advertising and promotions, including the promotion of excessive drinking, promoting alcohol in a way that has special appeal to minors, advertising free alcohol or discounts of 25 per cent or more, and offering free goods or services with the purchase of alcohol.[67]

3.4 Taxes and health costs

Excise taxes are collected from all local manufacturers of alcoholic beverages and all importers. The taxes are based not on the dollar value but on the quantity of the product.[68] Excise taxes have existed on alcohol in New Zealand since 1939, initially as an easy source of revenue.[69] In 1958, the government increased taxes on alcohol substantially (30 per cent) in order to reduce the fiscal deficit.[70] While excise taxes on alcohol were primarily for revenue purposes, in the 1970s the harmful effects of alcohol were raised as relevant to regulatory measures.[71] Now the Health Promotion Agency ('HPA') receives some funding through a levy on alcohol produced or imported for sale in New Zealand.[72] It has the following functions:

(a) giving advice and making recommendations to government, government agencies, industry, non-government bodies, communities, health professionals, and others on the sale, supply, consumption, misuse and harm of alcohol so far as those matters relate to HPA's general functions[;]
(b) undertaking or working with others to research the use of alcohol in New Zealand, public attitudes towards alcohol, and problems associated with, or consequent on, the misuse of alcohol.[73]

4 Unhealthy food regulation

Two main regulatory measures apply to unhealthy foods in New Zealand, with respect to labelling and advertising. Health Minister, Tony Ryall, said in 2012 that New Zealand would not place an excise tax on unhealthy food.[74]

Unlike most regulation of tobacco and alcohol, where there are just a few commonalities between the trans-Tasman nations, the food labelling regulations and their administration are a uniquely trans-Tasman regime. The governments of New Zealand and Australia entered into the *Food Standards Treaty* ('FST'), which came into force on 5 July 1996.[75] The objectives of the FST include 'to adopt a joint system for the development and promulgation of food standards'.[76]

The FST established the first trans-Tasman bi-national regulatory agency, the Australia New Zealand Food Authority, now known as Food Standards Australia and New Zealand ('FSANZ').[77] FSANZ is an independent statutory agency[78] authorised to make food standards for the Australia New Zealand Food Standards Code ('joint code').[79]

A key feature of the FST is that it preserves important national policy space and contains provisions allowing either country to opt out[80] of a joint food standard for exceptional reasons relating to health, safety, environmental concerns or cultural issues.[81] As well as FSANZ, an independent statutory agency – the New Zealand Food Safety Authority ('NZFSA') – has primary responsibility for developing food safety standards for New Zealand.[82]

The governing Act provides that the primary objective of FSANZ, in developing or reviewing food standards and variations of food standards, is to protect public health and safety.[83] Other objectives include the provision of adequate information relating to food to enable consumers to make informed choices, and the prevention of misleading or deceptive conduct.[84]

FSANZ does not expressly address unhealthy foods, but does deal with issues such as production, composition, contaminants and labelling.[85] The joint code generally requires that packaged food for retail sale include a panel containing nutritional information including the amount of energy, protein, fat, saturated fat, carbohydrate, sugars and sodium contained in an average serving and also per 100g/100mls consumed.[86] Additional labelling requirements apply if a product makes a specific nutrition claim such as 'good source of calcium, high in dietary fibre' or 'reduced salt'. In such instances, the name and average amount of any claimed nutrient or biologically active substance in the food must be shown in the nutrition panel.[87] However, this is arguably ineffective, as studies show that consumer understanding of nutritional information is poor, limiting the value of nutrition labels as a tool for making healthy choices. Also, research has shown that Māori, Pacific and low-income New Zealanders rarely make use of nutrition labels to inform their food purchases.[88]

A review of New Zealand food labelling law and policy conducted in 2011 found that there was general, but not complete, compliance with labelling requirements. The review suggested more active monitoring and enforcement as 81 per cent of New Zealanders regard food labels as their main source of information about the nutritional content of food. Currently, formal enforcement actions are limited to prosecutions, which are time consuming and expensive. The report recommended a more versatile, and hopefully therefore more effective, range of enforcement provisions, including the power to make orders or require user-paid compliance testing consequent on a breach; and the imposition of enforceable undertakings to adopt specific corrective action such as re-labelling, withdrawing products from sale, placing advertisements or otherwise informing consumers.[89]

As discussed above, the ASA is a voluntary industry body, responsible for the regulation of advertising. The ASA's codes of practice include the Children's Code for Advertising Food 2010,[90] which establishes the following principles (each of which is followed by guidelines):

> **Principle 1** – All advertisements should be prepared with and observe a high standard of social responsibility to consumers and to society. ...
> **Principle 2** – Advertisements should not by implication, omission, ambiguity or exaggerated claim mislead or deceive or be likely to mislead or deceive children, abuse the trust of or exploit their lack of knowledge. ...
> **Principle 3** – Persons or characters well-known to children shall not be used in advertisements to promote food in such a way so as to undermine a healthy diet as defined by the Food and Nutrition Guidelines for Healthy Children. ...[91]

5 Commonalities and differences in the regulation of tobacco, alcohol and unhealthy foods

Perhaps unsurprisingly, in New Zealand tobacco is overall more stringently regulated than alcohol, and alcohol is more stringently regulated than unhealthy food. Advertising bans are more comprehensive in relation to tobacco than alcohol, and the advertising codes for alcohol are more detailed than those relating to unhealthy food. Some of the regulatory mechanisms used to address tobacco and alcohol are similar, such as taxes and trading restrictions. No such measures are presently intended to address concerns about unhealthy food.

The use of similar regulatory devices, however, does not mean that the control of tobacco and the control of alcohol are identical or even closely analogous policy problems. For example, excess alcohol use in conjunction with driving is a problem. Tobacco use is a problem, but when associated with driving the nature of the problem does not change (in the absence of passengers). Additionally, the history of the regulation of both tobacco and alcohol does not reveal clear and consistent government policy about what problems the regulations are designed to address. Now, however, in relation to the Smokefree 2025 campaign, the goal is arguably much clearer. The government has described this as an 'aspirational' goal. Its plan so far, in addition to existing regulatory measures, is to adopt plain packaging legislation along the lines of that found in Australia and to fund projects to achieve the goal.[92]

Given that people smoke, in spite of the known ill-health and potentially fatal effects (and that there remain many social problems associated with excess alcohol consumption) one possible conclusion is that the regulation to date has not been sufficient to eliminate the problems of smoking. There has been a reduction in smoking rates overall in the general population. In a 2011–12 report by the New Zealand Ministry of Health, 17 per cent of those surveyed identified as smokers, whereas in 1996–7 the number was 25 per cent.[93] However, the report also found that 41 per cent of adult Māori smoke – a figure that has been relatively constant – and that 26 per cent of Pacific Islanders reported that they smoke.[94]

As detailed monitoring, review and evaluation of regulation is relatively rare, even though tobacco regulation has been progressively amended, it is difficult to pinpoint the success or otherwise of regulation.[95] What perhaps is clear is that the large array of measures designed to reduce smoking has not been enough to reduce smoking rates among Māori. That seems to be, in part, because the existing regulatory measures in relation to tobacco were not based directly on evidence about how to reduce Māori smoking rates in particular. The proposal for plain packaging regulation is also based on targeting the general population and does not consider whether extra measures are appropriate to reduce Māori smoking, although the Māori Affairs Committee supports the adoption of plain packaging measures.[96]

From a regulatory viewpoint, it is important to bear in mind that just as identical regulatory tools will often not achieve different goals, not all regulations are necessarily culturally transferable between Australia and New Zealand, or from the rest of the world to Australasia. Both New Zealand and Australia are susceptible to adopting regulatory regimes from overseas. Sometimes this works, and at other times the adopted regime fails because it is devised for different cultural circumstances and is based on jurisdictionally specific evidence. As Kate Tokeley has explained:

> Policy makers should proceed with caution when applying overseas research on regulatory issues to the New Zealand context … Some overseas findings will not apply to the specifics of the New Zealand situation. For example, international studies have shown that alcohol consumption lowers when prices are higher. Taxation of alcohol is therefore recognised internationally as an effective tool in reducing alcohol-related harm within the drinking population. This international research has led New Zealand economists to the logical conclusion that raising the excise tax on alcohol in New Zealand will contribute to reducing alcohol-related harm to our young people; but a recent study of Australian and New Zealand students suggests that alcohol consumption by Australian and New Zealand young people might be relatively unaffected by price increases. This study indicated that an increase in price of alcohol by as much as 25 per cent will not significantly reduce consumption. The conclusion was that taxation would have to be very high to result in a decrease in alcohol consumption among New Zealand and Australian youth. One possible explanation for this is that cultural norms

around drinking might play a stronger part in New Zealand and Australia than in other parts of the world.[97]

The above passage suggests that the Australian and New Zealand cultural approaches to alcohol may be the same. Whether or not that is true, the Australian and New Zealand regulatory interests are not always the same. Consequently, harmonisation with Australia (or even other countries) should not be presumed to be a solution; rather, the evidence should be assessed to determine the likelihood of it being so.

In addition to requiring supporting evidence, regulation costs money and resources, and any government is likely to decide if the cost of regulation is worth it.[98] Costs are incurred in all regulatory phases including design, implementation and enforcement. Costs may appear to be saved if another country designs the measure, but in the long-term costs of enforcement are higher (if enforcement is pursued) if the regulatory design by another country is ill suited to addressing the problem in New Zealand.

6 Regulation of tobacco, alcohol and unhealthy foods and the trans-Tasman relationship: moving forward

From the New Zealand perspective, regulatory coordination with Australia is often desirable but also entails complex practical and political questions. Frequently the politics will drive the outcome.[99] As the Organisation for Economic Co-operation and Development ('OECD') has said:

> An ongoing push for greater regulatory harmonisation, mutual recognition and integrated institutions, where appropriate, would continue to reduce spatial transaction costs between New Zealand and Australia and mitigate the negative impact of economic geography. As such, the recent Memorandum of Understanding between the New Zealand and Australian governments, which encourages more cooperation between regulators and policymakers and sets out a range of co-ordination initiatives to deepen business integration, is most welcome. ... However, as with all significant regulatory changes, it is important that harmonisation initiatives be consistent with New Zealand's own objectives and circumstances.[100]

As Australia is New Zealand's largest trading partner, some regulatory coordination is desirable, even for Australian exporters. The main areas in which regulatory cooperation is embedded between Australia and New Zealand are foods standards and labelling and, most relevant to this chapter, mutual recognition of goods.[101] Coordination in these areas may arise in part because food safety and mutual recognition of goods (including labelling and packaging) are trade issues relevant to the relationship between the nations, whereas age restrictions and taxes have less of a direct joint interest.

The countries have also aligned somewhat in connection with tobacco regulation.[102] Health warnings on cigarette packages were implemented in New Zealand following their adoption in Australia.[103] But this New Zealand adoption of Australian regulation is not the same as the cooperation that led to a combined agency for food products or the goods mutual recognition arrangements. Australian regulation that has been designed without New Zealand input is (unsurprisingly) less likely to include New Zealand interests. Consequently, I (and a co-author) have elsewhere concluded that:

> New Zealand and Australia's joint efforts with respect to food safety are an example of bottom-up regulation being well-suited to New Zealand's circumstances. New Zealand and Australia share common objectives and values with respect to much of the food safety regime, meaning that New Zealand did not have to sacrifice its policy preferences. Furthermore, the opt-out provisions preserve policy space for the aspects of the regime where New Zealand and Australia's policy preferences diverge. The scheme as a whole allows New Zealand to recognise significant cost savings, and such savings do not come at an unacceptable price.[104]

The success of the trans-Tasman joint food regime can be contrasted to the so far failed attempts to coordinate the safety regulation of pharmaceuticals under a joint body (with the proposed name of Australia New Zealand Therapeutic Products Agency ('ANZTPA')). Among the reasons that ANZTPA did not receive New Zealand political approval was the perceived lack of sovereignty for New Zealand in the arrangement (even though the proposed agency arose from a trans-Tasman negotiation).[105] Yet the same threat to sovereignty is usually not aired when a regulation is adopted (or proposed) and there has been no express New Zealand interest factored into its design. The plain packaging proposal is such an example. This may be because the health effects of smoking are analogous no matter what a person's nationality. Even if plain packaging is an appropriate[106] health-related measure, as discussed above, the regulatory design does not address the disproportionate rate of Māori smoking. I do not suggest that this is a reason not to introduce plain packaging; rather, what is apparent is that measures targeted at the general population do not reduce Māori smoking levels as effectively as those of other groups. So, perhaps more New Zealand money should be invested into addressing that starkly identified problem. In addition to potentially aiding the fight against people smoking, plain packaging measures have other impacts, which were partially discussed in the relevant policy papers. The Regulatory Impact Statement about plain packaging does not confirm any New Zealand interest in the manufacturing and packaging processes of cigarettes.[107] The Māori Affairs Committee has said that 85 per cent of tobacco products sold in New Zealand are packaged in Australia.[108] Thus, the adoption of plain packaging also potentially helps Australian cigarette exporters sell their product to New Zealand.

Labelling and packaging requirements are relevant to all trans-Tasman food, alcohol and tobacco trade. Under the *New Zealand Trans-Tasman Mutual Recognition Act 1997* (NZ) ('TTMRA') all goods that can legally be sold in Australia may also be legally sold in New Zealand, and vice versa, under the Australian equivalent legislation of the same name.[109] In accordance with s 10 of the Australian TTMRA there is no requirement that the imported goods meet the local standards for packaging.[110] Therefore, at first blush tobacco companies could avoid plain packaging laws by importing products from New Zealand, where the same plain packaging restrictions do not yet exist. However, under s 109 of the *Tobacco Plain Packaging Act 2011* (Cth) ('TPPA'), the Governor-General is permitted to make regulations declaring the TPPA exempt from the operation of the TTMRA. Under s 46 of the TTMRA, this exemption is only allowed to last for 12 months. Therefore a 'permanent solution' would involve either Australia seeking a permanent exemption from the TTMRA for tobacco products, or New Zealand enacting equivalent plain packaging laws to that of Australia. At present the New Zealand government proposes introducing equivalent laws, but the reason and timing for the equivalence may be overwhelmingly driven by the TTMRA issue. The current tobacco control objective for New Zealand is that New Zealand is smoke free by 2025. Plain packaging measures are likely consistent with that goal. But based on the history of tobacco regulation, other measures may be necessary to reach that goal or indeed, as discussed above, to target the reduction of Māori smoking in particular.

Trade mark law is also important in the context of labelling and packaging. There are some very important differences between New Zealand and Australian trade mark law. The starkest is that culturally offensive marks are not registrable in New Zealand[111] and are more likely to be registered in Australia.[112] As far as the relationship between plain packaging and trade marks are concerned, the culturally offensive provisions in New Zealand law are not directly involved, but the Australian plain packaging law will in effect achieve the non-use of some culturally offensive trade marks in Australia, where those trade marks relate to tobacco. That is a small and an entirely inadvertent Australian concession to the protection of indigenous people's rights. Some of the most well-known culturally offensive trade marks, which are no longer registered in New Zealand, have related to tobacco.[113] Such trade marks may not as a practical matter be registered in Australia (even though the law permits such registration) because of their obvious New Zealand nature, but many such offensive trade marks are found in relation to indigenous peoples around the world.[114] In this area New Zealand and Australian policy is quite different, but this has not prevented a single economic market negotiation to bring the trade mark laws closer together.[115] The approach of negotiating the hard topics together has, as discussed above, worked well in some instances and may well be an approach that could be extended to unhealthy food regulation.

As far as unhealthy food regulation goes, the current approach of light-handed regulation (and relying on consumer choice) could be detrimental. Some may consider that consumers should be free to choose to eat what they want.[116] The lessons from tobacco and alcohol regulation should be comprehensively evaluated while there is a chance to learn from the past and adapt for the future.[117] One lesson is that the regulation of unhealthy foods may be an area in which greater things could be achieved if Australia and New Zealand cooperated and worked out their interests together.

Notes

* Thanks to Thomas McKenzie and Danielle Thorne for research assistance.

1 See, in particular, *Australia New Zealand Closer Economic Relations Trade Agreement*, signed 28 March 1983, [1983] ATS 2 (entered into force 1 January 1983); *Protocol on Trade in Services to the Australia New Zealand Closer Economic Relations Trade Agreement*, signed 18 August 1988, [1988] ATS 20 (entered into force 1 January 1989). The CER is today often referred to as the single economic market and includes discussions about trade mark coordination (see below Part 5).

2 The Ministry of Health, for example, has said: 'The continued ability of the tobacco industry to use packaging in a way that allows advertising and promotion of tobacco products undermines the effectiveness of measures already taken to ban tobacco products promotion and advertising. It also undermines the effectiveness of other tobacco control initiatives': Ministry of Health (New Zealand), *Regulatory Impact Statement: Plain Packaging of Tobacco Products* (28 March 2012) <http://www.health.govt.nz/system/ files/documents/pages/regulatory-impact-statement-plain-packaging-tobacco- products.pdf> 2–3.

3 Ministry of Health (New Zealand), *The Health of New Zealand Adults 2011/12: Key Findings of the New Zealand Health Survey* (12 December 2012) <http://www.health.govt. nz/system/files/documents/publications/health-of-new-zealand-adults-2011-12-v2. pdf>.

4 Cancer Control Council of New Zealand, *Tobacco Control in New Zealand: A History Cancer* (27 June 2008) <http://cancercontrolnz.govt.nz/sites/default/files/tobacco_ control.pdf> ('*Tobacco Control in New Zealand*'). See *Juvenile Smoking Suppression Act 1903* (NZ) s 3.

5 Cancer Control Council of New Zealand, above n 4. See also *Toxic Substances Act 1979* (NZ) s 72.

6 See also Ministry of Health (New Zealand), *Smoke-free Environments Act* (27 May 2005) <http://www.health.govt.nz/our-work/regulation-health-and-disability-system/ smokefree-law/smoke-free-environments-act>.

7 Cancer Control Council of New Zealand, above n 4, 28.

8 *Smoke-free Environments Amendment Act 1997* (NZ) s 9.

9 *Smoke-free Environments Amendment Act 2003* (NZ) s 21.

10 *Smoke-free Environments Amendment Act 2003* (NZ) s 22.

11 *Smoke-free Environments (Control and Enforcement) Amendment Act 2011* (NZ) s 38C. This Act increases the penalties for selling tobacco products to minors. The NZ$2000 fine for an individual has increased to NZ$5000, and a business can now be fined up to NZ$10,000.

12 Cancer Control Council of New Zealand above n 4, 28.

13 *Smoke-free Environments Amendment Act 2003* (NZ) s 23A.

14 *Smoke-free Environments (Control and Enforcement) Amendment Act 2011* (NZ) s 22.

15 *Smoke-free Environments (Control and Enforcement) Amendment Act 2011* (NZ) s 23.

16 Cancer Control Council of New Zealand, above n 4, 18.

17 This was not done by legislation.

18 *Smoke-free Environments Act 1990* (NZ) s 22.

19 Cancer Control Council of New Zealand, above n 4, 27. See also *Smoke-free Environments Amendment Act 1993* (NZ) s 3.

20 *Smoke-free Environments (Control and Enforcement) Amendment Act 2011* (NZ) s 10; see also Health Promotion Agency (New Zealand), *Smokefree: History of Tobacco in New Zealand 2000–2012* <http://smokefree.org.nz/2000-2012>.

21   Cancer Control Council of New Zealand, above n 4, 20.

22   *Smoke-free Environments Act 1990* (NZ) ss 9, 12 and 13. For further information see Ministry of Health (New Zealand), *Smoke-free Environments Act* (27 May 2005) <http://www.health.govt.nz/our-work/regulation-health-and-disability-system/smokefree-law/smoke-free-environments-act>; Ministry of Health (New Zealand), *A Guide to the Smoke-free Environments Act 1990* (1 November 2004) Health Ed <https://www.healthed.govt.nz/system/files/resource-files/HE1608.pdf>.

23   See Nick Wilson and George Thomson, 'Tobacco Tax as a Health Protecting Policy: A Brief Review of the New Zealand Evidence' (2005) 118 *The New Zealand Medical Journal* 1403. On 28 April 2010, the tax on tobacco was increased by 24 per cent for loose-leaf tobacco and 10 per cent for factory made cigarettes. This was the first tax increase above the CPI for over a decade. Between 1 January 2011 and 1 January 2012, excise tax rose by another 10 per cent. The most recent tobacco tax occurred on 1 January 2013; again it was a 10 per cent increase.

24   Cancer Control Council of New Zealand, above n 4, 18.

25   Ibid 20.

26   *Smoke-free Environments Amendment Act 1997* (NZ) s 9.

27   *Smoke-free Environments Amendment Act 2003* (NZ) s 24.

28   *Smoke-free Environments Regulations 2007* (NZ) sch 1; see also Ministry of Health (New Zealand, *Graphic Health Warnings on Tobacco* (20 March 2013) <http://www.health.govt.nz/our-work/regulation-health-and-disability-system/smokefree-law/graphic-health-warnings-tobacco>.

29   See Ministry of Health (New Zealand), *Proposal to Introduce Plain Packaging of Tobacco Products in New Zealand* (23 July 2012) <http://www.health.govt.nz/system/files/documents/publications/proposal-to-introduce-plain-packaging-tobacco-products-in-nz-consultationjul31.pdf>.

30   Tariana Turia, 'Government Moves Forward with Plain Packaging of Tobacco Products' (Press Release, 19 February 2013).

31   Ministry of Health (New Zealand), above n 2, [23].

32   Tariana Turia, 'Biennial Oceania Tobacco Control 2013' (Press Release, 23 October 2013) <http://www.beehive.govt.nz/speech/biennial-oceania-tobacco-control-2013>.

33   Ibid.

34   Other regulation includes the ban of chewing tobacco. The *Smoke-free Environments Act 1990* (NZ) s 39 gave the government the ability to control and enforce the disclosure of the contents of tobacco products. The *Smoke-free Environments (Controls and Enforcement) Amendment Act 2011* (NZ) s 17 clarified the regulatory powers of the government to limit the harmful constituents in tobacco products. It gave greater control of tobacco contents to regulators however, this has remained largely unenforced. The *Smoke-free Environments Amendment Act 2003* (NZ) ss 24–5, requires tobacco manufacturers and importers to test products and provide annual returns. The Director-General of Health is required to ensure returns and reports are publicly available on a website.

35   Health Promotion Agency (New Zealand), above n 20.

36   Ibid.

37   Cancer Control Council of New Zealand, above n 4, 37.

38   Māori Affairs Committee, New Zealand Parliament, *Inquiry into the Tobacco Industry in Aotearoa and the Consequences of Tobacco Use for Maori* (2010) 10.

39   See Health Promotion Agency (New Zealand), *Smokefree 2025* <http://smokefree.org.nz/smokefree-2025>.

40   *Sale of Liquor Amendment Act 1969* (NZ) s 2.

41   *Sale of Liquor Amendment Act 1999* (NZ) s 90. For more information see Ministry of Justice (New Zealand), *Amendments to the 1989 Sale of Liquor Act* (December 1999) <http://www.justice.govt.nz/publications/publications-archived/1999/amendments-to-the-

1989-sale-of-liquor-act/publication>. The *Sale and Supply of Alcohol Act 2012* (NZ) s 257 makes it an offence to present a fake ID, use someone else's ID to buy alcohol or give or lend an ID to an underage person who subsequently uses it to buy alcohol.

42 For a full discussion see Paul Christoffel, *Removing Temptation: New Zealand's Alcohol Restrictions, 1881–2005* (PhD Thesis, Victoria University of Wellington, 2006).

43 For a discussion of monitoring, review and evaluation of regulation see Derek Gill and Susy Frankel, *Learning the Way Forward: Monitoring, Evaluation and Review* (2013) Regulatory Reform Toolkit http://www.regulatorytoolkit.ac.nz/resources/pdfs/book-3/learning-the-way-forward-final.pdf.

44 A majority of three-fifths of the district had to vote in favour of restoring licences for a dry area to become wet again. In 1990, the threshold to restore a licence was only a 50 per cent majority. See *Alcoholic Liquor Sales Control Act 1893* (NZ) s 15.

45 *Sale of Liquor Amendment Act 1999* (NZ).

46 *Licensing Amendment Act 1948* (NZ) s 3.

47 *Sale of Liquor Act 1962* (NZ) s 54.

48 *Sale of Liquor Act 1962* (NZ) s 184.

49 *Sale of Liquor Amendment Act 1976* (NZ) s 26.

50 The *Sale of Liquor Act 1989* (NZ) reduced the categories of licences from 29 to 4, including on-licences, off-licences, club licences and special licences (for on-licence sales at events). The licence categories are set out in ss 7, 29, 53 and 73 respectively. See also Ministry of Justice (New Zealand), 'Liquor Review 1996 – A Discussion Paper' (Discussion Paper, Ministry of Justice (New Zealand), July 1996) <http://www.justice.govt.nz/publications/publications-archived/1996/liquor-review-1996-a-discussion-paper/publication>.

51 *Sale of Liquor Amendment Act 1999* (NZ) s 30.

52 See discussion in New Zealand Law Commission, *Alcohol in Our Lives: Curbing the Harm*, Report No R114 (2010) 117–18.

53 *Sale and Supply of Alcohol Act 2012* (NZ) s 105.

54 *Sale and Supply of Alcohol Act 2012* (NZ) ss 51–4, 110.

55 *Licensing Amendment Act 1910* (NZ) sch 6.

56 *Sale of Liquor Restriction Act 1917* (NZ) s 3. This law exempted boarders and guests staying in hotels from the post-6:00pm purchase ban. Diners at restaurants situated in a hotel could buy wine or beer until 8:00pm. Other restaurants, however, could not serve alcohol at all.

57 *Sale of Liquor Amendment Act (No 2) 1967* (NZ) sch 1.

58 Off-licences had no set trading hours and club licence trading hours were determined based on an assessment of the club's activities. *Sale of Liquor Act 1989* (NZ) s 14.

59 *Sale and Supply of Alcohol Act 2012* (NZ) s 43. For further discussion see Ministry of Justice (New Zealand), *Sale and Supply of Alcohol* <http://www.justice.govt.nz/policy/sale-and-supply-of-alcohol>.

60 Alcohol Advisory Council of New Zealand, *The History of Alcohol Advertising on Radio and Television* [6] <http://www.alcohol.org.nz/sites/default/files/research-publications/pdfs/HistoryofalcoholAdverts.pdf>.

61 Ibid [7].

62 Ibid [7].

63 The ASA administers a code for the naming, labelling, packaging and promotion of liquor. Membership of ASA ensures the codes apply to advertising agencies, newspaper publishers, television, cinema, outdoor advertising and radio. It funds the Advertising Standards Complaints Board, established in 2010, to consider any complaints that may breach the code.

64 See Mike MacAvoy, *The History of Alcohol Advertising on Radio and Television* (2004) Health Promotion Agency (New Zealand), [14] <http://www.alcohol.org.nz/sites/default/files/research-publications/pdfs/HistoryofalcoholAdverts.pdf>.

65 See New Zealand Law Commission, above n 52, 334.

66 Advertising Standards Authority (New Zealand), *Code for the Naming, Labelling, Packaging and Promotion of Liquor* (1 October 2009) <http://www.asa.co.nz/code_liquor.php> (emphasis added).

67 *Sale and Supply of Alcohol Act 2012* (NZ) s 237. For further information see Ministry of Justice (New Zealand), *Sale and Supply of Alcohol* <http://www.justice.govt.nz/policy/sale-and-supply-of-alcohol>.

68 New Zealand Law Commission, above n 52, 291.

69 See Brian Easton, 'The Economic Regulation of Alcohol Consumption in New Zealand' (Paper presented at Conference on the Social Cost of Alcohol Abuse, University of Neuchatel, Switzerland, 24–5 October 2003) <http://www.eastonbh.ac.nz/2003/10/the_economic_regulation_of_alcohol_consumption_in_new_zealand/>.

70 *Customs Acts Amendment Act 1958* (NZ) s 3.

71 Easton, above n 69.

72 *Public Health and Disability Amendment Act 2012* (NZ) s 6. Its predecessor, the Alcohol Advisory Council ('ALAC'), was founded following the 1975 Royal Commission on the Sale of Liquor.

73 *New Zealand Public Health and Disability Act 2000* (NZ) s 58(2).

74 Stacy Kirk, 'Whopper Fat Tax Could Soak Up Health Issues', *Stuff* (online), 16 May 2012 <http://www.stuff.co.nz/national/health/6933884/Whopper-fat-tax-could-soak-up-health-issues>.

75 *Agreement between the Government of Australia and the Government of New Zealand Establishing a System for the Development of Joint Food Standards*, signed 5 December 1995 (entered into force 5 July 1996).

76 Ibid art 2(b).

77 See Ministry of Foreign Affairs and Trade (New Zealand), *The Australia-New Zealand Closer Economic Relationship Booklet* (2005) 26 <http://www.mfat.govt.nz/downloads/trade-agreement/australia/australia-booklet.pdf>.

78 FSANZ's powers and functions are governed by the *Food Standards Australia New Zealand Act 1991* (Cth) s 7. For a more detailed discussion of the institutional set up see Chris Nixon and John Yeabsley, 'Australia New Zealand Therapeutic Products Authority: Lessons from the Deep End of Trans-Tasman Integration' in Susy Frankel (ed), *Learning from the Past, Adapting for the Future: Regulatory Reform in New Zealand* (LexisNexis, 2011) 491.

79 In New Zealand the Parliamentary Secretary to the Minister for Health has executive responsibility for FSANZ. See also Food Standards Australia New Zealand, *About FSANZ* (2011) <http://www.foodstandards.gov.au/scienceandeducation/aboutfsanz/>.

80 As to the importance of the opt-out provision see Nixon and Yeabsley, above n 78.

81 Food Standards Australia New Zealand, *Background* (2011) <http://www.foodstandards.gov.au/about/background/Pages/default.aspx>.

82 New Zealand Food Safety Authority, *The New Zealand Food Regulatory Environment* (March 2008) 2 <http://www.foodsafety.govt.nz/elibrary/industry/NZ_Food_Regulatory_Environment_March_2008.pdf>.

83 *Food Standards Australia New Zealand Act 1991* (Cth) s 18(1)(a).

84 Ibid ss 18(1)(b), (c).

85 *New Zealand (Australia New Zealand Food Standards Code) Food Standards 2002* (NZ).

86 *Australia New Zealand Food Standards Code* (Cth) Standard 1.2.8.

87 Ibid.

88 Ministry of Health (New Zealand), *Food and Nutrition Guidelines to Healthy Children and Young People (Aged 2–18 years): A Background Paper* (2012) 95 <http://www.health.govt.nz/system/files/documents/publications/food-and-nutrition-guidelines-for-healthy-children-and-young-people-aged-2-18-years.pdf>.

89 Neal Blewett et al, *Labelling Logic: Review of Food Labelling Law and Policy* (Commonwealth of Australia, 2011) 136 <http://www.foodlabellingreview.gov.au/internet/food labelling/publishing.nsf/content/48c0548d80e715bcca257825001e5dc0/$file/labelling%20logic_2011.pdf>.

90 Advertising Standards Authority (New Zealand), *Children's Code for Advertising Food 2010* <http://www.asa.co.nz/code_children_food.php>.

91 Ibid.

92 See Ministry of Health (New Zealand), *Pathway to Smokefree New Zealand 2025 Innovation Funding – Successful Projects* (4 July 2013) <http://www.health.govt.nz/news-media/news-items/pathway-smokefree-new-zealand-2025-innovation-funding-successful-projects>.

93 Ministry of Health (New Zealand), above n 3, 130.

94 Ibid 22–3.

95 See generally Gill and Frankel, above n 43. There have been reviews of both tobacco and alcohol regulation as discussed in this chapter.

96 Māori Affairs Committee, above n 38.

97 Kate Tokeley, 'Consumer Law and Paternalism: A Framework for Policy Decision Making – Further Analysis' in Susy Frankel and Deborah Ryder (eds), *Recalibrating Behaviour: Smarter Regulation in a Global World* (LexisNexis, 2013) (footnotes omitted).

98 Of course, a government may regulate for political reasons even if it doubts the regulation is cost-effective. For a discussion of quantitative tools in regulation see Chris Nixon and John Yeabsley, *Voyage of Discovery: How Do We Bring Analytical Techniques to State Driven Behaviour Change?* (2013) Regulatory Reform Toolkit <http://www.regulatorytoolkit.ac.nz/resources/pdfs/book-3/voyage-of-discovery-final.pdf>.

99 Susy Frankel and John Yeabsley, *Features of the Uniqueness of New Zealand and Their Role in Regulation* (2013) Regulatory Reform Toolkit <http://www.regulatorytoolkit.ac.nz/resources/pdfs/book-3/unqiueness-of-nz-final.pdf>.

100 Paul Conway, 'How to Move Product Market Regulation in New Zealand Back Towards the Frontier' (Working Paper No 880, OECD Economics Department, 13 July 2011) <http://www.oecd-ilibrary.org/economics/how-to-move-product-market-regulation-in-new-zealand-back-towards-the-frontier_5kg89j3gd2r8-en>.

101 Mutual recognition is governed by the *Trans-Tasman Mutual Recognitions Act 1997* (NZ) and *Trans-Tasman Mutual Recognitions Act 1997* (Cth).

102 See Donley Studlar, 'The Political Dynamics of Tobacco Control in Australia and New Zealand: Explaining Policy Problems, Instruments, and Patterns of Adoption' (2006) 40 *Australian Journal of Political Science* 255.

103 The *Smoke-Free Environments Act 1990* (NZ), discussed above, was based on the *Tobacco Act 1987* (Vic).

104 Susy Frankel and Meredith Lewis, 'Trade Agreements and Regulatory Autonomy: The Effect on National Interests' in Frankel, *Learning from the Past*, above n 78, 436.

105 Some were opposed because they saw it as a cost for New Zealand businesses. These points are highly contested. For a general discussion see Nixon and Yeabsley, above n 78.

106 I say 'appropriately' because I do not purport to weigh the evidence about whether regulatory measures, such as plain packaging, will work to improve public health (that must be done by relevant experts). I make a similar comment with a co-author in Susy Frankel and Daniel Gervais, 'Plain Packaging and the Interpretation of the TRIPS Agreement' (2013) 46(5) *Vanderbilt Journal of Transnational Law* 1149.

107 The Regulatory Impact Statement said that if New Zealand companies were involved in producing tobacco packages it would be 'unlikely that they would need to alter their premises to meet requirements': see Ministry of Health (New Zealand), above n 2, [23].

108 Māori Affairs Committee, above n 38, 16.

109 *New Zealand Trans-Tasman Mutual Recognition Act 1997* (Cth).

110 The equivalent provision is s 10(2)(b) of the New Zealand Act: *New Zealand Trans-Tasman Mutual Recognitions Act 1997* (NZ).

111 *Trade Marks Act 2002* (NZ) s 17(1)(b).

112 This is an issue in the context of a single trade mark proposal for Australia and New Zealand: see Susy Frankel and Megan Richardson, 'Trans-Tasman Intellectual Property Co-ordination' in Frankel, *Learning from the Past*, above n 78, 527; Susy Frankel et al, 'The Challenges of Trans-Tasman Intellectual Property Coordination' in Frankel and Ryder above n 97, 101.

113 See Intellectual Property Office (New Zealand), *4.2 Likely to Offend Maori* (19 December 2008)   <http://www.iponz.govt.nz/cms/trade-marks/practice-guidelines-index/practice-guidelines/04-absolute-grounds-general-2/4-offensive-trade-marks/4-2-likely-to-offend-maori>.

114 This is an area where arguably the best solution would be for Australia to follow the New Zealand policy example, although we acknowledge there is no political will to do so: see Frankel et al, above n 112.

115 Ibid.

116 See discussion in Kate Tokeley, 'Consumer Law and Paternalism: A Framework for Policy Decision-making' in Frankel, *Learning from the Past*, above n 78, 267. Children and those without means do not always have such freedom.

117 This title comes from Frankel, *Learning from the Past*, above n 78, which is part of the New Zealand Law Foundation Regulatory reform project: <www.regulatorytooklkit.ac.nz>.

16 Australia

Sondra Davoren, Caroline Mills and Alexandra Jones

1 Introduction

Australia is a large country approximately equal in geographic area to the United States, with a population of approximately 23 million.[1] Extensive immigration has made Australia culturally diverse, with nearly half the population having at least one parent born overseas.[2] Indigenous Australians make up only 2.4 per cent of the total population.[3]

While Australia's smoking rates are comparatively low, rates of alcohol consumption, obesity and sedentary lifestyle are relatively high,[4] and Australia's ageing population will compound the increasing disease-burden of these conditions.[5] Health spending is projected to increase by 78 per cent between 2009–10 and 2049–50, partly due to the projected increase in preventable non-communicable diseases.[6]

Cancer is Australia's leading broad cause of disease burden (19 per cent of the total burden) followed by cardiovascular disease (16 per cent).[7] While death rates for some chronic diseases – including cancer and cardiovascular disease – are falling,[8] there have been increases in other chronic conditions, such as diabetes.[9]

Risk factors, including tobacco and alcohol use and unhealthy diet, contribute to over 30 per cent of Australia's total burden of death, disease and disability.[10] One third of all cancer deaths in Australia are caused by avoidable risk factors.[11]

Significant disparities exist between the health status of Aboriginal and Torres Strait Islander people and the general Australian population.[12]

2 Policy interventions to modify behavioural risk factors

Australia's public health policy landscape is informed by a three tiered governmental structure comprising a central federal government, seven state and territory governments and numerous local councils within each state. Each level of government is endowed with its own law making powers and areas of jurisdiction.

In Australia, a combination of legislative and regulatory interventions at all levels of government, together with comprehensive and sustained social marketing campaigns, have dramatically reduced smoking rates. In the last decade alone,

Australia has experienced a fall in the number of daily smokers of more than half a million people.[13]

Despite a demonstrated ability to leverage law and policy to address the health challenges caused by tobacco, the introduction of equivalent reforms to target harmful alcohol use and overweight and obesity is lagging. Efforts to address the acute rather than chronic effects of alcohol have dominated policy developments, while the framing of alcohol harm as a problem affecting only certain sections of society (young people/problem drinkers/indigenous people) allows many to disassociate from the issue of alcohol harm. The more complicated matrix of factors contributing to overweight and obesity levels[14] has engendered a climate of regulatory inertia, inflating the impact of individual choice and personal responsibility while downplaying environmental drivers of unhealthy diet.

In this chapter we present a case study of major Australian policy initiatives undertaken to address the burden of disease associated with tobacco, alcohol and obesity.

2.1 Tobacco

2.1.1 The history of tobacco control in Australia

As in many Western countries, smoking was ubiquitous in mid-20th century Australia. In 1945, more than three out of every four men and one in every four Australian women was a regular smoker.[15] Although rates declined in the 1950s and 1960s in the wake of concerns about smoking's health effects, an influx of televised tobacco advertising and a growing number of female smokers saw smoking prevalence remain at 36 per cent among Australian adults in 1977.[16] Since the early 1970s, the Australian federal government has acted in conjunction with state and territory governments to progressively implement a range of targeted measures to reduce smoking.

Restrictions on advertising and promotion have been at the forefront of these reforms. Over time, tobacco advertising and promotion has been successively restricted, commencing with the phasing out of direct cigarette advertising on television and radio between 1973 and 1976.[17] Advertising in newspapers and magazines was prohibited in 1990.[18]

Introduction of the *Tobacco Advertising Prohibition Act 1992* (Cth) in 1992 brought with it the first national standard for tobacco advertising, and included comprehensive restrictions on advertisements across print media, film, radio, television, and advertising on billboards and public transport. Successive governments at Commonwealth, state and territory level progressively expanded these restrictions, culminating in the prohibition of tobacco sponsorship for sporting and cultural events.[19] In 2001, the comprehensive nature of Australia's legislation in this area led British American Tobacco officials to comment that Australia had 'one of the darkest markets in the world' in which to market tobacco products.[20]

Despite Australia's strict regime, industry marketing efforts have continued through event promotions, trade shows, innovative packaging and in-store displays.[21] In response, many Australian states and territories have introduced bans on the retail display of tobacco products.[22]

The first mandatory health warnings on tobacco appeared in Australia in 1973, and Australian governments at all levels have cooperated to ensure health warnings have been successively strengthened since that time despite strong industry opposition.[23] Since 2006, pictorial images, including the graphic display of the harms and distressing effects of smoking, have been mandatory on almost all forms of tobacco imported or manufactured in Australia. Health warnings in place between 2006 and 2012 included graphics that covered 30 per cent of the front and 90 per cent of the back of packs, along with details of a national 'Quitline' counselling service.[24] Evaluation after 2006 found the warnings had effectively increased consumer knowledge of the health effects of smoking, discouraged uptake, encouraged cessation and helped to de-glamorise smoking.[25] Terms such as 'light', 'mild' and 'low tar' have been banned on Australian cigarettes since 2006,[26] consistently with international consensus that such classifications provide no meaningful reduction in harm.[27]

Other significant components of Australia's tobacco control program since the 1970s have included a statutory minimum purchase age of 18 years, progressive price increases through excise taxes, and mandated minimum pack sizes to make cigarettes less affordable, particularly to young people.[28] Taxes in Australia now make up about 60 per cent of the final price of a typical packet of cigarettes, with the price of cigarettes in Australia now among the most expensive in the world; cheaper only than those in Norway.[29] At a state and territory level, most Australian states have now also introduced a scheme of retail licensing for those selling tobacco.[30]

Anti-smoking mass media campaigns have been prevalent since the 1970s. Evidence-based campaigns in states, territories and, more recently, at a federal level, have become a key component of tobacco control efforts. Against a backdrop of stalling reductions in smoking prevalence in the early 1990s, Australia's first National Tobacco Campaign was launched in 1997.[31] Between 1997 and 2000, six health advertisements (known as 'Artery', 'Lung', 'Tumour', 'Brain', 'Eye' and 'Tar') were produced with the aim of encouraging smokers to quit.[32] Subsequent evaluation of these advertising campaigns was highly favourable,[33] with several of the advertisements internationally recognised and adapted by other countries for use.[34]

Increasing scientific evidence of the harms of second hand smoke, together with mounting public support and political will, have enabled incremental smoking bans to be implemented in Australian legislation.[35] By the mid-1990s, recognition of second hand smoke as a concern for both public health and occupational health and safety resulted in a proliferation of smoke-free policies across both public and private sectors. Government offices at both Commonwealth, state and territory levels became smoke free,[36] while restrictions were also introduced in indoor public spaces such as shopping centres, hospitals, schools, childcare settings, public transport and entertainment venues.[37] Every state and territory now bans smoking in enclosed public places,[38] although great variability remains between states, regions and at local levels in the regulation of smoking in outdoor spaces.

Australia was one of the first parties to sign and ratify the *WHO Framework Convention on Tobacco Control* ('WHO FCTC'),[39] which came into force on 27 February 2005. Australia must comply with the terms of the WHO FCTC, as a binding international treaty, including by implementing a range of specific tobacco control measures. Australia's commitment to the WHO FCTC has strengthened and supported national, state and territory tobacco control priorities, deepening the connections between domestic and international tobacco control policy.[40]

2.1.2 *The current state of tobacco control*

The measures outlined above helped to reduce the prevalence of adult smoking in Australia from 36 per cent in 1977[41] to 17.5 per cent in 2010.[42] Despite this, tobacco remains a significant cause of death and disease in Australia. More than 3.3 million Australians over the age of 14 continue to smoke daily or weekly,[43] and an estimated 15,000 people die annually of smoking-related illness.[44] The rate of daily smoking among Aboriginal and Torres Strait Islander populations was 45 per cent in 2008: more than twice that of the general population.[45]

In 2008, the Commonwealth and all state and territory governments signed the National Healthcare Agreement, which contained the ambitious goals of reducing adult daily smoking prevalence to 10 per cent, and halving adult daily smoking among Aboriginal and Torres Strait Islanders by 2018.[46] The National Preventative Health Strategy, released in the same year, included a comprehensive set of proposed reforms targeting tobacco.[47]

On 29 April 2010, the federal government announced its decision to adopt several reforms in what it characterised as the 'world's strongest tobacco crackdown'.[48] Changes included a 25 per cent increase in excise tax effective immediately, raising the price of an average pack of 30 cigarettes to over AU$15. This measure alone was predicted to reduce adult smoking prevalence by 2 to 3 per cent. Significant additional funds were also dedicated for new general and targeted social marketing campaigns, programs aimed at reducing indigenous smoking and further subsidies of cessation aids.

In a world first, the federal government also announced that it would remove one of the last remaining vehicles for tobacco advertising by developing legislation that would mandate plain packaging for tobacco products from 1 January 2012, to be fully implemented later that year. In light of its international significance, the development and implementation of plain packaging through the *Tobacco Plain Packaging Act 2011* (Cth) will be discussed in detail in Chapter 17 of this volume. Despite strong ongoing industry opposition at national and international levels, these reforms were successfully implemented. All cigarettes in Australia have been sold in logo-free, drab dark brown packaging since 1 December 2012.

2.1.3 *Lessons from tobacco control in Australia*

Studies have attributed reductions in Australian smoking prevalence to increasing taxation,[49] increasing expenditure on social marketing campaigns[50] and smoke-free policies.[51] Price increases in particular have been shown to have a strong effect on adolescent smoking behaviour.[52] In fact, much of the decline in Australian smoking prevalence since the late 1990s has been attributed not to more people quitting, but to fewer young people taking up smoking in the first place.[53]

Perhaps most importantly, and as longitudinal studies suggest, smoking is a multi-factorial problem that requires a comprehensive, multi-factorial response.[54] Of the many and varied tobacco control measures taken by Australia, some are recognised to have contributory rather than independent effects, and many are difficult to capture in standard statistical analysis. This notwithstanding, the combined effect of the strategy has been to reduce the glamour and appeal of tobacco products, increase knowledge of health effects and the quitting process, reduce cues and opportunities to smoke, and reduce the social acceptability of smoking. The value of continued implementation of comprehensive, multi-sectoral strategies is recognised as one of Australia's primary obligations under the WHO FCTC[55] and was recently endorsed at a state and territory level in the National Tobacco Strategy 2012–18, which aims to strengthen and extend all major streams of tobacco control over the next six years.[56]

While Australia's track record is impressive, ongoing progress will require continued political momentum to ensure the strength of the government response is not undermined by the continued efforts and investments of industry.

2.2 Alcohol

2.2.1 Alcohol in Australia

Australia is ranked within the top 30 highest alcohol-consuming nations, although this has not always been the case.[57] Total per capita alcohol consumption early in the 20th century was low (2.5 litres per capita in the 1930s), but rose sharply in the 1970s, peaking at 13.1 litres per capita in 1974–5. Per capita consumption has been relatively stable since then.[58] In 2010–11, the Australian Bureau of Statistics estimated per capita consumption in Australia to be 10.0 litres of alcohol, which is considered high by world standards.[59] Although consumption rates have remained steady in recent times, alcohol-related hospitalisations and emergency department presentations may be increasing,[60] suggesting changes in harmful drinking practices that are not adequately captured in survey-based consumption data.[61]

The prevailing causes of alcohol-related deaths in Australia are road trauma, cancer and alcoholic liver cirrhosis, and although a greater number of Australians die from acute rather than chronic alcohol-related conditions, the burden of disease and illness associated with alcohol, and the range of harm to others, is significant.[62] Alcohol consumption accounted for 3.2 per cent of the total burden of disease and injury in Australia in 2003, with a net impact of 2.3 per cent (taking into account the possible preventive health benefits in relation to cardiovascular disease).[63]

Rates of alcohol consumption and harm vary across population sub-groups.[64] The burden of disease is higher in men than in women (4.9 per cent compared to 1.6 per cent),[65] while rates of risky drinking and alcohol-related harm are higher among people living in rural and remote areas, indigenous Australians and young people.[66]

In 2009, Australia's National Preventative Health Strategy recommended a suite of alcohol policy and legal interventions to reduce rates of long-term, high risk drinking.[67] Recognising that the prevention and control of alcohol-related non-communicable diseases requires the implementation of policies that shift patterns of population consumption downwards, the strategy's key recommendations related to policy interventions affecting alcohol availability, affordability and promotion in Australia.[68]

2.2.2 *Availability: regulating the sale and supply of alcohol*

In general terms, there is an association between reduced availability of alcohol and reductions in alcohol-related harm, including rates of chronic disease.[69] Yet, while research has identified best practice policies that are effective and cost-effective at regulating the sale and supply of alcohol,[70] the potential for licensing laws to reduce chronic disease depends on the extent to which these laws impact on consumption levels.

In Australia, the principal source of alcohol availability regulation is in state and territory liquor licensing laws. Although the impact of specific liquor licensing laws on rates of long-term alcohol harm is not well known, an increasing body of evidence suggests certain policy approaches have greater potential to reduce long-term health impacts than others, as follows.

2.2.2.1 TRADING HOURS: LOCKOUTS AND LICENCE FREEZES

Trading hours for specific licence categories are set in liquor licensing legislation and vary across Australian jurisdictions.[71] Reductions in trading hours across the board have been rare, although some states and territories have adopted lockouts (refusing patrons entry after a designated time) and moratorium periods on the issue of late-night trading licences.[72]

2.2.2.2 OUTLET DENSITY

Awareness of the public health implications of high liquor outlet density – broadly, that higher rates of harm are associated with greater density of outlets and, in particular, increased rates of chronic disease are associated with packaged liquor density[73] – has resulted in emphasis on measures to address the cumulative impact of outlets. Many states and territories now require a cumulative impact assessment as part of planning and/or liquor licensing applications. In Western Australia and the Northern Territory, there is an evidentiary burden on a licence applicant to satisfy the licensing authority that granting a licence is in the public interest.[74]

2.2.2.3 SUPPLY OF ALCOHOL TO MINORS

Restricting the supply of alcohol to minors has been a key focus in almost all Australian jurisdictions in recent years. New South Wales, Queensland, Tasmania and Victoria have all introduced laws that make it an offence for a person who is not a parent, or an adult acting in the place of the parent, or with the formal approval of the parent, to supply a minor with alcohol in a private residence.[75] In Queensland and Tasmania it is also an offence to supply liquor to a minor without proper supervision.[76]

2.2.2.4 RISK-BASED LICENSING

Some Australian jurisdictions have adopted systems of risk-based licensing, rewarding or penalising venues based on their compliance history. Currently, the Australian Capital Territory, Queensland and Victoria operate risk-based licensing schemes in which annual licensing fees are set based on levels of risk, determined by reference to measures such as late night trading hours and prior infringements.[77]

2.2.3 *Affordability*

A key driver of alcohol consumption is the affordability – that is, price relative to income – of alcohol;[78] yet, as a way of decreasing population alcohol consumption, fiscal alcohol policies have been underutilised in Australia. The real price of alcohol in Australia is relatively low compared to other commodities and in some cases has been decreasing over time.[79]

In Australia, alcohol prices are determined by the imposition of duties under customs and excise regulations, the Wine Equalisation Tax ('WET'), and a 10 per cent Goods and Services Tax ('GST') applied to retail alcohol sales.[80] Excise taxes apply to beer and spirits based on the volume of alcohol contained in the product,[81] while the WET applies to wine and is calculated according to the wholesale price of the product.[82]

The effect of this arrangement – in which some alcohol products are taxed according to alcohol content, while others are not – has been to distort the alcohol beverages market, particularly by encouraging the production of large volumes of cheap wine.[83]

A 2010 federal Treasury review of Australia's tax system decried the current alcohol tax and subsidy arrangements – particularly the WET, described as ill-suited to reducing social harm – and recommended a volumetric tax on all alcoholic beverages.[84]

These broad recommendations have not been taken up by the federal government.[85] However, limited interventions have been employed to address specific adverse effects of the current alcohol tax system, as follows.

2.2.3.1 ALCOPOPS

Until 2008, ready-to-drink, spirits-based alcohol beverages ('alcopops') were cat-egorised separately in excise and customs legislation, and taxed at a proportionally lower rate than straight spirits.[86] The comparatively low prices of these products, together with heavy promotion, pushed up consumption of alcopops and, cor-respondingly, rates of harm in young people.[87] In 2008, the federal government increased the tax on alcopops by 69 per cent – a price increase of up to AU$1.00 per product – in order to address rates of harm.[88]

Following the introduction of the tax, consumption of alcopops fell by 30 per cent.[89] Although there was some substitution to other beverage types, the increase in these categories was not enough to offset the reduction in alcopops consump-tion, resulting in a 2 per cent reduction in alcohol per capita consumption: the first in Australia in four years.[90]

The success of the alcopops tax was limited; inconsistencies in the tax regime remain. For example, there has been a sharp increase in the consumption of alco-holic cider in recent years (150 per cent between 2007 and 2011),[91] driven in part by the low tax rate on 'traditional cider' (AU$0.23 per standard drink), which is taxed under the WET.[92] By comparison, the tax on flavoured ciders is AU$0.95 per standard drink,[93] the same tax as alcopops and spirits, despite flavoured and traditional ciders having roughly the same alcohol content.

2.2.3.2 COMMUNITY-BASED RESPONSES TO CHEAP ALCOHOL

Some remote communities have introduced price restrictions on, or banned the sale of, cheap wines. Such policies have effectively operated as a de facto increase in the minimum price of alcohol. An evaluation of these restrictions found reduc-tions in overall harm,[94] but significant substitution to fortified wines (the next cheapest beverage).[95]

A 2012 Australian National Preventive Health Agency review of the public interest case for introducing a minimum floor price in Australia recommended against so doing but strongly recommended changes to the alcohol tax system to remove the WET.[96]

2.2.4 *Advertising*

Sophisticated marketing techniques, combined with the availability of mass, online and social media, and the advent of new communications technologies, makes regulating alcohol marketing a major challenge for governments, Australia included.

Responsibility for advertising regulation rests primarily with the federal govern-ment, although there are limited powers to control alcohol advertisements in state and territory liquor licensing legislation. For example, some states may prohibit venue-based promotions that encourage excessive consumption,[97] eg 'all you can drink' specials, extended 'happy hour' periods and drinking games.[98]

The Australian Communications and Media Authority ('ACMA') is an independent statutory authority that oversees licensing, planning, ownership and control of broadcasting and telecommunication services; supervises the content of commercial, community, subscription and national radio and television; and regulates online content, including internet and mobile phone content. ACMA's responsibilities include the promotion of self-regulation in the communications industry.[99]

Unlike tobacco (but much like food marketing), there is no legal regulation of alcohol advertising in Australia. Rather, alcohol advertising is predominantly self-regulated, through an amalgam of voluntary industry and media codes of practice and the Alcohol Beverages Advertising Code ('ABAC'), which sets content standards in relation to broadcast and internet alcohol advertising, packaging and labelling of alcoholic beverages and, to a limited extent, alcohol sponsorship (specifically, promotion of alcoholic beverages at events).[100]

In addition to the ABAC, alcohol regulations prohibit alcohol advertisements between 5.00am and 8.30pm, unless accompanying a live sporting broadcast on the weekend or public holidays;[101] limit alcohol advertising within a 150-metre sight line of a primary or secondary school, unless the school is in the vicinity of a licensed premises;[102] prohibit the use of features that are appealing to children and young people; and require an alcohol responsibility message to be included in alcohol advertisements.[103]

Experience (Australian and international) has shown that systems that rely on complaints from the public or industry interpretation and enforcement of alcohol advertising – such as exists in Australia – seldom have any effect on the appeal and nature of alcohol advertising content.[104] Amid increasing concern about the impact of alcohol advertising exposure on children and young people, the lack of effective alcohol advertising controls in Australia is in sharp focus.

2.3 Obesity

2.3.1 Obesity in Australia

In 2011–12, 63.4 per cent of Australians aged 18 years and over were overweight or obese.[105] The prevalence of overweight and obesity in Australian adults increased to that figure from 61.2 per cent in 2007–08 and 56.3 per cent in 1995.[106] The prevalence of overweight and obesity in children aged 5–17 remained stable at 25.3 per cent.[107] Posited contributors to increasing rates of overweight and obesity include the explosion in the availability and convenience of manufactured energy-dense foods,[108] ubiquitous marketing[109] and the relative affordability of energy-dense products.[110] The prevalence of overweight and obesity has contributed to increasing rates of non-communicable diseases, with the prevalence of cardiovascular disease, diabetes[111] and preventable cancers[112] expected to continue to rise.

Major national policy initiatives undertaken to address overweight and obesity in Australia have included the commissioning in 2008 by the federal government of the National Preventative Health Taskforce to make evidence-based recommendations on health policy initiatives,[113] the federal government's 2009 investigation into obesity in Australia,[114] and a review of food labelling law undertaken by the Australian and New Zealand Food Regulation Ministerial Council, headed by Dr Neal Blewett AC ('the Blewett Review').[115] The findings of these investigations and the degree to which recommendations have been translated into policy and law will be further considered below.

2.3.2 *Food standards and labelling law*

2.3.2.1 LEGAL FRAMEWORK AND REGULATORY BODIES

Australian food standards and labelling law is regulated by Food Standards Australia New Zealand ('FSANZ'), a central agency created through collaboration between the Australian federal government, the New Zealand government and Australian state governments.[116] Governed by the *Food Standards Australia New Zealand Act 1991* (Cth) ('Act'), FSANZ administers the principal instrument for food standards and labelling regulation in Australia: the Australia New Zealand Food Standards Code ('Food Code').[117] The Act's broad objectives include protecting public health and providing adequate information relating to food to enable consumers to make informed choices.[118] The Food Code gives effect to the Act's objectives through a range of measures and is adopted almost uniformly throughout Australia by state-level legislation.[119]

2.3.2.2 NATIONAL REGULATION OF FOOD LABELLING: NUTRITION INFORMATION

The Food Code currently sets out minimum standards for display of nutrition information on packaged foods, requiring ingredients to be listed in descending order according to weight.[120] It also requires that packaged foods have nutrition information panels, which display the average amount of energy (measured in kilojoules), protein, fat, saturated fat, carbohydrate, sugars and sodium in the food per serving size (which is not standardised) and per 100 grams or millilitres of product.[121] Information about any nutrients which are the subject of claims on the package (eg 'rich in calcium') must also appear in the nutrition information panel, and the product must meet certain other criteria.[122] Currently, these provisions do not apply to food from fast food chains and coffee shops because those products are not defined as 'packaged food'.[123]

In most instances within Australia, the provisions of the Food Code, as incorporated into state legislation, represent the sole regulatory instrument for food labelling. However, certain jurisdictions have separately legislated to impose more rigorous standards. For example, since February 2012, New South Wales amendments to the *Food Act 2003*[124] and associated regulations have required mandatory display of energy values of food items in food chains that have 20 or more outlets in New South Wales or 50 or more nationally, a description extending to many fast food chains and large supermarkets.[125]

The Blewett Review recommended, among other measures, the development and incorporation of a multiple traffic light system into front of pack labelling, using traffic light signposts to indicate the levels of ingredients including fat, saturated fat, sugar and sodium in the product.[126] A voluntary scheme for front of pack labelling remains under development by government, in conjunction with industry and public health stakeholders. The Australian Food and Grocery Council ('AFGC'), an industry association representing packaged food and beverage manufacturers, continues to lobby against traffic light labelling.[127]

2.3.2.3 NATIONAL REGULATION OF FOOD LABELLING: HEALTH CLAIMS

Health claims about the nutritional benefits of packaged foods are also regulated under the Food Code.[128] Health claims as defined in the Act include high level health claims, where a relationship is claimed between a nutrient and a serious disease or a biomarker of a serious disease (such as 'reduces cholesterol'), and general level health claims (for example '99 per cent fat free').[129] The Food Code provides that products may base a general level health claim on a pre-approved food-health relationship,[130] or may self-substantiate the food-health relationship. To carry a health claim, the product must also meet nutrient profile scoring criteria contained within the applicable standard, to prevent health claims appearing on foods high in saturated fat, sugar or salt.[131]

2.3.3 *Self-regulation of food and beverage advertising*

Advertising of foods, in particular marketing aimed at children, remains largely unregulated. Self-regulation systems by food industry associations and broadcast authorities set standards and adjudicate disputes, though these systems have been criticised by public health groups for ineffectively restricting children's exposure to material promoting unhealthy food products.[132]

The three voluntary codes largely responsible for regulating advertising standards for food products are the Responsible Children's Marketing Initiative ('RCMI') (developed by the AFGC),[133] the Quick Service Restaurant Industry Initiative for Responsible Advertising and Marketing to Children ('QSRI'),[134] which is subscribed to by many large fast food chains, and the Australian Association of National Advertisers' Food and Beverage Advertising and Marketing Communications Code ('AANA Food Code').[135] Complaints about alleged breaches of all three codes are administered by the Advertising Standards Bureau ('ASB'). Because the ASB is not a statutory authority, parties dissatisfied with the results of ASB review have no legal recourse.

The codes contain similar provisions controlling advertising to children. For example, the RCMI prohibits participants from advertising food and beverage products to children under the age of 12 on television, in print or by other means directed primarily to children, unless the product represents a healthier dietary choice and the advertising promotes a healthy lifestyle.[136] The AANA Food Code contains similar provisions, as well as an overarching requirement that advertising communications of all types meet prevailing community standards.[137]

ACMA has broad responsibility to regulate advertising standards, including administering the Children's Advertising Standards 2009, which operate under the *Broadcasting Services Act 1992* (Cth). The standards set out some general, minimum requirements for the content of advertising broadcast during programs classified for children and young people, as well as for the use of endorsements by popular personalities or characters and the promotion of competitions.

The possibility of national-level legislative regulation of food and beverage advertising to children has been considered, as Australian children's exposure to television food advertising is amongst the highest in the world.[138] In recent years federal legislative initiatives including the Protecting Children from Junk Food Advertising (Broadcast Amendment) Bill 2008 (Cth) and the Protecting Children from Junk Food Advertising (Broadcasting and Telecommunications Amendment) Bill 2011 (Cth) have been proposed to restrict children's exposure to marketing of unhealthy food. All such legislative measures have been defeated in Parliament.

The Australian Competition and Consumer Commission, a statutory consumer protection authority, may also take regulatory action to prosecute corporate misconduct in areas including product safety, labelling, unfair market practices and pricing.[139] To date, these laws have been infrequently used in the context of challenging advertising or labelling of unhealthy food and beverage products.[140]

2.3.4 Regulation of sale of unhealthy foods in schools

With education a largely state-administered matter, there is no uniform regulation of the supply and sale of food and beverages in Australian schools. An example of state-based regulation is seen in New South Wales, which for several years has had in place the Fresh Tastes NSW Healthy School Canteen Strategy,[141] under which schools may not sell high fat or high sugar foods or drinks through over-the-counter sales or vending machines. This approach was underpinned by a nutrient profiling system identifying 'red light' foods, the sale of which is very restricted. A ban on the sale of sugar sweetened drinks was put in place in New South Wales government schools from 2007.[142] Other Australian jurisdictions have introduced non-mandatory policy measures aimed at school canteens or have indicated an intention to do so.[143]

2.3.5 Taxes and the use of economic disincentives

Australia currently has what may be argued to be a partial 'unhealthy food tax', with the GST applying to most processed and packaged foods, but not fresh foods such as bread, meat, fruit, vegetables and milk.[144] The GST, introduced in 2000, was not implemented with a policy objective of disincentivising the purchase of unhealthy foods, but fresh and unpackaged foods were exempt from the GST, ensuring that such products would remain affordable for low-income families,[145] effectively increasing the price of processed foods relative to fresh foods. Although tax reforms have been considered,[146] their introduction as an obesity policy initiative has not been pursued.

3 Conclusion

Although Australia has been internationally recognised for its leadership within tobacco control, relatively few evidence-based laws to reduce the impact of alcohol use and overweight and obesity levels have been implemented compared to other developed international jurisdictions.

Effective lobbying by the powerful tobacco, alcohol, food and beverages industries in Australia poses an ongoing barrier to implementing policy initiatives. In a political environment that currently favours 'red tape' reduction to promote economic growth,[147] regulatory measures seen as 'anti-business' remain politically unpopular. The framing by industry bodies of harmful alcohol consumption as a youth problem, or overweight and obesity as a matter of personal (or parental) responsibility allows political moves to implement universal measures such as alcohol tax reform, or restriction of advertising of unhealthy foods, to be portrayed respectively as 'tax grabs' or paternalistic 'nanny state' regulation.

As experience from tobacco control also shows, no single policy initiative is of itself an effective solution. A critical element in the success of tobacco control was a multi-faceted policy approach, underpinned by well-funded mass media campaigns. However, whereas many tobacco policies were without precedent, similar initiatives in alcohol and food policy are vulnerable to 'lack of evidence' arguments[148] – in particular lack of *Australian* evidence of effectiveness – reflecting a political climate that demands an unrealistic level of certainty for new policy.

The existing multi-layered system of policy development for alcohol and food, which spreads responsibility vertically between national, state and local government, and horizontally across government departments, may also present a barrier to broad legislative and regulatory policy responses.[149] A renewed commitment to multi-sectoral arrangements and whole-of-government approaches beyond tobacco will be required for Australia to truly realise its potential in addressing the burden of non-communicable diseases.

Notes

1 Australian Bureau of Statistics, 'Australian Demographic Statistics: September Quarter 2012' (No 3101.0, Australian Bureau of Statistics, 18 April 2013).
2 Australian Bureau of Statistics, *2011 Census Quick Stats* <http://www.censusdata.abs.gov.au/census_services/getproduct/census/2011/quickstat/0>.
3 Ibid.
4 Australian Bureau of Statistics, *Australian Social Trends* (25 September 2012) <http://www.abs.gov.au/AUSSTATS/abs@.nsf/Lookup/4102.0Main+Features20Jun+2012>.
5 Commonwealth of Australia, *The 2010 Intergenerational Report* (January 2010).
6 Ibid.

7 Australian Institute of Health and Welfare, 'Australia's Health 2010' (Australia's health series No 12, Australian Institute of Health and Welfare, 2010) [132].

8 Ibid.

9 Ibid.

10 See Australian Institute of Health and Welfare, above n 7, [66].

11 Anthea Page et al, 'Australian and New Zealand Atlas of Avoidable Mortality' (Public Health Information Development Unit, University of Adelaide, 2006) [xix] <http://www.publichealth.gov.au/pdf/atlases/avoid_mortality_aust_2006/avoid_mortality_contents.pdf>.

12 See Australian Institute of Health and Welfare, above n 7, [22].

13 Australian Bureau of Statistics, *Australian Health Survey: First Results 2011–2012* (No 4364.0.55.001, 29 October 2012) <http://www.abs.gov.au/ausstats/abs@.nsf/Lookup/73963BA1EA6D6221CA257AA30014BE3E?opendocument>.

14 Christopher Reynolds, *Public Health Law and Regulation* (Federation Press, 2004) 208.

15 Stephen Woodward, 'Trends in Cigarette Consumption in Australia' (1984) 14(4) *Australian and New Zealand Journal of Medicine* 405, 405–7.

16 Australian Bureau of Statistics, 'Alcohol and Tobacco Consumption Patterns' (No 4380.0, 1977).

17 *Broadcasting Act 1942* (Cth) s 100(5A); Becky Freeman, Indra Haslam and Vicki Tumini, 'Tobacco Advertising and Promotion' in Michelle Scollo and Margaret Winstanley (eds), *Tobacco in Australia: Facts and Issues* (Cancer Council Victoria, 4th ed, 2012) ch 11 <http://www.tobaccoinaustralia.org.au/downloads/chapters/Ch11_Advertising.pdf>.

18 *Smoking and Tobacco Products Advertisements (Prohibition) Act 1989* (Cth).

19 *Tobacco Act 1987* (Vic); *Tobacco Products Control Act 1988* (SA); *Tobacco Products Act 1990* (WA); *Tobacco Advertising Prohibition Act 1992* (Cth).

20 Simon Chapman, Fiona Byrne and Stacey Carter, 'Australia is One of the Darkest Markets in the World: The Global Importance of Australian Tobacco Control' (2003) 12 (supplement 3) *Tobacco Control* iii1, iii1 <http://tc.bmjjournals.com/cgi/content/abstract/12/suppl_3/iii1>.

21 Stacey Carter, 'Going Below the Line: Creating Transportable Brands for Australia's Dark Market' (2003) 12 (supplement 3) *Tobacco Control* iii87, iii94 <http://tc.bmjjournals.com/cgi/content/abstract/12/suppl_3/iii87>.

22 See, eg, *Tobacco Act 1927* (ACT) s 10; *Public Health (Tobacco) Act 2008* (NSW) s 9; *Tobacco Control Legislation Amendment Act 2010* (NT) s 20; *Public Health Act 1997* (Tas) s 72A(4A); *Tobacco Amendment (Protection of Children) Act 2009* (Vic) ss 2 and 5; *Tobacco Products Control Act 2006* (WA) s 22.

23 Simon Chapman and Stacy Carter, '"Avoid Health Warnings on All Tobacco Products for just as long as We Can": A History of Australian Tobacco Industry Efforts to Avoid, Delay and Dilute Health Warnings on Cigarettes' (2003) 12 (supplement 3) *Tobacco Control* iii13 <http://tc.bmjjournals.com/cgi/content/abstract/12/suppl_3/iii13>.

24 *Trade Practices (Consumer Product Information Standards) (Tobacco) Regulations 2004* (Cth) sch 1.

25 See, eg, Victoria White, Bernice Webster, and Melanie Wakefield, 'Do Graphic Health Warning Labels Have an Impact on Adolescents' Smoking-related Beliefs and Behaviours?' (2008) 103 *Addiction* 1562; Ron Borland et al, 'How Reactions to Cigarette Packet Health Warnings Influence Quitting: Findings from the ITC Four-Country Survey' (2009) 104 *Addiction* 669; Patrick Shanahan and David Elliott, Department of Health and Ageing, *Evaluation of the Effectiveness of the Graphic Health Warnings on Tobacco Product Packaging 2008* (2009) <http://www.health.gov.au/internet/main/publishing.nsf/Content/F22B9115FD392DA5CA257588007DA955/$File/hw-eval-full-report.pdf>.

26 *Undertaking to the Australian Competition and Consumer Commission Given for the Purposes of Section 87B of the Trade Practices Act 1974 (Cth) by Philip Morris* (5 May 2005) <http:// transition.accc.gov.au/content/item.phtml?itemId=683563&nodeId=d8d8b4d2 05504c8ba89a3b0ec148a75d&fn=Undertaking.pdf>; *Undertaking to the Australian Competition and Consumer Commission Given for the Purposes of Section 87B of the Trade Practices Act 1974 (Cth) by British American Tobacco Limited* (11 May 2005) <http://transition. accc.gov.au/content/item.phtml?itemId=683582&nodeId=7306af763b82c856e53 27b54d21608c0&fn=Undertaking.pdf>; Jonathan Liberman, 'Tobacco Litigation in Australia' in Scollo and Winstanley, above n 17, ch 16 <http://www.tobaccoin australia.org.au/downloads/chapters/Ch16_Litigation.pdf>.

27 See, eg, WHO FCTC, art 11.

28 Michelle Scollo, 'Pricing and Taxation of Cigarettes' in Scollo and Winstanley, above n 17, ch 13.

29 The Economist Intelligence Unit, *Cigarette Prices in Selected Cities, 2011* (March 2012).

30 *Tobacco Products Regulation Act 1997* (SA) pt 2; *Tobacco Products Control Act 2006* (WA), pt 4; *Public Health Act 1997* (Tas), pt 4 div 3; *Public Health (Tobacco) Act 2008* (NSW), pt 5; *Tobacco Products (Licencing) Act 1988* (Qld).

31 Commonwealth of Australia, *Australia's National Tobacco Campaign: Evaluation Report Volume One* (May 1999) <http://www.health.gov.au/internet/main/publishing.nsf/ Content/health-pubhlth-publicat-document-metadata-tobccamp.htm/$FILE/tobc-camp.pdf>.

32 D Hill and T Carroll, 'Australia's National Tobacco Campaign' (2003) 12 (supplement 2) *Tobacco Control* ii9, Table 1.

33 See, eg, ibid.

34 See, eg, United Kingdom Health Promotion Agency, 'Every Cigarette is Doing You Damage' Campaign (2002) <http://www.healthpromotionagency.org.uk/Work/ Tobacco/campaigns1.htm>.

35 Katherine Bryan-Jones and Simon Chapman, 'Political Dynamics Promoting the Incremental Regulation of Secondhand Smoke: A Case Study of New South Wales, Australia' (2006) 6 *BMC Public Health* 192 <http://www.biomedcentral.com/1471-2458/6/192>.

36 See, eg, Australian Public Service Commission, *Public Service Board Memorandum 86/9055: Towards a Smoke-free Workplace – Guidelines for Achieving Smoke-free Working Environments in the APS* (1986).

37 Kathryn Barnsley and Becky Freeman, 'Smokefree Environments' in Scollo and Winstanley, above n 17, ch 15, [15.4] <http://www.tobaccoinaustralia.org.au/ chapter-15-smokefree-environment/15-4-overview-of-key-public-areas-and-environ ments>.

38 Ibid.

39 Opened for signature 16 June 2003, 2302 UNTS 166 (entered into force 27 February 2005).

40 Kylie Lindorff and Madeleine Heyward, 'The WHO Framework Convention on Tobacco Control' in Scollo and Winstanley, above n 17 <http://www.tobaccoin australia.org.au/chapter-18-ftct/18-9-what-the-fctc-means-for-australia>.

41 Australian Bureau of Statistics, above n 16.

42 Australian Institute of Health and Welfare, '2010 National Drug Strategy Household Survey' (Drug statistics series No 25, Australian Institute of Health and Welfare, 2011) 22.

43 Ibid.

44 Stephen Begg et al, 'The Burden of Disease and Injury in Australia 2003' (PHE No 82, Australian Institute of Health and Welfare, May 2007) 6.

45 Australian Bureau of Statistics, *The Health and Welfare of Australia's Aboriginal and Torres Strait Islander Peoples* (No 4704.0, Australian Bureau of Statistics, 29 October 2010)

Adult Health: Smoking <http://www.abs.gov.au/AUSSTATS/abs@.nsf/lookup/4
704.0Chapter755Oct+2010>.

46 Council of Australian Governments, *National Healthcare Agreement* (2008).

47 National Preventative Health Taskforce, *Australia: The Healthiest Country by 2020* (2008)
306.

48 Commonwealth of Australia, *Taking Preventative Action – A Response to Australia: The
Healthiest Country by 2020* (2010) 10.

49 International Agency for Research on Cancer, 'Effectiveness of Tax and Price Policies
for Tobacco Control' (2011) *14 IARC Handbooks of Cancer Prevention*.

50 Sarah Durkin, Emily Brennan and Melanie Wakefield, 'Mass Media Campaigns to
Promote Smoking Cessation among Adults: An Integrative Review' (2012) 21 *Tobacco
Control* 127.

51 International Agency for Research on Cancer, 'Evaluating the Effectiveness of
Smoke-free Policies' (2009) 13 *IARC Handbooks of Cancer Prevention*.

52 Victoria White et al, 'What Impact Have Tobacco Control Policies, Cigarette Price
and Tobacco Control Programme Funding Had on Australian Adolescents' Smoking?
Findings over a 15-year Period' (2011) 106 *Addiction* 1493.

53 Australian Institute of Health and Welfare, '2010 National Drug Strategy Household
Survey' (Drug statistics series No 25, Australian Institute of Health and Welfare,
2011), 24; Daniella Germain et al, 'The Long-term Decline of Adult Tobacco Use in
Victoria: Changes in Smoking Initiation and Quitting over a Quarter of a Century of
Tobacco Control' (2012) 36 *Australia and New Zealand Journal of Public Health* 17.

54 United States Department of Health and Human Services, *Reducing Tobacco Use: A
Report of the Surgeon General* (2000) ch 7 <http://www.cdc.gov/tobacco/data_statistics/
sgr/2000/complete_report/index.htm>.

55 See, eg, WHO FCTC art 5.1.

56 Intergovernmental Committee on Drugs, *National Tobacco Strategy 2012–2018*
(Commonwealth of Australia, 2012) <http://www.nationaldrugstrategy.gov.au/
internet/drugstrategy/publishing.nsf/Content/national_ts_2012_2018_html>.

57 National Preventative Health Taskforce, *Technical Paper 3: Preventing Alcohol-related
Harm in Australia* (2009) 5.

58 Ibid.

59 See, eg, National Preventative Health Taskforce, *Technical Paper 3*, above n 57; World
Health Organization, *Global Status Report on Alcohol and Health 2011* (2011) <http://
www.who.int/substance_abuse/publications/global_alcohol_report/msbgsrupro-
files.pdf>.

60 Michael Livingston, 'Recent Trends in Risky Alcohol Consumption and Related
Harm among Young People in Victoria, Australia' (2008) 32(3) *Australian and New
Zealand Journal of Public Health* 269.

61 Michael Livingston et al, 'Diverging Trends in Alcohol Consumption and Alcohol-
related Harm in Victoria' (2010) 34 *Australian and New Zealand Journal of Public Health*
368, 372.

62 See, eg, Wendy Loxley et al, *The Prevention of Substance Use, Risk and Harm in Australia: A
Review of the Evidence* (National Drug Research Institute and the Centre for Adolescent
Health, 2004). Research from 2010 estimated that the total known costs of all alcohol-
related harms in Australia, including harm to others, was AU$36 billion annually:
Anne-Marie Laslett et al, *The Range and Magnitude of Alcohol's Harm to Others* (Centre for
Alcohol Policy Research, 2010) 214.

63 Begg et al, above n 44, 6.

64 National Preventative Health Taskforce, *Technical Paper 3*, above n 57, 15.

65 Ibid 11.

66 Ibid 15.

67 National Preventative Health Taskforce, *Australia: The Healthiest Country*, above n 47, 24.

68 Sally Casswell and Thaksaphon Thamarangsi, 'Reducing Harm from Alcohol: Call to Action' (2009) 373 *The Lancet* 2247, 2248.

69 Michael Livingston, 'Alcohol Outlet Density and Harm: Comparing the Impacts on Violence and Chronic Harms' (2011) 30 *Drug and Alcohol Review* 515.

70 See, eg, Thomas Babor et al, *Alcohol: No Ordinary Commodity* (Oxford University Press, 2nd ed, 2010) 196.

71 See *Liquor Regulations 2010* (ACT) reg 33; *Liquor Act 2007* (NSW) ss 12, 13, 20B, 25, 29; *Liquor Act* (NT) s 31; *Liquor Regulations* (NT) reg 4; *Liquor Act 1992* (Qld) ss 9, 86–90; *Liquor Regulation 2002* (Qld) reg 3A; *Liquor Licensing Act 1997* (SA) ss 32–40A, 44; *Liquor Licensing Act 1990* (Tas) ss 7–15, 19; *Liquor Control Reform Act 1998* (Vic) ss 8–15A, 17; *Liquor Control Act 1988* (WA) ss 97–8H.

72 Allan Trifonoff et al, *Liquor Licensing Legislation in Australia: Part 1 – An Overview* (National Centre for Education and Training on Addiction, 2011) 71.

73 Livingston, above n 69, 520.

74 Trifonoff et al, above n 72, 45.

75 See *Liquor Act 2007* (NSW) s 117; *Liquor Act 1992* (Qld) s 156A; *Police Offences Act 1935* (Tas) s 26; *Liquor Control Reform Act 1998* (Vic) s 119.

76 See *Liquor Act 1992* (Qld) s 156A(2); *Police Offences Act 1935* (Tas) s 26(2).

77 *Liquor Act 2010* (ACT); *Liquor (Fees) Determination 2013* (ACT); *Liquor Act 1992* (Qld) s 202; *Liquor Regulation 2002 (Qld)* regs 36–36D 3A; *Liquor Control Reform Regulations 2009 (Vic)* regs 17–30.

78 Ibid 10.

79 National Preventative Health Taskforce, *Technical Paper 3*, above n 57, 9.

80 See *Customs Act 1901* (Cth) ss 153AA–153AD; *Customs Tariff Act 1995* (Cth) vol 2 s IV ch 27; *Excise Act 1901* (Cth) pts VIIA–VIIAA; *Excise Tariff Act 1921* (Cth) sch; *A New Tax System (Wine Equalisation Tax) Act 1999* (Cth); *A New Tax System (Goods and Services Tax) Act 1999* (Cth).

81 *Excise Act 1901* (Cth) s 77FA.

82 *A New Tax System (Wine Equalisation Tax) Act 1999* (Cth) pt 2 div 5 s 5–5(3).

83 Commonwealth of Australia, *Australia's Future Tax System: Report to the Treasurer* (Department of Treasury, 2010) E5-2.

84 Ibid.

85 Australian Government, 'Tax Reform – Next Steps for Australia' (Tax Forum Discussion Paper, Commonwealth of Australia, 2011) 30 <http://www.futuretax. gov.au/content/Content. aspx?doc=TaxForum/Discussion_Paper.htm>.

86 *Excise Tariff Act 1921* (Cth) sch (superseded) (Act No 26 of 1921); *Customs Tariff Act 1995* (Cth) sch 3 (superseded) (Act No 147 of 1995).

87 Senate Standing Committee on Community Affairs, *Ready-to-drink Alcohol Beverages* (Parliament of Australia, 2008) 53.

88 *Customs Tariff Proposal (No 3) 2009* (Cth); *Excise Tariff Proposal (No 1) 2009* (Cth); *Excise Tariff Act 1921* (Cth) sch; *Customs Tariff Act 1995* (Cth) sch 3. See also Brian Vandenberg, Michael Livingston and Margaret Hamilton, 'Beyond Cheap Shots: Reforming Alcohol Taxation in Australia' (2008) 27 *Drug and Alcohol Review* 579, 579.

89 Steven Skov et al, 'Is the "Alcopops" Tax Working? Probably Yes but There is a Bigger Picture' (2011) 195 *Medical Journal of Australia* 84, 84.

90 Wayne Hall and Tanya Chikritzhs, 'The Australian Alcopops Tax Revisited' (2011) 377 *The Lancet* 1136, 1136.

91 Natacha Carragher, Anthony Shakeshaft and Christopher Doran, 'Here We Go Again: Cider's Turn to Highlight Anomalies in Australia's Alcohol Taxation System' (2013) 37 *Australian and New Zealand Journal of Public Health* 95, 95.

92 Ibid. See also *A New Tax Act (Wine Equalisation Tax) 1999* (Cth) ss 2.5, 31.1, 31.5.

93 Carragher above n 91. See also *Customs Tariff Act 1995* (Cth) vol 2 s IV ch 27; *Excise Tariff Act 1921* (Cth) sch.

94   Dennis Gray et al, 'Beating the Grog: An Evaluation of the Tennant Creek Liquor Licensing Restrictions' (2000) 24 *Australian and New Zealand Journal of Public Health* 39.

95   Eleanor Hogan et al, 'What Price Do We Pay to Prevent Alcohol-related Harms in Aboriginal Communities? The Alice Springs Trial of Liquor Licensing Restrictions' (2006) 25 *Drug and Alcohol Review* 207, 210.

96   Australian National Preventive Health Agency, *Draft Report – Exploring the Public Interest Case for a Minimum (Floor) Price for Alcohol* (November 2012) <http://www.anpha.gov.au/internet/anpha/publishing.nsf/Content/draft-report-minimum-price-alcohol>.

97   *Liquor Act 2010* (ACT) s 137; *Liquor Act 2007* (NSW) s 99; *Liquor Act 1992* (Qld) s 148A; *Liquor Control Reform Act 1998* (Vic) s 115A; *Liquor Control Act 1998* (WA) s 65B.

98   See Government of Western Australia, Department of Racing, Gaming and Liquor 'Responsible Promotion of Liquor on Licensed Premises and the Sale of Packaged Liquor' (Guideline, 31 January 2013) 3 <http://www.rgl.wa.gov.au/ResourceFiles/Policies/Responsible_promotion_of_liquor_for_Consumption_on_Premises.pdf>; *Liquor (Responsible Promotion of Liquor) Guidelines 2012 (No 1)* (ACT) (Notifiable instrument NI2012–127, 29 February 2012) <http://www.legislation.act.gov.au/ni/2012-127/current/pdf/2012-127.pdf>; Department of Justice (Vic) 'Guidelines for Responsible Liquor Advertising and Promotions' 12 <http://www.vcglr.vic.gov.au/resources/9f470ae4-b191-46ff-8a58-59211e71e5a6/doj-guide_for_advertising-promotions_lowres.pdf>; Office of Liquor, Gaming and Racing 'Liquor Promotion Guidelines' (July 2013) 12 <http://www.olgr.nsw.gov.au/pdfs/Liquor_promotion_guidelines.pdf>.

99   Australian Communications and Media Authority, *Regulatory Responsibility* (15 August 2013) <http://www.acma.gov.au/theACMA/About/Corporate/Responsibilities/regulation-responsibilities-acma>.

100   ABAC Scheme, *Alcohol Beverages Advertising (and Packaging) Code* (1 March 2012) <http://www.abac.org.au/wp-content/uploads/2013/06/ABAC-Code-at-1-March-2012-.pdf>.

101   Australian Communications and Media Authority, *Commercial Television Industry Code of Practice* (1 January 2010) s 6.7 <http://www.freetv.com.au/media/Code_of_Practice/2010_Commercial_Television_Industry_Code_of_Practice.pdf>.

102   Outdoor Media Association, *OMA Alcohol Advertising Guidelines* (2013) OMA <http://oma.org.au/__data/assets/pdf_file/0012/2460/OMA_Alcohol_Guidelines.pdf>.

103   Publishers' Advertising Advisory Bureau, *Guiding Principle for Alcohol Beverage Advertising* Publishers Bureau <http://www.publishersbureau.com.au/resources/pdf/NEW_PAAB_Alcoholic_Beverage_Advertising.pdf>.

104   Babor et al, above n 70, 191.

105   Australian Bureau of Statistics, *Australian Health Survey: First Results, 2011–12*, (No 4364.0.55.001).

106   Ibid.

107   Ibid 'Key Findings'.

108   Adam Drewnowski and Nicole Darmon, 'The Economics of Obesity: Dietary Energy Density and Energy Cost' (2005) 82(1) *American Journal of Clinical Nutrition* 256S, 266S; see also B Crammond et al, 'The Possibility of Regulating for Obesity Prevention – Understanding Regulation in the Commonwealth Government' (2013) 14(3) *Obesity Reviews* 213, 213.

109   Janny Goris et al, 'Television Food Advertising and the Prevalence of Childhood Overweight and Obesity: A Multicountry Comparison' (2010) 13 *Public Health Nutrition* 1003, 1008–9.

110   Adam Drewnowski and Nicole Darmon, 'Food Choices and Diet Costs: An Economic Analysis' (2005) 135(4) *Journal of Nutrition* 900, 903; see also B Crammond et al, above n 108, 213.

111 WA Davis et al, 'The Obesity-driven Rising Costs of Type 2 Diabetes in Australia: Projections from the Fremantle Diabetes Study' (2006) 36 *Internal Medicine Journal* 155, 158.

112 Peter Baade et al, 'Estimating the Future Burden of Cancers Preventable by Better Diet and Physical Activity in Australia' (2012) 196(5) *Medical Journal of Australia* 337, 338.

113 National Preventative Health Taskforce, *Technical Paper 1: Obesity in Australia: A Need for Urgent Action* (2009) 21–47.

114 House of Representatives Standing Committee on Health and Ageing, *Weighing It Up: Obesity in Australia* (Commonwealth of Australia, 2009).

115 Neal Blewett et al, *Labelling Logic: Review of Food Labelling Law and Policy* (Commonwealth of Australia, 2011).

116 FSANZ was created under a treaty between Australia and New Zealand, *Agreement between the Government of Australia and the Government of New Zealand concerning a Joint Food Standards System*, signed in 1995 and updated several times since then. The participation of states in FSANZ followed the Inter-Governmental Food Regulation Agreement ('FRA'), to which the Commonwealth of Australia and all Australian states and territories are signatories. The Council of Australian Governments signed the FRA, bringing into effect the present system for food regulation on 3 November 2000.

117 *Food Standards Australia New Zealand Act* 1991 (Cth).

118 Ibid s 3.

119 See *Food Act 2001* (ACT); *Food Act 2003* (NSW); *Food Act 2006* (Qld); *Food Act 2003* (Tas); *Food Act 1984* (Vic); *Food Act 2008* (WA).

120 *Australia New Zealand Food Standards Code – Standard 1.2.4 – Labelling of Ingredients* (Cth).

121 *Australia New Zealand Food Standards Code – Standard 1.2.8 – Nutrition Information Requirements* (Cth). See discussion by Sarah MacKay, 'Legislative Solutions to Unhealthy Eating and Obesity in Australia' (2011) 125(12) *Public Health* 896.

122 *Australia New Zealand Food Standards Code – Standard 1.2.7 – Nutrition, Health and Related Claims* (Cth) pt 3 div 1.

123 *Australia New Zealand Food Standards Code – Standard 1.2.1 – Application of Labelling and Other Information Requirements* (Cth).

124 *Food Act 2003* (NSW), ss 106K–106R.

125 Food Regulations 2010 (NSW), reg 16R.

126 Blewett et al, above n 115, 4, 8, 123–5.

127 See, eg, Australian Food and Grocery Council, 'Nationals Signal Red to Traffic Light Labels' (Media Release, 29 August 2011).

128 *Australia New Zealand Food Standards Code – Standard 1.2.7 – Nutrition, Health and Related Claims* (Cth) div 1.

129 *Food Standards Australia New Zealand Act 1991* (Cth) s 4.

130 *Australia New Zealand Food Standards Code – Standard 1.2.7 – Nutrition, Health and Related Claims* (Cth) div 2.

131 Ibid div 4.

132 J Lumley, J Martin and N Antonopoulos, *Exposing the Charade: The Failure to Protect Children from Unhealthy Food Advertising* (Obesity Policy Coalition, 2012).

133 Australian Food and Grocery Council, *The Responsible Children's Marketing Initiative of the Australian Food and Beverage Industry* (January 2014).

134 Australian Food and Grocery Council, *Australian Quick Service Restaurant Initiative for Responsible Advertising and Marketing to Children* (January 2014).

135 Australian Association of National Advertisers, *AANA Food & Beverages Advertising & Marketing Communications Code* (August 2009).

136 Australian Food and Grocery Council, *Responsible Children's Marketing*, above n 133, 'Core Principles'.

137 Australian Association of National Advertisers, above n 135, 2.

138 National Preventative Health Taskforce, *Technical Paper 1*, above n 113, 27–31.

139 *Competition and Consumer Act 2010* (Cth) sch 2 ('The Australian Consumer Law').

140 In April 2009 the ACCC found an advertising campaign by Coca-Cola had the potential to mislead consumers: ACCC, 'ACCC Acts on Coca-Cola Myth-busting' (Media Release, NR 070/09, 2 April 2009) <http://www.accc.gov.au/media-release/accc-acts-on-coca-cola-myth-busting>.

141 Premier of New South Wales, 'New Recipe for Healthy Students' (News Release, 20 April 2004) <http://www0.health.nsw.gov.au/resources/publichealth/health-promotion/obesity/rel_hcanteens_pdf.asp>.

142 NSW Government, 'Sugar Sweetened Drink Ban for NSW Schools' (31 August 2006) <http://www0.health.nsw.gov.au/pubs/2006/softdrink_ban.html>.

143 For a description of measures implemented around Australia, see Jacqueline Crowle and Erin Turner, 'Childhood Obesity: An Economic Perspective' (Australian Government Productivity Commission Staff Working Paper, 2010) app B, 128–58.

144 Australian Taxation Office, *The GST Food Guide* (Commonwealth of Australia, 2012).

145 *A New Tax System (Goods and Services Tax) Act 1999* (Cth), as amended.

146 National Preventative Health Taskforce, *Technical Paper 1*, above n 113, 21–2.

147 Ibid 168.

148 Crammond et al, above n 108, 213.

149 J Shill et al, 'Government Regulation to Promote Healthy Food Environments – A View from Inside State Governments' (2012) 13(2) *Obesity Reviews* 162, 167.

Part IV

Case Study of a Legal Dispute

17 The High Court of Australia and the Marlboro Man: The Battle over the Plain Packaging of Tobacco Products

Matthew Rimmer

1 Introduction

In an episode of the television show *Mad Men*, Don Draper, the creative director of the advertising agency Sterling Cooper, engages in a pitch on the advertising potential of tobacco:

> This is the greatest advertising opportunity since the invention of cereal … How do you make your cigarettes? … Advertising is based on one thing: happiness. And do you know what happiness is? Happiness is the smell of a new car. It's freedom from fear. It's a billboard on the side of a road that screams with reassurance that whatever you're doing is OK. You are OK.[1]

The Mad Men of the tobacco industry have long used packaging to undermine health warnings, to engage in false and misleading advertising, and to encourage consumers to initiate and maintain the use of its addictive products.

In order to support the *WHO Framework Convention on Tobacco Control* ('WHO FCTC'),[2] the Australian government introduced the *Tobacco Plain Packaging Bill 2011* (Cth) and the *Trade Marks Amendment (Tobacco Plain Packaging) Bill 2011* (Cth). The House of Representatives Standing Committee on Health and Ageing held an inquiry into the plain packaging of tobacco products and published a report.[3] The Senate Legal and Constitutional Committee heard submissions on the *Trade Marks Amendment (Tobacco Plain Packaging) Bill 2011* (Cth) and wrote a report supporting the introduction of the measures.[4]

The chief advocate for the plain packaging of tobacco products was Nicola Roxon – first as Minister for Health and Ageing, and then as the Attorney-General of Australia.[5] In July 2011, Nicola Roxon introduced the *Tobacco Plain Packaging Bill 2011* (Cth) and the *Trade Marks Amendment (Tobacco Plain Packaging) Bill 2011* (Cth). She commented: 'This is a world-first initiative, designed to remove the last vestige of glamour from tobacco products'.[6] She contended: 'Plain packaging will remove one of the last remaining forms of tobacco advertising in Australia' and 'will restrict tobacco industry logos, brand imagery, colours and promotional text'.[7] Roxon discussed the olive colouring of the packaging: 'The packaging will be mandated to appear in a standard, drab dark-brown colour, which has been chosen based on research for the lowest appeal to smokers'.[8] Roxon commented:

> An update to the current graphic health warnings to increase the coverage on the front of the pack from the current 30 per cent to 75 per cent, along with updated imagery and warnings, will accompany the introduction of plain packaging so that, rather than being a marketing tool, the pack will only serve as a stark reminder of the devastating health effects of smoking.[9]

The Coalition of the Liberal Party and the National Party were divided on the topic of plain packaging of tobacco products. Three distinct positions were discernible. There was evidently a division between those politicians who favoured public health measures such as tobacco control, those who were keen to pragmatically deny the Australian Labor Party a victory on any policy topic, and those who supported the tobacco industry and opposed plain packaging of tobacco products. For the Coalition, Dr Andrew Southcott, the Liberal member for Boothby, a medical doctor and a proponent of health regulation, made one of the most thoughtful speeches in the Australian Parliament.[10] He stressed that 'the Coalition therefore supports plain packaging and the public health intent behind this proposal'.[11] In the end, the Coalition resolved to support the plain packaging of tobacco products, albeit with procedural objections about regulations accompanying the regime. The leader of the Coalition Opposition, Tony Abbott, acknowledged, 'This is an important health measure. It's important to get smoking rates down further'.[12]

The Australian Greens also supported the measure of plain packaging of tobacco products. In his second reading speech, Richard di Natale, health spokesman for the Australian Greens, discussed the significance of the plain packaging of tobacco products.[13] He reflected upon his experience as a general practitioner and a public health specialist dealing with the human costs of tobacco.[14] Richard di Natale complained of tobacco advertising on plain packaging: 'They are little billboards of nastiness, advertising their wares to passers-by – from pockets, from kitchen tables, on dashboards of cars – all round the country'.[15] di Natale was of the view that the measure of plain packaging would be an effective means of addressing tobacco addiction: 'In short, this bill aims to ensure that the packet of cigarettes is as ugly as the product itself'.[16] The Australian Greens argued that the Australian Parliament should go further in its efforts to address tobacco control. Richard di Natale argued that there was a need to regulate donations by the tobacco industry to political parties in Australia. He also maintained that the Future Fund should be banned from making tobacco investments.[17]

After the passage of the legislation through the Australian Parliament, Japan Tobacco International[18] and British American Tobacco[19] brought legal action in the High Court of Australia, complaining that the *Tobacco Plain Packaging Act 2011* (Cth) amounted to an acquisition of property on less than just terms under s 51(xxxi) of the *Australian Constitution*. Philip Morris Ltd and Imperial Tobacco intervened in the case[20] and supported their fellow tobacco companies.

The Australian federal government defended the constitutionality of the *Tobacco Plain Packaging Act 2011* (Cth).[21] In its defence, the Commonwealth was supported by the governments of the Australian Capital Territory,[22] the Northern Territory[23] and Queensland.[24] The Cancer Council Australia made written submissions[25] but was not given leave to intervene.[26]

The High Court of Australia heard arguments over three days from 17 to 19 April 2012.[27] The various parties enlisted battalions of lawyers. The proceedings received intense media attention, and the public galleries were packed.

On 15 August 2012, the High Court of Australia rejected the challenges by tobacco companies to the validity of the *Tobacco Plain Packaging Act 2011* (Cth) and awarded costs against them.[28] On 5 October 2012, the High Court of Australia published the reasons for its decision in respect of the challenge by Big Tobacco to Australia's regime for the plain packaging of tobacco products.[29] The High Court of Australia ruled in favour of the Australian government by a landslide majority of six to one. The majority was formed by judgments by French CJ, Gummow J, Hayne and Bell JJ, Kiefel J, and Crennan J. The judges rejected the arguments of the tobacco companies that there had been an acquisition of property on other than just terms under the *Australian Constitution*.[30] The judges variously described the case of the tobacco companies as 'delusive', 'synthetic', 'unreal' and suffering 'fatal' defects in logic and reasoning.[31] There was a dissenting judgment by Heydon J.

This chapter considers the politics of intellectual property in an examination of the Australian domestic conflict over the plain packaging of tobacco products. It focuses upon the written submissions and the oral arguments of the parties,[32] and the ruling of the High Court of Australia in the case of *JT International SA v Commonwealth; British American Tobacco Australasia Ltd v Commonwealth*.[33] This chapter deals with several themes. First, it considers the historical exploration by the High Court of Australia of health regulation, the use of health warnings, and tobacco control. Second, it considers the emphasis placed by the High Court of Australia on the importance of public policy in the interpretation of intellectual property law, policy and administration. Third, it provides a detailed examination of the High Court of Australia's consideration of the question of acquisition of property on just terms under constitutional law. Finally, this chapter contends that the ruling of the High Court of Australia will spark an 'Olive Revolution' – in which other countries will follow the lead of Australia and mandate the plain packaging of tobacco products.

2 'The skull and crossbones for the digital age': public health warnings and tobacco control

In written submissions and oral argument, the Commonwealth government mounted a strong defence of the legality and constitutionality of the plain packaging of tobacco products.[34] Their submissions explained that the measures were 'directed to informing, redressing and reducing harm to the public health that is caused by use of the tobacco products'.[35]

In its submission, the Commonwealth provides an overview of the public policy objectives served by the introduction of the plain packaging of tobacco products. Citing the work of the World Health Organization, and the reports of the Royal College of Physicians of London and the United States Surgeon General, the Australian government stressed that smoking tobacco products caused great harm.[36] The Commonwealth noted:

> Smoking is estimated to have killed 900,000 Australians from 1950 (when reports identifying smoking as a cause of lung cancer first began to emerge) to 2008 and annually in Australia, as at 2004–2005, to have caused about 15,000 deaths and to have cost about 750,000 bed days.[37]

The Australian government was worried that the tobacco industry targeted youth: 'Adolescence and young adulthood is a time when people are "uniquely susceptible" to influences to use tobacco and further when, in almost all cases, the process of addiction to cigarettes begins'.[38] The Commonwealth referred to the strong body of research on the efficacy of plain packaging.[39]

The Commonwealth argued that there was a long history of the use of health warnings, product standards and information standards by the government: 'There is also a very long history of the statutory regulation of the packaging and labelling of all sorts of products (including food, poisons, therapeutic goods, agricultural products, children's toys and industrial chemicals)'.[40] The Commonwealth noted that there have been previous instances of restricting sale to products in plain packaging. There was discussion of the *Margarine Act 1887* (UK),[41] which required the plain packaging of margarine and margarine-cheese. There was also a discussion of a plain packaging requirement in the media classification scheme in Australia under the *Classification (Publications, Films and Computer Games) Act 1995* (Cth), and accompanying state and territory enforcement legislation.

The Solicitor-General for the Commonwealth Stephen Gageler argued: 'This legislation is no different in principle from any other specification of a product standard or an information standard for products or, indeed, services that are to become the subject of trade in the future'.[42] He observed, 'The product information required to be placed on these products differs only in intensity from product information that is routinely mandated to accompany therapeutic goods, industrial chemicals, poisons and other products injurious to the public health'.[43] He commented, 'The mandatory graphic health warnings are the skull and crossbones for a digital age, nothing more'.[44]

The Solicitor-General said that 'to suggest that the tobacco packages become little billboards for government advertising is wrong'.[45] He denied the government was engaged in advertising, or derived any such benefit, and contended that a regulatory norm of conduct was not an acquisition of property. The government stressed the sale and packaging of cigarettes had long been regulated in Australia, and that plain packaging was but the latest step in this process.

Walker SC for Imperial Tobacco argued that a distinction could be drawn between health warnings and government advertising.[46] He maintained that there is a:

> difference between a message which can regulate commerce or sale or trade and can require trade packages to carry those regulatory statements, call them warnings or information, on the one hand, and on the other hand packages in lawful trade … which are required by the Commonwealth to carry the political admonition, you should not smoke.[47]

Walker observed: 'There is nothing wrong with advertising as a method of government getting their messages over, whether it be to eat more fresh food, to be involved in physical exercise or any other health message'. However, he objected to

> a trader who is told in order to comply with the law you must provide at your expense the messages chosen by the government from time to time overtly intended to prevent people – the word used is "discourage" – is to discourage people, put them off buying at all.[48]

Walker warned of the government engaging in advertising on packaging – 'one only has to see products in the market that are consumer kind, whether they be soft drink bottles, t-shirts or, we would say, cigarette packs, to know that those are obvious opportunities for bonsai billboards'.[49]

During the case, there were frequent comparisons between warnings on Ratsak poison[50] and health warnings on tobacco products. On the first day of oral argument, Crennan J asked Griffith QC, a barrister for Japan Tobacco International: 'Well, what about Ratsak, it could be a trademark?'[51] Crennan J wondered: 'Is there anything wrong with the law providing that you have to add to any label certain instructions as to what to do if humans, including children, accidentally ingest it?'[52] Hayne J asked a barrister for British American Tobacco: 'What is the difference between that and requiring the vendor of Ratsak to inscribe on the pack in type of a particular size, "Keep out of the reach of children"?'[53] On the second day, the Solicitor-General responded:

> If you say as a prescription for the sale of Ratsak that it cannot be packaged in a way that is attractive to children it would be incongruous to compensate a seller of Ratsak for being unable to continue to use the machine that makes the packaging that is attractive to children.[54]

On the third day, Griffith QC, the barrister for Japan Tobacco International invited the seven judges of the High Court of Australia to inspect the labelling on Ratsak, which he had bought at a local shop.[55] He commented: 'Your Honour, our point is as, of course, proprietors of poisonous substances have marks, here it is only this top corner, there is nothing else on the pack about usage; there are warnings'.[56] The Chief Justice declined the opportunity to inspect the poison.

The High Court of Australia closely considered the public health objectives of the plain packaging of tobacco products. In a compelling history of public health and tobacco control, Kiefel J commented that '[t]he objects of the Packaging Act include the improvement of public health by discouraging persons from using tobacco products'.[57] She noted that the *Tobacco Plain Packaging Act 2011* (Cth) 'seeks to achieve that object by further reducing the attractiveness of the packaging of the products and the recall of brand name and other distinctive marks'.[58] Kiefel J observed: 'Whether that object will be largely achieved cannot presently be known'.[59]

Contextualising the question at stake in the litigation, Kiefel J commented: 'Many kinds of products have been subjected to regulation in order to prevent or reduce the likelihood of harm'.[60] She observed: 'The labelling required for medicines and poisonous substances comes immediately to mind'.[61] To illustrate the point, she referred to the *Therapeutic Goods Order No 69 – General Requirements for Labels for Medicines* and the *Poisons Standard 2012*, both made under the *Therapeutic Goods Act 1989* (Cth). Kiefel J also noted: 'Labelling is also required for certain foods, to both protect and promote public health'.[62] She cited as an example the *Food Standards Australia New Zealand Act 1991* (Cth) and the *Australia New Zealand Food Standards Code*, Standard 1.2.1, Application of Labelling and Other Information Requirements. Kiefel J also noted that art 8(1) of the TRIPS Agreement[63] provides that:

> members of the World Trade Organization 'may, in formulating or amend-ing their laws and regulations, adopt measures necessary to protect public health and nutrition, and to promote the public interest in sectors of vital importance to their socio-economic and technological development,

provided the measures are consistent with TRIPS'.[64]

Providing a history of tobacco regulation in Australia, Kiefel J observed: 'In recent decades, there has been a progressive restriction of the promotion of tobacco products, which, although remaining legal to sell and use, have been recognised as seriously harmful to the health of those using them'.[65] Her Honour noted: 'The Commonwealth and the plaintiffs are agreed that one consequence of the level of restriction of advertising of tobacco products has been that the packaging of these products has become the main means of their promotion'.[66] Kiefel J provided a portrait of the progressive tightening of advertising and packaging restrictions on tobacco in Australia – tracing such landmarks as the introduc-tion of health warnings in 1973; the prohibition on the broadcasting of tobacco advertisements in 1976; and the 1990 prohibition on tobacco advertisements in the print media. She also noted:

> Legislation in the States and Territories has prohibited certain forms of the advertising of tobacco products since the 1980s and from the 1990s has pro-hibited or restricted the promotion of tobacco products at the point of retail sale, including by the display of such products.[67]

Her Honour emphasised that further restrictions were added in the new millennium:

> Under the 2011 Information Standard a cigarette pack must contain: on its front, a 'Warning Statement' and a 'Graphic'; on its back, a 'Warning Statement', a 'Graphic' and an 'Explanatory message'; and, on one of its sides, an 'Information message'.[68]

Crennan J noted that 'smoking tobacco is a cause of serious and fatal diseases such as lung cancer, respiratory disease and heart disease and that the risk of contracting such diseases is reduced by quitting smoking'.[69] She observed: 'The objects of the Packaging Act are to improve public health and to give effect to certain obligations that Australia has as a party to the World Health Organization Framework Convention on Tobacco Control'.[70] She observed that '[i]mproving public health encompasses discouraging people from taking up or resuming smoking or using tobacco products, encouraging people to give up smoking or using tobacco products, and reducing people's exposure to smoke from tobacco products'.[71]

Crennan J noted that the ambition of the Commonwealth:

> is to contribute to achieving these objects by regulating the retail packaging and appearance of tobacco products to reduce the appeal of such products to consumers, to increase the effectiveness of health warnings on the packaging of such products and to reduce the ability of the retail packaging of the products to mislead consumers about the harmful effects of smoking or using tobacco products.[72]

Crennan J commented:

> The plaintiffs' ability to place material on their packaging is and has for a long period been limited by law. Legislative provisions requiring manufacturers or retailers to place on product packaging warnings to consumers of the dangers of incorrectly using or positively misusing a product are commonplace. In these cases, the warnings are in relation to the intended use of the tobacco products, namely smoking, the effect of which activity has been the subject of admissions by the plaintiffs, as recorded above. Any decision of the plaintiffs to continue to sell tobacco products in retail packaging which complies with more stringent product and information standards, directed to providing more prominent information about tobacco goods, does not involve any diminution in or extinguishment of any property.[73]

Crennan J emphasised that the current regulatory regime of stringent product and information standards does not involve the acquisition of property under the *Australian Constitution*.

Hayne and Bell JJ commented: 'Statutory requirements for warning labels on goods will presumably always be intended to achieve some benefit: usually the avoidance of or reduction in harm'.[74]

Gummow J also considered the objectives of the plain packaging regime:

> Parliament desires to contribute to achievement of those objects by regulating the retail packaging and appearance of tobacco products to reduce their appeal to consumers, increasing the effectiveness of health warnings thereon and reducing the ability of retail packaging to mislead consumers about the harmful effects of using tobacco products.[75]

He also observed: 'Another object stated in s 3(1) is the giving of effect to certain obligations upon Australia as a party to the WHO Framework Convention on Tobacco Control, done at Geneva on 21 May 2003'.[76]

Even the dissenting judge, Heydon J, described tobacco manufacturers as purveyors of 'lies and death'.[77] Heydon J, though, maintained that 'improving (local) public health is not the fundamental concern of the impugned legislation'.[78] He argued: 'Its fundamental concern is to avoid paying money to those who will be damaged if that desire to improve (local) public health is gratified in the manner which the legislation envisages'.[79] Given the international and national origins of plain packaging of tobacco products, it would seem contrarian to deny that plain packaging was primarily a public health measure.

3 Intellectual property and public policy

An important theme of the ruling is that intellectual property law serves larger public policy considerations – it is not merely an instrument of private rights-holders.[80]

The tobacco companies adopted an ideological position of intellectual property maximalism, asserting that the purpose of intellectual property law was one of protecting private rights. Professor Peter Drahos has called such a credos 'proprietarianism': 'Proprietarianism is a creed which says the possessor should take all, that ownership privileges should trump community interests and that the world and its contents are open to ownership'.[81] Deploying rhetoric about piracy and counterfeiting,[82] the tobacco companies hoped that intellectual property rights would block government regulation in respect of tobacco control.

It was striking that the tobacco companies relied upon a wide range of species of intellectual property to protect their tobacco products. British American Tobacco – who sold the Winfield line of packets – claimed ownership of registered and unregistered trade marks relating to tobacco products and the packaging of tobacco products.[83] The tobacco company also claimed copyright in 'artistic and literary works' – including the packaging for 'Winfield Optimum Night', 'Winfield Blue', 'Winfield Red', 'Winfield Silver' and 'Winfield Gold'. This is contentious – given that copyright law is being used here to protect utilitarian works.[84] British American Tobacco also asserted that it had two patents registered pursuant to the *Patents Act 1990* (Cth).[85] There has been much debate about absurd patent applications in the last decade.[86] And in this case, British American Tobacco revealed that it has filed patent applications for packages for tobacco products. For instance, British American Tobacco has registered a patent for a 'soft cup package for tobacco products'.[87] What is novel, inventive or useful about a soft cup package for tobacco products? Patent law should be encouraging the progress of science and the useful arts – treatments and therapies for cancer, for instance – rather than cigarette boxes. British American Tobacco also noted that its trade dress and get-up for tobacco products could be protected under passing off. The company also claimed a design registered under the *Designs Act 2003* (Cth) for a 'ribbed pack'.[88]

Japan Tobacco International – which sold the Camel brand of cigarettes and the Old Holborn brand of hand rolled tobacco – relied upon both trade mark rights and an action for passing off and misleading and deceptive conduct in relation to its get-up.[89] In their various interventions, Philip Morris and Imperial Tobacco also made similar arguments – trying to boost their case with a bundle of intellectual property rights.[90] The tobacco companies argued that such various intellectual property rights had been acquired by the Commonwealth government with the advent of the plain packaging regime.

In its submission, the Commonwealth government argued that intellectual property rights served larger public purposes:

> The statutory rights created by the *Trade Marks Act 1995* (Cth), *Patents Act 1990* (Cth), *Designs Act 2003* (Cth) and *Copyright Act 1968* (Cth) … are susceptible to modification or extinguishment at least for the purpose of preventing or reducing harm to the public or public health.[91]

The Commonwealth maintained:

> The rights are intended at least in part to benefit the public, and, in respect of patents, copyright and designs, may involve new developments pushing the boundaries of knowledge, science or technology, the dangers or disadvantages of which may only become apparent over the course of time.[92]

Indeed, the Commonwealth noted that art 8 of the TRIPS Agreement recognised that 'members may, in formulating or amending their laws and regulations, adopt measures necessary to protect public health and nutrition'.[93]

In the plain packaging decision, the High Court of Australia emphasised the importance of public policy in matters of intellectual property law. In his judgment, French CJ emphasised the public policy dimensions of intellectual property law:

> There are and always have been purposive elements reflecting public policy considerations which inform the statutory creation of intellectual property rights. The public policy dimensions of trade mark legislation and the contending interests which such dimensions accommodate were referred to in

Campomar Sociedad, Limitada v Nike International Ltd. The observation in that case that Australian trade marks law has 'manifested from time to time a varying accommodation of commercial and the consuming public's interests' has application with varying degrees of intensity to other intellectual property rights created by statute. Intellectual property laws create property rights. They are also instrumental in character.[94]

French CJ cited Professor Peter Drahos' view that the interpretation of intellectual property does not depend upon 'diffuse moral notions about the need to protect pre-legal expectations based on the exercise of labour and the creation of value'.[95] His Honour commented:

> The statutory purpose, reflected in the character of such rights and in the conditions informing their creation, may be relevant to the question whether and in what circumstances restriction or regulation of their enjoyment by a law of the Commonwealth amounts to acquisition of property for the purposes of s 51(xxxi) of the *Constitution*.[96]

French CJ outlined the various species of intellectual property rights – trade mark law,[97] copyright law,[98] patent law,[99] designs law[100] and passing off – and highlighted the public policy objectives that they were intended to serve. He also emphasised in his broad overview the limitations and boundaries to intellectual property law. French CJ stressed that intellectual property rights are created by statute in order to 'serve public purposes':

> Registered trade marks, designs, patents and copyright in works and other subject matter give rise to, or constitute, exclusive rights which are property to which s 51(xxxi) of the Constitution can apply. They are all rights which are created by statute in order to serve public purposes. They differ in their histories, their character and the statutory schemes which make provision for them.[101]

French CJ emphasised that intellectual property rights are negative in character – they do not provide positive rights to use goods and services: 'It is a common feature of the statutory rights asserted in these proceedings that they are negative in character'.[102] He cited a number of authorities on intellectual property being a purely negative right – including *Pacific Film Laboratories Pty Ltd v Federal Commissioner of Taxation* for copyright law,[103] *Steers v Rogers*[104] and the *Grain Pool of Western Australia v Commonwealth*[105] on patent law, and Laddie, Prescott and Vitoria generally on intellectual property.[106]

In his judgment, Gummow J commented that the case of the tobacco companies suffers from a 'delusive exactness'.[107] To put it more bluntly, he suggested that the tobacco companies are deluded in treating property rights the same as intellectual property rights – without due regard for their distinctive character.[108] Gummow J was concerned that the tobacco companies sought to elide property rights and intellectual property rights. His Honour gave consideration to the special character of intellectual property. He observed: 'What primarily is at stake is the utilisation of the remaining space on the front of tobacco packages for the display of trade marks and product get-up without the restraints imposed by the Packaging Act'.[109] In his judgment, Gummow J made the important point that trade mark law does not confer a crude 'statutory monopoly':

> The issues which are presented in these cases respecting the 'taking' and 'acquisition' of proprietary interests are to be approached with an appreciation that trade mark legislation, in general, does not confer a 'statutory monopoly' in any crude sense. Rather, the legislation represents an accommodation between the interests of traders, in the use of trade marks in developing the goodwill of their businesses and turning this to account by licensing arrangements, and the interests of consumers, in recognising trade marks as a badge of origin of goods or services and avoiding deception or confusion as to that origin.[110]

Gummow J commented that 'trade mark registration systems ordinarily do not confer a liberty to use the trade mark, free from what may be restraints found in other statutes or in the general law'.[111] He cited *New South Wales Dairy Corp v Murray Goulburn Co-op Co Ltd*,[112] where Deane J observed that the 'registration of a trade mark does not ordinarily constitute a licence for what would otherwise be unlawful conduct'.[113] Gummow J reiterated that the *Trade Marks Act 1995* (Cth), 'like other trade mark legislation, does not confer on registered owners or authorised users a liberty to use registered trade marks free from restraints found in other statutes'.[114]

In her judgment, Crennan J offered a useful and helpful analysis of the semiotics of tobacco packaging. Her Honour provided a short history of the evolution of trade mark law and the rights and interests of a trade mark owner. Considering the substance and reality of proprietorship, Crennan J considered the role and function of trade mark law:

> Whilst the prime concern of the *Trade Marks Act* is with the capacity of a trade mark to distinguish the goods of the registered owner from those of another trader, trade marks undoubtedly perform other functions. For example, a trade mark can be an indicium of the quality of goods sold under or by reference to it and it may be accepted that distinctive marks can have a capacity to advertise, and therefore to promote, sales of products sold under or by reference to them. The advertising function of a trade mark is much more readily appreciated than it once was, and that function may be of great commercial value.[115]

Crennan J provided a thoughtful consideration of the semiotics of trade marks. Her Honour noted:

> Whilst potential assignees and licensees of registered trade marks may value, even highly, the advertising function of a trade mark, or associated product get-up, an exclusive right to generate a volume of sales of goods by reference to a distinctive brand name is a valuable right.[116]

Crennan J concluded that the *Tobacco Plain Packaging Act 2011* (Cth)

> restrictions, which effectively prohibit the plaintiffs from using their property for advertising or promotional purposes, while severe from a commercial viewpoint, do not operate so as to effect an acquisition of any proprietary right or interest by the Commonwealth, or by the owner of the Quitline services or trade mark.[117]

Kiefel J emphasised, too, that trade mark law provides negative rights, not positive rights, to a trade mark owner:

> Strictly speaking, the right subsisting in the owner of a trade mark is a negative and not a positive right. It is to be understood as a right to exclude others from using the mark and cannot be viewed as separate from the trade in connection with which it is used. It is for the protection of that trade in goods that property is recognised in a trade mark.[118]

She stressed, like Crennan J, that the legislation preserved the trade mark rights of the trade mark holders against allegations of non-use and that the trade mark was contrary to law.[119]

In his dissent, Heydon J maintained that the Commonwealth had acquired the intellectual property rights of the tobacco companies. His Honour argued that '[t]he Commonwealth acquired the right to have the cigarette packets of each proprietor presented in the course of trade in the get-up of its choice'.[120] In his view, '[t]he rights the Commonwealth acquired substantially correspond with those the proprietors lost'.[121] Heydon J commented: 'A newly acquired right arose in the Commonwealth to command the publication of messages it desires to have sent, without charge, to the public'.[122] His Honour very much conflates and confuses property rights and intellectual property rights. As such, his analysis can be quite artificial – especially in imputing rights of control to the Commonwealth.

The ruling of the High Court of Australia may be influential in other controversies over intellectual property and public health – such as the disputes over gene patents,[123] and access to essential medicines.[124]

4 The bedrock principle: Australian constitutional law and the acquisition of property on just terms

The tobacco companies challenged the validity of the *Tobacco Plain Packaging Act 2011* (Cth) under s 51(xxxi) of the *Australian Constitution*, which empowers the

Parliament to make laws with respect to 'the acquisition of property on just terms'. With much bluff and bluster, the tobacco industry and its allies argued that the plain packaging of tobacco products would amount to an acquisition of property and require billions of dollars of compensation. The right-wing think tank the Institute of Public Affairs outlandishly warned: 'The Federal Parliament should deeply consider whether they are prepared to gift up to $3 billion annually to big tobacco to pass plain packaging for tobacco products'.[125]

Foreshadowing his arguments in the High Court, British American Tobacco advocate, Myers QC, asserted that 'the *Trade Marks Amendment Bill* and the *Trade Marks Amendment (Tobacco Plain Packaging) Bill* are unfair and badly drafted' and 'will cause harm within Australia and will damage Australia's international standing without any proven countervailing benefits'.[126] He argued that the legislation amounted to an acquisition of property without just compensation: the law 'does not just diminish the value of the trade mark; it diminishes the value because it prevents the exercise of the property right – that is, to use the trade mark in association with one's goods'.[127] Myers QC maintained that the legislation would be in breach of the TRIPS Agreement and the *Paris Convention for the Protection of Industrial Property*.[128] He also questioned whether the WHO FCTC necessitated the introduction of plain packaging legislation.

In court, tobacco companies struggled with their argument that the introduction of the plain packaging of tobacco products amounted to an acquisition of property on other than just terms. There was much discussion as to whether the Commonwealth had indeed effected an 'acquisition' of the tobacco trade marks. Japan Tobacco International's barrister, Griffith QC, argued: 'The Commonwealth law by its terms abrogates the power to substitute any message the Commonwealth chooses on what we say is our billboard'.[129] The tobacco companies argued for a broad view of property under the *Australian Constitution*, and claimed to hold various forms of intellectual property in relation to tobacco packaging, including trade marks, patents, designs, copyright and passing off. Their barristers said the intellectual property rights of tobacco companies had been extinguished, or at least severely impaired. Griffith QC said: 'On our analysis, everything has been taken'.[130]

Authorities in constitutional law and intellectual property law were sceptical of such aggressive demands for compensation under the acquisition of property on just terms clause.[131] In his article, 'Plainly Constitutional', Jonathan Liberman provided a useful analysis and summary of key themes in the judgments on acquisition of property and public health.[132] He commented that the majority were unconvinced by a number of the creative arguments by the tobacco industry about acquisition of property:

> On analysis, a number of these arguments strike as somewhere on the spectrum between tortuous and absurd, particularly those that assert that it is the very pursuit or achievement of the objects of the legislation that should entitle the tobacco companies to 'just terms' and thus render the legislation invalid.[133]

The Commonwealth argued that there had been no acquisition of property under the plain packaging of tobacco products regime.[134] The Commonwealth noted that 'taking of property is not acquisition of property'.[135] The Commonwealth maintained: 'Neither improving public health nor giving effect to international obligations can possibly be described as a benefit in the nature of property to another person'.[136] Moreover, nor could 'reducing the appeal of tobacco products or reducing the potential for retail packaging to mislead'.[137]

The Solicitor-General also argued that the concept of just terms raised larger questions of fairness and justice under the *Australian Constitution*. The Commonwealth maintained that it would be incongruous to compensate the tobacco industry:

> For the Australian nation representing the Australian community to be required to compensate tobacco companies for the loss resulting from no longer being able to continue in the harmful use of their property goes beyond the requirements of any reasonable notion of fairness.[138]

The Attorney-General for the Australian Capital Territory made a lively submission as an intervener.[139] The Territory observed that 'it would make no sense to hold that just terms should be provided for' ... 'an inherently injurious and potentially lethal product' which 'may mislead the public as to the dangers of that product'.[140]

The majority of the High Court of Australia held that the plain packaging regime did not amount to an acquisition of property. This ruling is consistent with past precedents on intellectual property and constitutional law, such as the *Grain Pool* case,[141] the *Nintendo* case[142] and the *Phonographic* ruling.[143] The tobacco industry could not rely on the slender obiter dictum in the *Blank Tapes* case.[144]

In a judgment notable for its clarity and precision, Hayne and Bell JJ outlined the bedrock principle in the case on the acquisition of property:

> It is well established that s 51(xxxi) is concerned with matters of substance rather than form and that 'acquisition' and 'property' are to be construed liberally. It is equally well established that 'acquisition' is to be understood as a 'compound' conception, namely 'acquisition-on-just-terms'. But allowing, as one must, ample meaning to 'acquisition' and 'property' in s 51(xxxi), there remains a bedrock principle. There can be no acquisition of property without 'the Commonwealth or another acquir[ing] an interest in property, however slight or insubstantial it may be'. Giving a liberal construction to 'acquisition' and 'property' does not, and must not, erode the bedrock established by the text of s 51(xxxi): there must be an *acquisition* of *property*.[145]

The judges also warned against reading cases on acquisition of property out of context: 'It must be emphasised, however, that it would be wrong to take what has been said in earlier decisions, or in these reasons, and divorce the statement from the context in which it appears'.[146] Hayne and Bell JJ stressed:

'Above all, it must be recognised that it is the constitutional text and the cardinal principles that emerge from that text to which attention must always be given'.[147] The judges emphasised: 'It is the constitutional text and the fundamental principles based on that text which must guide consideration of the issue'.[148]

Hayne and Bell JJ commented that the *Tobacco Plain Packaging Act 2011* (Cth) 'neither permits nor requires the Commonwealth to use the packaging as advertising space'.[149] Moreover, '[t]he Commonwealth makes no public announcement promoting or advertising anything'.[150] Hayne and Bell JJ observed: 'But the benefit or advantage that results from the tobacco companies complying with the TPP Act is not proprietary'.[151] Hayne and Bell JJ concluded that the *Tobacco Plain Packaging Act 2011* (Cth) 'is not a law by which the Commonwealth acquires any "interest in property, however slight or insubstantial it may be"'.[152] The judges held that the *Tobacco Plain Packaging Act 2011* (Cth) 'is not a law with respect to the *acquisition* of property'.[153] Hayne and Bell JJ emphasised: 'The Commonwealth acquires no property as a result of their compliance with the TPP Act'.[154]

Two judges were of the view that, whilst there had not been an acquisition of property, there may have been a taking.[155]

On the question of acquisition of property, French CJ discussed the difference between taking and acquisition of property. On his view, '[t]aking involves deprivation of property seen from the perspective of its owner'.[156] By contrast, '[a]cquisition involves receipt of something seen from the perspective of the acquirer'.[157] French CJ observed: 'On no view can it be said that the Commonwealth as a polity or by any authority or instrumentality, has acquired any benefit of a proprietary character by reason of the operation of the TPP Act on the plaintiffs' property rights'.[158]

Quoting Supreme Court of Canada authority Binnie J from *Mattel Inc v 3894207 Canada Inc*,[159] Gummow J noted that registered trade marks operated 'as a kind of shortcut to get consumers to where they want to go, and in that way perform a key function in a market economy'.[160] He commented: 'The system established by the Packaging Act is designed to give the opposite effect to trade mark use, namely by encouraging consumers to turn away from tobacco products even if that otherwise is where they would "want to go"'.[161] Gummow J observed: 'The result is that while the trade marks remain on the face of the register, their value and utility for assignment and licensing is very substantially impaired'.[162] His Honour concluded that 'there is sufficient impairment, at least of the statutory intellectual property of the plaintiffs, to amount to a "taking", but there is no acquisition of any property'.[163]

Crennan J noted:

> Given the nature of the plaintiffs' pre-existing rights to use their property for advertising or promotional purposes, restricting or extinguishing those rights, with a possible consequential diminution in the value of the property or the associated businesses, did not constitute a taking amounting to an indirect acquisition.[164]

Kiefel J held: 'The central statutory object of the Packaging Act is to dissuade persons from using tobacco products'.[165] She observed: 'If that object were to be effective, the plaintiffs' businesses may be harmed, but the Commonwealth does not thereby acquire something in the nature of property itself'.[166]

In a dissent, Heydon J complained generally about the government encroaching upon the acquisition of property clause:

> After a 'great' constitutional case, the tumult and the shouting dies. The captains and the kings depart. Or at least the captains do; the Queen in Parliament remains forever. Solicitors-General go. New Solicitors-General come. This world is transitory. But some things never change. The flame of the Commonwealth's hatred for that beneficial constitutional guarantee, s 51(xxxi), may flicker, but it will not die. That is why it is eternally important to ensure that that flame does not start a destructive blaze.[167]

The fear in the dissent seems to be that the Commonwealth would seek to conspire and engage in over-reaching regulation – without a strong reading of the acquisition of property clause. The reasoning in the judgment, though, lacks clarity. The six majority judges were quite careful to emphasise that the ruling did not address the larger question of the government's power to engage in regulation of other activities for the greater good of society.

5 Conclusion: the olive revolution

As a result of the decision of the High Court of Australia, Australia will no longer be 'Marlboro Country',[168] the victim of packaging and advertising by the Mad Men of Big Tobacco.[169] The High Court of Australia ruling on the plain packaging of tobacco products is one of the great constitutional cases of the age. The decision will rightfully join the canon of landmark Australian constitutional cases[170] – such as the *Bank Nationalisation* case,[171] the *Franklin Dam* decision[172] and the *Mabo* case.[173] Equally comfortably, the case belongs to the canon of landmark Australian intellectual property cases.[174] The decision will be a touchstone of matters of public health – particularly in relation to the regulation of advertising, packaging and labelling. The decision is consistent with other superior courts dealing with questions of tobacco control. In a 2007 case, *Attorney-General v JTI-MacDonald Corp*, the Supreme Court of Canada noted: 'When commercial expression is used … for the purpose of inducing people to engage in harmful and addictive behaviour, its value becomes tenuous'.[175] In 2012, the South African Supreme Court[176] defended regulations on tobacco advertising under the WHO FCTC. The ruling will reinforce the position of Australia in respect of international conflicts over the plain packaging of tobacco products. The ruling is also of international significance – given the battles over the plain packaging of tobacco products in global fora, such as the World Health Organization, the World Trade Organization, investment tribunals and trade negotiations, such as the Trans-Pacific Partnership.[177] The decision has also given encouragement to other countries to join an 'Olive Revolution' and introduce plain packaging of tobacco products.[178]

Notes

1 Matthew Weiner, AMC, 'Smoke Gets in Your Eyes', *Mad Men*, Season 1, Episode 1, 19 July 2007 <http://www.imdb.com/title/tt1059578/>.

2 *WHO Framework Convention on Tobacco Control*, opened for signature 16 June 2003, 2302 UNTS 166 (entered into force 27 February 2005) ('WHO FCTC').

3 House Standing Committee on Health and Ageing, *Advisory Report on the Tobacco Plain Packaging Bill 2011 and the Trade Marks Amendment (Tobacco Plain Packaging) Bill 2011* (Parliament of Australia, 2011).

4 Senate Legal and Constitutional Affairs Legislation Committee, *Trade Marks Amendment (Tobacco Plain Packaging) Bill 2011* (Parliament of Australia, 2011).

5 For profiles of Nicola Roxon, see Anne Summers, 'The Protector: Nicola Roxon', *The Monthly*, June 2012 <http://www.themonthly.com.au/nicola-roxon-protector-anne-summers-5265>; Australian Broadcasting Corporation, 'Kicking the Habit', *Australian Story* (27 August 2012) <http://www.abc.net.au/austory/specials/kicking-thehabit/default.htm>. See also Nicola Roxon, 'Why Are Plain Packs Making Big Tobacco So Angry? Australia's World Leading Work to Combat Smoking' (Speech delivered at Georgetown University Law Center, Washington, DC, 17 May 2012); Nicola Roxon, 'Goodbye to All That: Why I Resigned', *The Monthly*, March 2013 < http://www.themonthly.com.au/why-i-resigned-goodbye-all-nicola-roxon-7640>.

6 The Hon. Nicola Roxon, 'Second Reading Speech on the *Tobacco Plain Packaging Bill 2011* (Cth)', Hansard, House of Representatives, 6 July 2011, 7708.

7 Ibid.

8 Ibid.

9 Ibid.

10 The Hon. Andrew Southcott, 'Second Reading Speech on the *Tobacco Plain Packaging Bill 2011* (Cth) and the *Trade Marks Amendment (Tobacco Plain Packaging) Bill 2011* (Cth)', Hansard, House of Representatives, Australian Parliament, 24 August 2011, 9163.

11 Ibid.

12 Australian Broadcasting Corporation, 'Tobacco Giants Launch High Court Challenge', *The World Today*, 17 April 2012 <http://www.abc.net.au/worldtoday/content/2012/s3479228.htm>.

13 Senator Richard di Natale, 'Second Reading Speech on *Tobacco Plain Packaging Bill 2011* (Cth) and *Trade Marks Amendment (Tobacco Plain Packaging) Bill 2011* (Cth)', Hansard, Senate, Australian Parliament, 9 November 2011, 8735.

14 Ibid.

15 Ibid.

16 Ibid.

17 Ibid. In 2013, the Future Fund agreed to divest its tobacco stocks, after much community pressure: Matthew Rimmer, 'Future Fund Drops Tobacco: Should Fossil Fuels Be Next?', *The Conversation*, 28 February 2013 <https://theconversation.com/future-fund-drops-tobacco-should-fossil-fuels-be-next-12337>.

18 JT International SA, 'Plaintiff's Submissions in *JT International SA v Commonwealth*', S409/2011, 26 March 2012 <http://www.hcourt.gov.au/assets/cases/s409-2011/JT_Plf.pdf>.

19 British American Tobacco Australasia, 'Submissions of the Plaintiffs in *British American Tobacco Ltd v Commonwealth*', S389/2011, 26 March 2012 <http://www.hcourt.gov.au/assets/cases/s389-2012/BAT_Plf.pdf>.

20 Philip Morris Ltd, 'Philip Morris Ltd's Submissions in *British American Tobacco*

Australasia v Commonwealth', S389/2011, 26 March 2012 <http://www.hcourt.gov.au/assets/cases/s389-2012/BAT_Phillip.pdf>; Van Nelle Tabak Nederland BV and Imperial Tobacco Australia Limited, 'Submissions in *British American Tobacco Australasia Ltd v Commonwealth*, S389/2011, 26 March 2012 <http://www.hcourt.gov.au/assets/cases/s389-2012/BAT_VanNelle.pdf>.

21 Commonwealth, 'Submissions in *British American Tobacco Australasia Ltd v Commonwealth*', S389/2011, 5 April 2012 <http://www.hcourt.gov.au/assets/cases/s389-2012 BAT_Def.pdf>; Commonwealth, 'Submissions in *JT International SA v Commonwealth*', S409/2011, 5 April 2012 <http://www.hcourt.gov.au/assets/cases/s409-2011 JT_Def.pdf>.

22 Attorney-General (ACT), 'Submissions in *British American Tobacco Australasia Ltd v Commonwealth*', S289/2011, 4 April 2012 <http://www.hcourt.gov.au/assets/cases/s389-2012/BAT_AGACT.pdf>.

23 Attorney-General (NT), 'Submissions in *British American Tobacco Australasia Ltd v Commonwealth*', S389/2011, 26 March 2012 <http://www.hcourt.gov.au/assets/cases/s389-2012/BAT_AGNT.pdf>.

24 Attorney-General (Qld), 'Submissions in *British American Tobacco Australasia Ltd v Commonwealth*', S389/2011, 26 March 2012, 2 <http://www.hcourt.gov.au/assets/cases/s389-2012/BAT_AGQld.pdf>.

25 Cancer Council Australia, 'Submissions in *British American Tobacco Australasia Ltd v Commonwealth*', S389/2011, 26 March 2012 <http://www.hcourt.gov.au/assets/cases/s389-2012/BAT_CancerSubs.pdf>; Cancer Council Australia, 'Submissions in *JT International SA v Commonwealth*', S409/2011, 26 March 2012 <http://www.hcourt.gov.au/assets/cases/s389-2012/BAT_CancerSubs.pdf>.

26 Mark Moshinsky SC and Kim Rubenstein, 'Amicus Applications in the High Court – Observations on Contemporary Practice' (Paper presented at Gilbert and Tobin Constitutional Law Conference, 15 February 2013) <http://www.gtcentre.unsw.edu.au/sites/gtcentre.unsw.edu.au/files/moshinsky_and_rubenstein.pdf>. In recent times, there has been a mixed response to amicus curiae interventions in intellectual property matters – *Stevens v Kabushiki Kaisha Sony Computer* (2005) 224 CLR 293; *IceTV Pty Ltd v Nine Network Australia Pty Ltd* (2009) 239 CLR 458; *Roadshow Films Pty Ltd v iiNet Ltd* [2012] HCA 16 (20 April 2012). It is notable that other superior courts – notably, the Supreme Court of the United States – have been somewhat more open to participation of amicus curiae in intellectual property matters: see, for example, *Association for Molecular Pathology v Myriad Genetics, Inc.* 133 US 2017 (2013).

27 Transcript of Proceedings, *JT International SA v Commonwealth; British American Tobacco Australasia Ltd v Commonwealth* [2012] HCATrans 91 (17 April 2012); Transcript of Proceedings, *JT International SA v Commonwealth; British American Tobacco Australasia Ltd v Commonwealth* [2012] HCATrans 92 (18 April 2012); Transcript of Proceedings, *JT International SA v Commonwealth; British American Tobacco Australasia Ltd v Commonwealth* [2012] HCATrans 93 (19 April 2012).

28 High Court of Australia, *JT International SA v Commonwealth; British American Tobacco Australasia Ltd v Commonwealth* (15 August 2012) <http://www.hcourt.gov.au/assets/publications/judgment-summaries/2012/projt-2012-08-15.pdf>.

29 *JT International SA v Commonwealth; British American Tobacco Australasia Ltd v Commonwealth* [2012] HCA 43 (5 October 2012).

30 *Australian Constitution* s 51(xxxi).

31 *JT International SA v Commonwealth; British American Tobacco Australasia Ltd v Commonwealth* [2012] HCA 43 (5 October 2012) [44], [47], [124], [300].

32 Matthew Rimmer, 'Big Tobacco's Box Fetish', *The Conversation*, 20 April 2012 <http://theconversation.edu.au/big-tobaccos-box-fetish-plain-packaging-at-the-high-court-6518>.

33 *JT International SA v Commonwealth; British American Tobacco Australasia Ltd v Commonwealth* [2012] HCA 43 (5 October 2012).

34 Commonwealth, 'Submissions in *British American Tobacco Australasia Ltd v Commonwealth*', S389/2011, 5 April 2012 <http://www.hcourt.gov.au/assets/cases/s389-2012/BAT_Def.pdf>.

35 Ibid.

36 Ibid 7–10.

37 Ibid 10.

38 Ibid 10.

39 Melanie Wakefield has conducted a number of empirical studies on the plain packaging of products and health warnings. See, eg, Melanie Wakefield et al, 'The Cigarette Pack as Image: New Evidence from Tobacco Industry Documents' (2002) 11 *Tobacco Control* 77; Melanie Wakefield, Daniella Germain and Sarah J Durkin, 'How Does Increasingly Plainer Cigarette Packaging Influence Adult Smokers' Perceptions about Brand Image? An Experimental Study' (2008) 17 *Tobacco Control* 416; Daniella Germain, Melanie Wakefield and Sarah Durkin, 'Adolescents' Perceptions of Cigarette Brand Image: Does Plain Packaging Make a Difference?' (2010) 46(4) *Journal of Adolescent Health* 385; Melanie Wakefield et al, 'The Silent Salesman: An Observational Study of Personal Tobacco Pack Display at Outdoor Café Strips in Australia' (2013) *Tobacco Control* <http://tobaccocontrol.bmj.com/content/early/2013/02/19/tobaccocontrol-2012-050740.full>.

40 Commonwealth, 'Submissions in *British American Tobacco Australasia Ltd v Commonwealth*', S389/2011, 5 April 2012, 27 <http://www.hcourt.gov.au/assets/cases/s389-2012/BAT_Def.pdf>.

41 *Margarine Act 1887* (UK) (50 51 Vict C 29).

42 Transcript of Proceedings, *JT International SA v Commonwealth; British American Tobacco Australasia Ltd v Commonwealth* [2012] HCATrans 92 (18 April 2012).

43 Ibid.

44 Ibid.

45 Ibid.

46 Transcript of Proceedings, *JT International SA v Commonwealth; British American Tobacco Australasia Ltd v Commonwealth* [2012] HCATrans 91 (17 April 2012).

47 Ibid.

48 Ibid.

49 Ibid.

50 Ratsak is a poison designed for mice and rats, sold in Australia: see *Ratsak* <http://www.ratsak.com.au/>.

51 Transcript of Proceedings, *JT International SA v Commonwealth; British American Tobacco Australasia Ltd v Commonwealth* [2012] HCATrans 91 (17 April 2012).

52 Ibid.

53 Ibid.

54 Transcript of Proceedings, *JT International SA v Commonwealth; British American Tobacco Australasia Ltd v Commonwealth* [2012] HCATrans 92 (18 April 2012).

55 Transcript of Proceedings, *JT International SA v Commonwealth; British American Tobacco Australasia Ltd v Commonwealth* [2012] HCATrans 93 (19 April 2012).

56 Ibid.

57 *JT International SA v Commonwealth; British American Tobacco Australasia Ltd v Commonwealth* [2012] HCA 43 (5 October 2012) [371].

58 Ibid.

59 Ibid.

60 Ibid [316].

61 Ibid.

62 Ibid.

63 *Marrakesh Agreement Establishing the World Trade Organization*, opened for signature 15 April 1994, 1867 UNTS 3 (entered into force 1 January 1995) annex 1C ('*Agreement on Trade-Related Aspects of Intellectual Property Rights*') ('TRIPS Agreement').

64 *JT International SA v Commonwealth; British American Tobacco Australasia Ltd v Commonwealth* [2012] HCA 43 n 420.

65 Ibid [318].

66 Ibid.

67 Ibid [320].

68 Ibid [323].

69 Ibid [254].

70 Ibid [253].

71 Ibid.

72 Ibid.

73 Ibid [301].

74 Ibid [188].

75 Ibid [145].

76 Ibid [146].

77 Ibid [193].

78 Ibid.

79 Ibid.

80 Sam Ricketson, 'Plain Packaging Legislation for Tobacco Products and Trade Marks in the High Court of Australia' (2013) 3(3) *Queen Mary Journal of Intellectual Property* 224.

81 Peter Drahos, *A Philosophy of Intellectual Property* (Dartmouth Publishing Company, 1996) 202.

82 William Patry, *Moral Panics and the Copyright Wars* (Oxford University Press, 2009).

83 British American Tobacco Australasia, 'Submissions of the Plaintiffs in *British American Tobacco Ltd v Commonwealth*', S389/2011, 26 March 2012 <http://www.hcourt.gov. au/assets/cases/s389-2012/BAT_Plf.pdf>.

84 Jessica Litman complains about the use of copyright law to protect merely utilitarian works: see Jessica Litman, 'The Exclusive Right to Read' (1994) 13(1) *Cardozo Arts and Entertainment Journal* 29.

85 British American Tobacco (Investments) Ltd, *Smoking Article Packaging*, Australian Patent No 2001258572.

86 Adam Jaffe and Josh Lerner, *Innovation and Its Discontents: How Our Broken Patent System is Endangering Innovation and Progress, and What To Do about It* (Princeton University Press, 2004); James Bessen and Michael Meurer, *Patent Failure: How Judges, Bureaucrats and Lawyers Put Innovators at Risk* (Princeton University Press, 2008); Dan Burk and Mark Lemley, *The Patent Crisis and How the Courts Can Solve It* (University of Chicago Press, 2009); Robin Feldman, *Rethinking Patent Law* (Harvard University Press, 2012).

87 British American Tobacco (Investments) Ltd, *A Package for Tobacco Products*, World Intellectual Property Organization Application Number WO/2011/023983.

88 British American Tobacco (Investments) Ltd, *Ribbed Pack*, Australian Designs Registration Number 323481.

89 JT International SA, 'Plaintiff's Submissions in *JT International SA v Commonwealth*', S409/2011, 26 March 2012 <http://www.hcourt.gov.au/assets/cases/s409-2011/ JT_Plf.pdf>.

90 Philip Morris Ltd, 'Submissions in *British American Tobacco Australasia v Commonwealth*', S389/2011, 26 March 2012 <http://www.hcourt.gov.au/assets/cases/s389-2012/BAT_Phillip.pdf>; Van Nelle Tabak Nederland BV and Imperial Tobacco Australia Ltd, 'Submissions in *British American Tobacco Australasia Ltd v Commonwealth*', S389/2011, 26 March 2012 <http://www.hcourt.gov.au/assets/cases/s389-2012/ BAT_VanNelle.pdf>.

91 Commonwealth, 'Submissions in *British American Tobacco Australasia Ltd v Commonwealth*', S389/2011, 5 April 2012, 27–8 <http://www.hcourt.gov.au/assets/cases/s389-2012/BAT_Def.pdf>.

92 Ibid.

93 Ibid 28.

94 *JT International SA v Commonwealth; British American Tobacco Australasia Ltd v Commonwealth* [2012] HCA 43 (5 October 2012) [30] (citations omitted).

95 Drahos, above n 81.

96 *JT International SA v Commonwealth; British American Tobacco Australasia Ltd v Commonwealth* [2012] HCA 43 (5 October 2012) [30].

97 Mark Davison and Ian Horak, *Shanahan's Australian Law of Trade Marks and Passing Off* (Thomson Reuters, 5th ed, 2012). On the philosophy of trade mark law, see also: Lionel Bently, Jennifer Davis and Jane Ginsburg (eds), *Trade Marks and Brands: An Interdisciplinary Critique* (Cambridge University Press, 2008); Graeme Dinwoodie and Mark Janis, *Trademark Law and Theory: A Handbook of Contemporary Research* (Edward Elgar Publishing, 2008).

98 The High Court of Australia has also explored the role and purpose of copyright law in the cases of *Stevens v Kabushiki Kaisha Sony Computer Entertainment* (2005) 224 CLR 293; *IceTV Pty Ltd v Nine Network Australia Pty Ltd* (2009) 239 CLR 458; *Roadshow Films Pty Ltd v iiNet Ltd* [2012] HCA 16 (20 April 2012); *Phonographic Performance Company of Australia Ltd v Commonwealth* (2012) 246 CLR 561.

99 William Cornish, David Llewellyn and Tanya Aplin, *Intellectual Property: Patents, Copyright, Trade Marks and Allied Rights* (Sweet & Maxwell, 7th ed, 2010).

100 Sam Ricketson, *The Law of Intellectual Property* (Law Book Company, 1984).

101 *JT International SA v Commonwealth; British American Tobacco Australasia Ltd v Commonwealth* [2012] HCA 43 (5 October 2012) [35].

102 Ibid [36].

103 *Pacific Film Laboratories Pty Ltd v Federal Commissioner of Taxation* (1970) 121 CLR 154.

104 *Steers v Rogers* [1893] AC 232.

105 *Grain Pool of Western Australia v Commonwealth* (2000) 202 CLR 479.

106 Mary Vitoria et al, *Laddie, Prescott and Vitoria: The Modern Law of Copyright and Designs* (LexisNexis, 4th ed, 2011).

107 *JT International SA v Commonwealth; British American Tobacco Australasia Ltd v Commonwealth* [2012] HCA 43 (5 October 2012) [47].

108 Ibid.

109 Ibid [53].

110 Ibid [68].

111 Ibid [78].

112 *New South Wales Dairy Corp v Murray Goulburn Co-op Co Ltd* (1990) 171 CLR 363, 396-7.

113 *JT International SA v Commonwealth; British American Tobacco Australasia Ltd v Commonwealth* [2012] HCA 43 (5 October 2012) [78].

114 Ibid [137].

115 Ibid [286].

116 Ibid [293].

117 Ibid [306].

118 Ibid [348].

119 Ibid [351].

120 Ibid [218].

121 Ibid.

122 Ibid.

123 See Matthew Rimmer, *Intellectual Property and Biotechnology: Biological Inventions* (Edward Elgar Publishing, 2008); Matthew Rimmer and Alison McLennan (eds), *Intellectual Property and Emerging Technologies: The New Biology* (Edward Elgar Publishing, 2012); *Cancer*

Voices Australia v Myriad Genetics Inc [2013] FCA 65 (15 February 2013). The *Cancer Voices Australia* case is currently under appeal, see Amy Corderoy, 'BRCA1 Gene Patent Ruling to be Appealed', *The Sydney Morning Herald*, 3 March 2013 <http://www.theage. com.au/national/brca1-gene-patent-ruling-to-be-appealed-20130304-2fg1f.html>.

124 Thomas Pogge, Matthew Rimmer and Kim Rubenstein (eds), *Incentives for Global Public Health: Patent Law and Access to Medicines* (Cambridge University Press, 2010); Matthew Rimmer, 'Julia Gillard, Big Pharma, Patent Law, and Public Health', *The Conversation*, 27 November 2012 <https://theconversation.edu.au/julia-gillard-big-pharma-patent-law-and-public-health-10226>; Productivity Commission, *Compulsory Licensing of Patents*, Productivity Commission Inquiry Report No 61 (2013) <http:// www.pc.gov.au/projects/inquiry/patents>.

125 The Institute of Public Affairs, 'Plain Packaging May Require up to $3.4 Billion Taxpayer Gift Annually to Big Tobacco and Film Companies' (Media Release, 26 April 2010) <http://www.ipa.org.au/library/publication/1272344059_document_ governing_in_ignorance_-_26042010.pdf>.

126 Evidence to Senate Legal and Constitutional Affairs Legislation Committee, Parliament of Australia, Canberra, 13 September 2011 (Allan Myers) 3.

127 Ibid 7.

128 *Paris Convention for the Protection of Industrial Property*, opened for signature 14 July 1967, 828 UNTS 306 (entered into force 26 April 1970).

129 Transcript of Proceedings, *JT International SA v Commonwealth; British American Tobacco Australasia Ltd v Commonwealth* [2012] HCATrans 91 (17 April 2012).

130 Transcript of Proceedings, *JT International SA v Commonwealth; British American Tobacco Australasia Ltd v Commonwealth* [2012] HCATrans 93 (19 April 2012).

131 See Evidence to Senate Legal and Constitutional Affairs Legislation Committee, Parliament of Australia, Canberra, 13 September 2011 (Simon Evans); Simon Evans and Jason Bosland, 'Plain Packaging of Cigarettes and Constitutional Property Rights' in Tania Voon, Andrew Mitchell and Jonathan Liberman with Glyn Ayres (eds), *Public Health and Plain Packaging of Cigarettes: Legal Issues* (Edward Elgar Publishing, 2012) 48; Mark Davison, 'Plain Packaging Bill to Extinguish Some Tobacco Marks', *The Drum*, 15 April 2011 <http://www.abc.net.au/unleashed/56666.html>; Mark Davison, 'The Legitimacy of Plain Packaging under International Intellectual Property Law: Why There is No Right to Use a Trademark under either the *Paris Convention* or the *TRIPS Agreement*' in Tania Voon, Andrew Mitchell and Jonathan Liberman with Glyn Ayres (eds), *Public Health and Plain Packaging of Cigarettes: Legal Issues* (Edward Elgar Publishing, 2012) 81; George Williams, 'Plain Packaging Challenge Could Go Up in Smoke, but You Never Know', *The Sydney Morning Herald* (online), 7 June 2011 <http://www.smh.com.au/opinion/society-and-culture/plain-packaging-challenge-could-go-up-in-smoke-but-you-never-know-20110606-1fp92.html>

132 Jonathan Liberman, 'Plainly Constitutional: The Upholding of Plain Tobacco Packaging by the High Court of Australia' (2013) 39 *American Journal of Law and Medicine* 361.

133 Ibid 372.

134 Commonwealth, 'Submissions in *British American Tobacco Australasia Ltd v Commonwealth*', S389/2011, 5 April 2012 <http://www.hcourt.gov.au/assets/cases/s389-2012/ BAT_Def.pdf>.

135 Ibid 32.

136 Ibid.

137 Ibid.

138 Ibid 44.

139 Attorney-General (ACT), 'Submissions in *British American Tobacco Australasia Ltd v Commonwealth*', S289/2011, 4 April 2012 <http://www.hcourt.gov.au/assets/cases/ s389-2012/BAT_AGACT.pdf>.

140 Ibid 10.
141 *Grain Pool of Western Australia v Commonwealth* (2000) 202 CLR 479.
142 *Nintendo Co Ltd v Centronics Systems Pty Ltd* (1994) 181 CLR 134.
143 *Phonographic Performance Company of Australia Ltd v Commonwealth* (2012) 246 CLR 561.
144 *Australian Tape Manufacturers Association Ltd v Commonwealth* (1993) 176 CLR 480.
145 *JT International SA v Commonwealth; British American Tobacco Australasia Ltd v Commonwealth* [2012] HCA 43 (5 October 2012) [169] (emphasis in original).
146 Ibid [190].
147 Ibid.
148 Ibid [191].
149 Ibid [188].
150 Ibid.
151 Ibid.
152 Ibid [189].
153 Ibid (emphasis in original).
154 Ibid [188].
155 Ibid [44] (French CJ); [101], [141] (Gummow J). However, such comments are obiter. As Hayne and Bell JJ noted, 'the relevant constitutional question is whether there has been an *acquisition* of property, not whether there has been a *taking*' [164] (emphasis in original).
156 Ibid [42].
157 Ibid.
158 Ibid.
159 *Mattel Inc v 3894207 Canada Inc* [2006] 1 SCR 772.
160 *JT International SA v Commonwealth; British American Tobacco Australasia Ltd v Commonwealth* [2012] HCA 43 (5 October 2012) [139].
161 Ibid.
162 Ibid.
163 Ibid [101].
164 Ibid [296].
165 Ibid [372].
166 Ibid.
167 Ibid [241].
168 *Australian Marlboro Man 1966* (12 August 2010) YouTube <http://www.youtube.com/watch?v=Uh5lq-zAa0s>.
169 Matthew Rimmer, 'Tobacco's Mad Men Threaten Public Health', *The Conversation*, 23 September 2011 <https://theconversation.edu.au/tobaccos-mad-men-threaten-public-health-3450>.
170 See HP Lee and George Winterton (eds), *Australian Constitutional Landmarks* (Cambridge University Press, 2003).
171 *Bank of New South Wales v Commonwealth* (1948) 76 CLR 1.
172 *Commonwealth v Tasmania* (1983) 158 CLR 1.
173 *Mabo v Queensland (No 2)* (1992) 175 CLR 1.
174 See Andrew Kenyon, Megan Richardson and Sam Ricketson (eds), *Landmarks in Australian Intellectual Property Law* (Cambridge University Press, 2009).
175 *Attorney General v JTI-Macdonald Corp* [2007] 2 SCR 610.
176 *British American Tobacco South Africa (Pty) Ltd v Minister of Health* [2012] 3 All SA 593 (Supreme Court of Appeal).
177 See Dr Margaret Chan, 'Global Governance of Tobacco in the 21st Century' (Speech delivered at the Harvard University Conference on Governance of Tobacco in the 21st Century: Strengthening National and International Policy for Global Health and Development, Cambridge, MA, 26 February 2013) <http://www.who.int/dg/speeches/2013/tobacco_20130226/en/index.html>; Jane Kelsey,

Hidden Agendas: What We Need to Know about the Trans-Pacific Partnership Agreement (BWB Books, 2013); Matthew Rimmer, 'Plain Packaging for the Pacific Rim: The Trans-Pacific Partnership and Tobacco Control' in Tania Voon (ed), *Trade Liberalisation and International Co-operation: A Legal Analysis of the Trans-Pacific Partnership Agreement* (Edward Elgar Publishing, 2013); Jessa Boehner, 'Bloomberg, Health Experts Denounce Obama's Gift to Big Tobacco in the Trans-Pacific Partnership', Public Citizen, *Eyes on Trade*, (22 August 2013) <http://citizen.typepad.com/eyesontrade/2013/08/health-advocates-denounce-obama-for-caving-to-big-tobacco-in-tpp.html>; Mike Bloomberg, 'Why is Obama Caving on Tobacco?', *The New York Times* (online), 22 August 2013.

178 Matthew Rimmer, 'The Olive Revolution: Australia's Plain Packaging Leads the World', *The Conversation*, 15 August 2012 <https://theconversation.com/the-olive-revolution-australias-plain-packaging-leads-the-world-8856>.

Bibliography

Books

Alemanno, Alberto and Garde, Amandine (eds), *Regulating Lifestyle Risks: Europe, Alcohol, Tobacco and Unhealthy Diets* (Cambridge University Press, forthcoming).

Alston, Philip, Goodman, Ryan and Steiner, Henry, *International Human Rights in Context: Law, Politics, Morals* (Oxford University Press, 2008).

Babor, Thomas et al, *Alcohol: No Ordinary Commodity* (Oxford University Press, 2nd ed, 2010).

Barendt, Eric, *Freedom of Speech* (Oxford University Press, 2nd ed, 2005).

Bently, Lionel, Davis, Jennifer and Ginsburg, Jane (eds), *Trade Marks and Brands: An Interdisciplinary Critique* (Cambridge University Press, 2008).

Bessen, James and Meurer, Michael, *Patent Failure: How Judges, Bureaucrats and Lawyers Put Innovators at Risk* (Princeton University Press, 2008).

Bethlehem, Daniel et al (eds), *The Oxford Handbook of International Trade Law* (Oxford University Press, 2009).

Beyer, Joy de and Waverley, Linda (eds), *Tobacco Control Policies: Strategies, Successes and Setbacks* (RITC and World Bank, 2003).

Biondi, Andrea and Eeckhout, Piet (eds), *EU Law After Lisbon* (Oxford University Press, 2012).

Bonnie, Richard, Stratton, Kathleen and Wallace, Robert (eds), *Ending the Tobacco Problem: A Blueprint for the Nation* (National Academies Press, 2007).

Brownson, Ross, Colditz, Graham and Proctor, Enola (eds), *Dissemination and Implementation Research in Health: Translating Science to Practice* (Oxford University Press, 2012).

Burchell, Graham, Gordon, Colin and Miller, Peter (eds), *The Foucault Effect: Studies in Governmentality* (University of Chicago Press, 1991).

Burk, Dan and Lemley, Mark, *The Patent Crisis and How the Courts Can Solve It* (University of Chicago Press, 2009).

Calster, Geert van and Prévost, Denise (eds), *Research Handbook on Environment, Health and the WTO* (Edward Elgar Publishing, 2013).

Clapham, Andrew and Robinson, Mary (eds), *Realizing the Right to Health* (Rüffer & Rub, 2009).

Cordonier Segger, Marie-Claire, Gehring, Markus and Newcombe, Andrew (eds), *Sustainable Development in World Investment Law* (Wolters Kluwer, 2011).

Cornish, William, Llewellyn, David and Aplin, Tanya, *Intellectual Property: Patents, Copyright, Trade Marks and Allied Rights* (Sweet & Maxwell, 7th ed, 2010).

Correa, Carlos, *Trade Related Aspects of Intellectual Property Rights* (Oxford University Press, 2007).

Craig, Paul, *The Lisbon Treaty – Law, Politics and Treaty Reform* (Oxford University Press, 2010).

Davison, Mark and Horak, Ian, *Shanahan's Australian Law of Trade Marks and Passing Off* (Thomson Reuters, 5th ed, 2012).

Dinwoodie, Graeme and Janis, Mark, *Trademark Law and Theory: A Handbook of Contemporary Research* (Edward Elgar Publishing, 2008).

Dolzer, Rudolf and Schreuer, Christoph, *Principles of International Investment Law* (Oxford University Press, 2nd ed, 2013).

Downie, Jocelyn and Gibson, Elaine (eds), *Health Law at the Supreme Court of Canada* (Irwin Law, 2007).

Drahos, Peter, *A Philosophy of Intellectual Property* (Dartmouth Publishing Company, 1996).

Eskridge, William, Garrett, Elizabeth and Frickey, Philip (eds), *Statutory Interpretation Stories* (Foundation Press, 2010).

Feldman, Robin, *Rethinking Patent Law* (Harvard University Press, 2012).

Fidler, David, *International Law and Infectious Diseases* (Clarendon Press, 1999).

Frankel, Susy (ed), *Learning from the Past, Adapting for the Future: Regulatory Reform in New Zealand* (LexisNexis, 2011).

Frankel, Susy and Ryder, Deborah (eds), *Recalibrating Behaviour: Smarter Regulation in a Global World* (LexisNexis, 2013).

Garde, Amandine, *EU Law and Obesity Prevention* (Kluwer Law International, 2010).

Gormley, Laurence and Shuibhne, Nic (eds), *From Single Market to Economic Union – Essays in Honour of John Usher* (Oxford University Press, 2012).

Gostin, Lawrence, *Public Health Law: Power, Duty, Restraint* (University of California Press, 2nd ed, 2008).

Grando, Michelle, *Evidence, Proof, and Fact-Finding in WTO Dispute Settlement* (Oxford University Press, 2009).

Hawkes, Corinna et al (eds), *Trade, Food, Diet and Health: Perspectives and Policy Options* (Wiley-Blackwell, 2010).

Heron, Craig, *Booze: A Distilled History* (Between the Lines, 2003).

Howells, Geraint, *The Tobacco Challenge* (Ashgate Publishing, 2011).

Jaffe, Adam and Lerner, Josh, *Innovation and Its Discontents: How Our Broken Patent System is Endangering Innovation and Progress, and What to Do about It* (Princeton University Press, 2004).

Kagan, Robert, *Adversarial Legalism: The American Way of Law* (Harvard University Press, 2001).

Kahn, Philippe and Walde, Thomas (eds), *New Aspects of International Investment Law* (The Hague Academy of International Law, 2007).

Kelsey, Jane, *Hidden Agendas: What We Need to Know about the Trans-Pacific Partnership Agreement* (BWB Books, 2013).

Kelsey, Jane (ed), *No Ordinary Deal: Unmasking the Trans-Pacific Partnership Free Trade Agreement* (Allen & Unwin, 2010).

Kenyon, Andrew, Richardson, Megan and Ricketson, Sam (eds), *Landmarks in Australian Intellectual Property Law* (Cambridge University Press, 2009).

Kessler, David, *A Question of Intent: A Great American Battle with a Deadly Industry* (Public Affairs, 2001).

Kingdon, John, *Agendas, Alternatives, and Public Policies* (Pearson, 2nd ed, 2010).

Kouri, Robert and Régis, Catherine (eds), *Les grands défis en droit et politiques de la santé* [*Grand Challenges in Health Law and Policy*] (Editions Yvon Blais, 2009).

Lane, Eric, *Clean Tech Intellectual Property: Eco-marks, Green Patents, and Green Innovation* (Oxford University Press, 2011).

Lee, HP and Winterton, George (eds), *Australian Constitutional Landmarks* (Cambridge University Press, 2003).

Lester, Simon and Mercurio, Bryan (eds), *Bilateral and Regional Trade Agreements: Commentary and Analysis* (Cambridge University Press, 2009).

Lim, CL, Elms, Deborah and Low, Patrick (eds), *The Trans-Pacific Partnership: A Quest for a Twenty-first Century Trade Agreement* (Cambridge University Press, 2012).

Maletic, Isidora, *The Law and Policy of Harmonisation in Europe's Internal Market* (Edward Elgar Publishing, 2013).

McGrady, Benn, *Trade and Public Health: The WTO, Tobacco, Alcohol, and Diet* (Cambridge University Press, 2011).

McGrady, Benn, *Confronting the Tobacco Epidemic in a New Era of Trade and Investment Liberalization* (World Health Organization, 2012).

Mercurio, Bryan and Ni, Kuei-Jung (eds), *Science and Technology in International Economic Law: Balancing Competing Interests* (Routledge, 2013).

Patry, William, *Moral Panics and the Copyright Wars* (Oxford University Press, 2009).

Pauwelyn, Joost, *Conflict of Norms in Public International Law: How WTO Law Relates to Other Rules of International Law* (Cambridge University Press, 2003).

Piris, Jean-Claude, *The Lisbon Treaty – A Legal and Political Analysis* (Cambridge University Press, 2010).

Pogge, Thomas, Rimmer, Matthew and Rubenstein, Kim (eds) *Incentives for Global Public Health: Patent Law and Access to Medicines* (Cambridge University Press, 2010).

Rabin, Robert and Sugarman, Stephen (eds), *Smoking Policy: Law, Politics and Culture* (Oxford University Press, 1993).

Rabin, Robert and Sugarman, Stephen (eds), *Regulating Tobacco* (Oxford University Press, 2001).

Reynolds, Christopher, *Public Health Law and Regulation* (Federation Press, 2004).

Ricketson, Sam, *The Law of Intellectual Property* (Law Book Company, 1984).

Rimmer, Matthew, *Intellectual Property and Biotechnology: Biological Inventions* (Edward Elgar Publishing, 2008).

Rimmer, Matthew and McLennan, Alison (eds), *Intellectual Property and Emerging Technologies: The New Biology* (Edward Elgar Publishing, 2012).

Rose, Geoffrey, *The Strategy of Preventive Medicine* (Oxford University Press, 1992).

Sassi, Franco, *Obesity and the Economics of Prevention: Fit not Fat* (OECD, 2010).

Schütze, Robert, *European Constitutional Law* (Cambridge University Press, 2012).

Scollo, Michelle and Winstanley, Margaret (eds), *Tobacco in Australia: Facts and Issues* (Cancer Council Victoria, 4th ed, 2012).

Shuibhne, Nic (ed), *Regulating the Internal Market* (Edward Elgar Publishing, 2006).

Stalford, Helen, *Children and the European Union – Rights, Welfare and Accountability* (Hart Publishing, 2012).

Trebilcock, Michael and Epps, Tracey (eds), *Research Handbook on the WTO and Technical Barriers to Trade* (Edward Elgar Publishing, 2013).

Tudor, Ioana, *The Fair and Equitable Treatment Standard in the International Law of Foreign Investment* (Oxford University Press, 2008).

Tyler, Tom, *Why People Obey the Law* (Princeton University Press, 2006).

Vitoria, Mary et al, *Laddie, Prescott and Vitoria: The Modern Law of Copyright and Designs* (LexisNexis, 4th ed, 2011).

Voon, Tania (ed), *Trade Liberalisation and International Co-operation: A Legal Analysis of the Trans-Pacific Partnership Agreement* (Edward Elgar Publishing, 2013).

Voon, Tania, Mitchell, Andrew and Liberman, Jonathan with Ayres, Glyn (eds), *Public Health and Plain Packaging of Cigarettes: Legal Issues* (Edward Elgar Publishing, 2012).

Wagenaar, Alexander and Burris, Scott (eds), *Public Health Law Research: Theory and Methods* (Jossey-Bass, 2013).

Wogalter, Michael (ed), *Handbook of Warnings* (CRC Press, 2006).

Wolfson, Mark, *The Fight Against Big Tobacco: The Movement, the State, and the Public's Health* (Aldine De Gruyter, 2001).

Journal articles

Albers, Alison et al, 'Relation between Local Restaurant Smoking Regulations and Attitudes towards the Prevalence and Social Acceptability of Smoking: A Study of Youths and Adults Who Eat Out Predominantly at Restaurants in Their Town' (2004) 13(4) *Tobacco Control* 347.

Alemanno, Alberto, 'The Better Regulation Initiative at the Judicial Gate: A Trojan Horse within the Commission's Walls or the Way Forward?' (2009) 15(3) *European Law Journal* 382.

Alemanno, Alberto, 'A Meeting of Minds on Impact Assessment: When Ex Ante Evaluation Meets Ex Post Judicial Control' (2011) 17(3) *European Public Law* 485.

Alemanno, Alberto, 'The Legality, Rationale and Science of Tobacco Display Bans after the Philip Morris Judgment' (2011) 4 *European Journal of Risk Regulation* 591.

Alemanno, Alberto, 'Out of Sight Out of Mind: Towards a New European Tobacco Products Directive' (2012) 18 *Columbia Journal of European Law* 197.

Alemanno, Alberto, 'The HOB-vín Judgment: A Failed Attempt to Standardise the Visual Imagery, Packaging and Appeal of Alcohol Products' (2013) 1 *European Journal of Risk Regulation* 101.

Alemanno, Alberto and Bonadio, Enrico, 'The Case of Plain Packaging for Cigarettes' (2010) 3 *European Journal of Risk Regulation* 268.

Alemanno, Alberto and Garde, Amandine, 'The Emergence of an EU Lifestyle Policy: The Case of Alcohol, Tobacco and Unhealthy Diets' (2013) 50 *Common Market Law Review* 6.

Alleyne, George et al, 'Embedding Non-communicable Diseases in the Post-2015 Development Agenda' (2013) *The Lancet Non-Communicable Diseases Series* 4, 7.

Anis, AH et al, 'Obesity and Overweight in Canada: An Updated Cost-of-illness Study' (2010) 11(1) *Obesity Reviews* 31.

Arden, The Right Honourable Lady Justice, 'Proportionality: The Way Ahead?' [2013] *Public Law* 489.

Baade, Peter et al, 'Estimating the Future Burden of Cancers Preventable by Better Diet and Physical Activity in Australia' (2012) 196(5) *Medical Journal of Australia* 337.

Bae, Jin Yung et al, 'Child Passenger Safety Laws in the United States, 1978–2010: Policy Diffusion in the Absence of Strong Federal Intervention' (2014) 100 *Social Science & Medicine* 30.

Baicchi, Carol, 'Why Study Problematizations? Making Politics Visible' (2010) 2 *Open Journal of Political Science* 1.

Bartholomew, Kay, Parcel, Guy and Kok, Gerjo, 'Intervention Mapping: A Process for Developing Theory – and Evidence-based Health Education Programs' (1998) 25(5) *Health Education and Behavior* 545.

Bartlett, Oliver and Garde, Amandine, 'Time to Seize the (Red) Bull by the Horns: The

EU's Failure to Protect Children from Alcohol and Unhealthy Food Marketing' (2013) 38 *European Law Review* 498.

Basu, Robin, 'The RJR-JTI Saga – Lessons Learned and Unresolved Issues' (2007) 23 *National Journal of Constitutional Law* 107.

Berger, Dale and Marelich, William, 'Legal and Social Control of Alcohol-impaired Driving in California: 1983–1994' (1997) 58(5) *Journal of Studies on Alcohol and Drugs* 519.

Bernitz, Ulf, 'Logo Licensing of Tobacco Products – Can It Be Prohibited?' (1990) 4 *European Intellectual Property Review* 137.

Bloom, Bernard, 'Effects of Continuing Medical Education on Improving Physician Clinical Care and Patient Health: A Review of Systematic Reviews' (2005) 21(3) *International Journal of Technology Assessment in Health Care* 380.

Borland, Ron, 'A Strategy for Controlling the Marketing of Tobacco Products: A Regulated Market Model' (2003) 12(4) *Tobacco Control* 374.

Borland, Ron et al, 'How Reactions to Cigarette Packet Health Warnings Influence Quitting: Findings from the ITC Four-Country Survey' (2009) 104 *Addiction* 669.

Brennan, Laura et al, 'Accelerating Evidence Reviews and Broadening Evidence Standards to Identify Effective, Promising, and Emerging Policy and Environmental Strategies for Prevention of Childhood Obesity' (2011) 32 *Annual Review Public Health* 199.

Brenncke, Martin, 'Case Law' (2010) 47 *Common Market Law Review* 1793.

Briss, Peter et al, 'Developing an Evidence-based Guide to Community Preventive Services – Methods: The Task Force on Community Preventive Services' (2000) 18 (supplement 1) *American Journal of Preventive Medicine* 35.

Brownson, Ross et al, 'Researchers and Policymakers: Travelers in Parallel Universes' (2006) 30(2) *American Journal of Preventive Medicine* 164.

Brownson, Ross, Chriqui, Jamie and Stamatakis, Katherine, 'Understanding Evidence-based Public Health Policy' (2009) 99(9) *American Journal of Public Health* 1576.

Burris, Scott et al, 'Making the Case for Laws that Improve Health: A Framework for Public Health Law Research' (2010) 88(2) *The Milbank Quarterly* 169.

Burris, Scott and Anderson, Evan, 'Legal Regulation of Health-related Behavior: A Half-century of Public Health Law Research' (2013) 39 *Annual Review of Law and Social Science* 95.

Cabrera, Oscar and Madrazo, Alejandro, 'Human Rights as a Tool for Tobacco Control in Latin America' (2010) 52(2) *Salud Pública de México* 288.

Cabrera, Oscar and Gostin, Lawrence, 'Human Rights and the Framework Convention on Tobacco Control: Mutually Reinforcing Systems' (2011) 7(3) *International Journal of Law in Context* 285.

Cabrera, Oscar and Carballo, Juan, 'Tobacco Control Litigation: Broader Impacts on Health Rights Adjudication' (2013) 41(1) *Global Health and the Law* 147.

Campbell, Donald and Ross, Laurence, 'The Connecticut Crackdown on Speeding: Time-series Data in Quasi-experimental Analysis' (1968) 3(1) *Law and Society Review* 33.

Carande-Kulis, Vilma et al, 'Methods for Systematic Reviews of Economic Evaluations for the Guide to Community Preventive Services: Task Force on Community Preventive Services' (2000) 18 (supplement 1) *American Journal of Preventive Medicine* 75.

Carragher, Natacha, Shakeshaft, Anthony and Doran, Christopher, 'Here We Go Again: Cider's Turn to Highlight Anomalies in Australia's Alcohol Taxation System' (2013) 37 *Australian and New Zealand Journal of Public Health* 95.

Casswell, Sally, 'Current Status of Alcohol Marketing Policy – an Urgent Challenge for Global Governance' (2012) 107 *Addiction* 478.

Casswell, Sally and Thamarangsi, Thaksaphon, 'Reducing Harm from Alcohol: Call to Action' (2009) 373 *The Lancet* 2247.

Centers for Disease Control and Prevention, 'Ten Great Public Health Achievements – United States, 1900–1999' (1999) 48(12) *Morbidity and Mortality Weekly Report* 241.

Chapman, Simon, Byrne, Fiona and Carter, Stacey, 'Australia is One of the Darkest Markets in the World: The Global Importance of Australian Tobacco Control' (2003) 12 (supplement 3) *Tobacco Control* iii1.

Chapman, Simon and Carter, Stacy, '"Avoid Health Warnings on All Tobacco Products for just as long as We Can": A History of Australian Tobacco Industry Efforts to Avoid Delay and Dilute Health Warnings on Cigarettes' (2003) 12 (supplement 3) *Tobacco Control* iii13.

Chrisman, Sara, Schiff, Melissa and Rivara, Frederick, 'Physician Concussion Knowledge and the Effect of Mailing the CDC's "Heads Up" Toolkit' (2011) 50(11) *Clinical Pediatrics* 1031.

Clark, Helen, 'NCDs: A Challenge to Sustainable Human Development' (2013) *The Lancet Non-Communicable Diseases Series* 4, 2.

Colby, David et al, 'Research Glut and Information Famine: Making Research Evidence More Useful for Policymakers' (2008) 27(4) *Health Affairs* 1177.

Colley, Rachel et al, 'Physical Activity of Canadian Children and Youth: Accelerometer Results from the 2007 to 2009 Canadian Health Measures Survey' (2011) 22(1) *Health Reports* 15.

Collins, Michael et al, 'Cumulative Effects of Concussion in High School Athletes' (2002) 51(5) *Neurosurgery* 1175.

Collins, Michael et al, 'Alcohol in Moderation, Cardioprotection, and Neuroprotection: Epidemiological Considerations and Mechanistic Studies' (2009) 33(2) *Alcoholism: Clinical & Experimental Research* 206.

Corrigan, Oonagh, 'Empty Ethics: The Problem with Informed Consent' (2003) 25 *Sociology of Health and Illness* 768.

Cotula, Lorenzo, 'Reconciling Regulatory Stability and Evolution of Environmental Standards in Investment Contracts: Towards a Rethink of Stabilization Clauses' (2008) 1(2) *Journal of World Energy Law & Business* 158.

Craig, Paul, 'Subsidiarity: A Political and Legal Analysis' (2012) 50 *Journal of Common Market Studies* 72.

Crammond, B et al, 'The Possibility of Regulating for Obesity Prevention – Understanding Regulation in the Commonwealth Government' (2013) 14(3) *Obesity Reviews* 213.

Crow, Melissa, 'Smokescreen and State Responsibility Using Human Rights Strategies to Promote Global Tobacco Control' (2004) 29 *Yale Journal of International Law* 209.

Dashwood, Alan, 'The Relationship between the Member States and the European Union/European Community' (2004) 41 *Common Market Law Review* 2.

Davis, Ronald, 'Moving Tobacco Control Past the "Tipping Point"' (2000) 321 *British Medical Journal* 309.

Davis, WA et al, 'The Obesity-driven Rising Costs of Type 2 Diabetes in Australia: Projections from the Fremantle Diabetes Study' (2006) 36 *Internal Medicine Journal* 155.

Davison, Mark, 'Plain Packaging and the TRIPS Agreement: A Response to Professor Gervais' (2013) 23 *Australian Intellectual Property Journal* 160.

Davison, Mark and Emerton, Patrick, 'Rights, Privileges, Legitimate Interests, and Justifiability: Article 20 of TRIPS and Plain Packaging of Tobacco' (2014) *American University International Law Review* (forthcoming).

DeKosky, Steven, Ikonomovic, Milos and Gandy, Sam, 'Traumatic Brain Injury: Football, Warfare, and Long-term Effects' (2010) 93(12) *New England Journal of Medicine* 46.

Doll, Richard et al, 'Mortality in Relation to Smoking: 40 Years' Observations on Male British Doctors' (1994) 309 *British Medical Journal* 901.

Dresler, Carolyn and Marks, Stephen, 'The Emerging Human Right to Tobacco Control' (2006) 28 *Human Rights Quarterly* 599.

Drewnowski, Adam and Darmon, Nicole, 'The Economics of Obesity: Dietary Energy Density and Energy Cost' (2005) 82(1) *American Journal of Clinical Nutrition* 256S.

Drewnowski, Adam and Darmon, Nicole, 'Food Choices and Diet Costs: An Economic Analysis' (2005) 135(4) *Journal of Nutrition* 900.

Durkin, Sarah, Brennan, Emily and Wakefield, Melanie, 'Mass Media Campaigns to Promote Smoking Cessation among Adults: An Integrative Review' (2012) 21 *Tobacco Control* 127.

Farley, Thomas et al, 'New York City's Fight over Calorie Labeling' (2009) 28 *Health Affairs* 1098.

Feit, Michael, 'Responsibility of the State under International Law for the Breach of Contract Committed by a State Owned Entity' (2010) 28 *Berkeley Journal of International Law* 142.

Fielding, Jonathan and Briss, Peter, 'Promoting Evidence-based Public Health Policy: Can We Have Better Evidence and More Action?' (2006) 25(4) *Health Affairs* 969.

Fish, Morris, 'The Effect of Alcohol on the Canadian Constitution … Seriously' (2011) 57 *McGill Law Journal* 189.

Flegal, Katherine et al, 'Excess Deaths Associated with Underweight, Overweight, and Obesity' (2005) 293(15) *Journal of the American Medical Association* 1861.

Forsetlund, Louise et al, 'Continuing Education Meetings and Workshops: Effects on Professional Practice and Health Care Outcomes' (2009) (2) *Cochrane Database Systematic Review* CD003030.

Frankel, Susy and Gervais, Daniel, 'Plain Packaging and the Interpretation of the TRIPS Agreement' (2013) 46(5) *Vanderbilt Journal of Transnational Law* 1149.

Freeman, Becky, Chapman, Simon and Rimmer, Matthew, 'The Case for the Plain Packaging of Tobacco Products' (2007) 103(4) *Addiction* 580.

Garde, Amandine, 'Freedom of Commercial Expression and the Protection of Public Health in Europe' (2010) 12 *Cambridge Yearbook of European Legal Studies* 225.

Garde, Amandine, 'Advertising Regulation and the Protection of Children-Consumers in the European Union: In the Best Interest of … Commercial Operators?' (2011) 19 *International Journal of Children's Rights* 523.

Garriguet, Didier, 'Canadians' Eating Habits' (2007) 18(2) *Health Reports* 17.

Germain, Daniella, Wakefield, Melanie and Durkin, Sarah, 'Adolescents' Perceptions of Cigarette Brand Image: Does Plain Packaging Make a Difference?' (2010) 46(4) *Journal of Adolescent Health* 385.

Germain, Daniella et al, 'The Long-term Decline of Adult Tobacco Use in Victoria: Changes in Smoking Initiation and Quitting over a Quarter of a Century of Tobacco Control' (2012) 36 *Australia and New Zealand Journal of Public Health* 17.

Gervais, Daniel, 'Plain Packaging and the TRIPS Agreement: A Response to Professors Davison, Mitchell and Voon' (2013) 23 *Australian Intellectual Property Journal* 96.

Gessel, Luke et al, 'Concussions among United States High School and Collegiate Athletes' (2007) 42(4) *Journal of Athletic Training* 495.

Goris, Janny et al, 'Television Food Advertising and the Prevalence of Childhood Overweight and Obesity: A Multicountry Comparison' (2010) 13 *Public Health Nutrition* 1003.

Gostin, Lawrence and Taylor, Allyn, 'Global Health Law: A Definition and Grand Challenges' (2008) 1 *Public Health Ethics* 53.

Gray, Dennis et al, 'Beating the Grog: An Evaluation of the Tennant Creek Liquor Licensing Restrictions' (2000) 24 *Australian and New Zealand Journal of Public Health* 39.

Green, Lawrence et al, 'Diffusion Theory and Knowledge Dissemination, Utilization, and Integration in Public Health' (2009) 30 *Annual Review of Public Health* 151.

Greenhalgh, Trisha et al, 'Diffusion of Innovations in Service Organizations: Systematic Review and Recommendations' (2004) 82(4) *The Milbank Quarterly* 581.

Guerin, Diana and MacKinnon, David, 'An Assessment of the California Child Passenger Restraint Requirement' (1985) 75(2) *American Journal of Public Health* 142.

Guskiewicz, Kevin et al, 'Epidemiology of Concussion in Collegiate and High School Football Players' (2000) 28(5) *American Journal of Sports Medicine* 643.

Haan, Tanguy de, 'Plain Packaging: Expropriation and Disproportion' (2013) 35 *European Intellectual Property Review* 497.

Haddon, Jr, William, 'Advances in the Epidemiology of Injuries as a Basis for Public Policy' (1980) 95(5) *Public Health Reports* 411.

Hall, Wayne and Chikritzhs, Tanya, 'The Australian Alcopops Tax Revisited' (2011) 377 *The Lancet* 1136.

Hammond, David, Daniel, Samantha and White, Christine, 'The Effect of Cigarette Branding and Plain Packaging on Female Youth in the United Kingdom' (2013) 52(2) *Journal of Adolescent Health* 151.

Harris, Jennifer and Graff, Samantha, 'Protecting Young People from Junk Food Advertising: Implications of Psychological Research for First Amendment Law' (2012) 102(2) *American Journal of Public Health* 214.

Harvey, Hosea, 'Reducing Traumatic Brain Injuries in Youth Sports: Youth Sports Traumatic Brain Injury State Laws: January 2009–December 2012' (2013) 103(7) *American Journal of Public Health* 1249.

Harvey, Hosea, 'Refereeing the Public Health' (2014) 14(1) *Yale Journal of Health Policy, Law, and Ethics* (forthcoming).

Haynes, Abby et al, 'Galvanizers, Guides, Champions, and Shields: The Many Ways that Policymakers Use Public Health Researchers' (2011) 89(4) *The Milbank Quarterly* 564.

Henckels, Caroline, 'Balancing Investment Protection and the Public Interest: The Role of the Standard of Review and the Importance of Deference in Investor–State Arbitration' (2013) 4 *Journal of International Dispute Settlement* 197.

Heung, Carly, Rempel, Benjamin and Krank, Marvin, 'Strengthening the Canadian Alcohol Advertising System' (2012) 103 *Canadian Journal of Public Health* 263, 264.

Hill, D and Carroll, T, 'Australia's National Tobacco Campaign' (2003) 12 (supplement 2) *Tobacco Control* ii9.

Hoffman, Steven and Røttingen, John-Arne, 'Dark Sides of the Proposed Framework Convention on Global Health's Many Virtues: A Systematic Review and Critical Analysis' (2013) 15(1) *Health & Human Rights Journal* 117.

Hogan, Eleanor et al, 'What Price Do We Pay to Prevent Alcohol-related Harms in Aboriginal Communities? The Alice Springs Trial of Liquor Licensing Restrictions' (2006) 25 *Drug and Alcohol Review* 207.

Innvaer, Simon et al, 'Health Policy-makers' Perceptions of Their Use of Evidence: A Systematic Review' (2002) 7(4) *Journal of Health Services Research and Policy* 239.

Jacobson, Peter and Soliman, Soheil, 'Co-opting the Health and Human Rights Movements' (2000) 30(4) *Journal of Law, Medicine & Ethics* 605.

Jewell, Christopher and Bero, Lisa, 'Developing Good Taste in Evidence: Facilitators of and Hindrances to Evidence-informed Health Policymaking in State Government' (2008) 86(2) *The Milbank Quarterly* 177.

Johnston, Lorraine, Robinson, Sarah and Lockett, Nigel, 'Recognising "Open Innovation" in HEI-industry Interaction for Knowledge Transfer and Exchange' (2010) 16(6) *International Journal of Entrepreneurial Behaviour & Research* 540.

Kirkwood, Michael, Yeates, Keith and Wilson, Pamela, 'Pediatric Sport-related Concussion: A Review of the Clinical Management of an Oft-neglected Population' (2006) 117(4) *Pediatrics* 1359.

Koch, Ida, 'Dichotomies, Trichotomies or Waves of Duties?' (2005) 5(1) *Human Rights Law Review* 81.

Kur, Annette, 'The Right to Use One's Own Trade Mark: A Self-evident Issue or a New Concept in German, European, and International Trade Mark Law?' (1996) 4 *European Intellectual Property Review* 203.

Kuran, Timur and Sunstein, Cass, 'Availability Cascades and Risk Regulation' (1999) 51(4) *Stanford Law Review* 683.

Lancet, The, 'A Framework Convention on Alcohol Control' (2007) 370 *The Lancet* 1102.

Lancet, The, 'Urgently Needed: A Framework Convention for Obesity Control' (2011) 378 *The Lancet* 741.

Lane, Eric, 'Building the Global Green Patent Highway: A Proposal for International Harmonization of Green Technology Fast Track Programs' (2012) 27(3) *Berkeley Technology Law Journal* 1119.

Langlois, Jean, Rutland-Brown, Wesley and Wald, Marlena, 'The Epidemiology and Impact of Traumatic Brain Injury: A Brief Overview' (2006) 21(5) *Journal of Head Trauma Rehabilitation* 375.

Langlois, Kellie and Garriguet, Didier, 'Sugar Consumption among Canadians of All Ages' (2011) 22(3) *Health Reports* 1.

Lavis, John, 'Research, Public Policymaking, and Knowledge-translation Processes: Canadian Efforts to Build Bridges' (2006) (26) *The Journal of Continuing Education in the Health Professions* 37.

Lavis, John et al, 'How Can Research Organizations More Effectively Transfer Research Knowledge to Decision Makers?' (2003) 81(2) *The Milbank Quarterly* 221.

Liberman, Jonathan, 'The Future of Tobacco Regulation: A Response to a Proposal for Fundamental Institutional Change' (2006) 15(4) *Tobacco Control* 333.

Liberman, Jonathan, 'Four COPs and Counting: Achievements, Underachievements and Looming Challenges in the Early Life of the WHO FCTC Conference of the Parties' (2012) 21 *Tobacco Control* 215.

Liberman, Jonathan, 'Combating Counterfeit Medicines and Illicit Trade in Tobacco Products: Minefields in Global Health Governance' (2012) 40 *Journal of Law, Medicine & Ethics* 326.

Liberman, Jonathan, 'Plainly Constitutional: The Upholding of Plain Tobacco Packaging by the High Court of Australia' (2013) 39(2) *American Journal of Law and Medicine* 361.

Liberman, Jonathan, 'Alternative Legal Strategies for Alcohol Control: Not a Framework Convention – at Least Not Right Now' (2013) 108 *Addiction* 456.

Liberman, Jonathan and Mitchell, Andrew, 'In Search of Coherence between Trade and Health: Inter-Institutional Opportunities' (2010) 25 *Maryland Journal of International Law* 143.

Litman, Jessica, 'The Exclusive Right to Read' (1994) 13(1) *Cardozo Arts and Entertainment Journal* 29.

Livingston, Michael, 'Recent Trends in Risky Alcohol Consumption and Related Harm among Young People in Victoria, Australia' (2008) 32(3) *Australian and New Zealand Journal of Public Health* 269.

Livingston, Michael, 'Alcohol Outlet Density and Harm: Comparing the Impacts on Violence and Chronic Harms' (2011) 30 *Drug and Alcohol Review* 515.

Livingston, Michael et al, 'Diverging Trends in Alcohol Consumption and Alcohol-related Harm in Victoria' (2010) 34 *Australian and New Zealand Journal of Public Health* 368.

MacKay, Sarah, 'Legislative Solutions to Unhealthy Eating and Obesity in Australia' (2011) 125(12) *Public Health* 896.

Maisonneuve, Herve et al, 'Continuing Medical Education and Professional Revalidation in Europe: Five Case Examples' (2009) 29(1) *The Journal of Continuing Education in the Health Professions* 58.

Mann, Jonathan et al, 'Health and Human Rights' (1994) 1 *Health and Human Rights* 6.

Mayer, Robert, 'Protectionism, Intellectual Property and Consumer Protection: Was the Uruguay Round Good for Consumers?' (1998) 21 *Journal of Consumer Policy* 195.

McCrea, Michael et al, 'Unreported Concussion in High School Football Players: Implications for Prevention' (2004) 14(1) *Clinical Journal of Sports Medicine* 13.

McCrea, Michael et al, 'Effects of a Symptom-free Waiting Period on Clinical Outcome and Risk of Reinjury after Sport-related Concussion' (2009) 65(5) *Neurosurgery* 876.

McCrory, Paul et al, 'Consensus Statement on Concussion in Sport: The 4th International Conference on Concussion in Sport Held in Zurich, November 2012' (2013) 47(5) *British Journal of Sports Medicine* 250.

McGrady, Benn, 'Necessity Exceptions in WTO Law: Retreaded Tyres, Regulatory Purpose and Cumulative Regulatory Measures' (2009) 12(1) *Journal of International Economic Law* 153.

McGrady, Benn, 'Philip Morris v. Uruguay: The Punta del Este Declaration on the Implementation of the WHO Framework Convention on Tobacco Control' (2011) 2 *European Journal of Risk Regulation* 254.

McGrady, Benn, 'Panel Report US – Clove Cigarettes' (2011) 4 *European Journal of Risk Regulation* 600.

Mitchell, Andrew and Voon, Tania, 'Patents and Public Health in the WTO, FTAs and Beyond: Tension and Conflict in International Law' (2009) 43(3) *Journal of World Trade* 571.

Mitchell, Andrew and Voon, Tania, 'Implications of the World Trade Organization in Combating Non-communicable Diseases' (2011) 125 *Public Health* 832.

Mitton, Craig et al, 'Knowledge Transfer and Exchange: Review and Synthesis of the Literature' (2007) 85(4) *The Milbank Quarterly* 729.

Moher, David et al, 'Epidemiology and Reporting Characteristics of Systematic Reviews' (2007) 4(3) *PLoS Medicine* e78.

Mokhiber, Russell, 'Gerber Uses Threats of GATT Sanctions to Gain Exemption from Guatemalan Infant Health Law' (1996) 10(14) *Corporate Crime Reporter* 6.

Mold, James and Peterson, Kevin, 'Primary Care Practice-based Research Networks: Working at the Interface between Research and Quality Improvement' (2005) 3 (supplement 1) *The Annals of Family Medicine* S12.

Moodie, Rob et al, 'Profits and Pandemics: Prevention of Harmful Effects of Tobacco, Alcohol, and Ultra-processed Food and Drink Industries' (2013) 381 *The Lancet* 670.

Morain, Stephanie and Mello, Michelle, 'Survey Finds Public Support for Legal Interventions Directed at Health Behavior to Fight Noncommunicable Disease' (2013) 32(3) *Health Affairs* 486.

Moulton, Anthony et al, 'The Scientific Basis for Law as a Public Health Tool' (2009) 99(1) *American Journal of Public Health* 17.

Murnaghan, Donna, 'Knowledge Exchange Systems for Youth Health and Chronic Disease Prevention: A Tri-provincial Case Study' (2013) 4 *Chronic Diseases and Injuries in Canada* 257.

Paradis, Catherine, Demers, Andrée and Picard, Elyse, 'Alcohol Consumption: A Different Kind of Canadian Mosaic' (2010) 101 *Canadian Journal of Public Health* 275.

Patra, Jayadeep et al, 'Substance-attributable Morbidity and Mortality Changes to Canada's Epidemiological Profile' (2007) 98 *Canadian Journal of Public Health* 228.

Pawson, Ray, 'Evidence-based Policy: The Promise of "Realist Synthesis"' (2002) 8(3) *Evaluation* 340.

Potestà, Michele, 'Legitimate Expectations in Investment Treaty Law: Understanding the Roots and Limits of a Controversial Concept' (2013) 28(1) *ICSID Review* 88.

Powell, John and Barber-Foss, Kim, 'Traumatic Brain Injury in High School Athletes' (1999) 282(10) *Journal of the American Medical Association* 958.

Punnoose, Ann, 'Study Raises Concerns about "Heading" in Soccer, but Jury is Still Out on Risks' (2012), 307(10) *Journal of the American Medical Association* 1012.

Reiner, Miriam et al 'Long-term Health Benefits of Physical Activity – A Systematic Review of Longitudinal Studies' (2013) 13 *BMC Public Health* 813.

Ricketson, Sam, 'Plain Packaging Legislation for Tobacco Products and Trade Marks in the High Court of Australia' (2013) 3(3) *Queen Mary Journal of Intellectual Property* 224.

Ries, Nola and Tigerstrom, Barbara von, 'Legal Interventions to Address Obesity: Assessing the State of the Law in Canada' (2011) 43 *UBC Law Review* 401.

Room, Robin et al, 'International Regulation of Alcohol' (2008) *British Medical Journal* 337.

Sadeleer, Nicolas de, 'Procedures for Derogations from the Principle of Approximation of Laws under Art. 95 EC' (2003) 40 *Common Market Law Review* 889.

Samet, Jonathan and Wipfli, Heather, 'Unfinished Business in Tobacco Control' (2009) 302 *Journal of the American Medical Association* 681.

Sewell, C Mack et al, 'Child Restraint Law Effects on Motor Vehicle Accident Fatalities and Injuries: The New Mexico Experience' (1986) 78(6) *Pediatrics* 1079.

Shield, John and Evans, Bryan, 'Building a Policy-oriented Research Partnership for Knowledge Mobilization and Knowledge Transfer: The Case of the Canadian Metropolis Project' (2012) 2(4) *Administrative Science* 250.

Shill, J et al, 'Government Regulation to Promote Healthy Food Environments – A View from inside State Governments' (2012) 13(2) *Obesity Reviews* 162.

Shipan, Charles and Volden, Craig, 'Policy Diffusion: Seven Lessons for Scholars and Practitioners' (2012) *Public Administration Review* 788.

Sivaramakrishnan, Kavita and Parker, Richard, 'The United Nations High Level Meeting on the Prevention and Control of Noncommunicable Diseases: A Missed Opportunity?' (2012) 102 (11) *American Journal of Public Health* 2010.

Skov, Steven et al, 'Is the "Alcopops" Tax Working? Probably Yes but There is a Bigger Picture' (2011) 195 *Medical Journal of Australia* 84.

Stockwell, Tim et al, 'Does Minimum Pricing Reduce Alcohol Consumption? The Experience of a Canadian Province' (2011) 107 *Addiction* 912.

Stockwell, Tim et al, 'The Raising of Minimum Alcohol Prices in Saskatchewan, Canada: Impacts on Consumption and Implications for Public Health' (2012) 102 *American Journal of Public Health*, e103.

Studlar, Donley, 'The Political Dynamics of Tobacco Control in Australia and New Zealand: Explaining Policy Problems, Instruments, and Patterns of Adoption' (2006) 40 *Australian Journal of Political Science* 255.

Stumberg, Robert, 'Safeguards for Tobacco Control: Options for the TPPA' (2013) 39 *American Journal of Law & Medicine* 382.

Sweet, Melissa and Moynihan, Ray, 'Improving Population Health: The Uses of Systematic Reviews' (2007) *The Milbank Quarterly* 1.

Sykes, Alan, 'Comparative Advantage and the Normative Economics of International Trade Policy' (1998) 1 *Journal of International Economic Law* 49.

Taylor, Allyn, 'Governing the Globalization of Public Health' (2004) 32 *Journal of Law, Medicine & Ethics* 500.

Taylor, Allyn and Dhillon, Ibadat, 'An International Legal Strategy for Alcohol Control: Not a Framework Convention – at Least not Yet' (2013) 108 *Addiction* 450.

Teixeira, Luiz Antonio and Jaques, Tiago Alves, 'Legislation and Tobacco Control in Brazil' (2011) 57(3) *Brazilian Journal of Cancerology* 295.

Teret, Stephen et al, 'Child Restraint Laws: An Analysis of Gaps in Coverage' (1986) 76(1) *American Journal of Public Health* 31.

Terrell, Thomas et al, 'Genetic Polymorphisms, Concussion Risk, and Post Concussion Neurocognitive Deficits in College and High School Athletes' (2013) 47 *British Journal of Sports Medicine* E1.

Thow, Anne Marie and Priadarshi, Shishir, 'Aid for Trade: An Opportunity to Increase Fruit and Vegetable Supply' (2013) 91 *Bulletin of the World Health Organization* 57.

Treschan, Tanja et al, 'The Influence of Protocol Pain and Risk on Patients' Willingness to Consent for Clinical Studies: A Randomized Trial' (2003) 96 *Anesthesia and Analgesia* 498.

Vandenberg, Brian, Livingston, Michael and Hamilton, Margaret, 'Beyond Cheap Shots: Reforming Alcohol Taxation in Australia' (2008) 27 *Drug and Alcohol Review* 579.

von Tigerstrom, Barbara, 'Mandatory Nutrition Disclosure for Restaurants: Is Menu Labelling Coming to Canada?' (2010) 28 *Windsor Review of Legal & Social Issues* 139.

Voon, Tania, 'International Decision: *United States – Measures Affecting the Production and Sale of Clove Cigarettes*' (2012) 106(4) *American Journal of International Law* 824.

Wagenaar, Alexander, Webster, Daniel and Maybee, Richard, 'Effects of Child Restraint Laws on Traffic Fatalities in Eleven States' (1987) 27(7) *Journal of Trauma, Injury, Infection and Critical Care* 726.

Wakefield, Melanie et al, 'The Cigarette Pack as Image: New Evidence from Tobacco Industry Documents' (2002) 11 *Tobacco Control* 77.

Wakefield, Melanie, Germain, Daniella and Durkin, Sarah J, 'How Does Increasingly Plainer Cigarette Packaging Influence Adult Smokers' Perceptions about Brand Image? An Experimental Study' (2008) 17 *Tobacco Control* 416.

Wakefield, Melanie et al, 'Do Larger Pictorial Health Warnings Diminish the Need for Plain Packaging of Cigarettes?' (2012) 107(6) *Addiction* 1159.

Wakefield, Melanie et al, 'Introduction Effects of the Australian Plain Packaging Policy on Adult Smokers: A Cross-sectional Study' (2013) 3 *BMJ Open* e003175.

Weiss, Carol, 'Research for Policy's Sake: The Enlightenment Function of Social Research' (1977) 3 *Policy Analysis* 531.

Weiss, Carol, 'The Powers of Problem Definition: The Case of Government Paperwork' (1989) 22(2) *Policy Sciences* 97.

White, Victoria, Webster, Bernice and Wakefield, Melanie, 'Do Graphic Health Warning Labels Have an Impact on Adolescents' Smoking-related Beliefs and Behaviours?' (2008) 103 *Addiction* 1562.

White, Victoria et al, 'What Impact Have Tobacco Control Policies, Cigarette Price and Tobacco Control Programme Funding Had on Australian Adolescents' Smoking? Findings over a 15-year Period' (2011) 106 *Addiction* 1493.

Williams, Allan and Wells, JoAnn, 'The Tennessee Child Restraint Law in its Third Year' (1981) 71(2) *American Journal of Public Health* 163.

Williams, Allan and Wells, JoAnn, 'Evaluation of the Rhode Island Child Restraint Law' (1981) 71(7) *American Journal of Public Health* 742.

Wilson, Nick and Thomson, George, 'Tobacco Tax as a Health Protecting Policy: A Brief Review of the New Zealand Evidence' (2005) 118 *The New Zealand Medical Journal* 1403.

Woodward, Stephen, 'Trends in Cigarette Consumption in Australia' (1984) 14(4) *Australian and New Zealand Journal of Medicine* 405.

Yach, Derek, McIntyre, Di and Saloojee, Yusuf, 'Smoking in South Africa: The Health and Economic Impact' (1992) 1 *Tobacco Control* 272.

Young, Linda and Willie, Reynold, 'Effectiveness of Continuing Education for Health Professionals: A Literature Review' (1984) 13(2) *Journal of Allied Health* 112.

Zaza, Stephanie et al, 'Data Collection Instrument and Procedure for Systematic Reviews in the Guide to Community Preventive Services: Task Force on Community Preventive Services' (2000) 18 (supplement 1) *American Journal of Preventive Medicine* 44.

Index